Outsourcing Agreements

D1806853

Outsourcing Agreements

A Practical Guide

George Kimball

OXFORD
UNIVERSITY PRESS

OXFORD

UNIVERSITY PRESS

Great Clarendon Street, Oxford OX2 6DP

Oxford University Press is a department of the University of Oxford.
It furthers the University's objective of excellence in research, scholarship,
and education by publishing worldwide in

Oxford New York

Auckland Cape Town Dar es Salaam Hong Kong Karachi
Kuala Lumpur Madrid Melbourne Mexico City Nairobi
New Delhi Shanghai Taipei Toronto

With offices in

Argentina Austria Brazil Chile Czech Republic France Greece
Guatemala Hungary Italy Japan Poland Portugal Singapore
South Korea Switzerland Thailand Turkey Ukraine Vietnam

Oxford is a registered trade mark of Oxford University Press
in the UK and in certain other countries

Published in the United States
by Oxford University Press Inc., New York

British Library Cataloguing in Publication Data

Data available

Library of Congress Cataloging in Publication Data

Data available

Typeset by Cepha Imaging Private Ltd, Bangalore, India
Printed in Great Britain
on acid-free paper by
CPI Antony Rowe

ISBN 978–0–19–957522–0

3 5 7 9 10 8 6 4 2

Contents—Summary

Contents

Preface

More than two decades ago, a colleague strolled into my office with a request. A client selling businesses had agreed to provide buyers with what was then called data processing for a year or two after the closing. Since I had a personal computer in my office (odd in those days) perhaps I could prepare a contract? This was my introduction to outsourcing.

Since then, outsourcing has become the bread and butter of my law practice, an important business trend and, at times, a political issue. In a 'flat' world, companies routinely entrust critical operations to outsiders, moving them outside and often offshore to Asia or Eastern Europe. Companies are transforming themselves from integrated businesses into extended enterprises with worldwide operations, outside as well as beneath the corporate umbrella, all stitched together by broadband communications and (more to our point) contracts written in English and governed by common law principles.

For the executives, managers, and lawyers asked to build, sustain, manage, and (at least occasionally) unwind these relationships, the process can be disconcerting, even bewildering; and for many directly affected or displaced, traumatic. Companies new to the game often ask their lawyers and consultants to train interested executives, managers, and lawyers. What follows has evolved, in part, from many such training sessions. The purpose is to distill fifteen years' experience into a coherent and (it is hoped) readable guide to the process, risks, contract terms, and other lore.

There are differences among outsourced functions, as among particular companies and industries. Yet common themes predominate. Good contracts define the scope of service, assure quality, and adjust scope and charges as conditions change. If things go badly wrong, remedies are essential. There are also differences in applicable law, but most outsourcing contracts are written in English under legal principles broadly familiar wherever business is conducted in English. Commercial realities are much the same everywhere.

Practicing lawyers serve clients. Although we are not reptiles (contrary to some popular impressions) we do assume the colors of our surroundings. Every client, situation, and transaction is, to some extent, unique, with particular goals, priorities, and complexities. The views expressed do not necessarily reflect those of any firm or client, and might vary in particular situations for a host of reasons.

Examples in the text are drawn from experience, but without revealing specifics. As in television or on the screen, names and other particulars have been changed (or omitted) to protect the innocent and, for that matter, the guilty.

There is a distinct, consistent point of view in favor of clarity, simplicity, and balance. Outsourcing contracts can fill large binders, but, although some complexity is unavoidable, bulk is not always necessary or desirable. In negotiation, long hours may be devoted to nuances, details, and remote contingencies for which business people have scant patience. Endless complexity may be an interesting intellectual exercise for the specialist, but is more likely to confuse than to fascinate the poor client who must later make sense of what the lawyers leave behind.

Outsourcing involves elements of other, more familiar, transactions. Yet outsourcing differs from those patterns in important respects, because of the outsourcer's unique position within and without the customer's organization and, above all, the imperatives of mutual success through collaboration. Conventional adversarial thinking (so common among lawyers) often proves counterproductive. 'Scorched earth' tactics singe both sides. Concessions may come more readily when negotiations are cordial and used as an opportunity to build working relationships rather than seek unilateral advantage. Stringent, overreaching terms—of the kind still found in too many ostensibly 'standard' forms—are rarely acceptable. Time wasted crab-walking toward sensible middle ground is expensive, not only in legal and consulting fees, but lost goodwill and distractions from more important practical issues.

For these reasons, the reader will see a clear preference for reasonably balanced terms that respect both sides' interests, permit both sides to succeed, and, in general, motivate them to preserve the business relationship for mutual benefit. This is not, of course, the only possible approach, and many respected professionals seek more stringent terms with different tactics, but observation of clients and results over the years has led this writer to believe that kinder and gentler often proves wiser.

The philosophy and other views are my own. Errors, too, are entirely my responsibility, but profuse thanks are in order to many friends and colleagues who have assisted me along the way, answering questions, pointing me to good sources, serving as sounding boards and especially reading and commenting upon the manuscript—to its benefit and mine. Several of my Baker & McKenzie colleagues have kindly found time to read and comment upon portions of the manuscript, including Tina Gavel, Peter George, Brian Hengesbaugh, Steve Holmes, Ute Krudewagen, Ross McKean, Michael Mensik, Ali Mojdehi, and Harry Small.

I have been fortunate to find many friends willing to read and comment upon the manuscript, or to advise and otherwise assist upon particular topics or points of law, including Edward Arnold, Michael Cammarota, Sameer Desai, Harry Glasspiegel, Navneet Hrishikesan, Andy Johnson, Dave Leonard, Michael Murphy, and Mark Ross. Luke Adams and Clódagh McAteer of Oxford University Press, and their predecessors, Chris Rycroft and Kirsty Allen, provided indispensable guidance and wise counsel along the way, together with liberal doses of confidence, enthusiasm and encouragement. Fiona Stables and Alison Floyd provided invaluable and expert assistance editing the text, which Wendy Telfer skilfully proofread. Special thanks go to my friend and former colleague Andrew Hooles, who started all this by suggesting that Oxford ask me to review a book proposal. Thanks are also in order to many unnamed friends with whom I have been privileged to work over the years—clients, colleagues, consultants, professional peers, and business people on all sides—from whom I have learned much. To anyone inadvertently overlooked in these acknowledgements go my regrets as well as my thanks.

My wife Diana tolerated nights and weekends devoted to the book with remarkable equanimity, then volunteered to proofread the manuscript—once more saving her husband from the error of his ways. Our daughters, Katie, Kelley, and Susan, have wisely eschewed the law, but offered unstinting moral support.

George Kimball
June 2009
Seal Beach, California

Abbreviations

AAA	American Arbitration Association
ADM	applications development and maintenance
ARC	additional resource charge—the incremental charge for additional chargeable resources (for example so many dollars for each additional network connection, help desk call, or gigabyte of storage)
BPO	business process outsourcing—the outsourcing of HR, purchasing, logistics, or other functions (excluding IT)
COLA	cost-of-living adjustment
F&A	Finance and accounting
FFIEC	Federal Financial Institutions Examination Council (US)
FINRA	Finance Industry Regulatory Authority (US)
FSA	Financial Services Authority (UK)
FTC	Federal Trade Commission (US)
FTE	full-time equivalent
GST	goods and service tax
HIPAA	Health Insurance Portability and Accountability Act of 1996 (US), Pub L No 104-191, 110 Stat 1936 (1996)
HRO	human resources outsourcing—the outsourcing of payroll, benefits administration, and a wide variety of other HR functions
ICC	International Chamber of Commerce
ITO	information technology outsourcing—the outsourcing of data centers, networks, help desks, PC support, software development and maintenance, and other IT operations. Sometimes the term refers to the outsourcing of IT infrastructure, as opposed to applications maintenance and development (ADM)
KPI	key performance indicator
LPO	legal process outsourcing
MACs	moves, adds, and changes
MiFID	Refers to two directives concerning markets in financial instruments, Directive (EC) 2004/39 and Directive (EC) 2006/73
RFP	request for proposals

RRC   Reduced resource credit—the incremental credit received by
             the customer for reduced consumption of chargeable resources
             (for example so many dollars for each server or PC withdrawn from
             service)
SEC   Securities and Exchange Commission (US)
UNCITRAL   United Nations Commission on International Trade Law
WARN Act   Worker Adjustment and Retraining Notification Act of 1988 (US),
             Pub L 100-379, 102 Stat 890 (1988), 29 USC §§ 2101 *et seq*

Glossary

Outsourcing has its own peculiar jargon. Here are a few terms in common use.

Additional Resource Charge (ARC)	The incremental charge for additional chargeable resources (for example, so many dollars for each additional network connection, help desk call or gigabyte of storage).
Annual service charge	This means just what it says, but may be a fixed fee (divisible by twelve to compute monthly charges) or (more often) an estimate derived from baseline consumption, and likely to be adjusted up or down as the year progresses, based upon actual consumption or agreed changes. The most common adjustments are ARCs and RRCs.
Applications Development and Maintenance (ADM)	Outsourced software development and maintenance services, often performed in India or other offshore destinations.
Base case	Budget for outsourced activities, derived from the customer's historic cost data.
Baseline	Estimated consumption, usually based upon recent, current, or anticipated consumption, and often used as the touchstone for base charges and adjustments.
Benchmarking	The independent assessment of quality and cost against current market standards, generally performed by an independent firm.
Best of breed	This catch-phrase refers to the selective outsourcing of various functions among several service providers (as opposed to outsourcing to a single prime contractor).
Business Process Outsourcing (BPO)	The outsourcing of HR, purchasing, logistics or other functions (excluding IT).

Change control	(or 'change management') disciplined, written process for proposing or requesting, reviewing, and then authorizing changes. Often these processes involve the preparation of a proposal or change request, and then approval of a change order. Sometimes, contracts classify various kinds of changes, such as technical or operational changes, as opposed to contract changes.
Dead band	A narrow band on either side of the baseline, within which charges are fixed.[1]
Disaster and disaster recovery	Fires, hurricanes, earthquakes, and other similar events that may destroy facilities and otherwise disrupt or interrupt the performance of services. Sophisticated customers and suppliers have elaborate plans to restore services, or at least critical services, promptly following a disaster, often from a remote facility. These plans should be kept up-to-date, tested periodically, and coordinated with overall business continuity plans to carry on the customer's business.
Earn-back	Recovery or reversal of service credits, usually based upon sustained satisfactory or superior performance following a failure.
Key Performance Indicator (KPI)	Measure of service quality that is measured and reported at regular intervals, but generally without exposing the supplier to liability for service credits in the event of unexcused failures to meet desired levels.

---

[1] eg if a customer agrees to pay (i) US$100 per month for baseline consumption of 100 units, with (ii) incremental charges (ARCs) and credits (RRCs) of $1 per unit, and (iii) a two per cent (2%) 'dead band,' then the customer would pay $100 per month whenever consumption fell between 98 and 102 units. Outside those limits, ARCs and RRCs would apply. They could be added or deducted from the outer limits of the 'dead band', so that the 103rd unit raises the monthly charge to $101 ($100+$1), or 97 units cost $99 ($100–$1). Alternatively, they could be added to or deducted from the 100 unit baseline, so that 105 units would cost $105 and 95 units would cost $95.

Legal Process Outsourcing (LPO)	Outsourcing of legal support services of various kinds, such as document review, patent searches, and legal research, among others.
Most-favored customer	Charges and other terms at least as favorable as the supplier offers to any other customer for the similar volumes of the same or similar services.
Moves, Adds and Changes (MACs)	Installations, relocation, removal or modification of computers and other devices, individually or in groups, usually by dispatching technicians ('physical MACs') although some software upgrades and modifications may be installed remotely ('logical MACs').
Near-shore	The performance of services in neighboring countries. For US companies, this usually means Canada or Mexico, rather than, say, India. For Western European companies, this may mean an Eastern European country.
Offshore	The performance of services in remote countries, oceans apart from the customer's operations.
Project	Discrete, non-recurring tasks or other services that are in addition to the normal performance necessary to meet service levels. Generally, projects are separately authorized and may be separately managed.
Reduced Resource Credits (RRC)	The incremental credit received by the customer for reduced consumption of chargeable resources (for example, so many dollars for each server or PC withdrawn from service).
Refresh	Periodic replacements of hardware or software. Software is often required to be kept on current, or near-current releases.
Schedule	A common term for exhibits, attachments, and other documents related to an outsourcing contract that may be incorporated by reference and form part of the larger agreement. The most important describe the scope of service

	('statement of work' or 'service description'), service levels and credits, and the computation of charges. Other examples may include a transition plan; lists of assets, personnel, ongoing projects, approved subcontractors, and locations; security policies; disaster recovery requirements; financial or performance guarantees (for example from a supplier's parent company); and contract documents for related transactions (for example contracts, bills of sale, and the like for purchases of facilities and assets, or assignments of third party contracts transferred to the supplier).
Service credit	An amount payable by the service provider for unexcused failures to meet service levels. Business people commonly refer to these as 'penalties,' but, technically, they should be characterized as 'liquidated damages' or reductions in charges, rather than penalties (since the law generally declines to enforce penalties).
Service levels	Objective performance standards that suppliers measure and report periodically, and for which they may pay service credits in the event of unexcused failures. Typical examples include response times, availability of systems (measured as a percentage of scheduled availability), and mean times to respond to or resolve incidents.[2]
Termination assistance	Support provided by an incumbent supplier to effect a smooth transition (or 'reverse transition') when an outsourcing contract expires or terminates for any reason.
Tower	A common description for large categories of service (such as data center operations, help

[2] Service levels are sometimes referred to as 'service level agreements,' a term that originally referred to performance commitments of corporate IT departments. Specific service levels are not, strictly speaking, agreements, but performance commitments; and the tables and metrics attached to outsourcing contracts are not separate contracts. The term nevertheless persists, and both suppliers and users commonly refer to 'service level agreements' and 'SLAs.'

desks, or software maintenance). In large relationships, these may be documented and to some extent administered separately. This author prefers more descriptive terms, such as 'service category.'

Transition

The process of transferring operations from the customer to a supplier during the first few months after a contract is signed. This may involve on-site or remote management of the customer's operation ('facilities management'); the relocation of operations to the supplier's site ('lift and shift'); or the transformation of operations to a wholly-new model (such as the replacement of conventional procurement forms and processes with web-based catalogs and automated processes). Transformation generally involves the relocation of some or all operations to the supplier's facilities. Contract documents commonly include a transition plan.

1

WHAT'S IT ALL ABOUT?

1.1 GENESIS AND EVOLUTION

Outsourcing began more than forty-five years ago with a shrewd, ambitious Texan, Ross Perot. Then an IBM salesman, Perot proposed to operate, rather than merely equip, customer data centers. When IBM demurred, Perot left to found EDS and make his name and fortune. Perot's essential insight was to offer technology as a service.

Perot's success inspired imitators and competitors. Since those early days, outsourcing's reach has extended from the operation of data centers to include a wide array of service offerings in HR, procurement, logistics, finance and accounting, and other spheres. The 1990s brought the so-called 'mega-deal'— very large scale contracts to provide comprehensive IT services for such companies as Kodak, Xerox, and, eventually, many others. The century's end brought fears about the year 2000 and millennium bug; extensive, efficient and successful corrective work performed in India and elsewhere; and Exult's pioneering contract to deliver HR services to British Petroleum. Thus began 'business process outsourcing' (BPO) and the stampede offshore. Although outsourcing has moved beyond IT operations to embrace all manner of back-office and support operations, most solutions offered in the marketplace are still built around technology—some combination of computers, software, networks, and skills that offer customers better service at lower cost than the customers' own internal operations. Outsourced services are, in the dreadful jargon, 'IT-enabled.'

1.2 WHAT IS IT, EXACTLY?

Outsourcing may be defined as a long-term collaborative relationship that entrusts business functions or processes to a contractor (the supplier) through a long-term service contract.[1] Rather than operate their own data centers, networks, or various back-office functions, companies engage a supplier to do so. The supplier largely displaces former internal capabilities. Outsourced operations are extensions of the customer's business. The business relationship between customer and supplier, though not the legal structure, resembles a partnership or joint venture: prolonged, inter-dependent, and (it is hoped) cooperative and mutually beneficial.

Outsourced operations often go offshore, but should be distinguished from 'captive' offshore operations. Captives may be subsidiaries, affiliates, joint ventures, or 'build-operate-transfer' arrangements with offshore companies which set up operations in faraway places for later transfer to the customer. Captive operations, such as shared-service centers, offer many of the attractions of outsourcing (notably, access to lower cost talent) but the legal structure is quite different. In pure captives, the user is a parent company able to exercise complete control and willing to assume all of the costs, risks, and responsibilities associated with building, managing and supporting an offshore business.

Outsourcing is something else—a contractual and business relationship between unrelated companies from which both expect to profit. The legal foundation is a service contract—an outsourcing agreement—committing the supplier to deliver specific services and meet various quality standards for a price over a term of several years or more. Outsourcing agreements generally consist of an umbrella or master service agreement, supplemented by contract documents that describe the scope of service, performance standards, charges, and other particulars. Services may be performed in the customer's homeland ('onshore'); in a neighboring country ('near-shore') such as Canada, Mexico, or Costa Rica for US companies (or Poland for Western European companies); or in such remote ('offshore') destinations as India or the Philippines. Equity relationships (though not unheard of) are comparatively rare. The agreements—their making, contents, and management—are our focus.

---

[1] Thanks for this apt, succinct definition—outsourcing as long-term collaboration between organizations—go to the author's good friend and former partner, Ira Moskatel.

1.3 WHAT'S REALLY GOING ON?

Outsourcing and offshore captives are part of a trend toward disaggregated operations, made possible by broadband technology and global markets—now largely freed from exchange controls, state planning, and other artificial constraints. These conditions have given relatively free rein to the law of comparative advantage. Companies may obtain services worldwide, just as manufacturers obtain parts and fabricate products through worldwide networks of affiliates and suppliers. The typical personal computer may sport a familiar label, but inside are Intel or AMD microprocessors (made in the US), with disc drives, screens, and components from several Asian countries, and assembled in China, Mexico, or the Philippines. In much the same way, a company's support functions may now involve a domestic data center, monitored from Asia or Latin America, with orders taken by an Indian call center and fulfilled by a domestic contractor who delivers products to customers. Outsourcing contracts tie these relationships together.

Outsourcing is part of a larger paradigm shift in the economy. Early industrial barons built integrated businesses. John D Rockefeller's Standard Oil drilled for, extracted, and refined petroleum, then distributed kerosene. Standard Oil controlled virtually every link in the supply chain, from the wellhead to the customer's lamp. Henry Ford's River Rouge factory—a marvel of the early twentieth century—received shiploads of coal and iron; made its own coke, electricity, and steel; fabricated parts; then built and shipped new Fords to dealers. As Ford explained to one of his executives, he 'wanted raw material coming in on one end of the Rouge plant and the finished cars going out on the other end.'[2] Coal and iron ore came from Ford's own mines, transported on Ford ships or trains. Ford's methods assured consistent quality, efficiency, and, above all, economies of scale. His cheap, sturdy, reliable car put the world on wheels.

Eighty years later, in a borderless information economy, companies are reversing this process, for both manufacturing and services, in the never-ending pursuit of efficiency and lower cost. The emerging paradigm is something quite different from Detroit in its heyday: extended, global enterprises, with (i) scattered, worldwide operations; (ii) networks of subsidiaries, suppliers, and outsourced operations; (iii) all stitched together by broadband communications, data systems, and contracts.

---

[2] D Brinkley, *Wheels for the World* (New York: Viking, 2003) 293.

1.4 ESSENTIAL ELEMENTS

This book focuses upon the contracts, and issues and risks common to all outsourcing. Much may vary depending upon the location, governing law, particular service, and other specifics. Data center operations differ from applications support; call centers from integrated HR, logistics, or procurement services.[3] Yet there are many common themes: defining and managing the scope or service; establishing and enforcing appropriate performance standards; measurement of and payment for service; governance amid continual change; assuring legal compliance; provision for various unpleasant contingencies, and remedies, among others. Whatever the function or service, essential issues common to virtually all outsourcing include the following:

- *Scope.* Precisely what will the supplier do for the agreed price? What responsibilities will the customer retain? What dependencies exist between supplier and customer, or with third parties? Clarity and precision are great virtues in service descriptions.
- *Cost.* What must the customer pay for basic service, changes, and new services? How are charges adjusted for changes in consumption, technology, or laws and regulations? Can charges be kept in alignment with market rates for the customer's protection, yet assure the supplier an adequate margin? Are there other costs, apart from the supplier's monthly charges? Good pricing metrics are adaptable to changing requirements and conditions in order to keep supplier costs, customer charges and volumes of service in reasonable harmony as conditions change.
- *Performance standards.* How well must the supplier perform? How is performance measured and reported? Outsourcing contracts commonly include objective measurement criteria or service levels. Unexcused failures to meet those service levels may have financial consequences (which business people call 'penalties,' despite their lawyers' preference for such terms as 'credits,' 'fee reductions' or 'liquidated damages').[4] Service levels measure specific activities. Where they do not apply, more general quality commitments may apply—for example, to meet good industry standards (whatever they may be).

---

[3] See Ch 14 below, for a discussion of salient differences among the various varieties.

[4] In most common law jurisdictions, case law or statutes preclude recovery of 'penalties,' but respect provisions for payment of reasonable 'liquidated damages' or price reductions for inferior quality service.

- *Intellectual property.* In a knowledge economy, this matters more than ever before. Many outsourced services involve software or other intellectual property of critical importance to both sides. Service may include the development of new or improved solutions which either or both parties may wish to use, exploit, or further refine, even after their relationship ends. Customers prefer to own whatever new wrinkles may be developed; suppliers want to provide similar solutions and service to other customers. Many business process services use proprietary systems that suppliers wish to protect from the prying eyes of competitors—yet they must allow customers to carry on after the contract expires, even if customers engage competing suppliers.
- *Governance.* Operations, scope, and the parties' relationship must be managed amid changing business conditions, commercial requirements, technology, and legal constraints. This requires formal processes, effective communication, and constructive working relationships. Typically, large contracts call for executive sponsors on both sides, a joint management committee, and account or project managers on both sides, with supporting casts, regular meetings, and disciplined (meaning written) change management procedures. Outsourcing relationships are not partnerships, but, in some respects, governance may resemble a joint venture. Outsourcing's essence is long-term collaboration between organizations.
- *Compliance.* In a world of changing, increasingly stringent regulation, where outsourcing may be controversial and attract public and official attention, bland commitments to comply with applicable laws rarely suffice. Everyone must obey the law, but laws and regulations are complicated and subject to change. Such matters as taxation, employment, audit, and protection of employee and customer data (among others) may require detailed provisions, including adjustments to scope and charges as requirements evolve. Regulatory issues vary among industries, but there are common concerns, notably the privacy of personal data. Regulatory responsibilities cannot be delegated (although some costs and risks may be apportioned) and regulatory changes must be accommodated, financially and operationally. When laws change, services, and perhaps charges for those services, may also have to change.
- *Remedies.* What recourse exists in case of difficulty? Outsourcing contracts commonly provide a familiar armory, including representations, warranties, indemnities, audit rights, withholding, set-off, termination, and legal proceedings or arbitration. These address various 'worst cases'—remote, but dire, contingencies for which good contracts must provide, subject in most cases to some intensely negotiated limitations upon the parties' liability. Customers can usually terminate for poor performance or, without cause, for

what is euphemistically called 'convenience' (which generally costs money, in the form of a termination charge). Suppliers' termination rights are often limited to non-payment and other specific situations, so that suppliers cannot credibly threaten to shut down the customer's business. So long as bills are paid, the supplier must carry on. Whatever the situation, termination is a drastic, disruptive, costly exercise—a bit like parachuting from an aircraft: disorienting, hazardous, and not for the faint-hearted, but sometimes necessary and certainly preferable to a crash landing.

• *Transition and disengagement.* Good contracts provide for orderly transitions, including transfers of knowledge, data, intellectual property, and (sometimes) employees, as well as the testing and execution of elaborate plans to relocate operations, without interrupting or disrupting the customer's business. Transferring operations is a complicated exercise that requires good planning, testing, and collaboration, especially if some or all operations move offshore. Good contracts make similar provisions for disengagement (or 'reverse transition') when the contract expires or terminates. Transition to another outside supplier may be easier than reconstituting internal organizations and capabilities, but both are possible. Incumbent suppliers have every reason to cooperate in an orderly transition, whatever the circumstances, for doing otherwise would tarnish their reputations.

1.5 COMPETING AND COMPLEMENTARY GOALS

What are the parties trying to accomplish?

1.5.1 Customer goals

Companies outsource for many reasons, or so they say. Saving money is by far the most important. Other reasons may also matter. Outsourcing may expedite business transformations, introduce new technology, improve service, free management to focus attention upon fundamentals (the so-called 'core competencies'), and transform fixed investments into variable costs, whose consumption can be monitored and managed. Entrusting important functions to an outside supplier may allow the customer to shed assets, avoid ongoing capital expenditures, and manage costs more effectively, especially if charges are tied to consumption and passed through to business units. A supplier whose core competence is technology, HR, or logistics can help the customer to devote more of its scarce capital, energy, and management attention to its own products and customers. Capable outside suppliers may be qualitatively superior to internal operations (although bid documents and contract recitals rarely phrase this goal quite so frankly).

These are worthy goals, but costs are the proverbial elephant in the room. Rarely, one may be sure, do companies outsource without some prospect for savings. Outsourcing initiatives go nowhere without blessings from keepers of the corporate purse. Competitive and other pressures compel them to scrub operations for potential savings. Outsourcing is a proven way to squeeze costs out of support operations that do not produce products, serve customers, or generate revenue. For the customer, outsourcing is almost always about saving money. Outsourcing saves money in several ways.

- Outsourced solutions should be cheaper, because of the supplier's efficiencies, methods, economies of scale, and offshore operations.
- Charges can be passed through to business units, motivating users to conserve. Outsourced functions are no longer invisible overhead like running water for which no invoice or budget line ever appears. The psychology is primitive, but effective.
- Outsourcing transforms some fixed costs into variable charges that fluctuate with consumption, so that customers need not invest in or shed capacity on account of mergers, acquisitions, or changes in market conditions. Instead, the supplier must provide as much or as little as the customer needs, with rates that reflect changing marginal costs.

Outsourcing is not alchemy. Suppliers also have staff to pay, investments to make in hardware, software and facilities, overhead, and (they hope) margins. If a customer's internal operations are efficient and up-to-date, potential savings from outsourcing may be modest, even negligible. In the mature IT business, as internal operations have improved and technology has shifted away from mainframe data centers (which may offer substantial economies of scale), cost advantages from outsourcing seem to have eroded. The low-hanging fruit has already been harvested. On the other hand, there may be large savings when such labor-intensive functions as software development or maintenance go offshore, where prevailing salaries are much lower than in the US or Western Europe (although that gap has narrowed with time). For similar reasons, HR operations or procurement based upon online internet systems and offshore call centers may offer large savings over conventional paper processes and on-site staffs.

1.5.2 Supplier goals

Suppliers, like customers, are commercial enterprises, in business to make money for their shareholders. How exactly can suppliers both deliver savings to customers and make money? They must do the work better, faster, and cheaper, and recoup marketing and transition costs, plus any investment in assets, through an enduring business relationship. Bid, proposal, and transition costs may mean little or no margin for a year or more after signing. Over the life of the contract, as suppliers wring costs from operations with better technology, processes, and other efficiencies, they hope that margins will grow—especially if the customer buys additional higher-margin services, such as consulting services or development projects. The suppliers' own economics depend upon standardization, economies of scale, and, increasingly, the ability to shift operations to countries where labor costs less. Scale, efficiency, consistency, and labor arbitrage are the keys to their success. So are satisfied customers, who may expand or renew existing contracts, and provide favorable references to potential customers. The suppliers' cost models, operations, and technical solutions may be complex, but the essentials are straightforward.

1.6 OUTSOURCING IS DIFFERENT

Contracts allocate risks. Contract negotiation largely consists of allocating risks. Zealous lawyers usually attempt to shift as much risk as possible to the adversary, while minimizing their own client's exposure. This is hardly surprising, but in outsourcing, as the parties begin a prolonged, intimate (or at least entangled) business relationship, other considerations come into play.

Equity and balance matter. People are more likely to accept, and live with, allocations of risk that they regard as essentially fair and for which they bargained. Even relatively unpalatable results may be tolerable if they approximate an equitable division of responsibilities or represent honest compromises with benefits for both sides. The customer may dislike an expensive change order, yet approve it if the additional work falls outside the scope that was understood, documented, bargained for, and priced. Conversely, a supplier may be willing (as well as obliged) to perform more work without additional charge, if the work falls within agreed scope that was understood, bargained for, and priced. Attitudes and relationships are entirely different if one party is obliged to bear liability disproportionate to its actual responsibility, or trapped by unfavorable terms as a result of bullying, sharp tactics, or the exercise of unusual (often transitory) leverage.

In outsourcing, 'closing' (formal signing of contract documents) is a misnomer. The closing is just the beginning. When real estate is sold, the deal is complete when papers are signed, the deed is recorded, and funds are released. The parties rarely contemplate further dealings. They hope that any surviving obligations (indemnities, for instance) will lapse uneventfully. When goods and commodities are purchased, the relationship ends with payment, delivery, and perhaps expiration of a warranty. With outsourcing, signing begins a collaborative relationship meant to last years. The customer expects good service for a fair price, and cannot quickly or easily reverse its decision to outsource. The supplier expects to deliver service profitably. In practice, neither will succeed unless both succeed. Unhappy customers rarely renew contracts and make poor references. Suppliers with minuscule margins are tempted to cut corners, work to the letter of the contract, and bombard the customer with change requests. These outcomes are recipes for trouble. Lopsided contracts usually come to grief. Ultimately, the relationship matters as much as the contract; and each should reinforce the other. The contract should motivate both parties to perform even (or perhaps especially) when things go awry (as they are bound to, at least occasionally). Zero-sum thinking and adversarial tactics are almost always counterproductive, during contract negotiations and afterwards. This is not to say that outsourcing is a kind of love feast or New Age happening, where contentious issues disappear amid radiant goodwill and fellowship. Not at all—these are unsentimental commercial transactions, largely propelled by self-interest. But enlightened self-interest recognizes the importance of mutual success and, as always, fair play is good business.

Lawyers schooled in the adversary process should sometimes remind themselves that contracts are not bundles of remedies—armories, in effect—that work because of the risk (or threat) of such consequences as termination, legal proceedings, and awards of damages. Legal remedies matter, of course, and have their uses when things go badly wrong; but they are remote contingencies, unlikely to be exercised except as a last resort. Fear alone cannot motivate excellence. In reality, companies perform contracts for the same reason that nations observe treaties—not simply for fear of hostilities, but because it is in their interests to perform. The goal in negotiations, therefore, is not simply to provide adequately for the 'worst cases'—such as non-payment, non-performance, termination, or other calamities—but to achieve a kind of equilibrium, by allocating risks in ways that motivate both parties to perform, do the right thing, and sustain the business relationship.

2

MAKING THE DEAL

Outsourcing major operations may take a year or more, from start to finish. Companies must decide whether and what to outsource, select a supplier, and negotiate complex agreements spelling out the scope of service, performance standards, charges, and countless other terms and conditions—all the while preparing for the transition to outsourced operations. In its complexity, the process resembles a merger or divestiture, where preparations for separation or assimilation proceed in parallel with the dealmakers' minuet.

How deals are made may affect results. Outsourcing is as likely to go wrong (or at least disappoint) from errors at inception, as from errors in execution. All participants must balance the desire to expedite completion against the hazards of haste. Customers are anxious for promised benefits. Suppliers await revenues that can only begin after signing. People are anxious to return to their 'day jobs' or move on to new responsibilities or the next deal or project. No one wants to carry on paying lawyers and consultants any longer than necessary. Yet genius largely consists of an infinite capacity to take pains, and effective orchestration of the entire process, including some of the subtler details, helps to assure good outcomes. Errors have long lives, and customers' leverage diminishes after the contract is signed, the supplier takes charge of operations, and the customer's advisors go home.

Tone also matters, during negotiations and afterward. In the long run, trust and civility usually trump belligerence; and, in outsourcing, signing marks commencement rather than completion. So the process, despite its inevitable pressures and tension, should be harnessed constructively, to build and reinforce working relationships for the long term.

2.1 CONTRASTS WITH OTHER TRANSACTIONS

Outsourcing contracts commonly consist of a services agreement, supplemented by documents that describe the services, service level commitments, charges, transitional arrangements, and other particulars. When operations are global, there may be 'companion' agreements for particular countries or regions, in order to accommodate legal, operational, and cultural differences; facilitate effective tax planning; and effect transfers of employees and assets. The bulk and complexity of the documentation, and many contract terms, resemble those in mergers, acquisitions, joint ventures, or other complex transactions. However, important differences between outsourcing and other transactions affect not only the substantive terms, but also the negotiating process. Facile analogies to other kinds of transactions and relationships may easily mislead. Outsourcing agreements are not partnerships, joint ventures, mergers, or acquisitions. Differences in custom, practice, and documentation reflect commercial realities and accumulated experience.

First, negotiation lays the foundation for enduring business relationships. Scorched earth tactics and gamesmanship can poison those relationships and are best avoided. The relationship is fundamental. So is the deal—the essential business understanding or rationale for the transaction. Both the relationship and the deal are at least as important as the contract. All three—relationship, deal, and contract—matter and must be aligned; but the relationship is indispensable, perhaps paramount, especially when one considers that initial baselines, historic data, and forecasts are imperfect and that governance involves ongoing negotiation of innumerable details.

Second, the customer's leverage erodes after selection of a supplier. Suppliers may not feel obliged to offer further concessions after their competitors go home. Many affected staff may see their futures elsewhere, perhaps with the chosen supplier. This naturally affects attitudes, loyalty, and behavior. Some may jump ship, leaving the customer short-handed and, in extreme cases, unable easily to carry on independently if negotiations should falter. The process acquires momentum and becomes difficult for a customer to reverse. Well-advised customers therefore attempt to button down key terms early through a detailed letter of intent, term sheet, or other similar document that—even if not legally binding—effectively commits the supplier to price, scope, service levels, and other key terms.

Third, although outsourcing is not irreversible, it is difficult and expensive to unwind, either by bringing operations back in-house or shifting to another supplier. However robust the contractual remedies, however serious any difficulties may be, few companies can stomach the prospect of starting afresh (and, at least implicitly, admitting failure). Termination is a kind of tactical nuclear weapon, likely to scorch both sides.

2.2 THE PLAYERS

For major transactions, both sides assemble large teams. Their makeup varies somewhat from one supplier to the next, and among customers, depending upon the organization and outsourced functions; but in large transactions, the allocation of responsibilities often approximates the following:

2.2.1 Supplier teams

Supplier teams are usually led by sales executives who serve as the customer's primary point of contact and must account for substantial bid and proposal costs if the pursuit proves unsuccessful. Their supporting cast includes: (i) a proposal manager; (ii) a financial analyst; (iii) a solution architect; (iv) subject matter or operational experts to conduct investigations (with 'due diligence') and prepare proposals; and (v) a lead negotiator, who may or may not be a lawyer, but if not, is supported by a lawyer.[1] Their responsibilities break down as follows:

- *Lead negotiators* enter the fray as emphasis shifts from sales to negotiation. Suppliers recognize that sales and negotiation are complementary, but different,

---

[1] Business people on both sides sometimes imagine that they help themselves by 'keeping the lawyers out of the room.' Cost considerations naturally and appropriately constrain use of counsel; but (unless the lawyers are antagonistic) judicious use of counsel throughout negotiations can expedite a satisfactory conclusion by, among other things, eliminating any risk of re-negotiation when, eventually, the documents receive legal review. Experienced counsel help suppliers to be responsive, and customers to understand what is required for both sides to succeed. Customers are usually wise to require suppliers to bring their counsel to the principal meetings, or else risk having settled points reopened during later, inevitable legal review.

skills, and have learned from experience that sales executives are at least occasionally overcome by the scent of sales commissions and may not say 'no' when perhaps they should.

- *Proposal managers* are the chief lieutenants for both sales executives and lead negotiators, orchestrating and overseeing the seemingly infinite number of documents and details that go into a proposal. While sales executives sell and negotiators negotiate, the proposal manager oversees everything and everyone else, chasing each and every figure and bit of paper. If the sales executive or lead negotiator are captains of the ship, the proposal manager is the executive officer, who watches the bridge, engine room, and everything below decks. Good proposal managers obsess about details and may be insomniac (or at least heavily caffeinated).

- *Financial analysts* are keepers of the cost models used to develop pricing, and metrics to adjust prices as consumption and other circumstances evolve and emerge over the life of the relationship. They must balance the sales team's desires to meet the competition, win the business and please the customer with management's insistence upon adequate margins. In this respect they must, like the supplier's lawyer, act as a kind of friendly policeman—cordial and responsive to the customer, while protecting their own company's economic interests.[2]

- The *solution architect*, with a supporting cast of subject matter experts, determines precisely how the supplier will fulfill the customer's requirements. In outsourcing, 'solution' refers to the particular combination of facilities, technologies, staff, and other resources offered up to meet customer requirements. Solution architects map those requirements against the supplier's capabilities, seeking a combination that will meet the competition, satisfy the customer, and yield acceptable returns.

Finally, wise customers insist that the supplier's team include (at least after a preliminary selection) the proposed account executive and delivery manager. Nomenclature varies from one supplier to the next, but these are the people who take charge after signing, manage the relationship, and oversee actual delivery of service, at least for the first year or two. There are few better ways to evaluate the most important members of the proposed delivery team than bringing them to the negotiating table. Customers want to size up the account executive and

---

[2] One of the author's favorite clients used to refer to the financial experts, with respect and affection, as the 'inter-galactic financial police.' The witticism contained a germ of truth.

delivery manager for the same reason that companies retaining counsel for litigation insist on meeting the trial team. Bringing the people responsible for performance into the room may also reduce any temptation the supplier's sales team might otherwise feel to propose 'whatever it takes.' The account team must answer to the customer for performance and to their own management for profitability. They are unlikely to promise more than they can deliver.

Suppliers have sophisticated policies and procedures to evaluate opportunities, review proposals, and adjust pricing and other commitments as negotiations proceed. Usually, a senior executive oversees the entire effort and is consulted about key decisions. Significant deviations from supplier policies may require executive approvals, and decision makers seek consensus among sales, delivery, and other responsible business units within the supplier's organization. Complex cost models are used first to generate and then to refine or adjust pricing proposals. When customers require substantial investments in transition or infrastructure, impose unusual risks, or insist upon stringent service levels, there are corresponding increases in contingency allowances, amortization, and charges.

2.2.2 Customer teams

The makeup of the customer's team will vary from one company and situation to the next, but commonly includes: (i) a designated leader who reports to responsible executives, (ii) subject matter experts, (iii) business unit representatives, (iv) someone from purchasing, and (v) members of the team designated to manage the relationship after signing. These are the people who will live with the deal and the supplier's account team. The sooner they get acquainted and begin to work together, the better. Many customers overlook or underrate the importance of relationship management, and do not build a team with sufficient resources or appropriate skills. Managing a contract is not the same as managing operations—just as managing a construction contractor is not the same as erecting a building. When contracts go wrong, or fall short of expectations, poor relationship management is often to blame. Customer management should therefore begin to identify and build the right team as soon as they decide to outsource.

Customers and suppliers rely on supporting casts. For the customer, these often include outside consultants and legal counsel (who participate in negotiations) and (behind the scenes) executive sponsors and an array of supporting functions, such as audit, HR (to deal with employees displaced or transferred), regulatory compliance, and IT (even when other functions are outsourced, because most outsourced solutions depend upon networks, software, and other technology).

Outsourcing initiatives almost invariably involve one or more experts from the customer's purchasing department, but all concerned should bear in mind important differences between outsourcing relationships and procurement of commodity products and services. To begin with, IT services, web-enabled business processes, and other 'staples' of large scale outsourcing are not, strictly speaking, commodities. They involve combinations of rapidly-changing, sometimes unstable technologies, supported by large numbers of skilled personnel. The solutions offered may vary substantially from supplier to supplier, from one deal to the next, and evolve over the life of the relationship. They are changeable, and may not be completely interchangeable. Sometimes, key elements are under development when contracts are written. Disengagement is complicated and time-consuming. Sophisticated IT and business process services therefore differ fundamentally from such commodity services as laundry, catering, or utility service, let alone such commodity products as office supplies. Terms, forms, and processes developed for bulk purchases of standard, interchangeable products at the lowest possible cost are not necessarily useful or effective for sophisticated outsourced services. Price alone, though crucial, is rarely all-important. Lowest price may not equate with best value, or even lowest total cost.

Responsible executives should oversee the process and participate in major decisions. IT outsourcing inevitably involves the chief financial officer and chief information officer. Business process outsourcing initiatives in such realms as HR or procurement often involve wider constituencies, including heads of relevant functions or business units, as well as IT, HR, and finance. The process of assessment, preparation, selection, and negotiation affords the customer a unique opportunity to involve all affected business units and functions, and build a strong consensus behind the outsourcing initiative. There are challenges enough when all sing from the same hymnal. When headquarters, business units, and others pursue separate agendas or are not consulted, failure is likely.

Supporting the effort are the company's legal counsel and, in many transactions, outside consultants to assist with assessments, solicitation and evaluation of proposals, and ultimate negotiation of a contract. When outside lawyers are engaged (usually for similar reasons), the team should (indeed, must, if at all possible) include an inside lawyer, who knows the customer's business better than any outsider and can become prepared to support the relationship on a regular basis after signing.

2.3 HIRED HELP—CONSULTANTS AND LAWYERS

Companies that have not outsourced extensively often engage outside advisors: consultants and lawyers who do this for a living, know the suppliers, market trends, and other 'lore' and are thus able both to educate the customer's team and help assure a level playing field when dealing with experienced supplier teams. Suppliers regularly see the same advisors, and have good reasons—win or lose—to maintain good relations with those they call 'intermediaries.'

2.3.1 Sourcing consultants

In the beginning, Ross Perot and the other pioneers had more or less free rein, but advisors to customers—outside lawyers and consultants—soon introduced competitive bidding, a process familiar in public contracts, construction, and other very large scale procurements. Customers arrived at the negotiating table with sophisticated outside business and legal advice. Lawyers and consultants play complementary roles that may to some extent overlap—there being no bright demarcation line between business and legal issues—but broadly speaking, consultants advise upon operational and business issues, including the selection process, while the lawyers focus upon the contract documents, legal compliance, and other legal and contractual issues. Specialist consultancies have grown up that focus largely or even exclusively upon outsourcing (although some of those specialists reside within broader gauge consulting firms). Their working professionals include veterans of the big technology consultancies, major outsourcers, and corporate IT or other departments that have outsourced. The best consultants offer a valuable combination of market knowledge, strategic insight, practical experience, and good judgment.

Methods vary from one consulting firm to the next (although less than the variety of labels might lead a casual reader to suppose) and typically involve: (i) an initial assessment of the client's operations and requirements; (ii) development from that assessment and historic data of a 'base case' financial model; (iii) processes to decide what (if anything) to outsource; (iv) preparation of a request for proposals (RFP); (v) solicitation and evaluation of proposals; and, after (vi) selection (often referred to as 'down-select'); (vii) the negotiation of contract documents with one, and possibly two, finalists. Throughout, advisors help customers' management and deal teams to understand the process, the suppliers' business, the risks, and effective ways to contain and manage those risks.

The advisors' methods have had important consequences—intended and unintended—for individual customers, and for outsourcing generally. Advisors and their methods have altered the landscape, educating customers, securing more favorable terms, and building the basis for durable relationships on foundations of thorough preparation and realistic expectations. Many contract terms that are now widely accepted—concerning pricing, benchmarking, service levels, liability limits, and other important and often contentious terms—reflect a kind of marketplace consensus that owes much to the advisors' creativity and the leverage their clients possess when dangling large opportunities before eager sales teams. Without doubt, contract terms have shifted in the customers' favor during the past fifteen or more years, thanks in part to the customers' consultants and lawyers.

Companies even considering outsourcing, especially for the first time, are well advised to seek experienced consultants who know the market, and are known to the market. Good consultants do not come cheap, but pay for themselves several times over in lower prices, more favorable terms, and expensive mistakes avoided. Suppliers prefer sole source opportunities (without annoying experts poking at their proposals, or pesky competitors) but respect the consultants and (at least privately) their contribution to the process. Suppliers understand that consultants cost money, so their engagement indicates that the customer is serious and not 'just browsing.' Consultants speak their language, use familiar processes, and help to assure that the process is conducted impartially, with adequate factual foundations and other preparation. Consultants and the suppliers' sales executives inhabit the same professional world, attend the same conferences, and often cross paths fairly regularly. These relationships are useful lubricants in negotiations, and can help to attract qualified bidders, who have their own internal processes to qualify and select opportunities to spend scarce bid and proposal budgets. Suppliers value their relationships with intermediaries, who invite bidders to participate and may influence customer decisions.

2.3.2 Unintended consequences of competitive bidding

However, the advisors' methods have had some repercussions:

- Competition may deter variety and innovation. The usual bidding instructions compel suppliers to meet a fixed set of requirements. Anything else may be disregarded, and could disqualify the bid. This assures 'apples to apples' comparisons among bidders, but tends to discourage suppliers from proposing alternatives that may be superior. Alternatives may be disregarded, and in any event, time and other constraints get in the way. It is difficult enough for bidders to assemble a proposal, run cost models, and obtain internal approvals in time, without repeating the exercise for variations or alternatives that may not be seriously considered. For sales teams, the paramount objective is to win the competition. For this purpose, alternatives may be a distraction that they might raise later (by which time there may be too much momentum behind the basic requirements and the customer's underlying business case for the customer even to consider anything else). More collaborative processes have begun to invite and accommodate greater flexibility, particularly in business process engagements, where supplier solutions tend to evolve during analysis, selection, and negotiation.

- Competitive bidding appears to focus competition on price, but this appearance may mislead. Suppliers pressed to 'sharpen their pencils' often conclude that nothing else matters, but competitive bidding often yields a dead heat: two well-qualified suppliers, offering credible solutions, reasonable terms, and perhaps an incentive or two. In the end, slight differences in price projections (which brim with uncertainty) may matter less than considerations of corporate culture, favorable references, and impressions left by the proposed account team, rather than numbers in a pricing roll-up or a scorecard. These may be decisive when choosing between reputable suppliers with credible proposals and comparable pricing. Numeric scoring of intangibles may mask unavoidable subjectivity. As in job interviews and other evaluations, if everything else is roughly equal, people tend to choose others they like, with whom they feel comfortable. This is not just human nature at work, but good business, for in the end the customer buys not just a solution, price, and set of performance commitments, but a professional relationship in which such things as trust, integrity, consistency, and responsiveness matter more than a few pennies' difference in some cost metric.

- Competitive bidding tends to drive the business toward commodity—or essentially standard—services, with commodity pricing and margins. There are of course other reasons for these trends, including the maturity of relevant technologies and supplier solutions. Standard service offerings mean economies of scale, lower cost, and perhaps more consistent quality in actual delivery of service. Competition squeezes margins. However, many IT and business process services are not commodities in the usual sense. Commodity margins may make the suppliers' capital-intensive businesses relatively less attractive to investors—ultimately, a dubious outcome for all concerned.

The consultants' and lawyers' methods, forms, and terms have tended to become standards. This is, on the whole, a good thing to the extent that their ways embody accumulated, collective experience. For professional service firms, standard methods, and forms—sometimes derided as 'recipe books'—are keys to consistency, and also the leverage on which their own profitability depends. Armed with the wisdom of the ages, encapsulated in forms, an experienced data center manager is soon a full-fledged consultant; and a young lawyer can become more or less fully billable, without undue risk of grievous error. Many customers take comfort from using proven methods and advisors. It is often said that no one has ever been fired for picking IBM; and it may be equally true that no one has ever been fired for engaging a respected law firm or consultancy. However, outsourcing is not like buying socks—one size does not fit all. Client requirements, goals and cultures vary. What works for an oil company may not necessarily apply to a grocer or hospital. 'Standard' methods, forms, and terms should not be thoughtlessly adopted simply because others have done so, or because they are convenient. Innovations, or at least variations upon conventional wisdom, are often advisable, and the best advisors know how to pick, choose, and adapt their forms and methods to serve the client.

The consultants, of course, continue to refine their methods. In hopes of streamlining the process to save time and money, and accelerate the benefits of outsourcing, some consultants now prefer to limit competition to a shortlist of bidders. Doing so also allows more time to interact with and evaluate the suppliers, by saving time that would otherwise be devoted to the 'also rans' (who, for their part, are spared futile bid and proposal expense). Since suppliers' strengths vary, some consultants now develop requirements through collaborative sessions with competing suppliers, rather than simply prescribe a fixed set of requirements for all bidders. This can make comparisons more challenging, but permits suppliers to play to their particular strengths and allows customers to examine a variety of potential solutions.

2.3.3 Lawyers

The lawyers' role is modest at first—advising on structural and strategic issues, preparing or (for suppliers) responding to term sheets and other preliminary documents—but grows during the latter phases of selection before peaking during negotiations, when the details must be ironed out and reduced to writing. Major suppliers tend to rely upon inside legal departments, and engage outside lawyers only occasionally, if at all. Customers are more likely to select outside counsel with deep outsourcing experience, unless they have already outsourced extensively, and even then they may engage outside counsel to advise on tax, employment, or other specific issues. Once a fairly rare (not to say arcane) specialty, outsourcing has become a staple of corporate and technology practices in many law firms. Experienced counsel who know the business, process, and interplay among contract terms and business issues (and are usually known to the suppliers and consultants) can be invaluable to both management and the customer's legal department.

How can the customer get value for money from outside lawyers? Start by understanding the lawyer's various roles: as counselor, advocate, negotiator, scrivener, and (perhaps least understood) facilitator, drawing upon experience to understand and reconcile both sides' competing interests. The law is not science, but combines judgment, experience, and intuition. Justice Oliver

Wendell Holmes, Jr famously said that the life of the law is not logic but experience.[3] Lawyers cannot predict outcomes as precisely as engineers calculate loads or capacities. One can rarely be sure how a judge (let alone US jurors) may read a contract. Good lawyers are not 'deal-killers' but earn their keep by, among other things, anticipating what can go wrong, and asking difficult questions.

Experience suggests that clients get best value from outside lawyers by remembering the following:

- *Remember who is in charge.* Lawyers sometimes flatter themselves that they 'run the deal.' If true, this is a mistake. The business is the client's business, and the client will have to live with the results. Lawyers dispense advice and provide service. Clients give instructions and make decisions. Those who forget these distinctions, and 'turn it over to the lawyers' do so at their peril, and risk abdicating their responsibility. The lawyers' standard forms and processes offer valuable experience, but every client's business is different, and every transaction has unusual wrinkles.

- *Call early.* Usually, it is wise to involve the lawyers before making fundamental decisions that may be difficult and expensive, or impractical, to reverse. Opportunities for imagination and flexibility, once lost, may never recur. A few hours spent on the term sheet, letter of intent, or other preliminaries can save time, money and grief later on. When paying hourly fees, preliminary consultations may be both the cheapest and most valuable part of the assignment. Calling after the essentials are settled is usually false economy.

- *Keep them informed.* Without the full picture of the organization and its requirements, the lawyers cannot accurately assess the situation, or provide the best possible advice. By law, lawyers must keep secrets, so clients should give them the whole story, 'warts and all,' including organizational quirks and tensions. They must understand the company's business and the real reasons for outsourcing, which may be more complex (and less flattering) than ritual platitudes in the bid documents (which do not and should not wash dirty linen in public). Negotiation involves trade-offs, and therefore requires a clear sense of priorities.

- *Manage them effectively.* Clients expect good service, clear advice, and integrity for a fair fee. To help achieve these goals, there should be a realistic work plan, time schedule, and budget, with reasonable allowances for contingencies.

- *Pay attention.* Good legal advice includes clear explanations of the reasons, risks, and unknowns, as well as recommendations. In outsourcing, the devil

---

[3] OW Holmes, Jr, *The Common Law* (Boston: Little Brown, 1963 edn) 1.

really is in the details, and the most important issues are often scope, service, technical, and financial issues that the lawyers, working with consultants and business people, attempt to translate into contract documents. Only the client can determine whether contract documents capture its intentions.

- *Legal issues are business issues.* Often, lawyers and clients think of legal and business issues as though they were separate, when, in fact, they are points on a continuum. All 'legal' issues involve costs and allocations of risk; and all 'business' issues have to be resolved in clear, unambiguous and legally enforceable language.

- *Value for money means more than rates.* Discussions of legal and other professional costs often emphasize rates, but rates are less important than total cost or the ultimate value received, measured against the transaction's importance, or the potential costs of failure. Over time, lawyers should save more than they cost, although their contribution is difficult to quantify. Problems solved or avoided in negotiations may never hit the books and therefore defy any precise appraisal. When budgets are tight, clients and the lawyers should decide what matters most, then concentrate effort accordingly, with a sense of proportion. Not every issue calls for 'search and destroy' treatment. Sometimes, short documents can cover the essentials adequately, in a fraction of the time, cost, and verbiage. Sometimes, outside legal support consists of background advice, consultation with inside lawyers, and review of key documents. Arbitrary limits or instructions to confine attention to specific terms may not necessarily provide the best return on a limited outlay.

2.4 PRIME CONTRACT OR PORTFOLIO?

Once a company decides to outsource, it must consider whether to engage a single contractor to assume primary responsibility for all outsourced operations, or a more selective strategy, with different suppliers for particular functions. Early 'mega-deals' fit the former pattern: contracts with a single supplier for comprehensive IT services. More recently, many companies have outsourced selectively, even within a single functional area such as information technology. One company may operate the data center, while another maintains software applications, and yet another supports personal computers and answers calls at the help desk. Companies that outsource many operations tend to engage different suppliers for different functions.

Each approach—single source or 'best of breed'—has its attractions. There are no right or wrong answers, only choices and consequences. Prime contracts offer the attractions of simplicity. There is (or was, before business casual attire banished neckties) just 'one throat to choke'—a single contractor accountable for everything. For essentially similar reasons, general contractors are engaged to construct buildings. Few but the most sophisticated owners care to orchestrate deliveries of materials, building trades, permits, inspections and the rest; and fewer still have the ability to do so successfully. In outsourcing, as in the aircraft industry (to use another analogy), prime contractors can integrate and manage scattered, complex operations, including subcontractors. Boeing or Airbus fabricate surprisingly small portions of a jetliner, but know how to assemble the airframe, engines, undercarriage, and avionics so that the aircraft will fly and (most important to passengers) land safely. In somewhat the same way, a supplier's account team must oversee and coordinate customer requirements, its own delivery organization, subcontractors and third party suppliers.

On the other hand, no single organization, however experienced, sophisticated, and able, is likely to be the best in every line of business. No company is (or perhaps can be) best across the board. The supplier with the most efficient data centers does not necessarily operate the best call center, or offer the most attractive rates for software maintenance. Nor does the familiar supplier of IT services necessarily offer the best HR or procurement solution. Within HR, not all suppliers excel at recruiting. Many companies therefore select different suppliers for different functions. This can assure better service, and perhaps lower cost, but adds complexity for all concerned. The customer must play the role of the general contractor, and at least occasionally act as umpire or referee among suppliers who may not be accustomed to this kind of collaboration and are sometimes competitors. Like a good kindergarten teacher, the customer must take pains to see that the children 'play well together.' Outsourced HR operations, for example, may rely upon networks and systems supplied by another company, and both must adhere to common technical standards and security procedures. All this generally requires the customer to have (or often, create) a larger, more sophisticated, and more expensive organization to oversee outsourced operations. For lawyers called upon to negotiate and document the transactions, selective strategies may mean (among other things): (i) common patterns for service agreements; (ii) different, more elaborate governance arrangements (often including multilateral operating agreements among customers and individual suppliers);[4] and (iii) common procedures for

---

[4] See Appendix 13 below.

managing changes, disputes, regulatory compliance, data protection, and much else.

2.5 PHASES—ASSESSMENT, SELECTION, NEGOTIATION

Often, contracts are awarded through formal competition, although many also result from sole-source negotiations (often, extensions of longstanding relationships with hardware or consulting firms whose repertoires now include outsourced services). Generally, competition works to the customer's advantage, as competing suppliers refine their service offerings, adjust technical solutions, and improve financial terms. Sole source contracts tend to be less favorable to the customer, and may rest upon less preparation, since sole-source transactions do not necessarily require preparation of detailed requirements or requests for proposals (although similar disciplines and processes can be very beneficial and are often recommended). On the other hand, sole source transactions can be completed more quickly and accelerate the anticipated benefits of outsourcing, while reducing transaction costs.

Advisors to customers invariably recommend competitive selection. Customers who prefer to proceed with a single supplier may use the prospect of formal competition to obtain competitive terms. Favored suppliers are told that unless they offer market-standard terms, they will face competitive bidding. Recently, in order to save time and money, some consultants have begun to recommend selective, more collaborative, and less formal competition among a handful of qualified suppliers believed to be the likeliest candidates. With fewer participants, there is more time to become familiar with the suppliers, their methods, and personnel, and to negotiate variations upon standard requirements based on the competing suppliers' individual strengths and strategies.

Whatever the process, well-advised customers take time to assess current performance and costs, and attempt to reach agreement in principle upon all essentials before final negotiation of contract documents for a host of obvious reasons—and one that may be less obvious: momentum. Once an outsourcing initiative is announced, and especially after affected employees are aware, loyalties begin to shift and momentum builds. As in mergers and acquisitions, distraction from the business at hand may affect efficiency and performance. Morale may suffer. Employees likely to be displaced may head for the doors or focus upon job searches. After selection of a supplier, all this accelerates, and the process may become virtually irreversible.

Competitive selection involves the following phases, which may be adapted for informal competition, or even sole source negotiations.

2.5.1 Assessment

To begin with, customers must analyze existing operations and costs, then determine what services (if any) to outsource, and define a set of requirements for those services. Consultants are often engaged to assemble and analyze documents and data, and then help to define scope, and identify potential destinations and suppliers (sometimes through formal requests for information from potential suppliers). Crucial exercises include analysis of current operations and development of a 'base case' budget or financial model of current expenditures—a model that is generally disclosed to bidders and used as a basis for comparisons before, during, and after contract negotiations. However, base cases are not scripture. Companies may or may not know how much current operations actually cost, or how current performance compares with competitive standards. This is especially true for scattered, back-office operations that have never been fully documented or separately organized. Costs may be squirreled away in obscure places for historic reasons. Internal operations may not have been rigorously measured. Data centers tend to be somewhat more rigorous than other candidates for outsourcing, because computers were historically entrusted to a separate priesthood who use standard technologies and are accustomed to regular measurements and disciplined, formal procedures. The essential point is to determine what services, if any, might be better and more cheaply performed by an outside supplier. Generally, those services are support functions—non-strategic, but important and often critical operations outside the company's core competence.

From this assessment emerges a request for proposals and other bid and proposal documents. Often, RFPs include more or less detailed 'term sheets'—spreadsheets or other forms that spell out customer business, technical, operational, and other requirements in some detail, and require bidders to respond (generally by acceptance, conditional acceptance, rejection, or counterproposal).[5]

The lawyers' role in this first phase is modest but important, for the bid documents should include all of the fundamental commercial and contractual terms of the ongoing relationship. The proposed form of agreement may or may not be distributed to bidders, but at a minimum, essential terms must be developed, analyzed internally, and presented in summary form so that bidders can gauge

---

[5] Customers and their advisors often comment unfavorably upon extensive responses, but when advising customers, one should not necessarily fault suppliers' deal teams and lawyers for thorough comments. Brevity and succinctness are always virtues, but nervous sales executives need not overreact to hints that comments are excessive or competitors have accepted every requirement. Rarely is that the whole story.

the opportunity and price their proposed 'solutions.' The customer should consider opening positions, desired outcomes, and relationships among issues. Compelling a supplier to purchase existing assets, for example, will increase charges for convenience termination (since the supplier who amortizes its investment over the contract term will seek to recover the unamortized portion of its investment if the contract ends prematurely). For companies new to outsourcing, the assessment phase offers an opportunity to educate deal teams and management unfamiliar with outsourcing, so that they are better prepared not only to match wits with the suppliers' sales teams (who do this for a living) but (more important) to manage the crucial transition phase that follows signing and then oversee outsourced operations. Consultants and lawyers may be asked to prepare extensive briefing or training sessions about the process, issues, negotiation strategies, and tactics. Time spent understanding the process, issues, and relationships is time wisely invested.

2.5.2 Selection

Consultants working with the customer's team or internal purchasing professionals distribute an RFP or term sheet, hold bidders' conferences, answer questions, clarify or refine requirements, oversee preliminary disclosures, and generally manage the competitive bidding process, culminating in submission of elaborate written proposals, which are reviewed internally and then in meetings with bidders (known as 'orals,' perhaps because of the resemblance to the oral examination of graduate students). The customer's lawyers support this effort by drafting (in consultation with the client and other advisors) proposed contract terms, reviewing responses received, and supporting preliminary negotiations with suppliers. Contract terms may be presented in more or less detailed term sheets or through a proposed form of agreement. Essential terms may be reduced to a dozen or more pages, comparable to a detailed letter of intent; but some clients (and advisors) prefer to present complete agreements (or term sheets in equivalent detail), in order to 'smoke out' all objections and secure agreement before selection, while the customer's leverage is at its peak. There are advantages and disadvantages to each approach.

Brief summaries of terms save time and money. Discussions of terms are more likely to be business discussions with the supplier's sales executive than a debate with lawyers (who will dig into details and may just dig in). Brevity, however, may defer some potentially contentious details for a later date, after selection, when the customer's leverage has diminished. Translation of a letter of intent, term sheet, or heads of agreement into a much more elaborate contract inevitably creates openings for negotiation and even misunderstanding. On the other hand, by deferring the details, the customer reserves some flexibility to adjust its position based on lessons learned during preliminary discussions (for example to request concessions secured from other bidders).

Draft contracts do put all issues in play, abbreviate later negotiations, and help to cut off any objections. In this respect, a draft contract serves the same purpose as the familiar admonition that wedding guests should 'speak now or forever hold their peace.' On the other hand, contract forms, once circulated, may become difficult to strengthen. Suppliers confronted with additional terms may protest that their price and other commitments were predicated on a different understanding. Harsh terms may deter some bidders, unless the customer is a multinational Goliath whose business all suppliers will covet.[6]

Selection decisions are based upon review of proposals, and preliminary negotiation of scope, price, and other key issues. Since the customer's leverage declines after selection, it is imperative that customers confirm commitments in writing before awarding the business, even tentatively, to one bidder. Selection often involves parallel negotiation of a term sheet or detailed letter of intent with at least two finalists. Decision makers focus, appropriately, upon price, service levels, solutions, and quality. Rarely does selection turn upon contract terms. Most suppliers will, in the end, accept industry standard terms, with modest variations, although some suppliers are more flexible than others and some have distinct philosophies on particular issues. Second-tier suppliers or newcomers may be more flexible than market leaders; but customers should beware of new-comers who raise few objections and offer dramatically lower prices in an effort to 'buy business,' often without knowing what performance will cost. No one cares to be a surgeon's first patient.[7]

Usually, price, performance, and other criteria—but especially price—are decisive. However, when the finalists' bids are close (as often they are), the decision may turn upon other, less tangible considerations—such as quality, collaboration, responsiveness, and the proposed account team. Slight percentage differences in rates and charges may not be significant when projected over

---

[6] Requesting the supplier's standard form may offer clues about supplier policies, positions, and sensibilities, but customers rarely agree to work from supplier forms.

[7] Working with a new supplier, or even an experienced one in a wholly new line of business, creates both challenges and opportunities. A 'pioneer' customer may enjoy unusual leverage to shape service offerings, secure the supplier's best talent, and obtain favorable terms, but should bear in mind the risks of unproven solutions and uncertain costs, which may jeopardize the supplier's performance and profitability. In the worst cases, liberal termination rights at low cost are essential. At times, the customer may feel like a user of 'beta' software. If the price is right and the solution is both promising and tested (though not with live customers) the risk may be acceptable. 'Alpha' solutions designed on the customer's time and, at least to some extent at the customer's risk, are more hazardous.

the contract term, with appropriate allowances for the uncertainty inherent in any forecast. Customers should consider total cost, including not only the supplier's charges, but expenses retained, reimbursed, or passed through, inflation and currency risks, and costs of managing the relationship (which are often overlooked or underestimated).

During evaluation, competing proposals are often scored, using numeric scales and other tools beloved by consultants. These are excellent ways to focus discussions, compel decision makers to apportion weightings among various criteria, and facilitate comparisons; but they may also introduce a false sense of precision, for the scores (like examination marks in school) are often numeric labels for largely subjective evaluations. Slight differences in score sheets may or may not reflect actual differences in suppliers' probable performance, or the customer's ultimate satisfaction. Score sheets are not as precise as micrometers.

When a single finalist is chosen for contract negotiation, the selection should be confirmed in writing through a detailed letter of intent, or a shorter version that adopts the proposal or term sheet, as supplemented during or after orals, as the basis for further discussion. Simple letters reciting an intention to negotiate, sometimes favored by salesmen, are rarely in the customer's interests, because the customer's leverage erodes after selection. Letters of intent are rarely binding (except to the extent that they affirm non-disclosure obligations, or commit the customer to pay for some interim service), yet they have considerable practical value. Scope, pricing, performance, and other commitments affirmed by an executive's signature on a letter of intent are unlikely to be retracted. To begin with, the supplier's management usually consists of serious people who honor commitments and, even if otherwise tempted, recognize the hazards to relationships with customers and intermediaries, and to their reputation in the marketplace.

2.5.3 Contract negotiation

This final phase may take weeks, even months, depending upon the scale of the transaction, the process pursued and other factors. Three or four cycles or 'turns' are typical for the principal documents (master agreement, statement of work, service levels, and charges). To the extent that detailed documents were agreed during selection, the process may move more quickly, but almost invariably some further issues emerge from the supplier's investigation (or 'due diligence') and the evolution of customer requirements. Time may also be needed to resolve complex technical issues (such as privacy, audit, employment laws, and taxation) and to prepare for transition. Haste may prove expensive, particularly for the customer, who is less familiar with the process. Time pressures may further diminish the customer's declining leverage. Parties are well advised to set and keep realistic deadlines, rather than announce aggressive dates, miss them, and fuel rumors of trouble.

Some consultants recommend picking two finalists for a final round of parallel, intensely competitive negotiation—including negotiation of complete sets of closing documents—and deferring selection until the last minute. This 'horse race' preserves the customer's leverage until the very end, but has other less desirable consequences. Parallel negotiation compounds the cost of outside consultants and lawyers, as well as the internal turmoil and distraction. It also extends the schedule. Outside law or consulting firms may be able to summon reinforcements, but the customer generally has only one deal team, which must work closely with both finalists in order to make sound comparisons and an ultimate selection. Parallel negotiations may exacerbate internal tensions—for example if employees to be transferred prefer one supplier, but the other offers better price and terms. Transitions must be planned for two different suppliers, with different solutions. There is also some danger that the horse running second may give up the chase, rather than continue to spend tens of thousands of dollars every week in salaries, travel, and other costs. If that happens, the customer's leverage evaporates and the remaining competitor wonders just why the 'other guys' (whom they may privately respect, even fear) dropped out. Did they discover something that the remaining competitor missed? Did they run up against unacceptable terms or margins? Parallel negotiations may repay additional expenditures of time and money in very large transactions where the finalists are evenly matched; but usually, selection based on proposals and a detailed letter of intent or term sheet will assure the benefits of competition, through a shorter, less costly process.

During negotiations, multiple threads must proceed in parallel—contract negotiation, drafting of schedules and exhibits, the supplier's investigation, reference checks, pre-transition activities (such as review of a transition plan), price negotiations, calibration of service levels, and so on. Time spent coordinating these activities is time well spent. Clients expect their lawyers and advisors to manage and administer the process effectively, so that a consistent set of contract documents is ready for signature shortly after agreement is reached on all issues. Regular status calls or meetings with client teams and both sides are indispensable. So are complete, accurate checklists of open issues, documents, and other details.

2.5.4 Selection—the last dance

At the end of the selection phase (or, when parallel negotiations conclude) comes the time for decision. A winner must be chosen. For the customer, this can be a difficult juncture. If the competition is close, each contestant may have its partisans; no proposal or team is ideal; and delivering bad news to the loser is rarely an appetizing chore. Moreover, unless signature documents are ready, the loser may not be entirely out of the running. Rarely will the chosen supplier falter after selection, but it can happen and occasionally does. Therefore, runners-up are often asked to remain 'on call,' in the event the customer does not expeditiously complete negotiations with the declared winner. Sometimes, for a variety of reasons—including perceived strengths and a desire to spread one's bets—customers may award portions of their business to each of two or three finalists.

Customers recognize that selection effectively ends leverage, so often wrap their decisions in conditions. Rather than simply congratulate the winner, there will be a telephone conversation to the effect that the competition is excruciatingly close but the relevant team or committee is prepared to recommend the favored supplier's selection if they can agree to a very few, carefully chosen concessions. If the list is not too lengthy, and does not appear likely to derange the supplier's financial models, the supplier eager to see off the competition may just find a way to accommodate most of the items on that shortlist.[8]

2.6 DRAFTING TACTICS

Both sides prefer document control for the usual reasons. At the margins, editorial control may confer some tactical and even substantive advantage (albeit at some cost to clients paying by the hour). Most lawyers believe, with reason, that they are more effective working with documents whose every word and nuance they know (although specialists become familiar, over time, with the forms and methods of leading law firms and consultancies). On either side, integrated sets of form documents are designed, in part, to serve the particular side's interests. Many consultants prefer that they, on the customer's behalf, control essentially all documents other than the master agreement, which is entrusted to the customer's lawyer. Sometimes, the customer's lawyers control the

---

[8] Runners-up routinely request meetings to learn the reasons for the customer's decision, in hopes they can do better the next time. This is a common professional courtesy, but explanations should be discreet and respect the confidentiality of all bidders' proposals, pricing, and positions. 'Loss reviews' (as suppliers call them) or debriefings are not appeals or opportunities for reconsideration and often take place after negotiations conclude.

contract, and the supplier (with its experienced team) prepares initial drafts for, and retains editorial control of, some of the key schedules defining scope, service levels, charges, and transition planning. Whatever the division of labor, lawyers retain editorial control of contracts, but consultants or business people may have primary responsibility for schedules concerning operational, financial, and technical issues (with legal review and at least occasional editorial assistance). Schedules or exhibits concerning legal or contractual issues, such as employment or privacy compliance, may be left to the lawyers.

Consultants' forms for statements of work, service levels, and other working documentation are often of high quality, but customer-oriented; just as lawyers' contract forms favor one side or the other, and suppliers' forms favor the suppliers. No matter what the source, statements of work and other documents tailored to the particular transaction tend to take more time than master contracts, which are more nearly standard, for all customers and kinds of service. The phrasing of indemnities, change control procedures, and other familiar terms do not vary dramatically from one deal to the next, or for business process services, as opposed to IT. By contrast, services, service levels, solutions, pricing terms, transitions, and other operational and financial details may vary a good deal. As noted above, participants should expect three or four cycles of drafting, negotiation, and revision for all of the principal documents. To the extent that at least some key documents are lifted more or less verbatim from term sheets and proposals, the process may go faster.

Considerations of time and efficiency may dictate parallel work streams, as different groups negotiate contract terms, scope, pricing, service levels, and other issues. Coordination is therefore at a premium. Many issues appear in multiple documents, and there may be complex financial or operational dependencies. More robust service levels, for example, tend to raise prices. Changes in termination language may lead to adjustments in termination charges. Scope changes may be linked to service levels and pricing. Very little proceeds in isolation. Usually the most important financial, contractual, and operational issues tend to be resolved at a 'top table' in discussions that involve senior representatives from both sides and their lawyers.

Sometimes, impatient souls recommend drafting 'at the table.' This may work for a key phrase or two, but is rarely efficient or advisable, since language discussed in isolation may have ripple effects elsewhere in the contract documents, and business people quickly become impatient with what they perceive as wrangling over words (even when the words have important operational, financial, or legal implications). When working upon a few key issues with a small group (such as opposing counsel and advisors) familiar with complex contracts, editing key paragraphs projected upon a screen may be effective (though painfully slow). Generally, it is best to separate drafting from negotiation, and focus discussion during negotiations upon business, operational, and financial issues, rather than legal wording which bores clients and can contribute to impatience—sometimes with unfortunate consequences. Where working relationships between the lawyers are good, words can be left for them to sort out. Good lawyers can be depended upon to craft language that accurately reflects negotiated conclusions, including their client's concessions (and those tempted to do otherwise should pause to consider the effect upon their credibility, and that of their clients).

Sometimes, statements of work or other contract documents are written by committees or large working groups. Rarely are the results very satisfactory. Everyone has something to say and words are piled upon words, in the interests of collaboration rather than clarity. There is more than a germ of truth in the old witticism that camels or zebras are horses designed by committees. Generally, a competent (and trustworthy) draftsman on one side or the other should have primary responsibility for capturing negotiated changes, then recording them with appropriate cross-references, definitions, and the rest for further discussion with his or her counterpart.

On both sides, business people should resist any desire to leave the contract or other key documents entirely to the lawyers or outside consultants. The lawyers can (and should) resolve many points of language and detail between themselves, but business and legal issues are closely related. Documents affecting scope, service levels, and charges, in particular, must capture the business understanding. Paging through schedules can be sheer tedium, but it is important tedium.

2.7 NEGOTIATION TACTICS

At the risk of stating the obvious, suppliers seek to win opportunities on acceptable terms, that they can perform successfully and profitably. Customers want to complete the deal on time, with favorable terms and as little operational, financial, and other risk as possible. During selection or parallel negotiations, the customer's advisors may have a closely-related, but slightly different, agenda: to present their client with at least two qualified, attractive, essentially similar bids, then let the client choose. So they press the contestants to 'improve' their bids—shave costs, improve performance, accept greater risk, and concede more favorable terms. Occasionally, customer advisors and suppliers have at least one eye on precedents that might be established for future dealings with the particular supplier or suppliers generally. Suppliers, who are well aware of this tendency, may be all the more reluctant to vary the usual bottom-line positions, lest concessions come back to bite them on future transactions led by the same advisors.

Whether or not there are parallel negotiations, there are likely to be (as noted above) parallel discussions of: (i) contract terms; (ii) scope, solution, and service levels; (iii) pricing; and (iv) other critical issues, such as personnel or transition (which may overlap or be combined with master terms.) This method poses the following tactical challenges, to some extent for both sides:

- Piecemeal, incremental concessions—slicing the salami, as it were, a millimeter at a time, without securing anything in return. The usual tactical response is to table specific issues and attempt to resolve important issues, especially related issues, together—relaxing selected requirements, for example, in exchange for financial concessions. Good negotiators understand that to get something, they must usually give something in return. Opening positions on both sides usually include some room for maneuver and even 'trade bait'—positions known to be unacceptable that can be traded away.
- Resolution of issues in isolation, even though many issues affect others that arise elsewhere. An HR issue, for example, may have price and contractual dimensions.
- Tedium and detail breed impatience and frustration, especially among customer personnel not accustomed to contract negotiations. No one (not even the lawyers) actually enjoys endless debates over contract language. Indemnities are rarely exciting, until they are invoked. Impatience, frustration, and emotions are rarely good bases for decisions.

On both sides, there may be some tendency to posture about what is 'standard' or what others have supposedly accepted (without, of course, disclosing details). All this should be taken with the proverbial pinch of salt. Supplier teams who claim that their company has never agreed to a particular point often lack complete information. Most of their companies have at one time or another agreed to some variant of every term. Indeed, painful experience may be the very reason they now reject particular requests. Not all sophisticated customers necessarily buy the supplier's ostensibly 'standard' position. Similarly, other suppliers chasing an opportunity do not necessarily agree to everything on the customer's wish list.[9] If another competitor conceded a particularly contentious point, it may

---

[9] What the supplier has agreed on other occasions with other customers is, and should remain, confidential. Customers' lawyers may, of course, discuss prior dealings freely with the suppliers (outside their client's presence) and may advise customers about market standards and trends (without revealing other clients' confidences).

have done so in exchange for reciprocal (but undisclosed) concessions from the customer. More often than not, competing suppliers raise essentially similar points, albeit with differences in emphasis and occasional differences in substance. One supplier may accept some requests to which another objects, but usually, all bidders push back on more or less the same issues, so that competing responses are almost interchangeable. To win the business and close the deal, both sides generally compromise at least a few key issues.

Usually, candid and civil discussions of the parties' competing interests are more productive than debates about a particular customer's 'requirements' or the supplier's 'standard position.' A customer whose last experience with outsourcing ended with weeping and gnashing of teeth may seek liberal termination rights and ironclad commitments concerning disengagement. Where existing service is ragged, improving customer service and measuring users' satisfaction may have overriding importance. A supplier with a large portfolio of commercial hardware and software products is unlikely to agree that all manner of innovations can be patented by the customer. Big companies on either side do not, and cannot, lightly alter settled policies approved by their lawyers and auditors. In some respects, the process resembles a sort of dance, and elephants cannot dance as nimbly as ballerinas.

Outside the negotiation sessions, private 'coaching' of suppliers about perceived strengths and weaknesses may involve posturing but can be helpful. Sometimes, this is an effort to keep competing bids even—to improve or strengthen the bids and meet the competition. So long as specifics about other bids are kept confidential, this is helpful and appropriate. To be constructive and effective, coaching must also be scrupulously accurate. Oblique hints that the competition has offered dramatic concessions will raise eyebrows, to be sure, but sophisticated suppliers who know their marketplace (including their competitors' strengths and proclivities) will wonder what (unmentioned) inducements or concessions were offered in return—if indeed the 'other guys' were so accommodating.

Both sides occasionally engage in 'divide and conquer' tactics. Customers or their advisors may whisper to the supplier's sales executive that the supplier's lawyers are raising too many issues, or they may approach executive sponsors seeking concessions. Suppliers sometimes reciprocate by going around the deal team direct to the client's management in order to resolve key issues (perhaps saying similar things about the customer's overly zealous advisors). Occasionally, these methods are appropriate, even essential, but it is usually more effective to work within whatever ground rules have been laid down and minimize any risk of giving offense or, worse, making enemies among decision makers. Complaints about individuals are especially hazardous—unlikely to be acted upon and certain to leak.

Suppliers should not be faulted for raising legitimate issues. Scolding suppliers for objections and comments may tempt sales teams to bury issues in brief, cryptic responses, or omit them altogether; but serious issues do not go away simply because they are ignored. Thoughtful customers and their advisors respect sophistication and discipline in prospective suppliers, and sometimes pause to wonder whether the supplier who just smiles and says 'yes' can actually perform or even understands the issue. Supplier resistance to particular terms sometimes reflects lessons learned from painful experience that the customer would prefer to avoid.

Customers and their advisors understand very well the pressures upon sales teams. Sales executives are paid to win, and not simply rack up hundreds of thousands of dollars in travel, lodging, and other bid and proposal costs. However, the customer and its advisors also face pressures—to complete a transaction that management can approve, meet deadlines, and achieve financial goals. They must keep qualified bidders in the game until selection. They know perfectly well that some supposed 'requirements' will be unacceptable to bidders. If leading bidders walk away, the whole exercise can collapse, leaving the customer unattractive choices amidst an expensive, disruptive process that is difficult to reverse. For the customer and its advisors, this would be an embarrassing outcome that could, in extreme cases, affect the advisors' ability to collect a large receivable. Suppliers rarely walk away from serious opportunities, but could do so, and their leverage is greater than is commonly supposed. Horse races require at least two contestants. Moreover, sophisticated customers and their advisors do understand that there are points beyond which bidders cannot be pushed. Well-reasoned firmness on important issues reflects organizational and financial discipline, which customers should respect (even if they might prefer greater flexibility). At some point, the bidder who always says 'yes' will invite doubts about his ability to perform.

Experience suggests that the following tactics are usually effective, not only in completing the transaction, but doing so in a way that contributes to long-term success:

- Start negotiations—or better yet, selection—with an 'all-hands,' face-to-face meeting that begins with a discussion of tone and philosophy. Allow individuals to introduce themselves. Organizations consist of individuals—men and women, not 'resources.' Emphasize the importance of underlying business concerns and interests, rather than positions. Forswear extremes that no prudent person would accept. When differences appear, as they will, seek explanations and alternatives. Invite creativity about alternatives. Discuss both sides' long-term goals for the relationship. Listen, and treat the other side's interests and effort with respect. Review agendas, time schedules, and other ground rules. An afternoon spent getting acquainted and discussing these larger themes helps to ease initial suspicions and tensions on both sides and to lay foundations for successful negotiations and solid working relationships after the contract is complete.

- Start negotiating sessions with some brief, thoughtful, and well-focused opening remarks about the situation, an overview of significant issues and key philosophical or other themes. Wrap up each session with a similar summary of the day's accomplishments, next steps and concerns or suggestions about unresolved issues. Openings and conclusions often leave the most lasting impressions, as much for their tone as for specific content. Behind the detail, tactics, and immediate issues stands a decision maker who generally wants to get something done and is likely to respect candor, recognition of the decision maker's interests, and a willingness to listen and accommodate.

- Teams must prepare beforehand, and coordinate between sessions to be sure that all parts of teams know the inter-relationships among issues, what they can and cannot concede, and where they must consult with others before resolving critical issues. Both sides should expect some issues to be referred to the proverbial 'head table' or, occasionally, to senior management.

- Present a united front. Inevitably, business units, advisors, lawyers, and the financial professionals may have different perspectives about common goals. Within one's own camp, frank and vigorous internal discussion is helpful, but in open sessions teams should stand together and speak respectfully of competing considerations ('I'd like to find a way through this, but am concerned about what our financial analysts/HR department/lawyers are saying....'). For similar reasons, both sides should keep senior management and affected business units apprised and involved, so that whatever deals are struck prove sustainable and management can make informed decisions about any points that must be referred upstairs for decision.

- To the extent possible, focus upon substance rather than details or language. Look beneath the words on the page to understand the real business risks and issues—financial, operational, and technical. Discuss interests rather than formal positions. Ask why, then listen. Tiresome debates about language or allegedly 'standard' terms tend to bore and to annoy. Where business people agree, competent lawyers will find words.

- When agreement upon a particular item cannot be reached within a reasonable time (say, 10 to 15 minutes), issues may be tabled for the time being, so that discussion can proceed. This keeps things moving, avoids any appearance of impasse, and effectively builds a shortlist of major issues that might be resolved together, as a package, through mutual accommodation. Resolution of all issues on the first pass is almost inconceivable. Important or related issues tend to be resolved in groups.

- Commitment to mutual success means conceding (even offering) what the other side should fairly expect, and voluntary correction of obvious errors. Nothing is more disarming or reassuring than statements that begin: 'we don't think you really meant to give. . . .' Integrity is all.

- Keep a positive tone. Impasses are issues yet to be solved. One man's obstacle is another man's challenge. If one cannot do what they ask, what else might be suggested? Lawyers understand that their clients want to hear not simply what the law prohibits, but how to reach their goals and comply with the law without excessive risk. It's much the same here: each side knows that the other will not always agree, but when agreement is not possible, there are usually alternatives. For similar reasons, remember the value of civility, courtesy, respect, and good humor—especially in circumstances where both sides work long hours alongside one another, and must continue to collaborate after signing.

For participants new to the negotiation of complex contracts (generally on the customer's side of the table), it can all seem a bit overwhelming or bewildering— yet another reason to enlist advisors who do this for a living—but the essential principles of effective negotiation are straightforward:

- *Tell the truth.* The Eighth Commandment has not been amended or improved upon (despite centuries of effort). Apart from considerations of personal and corporate integrity (which are reason enough), anything else will be found out, discrediting everything else said, and possibly tarnishing or even poisoning business relationships. This does not mean laying all cards on the table or opening discussion with 'bottom line' positions, but effective negotiation requires integrity, not guile.

- *Understand bargaining strength.* Customers enjoy substantial leverage when competing suppliers bid for their business. That leverage diminishes after selection. Other circumstances may affect the parties' motivations or sense of urgency. Recession may mean that suppliers are particularly eager to close new business, or that the customer is anxious to achieve savings quickly.

- *Know your agenda, priorities, and authority, and those of the other side.* This means, above all, understanding the parties' complementary and competing interests. To understand the other side's interests, ask questions and listen closely. Many advisors to customers know from experience how suppliers are likely to think and respond, and can help to separate authentic requirements from mere desires.

- *Remember that good deals are good for both sides.* Long-term business engagements like outsourcing rarely succeed unless both sides succeed.
- *To make a good deal, know when to walk away.*   Each side should have and know its alternatives. Without alternatives one has no leverage, but no deal is almost always better than a bad one. A supplier can go home, write off pursuit costs, and go on to the next opportunity. A customer can carry on without outsourcing or find another supplier.

2.8 NEGOTIATION LOGISTICS

Practical arrangements for negotiation deserve more thought than they sometimes receive.

2.8.1 Location—my place or yours?

Negotiations tend to take place at the customer's offices. Customers have most of the leverage, initially; sales people are always anxious to please; and customer representatives are already there. However, at least during the more intense negotiation phase, there is something to be said for meeting at a neutral location—a hotel conference room, law office, or some other place where negotiations will have the full attention of all the participants, and are less likely to be interrupted. Wherever possible, and especially during the early stages, face-to-face meetings are better than conference calls. Facial expressions, body language, and the like communicate much more than disembodied, electronic voices; working relationships develop more easily; and it is far easier to caucus privately, set an appropriate tone, and assess the dynamics across the table.

2.8.2 The meeting room

Courtesy as well as practicality would suggest that, if possible, there should be a comfortable conference room, perhaps equipped with such conveniences as whiteboards, network connections, printers, projectors, and the like. Whether so much technology should be available is debatable. Instant network communications are an excellent way to share documents, but someone in the room is virtually guaranteed to have only one eye and ear on the business at hand while perusing incoming e-mail messages. For similar reasons, it may be desirable (if not always possible) to banish (or at least switch off) cell phones and Blackberries. Projecting contract language on the screen invites drafting by committee, which tends to slow down the process and produce problematic results. An adjacent room for private caucuses is helpful.

2.8.3 Teams and agendas

Often, both sides bring full negotiating teams to most meetings; but efficiency may be well served if, at least during the negotiation of details, the larger group breaks down for smaller working sessions. However, when the customer largely depends upon one or two people to make decisions and manage the process, this may not be possible.

Generally, discussion proceeds in essentially the same manner as for any other negotiation. Negotiating teams are usually of roughly equal size, and led by individuals of comparable seniority and authority—ideally, authority sufficient to decide all substantive issues, or all but a few issues that must be referred to senior management (such as major changes in financial terms, liability limits, or other fundamentals). Where one side is empowered and the other is not, the outcome is likely to include frustration (and perhaps some tactical disadvantage).

Whatever the size of the team, there are roles to be played on each side:

- *Leader and decision maker.* Usually, the supplier's sales executive and the senior manager present for the customer.
- *Negotiator.* For the customer, this is often a lawyer or consultant experienced in these negotiations; for the supplier, this is the role for the lead negotiator or sometimes the attorney. Letting someone else take the lead insulates the decision maker from any need to make on-the-spot decisions that may not be easily altered or retracted. Consultants, lawyers and lead negotiators (who depart after the signing) make better lightning rods, to the extent that awkward questions must be asked, or firm but unwelcome positions taken.
- *Scribe.* Someone on each side should take accurate notes of the parties' changing positions, resolutions of issues, lists of open issues, documents requested and delivered, and other important documents and details. Sometimes the individual chosen will also be librarian and keeper of a website where drafts and other documents are available. Detailed minutes quickly become a distraction, but each side should keep its own notes or daily file memoranda, summarizing the day's discussion and resolutions reached. Joint lists of open issues or action to be taken are very helpful.
- *Observer.* Assigning one team member, possibly the scribe, to watch the changing cast of characters and their attitudes—impatience, boredom, frustration, whatever it may be—is often wise. The lead negotiator is generally too busy to do this, and may easily miss cues visible to someone else at the end of

the table. Negotiations, like contests in sports, often develop momentum because of time pressures, personalities, and other intangibles. There are times to stand firm, take time out, seize the initiative, or press for resolution. Paying close attention to the temperature in the room, the mood of the participants, and other such 'atmospherics' (as Henry Kissinger would have called them) helps to achieve good results and avoid errors.

As for the agenda or plan of attack, there are no hard-and-fast rules, other than to think ahead, understand both sides' priorities, and have a plan, so that both parties can be prepared, productive, and work toward a common understanding concerning outcomes and timetables. Intuition is invaluable, but pure improvisation invites error. False or overly ambitious deadlines may appear to offer tactical advantages, but are more likely to yield incomplete resolutions or misunderstandings (no one will have read the documents) as well as mistakes through oversight or haste. At some point, one cannot avoid paging through the documents, one issue at a time, but doing so risks piecemeal concessions, inconsistencies, or neglect of inter-connections among related issues elsewhere in the documents. Often, the most important issues are resolved in groups and, in principle, among a smaller group of senior team members, rather than in plenary sessions. Parties may be more flexible about a particular contract term if offered some accommodation on scope or price. Trade-offs may be more difficult to achieve when paging through documents, paragraph by paragraph, line-by-line.

2.9 DISCLOSURES AND DILIGENCE

The importance of preparation is difficult to exaggerate. Experience suggests that the following preparatory work should begin as soon as a company begins seriously to consider outsourcing, during the assessment phase:

- Identify and begin to build a capable team to manage outsourced operations, then involve them in the process of assessment, selection, and negotiation. Starting early helps to avoid unprepared, under-strength management of outsourced operations—the single most common (and most easily avoided) error among companies that outsource important functions.
- Require potential bidders to sign confidentiality agreements before the first disclosures.
- Examine the numerous legal and contractual compliance issues presented by outsourcing (and remember that even preliminary disclosures of sensitive information—concerning individuals, for example—may be subject to privacy, data protection, and other laws and regulations).

Crucial legal and contractual compliance issues generally include the following:

- *Audit.* What controls must an outsourcer implement? What reports and certifications must an outsourcer provide to satisfy Sarbanes-Oxley and other requirements? What aspects of outsourced operations must be examined by the customer's auditors or regulatory agencies?
- *Contracts.* Many outsourced services require access to licensed technologies, leased equipment, and other assets or services provided by third parties. What consent requirements, use restrictions, or other terms may inhibit the necessary flexibility? Merely collecting and reviewing relevant contracts may prove a challenge, especially in companies that have experienced mergers, relocation, or other events that tend to scatter records.
- *Data protection and privacy.* Most outsourced services involve access to and use of sensitive personal data about employees and customers. Transfers of such data between countries may be regulated, particularly transfers within and from the European Union (whose directives have been models for legislation in some other countries). Before discussing compliance requirements with suppliers, it is helpful to be sure that the customer's present arrangements are in order and if (as is often the case) everything is not precisely as it should be, corrective measures must be undertaken.
- *Export control.* Transfers of software and technical information to offshore suppliers will implicate regulations under the US Export Administration Act or corresponding legislation elsewhere. Many business people forget, if ever they knew, that regulated 'exports' involve more than loading containers on ships. Transmission of technical data, or sharing of sensitive technologies with offshore companies may constitute exports for which licenses are required. Do any relevant technologies (encryption, for example) have military, intelligence, or other sensitive uses to which special requirements apply?
- *Invoicing and taxation.* What is the most tax-efficient way to receive invoices and pay for services? Suppliers are likely to seek to recover value-added taxes that apply to the services rendered, even if these taxes are incurred on inter-company charges. Accordingly, an informed customer should investigate the incidence of such taxes and consider invoicing structures that minimize their non-recovery and overall compliance costs. Other tax issues relate to withholding taxes that may apply on the customer's own charge-backs to foreign subsidiaries in cases where invoices are paid centrally, as well as possible creation of a taxable 'permanent establishment'.
- *Legal compliance.* Data protection and export control are merely two examples of a larger challenge: making sure that outsourced services continue

to comply with all of the customer's numerous legal obligations. How, for example, does a customer allocate responsibility for compliance with wages, hours, payroll withholding, and other employment-related laws when HR functions are outsourced? Customers in regulated industries must comply with regulations peculiar to their businesses. Ultimate responsibility to regulatory agencies cannot be delegated to an outsourcer (or anyone else), but an outsourcer may assume some operational responsibilities, and be accountable to the customer for adherence to approved procedures. Negotiated allocations of responsibility and risk should begin with an understanding of regulatory obligations and current compliance programs.

- *Employment.* Outsourcing may displace or transfer many employees. In the US, the outsourcer may wish to interview and recruit some affected employees. Notice may need to be given under the federal plant closure law, known as the Worker Adjustment and Retraining Notification (WARN) Act or similar state laws, which may have different or more stringent requirements.[10] In the European Union, employees displaced may transfer directly to the supplier, by operation of the EU Acquired Rights Directive and implementing legislation within the Member States. Some other countries have followed the European pattern, and many countries have laws affecting dismissals, severance pay, and the like. Requirements are complex, and require expert advice as well as considerable lead times (notably, to satisfy consultation requirements with works councils and unions). Companies considering outsourcing should therefore consider which employees may be affected, examine applicable legal requirements, and determine what filings, notices, consultation, or other action may be required before any contract is signed.

- *Asset transfers.* When equipment and facilities are transferred, the usual preliminaries are required, such as lien searches, title reports, environmental diligence, and review of contracts that may be transferred. Review of software licenses, equipment leases, and other third party contracts is generally entrusted to paraprofessionals, but the lawyers may be asked to advise concerning transferability and consent requirements.

Suppliers will, appropriately, request and customers will want to disclose much of the information collected as part of the customer's assessment of internal operations. Lawyers rarely participate in the suppliers' investigations, which include review of data, inspections of facilities, and meetings with key operational staff. Suppliers entrust this to experienced teams. Customers routinely

---

[10] 29 USC §2101 *et seq.*

request briefings on the supplier's diligence findings, which may reveal things not previously known or suspected, even by the customer's own management.

Where data are incomplete or appear unreliable, suppliers often seek some rights to verify or adjust scope after signing (for example after inventories are performed). Customers resist this, in part because their leverage evaporates after signing, when the supplier assumes control over operations. Sometimes adjustments are agreed, at least in limited spheres, or the contract may make some provision for adjusting inventories and charges for matters identified after signing.

Customers are well advised to make full, complete, and accurate disclosures. Occasionally, customers are reluctant to do so and, inevitably, at least some records are incomplete or missing. The better the disclosure, the more likely the supplier is to forego any opportunity for post-closing adjustments. More important, the better the disclosure, the more likely both sides are to succeed because charges, cost models, performance metrics, and baselines are calibrated accurately. Lawyers and consultants should be alert for internal politics and hidden agendas, especially where some business units or affected operations oppose outsourcing and prefer an internal alternative. These situations sometimes tempt customers to 'game' disclosure or withhold information, which would be both wrong and foolish. Gamesmanship undermines trust and could (in extreme cases) invite fraud, misrepresentation, or other claims.

2.10 ADVISORS AS FACILITATORS

During negotiations, lawyers and consultants serve as facilitators.

Not everyone fully appreciates the importance of this intermediary function. Good lawyers are much more than advocates, scriveners, and counsellors. Lawyers help clients to succeed not only by advocating their interests and drafting to secure their interests and even advantage, but also by focusing on long-term success; facilitating workable, fair resolution of contentious issues; displaying conspicuous fairness to the adversary; and maintaining a constructive, civil tone throughout. For the lawyers, each side of an outsourcing deal presents distinct challenges.

When advising customers, lawyers should be prepared to explain the process, its risks and potential benefits, the rationale behind customary terms, and the supplier's business, perspective, and legitimate interests. Lawyers and consultants play complementary roles and help to educate customers, especially first-time customers. Customers exert maximum leverage during selection and must resist the temptation to overreach, for uneconomic, unbalanced terms may prove painful and expensive later on. One may need to rein in more exuberant members of the customer team, and damp down unrealistic expectations and requests. Not every function requires 'fail-safe' reliability or gold-plated service. Sometimes, extravagant requests (which raise costs) and erratic disclosures mask opposition to outsourcing or other unstated agendas. Discussion of risks need not be alarmist, or fuel unrealistic insistence upon 'bulletproof' terms. Often, the operational and other risks of outsourced operations are no worse than those that exist within the customer's own internal operations; but they may be different and cannot be eliminated entirely. Sometimes, suppliers are better equipped to manage particular risks.

Supplier teams invariably include a lawyer (usually an inside lawyer) whose job it is to protect the company's interests, while complementing sales efforts and, at least occasionally, reining in the sales team. The best strike a balance between firmness and flexibility, saying 'no' graciously, only when necessary and never antagonizing the customer. Curmudgeons need not apply. When advising suppliers, lawyers are, in part, advocates or—as their clients might say—sales support. The outsourcers require little coaching, and less legal and other support than their customers. They have done this before, understand the business, and (one hopes) their cost models. On the other hand, robust representation must also be diplomatic in order to complement the sales effort, maintain the sales team's confidence, and forestall predictable whispers that the lawyers are being 'too difficult' and 'getting in the way' of the deal. Occasionally, the lawyers' experience as advocates helps sales teams to refine their messages and reminds sales executives that their lawyer is an ally, rather than an obstacle. Lawyers for suppliers should also be alert for occasional internal tensions within the supplier— for example, between sales and delivery organizations, or between deal teams and headquarters. Salesmen cherish their commissions; headquarters likes to report 'wins' and backlogs; delivery frets about operations and margins. The lawyers serve the company and try to get along with everyone.

Whichever side a lawyer or advisor represents, experience on the other side (or at least comprehension of the other side's interests) is helpful. Few customers fully appreciate suppliers' disciplined processes for cost models, bid reviews and approvals. Suppliers easily forget the first-time customer's apprehension about sending internal operations outside and offshore. Inevitable attention to 'worst case' scenarios may exacerbate customer fears.

On both sides, good lawyers seek simplicity and clarity. 'Keep it simple' is a fine maxim, but probably not a realistic one in transactions and relationships as complex as outsourcing. When companies entrust major operations to others, some complexity is unavoidable. No one should expect to compress an outsourcing contract into a dozen pages, or write charging metrics and service levels on the back of an envelope. Nonetheless, lawyers should keep things as simple as reasonably possible and avoid overwhelming the clients with verbiage and detail. With time and technology, documents have tended to grow longer and more complex. Lawyers are trained to identify all issues, resolve them, and document understandings with layers of words and procedures. The end result may be a contract as thick as a telephone directory that defies easy comprehension or administration—especially by customer clients new to outsourcing. Clients value clarity and plain English. No one can anticipate (let alone provide for) all contingencies, and issues arising after transition rarely surface in quite the way originally anticipated. Processes may be more important than rules, especially when reinforced by allocations of risk and responsibility that provide incentives to preserve and sustain the relationship. Documents need to be clear not only to the participants, but to successors who may sit in their places a year or two later.

2.11 PRIVILEGES AND PROFESSIONAL RESPONSIBILITY

Communications between lawyers and clients concerning legal matters are generally protected by the privilege. In some countries, this privilege may not extend to inside lawyers employed by a company. When working with large teams on an outsourcing contract, not all communications may be protected, for a variety of reasons including:

- Lawyers' participation in discussions of business, operational, or technical matters that have little or no relation to legal matters or legal advice.
- The involvement of large teams in many meetings and communications. Communications with consultants may inadvertently compromise the privilege. For similar reasons, communications with large groups of employees outside the usual management group may compromise the privilege (either directly or through thoughtless forwarding or broadcast of otherwise privileged communications).

In order to protect the privilege, it is generally good practice to: (i) explain privilege issues to the deal team; (ii) keep discussion of especially sensitive topics within a limited circle (such as knowledgeable management); and (iii) make appropriate use of privileged legends on communication and drafts. In the event of litigation, negotiation history becomes evidence, and participants (including the attorneys) may become witnesses. All the more reason to take pains that crucial advice is protected.

Many customers engage expert consultants to assist them with assessments, selection, negotiation, and even management of outsourced operations. Their work parallels and complements the legal work, and concerns a host of issues that must be captured in the contract documents. Many contract documents, particularly the crucial schedules defining scope, service levels and pricing, may be based on bid documents prepared by the consultants. Some consultants' activities may come close to the practice of law, although good consultants take pains not to give legal advice and rarely attempt to draft the contracts themselves. When reviewing or editing contract documents prepared by consultants, lawyers should always assume that they will be held accountable for the documents and related legal advice.

A few law firms which specialize in this field have affiliated consulting practices. Non-lawyer consultants do the usual consultants' work, often under the supervision of partners who act as the customer's primary outside advisors. This arrangement offers the client an integrated service, or 'one-stop shopping,' with professionals who know one another's methods and standard documents. However, when lawyers employ consultants or act as consultants, communications with the supplier's team are also, strictly speaking, communications with a represented party that should not take place without the participation or at least the consent of the supplier's lawyers.

Whoever employs the consultants, there may be too many meetings in too many different places for both sides to be represented, and many discussions concern arcane technical or operational matters to which lawyers add little. Clients are rarely sensitive to what may appear to be obscure (even mindless) professional etiquette, so the lawyers on both sides are well advised to work out acceptable 'rules of engagement.' Where working relationships between the lawyers are good, they may agree that lawyers may attend meetings even when their counterparts are unavailable. Nonetheless, in such situations, negotiation of contract terms and legal issues must be reserved for meetings where both sides have counsel, and business people must be free to reserve or revisit issues when their counsel are available. Scrupulous lawyers should not meet with the other side unless their lawyer is present or has consented. Even then, pains should be taken to keep opposing counsel informed and make sure there is ample opportunity to consult their counsel. Where consultants are employed by the customer's law firm, prudent suppliers may instruct their employees not to discuss contractual, negotiation, or other contentious issues without their lawyers.

3

WHAT RISKS?

Contracts allocate risk: that much is a truism, but what exactly are the risks? Too many lawyers and clients think of contracts as thick documents with familiar headings—recitals, definitions, representations, warranties, and the rest— without pausing to examine underlying risks and the purposes and effects of risk allocations.

Written contracts serve several purposes. They are memorials of business understandings, to which the parties may refer when issues arise. They create obligations that can be enforced through proceedings, and provide remedial rights that can be exercised without proceedings (to audit, withhold payment, and terminate, for example). In outsourcing—a prolonged, dynamic and inter-dependent business relationship—contracts also provide a framework or con-stitution for management of that relationship, and resolution of issues that are bound to arise from time to time. The written agreement is essentially fixed, although it may be amended, supplemented, and (occasionally) renegotiated. Much else will change: the customer's business requirements, market condi-tions, consumption of particular services, and the technologies and methods employed to deliver the service. Many factual assumptions and forecasts on which cost models, pricing, and plans were built are bound to be wrong. Foresight is imperfect. So are current data, however meticulous the customer's base case, however thorough the supplier's investigation. A good contract must help the parties to manage all of this uncertainty through processes that accommodate change and allocate risks appropriately.

Each side naturally prefers to push risks across the table, but without overwhelming bargaining leverage born of ignorance or desperation (or both), neither side is likely to impose all risks upon the other side. Ultimately, each side accepts some risk. How then to allocate risks, or from the customer's standpoint, to re-allocate risks that, before outsourcing, rest entirely with the customer. What, realistically, can be achieved at the negotiating table? How do risk allocations affect attitudes and performance after the contract is signed?

A good contract should not only limit potential exposure, but motivate both sides to perform and preserve the relationship so that goals can be achieved. In general, risk allocations should correspond with reality—with the parties' actual responsibilities and their ability to manage particular risks. Neither side writes insurance for the other. Overreaching terms, however obtained, breed resentment. Even the unskillful or overmatched may have excellent memories. If fooled, forced, or bullied, they will seek opportunities to reduce or avoid obligations improvidently assumed. Most business people recognize, at least privately, responsibility for their own operations, including errors and omissions. They also try to preserve business relationships and make them work, so long as doing so appears to be in the best interests of their company (all the more so, if doing so advances individual careers). Obligations, even disagreeable ones, are more likely to be honored if they are accepted as legitimate, bargained-for and consistent with long-run goals. Good contracts allocate risks in ways that harness these tendencies and help to achieve long-term objectives.

With these goals in mind, we may examine some of the risks. In outsourcing a great deal can go wrong. Business operations are transformed, transferred, and scattered; entrusted to largely (or wholly) new groups of people (often thousands of miles away); and changing combinations of occasionally quirky or unstable technology, all in the hope of saving money. At least occasionally, skeptics wonder why exactly consenting adults would hand over critical functions to outsiders who transfer operations to the proverbial far shore. But the risks, though numerous, are manageable and are offset by tangible benefits in savings, efficiency, and performance.

What, then, are the risks?

3.1 CUSTOMER PERSPECTIVES

Customers new to outsourcing approach the prospect with mixed emotions, attracted by the opportunities and potential savings, but wary of perceived hazards, including the following:

- *Loss of control.* Customers enjoy complete control over internal operations: locations, personnel, procedures, performance standards, and all the rest. Effecting change is a matter of giving instructions. After outsourcing, things are not so simple. A written contract governs the relationship. Instructions must be filtered through the supplier's account management. Changes are authorized through formal procedures, often at additional cost. Suppliers will say, with reason, that operations are theirs to manage, so long as they satisfy service level and other requirements. They answer for results, but enjoy a fair measure of autonomy in determining how best to deliver those results. To the customer all this may seem cumbersome, and far less flexible and adaptable than the proverbial 'old ways.' Good contracts must therefore balance the customer's understandable desire for oversight, control, and direction with the supplier's desire for reasonable autonomy in order to manage its business and, in particular, to standardize its services for the sake of efficiency and the economies of scale on which its price and margin may depend.

- *Transitional risks.* The customer's business may be at greatest risk during the initial transfer of operations. Experienced staff may be displaced or, even if not displaced, distracted, disgruntled, and inclined to seek opportunities elsewhere. Irreplaceable, unwritten knowledge and experience may walk out the door. Morale may suffer. So may operations, especially as they relocate from familiar surroundings within the customer's facilities to faraway places, at home or abroad, and the parties attempt to transfer knowledge through a process of debriefing, documentation, and training. The opportunities for errors and disruption resemble those associated with corporate relocations, but are compounded by changes in personnel and operational responsibility. Imagine for a moment moving a factory or headquarters while simultaneously completing a merger. Major transitions involve similar complexity. When the contract concludes—however it concludes, whether by exercise of termination rights or mere expiration of the term—the entire process must be repeated (if operations shift to another supplier) or reversed (if operations return to the customer).

- *Employment.* Outsourcing often displaces employees through transfer to the supplier or severance. These prospects are, understandably, huge distractions that may depress morale and have serious legal implications in all countries. Inadvertent or thoughtless action may have expensive consequences. When staff transfer, companies are concerned not only to satisfy legal obligations, but to retain, reward, and otherwise motivate experienced staff so that good service will continue. Essentially similar issues arise when the contract expires or terminates, and the customer (or a successor supplier) may wish to retain the workforce. Employment legislation may impose large costs (such as severance payments) as well as potential liabilities if legal requirements are not scrupulously observed.

- *Operational risks.* Outsourced operations rarely touch the customer's core competencies (such as product design) but most are essential, even critical. Imagine for a moment operating without electronic mail or payments during a prolonged network outage; customers' ire when they are unable to make reservations, place orders, or obtain support from an outsourced call center; or employee morale if outsourced payroll is late. Apart from the risks of serious disruptions in service, what of the risks of mediocrity, which can erode goodwill among users of outsourced services? Lacking direct operational control, customers are understandably concerned to assure good quality service— usually, service that meets or even exceeds the standards of the customer's former operations. What recourse do they have if service deteriorates after operations have more or less irreversibly moved outside or offshore?

- *Scope.* This may be the single most frequent source of friction after signing. Do the supplier's service obligations and base charges cover everything formerly done internally? Costly change orders could easily erase anticipated savings. However, even the best statements of work cannot capture all aspects of business operations, and customers' internal operations are not always well documented. Must the customer reach for his checkbook whenever and wherever the statement of work is silent, or omits an essential detail? Scope is, at bottom, both an operational and a financial issue.

- *Financial risks.* The business case for outsourcing is usually based on projected savings. Customers therefore fear paying too much because of unexpected change requests or excessive consumption. Charges for outsourced services by and large resemble bar tabs—thirsty customers pay more—and baselines are not always reliable. Apart from the supplier's bill, there may be other expensive surprises, in the form of costs retained or absorbed by the customer (to say nothing of the costs of managing the relationship, which are not trivial and are easily underestimated). Customers seek savings, certainty (or at least predictability), and the ability to manage costs by managing their own consumption. Thoughtful customers also ponder the supplier's financial health, especially when dealing with smaller, specialty, or startup suppliers (as opposed to such leviathans as the big computer hardware companies).

- *Legal, regulatory, and security risks.* Today, companies inhabit regulated fishbowls. Lapses have legal consequences, and are there for the world to watch (thanks to modern media), with the potential for immediate, dramatic effects upon reputations and share prices. Such regulated industries as banking, insurance, and health care have special concerns—the more so as regulators become attuned to the complexities of extended enterprises with outsourced operations. Most companies' principal assets include intellectual property that must be protected, along with sensitive personal data about employees and customers. Outsourcing adds complexity, by introducing a third party, as well as laws applicable to data transfers and operations in far-away countries. Who bears these risks? Can they be transferred or shared? Who is responsible for recognizing these issues when they arise, enforcing appropriate standards and procedures, and paying for violations and corrective action?

- *Extraordinary risks.* Negotiations devote disproportionate, sometimes disconcerting, attention to a variety of 'worst cases'—such remote, but potentially ruinous, contingencies as *force majeure* events (such as fires, floods, earthquakes, and terrorism), or ruptures in the relationship that might lead to termination or legal proceedings. Third parties (subcontractors, disgruntled employees, owners of intellectual property, or public agencies) may assert claims covered by one or more indemnities. Security might be breached, exposing consumers or employees to identity theft. Offshore operations may involve some measure of political risk. Could war on the Indian subcontinent affect operations in Bangalore or Chennai? Other less dramatic events may fundamentally alter the business relationships, such as enactment of restrictive laws, mergers, acquisitions, surges in consumption, or paradigm shifts in technology that supports the services, the customer's business, or both. Suppose the supplier's business is sold and its management replaced?

This 'parade of horribles' is not exhaustive, but illustrates the range of circumstances for which a good contract should provide, through (i) customary contract terms, such as representations, warranties, indemnities, termination rights, and other remedies; (ii) processes to prevent (or at least mitigate) unpleasant contingencies; and (iii) the allocation of residual risks between the parties.

3.2 SUPPLIER PERSPECTIVES

Suppliers have concerns of their own. Many are mirror images of the customer's worries.

Where customers worry about change orders that might erode expected savings, suppliers fear 'scope creep' that may erode their margins, if increasing volumes of service must be provided for a fixed price. Equally worrisome are risks of undiscovered, expensive surprises that may have been omitted from the customer's disclosures, or missed during the supplier's investigation of the customer's facilities and operations.

Customers hope to meet or beat savings targets written into business cases; suppliers' account managers feel corresponding pressure to deliver acceptable margins as well as good service. Just as customer deal teams build their business cases upon projected savings, suppliers' proposals are built upon cost models calculated to achieve profitability. On both sides, people must answer to higher-ups for financial results. Missing service levels tends to foreclose future business opportunities, as well as career opportunities for account executives and delivery managers.

Transition involves risk for both sides. The supplier has only one chance to make a good first impression. Success requires the customer's punctual and effective collaboration during a time of distractions and dislocation. Performance may depend upon transfers of personnel and the knowledge they possess. Whatever goes wrong—and in processes so complex, something is bound to go wrong—the supplier will be blamed, critics will feel vindicated, and the relationship may begin under a cloud.

When asked to absorb the customer's workforce, suppliers have the same concerns as any other employer, and want to be sure of sufficient work to keep new hires productive and profitable. They too fret about the maze of employment laws and potential liabilities, to say nothing of the possibility that, in a few years' time when the contract expires, some competitor will turn up asking to interview valued, well-trained staff. In EU countries, those people may transfer automatically, under the Acquired Rights Directive and implementing legislation in Member States—legislation that can impose substantial liability.

Suppliers understand the need to keep customers satisfied. Dissatisfied customers rarely award more business or renew their contracts. Credits assessed for poor service attract unwelcome attention, while simultaneously squeezing margins—a tough combination for the account manager who may have had little say in performance commitments or financial arrangements. If the sales team promised more than the supplier could, with confidence, deliver, or offered up some untested combination of products and services, the account team will take the heat when difficulties occur.

Pricing commitments over a lengthy contract term involve calculated risks about inflation, exchange rates and costs of the facilities, hardware, software, talent, and other resources required to deliver service. The supplier generally has little ability to adjust charges to its advantage, even though the customer may use 'benchmarking' and other rights to keep charges in line with the market, if market rates decline. Lacking clairvoyant powers, financial analysts are bound to get some of this wrong. With luck, errors will offset one another and contingency allowances will prove sufficient so that, overall, margins meet expectations, but there are no guarantees.

Suppliers, like customers, worry about increasingly stringent privacy and other laws that may increase both legal exposure and the costs of performance. Offshore suppliers may be mortified by the threat of protectionist legislation that could make their business models uneconomic, or even unlawful. Although suppliers are generally unwilling to assume primary responsibility for customers' compliance with laws and regulations that apply to the customer's business, suppliers understand perfectly well that non-compliance is bad news for both sides.

Where customers worry about lost control, suppliers worry about intrusive customers inclined to 'micro-manage' operations, who may insist upon variations from standard service offerings that add cost, increase opportunities for errors, and limit the economies of scale on which favorable pricing largely depends. Equally annoying, from the supplier's vantage point, is the customer who behaves like an adversary, so that discussions are debates, suspicion trumps trust, and both sides manage to the letter of the agreement—rarely a recipe for satisfaction or success. Suppliers enjoy this about as much as their customers appreciate receiving change requests for trivial adjustments in service.

One could go on, but these examples suffice to illustrate the complexities of these interdependent, collaborative relationships, and the risks underneath the closely-typed terms of an outsourcing agreement. Risk assessment begins by asking what could go wrong. Any sober assessment will recognize that a great deal could go wrong when critical operations move outside and offshore. However, doing nothing has risks too, especially if existing operations are inefficient, expensive, or out-of-date. For the customer, most of the risks are remote and manageable. Risks exist whoever performs the particular service—systems can fail, employees may err, sensitive data may be compromised. Sometimes, outside suppliers can better manage some of the 'worst case' risks. For example, suppliers who support the military, the police, and intelligence agencies, can deliver excellent security. Global technology companies offer greater disaster recovery capability than all but the largest companies. Assessment of risks is essential, but exaggeration of risks can either paralyze decision makers or tempt customers to seek excessive control or costly gold-plated solutions. These too have costs and consequences. Lawyers tend to think of risks as dangers (as they are) but for business people risks are facts of life that have to be managed effectively.

4

FOUNDATIONS AND FRAMEWORKS

Builders understand that before framing a building, one must lay foundations. In contracts, those foundations include recitals and objectives, rules of interpretation, the duration or term of the relationship, terminology, and the organizational structure of the contract documents. These terms, like the miscellaneous 'boilerplate' terms buried in the final pages of most agreements, have important, occasionally subtle, effects upon performance, as well as key contract terms, including scope and price.

4.1 CONTRACT ORGANIZATION

Outsourcing agreements may be written as self-contained documents, with contract terms, service descriptions, performance standards, transitional arrangements, pricing, and other essentials combined in a single comprehensive (if lengthy) document. For the lawyers, this may seem ideal. Tidiness has its attractions, and one of those attractions is consistency, which may be easier to assure when virtually everything that matters is rolled up into a single document.

Alas, what suits the lawyers may seem unwieldy, inconvenient, and inefficient to clients who have to live with and make sense of the lawyers' handiwork.

Those who work with documents after signing are more likely to focus attention on specific operational, financial, or other issues than, one would hope, indemnities. For their sake, self-contained exhibits describing the scope of particular services, relevant service levels, the calculation of charges, and other specifics are much more useful than comprehensive documents that compel users to thumb through fat binders searching for a particular responsibility matrix or pricing metric. For these purposes, separate, topical documents (and separate tabs in the binder) are more convenient.

Separate documents are also more efficient to prepare, negotiate, and maintain. In negotiations, discussions of price, service levels, and contract terms, for example, are likely to involve different groups of people. Separate documents facilitate more efficient parallel discussions. Moreover, service descriptions, transition plans, and other operational and technical documents are likely to be prepared and negotiated by business people or consultants (with legal review), where lawyers tend to write, edit, and negotiate the contracts. Combining everything in the lawyers' contract form may slow the process and (if private lawyers are retained) add legal costs without corresponding benefits. Later on, working documents such as service descriptions are far more likely to be amended or supplemented than, say, the audit, indemnification, liability, or intellectual property provisions of the master contract. Better, therefore, to keep the working documents separate, for the parties' convenience.

For these reasons, most outsourcing agreements consist of a master services agreement, supplemented by a dozen or more attachments or schedules. Of these, the most important are usually the statement of work or service description, pricing, service levels, and transition plan; although others concerning such matters as employee transfers, disengagement, governance, and disaster recovery (among others) are also important and may be heavily negotiated. Keeping them reasonably consistent with one another may pose challenges, especially in the final dash toward the finish line.

4.2 CONTRACT STRUCTURES

For purely domestic transactions, a single contract will suffice. If a domestic customer entrusts its data center operations to a domestic contractor, there need be only one contract, with a single set of attachments, even if the supplier proposes to relocate operations from pricey California to Oklahoma or Texas. A single contract may also suffice when the domestic customer relocates an entire function, such as software maintenance, to a single offshore destination, such as India (assuming no tax or other complexities).

The picture is more complex with genuinely multinational transactions—for example comprehensive IT services for a multinational customer operating in North America and Europe, with outsourced operations performed by a multinational supplier operating on both continents, in several countries, and service centers in India or other Asian countries. The parties may do business through many business entities. Different legal and regulatory constraints apply. Services may be delivered at different times, in different languages, and paid for in other currencies.

Many structures are possible, and details will depend upon specific operational arrangements, the parties' legal structures, and tax planning considerations. One can, for example, write a set of parallel service agreements, pairing the customer's mainland and offshore companies with the supplier or its relevant offshore affiliates, all under an umbrella or framework agreement governing the overall relationship. The UK customer contracts with the supplier's UK company; the customer's US subsidiary with the supplier's US company; and so forth for France, Germany, and other countries.

However, where essentially similar services are delivered in many countries, it may be simpler (and more convenient) to negotiate a single master agreement, and supplement it with brief local or companion agreements. The parties agree on a basic master agreement—say, for North America—with all relevant terms and schedules. If the relationship extends to the UK, there will be a brief companion agreement between the parties (or their UK affiliates) adopting the master agreement, but with appropriate provisions for UK taxes, employment laws, intellectual property laws, privacy legislation, payment in sterling, and any variations in the service offerings, performance standards, and other obligations. Hours of service, for example, may differ, and the British company is unlikely to observe July 4th, America's Independence Day, when rebel colonists dispensed with George III. These companion agreements, with exhibits, are generally brief, amounting to a few pages each. Negotiations are limited to the few terms that must vary from place to place, and both master and companion agreements come under a single governance structure in order to assure coherence and (importantly) resolve disputes between the parent companies (rather than through a multiplicity of local, possibly tactical, proceedings). From the customer's standpoint, this approach may reinforce management's usual desire to standardize operations worldwide, to the extent practical, in the interests of consistency and lower cost.

4.3 RECITALS

Recitals, which are usually bland introductory statements, are evidence of intentions and can be useful aids to the interpretation of complex documents.

They may also be admissions (in the event of litigation), sometimes conflict with the contract documents, and do not always receive the scrutiny they deserve. Contract recitals, like legislative findings, summarize the factual premises for the transaction, provide some background information about its history, and state broad intentions. So, in many contracts, do more detailed lists of goals and objectives, which also serve as guides to interpretation of the contract.

Customers prefer broad statements of intention and goals: improvements in service, lower cost, flexibility, better technology, and others, according to the situation. Customer counsel and consultants sometimes propose flattering statements about the supplier's qualifications, experience, sophistication, and proposal (on which they have, naturally, relied) and the customer's expectations for 'world-class' performance and blissful satisfaction. These provide a nice gloss for scope documents and other terms. Contracts, after all, should be interpreted to give effect to the parties' intentions. In documents meant to last for years, and likely to be applied in circumstances no one foresees (unlike, for example, a loan agreement or lease), the recitation of goals and objectives is more than window-dressing to give the document a neat, self-contained appearance. To a court (and in the US, jurors) these sound like promises. The recital begins to resemble a warranty and the proposal, a representation.

Suppliers object to the loaded term representation (which may tee up allegations of fraud or misrepresentation that may not be subject to the usual limitations upon liability).[1] They prefer brief, muted recitals with at least a passing reference to the supplier's desire to make a profit. Suppliers are reluctant (with good reason) to refer to (let alone incorporate) the sales talk in their proposal, or to appear to guarantee business results. Usually, the supplier's proposal will be overtaken by events during negotiations, so that it no longer accurately reflects the proposed scope, price, and other particulars and—notwithstanding future tactical advantages in any dispute—it is best to have a single, comprehensive, accurate document. Suppliers abhor grand sales talk (about 'world-class' service or customer delight), even when lifted from sales presentations and pasted into the contract. Salesmen ought perhaps to be somewhat more specific and less exuberant. From the customer's standpoint, specific commitments are generally more useful than glowing generalities. A sensible, reasonably balanced contract may recite the following:

- Basic factual background, such as issuance of a request for proposals; selection of the supplier based upon its proposal, as supplemented during

---

[1] As discussed at 12.3 below, outsourcing contracts usually limit liability, but liability for fraud and certain other claims is often unlimited.

negotiation; and the parties' decision to engage on the terms contained in the agreement.

- Both parties' intentions in general, neutral terms. The customer may seek lower costs, better and more uniform service, transformation of its operations and whatever else actually drives the decision to outsource. The supplier, for its part, seeks an opportunity to earn a reasonable return through successful performance.

Supplementary language may usefully add that statements of intentions and objectives are not intended to expand or otherwise alter either side's obligations, or to vary any express term of the agreement. Where the agreement is silent, ambiguous, or contradictory (and even the most comprehensive agreements have inconsistencies and blind spots), it should be interpreted to give effect to the parties' intentions. That is why, from the supplier's standpoint, some reference to its goals matters, for the commitment to provide service is not philanthropy, and interpretation of doubtful points should respect such commercial realities as the supplier's need to recover costs and earn decent margins. Suppliers, for their part, should respect the customer's desire for some overarching rules or principles for the interpretation of contract texts that cannot be absolutely comprehensive, or foresee all contingencies. Customers buy more than just a rate card plus black letter text describing specific service obligations. Their desire to pin down ephemeral sales talk is understandable.

4.4 TERMINOLOGY

Lawyers pepper documents with abbreviations, acronyms and 'defined' or capitalized terms. Everything described by the statement of work or swept into scope by a 'dragnet' clause becomes a 'Service.' Mandatory 'Service Levels,' measured and reported monthly, are distinct from general 'performance standards,' such as the obligation to deliver good service that meets industry standards. Although this apparent fetish for definitions (and the terms themselves) may bore clients, the practice represents good draftsmanship and helps to assure clarity, consistency, and precision. What Fowler's *Modern English Usage* would call 'elegant variation' is hazardous in agreements, where the use of different words may be presumed to convey different meanings. So 'Services' are the particular services to be delivered under the contract for the negotiated price—those services, and no others. 'Service Levels' are the ones attached to the contract.

There can be too much of a good thing. Sometimes, contracts are burdened with acronyms and jargon rivaling government contracts, as if written in an inscrutable dialect intended to baffle ordinary readers of English. Would anyone recognize an 'Eligible Non-ARD In-Scope Employee' on the street corner? Not likely—and this kind of verbiage can make contract documents unintelligible to business people. As so often, plain words work best.

More fundamentally, labels shape thinking. Sales presentations often refer to 'partnership,' a term that lawyers dislike because it implies joint ownership, agency, and liability (even though the business relationship may and perhaps should resemble a kind of partnership). But if outsourced services are more than commodities, should documents refer to suppliers as 'Vendors'—as though they were purveyors of paper clips, lock washers, and wing nuts? 'Supplier' or 'Service Provider' are at least neutral, though impersonal. 'Customer' has favorable connotations (since all businesses claim to be 'customer-focused'), but why not just use company names? No company entrusting crucial operations to a contractor wants to think of itself as just another customer. No one refers to family members as 'Husband', 'Wife', or 'Offspring'; or addresses co-workers as 'Boss', 'Subordinate', 'Secretary', or 'Receptionist'. Good businesses that meet the public address their customers by name. So should good contracts.

Many contracts have dozens of definitions (including the sample at the back of this book). Some are straightforward and unlikely ever to be contentious; but many have scope, financial or other (often subtle) implications that bear close attention and will repay scrutiny. Often, there is no clear or preferred answer, but implications must be considered from the relevant party's perspective for the particular kind of service and business context. Key definitions often include some of the following (listed alphabetically) and others (this list is in no sense exhaustive):

- *Affiliates*, which sometimes include divested business units entitled to receive service, at least for a time, after divestiture, and may not be limited to those wholly-owned or controlled by the parties. This may not matter, but could.
- *Assets* of all kinds, if relevant, including hardware, software, contracts, and perhaps intangibles.[2] Are 'Assets' limited to those listed on an attachment? Or are the lists open-ended ('including, without limitation')? What about assets overlooked initially but identified after signing? Do they count, and must they be paid for if used or supported—or is the price fixed, no matter what later inventories disclose?

---

[2] Assets typically matter more in IT transactions (which often involve transfers of, or use of, particular equipment, facilities, and software) than in business process transactions. Listing assets in familiar categories helps to avoid oversight and confusion and limits the risk of supplier pricing and other errors that may arise from use of a customer's unique or subjective classifications.

- *Baselines*, meaning current or initial volumes, rates or other metrics, subject to later adjustment, which may drive pricing and require periodic adjustment as consumption grows or contracts.
- *Confidential information* may or may not include intellectual property, and may or may not have to be marked or otherwise identified as confidential. Confidential information usually excludes matters independently developed, lawfully obtained from others, or otherwise in the public domain. There may be classes of confidential information (for example for especially sensitive information about the business, its employees, or customers that may be subject to greater protection).
- *Control*, which is usually (but not necessarily) defined in terms of majority ownership, voting control, or equivalents.
- *Employees* who may fit into various categories, such as those displaced or otherwise affected ('Affected Employees'), those who transfer to the supplier ('Transferred Employees'), key staff whose appointments must be approved ('Key Employees'), or transferees assigned to support the customer ('Key Transferred Employees').
- *Equipment* may be limited to listed devices, described generically or even defined to include related contract rights (such as support contracts or licenses to use system software). As with 'Assets,' one must consider how to treat unlisted or undiscovered items.
- *FTE* (full-time equivalent), meaning the level of effort associated with a single employee for an entire year, with appropriate allowances for vacation time and perhaps training and other administrative activities.
- *Intellectual property* in its various forms, including new 'work product', whether created specifically for the customer or incidentally in the course of performance.
- *Parties* may (or may not) include subsidiaries and other affiliates.
- *Projects*, meaning discrete, non-recurring tasks, authorized from time to time that are not part of basic service or required to meet service levels and other basic requirements. Few terms cause more confusion than 'project,' because of its loose, varying usage in everyday operations. To some people, 'projects' are major, infrequent undertakings (such as development projects, or the introduction of wholly-new systems and processes); to others, virtually any service performed upon request (for example the installation of a new device or software update) is a project. In outsourcing, where the menu of services often includes a variety of more or less standard activities (such as installations of new equipment), the more limited definition suggested above is usually better (and simplifies discussion of billing issues, since there are usually rates and charges for standard, recurring activities ordered from a menu).

- *Resource units* used to measure consumption and calculate charges should be defined with care and precision. Will the customer pay per user or employee or, for some IT services, per supported device? When services are paid for on an hourly basis, what is the best way to define 'productive' or 'chargeable' hours? To what extent may they include training, administrative time, or travel?
- *Services*, meaning those described by the contract documents or captured by operation of a 'sweep' or 'dragnet' clause (described in section 5.1) incorporating similar services formerly performed by or for the customer. Services are sometimes grouped in categories (known for some reason as 'towers,' such as data center, network, PC support, and applications in IT, or payables, receivables, and general ledger for accounting services). There may be operational or financial dependencies among various services.
- *Software*, both application and system software, often classified as belonging to one party or the other, or to a third party. Records of third party licenses are rarely complete or current, so one faces the same questions as with assets. Is software limited to listed systems? Are the lists exclusive, illustrative, or open-ended? What about software identified after signing? Software is sometimes defined to include related technical and user documentation.
- *Time*, including dates, calculation of time periods using business or calendar days, and inclusion or exclusion of holidays observed in various places.
- *Users* who are entitled to receive services. These typically include customer employees and affiliates, but may also include contractors, suppliers and others, at least for some purposes. So long as the supplier receives payment for additional volume it may be quite content, but the documents should be clear. Sometimes individual 'users' are distinguished from business units entitled to receive service ('Service Recipients').

4.5 CONTRACT TERM

Ten-year contracts were once common, but technology and business change rapidly and comparatively few transactions now involve asset purchases (which suppliers prefer to amortize over long periods in order to minimize service charges). For these reasons, five to seven-year terms have become more typical, and three-year terms are not unusual. Suppliers still prefer longer terms. Suppliers like longer terms and bigger backlogs. Longer terms may permit more favorable pricing. Suppliers may make concessions for longer-term contracts. The longer the term, the greater the supplier's ability to spread costs and, in general, the larger the volume of business, the greater the supplier's flexibility to reduce prices.

Whatever the term, both sides should expect more or less continuous negotiation of scope, service, change orders, and other issues; plus significant re-negotiations every three to four years as issues arise, technology evolves, and business requirements change. From the customer's standpoint, the nominal initial term may matter less than commonly supposed, provided termination charges are modest after the first two or three years.

When considering longer or shorter terms, consultants and financial analysts must consider the effect of scheduled replacements ('refreshment') of assets upon both service and termination charges (which, among other things, recover unamortized investments in case of premature termination for the customer's convenience).

4.5.1 Financial engineering and term

Once upon a time, IT infrastructure contracts almost invariably involved sales of hardware and other assets at book value. The customer received a tidy payment, disposed of assets without booking a loss, and entered into a long-term services contract. The economic and accounting logic resembled a sale and leaseback. This practice has faded in recent years, for a variety of reasons. Accounting practices appear to have grown more conservative, suppliers seem to have less ready cash, and customers and their advisors have discovered that 'financial engineering' may boil down to expensive financing that reduces future flexibility.

When assets are sold to the supplier, longer-term contracts permit the supplier to spread the cost over a longer time and reduce service charges. Financial engineering may permit a customer to unload assets without recording losses, but the supplier adds its cost of money (which may exceed the customer's) and profit to the price paid, then rolls everything into service charges in order to recover its investment, cost of money, and profit over the contract's term. Later, customer management may forget the benefit that they (or their predecessors) received, and discover (with ritual expressions of surprise) that their charges exceed market rates then prevailing. Moreover, investments in assets boost the supplier's termination charges, which include some allowance for unamortized investments and transition costs in the event of premature termination. Asset purchases may make termination a costlier option and so reduce a customer's future bargaining leverage. For these reasons, most customers treat 'financial engineering' skeptically. Many consultants now recommend that their customers retain all assets and related costs.

Business process outsourcing rarely involves transfers of assets, although financial engineering is sometimes considered as a way to spread heavy transition costs over the contract term by building those costs into service charges. The accounting treatment of such arrangements is best left to the accountants, but the economic consequence is, again, to increase both service and termination charges, since costs must be recovered through performance or, in case of premature termination, termination charges.

4.5.2 Renewals

Suppliers often propose 'soft' clauses: give notice, and then negotiate in good faith. Customers prefer flat renewal rights, without preconditions. Suppliers may propose to condition renewal options on the absence of any default, or circumstances that might constitute default, given sufficient time or notice, at both the time of notice and the effective date of renewal. Suppliers may also want cost-of-living and other price adjustments to apply during any extension period. In a business where costs have tended to decline, and many contracts are re-negotiated long before they expire, renewal options have modest practical importance. However, they can be useful to customers who dally, and leave insufficient time to investigate options before the contract expires—leaving no practical alternative to renewal on whatever terms the incumbent may offer. Notice and other time periods should be reviewed (and compared with termination assistance provisions) to be sure that the customer has sufficient time to find another supplier and disengage (a process that can easily take up to a year or more for the more complex contracts).[3] Decisions should be made well in advance of actual expiration, for in practice, as the deadline approaches, assigned staff will (understandably) begin looking for other opportunities inside the outsourcer or elsewhere. Attrition may affect performance.

Some supplier forms include 'evergreen' or automatic renewal provisions: unless the customer gives timely notice before the contract expires, it renews automatically and indefinitely, a year at a time. These are rarely in the customer's interest. Renewal should be a conscious decision, with an opportunity for reflection and, if necessary, adjustment, rather than an accident or the result of an oversight. Options to extend, even a month at a time, are a useful way to accommodate transition and other delays.

---

[3] Termination clauses often allow the customer to extend service, or selected services, for extended periods after the contract would otherwise lapse. These more limited extension rights permit the coordination of disengagement with transition to another solution.

4.6 EXCLUSIVITY

In an ideal world, suppliers would prefer the comfort of exclusive contracts, and in the early days, before customers routinely hired consultants and lawyers, many contracts were exclusive arrangements, often lasting the then-customary ten years. Apart from the obvious attractions of monopoly, exclusivity assures steady revenue, maintains the integrity of service offerings, and prevents 'cherry-picking.' Some services are more profitable than others, and the profitability of particular services is not always predictable. Many services are linked operationally. A help desk, for example, answers questions, maintains records of users and configurations, and dispatches particular kinds of support. Take it away, and both operations and cost models will change.

Customers abhor exclusivity. Rather than assure a comfortable life, they prefer that suppliers earn their business every day. They point out that if the supplier performs well (or even adequately) incumbency may assure a favored position. The proverbial 'devil you know,' enjoys obvious advantages over any competitor; and no supplier is equally capable across all services, or possesses all required skills. Monopolists can become complacent. For these reasons, exclusive contracts are now comparatively rare.

Suppliers, however, have a legitimate interest in assuring sufficient volume of business to justify pricing, investments in dedicated assets, and the assignment of dedicated account teams, whose costs must be spread over a reasonable volume of business. For the supplier, economies of scale are fundamental. Suppliers will not permit customers to avoid convenience termination charges by reducing scope and volume a millimeter at a time. Many contracts therefore include minimum revenue or volume commitments. If scope contracts or consumption declines below agreed minimum levels, the customer may offer the supplier additional work, 'top-up' payments on an annual or other periodic basis, or, if it wishes, terminate the contract for convenience and pay an agreed termination charge. Many customers dislike 'take or pay' minimum commitments, but in practice, if thresholds are comparatively low—for example, half or two-thirds of anticipated consumption—they are unlikely to be triggered. Dramatic contractions, if ever they occur, may be most likely amid other events—such as major divestitures—that would in any event compel the parties to re-evaluate and adjust their relationship.[4]

---

[4] For a fuller discussion, see 6.12 below.

The operational and financial integrity of supplier solutions may also be protected through:

- Assured opportunities to bid on new business related to the outsourced functions (but well-advised customers invariably reject rights of first refusal, which effectively deter competitors who know the incumbent can always match their bid).
- Partial termination rights that respect operational dependencies among related services. Related services must either be terminated together, or charges must be equitably adjusted to offset any inefficiencies. In practice, termination rights should be exercised in discrete, logical groups—for example by locations, functions, or business units.

Customers may fairly require suppliers to cooperate with other contractors, including their competitors. Suppliers generally agree, so long as such legitimate interests as intellectual property and security are protected, and they receive payment for significant additional effort in support of other contractors or, for that matter, the customer's own internal team.

Both sides usually recognize that, in practice, the incumbent—with its knowledge of the business, personnel on site, ongoing responsibilities, relationships throughout the customer organization, and other advantages—may enjoy *de facto* exclusivity, at least for the basic services, so long as performance is adequate. Bringing in others may be less efficient and more costly, but may also have the important benefit of keeping the incumbent alert and hungry.

4.7 LISTS

Many contract provisions enumerate performance obligations. Many schedules are lists of hardware, software, contracts, and other assets transferred, used, or otherwise affected by the transaction. These lists are rarely (indeed, almost never) complete or entirely accurate.[5] Statements of work often include lengthy lists of functions, operations, and other responsibilities. Some advisors to customers define 'include' (and its variants) to mean 'including, without limitation' wherever it appears. In other words, all lists are open-ended. This is advantageous for the customer and, if insisted upon, compels the supplier's counsel and team to scour the documents, and insert appropriate qualifications or limitations where necessary. Where time permits, it may be helpful for the parties

---

[5] See 5.3 below for discussion of the treatment of items discovered after the contract documents are signed.

jointly to review lists of performance obligations in particular, and discuss their appropriate extent and any relevant limitations, so that both sides walk away from negotiations with a common understanding. Often, open-ended lists are appropriate. In other situations, appropriate qualifications and limitations should be considered, such as:

- illustrative or generic limitations ('oranges, bananas, strawberries, and other fruits');
- specific exclusions ('oranges, bananas, strawberries, and other fruits, except lemons');
- specific or exclusive lists ('including only the following...');
- 'Containment' language (for example 'other incidental activities reasonably related to...').

Each of these variations (and, for that matter, open-ended lists) may be appropriate in particular situations. Some lists (of competitors and key personnel, for example) should be updated regularly during the contract term. Inventories or lists that drive scope and pricing (such as lists of supported users, facilities, or devices) are crucial.

4.8 RULES OF INTERPRETATION

The usual rules of contract interpretation apply to outsourcing agreements, as they do to other contracts. When the text is imprecise, silent, or inconsistent, the contract should be interpreted to give effect to the parties' stated intentions. Recital of those intentions is customary and appropriate, but they should not alter basic performance obligations or override clear language in the contract.

Agreements consist of many documents—often prepared in parallel by different hands and, perhaps inevitably, with insufficient time and imperfect coordination—so the parties or (in case of disputes) a court or arbitrators may have to reconcile differences among the master agreement, related schedules, and any companion agreements for services in particular countries. Generally, the master agreement should supersede any inconsistent terms in the accompanying service descriptions and other schedules. Conflicts between the agreement and schedules should be rare if the agreement refers to generic 'services,' and reserves operational, performance, financial, and similar specifics for the schedules. The master agreement is a kind of umbrella, and is more likely to have been drafted by lawyers, who may or may not comprehend technology and operations, but are supposed to get the legalities right. Schedules and exhibits, by contrast, are more often written by consultants and other experts who know the technology, operations, and financial commitments, but may not be accustomed to writing contracts. One of the lawyers' more important (if tedious) tasks is to reconcile all of the documents before signing, in order to assure consistency, particularly in the use of terminology and such operational mechanics as adjustments of charges, service levels, and baseline consumption.

To the extent that any difference might appear, it may be useful to add that specific, detailed descriptions of any particular service or other obligation supersede general references in the master agreement. For similar reasons, specific terms of a companion agreement concerning local law or service, will supersede inconsistent terms of the master agreement and its accompanying schedules. French users, for example, will expect help desk analysts to speak French.

5

THE SERVICES

Services are the essence of an outsourcing agreement. They are what the supplier contracts to deliver and the customer expects to receive for the agreed price. Documents describing those services—commonly referred to as statements of work or service descriptions—are, with related pricing, the most important contract documents (more important, usually, than the master contract). When difficulties arise after signing, differences of opinion regarding the scope of service may be the likeliest source of misunderstanding. If scope is too narrowly circumscribed, the customer may pay more than anticipated—writing checks and signing change orders for work the supplier's basic service should have included. Conversely, if scope is loose or elastic and tends to expand (or, as suppliers say, 'creep') without corresponding financial adjustments, the supplier's margins may erode very quickly.

Getting scope right therefore matters to both sides. In negotiations, the lawyers are, in part, advocates of clarity rather than adversaries, working with the parties to make sure that the documents accurately capture the business understanding, including any dependencies, qualifications, limitations, or exclusions. Good statements of work provide ready answers to basic questions: What, precisely, must the supplier deliver? When, where, how frequently, and in what volumes? What must the customer provide so that the supplier can perform? The ideal statement of work is clear to a reasonably proficient lawyer or business person on either side who did not participate in the original negotiation. Particular performance obligations are either within the agreed scope of service, or excluded. The best protection against misunderstanding is a combination of preparation and clarity: well-defined requirements, accurate cost data presented in a base case, full disclosure by the customer and thorough investigation by the supplier, culminating in a precise, comprehensive document with clear boundaries. These ideals are not always achieved. Time is usually short, information is incomplete, and even the best contracts must allocate risks for the unknown, such as undocumented service commitments or items omitted from the customer's disclosures and overlooked during the supplier's investigation. No document of reasonable size and clarity can describe each and every activity, and even the best documents are poor substitutes for diligence on both sides.

To avoid confusion (and inconsistencies between contract terms and statements of work) contracts commonly refer to 'Services' generically and define those 'Services' to include services described by statements of work, plus related incidental services captured by 'sweep' or 'dragnet' clauses, including (typically) services formerly performed by the customer and its displaced staff or an incumbent supplier. In theory, the same agreement could be attached to statements of work, pricing, and other exhibits for almost any outsourced service—from data center operations to logistics to catering—although in practice, many details within the agreement will vary at least slightly according to the particular function, industry, and other variables.[1]

5.1 'SWEEP' CLAUSES

Ideally, a supplier might prefer to limit services to those expressly described ('the following services, and no others'), so that everything else requires a change order at additional cost. Customers prefer broad generalities ('all services now performed, or performed by customer's staff during the twelve months preceding the date of the agreement'). Neither extreme is realistic or entirely fair. So-called 'general scope,' 'dragnet,' or 'sweep' clauses embrace functions not specified by the contract documents, but (i) inherent in functions described in general terms, (ii) formerly performed by displaced staff, or (iii) included in budgets or other disclosures to the supplier. In principle this seems fair where suppliers assume responsibility for whole functions, but reality is not always so neat. In practice, the effect is to shift to the supplier the risk for incidental, related services unmentioned in the statement of work and perhaps unnoticed in disclosures or investigations. As so often, the devil is in the details.

---

[1] For a discussion of differences among various kinds of outsourced services, see Ch 14 below.

No document can possibly describe all tasks and responsibilities. Customers want language to the effect that services include inherent, related or 'lesser-included' responsibilities implicit in general descriptions. Technicians repairing computers are expected to have tools, just as painting contractors have brushes, ladders, and other tools of their trade. Few suppliers object to references to implicit or inherent services, although they may suggest that the same principle should apply to customer responsibilities described in general terms.

Scope may fairly include services now performed, or included in a 'base case' or budget, but the supplier will want to exclude services that require different skills, services covered by other budgets, or services excluded, for whatever reason, from the proposal and price. Suppliers may also take pains to exclude miscellaneous services unrelated to the outsourced functions that may, for historical or organizational reasons, reside within outsourced budgets and departments. Consider who bears the burden of proof (especially when knowledgeable people transfer to the supplier or depart). Memories fade and sometimes seem malleable. A typical customer-oriented sweep clause might read as follows:

Throughout the Term, Supplier shall provide:
(a) The services, functions and responsibilities described in the Service Description(s), as they may be amended and supplemented from time to time pursuant to the Change Control Procedures;
(b) The services, functions and responsibilities performed during the twelve (12) months preceding the Effective Date by the personnel who were displaced or whose functions were displaced as a result of this Agreement;
(c) The services, functions and responsibilities performed by or for Customer under the base case; and
(d) Any services, functions or responsibilities not specifically described, but inherent in or necessary for the proper performance of the services, functions or responsibilities described above.
(For convenience, the foregoing, and any and all similar services performed by Customer prior to the Effective Date, are collectively referred to as the 'Services.')

Suppliers attempt to protect themselves by proposing specific qualifications, limitations, and exclusions from scope (in somewhat the same way that insurance polices cover some risks but exclude others), and circumscribing the sweep clause itself. Language may be heavily negotiated, and often includes at least some qualifications, such as:

• services 'reasonably related' to outsourced functions rather than 'all services;'
• related services regularly performed, during a discrete period, and not discontinued, in the manner and volume formerly performed—in other words, there are time horizons and at least loose limits upon volume;

- services disclosed by the base case or financial models, and reasonably related to those required by the statement of work—unrelated items buried in budgets do not slip into scope unless they are legitimate parts of the outsourced service offering;
- services not specified by the statement of work will be performed in accordance with the customer's past practice—again, this imposes at least a loose limitation upon the supplier's commitment;
- 'sunset' or 'cutoff' periods may oblige customers to identify overlooked or undocumented functions within a reasonable time after signing. This forestalls belated requests that suppliers do what was done long before, and may prompt the parties to perform a gap analysis while memories are fresh. Customers, naturally, would prefer that the supplier (whose experts have presumably conducted a thorough investigation) bear all risk of omissions and oversights. Unless gap analyses are actually performed within the time allowed, sunset clauses operate as statutes of limitation, cutting off claims for additional service.[2]

So a supplier might revise the sweep clause along the following lines:

Throughout the Term, Supplier shall provide:

(a) The services, functions and responsibilities described in the Service Description(s), as they may be amended and supplemented from time to time pursuant to the Change Control Procedures (*and subject to all qualifications to, limitations upon and exclusions from Services stated in the Service Description(s) or other Contract Documents*);

(b) The [eg, *information technology-related*] services, functions and responsibilities regularly performed during the twelve (12) months preceding the Effective Date by the personnel who were displaced or whose functions were displaced as a result of this Agreement *that were not discontinued before the Effective Date and are identified in writing to Supplier within twelve (12) months after the Effective Date*;

(c) The services, functions and responsibilities performed by or for Customer under the [budget or 'base case'] *reasonably related to the services, functions and responsibilities described by the Service Description(s) and identified in writing to Supplier within twelve (12) months after the Effective Date;* and

(d) Any services, functions or responsibilities not specifically described *or excluded from the Service Description(s)*, but inherent in or necessary for the proper performance of the services, functions or responsibilities described above.

To the extent that any of the foregoing provisions may require performance of services, functions and responsibilities not specifically described by a Service Description,

---

[2] After the contract is signed, gap analyses may be neglected in the onrush of other business. Customers who agree to 'sunset' limitations should add gap analyses to required transition activities, then follow through.

Supplier's obligations shall be limited to performance in substantially the manner and volumes formerly performed prior to the Effective Date. None of the foregoing provisions shall be construed to assign to Supplier any responsibility for performing services, functions or responsibilities designated as Customer responsibilities (or inherent in or necessary for the proper performance of services, functions or responsibilities identified as Customer responsibilities).

These sample provisions and possible edits by no means exhaust the possibilities, but illustrate some typical approaches to the issues. Customers seek inclusiveness; suppliers hope to contain their obligations; and in the end, both sides must accept a reasonable balance.

Each side should scrutinize the documents carefully to be sure they accurately reflect the parties' intentions. Customers must be sure that statements of work are reasonably comprehensive. Omissions may prove expensive. Suppliers must take pains to exclude responsibilities beyond the scope of their proposal and price, lest sweep clauses, other general language, or mere inertia extend commitments beyond intentions (or the underlying cost-model that supports the supplier's price). Scope documents should also specify the customer's responsibilities, and any related dependencies. Some of the supplier's responsibilities may depend upon timely performance by the customer. Sweep clauses help to fill gaps by providing agreed rules to allocate responsibility for activities neither expressly required nor excluded from statements of work, but they are not a substitute for complete disclosure by the customer, thorough investigation by the supplier, or painstaking discussion between the parties in order to be sure that the documents accurately describe a common understanding.

Sweep clauses first appeared some years ago, when the typical outsourcing contract transferred data center and other IT operations to an outsourcer, together with the customer's staff and, often, its facilities and equipment. Customers who handed over everything wanted to be sure that everything would, in fact, be done for the agreed price. Whatever had been done before had to continue. By and large—with qualifications like those described above—suppliers accepted this framework, for their comprehensive services were supposed to replace internal operations in all essentials.

More recently, the paradigm has begun to shift in some spheres. Selective outsourcing is common. Functions may be retained in part; entrusted to teams of suppliers; transformed with new technologies and processes; or largely replaced by an array of essentially standard services that may not correspond precisely to former internal operations. Staff and assets may not transfer to the supplier. In such circumstances, or when one outsourcer succeeds another, the original rationale may not apply, so conventional sweep clauses may be omitted, or narrowly focused upon inherent or lesser-included responsibilities.

5.2 STATEMENTS OF WORK

Forms for statements of work or service descriptions vary a good deal. The best describe *what* the supplier must do and deliver, without specifying *how* services are performed—for that is largely up to the supplier, and methods are likely to evolve. Usually, statements of work are drafted by consultants, suppliers, or other business people, although lawyers assist with editing, for clarity, precision, and consistency, as well as the negotiation of contentious issues. Few lawyers possess the kind of detailed operational and technical knowledge required to write thorough statements of work.

Statements of work may combine narratives, matrices, and lists. Some years ago, statements of work tended to be detailed narratives, describing operations and activities in detail roughly comparable to a cook book, with fairly detailed descriptions of the steps necessary to perform and complete particular operations. Detailed narratives offer the most precision. However, they take time to write, may be obscure or impenetrable, and (when written as customer requirements) may describe current operations within the customer's organization—operations likely to change when transferred to a supplier and to evolve thereafter. When differences arise concerning interpretation of the statement of work, accidental imprecision or inconsistency in complex narrative may tempt one side or the other to seek tactical advantage, even at the expense of bruising business relationships. Generally, summary descriptions of functions and outputs are preferable to minute descriptions of operations.

Narratives based upon current customer operations tend to introduce variations from the supplier's standard methods and procedures, which could add cost, while reinforcing some customers' tendency to micromanage operations, rather than effectively manage outputs and results. Suppliers often ask customers to adopt the suppliers' standard methods, nomenclature, and the like for standard services (such as help desk calls, service requests, and so on). Standardization and economies of scale are their game. Unless there are excellent business reasons to retain the customer's old ways, the supplier's standards may make sense, for the supplier should know its business and will probably charge less, perform better, and be more willing to be accountable for its standard methods.

Many suppliers and some consultants now prefer matrices or very general descriptions of each party's responsibilities. Many people find matrices easier to work with. They are simpler (and thus cheaper) to prepare, and neatly segregate or pair the parties' responsibilities for particular functions. Matrices may help to assure common-sense interpretations later, and minimize risks of gamesmanship, but the brief, occasionally cryptic phrases that appear in the tables may also risk imprecision. The parties could talk past one another without achieving a genuine meeting of minds. Joint review of matrices with separate columns for customer, supplier, and joint responsibilities usefully obliges customers to consider their own responsibilities, rather than assume (as some do) that everything passes over to the outsourcer.

Some advisory firms now recommend a 'value-chain' method that breaks down relevant operations in great detail, assigning one party or the other responsibility for specific resources, processes, and functions in complex charts. The exercise compels disciplined analysis on both sides, and may facilitate a common understanding, although it may be difficult to square with traditional methods of thinking, or general commitments to do what was formerly done by displaced staff. For example, IT professionals accustomed to thinking of particular classes of devices—mainframe, midrange, network, and so on—may not immediately adapt to the consultants' framework.

Whatever the form of the document, it is likely to include pages of dense text, obscure to all but the *cognoscenti*, detailing complex business operations. Given the complexity and potential for misunderstanding or confusion, a general introduction—written in plain English—describing the scope of service and the supplier's solution helps the reader (including executives, managers, and, if necessary, judges not regularly immersed in relevant disciplines) to make sense of what otherwise seems a jumbled collection of jargon and charts. Someone reading the introduction to a statement of work for IT services, should be able to learn that (for example) the scope includes the data center and wide area network but excludes local networks, voice telephony, and software maintenance without having to wade through the whole document.[3]

Drafting and negotiation of statements of work requires close collaboration between business people and consultants (who understand the operations but may not be accustomed to drafting contracts) and lawyers (who draft contracts for a living, but may be essentially clueless about technologies or operations). Observing the following guidelines can help to create documents that are reasonably comprehensible to all concerned, including those who inherit the relationship when original participants move on:

- Introduce the document with a clear, succinct description of the essentials.
- Use plain English and avoid jargon (although some technical language may be essential).

---

[3] For an example, see Appendix 4 below.

- Define all acronyms (lest the contract be mistaken for a government contract and bewilder the reader).
- Use active verbs (for example perform, deliver, install, operate).
- Avoid subjective terms (for example ensure, satisfy) and open-ended or infinitely elastic commitments (for example every, all, without limitation) unless charges are consumption-driven ('by the drink,' per FTE, time and materials).
- When ad hoc or non-specific services must be described, limit or contain the commitment in some fashion ('to the extent staff are available') or provide for payment 'by the drink' (on a time and materials, FTE or other basis that aligns effort with charges).
- Resist the temptation to seek tactical advantages (such as purely open-ended commitments) that yield momentary leverage without long-term benefit, because they merely defer rather than resolve issues.
- Functions that are especially sensitive or require complex interaction between the parties, or between the supplier and users or third parties, generally deserve more detailed treatment. HR or finance and accounting transactions, for example, may allocate some responsibilities for tax compliance to suppliers, while reserving others for the customer. Suppliers of HR or recruiting services communicate directly with employees and applicants, and those communications may create issues and liabilities for the customer. IT infrastructure contacts often require the supplier to manage and administer contracts for such crucial support as hardware and software maintenance—contracts for which the customer remains responsible. How then should the parties deal with notices, elections, or renewals or exercise various rights under those contracts (apart from day-to-day service requests)? Leaving these things to chance is not recommended.
- Above all, be sure that service descriptions are reasonably complete. Do they answer the cub reporter's basic questions: who, what, where, when, and how much? Qualifications, limitations, exclusions, dependencies, and customer responsibilities should be clearly stated.

Finally, customer teams should remember that, just as war is entirely too important to leave to the generals, statements of work are too important to leave to the consultants, lawyers, and other experts. Amid all that must be done to complete the transaction, time must be found for a thorough (meaning page-by-page) review of all service commitments, customer responsibilities, and dependencies, as well as any qualifications, limitations, or restrictions upon the parties' obligations. No words, however painstakingly prepared, can fully capture all that must be done, but the documents are more likely to capture the business understanding if time is taken to talk through the details and agree upon acceptable language. The process is tedious but essential. Thorough discussion not only improves the documents, but helps to assure common expectations and understandings—the more so when discussions include, as they should, the supplier's delivery team and their counterparts in the customer's organization, all of whom must live with the results.

Customers and their advisors occasionally suggest that supplier proposals be attached to and incorporated in contracts. This offers the tactical advantage of transforming sales talk into contractual commitments, but is rarely appropriate. Proposals often contain masses of general or background information that simply do not belong in the contract. The supplier's solution and other details evolve during investigation and negotiation, so that the proposal becomes outdated before the contract is signed. If attached to the contract, the proposal would surely conflict with the final statement of work.

Rather than attach the proposal, it is better practice to settle upon a single set of documents that define the parties' obligations—namely, the contract, statement of work, and accompanying schedules. These often reproduce tables, lists, and other material from the proposal, suitably edited and updated. Bid documents usually include matrices and other forms meant (when completed and negotiated) for inclusion in the contract binder. When sales presentations impress, customers should insist that statements of work and other contract documents describe the solution presented, capture expectations created, and (most importantly) include specific commitments. The presentations themselves are rarely precise or specific, and generally do not belong in the contract.

5.3 UNIDENTIFIED ITEMS (AND OTHER SURPRISES)

However thorough the supplier's investigation, and however comprehensive the customer's disclosures, some hardware, contracts, or other items are bound to be missed. Suppliers would prefer to charge more for each additional item. Customers prefer to keep charges fixed, and abhor adjustments after they surrender control of operations. Occasionally, customers simply suggest that the price be divided by a larger number of units, reducing per unit charges. In other words, the price is fixed, regardless. Suppliers might prefer to write change orders, and charge more for additional service. In effect, each would have the other absorb the entire risk. There are obvious objections to either extreme. In an ideal world, customers would make full disclosure, and suppliers would conduct exhaustive investigations and inspections, but these ideals are rarely achieved. The parties' competing positions may be reconciled through contract provisions for unidentified or unlisted resources. If assets or contracts were disclosed, or could or should have been discovered, they are included in scope and the supplier's price; if they were not disclosed and could not have been discovered, then the customer pays according to the relevant metric. Language may be heavily negotiated, especially concerning disclosure and presumptions. The essential problem resembles latent defects in a sale or lease of real estate: what was (or should have been) apparent from inspections?

5.4 PERFORMANCE OBLIGATIONS

What precisely does a supplier undertake by signing an agreement to deliver particular services? There is, of course, the duty to perform those services and to act in good faith (an implicit obligation in all agreements, and often stated explicitly). But what level of effort is required? Outsourcing contracts are replete with such phrases as 'reasonable efforts' (or 'reasonable endeavors') and such variations as 'diligent efforts,' 'commercially reasonable efforts,' or 'best efforts.' What do these terms mean? Do they mean anything more than acting in good faith to carry out the contract?

The answer, as so often with the common law, varies a good deal depending upon the jurisdiction, court, and context. None of the familiar terms is precise. Indeed they may be so vague as to be meaningless and, as a practical matter, unenforceable. 'Best efforts' are commonly thought to mean something more than business as usual, but how much more is difficult to articulate or quantify— and thus hard to enforce—without objective standards. Suppliers resist 'best efforts' commitments, which could imply exceptional efforts (conceivably, everything possible) without regard to the usual economic constraints.

In practice, 'best efforts' commitments are rarely agreed in outsourcing, apart from clauses concerning disaster recovery, *force majeure*, and other emergencies, where suppliers are generally willing to perform above and beyond the call of duty—working nights and weekends, bringing in reinforcements or experts as needed to restore service and sustain their customer's operations. For the rest, 'reasonable efforts' or 'commercially reasonable efforts' suffice. Those two terms seem roughly equivalent, although the term 'commercial' may help suppliers to resist any suggestion that uneconomic or heroic efforts are required. When contracts use a 'reasonable efforts' standard for everyday business as usual and 'best efforts' for emergencies, conventional rules of construction might suggest that the latter standard requires something more (perhaps much more) than 'reasonable efforts,' but only in exceptional situations. 'Reasonable efforts' commitments, when read alongside standard quality language that refers to good industry standards, would suggest that a supplier should be held to the standards of its competitors.

However, rather than relying upon rules of construction or any custom or usage, the parties might be well advised to define the terms. For example:

'Commercially Reasonable Efforts' means diligent performance in a manner consistent with good standards in Supplier's industry and the quality and performance standards in this Agreement, but shall not be construed to require unusual or exceptional expenditures or use or engagement of facilities, resources and staff not ordinarily available for performance of Services.

In other words, business as usual means diligent, conscientious performance consistent with industry standards, using the resources ordinarily available, for which the customer has agreed to pay. Extreme measures are not required. 'Best efforts' require more, though not heroic measures that might put the supplier at unacceptable risk:

'Best Efforts' means use of all of Supplier's available facilities, staff and other resources and capabilities in order to respond to emergencies and other urgent situations (such as, for example, execution of a disaster recovery plan, *force majeure* conditions or major outages, interruptions in service and corrective action) but without materially impairing Supplier's ability to serve other customers or its financial condition.

More or less stringent variations are possible, and the attempt to articulate clear standards may provoke spirited discussion—discussion worth having before a signing, rather than after an incident or misunderstanding.

6

FINANCIAL TERMS

In outsourcing, as in other transactions, few things matter as much as the price. The parties' interests seem directly opposed. Suppliers prefer to charge more; and customers, to pay less. Yet the competing interests of customer and supplier are more closely aligned than one might suspect, because of the parties' symbiotic relationship. Satisfied customers expect savings, meaning lower total cost than former internal operations or, if they have already outsourced, lower than their current supplier. Savings come directly, through lower total cost; and indirectly, by managing consumption and transforming costs (including fixed costs) into variable service charges. Historically, costs of such support functions as IT, HR, and accounting have been buried in overheads, so that users regard them as 'free,' and not costs that affect their business unit's bottom line. With outsourcing, there is a bill to pay. This can have salutary (if unsettling) effects.

Suppliers also need acceptable financial results—that is adequate returns—just as their customers need savings. Suppliers struggling to break even are unlikely to perform well. Troubled accounts may not attract the supplier's best talent. Sophisticated customers understand this, as well as the wisdom in such maxims as 'you get what you pay for.' Quality may not come cheap.

The parties' competing interests can be reconciled, if not aligned, if pricing assures both a competitive price for the customer and an adequate return for the supplier, while adjusting charges as consumption fluctuates to preserve this equilibrium. Healthy relationships require flexibility so that charges, underlying costs, and consumption remain in reasonable harmony; and the supplier earns decent margins at rates the customer believes to be fair and competitive. Revenues must cover costs of performance, overheads, and the original investment in the relationship through bid, proposal and marketing costs, and investments in assets or facilities.

6.1 PRELIMINARIES—THE BASE CASE

In order to measure potential savings, and compare outsourced alternatives, companies planning to outsource first prepare a detailed financial model (or 'base case') for the services proposed to be outsourced. Often, this essential chore is entrusted to outside consultants. Sometimes, the work is done internally. In either case the result is usually the foundation for both the supplier's pricing and the business case presented to management to support the proposed transaction. Pains must be taken to capture all relevant costs—for staff, hardware, software, facilities, telecommunications, third party products and services, overheads, travel, and all the rest. The quality of historic data may vary. Some costs are shared among business units. Others may be buried in odd places for historic reasons; just as budgets for operations proposed to be outsourced commonly include some activities likely to be retained.

The complexity and importance of this exercise is difficult to overstate, for the result tends to become the benchmark against which both initial proposals and future performance are measured. The customer's lawyers (and other participants not directly engaged in the financial analysis) should keep several points in mind:

- However thorough and meticulous the effort, historic data are rarely complete or completely accurate. This is especially true in the aftermath of mergers, acquisitions, or reorganizations.
- Collection and allocation of costs may be affected by organizational idiosyncrasies, subjective judgment, and, occasionally, individual or organizational preferences and agendas. No one is perfectly objective, of course, but objectivity must be the goal (and in this respect, engagement of outside consultants can help).

- Analyses of both current operations and future outsourcing must take pains to include all costs. This means comparison of total costs—including the costs of completing the transaction, costs retained by the customer after the deal is signed, and the costs of the organization that manages outsourced operations. Transition and relationship management costs are greater for offshore operations, or for portfolios of outsourced operations. Distance and complexity tend to add cost. Rarely will savings even approach crude differentials in salaries between, for example, Palo Alto, California, and Mumbai.

- Comparisons against historic data are instructive, but continuing trends (which are harder to measure) may be more important. It is helpful to know how the total costs of the outsourced solution compare with years gone by, but more useful to know how the outsourced solution compares with what the customer would pay if nothing changed and the customer simply carried on as before. When operations are to be transformed as well as outsourced—for example when the outsourcer is engaged to implement wholly-new systems and processes—comparisons with historic data are likely to be less meaningful.

6.2 RELEVANT TRENDS

Many outsourced solutions, even outside IT, are creatures of technology. In procurement, web-based catalogues may replace their printed predecessors. Outsourced business process services usually involve some combination of systems, web pages, call centers, and other substitutes for paper forms and manual processes. Prices for these services therefore depend, in part, upon costs for bandwidth and computing, which have tended to decline. Talent, by contrast, tends to become more expensive, especially in such prime locations as Northern California. That trend has been offset by the stampede offshore to India, Eastern Europe, the Philippines, and other such places—but there too, demand has begun to fuel rapid increases in wages and salaries. Currency fluctuations complicate this picture.

Apart from labor arbitrage, bandwidth, and hardware, some other savings have become more elusive. Ten or fifteen years ago, companies' internal IT operations tended to be less efficient than outsourced alternatives, and consolidation of mainframe operations into a supplier's data center offered economies of scale. With distributed systems, such savings are harder to find, and many companies' internal operations have become far more efficient. So handing off to someone else may not, by itself, save much money. When outsourcing, the customer pays the outsourcers' costs—hardware, software, staff, facilities, and the rest—plus the outsourcers' overhead, margin, and (lest we forget) the customer's not inconsiderable costs to manage the relationship. All this adds up. Nonetheless, because of long-term declines in the costs of computing, many customers expect charges for outsourced services to decline over the life of the agreement (in somewhat the same way that the chronic inflation seemed a fact of life during the 1970s).

6.3 DEAL ECONOMICS

However complex the service, the suppliers' economic goals are straightforward: to earn a profit from long-term service contracts. They recover initial bid, proposal, marketing, and transition costs over the life of the contract, and squeeze out costs through economies of scale, improvements in productivity, standard processes, and other efficiencies. Typically, they earn their money after the transition is complete. During the first year or two, they may do well to break even. Later, if all goes well, margins will grow, so that average returns for the whole contract term are acceptable. Customers seek savings. In a marketplace where the costs of technology have declined, pressures for savings do not relent after signing. On the contrary, customers tend to press their suppliers throughout the contract term, and their advisors often recommend such techniques as benchmarking—a kind of appraisal against current market—in order to squeeze further reductions from their suppliers.[1]

Here, then, is a basic, ongoing tension. Just when the supplier looks forward to earning its anticipated return, the customer will press for price cuts. This fundamental tension lies beneath all mechanisms for adjusting charges and, for that matter, other adjustments affecting costs of performance (such as adjustments related to regulatory changes or improved performance standards).

6.4 BASE CHARGES

Contracts generally specify charges for the basic service, with adjustments for fluctuations in volume, changes in scope, and other changes in circumstances. Generally, the charges should be all-inclusive, with limited exceptions for specific reimbursable expenses and costs retained by or passed through to the customer. Customers dislike surprises on invoices for essentially the same reason that suppliers dislike uncertain or unbounded scope. Scope and price are closely linked, and must be defined precisely.

---

[1] See 6.6 below.

Finding words for pricing, algorithms, and incremental adjustments may challenge the draftsman. Spreadsheets may not necessarily capture all terms or possible variations and contingencies. Descriptions sufficient for proposals or management review may not translate easily into contract language. Sample calculations are helpful, especially for complex adjustments. Whether or not the text includes sample calculations, the parties should perform sample calculations and sensitivity analyses to make sure that results match expectations.

Pricing methods and metrics can be complex, but at the risk of some oversimplification, the following approaches are common:

6.4.1 Fixed charges

Fixed charges—like monthly rent in a lease—are simplest. However, if consumption soars, the customer may pay too little to compensate the supplier fairly, or even cover its costs. If consumption falls substantially, the customer may pay too much, while the supplier enjoys a windfall (assuming, in both cases, that costs to perform fluctuate with consumption). Where operations, technology, and service volumes are stable, predictable, even static, charges can be fixed. More often, fixed charges are adjusted as consumption and other circumstances change. For example, fixed charges (so much per month, or one-twelfth of an 'annual service charge') may be paid for consumption within a narrow range (for example 95 to 105 per cent of estimated or 'baseline' consumption). Consumption-based adjustments (described below) generally apply outside these 'dead bands.' Baseline consumption forecasts may be fixed over the contract term, or incorporate forecasts of growth (when the customer's business may expand) or contraction (for example systems slated for retirement). Since forecasts are never perfect, adjustments may be as important as projections based upon those forecasts.

6.4.2 Consumption-based charges

Consultants and many outside professionals commonly work on daily, hourly, or other 'time and materials' rates. These have the merits of simplicity and flexibility, but may not provide much incentive for efficiency, other than incentives for the customer (who bears the risk) to manage its consumption of the service. Nonetheless, billing by the hour, day, or full-time equivalent remains common for many labor-intensive services, such as software maintenance and development.

Purely quantitative, consumption-based charges (so much per hour, transaction, user, or device) resemble charges for electricity and other utilities. The more the customer uses, the more the customer pays. Unit charges are usually linked to consumption of resources used to deliver the service and thus, the supplier's marginal cost. When scope is uncertain, or the customer anticipates occasional, unpredictable needs for a particular service, consumption-based charges may be the only sensible alternative.

However, marginal costs for many services vary with volume. To use an extreme example, supporting a handful of users is rarely economic, because of substantial fixed costs. Price quotations generally presume some regular volume of service, in order to cover such fixed costs as account management, recovery of initial investments, and basic infrastructure. These arrangements may therefore include minimum payment or volume obligations sufficient to cover the supplier's unavoidable costs. For this reason, so-called 'utility' or 'on-demand' pricing for some outsourced services does not, in practice, differ very much from the more conventional approach, with base charges and consumption-based adjustments. The customer's savings depend not only upon the supplier's efficiencies, economies of scale, and offshore operations, but also upon effective management of consumption. Granular, quantitative pricing driven by consumption may provide customers with excellent tools to manage costs— especially if billings are in sufficient detail to permit 'charge-backs' to business units. Charges based upon consumption are often billed based on estimates, subject to periodic reconciliation (quarterly or semi-annually).

Software development and maintenance and some other labor-intensive services are often charged based upon numbers of full-time equivalents (FTEs) or time and materials rates (often at a discount from standard rates because of long contract terms and service volumes). Fixed charges are sometimes agreed for the management of large portfolios of applications, but portfolios change over time, and packages or proprietary systems of varying complexity come and go. Pricing adjustments, such as changes in volumes or skills, present challenges and no consensus has emerged regarding how best to measure or quantify levels of effort. None of the other methods tried, including 'work units' and 'function points,' has proved entirely satisfactory. Essentially similar challenges arise with such business process services as general accounting. The number of quarterly and annual closings is, of course, fixed: but the amount of work to be done, and skills required, could vary for a number of reasons. Given these complexities, there is a tendency to fall back to FTEs, time and materials, and other familiar (if not entirely satisfactory) standbys. Business process services tied to numbers of employees, payments, shipments, or other transactions are better candidates for consumption-based charges. For example, accounts payable services—review and payment of invoices and related activities—are readily linked to numbers of invoices. Some HR services may be tied to numbers of employees supported.

6.4.3 'Open book' charges

'Open-book' or 'cost-plus' pricing is comparatively rare, arguably advantageous to the customer, and a very disarming marketing strategy since it seems transparent. Rather than pay so much per device, call, or transaction the customer agrees to pay the supplier's costs plus a percentage markup. Similar 'cost-plus' methods are used in some construction and government contracts. However, open-book pricing is complex and replete with opportunities for acrimony (for example concerning overhead allocations, 'allowable' costs, and other accounting issues). Administration of these contracts poses challenges. However skilled the customer's account team, and however robust the audit rights, no customer is likely ever to fully comprehend all the subtleties and mysteries of the supplier's accounts (assuming for the moment the customer's willingness to engage a platoon of accountants and analysts). Moreover, assured reimbursement eliminates the usual incentives to cut costs in a business where many costs have tended to decline over time. For this reason, few advisors to customers recommend 'open-book' contracts.

6.5 ADJUSTMENTS

6.5.1 Incremental charges and credits

The supplier's costs and charges to the customer should remain in reasonable harmony as usage fluctuates. When more service is required, more must be expended to provide the service and the customer will fairly expect to pay more. When consumption declines and resources are shed, the customer will expect to pay less. Increasing numbers of calls to a help desk, for example, mean more analysts, circuits, headsets, and work stations; and the reverse if usage declines. Either way, allowance also must be made for one-off expenses (such as additional facilities or capacity, when consumption increases; or the unamortized cost of equipment retired prematurely if consumption declines) and marginal costs. For some services, additional increments may cost less (where there are economies of scale); and below a certain level of consumption, marginal unit costs may increase, since fixed costs must be spread across fewer units of consumption. Imagine for a moment a mainframe computer running only a few cycles for a single customer, but still requiring cooling, power, raised floor space, maintenance, staff support, and system software.

The most common adjustments are incremental charges and credits (often known by the acronyms 'ARC' and 'RRC').[2] If the customer needs more, or fewer, servers, help desk calls, e-mail accounts, or other chargeable resources, bills are adjusted accordingly, often through a process of periodic reconciliation. Within a narrow range (or 'dead band') the charge may remain fixed. Outside that band, the customer pays more for each additional server, help desk call, man hour, or other chargeable resource. Conversely, if consumption falls below the lower limit of the dead band, charges decline accordingly.[3]

These incremental charges and credits generally apply within a wide range on either side of the baseline (say, ± 25 to 35 per cent). When consumption exceeds the upper limit, or falls below the lower limit: (i) there may be an equitable adjustment (as described below, generally based on the net change in costs or inputs); (ii) the parties may re-negotiate; or (iii) if there are minimum revenue commitments tied to the lower limit, the customer may either terminate the contract for convenience or make up the shortfall between actual consumption and the minimum obligation.

Most of these mechanisms are tied, directly or indirectly, to the supplier's consumption of various resources used to provide the service. This effectively links the supplier's costs with charges to the customer, and so helps to assure a reasonably equitable outcome. It also reinforces the tendency to 'build up' prices from cost models. Some suppliers, especially outside the relatively mature IT services business, have attempted (with mixed success) to improve their margins by offering charges based upon numbers of transactions processed, capitation (such as numbers of employees or users supported), or assured savings from the customer's current budget; but for the time being, resource and consumption-based pricing remains the most common method.

6.5.2 Cost of living adjustments and currency fluctuations

Inflation, the plague of the 1970s, has subsided, but cost-of-living adjustments to offset inflation persist in many contracts, including contracts for outsourced services. The parties' positions are predictable. Customers prefer smaller increases—with ceilings, 'collars,' low fixed increases, and the like—where

---

[2] 'Additional Resource Charges' and 'Reduced Resource Credits.'

[3] Those charges may be calculated from either the outer limit of the dead band, or the baseline, as the parties may agree. To use a simple example, if the customer pays US$100 per month for 100 units, $1 for each incremental unit, and there is a 5% dead band, 106 units might cost either (i) $101 ($100 for the first 105 units, plus $1 for the 106th) or (ii) $106–$1 for each additional unit above the baseline figure (1).

suppliers prefer more generous provisions that fully protect them against the risk of future increases in their costs. As salaries for IT professionals climb in India and elsewhere, and economists ponder the effects of pumping liquidity into the world economy during 2008–2009, cost-of-living increases may become an increasingly sensitive and contentious issue in offshore transactions.

Often the principal issues concern labor costs, including:

- The proportion of the charge subject to cost-of-living adjustments (which may be more appropriate for labor rates than for charges related to hardware or bandwidth).
- The selection of an appropriate index. Price indices come in many flavors and varieties, based upon geographic regions, the 'baskets' of goods and services measured, and other factors. Suppliers prefer indices tied to labor costs.
- When services are performed offshore, at least a portion of the charge may be subject to adjustment based upon an offshore index, or adjustments for currency fluctuations. For tax and other reasons, global services are often billed locally in local currency. Otherwise, currency risk is negotiable, and conversions (when necessary) are based upon rates published daily in such places as the *Wall Street Journal*, *Financial Times*, or various authoritative websites. Since suppliers seek flexibility to obtain services at varying offshore locations, customers are generally content to let them absorb the currency risk. Customers generally prefer pricing and billing in their own currency, and let the suppliers worry about and absorb whatever currency risks may be associated with their offshore operations.

6.5.3 Equitable adjustments

Greater uncertainties exist when there are large swings in consumption, often driven by such corporate events as mergers, acquisitions, or divestitures. When consumption is far above or below anticipated baselines (and, in practice, outside some reasonably wide band, such as ±25 per cent), many contracts adopt 'equitable adjustment' mechanisms originally developed in construction and government contracts. In those situations, there may be an adjustment, based upon net changes in costs of performance, in order to accommodate major changes in conditions and circumstances. If the contractor has to perform a great deal more work, it should be compensated for net additional costs, plus reasonable overheads and margins.

In outsourcing, adjustments may be based upon the net change in the cost of providing the service, with appropriate allowances for investments in new assets and facilities (or the unamortized costs of assets retired prematurely), cancellation and other one-time charges, plus overheads and profit. Since suppliers are reluctant to disclose costs, one may provide for disclosure of cost data to outside accountants or phrase the clause with reference to net changes in staffing, equipment, and other resources, rather than costs. In practice, sophisticated companies and their advisors can estimate probable costs with reasonable accuracy so long as incremental changes in those resources are disclosed. The essential point is to examine net changes and one-time expenses or savings, such as investments in additional equipment or facilities (when consumption surges) or premature dispositions (when consumption shrinks substantially).

Sometimes these equitable adjustment (or 'extraordinary event') clauses are 'soft' statements of intention obliging the parties to consult, and sometimes they are written to be binding (charges 'shall be adjusted') so that a judge or arbitrator can decide the matter, if necessary, using the framework laid down in the contract. That prospect can help people otherwise inclined to be sensible, if only out of fear that an outsider may decide the issue for them. Customers obliged to deal with incumbents generally prefer enforceable adjustment clauses.

Here is some sample language:

Charges (including termination charges) shall be equitably adjusted in the manner described below if an 'Extraordinary Event' occurs. A Extraordinary Event shall mean any event or series of related events which results (or can be reasonably expected to result) in use, during any single month, of less than seventy-five per cent(75%) or more than one hundred twenty-five per cent(125%) of the baseline quantity of any chargeable resource, together with [Customer's] [either Party's] reasonable projection that Customer's usage of that resource or consumption of any related Service(s) during the eleven (11) months thereafter will continue to vary from the baseline by at least the foregoing threshold percentages. If [Customer notifies Supplier] [either Party notifies the other] of the occurrence of a Extraordinary Event, the relevant charges shall be equitably adjusted to reflect: (i) increases in Supplier's cost of providing the Services because of the Extraordinary Event (including, without limitation, incremental costs associated with the use of additional Supplier personnel, acquisition of additional Equipment and procurement of additional Software licenses); (ii) decreases in Supplier's cost of providing the Services because of the Extraordinary Event (including, without limitation, savings arising from reductions in Supplier personnel, Equipment and Software used to provide the Services); and (iii) a reasonable allowance for profit. In addition, the relevant termination charges shall be equitably adjusted to reflect any acquisitions or dispositions of assets, severance, cancellation costs, and similar matters. The adjustment described in this Section shall take effect as of the first month following notice in which Customer's usage of the measured resource varies from the Baseline by at least the required percentage. Each Party shall make available to the other the information reasonably necessary to determine the equitable adjustments described in this Section. However, Supplier shall not be required to disclose its actual costs, profit or anticipated profit to Customer, unless the adjustment is disputed, in which case such information shall be disclosed, upon request and in confidence, to Customer's independent accountants or consultants (so that they may evaluate the reasonableness of proposed adjustments and advise Customer). The independent auditors or consultants shall execute a nondisclosure agreement with both Parties, and may not disclose Supplier's costs or profit margins to Customer, but may provide sufficient information for Customer to assess the proposed change or equitable adjustment. If the Parties are unable to agree upon such adjustments within sixty (60) days after delivery of Customer's notice, the adjustments shall be determined in accordance with the disputes procedures.

Many variations are possible. Should both parties have the right to invoke these adjustments, or merely the customer? Suppliers may prefer to measure net changes in inputs, rather than costs, and hesitate to reveal costs, even to the customer's auditors. Should this be enforceable ('shall be equitably adjusted'), or merely a commitment to talk (phrased as a commitment to exchange information, confer, and negotiate in good faith)? When should adjustments take effect— when thresholds are exceeded, the process is invoked, or its outcome is determined? These mechanisms are often invoked in uncertain economic times, when abrupt changes in business conditions or corporate transactions bring them into play. They provide an objective framework for negotiation, rather than a formula for calculation of adjustments, especially when cost data are not disclosed. The process can easily become contentious.

6.6 PRICE PROTECTION

Come what may, customers want the lowest price available. The bigger the contract, the keener this desire is likely to be, especially with long-term contracts for services the market price of which may tend to decline. Purchasing professionals expect this, especially in large companies. No one pays less for commodities than a major corporation, so (they reason) no one should pay less for outsourced services. Customers commonly seek at least one of two forms of price protection:

- 'most-favored customer' clauses obliging the supplier to charge the lowest rates then offered to or paid by others for the same services; and
- 'benchmarking' of rates, charges, and quality against current market standards through an independent assessment.

6.6.1 'Most-favored' pricing

Suppliers detest 'most-favored' pricing, seeing (correctly) a ratchet to reduce prices and margins, and introduce administrative complexities. For suppliers, most-favored pricing presents difficult (perhaps insoluble) compliance problems—problems an order of magnitude more difficult than those faced by suppliers of commodity products. Major suppliers may have no practical way of knowing what scattered sales teams have proposed, or what overseas contracts may contain. Services may be bundled in distinctive, even unique, combinations. Charges for essentially similar services may vary on account of asset transfers, contract duration, transition costs, and other variables. So comparisons are difficult, at best. In litigation, the very existence of 'most-favored' commitments invites extensive (and from the supplier's standpoint, intrusive) discovery. To assure 'apples to apples' comparisons, suppliers will insist that analyses be normalized to reflect asset purchases, personnel transfers, scope of services, volumes of services, geography, and other factors (which may just happen to reduce the universe of comparable contracts to near zero). Suppliers may also propose to limit comparisons to contracts entered into after, before, or between particular dates. Most suppliers reject 'most-favored' terms.

To be fully effective, 'most-favored' clauses require periodic certification from a knowledgeable corporate officer (who may be unable to certify compliance with complete information or much confidence), and permit confirmation, usually by an outside auditor (because of supplier sensitivity about disclosing costs, and the suppliers' confidentiality obligations to other customers). All of these complexities reduce the usefulness of 'most-favored' pricing on the comparatively rare occasions when it is agreed. For the customer, 'most-favored' pricing creates leverage in the event of controversy (if the supplier is out of compliance), but these provisions are rarely invoked and may not be very effective.

Nonetheless, customer advisors routinely propose 'most-favored' pricing. A few suppliers will agree, at least with respect to changes or new services, subject to some conditions. For example, a supplier may be willing to offer the best rates then quoted by a particular business unit within a particular region for similar volumes of the same service. Given the practical monopoly incumbents often enjoy, this may be useful protection. More important, merely proposing 'most-favored' pricing helps customers to negotiate meaningful benchmark clauses. Here is a sample 'most-favored customer' clause incorporating some of the points discussed above:

Charges payable from time to time by Customer under this Agreement shall not exceed those then paid by other Supplier customers under contracts signed after the Effective Date to whom Supplier provides services similar in duration, scope, and volume to the Services. The comparison of charges payable by Customer and such other Supplier customers shall take account of non-standard terms such as purchases of assets, transfers of personnel, and places of performance. If the prices charged to another Supplier customer are, considering the foregoing, lower than the charges to Customer, then the charges to Customer shall be equitably reduced to provide Customer the benefit of the lower charges, retroactive to the first date on which such lower charges to the other Supplier customer first became effective. Within thirty (30) days after the beginning of each Contract Year, a Supplier officer with executive responsibility for outsourcing services shall certify in writing to Customer that Supplier's charges to Customer comply with this Section. Upon request, Supplier shall provide to Customer's independent auditors the information reasonably necessary for Customer to verify compliance. The auditors shall inform Customer and Supplier whether Supplier's charges comply with this Section, but shall keep any information disclosed to them for this purpose in strict confidence.

6.6.2 Benchmarking

Competition among suppliers, advances in technology, and economic pressures have combined to increase customer interest in benchmarking, especially benchmarking with 'teeth' that directly or indirectly compels suppliers to match the market. Since comparisons require ample market data, and at least rough comparability among service offerings, benchmarking is, at least for the moment, somewhat more useful for IT services than in the less mature markets for various business process services. Where market data are insufficient, a benchmarker may construct a price from cost estimates, but this method is less reliable.

Benchmarking reports are ordinarily prepared by specialized, independent firms (but never the supplier's competitors). Benchmark firms are usually selected by the customer from a shortlist of reputable firms acceptable to both sides. Although suppliers dislike benchmarking, they are more willing to accept strong benchmark clauses if the process involves a reputable, independent firm. Benchmarkers may be required to sign strict confidentiality agreements, so that findings are held in confidence, and any data collected are used elsewhere only on a 'blind' basis without disclosing the parties.

Customers generally prefer a purely unilateral exercise, at their initiative, under their direction and at their expense. Suppliers sometimes propose a joint engagement in which they share the expense. Where costs are shared, and the parties jointly engage the benchmarker, there may be greater perceived objectivity, better cooperation, and fuller sharing of results with both sides. Whether this is advantageous may depend upon the particular situation, and one's point of view as customer or supplier.

Comparisons against market standards of quality and cost must be normalized to adjust for circumstances, including:

• *Unusual service or service level requirements.* Custom or 'fail-safe' service will cost more than ordinarily acceptable commercial service.

- *The caliber of the service provider.*   The top-tier providers of services are rarely the cheapest. They and their customers presumably perceive the difference as a cost of, among other things, overall quality and capability. With their cost structures, they do not accept comparisons against competitors operating from basements or garages.
- *Overhead allocations.*   Sometimes account management and other general or 'cross-functional' services are separately charged, and sometimes they are allocated among various services.
- *Transfers of assets and personnel.*   Some large transactions involve sales of millions of dollars worth of assets and transfers of large numbers of employees, who may be assured employment, at least for a time, with compensation comparable to that provided by the customer. These costs may be built into service charges and spread over the term of the contract; or a separate transition charge may be paid up front.
- *Volumes of service.*   Competitive pressures and economies of scale mean that very large consumers of service often pay less.
- *Geography.*   Charges reflect costs of hardware, software, infrastructure, bandwidth, and the like (which may tend to decline over time), but also scarce professional talent (which may grow more costly, especially in some regions). Suppliers increasingly attempt to serve customers from low-cost locations, at home, and overseas. Nonetheless, some services must be rendered where the customer operates. Services performed in Western Europe or North America will cost more than those performed in India or the Philippines.
- *'Financial engineering.'*   Unusual discounts, credits, 'loss leaders,' or other incentives inconsistent with customary notions of 'fair market' pricing may be recovered through service charges, and must be accounted for to assure fair comparisons.

Given the importance of benchmarking, many details of the process and language are intensely negotiated. Apart from those already mentioned, important issues include:

- *Scope.*   Usually all services, or discrete segments (by service category or region), in order to minimize the possibilities for 'cherry-picking.' In practice, margins vary among services, as in many businesses. Every diner knows that drinks and wine lists have larger margins than, say, appetizers. So too in outsourcing, where benchmarking the most profitable items on the menu could squeeze the supplier's margin.
- *Timing.*   Usually no more than annually, and often beginning only after the first or second year, when the parties are immersed in transition, need no other

distractions, and the original pricing remains reasonably current, especially when it results from competitive selection.

- *Sampling.* Issues include the size of the 'peer group,' comparison criteria for the 'peers,' and the benchmark firm's ability to consider adjusted in-house cost data as well as charges paid for outsourced services.
- *Competitiveness.* Customers generally prefer that charges fall within the lowest quartile of the benchmarker's sample, where suppliers believe that pricing near the median of the sample should suffice.
- *Consequences.* Customers favor termination rights and mandatory price reductions. Suppliers prefer to limit reductions to a very few per cent.

Of these, the most important and potentially contentious issue is the last: the customer's remedy if the benchmark is unfavorable. Suppliers readily agree to meet, confer, and consider adjustments in service levels, corrective action, or adjustments in charges. 'Soft' or 'meet and confer' clauses used to be the norm, and could, in fact, precipitate negotiated reductions. Findings that charges exceed market rates impose practical pressure upon both sides to make adjustments. Neither the customer's chief financial officer nor the supplier's account executive can easily ignore findings that charges significantly exceed market rates.

In any event, benchmarking clauses are now likely to have teeth, although the precise consequences of unfavorable findings are intensely negotiated. Suppliers are reluctant to agree to match market rates estimated by an outsider (which might cut margins excessively), or to allow the customer an inexpensive termination if that outsider determines that contract charges exceed current market rates. Common compromise resolutions include limited adjustments to charges (not to exceed some modest percentage) and discounts from the usual charge for convenience termination.

For customers, benchmarking has many attractions. In a business where quality has tended to rise, and costs to decline, customers seek assurances that market prices and service levels will remain competitive throughout the contract term. However, benchmarking can be time-consuming, expensive, and contentious. Comparisons involve fallible, debatable judgment. Even within a particular geographic region or industry, there may be wide variations among contracts. No two customers or contracts are exactly alike. Sources of market data are less extensive and reliable than, for example, public sales records used to appraise real estate. Data from internal corporate departments must be adjusted for comparison against outsourced services. Consultants and interested parties may honestly reach different conclusions. Debate may take on a life of its own, without any consensus emerging.

Suppliers suspect (understandably, from their standpoint) that the process is biased against them. Human nature, if nothing else, invites benchmarkers to focus upon opportunities for savings, or for service improvements that cost money to deliver. It is fair to say that, with general improvements in technology and market declines in many costs, benchmarking reports rarely recommend increases in charges (just as, when public agencies take property for public use, the property owner's appraisal always exceeds the government's offer). In any event—despite supplier requests—customers rarely agree that the supplier can invoke the process, or that favorable findings will justify increases in charges. Benchmarking is a one-way street.

Customers believe that nominally fixed charges (plus cost-of-living increases) may, over time, exceed the market rates, and yield overly generous profit margins. Ad hoc changes, effected after signing and under time pressures, without an opportunity to 'shop around,' are not always priced at the most competitive rates.

Each side has legitimate concerns. Usually, benchmarking prompts some reconsideration of charges and other financial terms. Whatever its limitations, benchmarking can be an effective catalyst for re-negotiations that raise service levels and reduce charges. In practice, it is most effective and most likely to strengthen business relationships when undertaken as part of a periodic review of the entire relationship that permits both parties to reconsider service levels, the supplier's solution, and other aspects of the transaction. With more to discuss than just the charges, the supplier may enjoy greater flexibility to meet market rates yet sustain margins if other cost-related elements of the transaction are in play. From the supplier's standpoint, price is not an independent variable, but linked to quality, hours of operation, performance standards, and other requirements that drive costs. Neither suppliers nor customers are wholly satisfied with the present state of the art, and the search for better or alternative methods continues.[4]

Here is a sample benchmarking clause:

Customer may [at any time] [once in every Contract Year] measure the quality, efficiency and cost of some or all Services against the market using an independent benchmarking firm retained by Customer ('Benchmarker'), which may not be a Supplier competitor. Benchmarker shall submit its draft findings to both Parties for review and comment by both Parties, consider comments received, and then deliver its final report in writing

---

[4] One approach is to re-open bidding periodically, on the theory that: (i) competing bids (including a fresh bid from the incumbent) are the best evidence of market rates; and (ii) the incumbent need never risk being forced to perform at a loss.

to both Parties. If the Benchmarker determines that Supplier's Charges materially exceed market rates for similar volumes of similar services (normalized, as provided below), then the Parties' representatives shall meet to discuss adjustments of the Charges. If the Parties are unable to agree upon adjustments in Supplier's Charges within sixty (60) days after receiving Benchmarker's report, then Customer may, at its option, terminate some or all relevant Services, or this Agreement, as Customer deems advisable, for convenience, as provided below, but no Termination Charge shall be paid. Customer's right to terminate shall expire one hundred eighty (180) days after receiving Benchmarker's final report. For purposes of this Section, 'materially exceed' shall mean that total charges for benchmarked Services exceed the [least expensive quartile] [median] of the benchmarked sample. Comparisons with market measures of quality and cost shall be normalized to account for investments in assets, transfers of personnel, variations in configurations, transition charges, reasonable overheads and profit, the place of performance, differences in service levels, unique or unusual Customer requirements, the place of performance and other, similar factors. Comparisons shall disregard unusual or uneconomic terms (such as introductory discounts).[5]

Suppliers often seek a variety of protections. Full consultation with both parties and review of a draft report is usually worthwhile, and can be a catalyst for resolution. Joint engagements reduce the cost to the customer, and may help to assure better collaboration among supplier, customer, and the benchmark firm. Normalization is entirely appropriate, as is an opportunity to negotiate adjustments—an opportunity certain to be taken and often successful. However, commitments merely to negotiate over the selection of the benchmark firm, the methodology, and even the result over an indeterminate (presumably long) period can deprive the exercise of most of its usefulness from the customer's standpoint. For similar reasons, customers generally resist any appeal right, at least in the absence of manifest error or serious abuses (in which case the supplier could presumably invoke the normal disputes mechanisms in the contract).

6.7 GAIN-SHARE

Sharing financial benefits, commonly referred to as 'gain-share,' can be an effective catalyst for innovation and change. Indeed, gain-share is an ideal example of a genuine 'win-win' proposition.

One flaw in the usual contract is the absence of incentives for the supplier either to exceed service levels or to find additional savings or revenue for the

---

[5] Bracketed provisions are alternatives.

customer. Suppliers are (for understandable reasons) unwilling to share savings from efficiencies or economies of scale in their own operations, since those savings are the basis for their profit and may in any event be squeezed by benchmarking or forward commitments to future reductions in price.

Gain-share can provide incentives. Customers must remember that sharing unexpected revenues or savings from innovations or exceptional performance is, in a sense, 'free'—to the extent that such incentives are paid from 'found' money the customer would not otherwise possess. If the customer accepts this point of view, it may be willing to offer the supplier more generous incentives to increase revenues and reduce costs. Gain-share can also ensure that the supplier has a stake in the outcome by linking the supplier's profit to results actually achieved. In other words, the parties' interests are aligned.

Examples of gain-share include:

- sharing cost savings (for example the cost per user of desktop services or lower cost procurement of computers through the supplier's bulk discounts);[6]
- sharing incremental revenues above the customer's existing revenues (such as sharing benefits from accelerated or improved collections); and
- allowing the supplier to earn a bonus for excellent performance in excess of contracted service levels, such as improved customer satisfaction surveys or improved sales.

The principle is rarely controversial. The devil is very much in the details. Customers approach bonuses with caution. Superior performance (beyond contracted service levels) may not translate into tangible benefits. If 99 per cent availability suffices, should the customer pay more for that last percentage point? On the other hand, sustained excellence across all service levels for extended periods may be worth rewarding, as an incentive for superior service. Canny customers may propose that a portion of any performance bonus be paid to the supplier's account team in order to motivate and reward individual perform-ance, and to attract and retain the supplier's best personnel. Not all suppliers' policies permit this, but if agreed, it can be an excellent incentive. Merely making the suggestion during negotiations may raise eyebrows among prospective members of the supplier's account team.

Unless performance standards are clearly defined, there is a risk of blurring the line between what the supplier should do on a 'business as usual' basis, and genuinely exceptional performance meriting some additional reward.

---

[6] Suppliers may not necessarily disclose actual discounts, but because they buy in bulk, they may still be able to offer lower prices than the customer could obtain, even after applying a markup.

For example, suppliers will generally include assumed cost savings for improved efficiencies and leveraged use of assets and third party contracts as part of the base charge. These need to be excluded from the scope of any gain-share arrangement—which is often far from straightforward, given most suppliers' reluctance to disclose costs.

In practice, the most common forms of gain-share therefore tend to be linked to benefits that do not require disclosure of the supplier's internal costs. For example, if the customer retains third party contracts used to provide in-scope services, the customer could agree to share savings achieved when the supplier obtains reductions in the cost or consumption of third party goods or services. Savings are transparent, since the customer generally retains these contracts, and either pays or reimburses costs. The supplier need not divulge its internal costs in order to determine shares of savings.

Another challenge is ensuring that the supplier is only rewarded for its own excellent performance, rather than improvements attributable to the customer's own efforts or those of third parties. This is particularly difficult where the supplier's performance depends in part upon the customer or on third parties, as it may in many complex business process outsourcings. Where dependencies exist, suppliers will press for gain-share or other incentive payments, when the supplier fully performed and would have exceeded relevant thresholds, but for customer or third party failures to perform.

Corporate amnesia presents another hurdle. Savings or benefits delivered in the first year of a five-year contract are unlikely to be remembered after the books are closed for the initial year. Customers can quickly grow to resent gain-share arrangements which generate significant revenues for the supplier. 'New' revenue streams or cost savings are soon taken for granted as part of the basic service. Specific gain-share arrangements therefore tend to have limited shelf lives, and are often limited to shares (declining shares, in some cases) of savings or additional revenue during the first year or two after a particular innovation.

6.8 INVOICES AND PAYMENT

Invoices present two basic issues—timing and detail.

Suppliers like to be paid quickly, even in advance. Customers prefer a more leisurely approach. No surprise there—all concerned understand the 'float,' and cost of money. Customers prefer to pay in arrears, after service is rendered. Suppliers prefer to bill (or better yet, be paid) in advance (at least for base charges or estimated base charges, subject to later reconciliation). Suppliers say they incur costs throughout the billing period, and prefer not to wait for their money, or extend credit. Billing on the first and payment on the 15th of every month approximates level payment. Supplier cost models commonly include imputed interest, often at rates higher than their corporate customers pay. Extended payment terms may oblige the supplier to add interest to its cost models and increase the customer's charges. Suppliers often propose to charge interest on late payments, if only to exert pressure. Customers may press for more favorable pricing in return for expedited payment.

The parties should agree, if possible in advance, upon the form and level of detail in the supplier's invoice. Customers may want billing by service, location, business unit, or other variations in order to charge costs back to business units. Supplier billing systems may or may not provide the desired level of detail, and variations in their systems, if feasible, may take time and money to create. In multinational transactions, tax-planning considerations may require local invoicing. For example, when support services are performed in European countries, the supplier's local affiliate may bill the customer's local business unit in order to minimize unrecoverable value added tax. These complexities deserve attention and should not be afterthoughts, to be sorted out after signing.

Customers sometimes insist that bills for services be presented, if at all, within a brief period (typically 60 to 90 days) after completion of the relevant service or billing period. This protects the customer from liability for stale invoices and cuts off belated claims for out-of-scope work that might otherwise surface much later, if controversy erupts. In complex outsourcing relationships, the supplier rarely performs in literal compliance with each and every requirement of the statement of work, and is likely to have done both more and less than a strict reading would require. In the event of a dispute, those variations may become issues, as the supplier seeks leverage by making claims for performance above and beyond literal requirements. Short cutoff periods for billing help to foreclose such claims.

6.9 COST REIMBURSEMENTS

Prices are not the whole story, for customers commonly pay or reimburse a number of other expenses, usually classified somewhat imprecisely as pass-through, retained, or reimbursable expenses. Generally:

- 'Pass-through' expenses are costs of third party products and services related to the supplier's service. For example, in an IT or network infrastructure contract, the supplier may manage the customer's relationship with a telecommunications carrier, review and approve the carrier's invoices, and then submit invoices to the customer for payment. Customers expect suppliers to be responsible for a prompt, thorough, accurate review of charges (including financial responsibility for errors and oversights, such as overpayments and lost discounts attributable to supplier delays).

- 'Retained' expenses are costs of third party products and services paid directly by the customer such as costs of applications software licensed to the customer and used by the supplier, or leases for equipment and facilities used by the supplier.
- Reimbursements are out-of-pocket costs incurred and paid by the supplier, but reimbursed by the customer (such as travel and living expenses for consultants and other itinerant professionals).

Why not incorporate all of these costs in the supplier's charges? Suppliers might do so if they saw significant potential for savings and efficiencies, but otherwise, their overhead and margin, when added to the underlying costs, would merely increase the total cost to the customer. Moreover, some of these costs may not be entirely predictable. If they were incorporated in base charges, with appropriate contingency allowances, the customer might pay more than necessary.

Travel and living expenses are often sensitive, partly because these costs (unlike the inner workings of the supplier's operations and cost models) are disclosed and well understood. One way or another, the customer will pay for travel, hotels, and other costs. However, predictable travel expenses incurred in the normal course of performance (such as travel to attend quarterly management meetings, or 'home leave' for onshore staff whose homes are abroad) are usually included in service charges, just like other predictable costs of performance. Unusual requests are another matter—for example when the supplier must summon experts from afar for a special project. Customers usually want rights to approve big ticket expenses (often, through budgets), compliance with approved travel policies (no limousines, hotel suites, or champagne), and, on request, documentation of expenses. Customers frown upon long-term detached duty (fly in Monday, fly home Friday) because they feel they pay a premium for less than a full week's work, and without a full commitment to their business. Sometimes, however, it may be the only way to get the right person, and the supplier's personnel have spouses, families, mortgages, and lives, just like everyone else.

To avoid misunderstandings, it is wise to identify all expenses retained or passed through in a chart or table (often referred to as a financial responsibility matrix) allocating responsibility for all manner of costs in considerable detail. This is especially important when representing suppliers, as customer-oriented contracts invariably provide that charges are all-inclusive, apart from any reimbursable costs expressly stated in the contract.

6.10 TAXES[7]

Tax is a cost. It has several elements: the tax itself; the cost of compliance; and the consequences of non-compliance. As with any other cost, a customer and provider can generally allocate these costs between them—deciding who will bear the tax, the cost of determining the applicable filing and other requirements, and any interest or penalties that may be due in case these determinations turn out to be incorrect or untimely. The parties also can—and usually do—allocate the costs of dealing with future changes in tax laws. Thus, for example, some customers and their advisors may propose that fees should include all taxes, regardless of any change in law. On the other side, some providers propose that all payments be grossed up to offset any applicable withholding tax.

Obviously, no private agreement can shift the legal duty to assess, collect, and pay applicable taxes. Some have observed, moreover, that sophisticated suppliers are well placed to quantify any attempt to transfer the tax burden or compliance risk from the customer to the provider, and will ultimately recover such costs from the customer, one way or another. Major suppliers generally have internal tax specialists who have seen it all before. Customers should understand the tax ramifications of any potential outsourcing relationship, otherwise they may bear tax costs or risks that could have been reduced or avoided.

A global outsourcing relationship typically raises at least three types of tax issues: (i) permanent establishment; (ii) withholding tax; and (iii) transactional tax. The permanent establishment inquiry generally focuses on whether the supplier creates a taxable presence for the customer in another country where the supplier performs some or all of the contracted services. The withholding tax inquiry focuses on whether any cross-border remittances attract withholding tax in the payor's country of residence. The transactional tax inquiry focuses on whether any payments, in-country or cross-border, attract value-added, sales, and use, or other similar tax. Addressing these issues may be relatively straightforward when hiring an offshore provider to maintain and develop software applications. By contrast, the exercise is more complex when hiring a global supplier to maintain IT infrastructure around the world.

The permanent establishment issue lies somewhat outside the control of the customer and supplier. Local tax authorities interpret the rules, even where they claim to follow internationally accepted standards. Under a typical tax treaty, the services that a supplier performs on behalf of its customer in a country should not give the customer a taxable presence in that country, so long as the supplier

[7] The author thanks his friend and colleague, Michael S Mensik, for his insight and assistance with this section and others concerning taxation.

qualifies as an 'independent agent... acting in the ordinary course of its business.' If the supplier does not meet this qualification, one key question—among many others—is whether it has and habitually exercises the right to bind its customer to contracts with other parties, among other things. If so, the customer may be deemed to have a local taxable presence. So, for example, a captive call center where operators regularly make commitments on behalf of the foreign parent may constitute a permanent establishment.

Most industrialized countries have entered into an array of tax treaties that generally conform to internationally accepted standards. On the other hand, less developed countries may only have executed a handful of treaties with other countries. In the absence of an applicable treaty, the local tax authorities are free to apply their own domestic 'doing business' or nexus standards to determine whether the customer has a local taxable presence as a result of the services that are being performed within the country. These standards are typically less refined than those contemplated under tax treaties and may have a broader reach. Understanding the applicable standards—whether derived from a treaty or domestic law—is obviously important in any offshore initiative. Moreover, these standards are not static. It is, therefore, equally important to monitor how local authorities may modify or reinterpret them over time.

In multi-country outsourcing transactions, the customer often presumes that a centralized invoicing structure will best serve its needs with a single global invoice for all services, wherever performed. It then concentrates its tax analysis on this payment stream. Its importance is obvious, but analysis should not stop there. It should extend to understanding the intercompany charge-backs that will (or should) occur within both its and the supplier's organization as a result of such an invoicing structure. This inquiry can reveal that charges recovered from the customer's foreign affiliates attract withholding tax, which the customer may or may not be able to credit against its own income tax liability. More significantly, the inquiry can reveal that the supplier will incur non-recoverable value-added or goods and services taxes (VAT and GST, respectively) or other similar taxes, which the customer may ultimately bear, explicitly or implicitly.

VAT and GST are not taxes that the customer should ultimately have to bear, at least outside the financial sector where banks and similar entities may not be authorized to charge those taxes to their customers. By design, these are taxes that generally should be passed along to, and ultimately borne by, the final consumer in the supply chain. Non-recoverable VAT and GST can often be avoided by locally invoicing at least certain in-country services. Tax paid for local services can be recovered through local sales of the customer's own products. Local invoicing, however, may not be feasible in all instances: the provider may not have a local presence; its local presence might lack the capability to issue invoices; or the in-country services might be subcontracted to a local independent agent that is not empowered to invoice the customer's local affiliate for various reasons. In such circumstances, the customer usually has solid ground to argue that the provider should bear any resulting non-recoverable VAT or GST.

There may well be other tax imperatives to reckon with in large scale outsourcing relationships, such as global tax planning—a complex subject beyond the scope of this book—but expert analysis of withholding and transactional tax issues is crucial, and can be a fruitful area for collaboration between the parties as they seek to manage tax liabilities, comply with legal requirements, and pursue legitimate planning opportunities.

6.11 PRICING ASSUMPTIONS

Pricing is often based upon specific factual assumptions. Customers prefer to reduce uncertainty and keep the assumptions to a minimum, or remove them altogether, which may or may not be possible or appropriate.

Many assumptions concern the customer's responsibilities, operations, and facilities. If the supplier expects to use the customer's office space, it is appropriate to say so, and compensate the supplier if, at a later date, circumstances change, and it must lease its own offices. If the supplier plans to use the customer's phone switch, the contract should say so, and compensate the supplier if it must provide its own. When services are performed locally and offshore, there may be an assumed ratio between the two, and different rates for increases (or reductions) in one place or the other, reflecting actual cost variations. Other assumptions may concern probable consumption. Depending upon the pricing methods and metrics, there may be factual assumptions about, for example, usage of particular services (such as numbers of calls or installations per user or per month). Whether these are appropriate and reasonable will depend upon the facts and circumstances of a particular transaction. Usually, there is a good deal to be said in favor of realism.

When there are written assumptions, the parties should decide how and to what extent charges may be adjusted if assumptions prove to be unfounded. Charges may be adjusted based upon increased consumption, using the usual metrics, or adjusted based upon net changes in costs, resources, or other objective criteria, as for other kinds of equitable adjustments.

6.12 MINIMUM COMMITMENTS

Minimum revenue commitments typically oblige the customer to spend at least half or two-thirds of anticipated baseline consumption every year. If total spending falls below the threshold, the customer must either make up the difference or terminate for convenience (and pay a termination charge), unless the parties renegotiate the contract. Customers instinctively dislike these 'take or pay' provisions, which could lock them into contracts and require payment for unnecessary, unperformed services. No one wants to write that check. In practice, few such checks are written and, one suspects, few suppliers actually want to receive them. They would much prefer growth, or to negotiate scope adjustments if circumstances change. Suppliers understand perfectly well the deterrent power of minimum payment obligations and termination charges, but there are other rationales, more palatable to their customers. Suppliers seek minimums in order to: (i) cover their investments, account management, basic infrastructure, and other fixed costs; (ii) support volume discounts; and (iii) assure favorable accounting treatment of their backlogs. In practice, if levels are set well below anticipated consumption, these provisions rarely come into play, and customers who foresee shortfalls can avoid 'topping-up' payments by engaging the supplier on some additional projects or other discretionary work.

Minimum payment terms may operate in various ways. The simplest put a percentage floor under revenue for every year of the term. Come what may, revenues must meet or exceed an agreed threshold, usually expressed as a percentage of anticipated total revenue (excluding, of course, any expense reimbursements). Otherwise the customer must make up the difference at year's end. More complex arrangements may impose minimum commitments for each service category (for example receivables, payables, and general accounting in a finance and accounting transaction) and for the entire relationship, across all services. Suppliers may prefer this approach when services are operationally independent or managed by different business units, each with its own profit, loss, and fixed costs.

To minimize the risk of paying for unwanted services, customers prefer to peg minimums as low as possible, and fix them in absolute terms, rather than as a proportion of scope, which might grow. Customers sometimes propose to meet minimum obligations through commitments that decline from year to year, but meet an overall threshold for the full contract term, while giving them substantial leeway to reduce scope and go elsewhere after the first two or three years.

6.13 SUPPLIER FINANCING

Some suppliers, especially smaller companies, may borrow against contract revenues to finance asset purchases and general operations. When they obtain this kind of project financing, and pledge anticipated revenues, lenders will look for:

- substantial minimum payments (sufficient to cover debt service and operating costs);
- restrictions upon set-offs and withholding;
- exclusivity (or other limitations on the customer's ability to take work in-house);
- assignment of payments to the lender;
- representations and warranties concerning title, liens, and condition of any equipment, facilities or other assets acquired to perform the contract, which become collateral for the loan;
- prompt, direct payments (often by wire transfer to a dedicated account);
- interest or late charges for late payments;
- optional or mandatory customer purchase of dedicated assets upon termination; and
- termination charges sufficient to retire the debt in the event of any termination (even default termination).

Many of these terms limit customers' flexibility and are therefore unattractive to customers, but they may be essential for the supplier to finance its investment in the relationship. To the extent that financing is primarily for asset purchases, and those assets are dedicated to the customer, it may be easier and cheaper for the customer simply to purchase the assets and make them available for the supplier's use. The supplier will expect to recover interest expense through service charges, thus increasing cost, even as the lenders' requirements increase termination charges and otherwise reduce the customer's flexibility.

AMITABH CHAKRABORTY.

7

PERFORMANCE STANDARDS

Quality may matter less than price, but quality matters. Suppliers tout quality. Internal sponsors of outsourcing reassure skeptics that the brave new world will be better, or at any rate no worse, as well as cheaper. When operations are outsourced, few things will shred reputations faster or more thoroughly than a perceived erosion of quality.

Outsourcing contracts generally treat quality in two ways: (i) through general quality commitments (for example to meet or exceed industry or historic standards); and (ii) a number of specific commitments, known as service levels. Service levels help to assure good service at reasonable cost as technology and customer requirements evolve. Service levels are quantitative measures of performance, such as system availability and user satisfaction. Unexcused failures may oblige the supplier to pay modest sums as liquidated damages or fee reductions. Service levels serve several purposes. They set expectations on both sides. They deter— and to some extent compensate the customer for—poor performance, although the modest amounts paid rarely equal actual damages for serious failures (let alone consequential damages, lost profits or lost revenues that can rarely, if ever, be recovered).[1] Nonetheless, customers committed to contracts lasting years

---

[1] See 12.3 below, concerning liability limits.

understandably insist that failures must have consequences. Fundamentally, service levels assure attention to customer priorities and help both sides to identify incidents and trends, manage performance, and, when necessary, take corrective action.

7.1 SERVICE LEVEL BASICS

Current practice grew (like so much else) from experience with information technology. Many years ago, corporate IT departments began to document, measure, and report performance to their internal customers. These internal commitments were called 'service level agreements.'[2] The practice spread to commercial outsourcing. Outsourcing contracts often include dozens of service levels. At least a few are usually labeled 'critical' and cost the supplier money if they are missed. Others are measured and reported for management purposes, but have minimal, if any, financial consequences. Serious failures must be investigated, in order to determine causes and prevent recurrence.

7.1.1 Common metrics for IT

Service level schemes vary, depending upon the scope and scale of the contract, customer requirements, and other factors. Generally, they are objective, quantifiable, repeatable measures of matters within the supplier's responsibility, such as the performance of systems, the resolution of incidents or service requests, or the volume and accuracy of transactions and other outputs. The following examples illustrate some of this variety, and are typical (but by no means exhaustive):

7.1.1.1 Systems and networks
Important factors include the following:

• *Availability* of systems, typically measured as a percentage of scheduled availability, excluding maintenance windows and other scheduled downtime. There may be separate measurements for various computing platforms or for specific applications. Precise definitions are essential. Availability may mean availability of a computer and operating system, or availability of applications with relevant data. It may be measured on an average basis (for example for all

---

[2] The term persists, although specific service levels are not, strictly speaking, agreements, and the tables and metrics appended to outsourcing contracts are not separate contracts. Nonetheless, people commonly refer to 'service level agreements' or 'SLAs.'

servers) or for individual machines, or both. It may be measured at the host computer, or across a network.

- *Network availability*, also expressed as a percentage of scheduled availability, and with precise definitions for the network and measurements.
- *Response time* for particular systems or functions, measured at the host computer or across a network.
- *Response time* for repairs, measuring the time required for technicians to respond to incidents, generally classified according to severity (for example x per cent of Priority 1 Incidents within one hour; y per cent of Priority 2 Incidents within four hours).
- *Resolution time*, meaning actual time not merely to respond, but to fix the problem. Resolution time is measured and reported in much the same way as time to repair, but with longer times (for example respond within two hours, and finish repairs within one business day).

7.1.1.2 PC support
PC support functions include:

- completion of moves, adds, and changes (MACs), measured as a percentage completed on schedule;
- installations of systems, or setup for new users, also measured as a percentage completed on schedule;
- inventory accuracy, measured by periodic reconciliation against physical inventory, expressed as a percentage; and
- response and resolution times for repairs and incidents (as described above).

7.1.1.3 Help desks and call centers
The performance of help desks and call centers can be assessed using the following criteria:

- the average time taken to answer calls, measuring the percentage of calls answered by a live analyst within a time limit (for example x% within y seconds);
- call abandonment, measuring the percentage of callers who hang up rather than remain 'on hold' in a queue (for example not more than x% of calls);
- first call resolution, measuring the percentage of problems resolved through a single call to the help desk, expressed as a percentage of calls (calculations may exclude calls incapable of resolution in a single call, such as those requesting the dispatch of a technician or multiple calls about a single outage); and
- for inquiries submitted by e-mail, similar measurements of response time and resolution on the first contact.

7.1.1.4 User satisfaction

Many customers consider user satisfaction exceptionally important. For suppliers, user satisfaction and surveys can be problematic, because users' opinions are subjective. Those who preferred the old ways may not stand up and cheer when, for example, remote call centers and dispatched technicians replace expensive on-site support. Initial dissatisfaction may reflect annoyance with the disciplines and processes imposed by outsourcing, or with the decision to outsource, rather than the quality of the service. Surveys may be conducted by outside firms, using questions approved by both sides, and measuring satisfaction against a baseline assessment conducted before or shortly after the contract was signed. Many suppliers perform surveys as a matter of course, in their own efforts to assure quality. Some surveys deal separately with ordinary users, the customer's contract management organization, and its executives. Often, questionnaires are developed jointly, or at least with approval from the other party. Comprehensive assessments of user satisfaction may include: (i) routine inquiries after service calls; (ii) blanket surveys of all users (which may yield useful information, especially from the discontented, although they are rarely statistically rigorous); and (iii) surveys of representative samples (which are more likely to give an accurate picture of overall performance). Some or all of these techniques may be useful in particular cases, but suppliers rarely risk payment of service credits for anything other than periodic surveys of representative samples.

Rating scales should be agreed in advance, and provide a reasonable range for assessment, somewhat like report cards for schoolchildren. Perfection should never be the standard, but from the customer's standpoint mediocrity may be nearly as bad as certifiably poor service. Ordinary users' impressions of routine service—such as help desk calls or PC repairs—may color (for better or for worse) the reputations of the supplier and the corporate sponsors of outsourcing.

During and immediately after transition, some 'teething troubles' should be expected. There may be difficulties hiring or relocating staff, and even knowledgeable professionals take time to learn the customer's particular policies and quirks. Customers should anticipate grumbles, because things go wrong, and most change (even necessary change) prompts some complaints. Sometimes grumbling means the process is working as it should. User satisfaction tends to decline at first, and then improve. Where user satisfaction is tracked (as a service level or otherwise), measuring satisfaction at or before commencement may minimize nostalgia for the 'good old days' and help to assure comparisons against reality, rather than rosy memories.

7.1.1.5 Transactions

Transactions—such as shipments, deliveries, or payments—can be excellent measures of performance, since they reflect actual impact on the business, and often capture the performance of several related functions. Punctual delivery of shipping instructions to a warehouse, for example, may require the efficient operation of servers, applications, networks, user workstations, and so on. If everything works, a very high percentage of customer orders should be shipped on time. Calibration should reflect the performance of the least reliable element in the chain. However, since these metrics are specific (even unique) to particular companies, they may be difficult to compare against any industry standards. On the other hand, because some of these activities are critical to the customer's business, failures may justify substantial financial consequences.

These are merely examples. The variety of potential metrics is enormous. As outsourcing has moved beyond data centers, networks, and other IT infrastructure to embrace a variety of business processes, the variety has grown; but many service levels have evolved from familiar IT metrics. Call centers, after all, are not so very different from IT help desks. Many outsourced services rely upon servers or software applications whose availability can be measured; just as processing times and accuracy can be measured for completion of transactions, or responses to incidents and correction of problems. However, not all business process services can or should be measured using IT metrics and, in all cases, the selection of appropriate metrics should reflect the underlying service, the customer's priorities, and the supplier's service offering.[3]

7.1.2 Measurement and reporting

Service levels are measured and reported periodically, usually monthly. Some are measured during business hours or other peak periods, and others are measured around the clock, seven days a week (excluding agreed maintenance periods). Many are measured automatically. Software, for example, tracks calls to a help desk, their duration, the time taken to answer, and other particulars. The supplier's 'trouble ticket' or tracking software will record when calls are received and incidents resolved. Many computers produce regular measurements and reports of their performance. Suppliers generally provide much of this data to the customer in monthly reports. Ideally, measurements should be objective, automatic, and inexpensive to obtain. Often, data are equally available to both sides, or can be provided to the customer's management in real time on a 'read-only' basis. In all cases, the parties should satisfy themselves that performance can be measured easily, inexpensively, and accurately.

---

[3] See Appendices 6 and 7, for sample service level documentation for IT infrastructure and finance and accounting services.

7.1.3 Establishing service levels

To negotiate effective service levels, the customer must first decide what matters to its business, and how relevant performance can be measured. Preparation should begin long before a contract is awarded, with thorough analysis of the company's present performance and needs, and users' preferences. Surveys of users before outsourcing provide a good yardstick for measuring a supplier's performance, and help the customer to know its own collective mind: What works well? Where is improvement needed? What matters most to individual users, senior management, or leaders of key business units? Armed with this information, the customer's negotiating team is better prepared to propose and negotiate service levels with prospective suppliers of outsourced services. There is, however, a tendency to excess, as users compile 'wish lists' with more stringent and numerous metrics than the business may actually require, or the suppliers are willing to provide for an acceptable price. Inundation with metrics and reports is not necessarily a key to success, or even very useful. Measuring and reporting numerous metrics takes time, effort, and other resources, and so contributes to costs and, thus, charges. More subtly, excessive attention to service levels and reports may focus attention on minutiae and historic performance, rather than larger strategic issues. Good drivers watch rear-view mirrors and instruments, but also surrounding traffic and the road ahead.

Whenever possible, service levels should be fixed before the contract is signed, rather than afterwards. Customers want tangible commitments to quality while they retain negotiating leverage, before an outsourcer assumes responsibility for operations. Quality costs money, so suppliers need to know what standards will apply before prices are fixed. Neither party will want to begin the relationship with a debate. There are several possible bases for the calibration of service levels, including:

- The customer's own operations, if adequately documented. This measure is generally most appropriate where the supplier takes over existing operations and keeps them in place using similar methods and technology—if existing quality is good. Where current operations are inefficient, historic data may set the bar too low. Sometimes, historic data are incomplete or missing, and suppliers are understandably reluctant to commit to meet undocumented memories of past performance. When services relocate, and methods and processes are transformed, historic data (if available) may have limited relevance.
- The supplier's own standards for services delivered to other customers. This is particularly appropriate for operations transferred to the supplier's service center. If the supplier's help desk routinely answers most calls within

thirty seconds, the customer will expect comparable performance (assuming comparable staffing, call volumes, and other appropriate parameters).

- Market standards, established as presumptive service levels, and validated during a transition period. Preliminary service levels are fixed at levels the parties think achievable, and then measured during the transition period. If they are consistently achieved, they become effective after the transition period. If not, the supplier recommends corrective action, which may require investment by the customer. If the customer declines to make those investments, service levels are fixed at levels that can be consistently achieved. This method is often suggested when historic data are lacking.

As a last resort, service levels can be agreed upon after signing, but the customer's negotiating leverage diminishes once the outsourcer assumes responsibility for operations. Where the parties disagree, mediation or other expert intervention may help and, in the worst case, the contract may permit early termination if satisfactory service levels cannot be agreed—but such a drastic, disruptive remedy will rarely be attractive or practical.

7.1.4 Classifying service levels

Of the dozens of service levels commonly measured and reported, only a few are usually identified as 'critical' service levels that, if missed, expose the supplier to significant liability—generally because failures would have serious effects upon the business. Network outages and failures of key systems that disrupt production exemplify the kinds of service levels often classified as 'critical.' Why so few? Partly, because relatively few things are really crucial, and partly because (as we shall see) suppliers limit their financial exposure in various ways. If that exposure is spread among large numbers of service level metrics, credits are quickly reduced to mere pinpricks, without deterrent effect.

In practice, critical service levels are rarely missed. Suppliers pay attention to critical services (at least in part because of the financial consequences), and never sign up for standards they cannot routinely meet. Difficulties more often arise with services of lesser importance, where mediocrity may irritate users, but cannot seriously disrupt the customer's operations or, except in extreme cases, constitute material breach sufficient to justify default termination. Long delays at the help desk, interruptions in electronic mail, random or careless errors processing transactions, bungled service calls, and other such irritants can cause almost as much frustration as more serious, but rare, failures of major systems. To police this risk, there may be a lower, sub-critical tier of service levels (denominated 'standard service levels' in the accompanying forms) that are measured and reported monthly, but bear only modest financial consequences. There may be a token payment, or a larger payment if the same standard service level is missed repeatedly, or large numbers are missed (*x* failures in any single month, or *y* failures within any *z* consecutive months). The principle is familiar to any motorist: parking offenses cost less than speeding, but are not free.

Sometimes service levels have tiers or thresholds, with minimums (which cannot be missed without consequences), normal or expected service levels (par, expected every month), and more aggressive targets (which might, if exceeded, permit the supplier to collect incentive payments or 'bank' credit against future failures). Thus 99.9 per cent availability may be the target, 99 per cent the norm, and 98 per cent the minimum, below which credits are paid. Occasionally, there are still lower thresholds (for example 95 per cent), for which larger credits are paid, because of potential impact on the customer's business.

Finally, incidents or failures are often classified according to priority or severity. Formulations vary, but usually there are at least three classes: (i) the most serious outages that shut down business operations; (ii) those affecting groups of users that disrupt but do not stop operations; and (iii) incidents affecting isolated users or without significant effects upon the performance of systems and services.

7.2 BUSINESS PROCESS SERVICE LEVELS

Business process services pose particular challenges because the markets are not yet mature. Service levels matter for the same reasons as in IT services. Customers wish to assure good performance, manage suppliers effectively, and deter poor performance. However:

- There may be few, or at least fewer, accepted standards. Major suppliers of IT services offer broadly similar services: data center operations, network management, help desk, PC support, and the rest. Over time, many metrics (such as those discussed above) have obtained broad acceptance among suppliers, customers, their outside advisors, and independent firms who assess and benchmark performance based on accumulated market data. Competing suppliers of business process services, by contrast, may offer very different solutions. There may be few established standards or sources of market data about performance and best practices, although these emerge as markets and supplier solutions mature.
- Many potential customers for business process services have not consistently measured the performance of existing operations in such spheres as HR,

logistics, or other candidates for outsourcing. Even if there were good historic data, its relevance might be marginal, since outsourcing may introduce wholly new processes. The outsourcing of IT operations transfers responsibility, and operations may relocate to the supplier's facility; but usually the same applications operate on similar machines. Not so with business processes, where, for example, an internal website and remote call center may supplant many functions formerly performed by an in-house department, using older systems, telephones, paper forms, and manual processes.

To manage business process services with effective service levels, companies may do some combination of the following:

- Adapt familiar metrics used for IT services. Many service offerings depend upon applications of IT, networks, and the internet. Familiar measurements of availability, response time, and the rest may be relevant. Call centers, for example, resemble IT help desks, so that familiar measures of responsiveness— average speed to answer, first call resolution, call abandonment rates, and the rest—may be useful. Measurements of timeliness, accuracy, throughput, response times, and resolution of incidents may be as useful for business processes as they are for IT, especially if (as is often the case) processes are based upon automated tools. As with IT, measurements closely related to results— transactions, shipments, payments, deliveries—matter more to most customers than technical information about devices and operations.
- Suppliers keep records of performance for their customers and facilities, and should offer consistent quality to all customers. A supplier's standard metrics and reporting may provide a good basis for discussion.
- Key transactions—shipments, payments, payrolls, and so on—can be identified, measured during an initial transition period, and then fixed as standards for the remaining term of the contract. Other metrics can also be developed, validated, and agreed as part of the transition period that follows signing. In an ideal world, or a mature market, this might not be necessary, but often, some collaborative effort to develop and refine service levels after signing may be unavoidable.

7.3 SERVICE CREDITS

All failures should be investigated, reported, and reviewed for appropriate corrective action. Failures to meet critical service levels cost money unless they are excused as consequences of *force majeure* events or the customer's acts and omissions. Business people commonly refer to these payments as 'penalties.' Most contracts refer to these payments as 'credits' and treat them either as liquidated damages or reductions in the supplier's charges, reflecting diminished quality and value. Liquidating damages may suggest that recovery is the customer's sole remedy for unexcused failures, but this result may be avoided by good draftsmanship, such as reservation of the right to recover additional damages when the incident constitutes material breach, by itself or in combination with other circumstances.

The amount paid may be a lump sum, a percentage of the monthly charge, or the product of a formula. However determined, the amount involves implicit or explicit weighting based upon the importance of a particular function or service to the customer's business. The more significant the failure, the more it will cost. Repeated or multiple failures may cost even more. For example, if the same failure recurs, or more than one critical service level is missed in a single month, there may be a surcharge. One common approach is to compute credits as percentages of an 'amount at risk' available for the payment of credits, expressed as a percentage of the supplier's monthly charge. Thus, if 10 per cent of the bill is 'at risk' and a particular service level bears a 40 per cent credit percentage, the credit paid for a failure would be 40 per cent of the 10 per cent at risk, or 4 per cent of the monthly charge.

However the credits may be calculated, potential exposure is typically circumscribed by limits upon:

• *Total liability.* This is the supplier's maximum financial exposure, typically expressed as a percentage of the monthly charge and often referred to as the 'amount at risk.' The outsourcer could miss several service levels, but never pay more in credits than this ceiling. Negotiated ceilings commonly approximate the supplier's expected profit margin and amount to high single digit, or low double digit, percentages of monthly charges.

• *Numbers of critical service levels.* Many service levels may be measured and reported, but usually only a few bear significant financial exposure. The appropriate number will vary with scope, scale, and other circumstances, but does not often exceed a dozen to fifteen, and may be less. Spreading exposure among too many critical service levels may transform hurdles into speed bumps.

• *Individual credits.* No single failure can cost more than an agreed percentage of the monthly charge, typically a fraction of the monthly maximum or amount at risk. If 10 per cent of the bill is at risk, for example, there may be a 3 to 4 per cent limit on any individual credit. Limits on individual credits help indirectly to assure that exposure is apportioned among all credits and services.

• *Gross ceiling—all credits.* The potential total of all credits will generally exceed the monthly maximum, but not a higher aggregate ceiling. For example, if there were ten critical service levels, averaging 3 per cent of the supplier's monthly charge, the aggregate maximum would be 30 per cent of the monthly charge (subject, of course, to the monthly maximum or amount at risk, which is typically in the 8 to 15 per cent range, with many negotiated variations). If the supplier missed all ten, it would only pay the monthly maximum (although the ceiling would provide no protection against other remedies, notably default termination).

Taken together, these limitations assure that credits 'bite' but are not punitive. A contract might provide, for example, that: (i) there can be no more than ten critical service levels; (ii) totaling 30 per cent of the monthly charge; (iii) payments in any single month cannot exceed 10 per cent of the monthly charge; and (iv) no single credit can exceed 5 per cent of the monthly charge. Where the contract structure is based upon largely separate categories of service (such as data center and desktop IT services, or receivables, payables, and general accounting services) these calculations could also be based upon charges for relevant services, rather than the supplier's total charge.

Credits may be the sole remedy, or at least the sole monetary remedy, for unexcused failures to meet service levels. Customers and their advisors commonly reject 'sole remedy' language, lest they be limited to the collection of pocket change for serious failures. However, they may agree that credits are the primary monetary remedy for occasional failures, so long as they reserve the right to recover their full damages (up to negotiated limits on liability) where those failures constitute or contribute to material breach of the entire agreement. In cases of material breach or default termination, the customer will want to recover more than the comparatively modest service credits.

7.4 EXCUSED FAILURES

Not all failures are the supplier's fault. Accordingly, no credits should be paid for failures beyond the supplier's control, such as:

- *Force majeure* events. Contracts may excuse interruptions and other failures to meet service levels, when they occur, and during emergencies, while operating from a recovery site.[4]
- Acts or omissions of the customer, its employees, agents, and contractors, such as user errors, violations of law, breaches of the agreement (including failures to discharge customer responsibilities), breaches of agreements with third

---

[4]   Many contracts include disaster recovery services, and oblige the supplier to restore service, or at least critical services, from a remote site after a calamity. Plans should be kept current and tested regularly. Service levels may or may not apply, and are often excused, at least initially.

parties, infringements, reductions requested or approved by the customer, customer failures to take corrective action, or make necessary investments that are reasonably necessary to keep its systems up-to-date, and meet unexpected surges in demand.

Not all of these are standard, and exceptions may be heavily negotiated, but most contracts limit the outsourcer's responsibility and exposure to matters within its reasonable control.

7.5 SERVICE LEVEL ADJUSTMENTS

Technology, business requirements, and much else will evolve during the contract term. Performance standards improve. Many PC users remember when 'ancient' 286, 386, or 486 chips were greyhounds. How then can a customer keep pace and have confidence that service represents current standards? Contracts often require suppliers to use current, or near-current, systems, but they may also contemplate, and even require, changes in specific measures of quality, including service levels.

Outsourcing contracts normally contemplate periodic (and at least annual) joint reviews of service level performance and possible adjustment by mutual agreement, often through approved changes. Sometimes these exercises are forgotten or overlooked after the contract is signed and filed away. Major changes, such as the introduction of new systems, often involve the adoption of new service levels by negotiation through a validation process.

Contracts often allow the customer to make modest adjustments unilaterally—for example to re-classify non-critical and critical service levels or adjust credit amounts, within limits. Suppliers may accept this flexibility, so long as overall exposure is unchanged. For example, a contract may allow the customer, once or twice a year, to adjust a limited number of service levels, or to re-classify some secondary service levels as critical, provided that: (i) the monthly ceiling remains in place; (ii) the aggregate total of all potential credits remains fixed; and (iii) the total number of critical service levels does not exceed an agreed figure. Changes are generally effective after a reasonable notice period.

Customers increasingly seek assurances that service will improve during the contract term. An agreed plan to upgrade technology may, for example, justify a schedule of progressive improvements. Occasionally, contracts automatically adjust service levels to reflect actual, sustained improvements in performance. If so, the suppliers will tend to insist upon some margin for error, or ceiling upon potential requirements. Otherwise several months of exceptional performance could become an overly aggressive standard. Months without an outage or incident do not necessarily make perfection an appropriate standard. Some assured improvements may be conditioned upon customer investments in its systems and infrastructure, or other dependencies.

7.6 SUPPLIER INCENTIVES

Suppliers often propose offsetting incentives, partly in the hope of mitigating their risks. These may take many forms, including the following:

- cash payments for superior performance, such as consistent achievement of service levels, or more aggressive 'target' levels—for example by beating expectations for six months or a year across all service levels, or within a service category, if there are no unexcused failures;[5]
- non-cash 'credits' that accumulate against future failures based on the consistent achievement of service levels;
- forgiveness for isolated failures—for example a solitary failure in an entire year; and
- 'earn-backs' that erase or forgive credits if failures are corrected in the months following a failure. If a service level is missed, but consistently achieved for several consecutive months thereafter, the credit may be reversed. Suppliers may propose forgiveness if they meet the mark during the following month; customers tend to expect more—not merely to climb out of the ditch, but stay out for several months (and without other unexcused failures in the meantime).

Many variations are possible. The greater the supplier's exposure, the greater its interest in incentives, earn-backs, or other mitigation of that exposure. The suppliers' objectives are straightforward: to limit their exposure if performance generally meets or exceeds agreed standards, and perhaps to earn some additional margin through consistently successful performance.

Sophisticated customers may tie incentives to tangible benefits to the business, such as more rapid collections or shipments. The difference between 99.5 and 99.9 per cent availability of an e-mail server may not translate into any benefit to the customer's business; however, sustained superior performance across all service levels may justify incentive payments, because a supplier who

---

[5] When cash incentives are paid, requiring the supplier to pay bonuses to staff assigned to the customer's account it can be an excellent way to attract, motivate, and reward the supplier's best people.

routinely meets or exceeds all service levels is likely to be performing well. Incentives for consistently outstanding service may be money well spent.

Usually, service levels are reported and credits paid on a monthly basis. However, when complex adjustments are contemplated, such as incentives for sustained excellence or forgiveness for consistent achievement after an incident, the parties sometimes agree upon annual or semi-annual reconciliation exercises that include reporting, calculation of all applicable credits and adjustments, and net assessment or payment of amounts due. This simplifies the administration of complex service level schemes, and may coincide with (or prompt) a useful annual review of service level performance and other issues. On the other hand, the prompt monthly payment of credits may help to assure immediate attention from the supplier's account team or management. Writing checks can concentrate minds.

7.7 DEFINITIONS—THE DEVIL IN THE DETAILS

Pains should be taken when defining service levels, and especially the ways in which they are measured—where, how, how often, with what tools, and so on. For example:

- System availability may mean the availability of the operating system or applications, with or without relevant data, measured at the host computer, or across a network. Customers naturally prefer more comprehensive metrics, for without any single link in the chain, the system may be effectively unavailable and useless. Suppliers prefer to limit their exposure to their sphere of responsibility. The supplier maintaining software applications, for example, is at the mercy of the hardware and network.
- Server availability may be measured in the aggregate (for example total time for all servers, less outages) or by machine. Averages may mask some dreadful performance. For example, 99 per cent availability sounds admirable, but if there are hundreds of machines, a few could be stone dead without tripping the service level. Many customers therefore propose aggregate and individual parameters (for example 99 per cent availability on average, but no more than x hours of unscheduled downtime for any one machine). Sometimes servers are grouped according to their importance, with higher standards for machines that host critical applications. Downtime excludes regular maintenance periods (commonly scheduled during off-peak periods, such as the small hours of weekend mornings).

- Calls to the help desk may mean telephone calls (measured by automatic equipment), or may include facsimiles, e-mail messages, and web inquiries. Each may be measured somewhat differently. Measurements of response or resolution time commonly commence when a help desk analyst logs the inquiry into its tracking software by opening a 'trouble ticket.'
- 'First call resolution' or 'first contact resolution' (ie the number of inquiries resolved on the first call or contact) commonly excludes requests to dispatch technicians and install new equipment, or other calls incapable of resolution in a single call, such as those transferred to a customer or third party support organization.
- Multiple failures attributable to a single outage (such as the failure of one computer or telecommunications device) generally count as one incident. Similarly, if two credits might be paid for one incident, only the greater is typically paid.
- Time measurements may exclude travel time (when technicians drive to remote locations), or time lost while waiting for a user to confirm that work has been satisfactorily completed. Measurements of completion or resolution time often permit the outsourcer to mark a trouble ticket or service request as complete if the technician reasonably believes the work is done, and the user is unavailable to accept or approve the work.
- Users or 'seats' may mean individuals (generally employees and others eligible to receive service) or may mean networked devices (which can be counted with software tools).
- Some definitions may vary when used for service levels, as opposed to billing. For example, the customer may pay for all inquiries to the help desk, but some service levels or metrics may apply only to telephone inquiries (excluding e-mail, facsimiles, and the like). Some call counts exclude multiple calls about a single outage, on the theory that there should be no additional payment merely because many users report an incident.

These are merely examples. Each and every definition requires close scrutiny, and the correct answer in a particular situation may depend upon the supplier's standard practices, customer requirements, and other operational details.

7.8 NEGOTIATION OF SERVICE LEVELS

Service levels are not negotiated in isolation. Often, they are among the most important, intensely negotiated issues, alongside scope, price, liability limits, and remedies, among others. The resolution of major issues involves reciprocal concessions. Pressing for stringent service levels is bound to affect the resolution of other issues. Negotiated concessions usually have a price. In assessing these trade-offs, one must consider the real importance of service levels with a clear eye. Quality always matters, but service levels and credits may not always matter quite as much as is commonly supposed. Suppliers negotiate service levels energetically. Failures affect margins, and possibly the careers of the supplier's account team. (Some customers overlook this point, but to a supplier's account executive or delivery manager, the black mark—or red pixels on an executive's 'dashboard'—may be at least as important as the few thousand dollars deducted from an invoice after an unexcused failure.) Risks of failures and credits figure in the cost models that suppliers use to evaluate and approve potential business.

In reality, critical service levels are rarely missed. Suppliers never agree to any service levels that they cannot meet consistently. Once the contract is signed and service commences, suppliers pay attention to potential failures that could cost money. Critical failures are rare, and even when they occur, customers do not always force the issue and collect credits. Viewed in this light, large credits, or high ceilings on the supplier's exposure may not have quite the practical importance of other issues affecting scope, quality, cost, or remedies. Intensely negotiated credit payments are not, for the most part, real money, because they are so rarely paid. Service levels, moreover, are not the only way to measure quality or even the most important. Many customers profess dissatisfaction, even when service levels are consistently achieved. Meeting service levels is necessary, but not sufficient—in somewhat the same way that good vital signs such as respiration, temperature, blood pressure, pulse, and the rest do not necessarily constitute good health.

Apart from questions of overall negotiating leverage, and the fundamental truth that neither side can expect all key issues to be resolved in its favor, lawyers and clients negotiating these transactions should keep some linkages in mind, including the following:

- *Quality and price.*   Quality costs money. More stringent service levels require more support, redundant systems, and so on, all at greater cost. To answer all help desk calls within 30, rather than 60, seconds, the supplier needs more analysts. To assure 99.95 per cent availability, the supplier may need a redundant machine, with applications, data and the rest ready to go instantaneously. For genuinely critical systems, such as patient care in a hospital or an airline reservation system, this kind of protection may be essential. Not every business function actually requires 'fail-safe' reliability. Similarly, if less obviously, unusual measurements or novel service levels cost money to measure, monitor, and report. Often, the supplier's standard service, metrics, and service levels may suffice, at lower cost.

- *Service levels and default termination.* Serious or repeated failures to meet service levels may constitute material breach, and entitle the customer to terminate, after notice and a cure period. Default termination clauses sometimes provide that repeated or multiple failures (for example x critical failures in one month, y critical failures in z consecutive months, or total credit payments above some threshold within any twelve months) constitute material breach and grounds for termination without further opportunities to cure. It is not always easy to agree upon these figures. Customers are wary of the implication that if n failures are too many, n-1 may be tolerable, even if the parties reserve (as they should) the right to assert that other or different combinations may or may not constitute material breach.

Finally, customers—and in particular, first time customers—should remember the value of simplicity. Service level schemes easily become intricate, with tiers, classifications, weightings, calculations, adjustments, incentives, earn-backs, and other wrinkles that do not necessarily justify the time, effort, and occasional bewilderment they can cause. The elegant charts and calculations may or may not be entirely clear to those managing the contract after the lawyers and consultants have gone home. Effectiveness includes clarity and ease of administration.

8

INTELLECTUAL PROPERTY

Most outsourced services depend upon software and other technologies protected as trade secrets, or by patents or copyright. Intellectual property rights therefore lie near the core of most outsourcing agreements. Each side seeks to protect what it already possesses. Each side may claim interests in any new developments created. Usually, the most important varieties of intellectual property are computer software and confidential information about the parties' businesses, personnel, customers, methods, and technologies. Other kinds of intellectual property matter—depending upon the industry, service, solution, and other circumstances—but, usually, software and secrets are the prime concerns.

8.1 LEGAL RUDIMENTS

For the benefit of readers unfamiliar with the complexities of intellectual property laws, a brief overview may be helpful, but it is only a sketch, nothing more. Much intellectual property law is both statutory and territorial, and so may vary a good deal, even among common law countries. Protection in one country does not usually extend beyond that country's borders.

In the US, patents and copyrights are, in part, creatures of constitutional law. Article I, section 8 of the Constitution empowers Congress to 'promote the Progress of Science and useful Arts, by securing for limited Times to Authors and Inventors the exclusive Right to their respective Writings and Discoveries.' In England, statutes have protected copyrighted work since the eighteenth century.[1]

Patents are twenty-year monopolies, granted in the US by the Patent and Trademark Office, for new and useful inventions or discoveries, including processes, devices, and new and useful improvements.[2] Once a patent issues and until it expires, anyone else who makes, uses, sells, or imports the patented matter is an infringer and may be enjoined, even if they developed the device or process independently and innocently. In the US, unlike many countries, computer algorithms and business methods may be patented, although the practice and policy are controversial, and are often disputed in the case of particular patent claims. In Europe, computer programs cannot be patented as such, although patent protection may be available if the program produces a 'technical effect' beyond mere interaction with computer hardware.

Copyrights protect less—essentially, the expression in 'works of authorship,' not underlying ideas—but for far longer: the author's lifetime plus seventy years.[3] Copyright holders enjoy, among other things, exclusive rights to reproduce and distribute copyrighted works and create derivative works,[4] but: 'In no case does copyright protection. . . extend to any idea, procedure, process, system, method of operation, principle or discovery. . ..'[5] The EU's Software Directive embodies the same principle: that 'Ideas and principles which underlie any element of a computer program. . . are not protected by copyright,' although computer programs generally enjoy the same copyright protection as literary works.[6] Thus, one who simply copies someone else's software infringes the copyright; but creation of essentially equivalent software without copying is lawful. In the US, registration with the Copyright Office is not required, but confers the right to sue infringers for damages.[7] Registration is not required in the UK.

The ownership of inventions and works of authorship rests initially with individual authors and inventors, with one important exception. In the US,

[1] The principal statute is now the Copyright, Designs and Patents Act 1988.
[2] 35 USC §§ 100–103, 154(a)(2), and 271 (basic statutory provisions concerning inventions, term of patent and infringement).
[3] 17 USC §302(a); Copyright, Designs and Patents Act 1988, s 12(2).
[4] 17 USC §106. English law is similar. See Copyright, Designs and Patents Act 1988, ss 2(1) and 16.
[5] 17 USC §102(b).
[6] Directive (EC) 2009/24 [2009] OJ L111/16.
[7] 17 USC §§ 411–412.

copyrights in 'works made for hire' belong to (i) employers of employee authors (to newspapers, for example, not the reporters they employ) and (ii) those who specially order or commission certain classes of works, including 'collective works' (such as periodicals and anthologies) if the parties concerned agree in writing that the work is 'made for hire.' For outsourcing customers, these rules have two important consequences:

- First, if rights in software or other work product are to transfer to the customer, the contract should say so, clearly and explicitly. Otherwise, if the 'authors' or 'inventors' work for the supplier, they or (more likely) their employer, the supplier, will own their handiwork. Suppliers generally have agreements in place to be sure that their employees' handiwork belongs to the company.
- Second, since application of the 'work made for hire' doctrine may be complicated and uncertain, when contracts contemplate customer ownership of new developments, the supplier should agree that its work is 'for hire' and assign its rights to the customer (in the event a court later determines that, despite the parties' intentions, the work was not a 'work made for hire').

English law contains nothing quite like the US 'work made for hire' doctrine, but employers are the first owners of copyrights in works made by employees in the course of employment.[8] Since many professionals are often engaged as independent contractors, rather than employees of the supplier, both parties will want to be sure that rights are assigned appropriately to one of the parties.

Trademarks and service marks—the distinctive symbols associated with particular products and services, such as Coca-Cola's familiar script upon a red disc or Ford's blue oval—may also be registered and protected, but they rarely matter much in outsourcing. Customers and suppliers readily agree to respect the others' names and marks. Suppliers sometimes register service marks for their particular service and may request permission to display customer names and marks in sales literature or on their web sites.

Copyrights, trademarks, and patents are authorized by governments and statutes, although basic copyright protections may exist without registration. They are therefore territorial, and effective within national boundaries. Copyright treaties protect copyrighted works in member countries on essentially the same basis as the member country's own citizens, but there are significant variations in copyright protection for software. Other treaties afford certain priorities to successful applicants for patents and trademarks. If they apply for

---

[8] Copyright, Designs and Patents Act 1988, s 11(2).

protection in additional countries within limited periods specified by treaty, eventual registration may relate back to the applicant's original filing date.

Trade secrets are creatures of contract and secrecy, recognized by law and enforceable in court, but not registered or approved by any public agency. Trade secrets are information, methods, processes, information, formulae, devices, and the like that have value because they are kept secret.[9] Trade secrets may last indefinitely, so long as they remain secret. Patent claims are published, but with trade secrets, secrecy is paramount. Food and drink companies, for example, protect their recipes and formulae almost as vigorously as nations guard military secrets. Thefts or misappropriation of trade secrets are actionable, and may be enjoined—stopped or reversed by court order—but the law affords no protection against honest imitation: the risk that some clever competitor may develop an equivalent, even through reverse engineering. So long as the competitor does nothing improper, he is free to imitate.

In the US, software may be patented, and is universally protected by copyright and as a trade secret. Software licenses therefore contain robust non-disclosure and other restrictions, as well as a copyright license. Merely loading software into a computer's memory may constitute copying.[10] Licensors rarely disclose source code used to generate the machine-readable object code that operates systems. They may entrust source code to neutral escrows empowered to release code to users if the product is abandoned, the licensor ceases operation, or other dire contingencies arise. However, the source code, if released, may have limited value without access to technical documentation and the development team.

8.2 CONFIDENTIALITY

Virtually all outsourced services involve access to, use of, or processing of sensitive information—for example about employees, customers, and operations. Non-disclosure issues arise at inception, when bidders are obliged to sign non-disclosure agreements covering the prospective customer's request for proposals, requirements, and all disclosures concerning the operations

---

[9] Uniform Trade Secrets Act, s 1(4), in effect in 47 US states, defines 'trade secrets' as 'information, including a formula, pattern, compilation, program device, method, technique, or process, that: (i) derives independent economic value, actual or potential, from not being generally known to, and not being readily ascertainable by proper means by, other persons who can obtain economic value from its disclosure or use, and (ii) is the subject of efforts that are reasonable under the circumstances to maintain its secrecy.'

[10] However, the owners of copies of software may make archival copies and copy software into computer memories for normal use or in order to maintain the computer (17 USC § 117). The EU's Software Directive permits authorized users to load, display, and run programs. Directive (EC) 2009/24, Art 1(2), Art 4(1)(a). See Copyright, Designs and Patents Act 1988, s 50C.

proposed to be outsourced. Bidders require confidential treatment of their technical proposals and pricing. None of this is surprising or controversial. Nor, for that matter, are reciprocal confidentiality obligations in outsourcing agreements. Suppliers understand perfectly well that data concerning the customer's business, operations, employees, customers, and much else must be protected; just as customers accept that their supplier's price quotations and critical technologies are not to be disclosed.

Although these principles are straightforward, details matter, including the following:

- *Designation of confidential information.* Must confidential documents and data be stamped or otherwise marked, or are all data in certain categories confidential? What about disclosures made in circumstances that a reasonable person would recognize as confidential—must they be identified or designated? Most lawyers prefer the broad brush, recognizing the risk that documents may not be marked and unguarded conversations or e-mail messages may reveal sensitive information. Most contract forms, whether supplier or customer-oriented, tend to define confidential information in broad terms that may be opaque to readers unaccustomed to reading contracts. It is therefore wise to call out points of specific concern clearly, without curtailing the scope of general protections. General definitions may therefore be followed by 'laundry lists' of examples for each side—such as business plans, customer lists, research projects, pricing, change proposals, service level reports, and other competition-sensitive information.[11]
- *Exclusions.* Most definitions of confidential information exclude matters that are not secret, such as information in the public domain, commonly known in relevant industries, independently developed, or legitimately obtained without breaching legal or contractual obligations. To comply with privacy laws, information about individuals may be treated confidentially, even if basic information may be available from such published sources as telephone directories.
- *Permitted uses.* Generally, confidential information should only be used for purposes related to performance, such as the storage and processing of customer data, performance of services, or evaluation of the supplier's price quotations. Disclosure is often restricted on a 'need to know' or similar basis. Employees and subcontractors with whom confidential information is shared may be required to enter into confidentiality agreements, but suppliers

---

[11] The definition of software and other intellectual property as 'confidential information' may have unintended consequences, such as conflicts with the licensing provisions of the contract.

usually resist having employees sign confidentiality agreements directly with customers. If the data are especially sensitive, then the customer may require a non-disclosure agreement for the customer's benefit, enforceable by the customer as a third party beneficiary (in the US and other jurisdictions that recognize third party beneficiary contracts). Written admonitions to staff about the sensitivity of the work and their confidentiality obligations are also helpful.[12]

- *Standard of care.*　Many contracts require compliance with stringent security policies, often based upon the customer's internal practices. At a minimum, or where such policies are silent or do not apply, the contracting parties are usually expected to treat information they receive in the same manner as their own similar information. Suppliers should, for example, treat data concerning a customer's employees with the same discretion and care as for their own personnel records.

- *Compulsory disclosure.*　Generally, contracts allow disclosure under sub-poena or other legal compulsion, but the recipient must give prompt notice, so that the owner of the information may seek court protection and take other appropriate measures. Recipients are generally obliged to cooperate, but disclosing parties bear the expense of seeking protective orders or other protection. When the customer is a public company, obliged to file 'material' contracts with the Securities and Exchange Commission, and the contract is sufficiently large, suppliers will propose that confidential treatment be requested for pricing, service levels, and other competition-sensitive terms.

- *Expiration and return of data.*　The return or destruction of documentation and data is generally required when a contract expires or terminates. This is not controversial, although there may be some need to retain selected information for archival, audit, and similar purposes. In the information age, implementing these requirements is more complicated than returning or shredding paper documents, and the customer may fairly request a certifica-tion with chapter and verse concerning steps taken to remove and return data, erase media, and destroy paper copies. The customer will require a waiver of any lien on its data, and an absolute obligation to return its data enforceable, if necessary, by court order in the form of a mandatory injunction compelling the return of the data. In this way, the customer may avoid, among

---

[12] When outsourcing to India, many customers enter into separate non-disclosure agreements with the Indian company performing the work (often the parent of the domestic company with whom the service contract is signed) that are governed by Indian law and enforceable in India. Although Indian courts are not known for speed in reaching final judgments, preliminary injunctions are available within a reasonable time.

other things, the assertion of any statutory or common law lien imposed on personal property held for the performance of a service. Laundries, tailors, garages, and others may retain property entrusted to them until services are paid for, and so could a data center; but outsourcing customers never agree that critical data can be, as they see it, held hostage.

8.3 OWNERSHIP—THE EMOTIONAL MORASS

Intellectual property rights are complicated; so are contractual provisions allocating those rights. Not all business people appreciate the complexities and subtleties. Discussions easily degenerate into emotional debates about owner-ship—itself a more complicated subject than is often understood. Customers wax indignant about owning what they pay for. Suppliers urge the importance of their accumulated skills and experience, and their need to offer similar services to other customers, which could be difficult if their stock in trade belonged to a swarm of former customers. Room temperatures and blood pressures rise, but little is accomplished. How then to square the circle?

First, both sides may need to be reminded that, legally, ownership means a bundle of rights that may be apportioned or shared in various ways to suit situa-tions and needs. One can shop and commute in a leased car, live happily in rental accommodation, even erect buildings on leased land; the name on the title may have no practical effect on rights of use. With intellectual property, ownership typically confers rights (and perhaps obligations) to enforce and otherwise protect those rights and to exploit them commercially through licenses and fur-ther developments. Portfolios of patents, copyrights, and other intellectual property may be valuable assets, especially for technology companies. On the other hand, a licensee may (depending on the terms of the license) enjoy essentially unfettered rights to use someone else's intellectual property in his business, in much the same way that a motorist may drive a leased car.

Second, when approaching intellectual property rights in an outsourcing contract, it is useful to consider some practical questions whose answers may help the parties to make sensible allocations of intellectual property rights that accommodate both sides' legitimate commercial interests.

• Why do we care? What business are we in? Is this particular technology an essential part of either party's business? Is it something that offers competitive advantage?

- Is technology a tool for performance of service, or an application? Is the technology a commercial product? If not, does it have any commercial potential? If so, which company is better positioned to exploit that potential?
- What rights does each side need during and after the contract term?
- Is the technology something that already exists, and might be improved, or something largely or wholly new? If it already exists, is it owned by the customer, the supplier, or a third party? If the technology is a new development, created during performance of the contract, is it custom work, created for the particular customer, an improvement of one party's existing system, or an incidental byproduct of performance?

Answers to these questions may vary according to the kind of service and commercial reality involved. It pays to look past ritual opening positions ('we own what we pay for' or 'we own whatever we develop') and consider what the parties need in order to succeed. Consider the following examples:

- *Applications development and maintenance.* Customers engaging a supplier to maintain the customer's proprietary applications, for example, fairly expect to own whatever modifications the supplier may devise and deliver, though not the supplier's proprietary tools and methodologies. The customers may want to use those tools after the contract expires, and the supplier may be willing (perhaps for a price) at least so long as its tools are not shared with the supplier's competitors (who have their own tools). Generally, each side expects to walk away with whatever it brought to the relationship, including improvements created during performance. Customers need their proprietary applications to do business; just as the suppliers need their proprietary tools, utilities, and applications. With applications services, ownership of wholly new developments usually presents the largest challenges. If the customer insists upon ownership, the supplier will want a license to use its handiwork for other customers (except perhaps the customer's competitors). If the parties agree that the supplier will own the work product, the customer will want a broad license to use the system for its business, to modify and further develop the system over time, and perhaps exclusive rights within its industry, at least for a time, lest its perceived competitive advantage be lost. However ownership rights may be allocated, the essential thing is the allocation of rights to use, exploit, and further develop any newly-developed system, whoever owns the underlying intellectual property rights.
- *IT infrastructure.* A supplier engaged to operate the customer's proprietary and third party applications in the supplier's data center will not expect to own those applications merely because operations transfer to the supplier's data center. On the other hand, suppliers who sell hardware and software

products are hardly likely to part company with rights in any proprietary technologies deployed to serve the customer. They will cheerfully sell their commercial products to the customer or even their own competitors after the contract expires. Most IT solutions are based upon standard technologies and commercial products, so that later transition to another supplier or repatriation of outsourced functions is comparatively straightforward. Customers prefer to avoid dependence upon any supplier's proprietary technologies, unless those technologies are commercial products, generally available in the marketplace on reasonable terms. Customers may therefore insist on the right to approve any use of proprietary and especially non-commercial products without customer consent (which may be conditioned upon assurances that the particular product or a commercial equivalent will be available when the contract expires).

- *Business process services.* Some business process offerings are built upon proprietary software and offered only as part of a bundled service offering. These suppliers are no more likely to make their software available to competitors than Colonel Sanders is to offer his secret blend of eleven herbs and spices to another fast food company. A suite of HR applications and tools, for example, may be offered only as part of a comprehensive service. On the other hand, many finance and accounting services are based upon customer implementations of third party solutions, rather than technologies owned by either party to the outsourcing contract. The supplier furnishes skills, experience, and inexpensive (meaning offshore) talent, rather than proprietary technology.

The discussion that follows applies this practical approach to customer, supplier, and third party intellectual property rights, as they appear in typical outsourcing relationships. The reader should keep in mind that many variations are possible, depending upon circumstances and the parties' bargaining leverage. The essential point is to break the problem into its constituent pieces, consider the parties' competing interests, identify the rights they need to do business together and carry on afterwards—then seek practical outcomes.

8.4 CUSTOMER INTELLECTUAL PROPERTY

Customers often license suppliers of IT or business process services to use the customer's proprietary systems during the contract term in order to support the customer's business. If the supplier maintains or modifies the customer's proprietary software, the rights licensed to the supplier must include rights to modify, enhance, and create derivative works for use performing services for the customer. These licenses expire when the contract expires and the customer usually retains all rights in modifications, enhancements, and derivative works. Each side tends to keep what it brings to the outsourcing relationship, including later improvements.

Variations may be appropriate where the supplier embeds its own technology in the customer's software or provides some particular innovation based upon its experience and distinctive skills. In such situations, the customer is likely to own its original intellectual property, and developments of its intellectual property; while the supplier retains its embedded technology, including improvements to that embedded technology. The supplier generally licenses the customer to use the supplier's technology after the contract expires, but customers' rights to use supplier technology are typically limited to support of the customer's business, excluding any use for third parties that might compete with the supplier. Customers commonly insist upon rights to approve use of any supplier technology that may be embedded in the customer's proprietary software or any new developments.

Each side has legitimate interests. The customer wishes to retain what it owns, including improvements, especially if the technology provides a competitive advantage. For example, a retail customer may care passionately about systems used to manage inventories or track customers' buying patterns. On the other hand, the supplier's skills and accumulated experience are its stock in trade. Those skills and experience are not static. Learning from a particular engagement can be put to good use on future engagements for other customers. The original customer may not mind, so long as that other customer is not a competitor. So, to extend the example, a retailer may prohibit re-use of its code, or redeployment of the design team to another retailer, yet agree that both may be made available to companies in other markets and industries.

8.5 SUPPLIER INTELLECTUAL PROPERTY

The suppliers' software portfolios often include tools, utilities, and applications. Sometimes, the portfolio includes some commercial products that are available to all comers (including competitors) willing to pay license and support fees. Other supplier software and intellectual property may be for internal use only, in the delivery of service and operation of the supplier's business, or offered only when 'bundled' with service offerings. All supplier software is generally licensed to the customer during the term, insofar as it is needed to receive and use the supplier's service. An HR service offering may, for example, include web-based tools for employee benefits elections—capability critical to the supplier's service offerings that it is unlikely to share with others, especially its competitors.

Customers are wary of dependence on any single supplier, solution, or product. Licenses to use suppliers' software and other intellectual property during the contract term are all very well, as far as they go. When the contract expires, however, the customer or a successor supplier may want the supplier's software (if available) or a substitute with essentially equivalent capabilities. For this reason, customers often propose and insist upon some combination of the following:

- Rights to approve the use of the supplier's proprietary software and other technologies *before* they are deployed or embedded in the customer's systems. Approval may be conditioned upon: (i) commitments to license the customer or a successor supplier to use the software or technology after the contract expires, or (ii) the availability of commercial alternatives on reasonable terms.
- Where the supplier's proprietary software and technologies are not available after the contract expires (as is often the case with business process services), the customer may: (i) insist upon the use of a commercial product during the contract term, or (ii) where proprietary technologies and services are bundled, propose a long disengagement period, extension rights, or other interim arrangements sufficient to assure continuity of service while a replacement solution is implemented.

Most IT service providers rely upon standard commercial products, including, for HP, IBM and some others, their own commercial products. Suppliers may furnish proprietary software for the customer's use during the term, and offer commercial products afterwards on standard terms. The customer must confirm that the supplier's software will be available to the customer (or another supplier) after expiration or termination, on commercially reasonable terms for support and upgrades. Suppliers with hardware and software businesses are usually willing to sell to their competitors, but this should be confirmed. If the product is not a commercial product, the supplier may make its software available on an 'as-is' basis, without warranties or support, or there may be commercial substitutes. Generally, suppliers prefer not to leave their proprietary tools behind, but competing suppliers who might take over have their own tools, or use commercial equivalents. The customer's concern is, in a word, reversibility—the ability to bring back outsourced functions or take them elsewhere when the contract concludes.

Special issues arise with business process services, which often involve combinations of proprietary software, tools, and methods. Generally, suppliers of business process services do not provide their software or tools, unless they are bundled with services. Licenses to customers are limited to rights of use during the term, in connection with receipt of services. They will not permit their customers (let alone their competitors) to have the proverbial 'keys to the king-dom,' which were, after all, designed for use in an integrated service offering. When the contract ends, for whatever reason, so do all rights to use the software. The customer must find some other solution. Disengagement may therefore be more complex and time-consuming for HR or procurement than for IT services delivered with familiar methods and standard commercial products. Customers protect themselves with extended disengagement periods, extension rights or perhaps licenses permitting usage for a limited period sufficient to assure an orderly reverse transition. Where business process services rely on familiar third party products, as licensed to and implemented by the customer (as is often the case with finance or accounting services) these issues are less significant (although extension rights and generous, flexible disengagement periods are generally advisable for a variety of unrelated reasons).

8.6 THIRD PARTY SOFTWARE

Consents for the supplier's use of third party software are a key issue, particularly with IT services, where the supplier is likely to support or operate large portfolios of applications. Early on, customers should collect all third party licenses and maintenance agreements, then review use restrictions, assignment clauses, and other restrictions. The parties must decide when they are free to transfer or make software available to an outsider, or whether they must obtain consent, use the outsourcer's umbrella license, or make other arrangements. There are usually at least two sets of issues: compliance with the contract and infringement of the licensor's copyright. If the contract permits use by the customer's employees, and users become the employees of the supplier, infringement issues may arise. If software is licensed only for use on the customer's machine, in its facility, trans-ferring that software to the supplier's machine will violate the license.

Generally, outsourcing contracts allow wide flexibility, so that a customer may assign third party licenses, sublicense, or otherwise make software available to the supplier through some other arrangement for access and use, subject in all cases to applicable licenses. Underlying licenses may restrict transfers, tie the software to a particular machine, restrict or prohibit assignments, or condition all transfers upon payment of fees. Invariably, the parties seek the cheapest compliant option.

The contract must say who pays for consents, licenses, and software mainten-ance. Often, the supplier pays for systems software and the customer pays for applications, but there are no hard and fast rules. Costs for consents or software paid by the supplier are, of course, buried somewhere in the supplier's service charges. Insistence that the supplier should absorb consent costs may just prompt the supplier to build an overly generous allowance into its cost model and price, raising total expense to the customer. Negotiated outcomes vary, and occasionally the parties agree to share costs, or share costs above some threshold built into the price. Whatever the resolution, customers should bear in mind that, in reality, nothing is 'free.'

During negotiations, the collection and review of contracts, consent requests, and related activities are usually entrusted to business people to manage, with some legal oversight in order to review key contract terms, prepare forms for consents, and assist with judgment calls. Suppliers, who know the process, often manage this effectively. If required to pay consent costs, suppliers will insist on control of the process. Suppliers often prefer to obtain rights of use, rather than assignments, which are likely to cost more and are more complicated to reverse when the contract ends.

Customers sometimes propose that when the contract concludes, all third party software licenses held by the supplier and used to support the customer should be transferred to the customer. If software licenses are not transferable, the supplier must obtain the customer's consent before using any third party products, and there is an opportunity to determine whether and on what terms those products are available to the customer or a successor supplier. Suppliers cannot transfer master licenses used to support many customers; nor can they predict or guarantee the terms on which third parties may license their products some years hence. In practice, the usual outcome is a provision that effectively compels the suppliers to use commercial products that are readily available on reasonable terms. For customers the essential point is, again, reversibility: the ability to unwind the original transition. Suppliers have no quarrel with the principle, but cannot know in advance just what products may be in use when the contract ends, or on what terms those products may be available to their successor or the customer. When consents are requested, the parties should request whatever future consents may be required in order to re-assign, restore, or reinstate licenses, and assure the customer's right to use on reasonable terms when the outsourcing contract expires.

8.7 NEW DEVELOPMENTS

Where scope includes software maintenance and development projects, ownership of intellectual property can be a sensitive and contentious issue. These issues may play out quite differently, depending upon the context.

Suppliers tend to insist on ownership of improvements to their tools, utilities, methods, and other proprietary technologies, including, of course, any commercial hardware or software products. They cannot agree that portfolios of some of their principal assets be covered, in effect, with customer fingerprints. Neither will customers agree that suppliers engaged to modify or maintain the customers' proprietary software own improvements, which the customers regard, legally and philosophically, as works made for hire.

With business process software and solutions, the supplier may insist on ownership, as improvements developed from performance for various customers are added to its bag of tricks, but variations are possible where the customer makes a substantial investment or contributes its own intellectual property. As noted above, suppliers of business process services rarely license proprietary software to former customers whose service contracts have lapsed.

Custom development—wholly new software written for a particular customer—is another matter altogether, which customers liken to a custom-made suit of clothes—including, incidentally, the patterns used by the tailor, who may not mind, so long as he can make similar suits for other customers. One must not stretch the metaphor too far, but there lies the rub—the essential tension between customers writing checks for custom work and suppliers anxious to preserve their rights to offer similar services and solutions to other customers.

Many customers start by demanding ownership of all new developments, including rights to obtain copyright, patent, and similar protection. So, for their own reasons, do the suppliers. In customer forms, new developments are customer property (and 'works made for hire' under US copyright law, with rights assigned to the customer to the extent that they are not 'works made for hire'). The customer may propose tough restrictive covenants, limiting work for competitors by members of the supplier's technical staff. Ideally, the supplier would prefer the reverse: supplier ownership of everything developed, with licenses for the customer to use new systems in the customer's business, and emphatically not in competition with the supplier. Suppliers resist outright ownership by customers. Conceding patent rights in particular may foreclose future opportunities because of the patent monopoly, if there should be any patentable inventions.

For custom developments, the usual resolution is for one party to own the work, and license the other party on terms that permit the licensee to achieve its reasonable expectations. If the parties agree that the customer owns new developments, the supplier may: (i) condition passage of title upon payment; (ii) obtain a royalty-free license to use (except for competitors of its customer, and excluding perhaps any features unique to the customer); and (iii) reserve all rights in its methods, architecture, design, and any objects, code, or components that it brought to the work. On the other hand, if the supplier retains ownership, it may license the customer, with full rights to modify, enhance, create derivative works, and otherwise freely exploit new developments, without accounting or royalty, for use in the customer's own business (and not, needless to say, in competition with the supplier). Customers may propose that their licensed rights be exclusive, at least for a time, within their particular industry. One may consider various other arrangements, including joint ownership, participation in earnings from use with third parties, or (as suggested above) a permanent, non-exclusive royalty-free license granting the other party extensive rights to exploit the technology. Often these issues are best considered on a case-by-case basis as projects are authorized, rather than in the abstract. The parties often agree that improvements to a particular party's proprietary system belong to that party, so that a manufacturer owns refinements to its 'just in time' inventory management system, and a supplier of HR services owns improvements to its payroll system.

Joint ownership often seems an attractive, collaborative compromise. Beneath the generous intentions, however, lie a welter of unattractive complexities. In the US, unless the parties otherwise agree, either co-owner may grant a non-exclusive license, although it must account for royalties received. In most European countries, this rule is reversed: neither co-owner may grant a non-exclusive license without the other's consent. So where this option is pursued, the contract must spell out all details concerning consents, reporting, shares of profits, and the rest. Making co-ownership work is difficult when the parties' relations are good, as everyone anticipates amid the goodwill of deal-making. After the relationship sours or the contract expires, difficulties are compounded. In practice, it is often wiser to make a commercial decision that one party or the other is better situated to exploit the particular technology, and so should own the technology and, perhaps, make some accommodation to the other. For example, the supplier that improves a particular software product at one customer's expense may make that product available, including support and future upgrades, on generous terms, or even offer some financial participation in future uses, but without introducing the complexities associated with co-ownership.

However ownership rights may be apportioned, the supplier will want to perform similar services for others, including perhaps the customer's competitors. One typical resolution involves (in addition to licensing arrangements) restrictions on key management and technical staff while engaged in work for this customer, and for a decent interval thereafter. Suppliers are concerned about handcuffing their staff and, as a practical matter, have difficulty policing restrictions in large organizations performing services for numerous customers nationwide and worldwide.

If the parties anticipate numerous development projects, they should consider negotiating a standard set of terms for those projects, including the usual terms found in systems integration or development contracts (project management, acceptance and testing, limitations on liability, warranties, termination rights, performance warranties, and the rest).[13] Where extensive new development is anticipated, and apportionment of interests between the parties may vary with the situation, they may wish to agree upon some well-defined alternatives, such as: (i) outright customer ownership; (ii) customer ownership, with a license for supplier use; and (iii) supplier ownership, with a license for customer use during and after the contract term. Writing the menu in advance reduces the risk of haphazard modification and uncertain outcomes when projects are undertaken without necessarily sorting out the subtleties of intellectual property rights.

Finally, too many contracts overlook the possibility of incidental developments—unplanned improvements created as byproducts of performance. Since provenance may be unclear, default rules may be useful, depending upon the nature and use of the improvement. Supplier and customer alike may claim that incidental improvements in their respective systems should be treated in the same manner as derivative works—so that incidental improvements to a supplier's processes and tools belong to the supplier, where incidental improvements in the customer's systems belong to the customer (perhaps with cross-licenses in each case). Both sides may also find some protection in conventional 'residuals' clauses, permitting the parties to use what their employees carry away in unaided memory (excluding of course matter that belongs to one party or the other, such as the customer's trade secrets).

8.8 OPEN SOURCE ISSUES

Open source software has been one of the more interesting phenomena of recent years—freely available, essentially 'free' software, often with capabilities to match the best commercial products. Linux, the increasingly popular operating system derived from Unix; Firefox, Mozilla's web browser; and Open Office, a suite of desktop applications developed by Sun Microsystems and compatible with Microsoft Office, are among the best known open source software. Support for many open source programs is now available not only from web-based communities of developers, but also from major technology companies.

However, contrary to the popular misimpression, open source software is copyrighted, but licensed under open source licenses (often referred to as 'copy-left') with peculiar terms. Unlike the usual commercial license for proprietary software, open source licenses such as the GNU general public licenses make source

---

[13] For an example, see Appendix II.

code available, and permit users to sublicense or transfer software to others, so long as they do so on the same liberal terms—licensing entire programs, including source code, without charge.[14] This requirement—the so-called viral effect—can effectively throw open proprietary systems otherwise protected as trade secrets, if open source and proprietary code are mingled. For this reason, most form outsourcing contracts now prohibit any introduction of open source code or systems into customer's systems, solutions, and environments, unless the customer expressly approves the introduction of an open source software product. Open source solutions and strategies have many attractions, but should never be accidental.

8.9 INNOVATION AND THE HOLY GRAIL

Outsourcing initiatives are often launched amid glowing talk and expectations of innovation. Suppliers advertise their prowess as innovators. Customers are beguiled, then disappointed at the supposed failure to deliver innovation after the sales team has gone away and glossy sales presentations have been largely forgotten. Why is this so, and can disappointment be prevented?

By and large, customers get what they pay for, and suppliers deliver what they contract to provide. Most of the time, for all the talk of innovation, customer requirements and business cases focus, above all, on price and savings. The exercise tends to look backward rather than forward, comparing pricing and total costs with historic costs, prospective performance with recent performance. Customers keen on innovation may not have an appetite for the premium rates charged for the suppliers' most senior experts—whose handiwork the supplier will insist upon owning. Competitive pressures, especially price pressures, tend to drive many suppliers toward a kind of commodity business model with standard offerings and modest margins. Suppliers eager for consistency, efficiency, simplicity, and economies of scale prefer to offer essentially standard services to all customers, using the same methods, processes, software, facilities, and personnel. Their ideal is not so much Baskin Robbins, with thirty-one different flavors of ice cream, as Henry Ford, who is supposed to have said that a customer could have his Model T Ford in any color he wanted, 'as long as it's black.' Ford's black paint dried faster than other colors, and the elimination of choice permitted Ford to accelerate his assembly line and reduce costs. [15]

---

[14] For a list of open source licenses, see <http://www.opensource.org/licenses>.
[15] D Brinkley, *Wheels for the World* (New York: Viking, 2003) 180–1.

Stringent service levels, curiously, may actually deter innovation. Supplier proposals and pricing are based upon proven, familiar methods certain (or virtually certain) to meet and exceed all service levels and avoid payment of credits for unexcused failures—credits that erode margins and, if paid very often, can abbreviate careers. Changes in operations and methods involve some risk of error, especially at first, so if errors can be penalized, there may be little incentive to change.

Customers seeking innovation must be prepared to accept some risk. Innovation is an uneven, unpredictable process. Progress may come in fits and starts, punctuated by occasional breakdowns and false starts. Innovation requires effort, and innovators may not come cheap. Where innovation is seriously wanted, relevant planning, development, and testing must be written into the contract scope and the additional effort will bear a price. Common techniques to stimulate innovation include, among others: (i) the designation of suitably qualified experts on the supplier's account team to review operations and make regular recommendations; (ii) supplier participation in annual or other periodic technology plans; and (iii) periodic briefings for customer management on trends, new product and service offerings, and market intelligence.

9

TRANSITIONS

In outsourcing, 'transition' refers to the elaborate process, often spread over several months, of transferring knowledge, assets, people, and operations from the customer to the supplier and, when the relationship concludes, either onward to another supplier or back to the customer. The latter process—sometimes called 'reverse transition' or 'disengagement'—is essentially similar.

Initial transitions and later disengagement are to outsourcing as take-offs and landings are to aviation. Seat belts should be fastened and, in the cockpit, pains should be taken to avoid accidents. In aviation, crashes are most likely at take-off or landing, and usually result from pilot error. So too with outsourcing.

9.1 PRELIMINARIES

Occasionally, work begins even before the contract is signed. Two situations are common:

- Incidental support may be needed for special projects or to fill gaps, like those that often appear in the ranks as outsourcing approaches—gaps that the customer cannot fill with new hires if positions are to be outsourced and operations transferred.

- Some preparatory activities may have to begin before signing in order to meet deadlines. For example, facilities may have to be prepared, and equipment and telecommunications circuits ordered from suppliers.

These situations are easily documented with letter agreements or other simple documents. Suppliers receive payment on a time and materials or similar basis for preliminary services, and if no contract is ultimately signed, customers must also cover unavoidable cancellation and other costs of equipment, materials, or facilities ordered in anticipation of a contract. Suppliers welcome any opportunity to begin performing chargeable work, and to position themselves 'inside the tent.' Customers recognize these situations as matters of convenience—and even necessity—that may make their decision to move forward with the chosen supplier nearly irreversible.

9.2 KINDS OF TRANSITION

Some years ago, many customers and suppliers favored a kind of 'big bang.' Contracts were negotiated in secret, signed, announced, and immediately implemented. In those days, outsourcing often meant facilities management, at least initially. The supplier's team showed up at daybreak to advise affected staff that they had a new employer and began operations. One may question whether this was ideal or wise, but it is no longer feasible in an era where operations are scattered (rather than confined to a data center), rumor mills are electronic, outsourcing often means going offshore, and relevant laws require notice to employees or public agencies, consultation, and other essential steps.

Now, most outsourced operations relocate elsewhere—often overseas—and many are transformed. Even if operations remain essentially unchanged, this kind of 'lift and shift' transition is a good deal more complicated than old-fashioned facilities management, where the supplier oversaw the same staff, operating the same systems in the same facilities. Operations continued much as before. Change, and perhaps relocation, might come later, but initially, little changed apart from employee badges and immediate supervision.

When operations move long distances, few, if any, knowledgeable staff transfer to the supplier. Rarely are employees inclined to expatriate themselves, even if entitled to do so. If operations are transformed to wholly new systems, complexities increase by orders of magnitude. Even if no employees transfer to the supplier, knowledge must transfer, through a disciplined process that captures not only formal procedures but unwritten 'tribal knowledge' and then trains successor staff. They should be competent, qualified, and knowledgeable in relevant technologies and disciplines, but the supplier's staff are unlikely to know corporate lore or users' idiosyncrasies. None of this means that transition should not succeed. Suppliers execute successful transitions regularly using proven methods. Transition is an essential competence for suppliers, but it is neither easy nor simple. From the customer's standpoint, the level of complexity—and the potential for chaos—roughly approximates that of relocation of headquarters or factories, or perhaps a divestiture. There is much to do, much can go wrong and the show (that is, operation of the customer's business) must go on.

9.3 TRANSITION PLANS

Detailed transition plans are essential, and among the most important contract documents. Usually, they are founded upon complex time lines and charts, with key milestones that may have financial as well as operational implications. If (as is usually the case) operations relocate to supplier facilities, there may be detailed plans for migration of operations, with further milestones, oversight, tests, and other protection. Suppliers deploy experienced specialists to manage transitions. Poor execution may tarnish the supplier's reputation almost irreparably, along with the reputations of those who recommended outsourcing and the particular supplier. There is only one opportunity to make a first impression and first impressions are durable. Generally, the better the preparation, planning and testing, the better the results. Delays, when they occur, are often matters of mutual responsibility, in particular, the inattention or unavailability of customer personnel required for knowledge transfer, testing, and other essential activities. Delays attributable to *force majeure* or the customer's own delays and errors are, of course, excused. Suppliers seek compensation for customer delays for the same reason that taxi meters run while waiting for customers. Where responsibility for delays is shared, partial or proportional compensation may be appropriate.

Few lawyers are asked to review the operational, technical, and other intricacies buried in the text and flowcharts. These are matters for the supplier's transition experts and those who know the customer's operations, facilities, and personnel. Experience suggests that the following measures are helpful:

- On both sides, someone must take charge and be accountable. For major transactions, suppliers generally appoint an experienced transition manager—someone who has done this repeatedly and successfully.

- The supplier's transition manager should have a counterpart, who is not likely to be a transition specialist, but knows the customer's organization and operations, acts as the primary contact, and possesses the authority to oversee and direct the customer's participation. When no such person is available, or has sufficient time, outside experts can be engaged for this purpose, with knowledgeable support from within the customer's organization.

- Communication is essential, in order to acquaint stakeholders and users with anticipated changes (which may not always correspond with what they think they remember from earlier briefings), monitor performance, make adjustments, and resolve occasional difficulties. Good transition plans include communication with users, regular reports to the customer's management, and frequent meetings. Communication plans explain not only changes in service, but changes in management and administration of services. Requests for service, new equipment, and all the rest may be processed differently. Work formerly done on-site may be done remotely, or on-site support may be replaced by dispatched support. Electronic 'forms' and web portals may replace paper. The end result may be superior as well as cheaper, but it has to be explained, clearly and frequently. For organizations as well as individuals, change can be disconcerting.

- Transition plans should map *both* sides' responsibilities in detail. Many customers prefer to think of transition as the supplier's responsibility. Suppliers are supposed to possess the relevant expertise and experience, but the process is collaborative, and replete with dependencies. Knowledge transfer, for example, cannot occur unless customer staff are available as and when needed, often including some employees slated for transfer, early retirement, or discharge, who may want financial incentives to remain for several additional weeks. Countless decisions have to be made, as in construction, where the contractor pours the concrete foundation, frames the structure, and finishes all interiors, but requires seemingly endless decisions and direction from the owner's project manager. Sales presentations and contract documents sometimes refer to 'seamless' transitions, as if no one will notice and nothing will go wrong. This is generally an aspiration and, to some extent, a delusion. Even the best executed transitions involve some dislocation and at least occasional errors.

- Time and pains taken for rehearsals, pilot operations, and tests are excellent investments. There is no better way to expose weaknesses in planning, without disrupting the operation of the customer's business. These are outsourcing's answer to test flights.

9.4 TRANSITION CHARGES, MILESTONES, AND DELAYS

Transitions are complex, labor-intensive, and expensive. Costs can either be paid as incurred, or absorbed into service charges and spread over the life of the relationship. The latter approach preserves initial savings, but increases service charges, makes benchmarking more difficult, and boosts termination charges (for in the event of premature termination, the supplier will insist upon recovery of its initial outlays). Burying transition costs in service charges also increases total cost, because supplier cost models include the costs of capital and a return. In other words, spreading or deferring transition costs is a kind of financing.

For these reasons, many customers pay substantial transition costs when incurred, either on a time and materials basis or by allocating a fixed charge among milestones. Customers tend to prefer fixed charges, which offer certainty; but often in transitions, there is enough uncertainty to make time and materials charges attractive. Any fixed fee would have to include a large allowance for contingencies, increasing total cost. Either approach permits the customer to impose financial consequences for supplier delays in the form of credits or liquidated damages, which may be assessed and withheld from payments in the event the supplier is both late and blameworthy—just as credits are assessed when service levels are missed. Delays on account of the customer's failures to perform, *force majeure* events, or other circumstances beyond the supplier's reasonable control should be excused. When suppliers absorb transition costs, fold them into service charges, and effectively spread the cost over the entire contract term, they are rarely willing to make significant payments for delays during transition.

Suppliers sometimes propose that if intermediate transition milestones are missed, and credits assessed, those credits may be recouped if the supplier makes up lost time and successfully meets the deadline for the completion of transition. The rationale, of course, is that recovery of credits paid provides an incentive for extra effort to meet the deadline—to pour on the coal, as it were. There is something to this, although serious delays along the way are likely to mean expensive disruptions on both sides.

When payments and credits are tied to milestones, contract language concerning acceptance matters a great deal. Since both sides are powerfully motivated to move forward on schedule, they can usually agree that completion means substantial completion, or completion in all material respects, and that acceptance will not be unreasonably withheld or delayed. Insistence on perfection invites delay, at a time when operations may be fragile, knowledgeable staff are leaving, and savings are expected after operations transfer to the supplier.

Customers almost universally stipulate that material failures during transition constitute a material breach of the contract, and thus grounds for termination. This is, in a sense, obvious, for there are few better examples of 'material' breach than a botched transition; but in reality, there could be no worse time to exercise termination rights than during a complex transition. The process, once started, is difficult to halt, let alone reverse. The customer who has begun to shut down former internal operations may have no short-term alternative and little willingness to declare failure by abandoning an outsourcing initiative begun with much effort and fanfare.

9.5 TRANSFERS OF ASSETS

In the early days, outsourcing meant selling data centers, computers, and the rest to an outsourcer, usually for book value. To the customer, this could offer an almost irresistible combination: better service and lower ongoing costs plus cash at signing, without having to record a loss on obsolete equipment with little market value.

Times have changed. Suppliers are less willing to pay, and customers increasingly recognize the hidden costs and consequences of asset sales. When suppliers buy assets, they must recover their investments through larger service charges and, in the event of early termination, larger termination charges. Suppliers always insist on the recovery of unamortized investments they had expected to recover over the full contract term. Total costs are likely to increase through what is, in essence, relatively expensive financing. Nonetheless, for a variety of commercial and operational reasons, a fair number of transactions—particularly IT infrastructure transactions—involve transfers of facilities, equipment, and other assets.

9.5.1 Transfers of facilities

Occasionally (if much less frequently than in the past), suppliers purchase data centers and other facilities from their customers, or take over existing leases. In these situations, the commercial, legal, and contractual issues are essentially similar to those in any other real estate transaction. Buyers seek assurances about title, the condition of the property, compliance with relevant laws and—especially in the US—the absence of environmental contamination. US laws may impose essentially unlimited liability for existing contamination upon any buyer, tenant, or operator of a facility. Prudent suppliers therefore take pains to investigate environmental conditions by engaging experts to search public records and other sources regarding historic uses, conduct inspections, and, if warranted, perform soils and other testing. Former industrial sites or military bases are often contaminated, and diesel tanks for emergency generators have been known to leak.

With leased premises, landlord consent may be required in order either to assign the lease or sublease space to the supplier. Landlords may or may not be able to withhold consent (or to condition their consent upon rent increases or other payments), depending upon the language of the lease and relevant law. Whenever consents are required, both parties would do well to consider what else may be needed—for example consents to remodel, to reassign the lease, or to transfer it to a future supplier—in order to avoid having to go back to the landlord, with check book in hand, on some future occasion.

Finally, many customers make space available for suppliers within their own facilities, but without transferring title or even creating a leasehold. Customers merely agree to provide office space with basic furnishings, equipment, utilities, and cleaning service. When supplier personnel must be on-site, and customers have sufficient space, this can be the cheapest alternative. Otherwise, supplier cost models will add overheads and margins to the costs of any facilities for which the supplier must pay. Customers also require compliance with access, security, and other policies. Premises must be clean when returned, subject to normal wear and tear. The supplier's occupancy is generally a license—in effect, simple use—revocable at will, and not a leasehold. If the customer requires the supplier to vacate the premises before the contract expires, the customer can expect to pay for relocation and substitute space. Detailed terms—for example concerning consent to any alterations—are rarely controversial. Use is generally limited to support of the particular customer and incidental administrative activities. Occasionally, suppliers seek flexibility to use staff located at customer sites to support multiple customers. Customers instinctively object, but such arrangements may mean that experts are housed on-site, and more readily accessible, even though their expertise will be shared with others.[1]

9.5.2 Transfers of equipment

These are no different than in any other asset purchase. Since computer and network hardware depreciates rapidly, its economic importance may be modest.

---

[1] Business people should consider the philosophical and operational implications of such practical steps as: (i) physically segregating the outsourcer's new employees from other staff; (ii) forms of badges; (iii) listings on the customer's internal phone directory; and (iv) access to corporate networks. Some formal separation is often desirable for many purposes (including building loyalty, effective management, and avoidance of joint employment issues, among others); yet wise customers try to minimize adversarial ('us-them') thinking. Outsourcing often works best when those involved consider themselves to be part of a joint team, serving the same customers within the customer's business.

Inventories are often inaccurate, and contract documents must provide for adjustments to account for assets located after closing.[2] Transfers of leased equipment may require the lessor's consent. Lessors usually consent readily, if the supplier has good credit, but may not release the original lessee. Equipment leases should be reviewed with care, as they sometimes contain traps for the unwary, such as punitive 'holdover' or renewal charges. Legal (or at least paralegal) review is advisable. Customers generally prefer to sell equipment 'as is' (where applicable law permits) and without warranties other than good title. Suppliers, if given an opportunity to inspect and to confirm that major hardware is under manufacturers' maintenance contracts, will usually accept this, rather than insist upon warranties that equipment is in good working order.

9.5.3 Transfers of contracts

Many outsourced services—particularly IT services—involve heaps of software licenses and other contracts with third parties. Some of these may be assigned or otherwise transferred to the supplier. Others, the customer may retain, while authorizing the supplier to manage or administer the relationship. For example, if a company has a service contract in place for its personal computers, it may retain the contract, pay all charges, and authorize the supplier, acting through its help desk, to request service calls, parts, and other support. In IT contracts, outsourcers often assume responsibility for system software (particularly on the supplier's own machines), while the customer pays for applications, but there are no hard and fast rules and many variations may be proposed or negotiated.

Software licenses, maintenance agreements, and other contracts to be transferred to or managed by the supplier should be collected and reviewed before any agreement is signed. In large organizations, merely finding complete, current copies may be a challenge. Many, perhaps most, of these contracts will restrict, condition, or prohibit transfers. Transfers often require consent or payment or both. Use by a supplier without consent may not only breach the contract, but (in the case of software licenses) infringe the licensor's copyright or other rights.

In all cases, the parties should consider the context. Will the supplier merely manage the contract, or actually exercise some or all of the customer's options, licenses, or other rights? Such distinctions may be critical when determining how to deal with third party contracts. Sometimes contracts are assigned to the supplier (who becomes the contracting party liable for performance and payment). At other times, the supplier is merely authorized to act on the customer's behalf

---

[2] This is particularly important where IT services are priced per user (or 'seat'), per server, or on some other basis driven by the inventory.

(for example to order parts and support) or allowed access in order to operate a system for the customer, who retains the contract and remains liable. Sometimes software licenses terminate and the customer operates under the supplier's master license for the term of the contract. In other situations, the customer may retain the primary license, and obtain a derivative license for the supplier, sufficient for its purposes. Choices among these various alternatives may depend in large part upon contract terms, and the potential costs of obtaining consents.

Review and solicitation of consents can be a joint endeavor, where the customer benefits from the supplier's experience. Each may be able to take advantage of the other's relationships. Neither has any particular interest in enriching the software licensors, so as between supplier and customer, the exercise is not likely to be contentious.

Costs of obtaining needed consents are, of course, a point for negotiation. Sometimes suppliers pay all or a portion of the costs of consent, expecting (of course) to recover the cost through the charges. Whatever the supplier pays must be built into the price. Ultimately, the customer pays, directly or indirectly. Options include:

- the payment of all consent costs by one side or the other;
- sharing consent costs (which can align incentives); and
- payment by the supplier, up to an agreed ceiling, with the excess to be paid by one party or the other, or shared.

When requesting consents, the parties should request whatever other rights may be needed in the future, such as the right to transfer to the customer or another supplier when the contract ends, without further payment. Sometimes, software licensors will throw in something of value in return for the consent charge (such as upgrades, maintenance, or training). Well-advised customers will seek some protection for the time of disengagement, although it is difficult for suppliers to provide complete protection. No one can predict what products may be in use several years hence, or on what terms they may be available. Nonetheless, when a customer decides to use the supplier's master license, it should investigate the cost of reinstating its own license when the contract expires. Obtaining consents takes time, so it is wise to start early.

9.6 PERSONNEL TRANSFERS

People are crucial, because of the knowledge they possess, their skills, and common humanity—to say nothing of the disruptive potential of attrition, unrest, and poor morale. For affected staff the process may be very disconcerting.

Some may be displaced, especially if operations relocate offshore. Some may be offered positions, at least for a time, with the outsourcer. In the US, large scale transfers of employees to the supplier were formerly typical, but are less so today, when many operations move offshore. Comparatively few displaced staff are willing to emigrate, even if invited or entitled to do so. Outside the US, affected employees may enjoy statutory protection (including severance), and in the EU and some other jurisdictions, they may have the right to claim that they are 'effectively transferred' to the supplier under 'acquired rights' legislation. They keep their jobs, salaries, benefits, and other rights, just like employees of companies whose stock is sold to new owners.

Essential business goals are much the same worldwide, as companies seek to reduce costs, including labor costs; preserve essential work forces; honor their obligations to employees; and comply with relevant laws. However, since employment laws vary a great deal, practice necessarily varies not only from one country to the next, but within federal states such as the US, where there are many variations among the fifty states. Everywhere, compliance is complex and errors may prove expensive, not only financially but also in the potential impact upon reputations. Here, only a general introduction is attempted. There is no substitute for expert advice about specifics.

9.6.1 US practice

US employment laws are an intricate quilt of state and federal statutes and common law. At bottom, unless otherwise agreed (and subject to many statutory protections and legal doctrines) employment is an 'at-will' relationship that either party may terminate at any time, for any reason or for no reason. Many employers have 'at-will' employment policies and confirm this point with simple offer letters describing the terms of employment, including the right to terminate at will. Many employers have severance policies, awarding some severance pay based upon length of service in the event of dismissal, but, in general, there are no statutory obligations to pay severance (as exist in many countries). Statutes protect employees against dismissal on account of race, age, disability, and other improper grounds. Employers who are arbitrary or unreasonable may risk claims of 'wrongful termination'—commonly premised upon violations of the covenant of good faith and fair dealing that the law implies into all contracts, even unwritten or implied contracts of employment.

When US companies outsource, employees may be laid off entirely or offered positions with the supplier. In either case, there is a termination of employment. When transfers of employees are desired, the supplier will generally interview eligible employees, extend offers of employment conditioned upon completion of the transaction, and then bring them on board, usually with comparable pay, benefits, and seniority. The process, however, is complex and full of pitfalls for the unwary.

9.6.1.1 Joint employment
One such pitfall is the legal doctrine of joint employment. When two companies supervise an employee, determine working conditions, evaluate performance, and, in case of difficulty, impose disciplinary measures, both may be deemed employers. Both are thus guaranteed seats at the defense table if an unhappy employee or former employee files suit. Joint employment risks are especially serious for employees who work on-site, alongside their friends and former colleagues at the customer's offices, and also during the process of selection, transfer, and transition.

To minimize these risks, collaboration between the parties on employment matters should generally be entrusted to the companies' personnel or HR experts, who are familiar with the risks, and should take pains to observe appropriate demarcation lines. The customer should never comment specifically on pay, benefits, or anything else about prospective employment by the supplier; just as the supplier should say nothing about the customer's severance policy, payment for accrued but unused vacation, or other details of the customer's arrangements with its employees. Each company should refer questions about the other company's policies to the other company's representatives. Often each side holds meetings for affected employees in order to explain transitional arrangements and answer questions. When, as is often the case, customers and suppliers are concerned to preserve a knowledgeable, experienced workforce, the supplier's upbeat 'town hall' meetings provide valuable reassurance and help to shore up fragile morale.

After the contract is signed, companies may largely eliminate the risk of joint employment liability by respecting contractual procedures and organizational boundaries. Customers should manage suppliers through the contract, and give instruction and directions through the supplier's account management team, not directly to individuals, as if they were still the customer's employees. Meddlesome 'micro-management' of operations is in any event poor practice. Employees delivering service are entitled to clear direction from a single source—meaning, for transferred employees, their new employer.

9.6.1.2 Disclosures
Before interviewing employees eligible for transfer, suppliers will commonly request basic information about candidates, including names, seniority, compensation, and other particulars. Some basic information, sufficient for

cost models and pricing, can be disclosed on a 'blind' (or 'anonymized') basis, without names or other individual specifics, but at some point the supplier will fairly expect particulars—name, position, seniority, and compensation, among other things. Often, depending upon company policy and applicable law, this information cannot be disclosed without individual consent (even in the US, where privacy laws are less stringent than in many other countries). Employee consent is usually forthcoming, since the employees generally want continued employment. Disclosure should generally exclude personnel files, which contain evaluations, disciplinary records, and other sensitive information. Keeping these records confidential permits the prospective employer to make its own decisions and assures the employee a fair opportunity and fresh start, while reducing the risk of joint employment liability or defamation claims if an employee receives no offer and later files suit. Disclosures of employment information should, of course, be strictly confidential. Lists of affected employees, salaries, and the rest should be protected with particular vigilance, and distributed on a 'need-to-know' basis.

9.6.1.3 Morale and secrecy

Companies considering outsourcing understandably prefer to keep their plans quiet, especially during the preliminary or exploratory phase, before any decisions are taken. Thereafter, word is almost bound to leak, however discreet management may be. Outsourcing is a major corporate event. For affected employees, it is still more jarring, because of obvious effects upon livelihoods, careers, families, and lives. Once the word is out, or even rumored, many become restless or distracted and begin to investigate other opportunities. This affects morale and productivity, among other things. Therefore, once decisions are taken, it is usually wise to keep employees as well informed as possible, and within the EU, consultation with employees and their representatives may be legally required before any decision to outsource.[3] Without accurate information, rumor mills run wild. Rumors are usually much worse than the truth. Silence fuels mistrust and there is no good substitute for telling people the truth.

9.6.1.4 Layoffs and statutory notice requirements

In the early days of IT infrastructure outsourcing, most (and often all) affected employees were offered opportunities to transfer to the supplier, generally for the same salary and often in the same location. Dislocation and relocation were comparatively rare. Not so today, when outsourced operations are often

---

[3] See 9.6.2 below.

transformed and transferred overseas. Even if job opportunities were offered, few would willingly become expatriates.

So outsourcing often involves reductions in the workforce. The risks to morale are comparable to the risks in any other layoff, and the risk of adverse publicity is, if anything, worse. Outsourcing may be controversial and attract unwelcome attention from reporters and politicians. All the more reason, therefore, to respect the dignity of departing employees, offer generous severance and outplacement benefits, and scrupulously comply with legal requirements, which may vary a good deal from state to state. Money spent to do right by longstanding employees is generally a better investment than legal fees paid for the consequences of shortcuts. As so often, doing the right and generous thing is usually good business.

Notice to employees and public agencies under federal and state plant closure laws are one legal requirement that may apply. The federal Worker Adjustment and Retraining Notification (WARN) Act[4] requires employers to give sixty days' advance notice when sufficient numbers of full-time employees will suffer an 'employment loss' because of a 'plant closing' or 'mass layoff,' as each of those terms is defined by the statute and regulations.

Definitions and thresholds complicate the application of the statute:

- 'Employers' subject to the statute have 100 or more full-time employees, or 100 or more full-time and part-time employees who work, collectively, at least 4,000 hours a week (excluding overtime).
- 'Employment loss' means dismissal (other than for cause), a layoff lasting more than six months, or a reduction to less than half-time employment for six months.
- 'Plant closing' means permanent or temporary shutdown of an employment site, or one or more 'facilities or operating units' at a single site where fifty or more full-time employees are dismissed within thirty days.
- 'Mass layoffs' are reductions in force (other than from plant closings) affecting either 33 per cent of full-time employees at a single site employing at least 100 full-time workers, or 500 full-time employees.[5]

Outsourcing scattered positions in various locations and business units may not be subject to the statute if too few affected employees are affected in any one place.[6] However, shutting a facility or shedding an entire business unit (such as,

---

[4] 29 USC § 2101 *et seq.*
[5] 29 USC § 2101(a)(1), (2), and (3).
[6] See, eg, *Finley v MW Kellogg Co* No H-96-0314, 1998 US Dist LEXIS 23506 (SD Tex 26 March 1998).

for example, an IT department) may constitute a 'plant closing.'[7] Notice, when required, must be given to state and local government agencies, to the local mayor, or other chief elected official, and to affected employees or their representatives, if any.[8]

It is not entirely clear whether the statute applies to outsourcing transactions when displaced employees are offered employment by the supplier and operations continue under the supplier's management. Arguably, there is no 'employment loss' for employees who carry on as before with a new employer. For that reason, the statute exempts sales of businesses, and the courts have so held, but the statutory exception refers only to sales of businesses—even if its logic is more extensive.[9] There can be no assurance that the courts would necessarily extend the exception to outsourcing, and the statute is likely to apply when sufficient employees are laid off, if the circumstances can be fairly treated as a 'plant closing' or 'mass layoff.' If insufficient numbers of employees are displaced, the statute does not, in any event, apply and notice should be unnecessary. Many states have similar notice laws, but with different requirements. Liability for violations may be substantial, and so in close or doubtful cases, it is usually wise to err in favor of compliance and give statutory notices.

9.6.1.5 Transfers of employees

Under US law, transfers of employees generally involve termination by the customer and essentially simultaneous hiring by the supplier. During the final few weeks, while the customer prepares final paychecks and conducts exit interviews, the supplier interviews some or all of the affected staff, with a view to offering them positions with similar compensation. Some may have only short-term positions, especially if the supplier relocates operations. If so, the parties should consider what severance, if any, is due. Customers prefer not to pay severance for employees who transfer to permanent positions, but company plans, policies, and obligations differ and merit close review. Sometimes, where there is particular concern to retain experienced, knowledgeable staff, suppliers may agree to pay retention bonuses, match customer severance programs, or

---

[7] 20 CFR § 639.3(b).

[8] 29 USC § 2102(a).

[9] 20 USC § 2101(b)(1) (exempting sales of businesses from the statutory definition of 'employment loss'). According to Senator Hatch, sponsor of the exception: 'It would seem fairly obvious that if the business continues on as before with no significant changes of any kind, that there would be no need to go through the formal notification process.' 134 Cong Rec 16,026 (1988). Some decisions support a 'practical, effects-driven analysis of whether a break in employment actually occurred.' *Gonzalez v AMR Services Corp* 68 F 3d 1529, 1531 (2d Cir 1995); *International Alliance of Theatrical and Stage Employees and Moving Picture Machine Operators v Compact Video Services, Inc* 50 F 3d 1464, 1467–68 (9th Cir 1995); *Moore v Warehouse Club, Inc* 992 F 2d 27 (3d Cir 1993).

pay severance based on total length of service (including years of service with the customer), but all this augments the price.

Offers of employment to transferred employees are generally conditioned upon the usual questionnaires and interviews, as well as signing of the services agreement. Routine background checks may be conducted, consistent with company policy and applicable law. Occasionally, drug tests may be required—again, consistent with company policy and applicable law. Customers may ask that these requirements be waived for transferring employees.[10] Offers from suppliers should be based upon an independent evaluation of appropriate, objective criteria, and not whispered recommendations from the customer and current employer, who should take pains to avoid acting as a joint employer.

Many suppliers are 'at-will' employers, and offers or employment letters will state this. Customers may seek assurances that transferred employees will, in fact, have jobs for at least a year or two after signing. Suppliers with 'at-will' policies are equally anxious not to guarantee employment for particular groups of employees. However, suppliers with 'at-will' policies can usually find other means to assure customers that experienced people are unlikely to be laid off—for example through generous severance commitments in the event of premature dismissal for reasons other than misconduct, deficient performance, or other good cause. Customers anxious to assure permanent employment for transferred staff in this way should be prepared to guarantee sufficient revenue and service consumption. If transferred staff are to be assured employment, there must be work to do for which the customer is prepared to pay. Sometimes, selected employees with critical knowledge (for example knowledge of existing, undocumented systems) must be committed to the customer's account on something like a full-time basis, at least initially. Lists of such employees should also be kept confidential.

9.6.1.6 Terms of employment for transferred employees

Invariably, transferred employees are offered wages or salaries that at least equal those formerly received while in the customer's employ. Comparability of total compensation is more complicated, since benefit programs vary. Suppliers readily agree to waive waiting periods, deductions, and other prerequisites for fringe

---

[10] On the other hand, customers sometimes propose that suppliers conduct background checks for supplier employees assigned to the customer's account, especially those assigned to work at the customer's facilities. Given companies' growing sensitivity about privacy, protection of personal data, and identity theft, there is an understandable desire to take all reasonable steps to exclude untrustworthy individuals who may become security risks. Applicable law varies, but relevant considerations often include some reasonable relationship between job requirements and the proposed background check or drug test—for essentially the same reasons that companies may impose more stringent requirements on employees who handle money or operate hazardous equipment.

benefits; recognize prior employment with the customer for seniority and other purposes; and treat newcomers generously. But suppliers' benefit programs are often leaner than those of their corporate customers (as one might expect, given the imperatives of lower cost). So rather than guarantee equivalent total compensation, suppliers prefer a looser standard, such as overall comparability across all affected wage and salary ranges, rather than equivalence for each and every transferred employee. Where the total package seems less attractive, or there are wide differences in key benefits, the supplier may propose that employees receive incentive bonuses to offset these differences and keep staff during transition (especially those without long-term futures).

Customers often expect suppliers to respect accrued, but unused vacation (except in such states as California, which require payment for unused vacation at termination).[11] Suppliers are generally willing to accommodate such requests, but may seek corresponding financial adjustments for vacation accrued before the employee's arrival—vacation, in effect, earned on the customer's watch, for which the supplier must pay, while meeting its service obligations. The parties should seek specialist advice regarding pension plans. Sometimes, transferred employees' balances can be distributed to them, or transferred to the outsourcers' plan. Wise customers consider whether employees' pension rights have vested, or might vest shortly after their employment would otherwise terminate and in such cases, consider deferring their transition. Employees on maternity, family, or military leave are generally permitted (consistent with applicable statutes) to return to work and then transfer to the supplier when their leave ends.

Customers generally indemnify suppliers against employee claims arising during employment by the customer, or upon termination by the customer just before closing. Suppliers are expected to reciprocate, indemnifying customers against employee claims arising after closing, during employment by the supplier and pre-contract interviews and screening. Each party is generally responsible for its own compliance with all employment laws and regulations. Well-drafted contracts routinely exclude third party beneficiaries, so that no employees (and for that matter, no subcontractors) can attempt to enforce the outsourcing contract for their benefit.

9.6.1.7 Unions
Unions represent only a small fraction of the American workforce[12] and are therefore less significant than in many other countries. As a practical matter,

---

[11] Cal Lab Code § 227.3.

[12] Just 12.4% of employed workers in 2008, and only 7.6% of private sector employees, according to the Labor Department's Bureau of Labor Statistics <http://data.bls.gov/cgi-bin/print.pl/news.release/union2.nr0.htm> (accessed 20 March 2009).

operations manned by members of collective bargaining units are rarely outsourced. Unions opposed to outsourcing, anxious to preserve union jobs and protected by collective bargaining agreements have little reason to cooperate with management desires to outsource; non-union suppliers have little interest in taking on bargaining units or inviting campaigns to organize their workforces. So within the US, 'union shops' are almost invariably excluded from the scope of outsourced operations.

9.6.1.8 'Poaching'[13]

Outsourcing contracts often restrict (or purport to restrict) each party's ability to recruit the other party's employees. In many US states, one may not practically, or even lawfully, restrict an employee's ability to seek greener pastures, and damages may be difficult to prove. Where meaningful deterrents are desired, the usual solution is a commitment not to recruit the other party's employees (apart from general solicitations such as advertising or public web postings), coupled with an obligation to pay liquidated damages for breach of this obligation. Liquidated damages, typically computed as a percentage of annual compensation, offset at least some of the costs of training and recruitment. Those who do apply in response to general advertising, or otherwise on their own initiative, must of course be treated fairly. Their applications should be considered in good faith.

In practice, poaching by customers may be bad business. Recruiting supplier staff (especially the customer's former employees) can affect business relationships, diminish the customer's ability to outsource other functions (if affected employees think they can easily return), and the outsourcer's ability to perform (if too many people 'go home'). Conversely, for a supplier to recruit its customers' staff would be poor customer relations. There is much wisdom in Poor Richard's admonition that good fences make good neighbors. In practice, barriers between companies are permeable, but restrictions backed by liquidated damages tend to encourage discussions that may lead to consent where there are extenuating circumstances or good business reasons to accommodate a particular transfer.

9.6.2 EU practice

Within the Member States of the EU, most transfers of employees in major outsourcings are governed by the Acquired Rights Directive[14] and implementing legislation in the Member States, which varies a good deal, and may be

---

[13] An allusion to cattle rustling in the Old West, rather than poached delicacies!
[14] Council Directive (EC) 2001/23 [2001] OJ L082/16.

more stringent than the governing Directive. In essence, the Directive treats outsourcing like other transfers of undertakings—sales of a company's stock, for example—so that employees transfer with the outsourced operations, and with their terms of employment, representation, and other rights intact and unchanged. Executives from US or other companies based elsewhere soon discover that, under these rules, outsourcing may not necessarily be a way to reduce headcount and labor costs.

The Directive governs transfers of undertakings, businesses, or parts of under-takings, including any 'organized grouping of resources which has the objective of pursuing an economic activity, whether. . . central or ancillary' whenever the 'business to be transferred is situated' within the EU.[15] Conspicuous silence regarding the place to which operations may be transferred may suggest an intention that this legislation should apply when operations are outsourced to destinations outside the EU, such as India.

All of the transferor's rights and obligations related to employment contracts and relationships transfer to the supplier, who becomes fully liable for existing obligations, and may become jointly and severally liable if Member State legisla-tion so requires.[16] Member State legislation may compel disclosure of employ-ment obligations, but failures to disclose do not diminish the new employer's obligations or its potential liability to transferred employees.[17] As transferees, suppliers must continue to observe the terms of union contracts, until they expire or are superseded by other collective agreements.

Transfers alone are not grounds for dismissal of transferred employees. Any such dismissals are likely to be 'unfair dismissals' bearing substantial liability, but the Directive does 'not stand in the way of dismissals that may take place for economic, technical or organizational reasons entailing changes in the work force.'[18] Where such reasons exist—for example because of the supplier's planned transformation of operations—the supplier may be able to effect dismissals after transfer and avoid 'unfair dismissal' liability, but the supplier will expect an indemnity for all potential liability, including its certain liability for

---

[15]   Directive (EC) 2001/23, Art 1. In *Ayse Suzen v Zehnacker Gebaudereinigung GmbH* [1997] ECR 1259 the European Court of Justice ruled that the original 1997 Directive applied if outsourced activities were economic activities in their own right, and there was a transfer of either significant tangible or intangible assets, or a major part of the workforce, measured by numbers or skills. Implementing regulations in the UK apply expressly to 'service provision changes,' defined as activities formerly performed internally, or by a contractor, on the customer's behalf and transferred to a new contractor. Transfer of Undertakings (Protection of Employment) Regulations 2006 (TUPE 2006), SI 2006/246, s 3(1)(b).

[16]   Directive (EC) 2001/23, Art 3(1).

[17]   ibid Art 3(2).

[18]   ibid Art 4(1).

whatever severance pay may be required under applicable contracts, policies, or law.

Suppliers and customers must inform and consult with affected employees (a larger group, potentially, than those to be transferred) or their representatives in unions or works councils regarding 'measures envisaged' and 'in good time' (meaning, in practice, time periods laid down by Member State legislation or a reasonable time, depending upon the impact) 'with a view to reaching an agreement.'[19] The Directive, like much EU legislation, is phrased in general terms, leaving much for courts and Member State parliaments to determine, and there is a good deal of variation in Member State legislation concerning time periods, remedies, and other matters, as well as ordinary employment law. Where the Directive does not apply, or employees are dismissed before or after transfer for economic, technical, or organizational reasons, other EU or national legislation may come into play, and require notice, consultation, and other procedures or payment of severance. For example, a 1998 Directive (amending and superseding earlier legislation) requires notice and consultation in the event of 'collective redundancies,' defined as the dismissal of more than twenty employees within ninety days, or numbers of dismissals that exceed certain numeric thresholds.[20] Extensive disclosures are required, followed by consultations with unions, works councils, or other representatives regarding the circumstances, reasons, selection criteria, and possible measures to avoid, reduce, or mitigate the effects of redundancies. National legislation in the Member States varies a good deal, may be more favorable to employees, or impose additional requirements—for example criteria for selection based upon length of service, hardship, or other criteria laid down by statute.

What does all this mean, in practice, for companies contemplating the outsourcing of European operations?

- Above all, they should plan ahead, collect basic information about affected employees, and obtain expert advice about (i) application of the Directive and implementing legislation, which covers most, but by no means all outsourcing;[21] (ii) consultation periods and other requirements under legislation implementing the Directive; and (iii) such important matters as unions,

---

[19] ibid Art 7(1) and (2).

[20] Council Directive (EC) 98/59 [1998] OJ L225/16 Article 1(a). The thresholds are: (i) 30 dismissals in establishments employing 20–99 workers; (ii) 10% of the workforce at establishments with 100–299 workers; and (iii) at least 30 dismissals at establishments employing 300 or more workers.

[21] eg the UK's TUPE Regulations do not apply to certain short-term projects, or outsourcings that involve no 'organized grouping of employees' for the 'principal purpose of carrying out... activities on behalf of the client.' TUPE 2006, s 3(3)(a). Other EU Member States, such as Italy, typically require some transfer of assets or goodwill, so may be less likely to apply the Directive to outsourcing.

pension rights, and potential severance liability under the usual national employment laws as well as acquired rights legislation. Financial projections must account for such costs as potential severance and other liability, plus salaries and benefits at current rates for employees who do transfer. [22]

- Some question remains about extraterritorial application of the Directive and implementing legislation when operations relocate outside the EU—to India, for example. In practice, affected employees may have more important concerns than a theoretical right to emigrate, but for the company sending operations offshore, there are large potential liabilities for unfair dismissal, severance, and failure to consult in a timely manner. In the past, many companies have disregarded acquired rights legislation in offshore outsourcing from Europe, in the belief that the Directive would not apply, and in any event few affected employees would particularly care. That strategy has grown riskier, for the Directive at least arguably appears to allow extraterritorial application and, in the UK, one recent decision of an employment appeals tribunal suggests that TUPE may apply to offshore transfers outside the EU.[23]

- Multinational companies with EU operations and headquarters elsewhere often outsource worldwide operations through a master agreement (in North America, for example) with corresponding local or companion agreements for European countries, with special provisions for local employment and other laws. These can only be signed and implemented after notice to employees or their representatives, consultation, and other steps required by acquired rights legislation. In practice, this means implementation in stages, first outside the EU, and then in various European countries at times that account for statutory time periods and other requirements.

- When the parties fully anticipate that employees will transfer—and even want them to transfer—the process is complex and expensive. If the supplier is not prepared to accept transferring employees, the customer may attempt to find positions for them elsewhere in the company, but if no roles exist that they can fill, the customer may face substantial potential liability for unfair dismissals.[24] Employees transfer to the supplier, who may have economic, technical, or organizational reasons to dismiss the employees, and will invariably request indemnification from the customer.

---

[22] This chapter attempts no more than an introduction to essential issues. The need for early, expert advice cannot be overemphasized. Variations among national legislation and regulations are numerous and substantial. Complexities abound, along with opportunities for expensive errors, liability, and unfavorable publicity.

[23] *Holis Metal Industries v GMB and Newell* [2007] UKEAT/0171/07/CEA (sale of business to an Israeli buyer and relocation of operations to Israel).

[24] eg in the UK, there may be liability of up to £72,900 for each employee.

- When the contract expires or terminates, acquired rights legislation may apply again, in reverse, to all supplier employees primarily engaged in performance for the customer, who may transfer back to the customer (if services repatriate) or on to a successor supplier.[25]

9.6.3 Employment outside the US and EU

Outside the EU, few countries have acquired rights legislation for compulsory transfer, but many countries require notice; consultation with unions, representative groups, or workers; and, in case of separation, substantial severance payments. In some countries, official approvals may be required and statutory criteria may govern the selection of employees for any group redundancy. Statutory criteria (such as seniority) rarely align with management preferences concerning transfer and retention. Some employees (pregnant women, for example, or union representatives) may enjoy special protection. US executives accustomed to 'at-will' employment are often astonished by the complexity and expense of this legal labyrinth. Again, companies contemplating outsourcing should, early in their planning, identify employees who may be displaced, and seek advice about local legal and other requirements, then estimate potential severance and other costs.

9.7 DISENGAGEMENT

However the relationship ends, well-drafted contracts contain detailed provisions for disengagement, including an attachment spelling out obligations to transfer equipment, personnel, and other resources to the customer or a successor supplier—reversing, in effect, the original transition. Whatever the circumstances—default or convenience termination, or expiration of the contract term—these things must be done in an orderly, businesslike fashion that maintains good service during the transitional period and minimizes any disruption of the customer's business. Since expiration or termination may be years away, the supplier's solution and customer requirements are bound to evolve, and the successor is unknown, the 'reverse transition' cannot be planned in detail. Essential commitments may, however, be defined and potential misunderstandings avoided or at least reduced. From the customer's standpoint, it is only prudent to settle these things in advance—at a time when everyone is cordial and

---

[25] The *cognoscenti* call this 'reverse acquired rights' or 'reverse TUPE.'

the supplier aims to please—rather than risk a potentially contentious exercise later on, when relations between the parties may be strained, and the supplier's attention may be focused upon other opportunities. For suppliers, anything other than an orderly conclusion puts the company's reputation at risk, and it matters, as always, to define clearly what precisely must be done for the agreed price.

When business processes such as HR, logistics, or procurement are outsourced, disengagement can be more challenging than in a conventional IT transaction, because: (i) the outsourcer will have transformed the customer's operations; and (ii) new processes may include proprietary elements that are unique to the particular supplier and may not be transferable. In these respects, IT can be easier, since leading suppliers use relatively mature technologies, familiar methods and commercial products. One supplier's help desk or data center is likely to resemble that of its competitor. Software development methodologies are essentially similar worldwide. Business process solutions and services, by contrast, may vary a good deal from one supplier to the next, so that repatriation to the customer, or transition to a competing supplier's proprietary solution, may be protracted and complex.

Good contracts should establish ground rules for timing, scope, and cost of disengagement. Since timing and other particulars for future service are unknown and unknowable when contracts are written, customers often propose to discontinue service in phases (by location, business unit, or some other logical sequence to be determined at the time) with relief from any minimum payment obligations during the final wind-up. Usually, basic service charges cover the cost of termination-related services ('termination assistance') until the contract ends. Thereafter, termination assistance or some or all normal services must be provided at contract rates, on a time and materials basis, or occasionally at a 'holdover' premium. Customers frequently have limited rights to extend the contract or selected services on a month-to-month basis for a few months after service would otherwise cease in order to accommodate reverse transitions.

Many customers propose catch-all commitments to provide whatever assistance is reasonably requested or required to effect a smooth transition. Given the unknowns, this is an understandable request, but suppliers are uneasy about open-ended, elastic obligations. Suppliers generally propose to be paid for additional effort, if the reverse transition requires additional manpower or special skills. The team ordinarily assigned is unlikely to include transition specialists, and staff engaged in knowledge transfer, rehearsals, and testing will have less time to spare for day-to-day operations. The customer can either pay for additional effort, or relieve the supplier from some operational or service level obligations, so that the transition can be completed without significant additional expense.

The supplier may propose that payments for termination assistance be protected from set-off or withholding, in order to insulate the orderly transition from any controversy then brewing. For the customer to withhold payments during disengagement might be very short-sighted, for one way or another, the supplier is likely to calibrate its efforts to match incoming revenue. The customer may insist that provisions for termination assistance be enforceable by mandatory injunction. In the unlikely event of termination by the supplier for non-payment, the supplier may condition further performance, including termination assistance, upon prepayment or other appropriate protection.

Whatever the circumstances or service offering, the contract (or an accompanying exhibit) should spell out detailed arrangements to wind up the relationship during the final few months of the contract term, or during the interregnum between delivery of a termination notice and cessation of service. During those last few months, service must continue so that the customer can conduct its business, while both parties prepare to disengage and either repatriate operations to the customer or transfer operations to another supplier. These termination-related services are essentially identical, whatever the reasons for termination or other circumstances. They resemble the initial transition and commonly include the following:

- Transfers of assets on customer premises or dedicated to the customer's exclusive use. Assets shared with other customers are rarely, if ever, transferred. Leases of dedicated equipment may be assigned. Assets owned by the supplier may be transferred at book value, or market value (which may be less, for many kinds of equipment). Price is a matter for negotiation. Convenience termination charges often include an allowance (generally undisclosed) for unamortized asset costs. If so, and termination charges are paid, assets may change hands for nominal consideration.

- Transfers of personnel, usually limited to personnel assigned to the customer's facilities or dedicated to the customer on a substantially full-time basis (often excluding the supplier's account executive, his or her immediate subordinates, and shared staff supporting multiple customers). In the US, the supplier cannot simply transfer people, but (if the contract so provides) must allow them to be interviewed by the customer or a new supplier. A well-managed, cooperative process (even if not entirely free from tension) may help to reduce uncertainty and attrition, and so help to maintain consistent quality. In the EU, dedicated employees may transfer by operation of law under acquired rights legislation, in essentially the same manner as the initial transition.

Many Indian suppliers, operating as they do in an intensely competitive labor market, resist recruitment of their staff, but may agree to make experienced members of the customer's account team available for extended periods, after the contract expires, on a time and materials or similar basis.

- Transfers of software, data, technical information, working documents, and other intellectual property necessary to continue performance, and to solicit bids from possible successors. Transfer of the customer's own data and other information is straightforward and rarely controversial (assuming that the successor is content to work with them in the form then maintained, without data conversion); but suppliers may be sensitive about transferring anything that contains their proprietary methods or other intellectual property, especially to competitors. In the IT business, a supplier's commercial software products may be available for license, even to competitors; but suppliers rarely share internal procedures and tools, especially with competitors. Business process suppliers rarely provide their proprietary tools, methods and software to competitors or former customers, since they are marketed only in conjunction with service offerings. Any new supplier will have its own bag of tricks, and competing solutions may or may not be as easily interchangeable as operations of data centers, networks, call centers, or other IT infrastructure that, by and large, use well-established, standard technologies.

- Transfers of third party contracts, such as equipment leases and software licenses. The latter may involve substantial transfer or reinstatement charges, so parties are well advised to decide in advance exactly who pays for what. Generally, the customer or successor supplier will assume primary responsibility for securing consents. Wise customers will have considered reversibility when the contract was signed and consents were obtained, so that contracts are more readily transferable, without major additional expense. The supplier's master subcontracts or licenses to support multiple customers are rarely transferable, although those licensors and suppliers may be perfectly willing to serve either the customer or a successor supplier.

- Cooperation with the new supplier or customer, as appropriate, in planning, testing and execution of a migration plan. Generally, the incumbent's role in these activities is secondary, but significant and, to some extent, indispensable—so much so that customers often insist that the supplier's obligations to provide transitional services be enforceable, if necessary, by court order.

- Completion, early termination, or transfer of special projects then under way, with appropriate transfers of work in process and intellectual property rights.

- Access to the supplier's facilities and staff to carry out all of the foregoing purposes—for example to interview affected employees, ask questions, support transition planning, and a myriad of other circumstances.

In general, little of this is controversial, although suppliers are sensitive about the disclosure of their software, proprietary methods, and other intellectual property, as well as recruitment of their staff. Suppliers understand that an orderly, well-executed transition is in both sides' interests. So long as scope is reasonably well defined, and any additional effort is paid for, they should be reasonably content.

10

GOVERNANCE

In outsourcing, making the deal is only the beginning. Making it work is more difficult, and was, until recently, a challenge that outside advisors tended to overlook. With their work done, the contract signed and their bills paid, the advisors would move on, leaving their clients to make the best of it.

Those left behind faced many challenges. The process began with a kind of upheaval known as transition. Customers soon discovered that they could no longer manage their operations directly. Managing a contract was something new, for which they were unprepared. Former employees sported different badges and no longer took instructions. Getting things done required new processes and approvals. Services that were once 'free' suddenly cost money. There might be hiccups in day-to-day performance. Everything had changed, and not always to universal acclaim. Organizations were unprepared, and surveys revealed some disappointment and dissatisfaction.[1] One common source of trouble was weak governance, including failure to prepare adequately for the challenge of managing outsourced operations.

---

[1] The extent of dissatisfaction is easily overstated. Most outsourcing relationships are reasonably successful. Few achieve all expectations, but few are outright failures either. Occasional difficulties should be expected, as with anything else so complex and challenging.

Participants now recognize that better management of these relationships yields better results. Consultants urge companies contemplating outsourcing to begin building governance capability long before a contract is signed. The consultants' service offerings extend beyond the closing date. Suppliers come to the table with their own sets of best practices for governance, which often resemble the consultants' charts and advice. Key ingredients include governance in depth on both sides, from executive sponsors through layers of management, reporting, and coordination; disciplined change management; and the effective management of costs.

10.1 LAYERS OF LEADERSHIP

Some years ago, customers routinely agreed to hand over entire IT operations to a single supplier, who would buy the facilities and equipment, hire the people, and agree to provide the same or better service, for less. Left behind was the customer's chief information officer, with a secretary and filing cabinet. Somewhere in the filing cabinet, gathering dust, lay the contract, with standard language (carried over from the first draft, but unread) describing a joint steering committee, whose minutes could never be found because it never met. Everybody was supposed to live happily ever after. Occasionally, perhaps they did.

More often, customers fell behind from the outset and never caught up. They attempted to direct operations that were no longer theirs to manage, while losing sight of longer-run goals amid day-to-day operational issues or occasional crises. The supplier, like the lonely chief information officer, often had to cope with dissonance among business units pulling in different directions. No one was happy with these results.

Today, relationship management and governance are widely recognized as the customer's most common, avoidable error: too few people, with the wrong skills, no clearly defined role within the organization, and (usually) insufficient support and authority. This is a recipe for disappointment—operationally, financially, and in every other respect.

The terms relationship management and governance are related and overlap, but are not quite interchangeable. As used here, 'governance' refers to formal organizational structures and processes; and 'relationship management' refers to management of the business relationship between organizations, including constructive attitudes and behavior, excellent communication, and good working relationships, led by attentive executive sponsors. One reinforces the other. Relationship management must be harnessed with orderly processes and organization. The organization and processes are most likely to be effective when the parties conduct business in a collaborative, constructive, fair-minded way.

Robust and effective structures for large scale outsourcing relationships include the following:

- *Executive sponsors* on both sides. For the customer, this may be the chief executive, chief financial officer, chief information officer, or (for business process contracts) the head of the relevant function (such as HR, purchasing, or logistics). Customers should require the supplier to identify an executive sponsor or 'guardian angel' as well—someone who will pay regular attention, and possess sufficient clout to resolve major issues if and when they arise.

- *Executive oversight* through a joint board or steering committee which meets regularly and, ideally, face-to-face (rather than by conference call, where there is no eye contact, and busy executives can press the mute button while answering e-mail). Visiting the other side's headquarters or other facilities on a regular basis is always a good idea. Committee members often include executive sponsors, account and operational management on both sides, and representatives from affected business units. Steering committees, like boards of directors, should deal with direction, policy and other 'big picture' topics, as well as any contentious issues that percolate up through the various layers of working management. Active committees and executive sponsors help to assure that few issues rise to that level, since few people on either side care to show their superiors lists of issues that they have been unable to resolve.

- The supplier's *account management*, generally consisting of an account executive (who manages the relationship, deals with major issues, and hopes to sell more business), one or more delivery managers (who oversee day-to-day performance of particular services), a finance manager (who prepares invoices, budgets, and forecasts), a contract administrator, subject matter experts for various service lines or projects, and, initially, a transition manager. The number, seniority, and experience of the supplier's team may correlate with the size of contract. Suppliers tend, naturally, to put their best, most experienced teams on their largest accounts. Thus the account's relative importance to the supplier may affect the delivery team and, for that matter, customer access to the supplier's most senior executives.[2] Smaller accounts may share account executives, delivery managers, and other key staff with other customers.

---

[2] This is not to suggest that the largest suppliers cannot effectively serve mid-sized or smaller companies. Quite the contrary—many of their most successful relationships are with customers outside the Fortune 500. The smaller customer, however, must recognize that it may not have quite the same clout or access to top management as a multinational company.

- The customer's *project management office*, including a senior representative (corresponding to the supplier's account executive) and a supporting cast responsible for operations, finance, contract administration, and various categories of service or business units, as appropriate. The number of people and the scope of individual responsibilities need not correspond precisely with the supplier's account team, but each function has a counterpart on the customer's side. The project management office forms part of the customer's larger retained organization, which also includes remaining internal operations.
- *Joint working groups or committees* to deal with planning, budgets, technical standards, change management, regulatory compliance, and specific projects or services. These foster effective communication, break down organizational walls, and can, with proper leadership, engender a broad sense that all concerned are part of a single team, serving the same customers (not adversaries or rivals, despite differences in perspective and, in some respects, commercial interests). As governments apply increasing scrutiny to outsourcing, and increasingly stringent laws and regulations restrict use of personal data, the regular review of compliance issues has become particularly important.
- *Periodic review* of the whole relationship—scope, charges, service levels, contract terms, everything—at least annually can permit a fresh look, re-calibration, and appropriate adjustments. Usually both sides have concerns, so there is plenty to discuss, even without full-blown re-negotiation. Occasional re-negotiation of some aspects of the relationship is common, simply because of changes in business conditions, requirements, and technology.

Apart from formal organization, administrative details deserve attention, including written operational procedures, regular meetings (with agendas, minutes, and appropriate follow-up) and good records, particularly of adjustments to scope, charges, and contract terms. Few things matter more to both sides than rigorous, disciplined change management, which should be coupled with good financial management—detailed, accurate invoices with appropriate backup information, closely and punctually reviewed by an attentive customer. These disciplines are not formalities or 'busywork', but essential tools for the management and control of a complex business relationship.

Where the governance structure must accommodate a portfolio of outsourced services (the so-called 'best of breed' strategy) there are added complexities, such as joint oversight or steering committees involving more than a single supplier, with corresponding working groups. Some suppliers to the same customer may be competitors and the customer must sometimes mediate or play referee.

Collaboration becomes an important criterion for evaluation and success. Internal shared service organizations may also be involved and should be held to the same standards as external suppliers. Common procedures may make the customer's life easier, especially where suppliers' responsibilities intersect (for example when outsourced business functions must use infrastructure operated by another supplier). Common procedures work best when developed collaboratively, rather than imposed, and should be tailored to suit the full range of outsourced services. Procedures developed for IT, for example, may not work exactly as written for business process services.[3] Where multiple suppliers must collaborate with one another and their common customer, a written agreement concerning working arrangements, compliance with common standards, and protection of confidential matter may be useful.[4]

Ideally, when the outsourcing of various related functions is undertaken as part of a broad strategy, there will be similar contract terms, service levels, governance procedures, and the rest, based upon a common set of contract documents, adapted to the particular functions. Negotiated outcomes will vary from one contract and function to the next. The supplier of one service may not, for example, agree to the same indemnities and liability limits as the supplier of some other service, but when the customer develops standard terms and documents, substantial commonality can be achieved and will simplify administration for all concerned.

Finally, the lawyers' and consultants' 'standard' forms for governance must be tailored to suit the situations and participants. Occasionally, in the rush to complete a transaction, governance does not receive the attention it deserves. Forms or templates are simply added to closing binders without much discussion or thought. Elaborate forms with colorful organization charts, meeting schedules, and committee structures are useless if ignored or set aside after signing. Then, anarchy reigns. Smaller-scale or isolated transactions do not require the governance structure required to manage comprehensive services for a global company or a portfolio of outsourced functions. Essential needs are much the same—executive leadership and oversight, solid account management, good communication, change management, financial discipline, and the rest—but formal arrangements may be simpler. Whatever the function or scale of the relationship, the parties should talk through particulars, consider how best to manage their mutual affairs, then document the particulars and (above all), follow through

---

[3] Customers who have outsourced a single major function, usually IT, often assume that other outsourced functions are just the same. This is not necessarily so. See Ch 14 below.

[4] For a sample cooperation agreement among suppliers and a single customer, see Appendix 13 below.

after signing by populating organization charts and committees, conducting regular meetings, keeping good records, addressing and resolving issues that might otherwise fester, and all the rest. Active and engaged governance on both sides is excellent preventive medicine.

10.2 ACCOUNT LEADERSHIP

After the contract is signed, the sales team disappears and the supplier's account team takes charge, usually led by an account executive (responsible for the overall relationship), one or more delivery managers (who oversee operations), and, initially, a transition manager (who leads that crucial process). The account executive becomes the customer's primary point of contact, acting as a kind of ambassador—the supplier's representative to the customer and a conduit for two-way communication. The account executive and his or her subordinates serve as the customer's advocates within the supplier's councils. They interact with the supplier's delivery organizations to recruit talent, obtain answers, secure additional capacity and resources, and solve problems. They are a kind of fulcrum and intermediary: buying products and services from delivery organizations within their company, which they re-sell, preferably without writing checks for service level failures or otherwise disappointing the customer.

The account team's counterparts in the customer's project management office interact regularly with the supplier's account team and exercise corresponding responsibilities. Companies outsourcing on a large scale are, as noted above, well advised to build organizations with the skills, training, and clout necessary to manage outsourced operations. Their functions—relationship and contract management, contract administration, change management, operational oversight, planning, and financial management—correspond at least approximately with those on the supplier's account team.

The customer's management, like the supplier's account team, also performs a kind of ambassadorial function. They interact with the customer's executives, management and business units, oversee and direct the supplier, and communicate the supplier's needs and concerns to their various constituents within the customer's organization. Suppliers fairly expect a single representative to speak for the customer, whose business units must speak with one voice through that representative—a representative whose job description should include maintaining consensus within the customer's organization. When business units pursue competing agendas, or are at odds with headquarters, trouble is virtually certain. In a sense, the customer's project management office and its leader resemble the coxswain in a racing shell, who must steer while keeping the oarsmen in rhythm.

10.3 KEY PERSONNEL

Since account leadership is crucial, customers seek approval rights for and long-term commitments from both the supplier's account executive and key subordinates. They may be designated as 'key personnel' who are committed to the customer's account for reasonable minimum periods. Their selection and replacements are often subject to customer approval. Common negotiating issues include the following:

- *How many?* Customers naturally prefer more, and suppliers, fewer, but on large transactions they usually agree upon a shortlist that includes the account executive, delivery managers, key technical leads, or subject matter experts (for example managers of key operations or facilities) and, initially, the transition manager. Customers may also propose that certain transferred employees—generally, those with specialized skills or knowledge of the business and systems—be dedicated to the customer's account, at least initially. Suppliers are generally receptive, provided sufficient work is assured. Occasionally, customers request the right to reclassify positions as 'key positions,' subject to approval and other requirements. So long as the total number of key or restricted positions is limited, this may be acceptable to suppliers. For smaller accounts, account managers and others may serve multiple customers, and some support services (billing and contract administration, for example) may be provided remotely.
- *How long?* Here again, there is a predictable tension between suppliers, who prefer shorter commitments, and customers who prefer to keep good team members as long as possible. In a business where turnover is rapid and capable people hope for promotion, commitments for a year or two are fairly typical. The supplier's usual undertaking is not to reassign key personnel on the supplier's initiative during the agreed period, although there remains some risk of resignation, removal for cause, or transfer at the key employee's own initiative.
- *Replacements.* Customers generally request an opportunity to interview proposed replacements, review *resumés* and check references. Some customers request extended orientation or transition periods, when newcomers work alongside their predecessors, or a formal succession plan. Customers' involvement in personnel matters is limited (as it should be, for a variety of reasons, including the risk of 'joint employment' exposure), but customers generally request a right to require suppliers to remove staff from any position, from the account manager to the lowliest technician or call center analyst, if the customer reasonably believes that the assignment is not in its best interests.

This general language covers a multitude of sins —poor performance, clashes of personality, and customer relations issues. Suppliers request an opportunity to consult with the customer and consider other corrective measures before replacing anyone. Customers disclaim responsibility for any personnel action that may be taken. In view of the potential risks of employment litigation, both sides should consult with their HR professionals and counsel when issues arise. Consultations between senior management and appropriate professionals may be more prudent than written notices, which could become exhibits in employment litigation.

- *Restrictions.* Since key members of the account team develop intimate knowledge of the customer's business, customers often propose to restrict their redeployment to any competitor's account. Suppliers resist this, pointing out that they cannot very well develop the industry knowledge customers demand without serving other clients. The usual resolution is a shortlist of key positions, and restrictions limited to short periods and specific competitors. The shorter the list of key employees subject to these restraints, the more likely the supplier is to accept restrictions. Similar restrictions on re-assignment may apply to some transferred staff who possess important (often undocumented) knowledge of the customer's systems and operations, as well as competition-sensitive information.

10.4 REPORTING AND REPORTS

Suppliers issue formal reports regularly, capturing a variety of statistics about service levels, consumption, and performance, among other things. Sometimes, current information is made available to customers and supplier executives through 'dashboard' software or read-only access to problem management systems, especially for more critical incidents or failures. Regular monthly reports should also be provided electronically, to save time and money.

Many customers request the kinds of reports to which they have been accustomed, as well as whatever other reports they may request from time to time. Suppliers prefer to stick to their standard reports, for which they have tools and procedures. Often, customers find that these are more than sufficient, particularly when inquiry tools allow suppliers to obtain whatever additional reports they may need. Suppliers prefer not to undertake extensive ad hoc reporting, on account of costs. Someone must compile the information, prepare, and then review reports before their submission to the customer. In the information age, systems can inundate all concerned with information, so care should be exercised to limit reporting to data that matter.

More important than the reports themselves are accompanying comments about changes, exceptions, deviations, incidents, corrective action, projects, and trends. Reports of past performance are, in a sense, 'old news,' but help to manage expectations and future performance. Joint groups and regular meetings between supplier account teams and their counterparts can also help to translate performance reports into information that is comprehensible and useful to business users, who care far more about the impact on their business than raw technical statistics. All concerned must learn how outsourced services support and affect the business. Relationships with users improve when users believe that support functions, including outsourced functions, listen, understand, and care.

Fundamentally, all of these things are intended to assure frequent, complete, and honest communication at all levels of the business relationship. Without good communication, effective collaboration is unlikely.

10.5 CHANGE MANAGEMENT

Few things matter more in governance than effective change management. Successful and enduring relationships must accommodate continual change in requirements, technology, and the parties' businesses. Yet the familiar written procedures are often neglected or misunderstood, and can be misused. Customers fear blizzards of change requests. Suppliers trapped in losing contracts may see changes as prescriptions to restore health. These related tendencies may be symptoms of more fundamental trouble with scope, pricing, or costs.

Change requests and change orders are, above all, a way to manage and document change. Good change discipline protects both sides against uncertainty, including the risks and consequences of casual or inadvertent amendment through informal understandings, exchanges of e-mail messages, conversations, or conduct. The essential message is a familiar one: put it in writing. Suppliers may insist upon signed documents before proceeding with significant changes, and customers may decline to pay for work not authorized in writing. In general, change management (or change control) for outsourcing resembles similar processes in construction, public contracts, and other complex service contracts.

10.5.1 Contract changes

Contracts sometimes divide changes into categories, separating technical or operational changes from contract changes or changes in scope. Alternatively, a single procedure can cover all kinds of changes (although purely technical changes may involve different processes for review and approval). The use of a single procedure can minimize metaphysical debates about distinctions among various kinds of changes. The usual categories overlap, nomenclature is easily misunderstood, and most changes (other than minor operational matters) do amend one or more of the documents that, taken together, constitute the contract between the parties.

Typical change clauses call for written requests, detailed change proposals (including costs, effects upon time schedules, service levels, and other particulars), a reasonable period for review, and acceptance by signing. Approved changes amend contract terms and appropriate schedules. Unless and until a change order is signed, the supplier has no obligation to perform additional work, and the customer has no obligation to pay. Sometimes, it makes sense to adopt (or at least adapt) the supplier's standard nomenclature and processes (especially for purely technical or operational changes) if they provide adequate protection for the customer and do not conflict with related contract terms. The suppliers' forms are, naturally, supplier-oriented.

Well-advised customers insist that the contract should specify how changes are priced—typically: (i) without charge if no additional resources are required; (ii) otherwise based on contract rates and metrics; or (iii) if no rate or metric applies, then net additional effort is priced at the supplier's standard rates, an agreed discount from those rates, 'most favored' rates, or by some other objective method. Suppliers sometimes prefer to leave pricing for later discussion, but customers fear the practical monopoly of incumbency and the risks of abuse, especially if supplier margins have eroded for unrelated reasons. Wise suppliers recognize that objective standards, like those in an agreed rate table, make it easier for the customer to engage the incumbent than to invite competitive bids.

This protection matters more for changes in existing services than for wholly-new services (as when a supplier of IT services extends its repertoire to HR administration). With the latter, the customer usually retains ample flexibility to invite bids, and the supplier's cost and pricing metrics for other services may be entirely different, so that extrapolation from the original contract may not make economic sense.

When new locations or affiliates are added, the customer often pays for one-off planning, implementation, and setup charges on a project basis (fixed price or time and materials) and then pays for additional service in the usual way at contract rates, based on numbers of users, devices, calls, transactions, and other appropriate criteria. Service in remote locations may be more expensive. Conversely, when locations or business units are sold off, the supplier should support the transition, be paid for one-off effort, and either provide service to the successor or phase out service in an orderly manner.

Suppliers may seek payment for major proposals. Weeks or months spent developing detailed estimates and requirements are not trivial exercises. Customers may therefore agree to pay, especially if the supplier agrees that the proposal (or at least newly defined requirements) may be put out to bid and the supplier first presents (free of charge, and quickly) a rough order-of-magnitude estimate of probable scope, time, and cost in order to help the customer decide whether or not to proceed further. Suppliers prefer not to prepare major proposals or sets of requirements free of charge, and then have them turned over to competitors to bid against them.

10.5.2 Operational changes

Disciplined, well-controlled and documented management of operational change is essential and not at all controversial. However, suppliers want ample discretion to make changes in operations, especially when they operate from shared facilities that support many customers and use standard methods for all customers. They say that the customer buys a services and results, and should not micro-manage operations, especially when the price depends upon economies of scale and standard processes. Suppliers' business models and quality standards largely depend upon standard processes and economies of scale. On the other hand, customers need to be sure that no material changes occur that affect their operations, adversely affect services, or raise costs, without the customer's consent. Changes with such potential effects generally require prior notice and customer approval.

10.6 PERIODIC REVIEW AND RE-NEGOTIATION

Most large scale outsourcing relationships involve regular, even continuous negotiation over changes, projects, service anomalies, disputed matters, and other miscellany. To provide a convenient framework for those discussions, governance provisions may call for regular review of contract terms (typically, every year or two) through a kind of 'meet and confer' process or what NASA engineers might call a 'mid-course correction.' These do not bind either side to do more than negotiate in good faith, but, in practice, both sides usually accumulate lists of issues that provide ample fodder for productive negotiations and mutual accommodation. When relationships seem headed for trouble, periodic reviews provide opportunities for reflection and repair before problems threaten the business relationship.

To be fully effective, periodic reviews should be well-prepared and examine all aspects of the relationship—scope, solution, technologies, personnel, pricing, service levels, contract terms, actual performance—in a word, everything. Customers may wish to consult outside experts for a sense of current market trends and advice concerning the latest and best practices. Suppliers may wish to recommend improved technologies, tools, and solutions. Both sides will have learned from experience, and each should ask what they and their counterparts might now do differently, based upon lessons learned. Periodic reviews are the best possible time for benchmark assessments, if desired, since with other aspects of the relationship under review, suppliers have greater flexibility to meet customers' changing financial goals through adjustments in scope, service levels, and the combination of commitments and resources that suppliers call their 'solution'. Repeating this exercise every year or two can help to cement good communications, keep the contract terms consistent with changing realities, and prevent the growth of routine differences into more serious difficulties.

In any event, whether or not the parties engage in regular reviews, many contracts are re-negotiated within a few years in order to accommodate changes in business requirements, service delivery, and technology, or such major corporate events as mergers or divestitures. Benchmarking charges against the current market often leads to re-negotiation of financial terms. Once that exercise begins, the parties usually bring other issues to the table, although re-negotiation is usually limited to a comparatively few areas or issues that, for one reason or another, require attention. Since contracts and situations differ, no formula or pattern applies, but the following themes are typical:

- Customers seek lower costs, especially when outsourced services involve hardware, bandwidth, and other resources whose costs have tended to decline. Many customers expect to consider lower cost offshore options. Customers seeking financial concessions because of their own difficulties may expect suppliers to condition any reductions in charges upon improved payment terms or changes to the scope of service, service levels, or the delivery model, that reduce the supplier's cost to perform. Charges are not independent variables.
- In exchange for concessions, suppliers may seek extended terms, greater scope, opportunities for higher margin business, and other accommodations that sweeten the deal from their standpoint. In order to offer lower prices, suppliers now prefer to offer standard services to all customers, with wide discretion to determine how and where they will perform—at home or abroad,

directly or through subcontractors. Flexibility and scale tend to reduce the suppliers' costs.

- Since the pendulum has tended to swing in the customers' favor in recent years, customers request more favorable (or, as they put it, 'market standard' terms) on such important and potentially contentious matters as benchmarking and service levels.
- Regulatory and legislative changes, or prospective changes, may affect scope, divisions of responsibility, and such important contract terms as regulatory compliance, change management, and remedies.
- Terms unaffected by changing conditions are left alone, in keeping with the principle that what is not broken need not be fixed. There may be no need for extensive, or indeed any, changes to the master services agreement.
- Where changes to contract documents are extensive, it is often helpful to amend and restate the entire contract or relevant schedules, updating all terms, and incorporating all accumulated ad hoc amendments. This involves a little more work for the lawyers, but leaves the parties with a single, up-to-date set of usable documents, rather than binders full of amendments and change orders with obscure cross-references.

Re-negotiation is an opportunity to repair whatever has gone wrong. Inevitably, something has. At least occasionally, re-negotiation is primarily a salvage mission. Curiously, practitioners find re-negotiation more challenging than wholly new contracts, even though such challenges as transition, personnel transfer, disclosure, and due diligence are long past. Re-negotiation is more difficult because the parties already know one another well, the honeymoon is over, and each has some accumulated grievances that have taken on lives of their own and assumed disproportionate importance in the minds of participants. Often, little has been forgiven or forgotten. This can be an indication that working relationships need as much attention as contract terms, scope, service levels, or charges. In those cases, amending the contract is unlikely, by itself, to fix the problems.[5]

10.7 RELOCATION

Relocation has become an increasingly important issue as operations have spread globally. Suppliers pressed to provide the most attractive rates seek maximum flexibility to shift work to cheaper locations. Customers, conversely, fear that knowledgeable employees may leave (taking critical knowledge with

---

[5] See 11.3 below.

them) when operations go offshore, or move from one country to another. There may be other concerns about some locations, such as accents, language proficiency, or political risks. Many customers therefore request approval rights before operations relocate at the supplier's initiative. The parties may agree that the relocation of at least some services from one supplier facility to another (or relocation offshore) requires customer consent. This means, in practice: (i) the prior approval of a comprehensive written migration plan, including rehearsals and testing; (ii) the execution of the plan at the supplier's expense; and (iii) sometimes: (a) credits for delays, interruptions in service, and other problems, or (b) agreement upon adjusted (presumably lower) charges. If the supplier relocates in order to save money, the customer may want to share in the savings by re-negotiating charges. Customers expect suppliers to absorb costs of any relocation undertaken at the supplier's initiative. Customers may also require that the supplier include specific provisions in any contract with a new subcontractor, even an affiliate, including third party beneficiary rights. When operations relocate offshore, customers should make sure that the original supplier (and not an affiliate or subcontractor in some remote place) is fully responsible, and provides every reasonable assurance of good service, with appropriate arrangements for security, change management, oversight, backups, regular deliveries of work product, business continuity, and communication during the customer's regular business day.

10.8 INTANGIBLES

Whatever formal arrangements are agreed, much depends upon intangibles, starting with the tone and example set from the top by executive sponsors, the supplier's account team, and the customer's project management office. Courtesy, civility, tact, integrity, real interest in the other side's business and point of view, a commitment to fair play; willingness to listen, learn, acknowledge errors and forgive (rather than 'keep score')—all of these matter as much as formal procedures. Good leaders must represent, advocate, accommodate, and reconcile. In a word, they must be diplomats. Sir Harold Nicolson, a distinguished British diplomat, memorably distilled the essence with these words:

These, then are the qualities of my ideal diplomatist. Truth, accuracy, calm, patience, good temper, modesty and loyalty. . . 'But,' the reader may object, 'you have forgotten intelligence, knowledge, discernment, prudence, hospitality, charm, industry, courage and even tact.' I have not forgotten them. I have taken them for granted.[6]

---

[6] H Nicolson, *Diplomacy* (Oxford: Oxford University Press, 3rd edn, 1969) 67.

This does not mean that relationship management requires heroic qualities, although there are no known substitutes for intelligence, integrity, good judgment, or good manners. Nor does it mean concealing or deferring hard questions. Candor is as essential as courtesy. Relationship management requires competence, knowledge of the organizations, the kinds of qualities described above, and—above all—an appreciation that the other side is not simply an adversary. Each will succeed if the other succeeds, and not otherwise. When America's Declaration of Independence was approved, Benjamin Franklin famously reminded members of Congress—rebels all—that they had to hang together or they would hang separately. The same principle applies here (albeit with somewhat less drastic consequences).

Each side must learn about the other side's business and organization. The supplier's account team must not only learn the customer's industry, but also the customer's structure, history, internal politics, goals, competitive pressures, and concerns. They must know what is on the minds of the customer's management, and especially what issues keep them awake at night. Good account executives and delivery managers focus on delivering good results, rather than opportunities to write change orders. When results are good, customers are more receptive to proposals for additional service or special projects.

In the same way, customers should try to understand the supplier's business and organization—especially the role played by the supplier's account team, who answer for performance, customer satisfaction, and profitability. Both sides should, while pursuing their own objectives, help their counterparts to succeed, collectively and individually. On both sides, people have careers, ambitions and reputations. When they perform, recognition can pay dividends in goodwill and otherwise, through favorable references or further opportunities (for the supplier) or some 'free' consulting or other service (for the customer).

Effective governance requires sound organization and procedures, consistently observed, and animated by constructive, collaborative attitudes and conduct.

11

TROUBLED CONTRACTS

In complex, long-term relationships such as outsourcing contracts, much can and sometimes does go wrong—but not often. During negotiations, all concerned worry about ugly risks that might lead to ruptures, contract terminations, or lawsuits. These are remote contingencies. Rarely do they actually occur. Outsourcing is no more prone to failure or litigation than other kinds of business. Nonetheless, these are risks for which participants should be prepared, especially companies outsourcing on a large scale for the first time.

11.1 SOURCES OF TROUBLE

Scope may be the single most common bone of contention. Statements of work can never be complete or comprehensive. In any event operations and solutions evolve. General scope clauses—to the effect that the supplier will do what was formerly done by displaced staff within 'base case' budgets—are by their nature imprecise. The customer's historic data and disclosure are rarely complete, and no supplier's investigation (or 'due diligence') uncovers everything. There are always at least a few surprises. No statement of work or service description could (or perhaps should) capture every last detail. Occasional misunderstandings should be expected. Boundaries between customer and supplier responsibilities are bound to be imprecise and—especially when either or both sides feel financial pressure—may become contentious.

Service and performance issues may be the second most common source of trouble. Major outages, meltdowns of key systems, and other 'worst case' situations are mercifully rare. Mediocrity, complacency, and irritating errors are, regrettably, much more widespread and, curiously, as difficult to tolerate as more serious, but infrequent, breakdowns in otherwise acceptable service. Incumbency tends to breed comfort and complacency, rather than alert attention to client needs. Delivery models involve scattered operations, complex systems, and fallible mortals. All are potential points of failure.

These two themes, however, hardly exhaust the possibilities. Consider the following situations:

- Optimism, rather than realism, about cost, timing, and performance. Sales executives have a natural inclination to promise what they hope can be delivered. Their audience may be equally tempted to believe sales talk, in the hope of impressing management with a brave new world of lower cost and superior performance. Actual contract requirements are not always aligned with expectations.
- Deficient disclosure, which is usually unintended and often results from haste, compounded by blind spots or chaos in records after mergers, acquisitions, or reorganizations.
- Project delays, overruns and failures, for all the usual reasons familiar to anyone who has remodeled a home. Rarely is either side blameless.
- 'Back of the envelope' understandings about particular terms, functions, or projects, reached when under time and other pressures, with excessive hopes, and insufficient information or discipline.
- Customer business units unable or unwilling to sing in tune. Not everyone necessarily agrees that outsourcing was a good idea, especially after trouble erupts.
- Poor technical decisions. Will new tools produce expected efficiencies? If not, trouble is likely. With IT services, or services that depend upon IT, customers should retain (or if necessary, create) strategy and architecture functions and then collaborate closely with suppliers of outsourced services.
- Mismatched objectives. Does the customer want a custom solution and red carpet service? For a commodity price? Does the contract actually require what the customer now wants (long after requirements were formulated)? The customer may say 'it's not what we want,' and hear the supplier object that 'it is what we contracted to provide.' Both may be right. There is abiding truth in the ancient maxim: 'fast, cheap, good—pick any two.'
- Transitions may go wrong. Successful transitions require good planning, realistic schedules, and both sides' attention and commitment. Haste invites trouble.

- Changes in personnel may mean changes in tone and direction. The sales team bows out in favor of account executives and delivery managers. The customer executive who made the deal may move on, and his or her successor may have different goals. Suppliers may reorganize, shuffling organizations and personnel. A merger or acquisition on either side may displace key personnel en masse.
- Occasionally, lopsided contracts are signed. The customer whose chief executive agrees to a ten-year, cost-plus exclusive contract without service levels may repent; just as the supplier who bids on a break-even basis in hopes of 'getting well' through growth, projects, or future business may be sorely disappointed. Generally, if one party is unhappy, both soon will be. Reality has an awkward way of exposing bad deals.
- Elaborate documentation and processes grow more complex through negotiated compromises, then baffle those who have to make them work. Clarity and simplicity are virtues. No one can manage a business with processes that resemble rules of civil procedure.
- A focus on immediate concerns may obscure longer-term opportunities. Rather than seek opportunities for 'nickel and dime' change proposals or small projects, wise account executives take a longer, strategic view of potential opportunities. Customers need to lift their eyes from current reports and operational details to look at far horizons. Each side should regularly ask how outsourced functions might contribute to the long-term success of each company's business.
- Antagonistic conduct usually makes matters worse. Literal-minded readings of contract requirements may score debating points or secure short-term advantage, but erode irreplaceable goodwill.

These examples suffice to illustrate some consistent, even chronic, themes. Many troubled relationships are rooted in, or aggravated by, some combination of human errors, adversarial thinking, poor (even non-existent) communication and inability (or unwillingness) to consider the other side's interests. Each side complains, at least privately, about the other. Customers tire of sales pitches and change requests (especially if those requests are frequent and small). Suppliers dislike having to sell in order to earn any additional business. Customers press for lower charges and wonder whether incumbency and complacency tend to inflate margins on changes or projects. Suppliers feel like unwilling participants in an ongoing auction, where requirements change continually, goodwill never accumulates, and nothing but price ever matters. Both sides feel misunderstood and at least slightly ill-used. Each believes it is blamed for difficulties the other side might have prevented or avoided.

Interestingly, both sides' complaints are remarkably similar and at least partly justified. Each suspects (often correctly) that the other side is not entirely candid. All this reinforces suspicions. Each tends to assume the worst of the other. So the parties begin to behave defensively, like wary swordsmen circling one another. Let's examine the realities beneath the comments:

- Some suppliers are tempted to charge, or propose change orders, for the most minute variations from contract scope.[1] If margins are squeezed, the pressures to do so may be powerful, despite the effect upon customer relations. Some customers behave as though nothing but price matters.
- Suppliers would like to sell additional business. No surprise there. Account teams are generally expected to do so and they are rewarded when they succeed. This is understandable and, to a point, appropriate; but their superiors should appreciate that long-run growth depends more upon successful, long-run relationships and customer satisfaction than salesmanship. Good salesmanship consists of establishing a history of good performance, then offering attractive proposals to fill actual needs, not peddling the flavor of the month.
- Although most suppliers would prefer the comfort of exclusivity, they understand the need to earn a customer's business. On the other hand, if suppliers consistently perform well and offer competitive terms, they appreciate loyalty as much as anyone else. From the customer's standpoint, there can be few better motivators for a supplier than prospects for new business, but those prospects should never resemble the artificial rabbit at the greyhound track—alluring, out of reach, and, in any event, inedible. Suppliers become annoyed when competitors not only compete, but receive sensitive information about the incumbent's solutions, performance, proposals, or quotations.
- On both sides, too little effort is expended either explaining one's own business, or learning the other side's business, industry, organization, competitive challenges and culture.
- Many customers and supplier transition teams devote too little time and effort to explaining new arrangements to those who actually receive the service—how, for example, to obtain what they need through new processes involving unfamiliar approvals and personalities. The contract ultimately signed may differ significantly from preliminary internal briefings that, unless updated, position users for misunderstanding and disappointment.
- In outsourcing, as in life, most people prefer to blame others for their difficulties. Managing and delivering service from and to scattered locations amid continual change is not easy. Success requires skill, effort, relentless

---

[1] This tendency can sometimes be detected in pre-contract reference checks.

attention to detail, and effective collaboration. At least occasionally, something is bound to go wrong and, with rare exceptions, when things go seriously wrong, both sides have erred. 'Blame games' are rarely the best way to determine precisely what went wrong, address the causes, and prevent recurrence.

How then to prevent these kinds of difficulties or, more precisely, how to prevent inevitable operational and technical difficulties from poisoning the relationship? Experience suggests that the following preventive measures are helpful:

- Put in place and use strong governance structures and processes like those recommended in Chapter 9 above, which are designed (among other things) to assure good communication on all levels.
- Be clear in all things—scope, responsibility, decisions, strategy, and expectations.
- Communicate early, often, and truthfully, even when the truth is uncomfortable. Bad news is rarely quite as bad as the other side's worst fears and never improves with time. Let nothing fester.
- Educate continuously. Suppliers and their customers' internal organizations must teach users new processes, then refresh and update that training and make support readily available. 'Friendly' websites and self-help tools are essential. So is easy access to live, knowledgeable people. Users' frustrations beget gossip and can easily tarnish perceptions of the whole outsourcing initiative.
- Recognize that when things go badly wrong, both sides usually share responsibility. It is sometimes said that victory has many fathers and defeat is an orphan. In fact, to make problems worse, one usually requires help. Be willing to acknowledge mistakes, absorb lessons and move forward without harping on the past. Forgiveness and contrition can be good for the soul. They can also be good business.
- Insist upon teamwork, team thinking, courtesy, and respect. In collaborative efforts, the importance of intangibles is difficult to overstate. Business is not war, fortunately, but there are few better examples of teamwork than the wartime alliance led by General Eisenhower. Even critics of his generalship recognized Ike's gifts as manager of an alliance—coping with such outsize personalities as Patton, Montgomery, Churchill, and de Gaulle. He insisted that there was but one team, and is said once to have sent an American officer home because he had referred to his counterpart as a British so-and-so. The oath did not bother the general (whose temper was legendary, though well controlled) but the reference to an ally's nationality was inexcusable. In somewhat the same way, leaders of collaborative business relationships like outsourcing should insist upon constructive, collaborative habits and respect for the other side.

11.2 FIXING 'BROKEN DEALS'

In outsourcing, litigation and default termination are comparatively rare. No one can be entirely sure why, but most suppliers deliver good service most of the time and even if service is ragged, customers appreciate that default terminations are unpleasant and disruptive. The supplier remains responsible for critical functions while the relationship unwinds and unravels. Legal remedies are cumbersome and rarely provide a complete or satisfactory remedy, especially in the absence of any ability to recover lost profits or consequential damages. Proceedings are an unpleasant, hideously expensive distraction for both sides. The supplier's liability is limited, and the grounds for claiming 'material breach' may be debatable. If the court or arbitrators should agree with the supplier that there were insufficient grounds for default termination, the exercise may be ruled a convenience termination, for which the customer must pay a substantial termination charge. Sometimes, suppliers have legitimate claims for services performed outside the contract's scope. In other words, both sides have much to lose.

For these reasons, ruptures are rare, and unsuccessful transactions often end through convenience or partial terminations (sometimes dressed up as 'restructuring') rather than default termination or open hostilities. If only a year or two remain before the contract expires, a dissatisfied customer may simply let the contract expire and spend the remainder of the contract term preparing to take its business elsewhere. When several years remain, what can a customer do when a relationship sours?

First, determine what has gone wrong. In difficult cases, customers may consider engaging counsel to conduct a thorough, dispassionate, and privileged internal investigation; and be prepared for the probability—verging upon certainty—that both sides have erred. Suppliers who make a mess of things usually have help. Pains should be taken to reassure all concerned that honest answers (and not scalps) are the goal. The lawyers' findings, if protected by privilege, need not be disclosed in the event of proceedings (although in some countries, the privilege may apply only to outside counsel, and not the company's own lawyers). A frank assessment is essential for sound decisions, but need not become evidence.

Customers should consider seeking an independent perspective from outside attorneys, consultants, or other advisors. Their experience with similar situations elsewhere can be illuminating. Troubles are rarely unique. Most of what goes wrong has happened before, somewhere else. Outsiders may be more willing to articulate unwelcome conclusions, uninhibited by organizational politics.

Since they are outside the corporate pecking order, their advice may be more palatable or persuasive than the views of interested executives or their business units. This emphatically does not mean an immediate rush to engage trial warriors. Their moment may come, but, initially, the lawyers' role is secondary: to investigate, evaluate, and advise, in the hope of helping management to find a solution.

Then, with the facts in hand, all the alternatives, their costs, potential consequences, advantages, and disadvantages should be considered. Default or convenience termination, legal proceedings, re-negotiation, repatriation, and preparations for renewed bidding may be complementary alternatives that can, at least initially, be pursued in parallel. Keeping choices open is good contingency planning that enhances customers' leverage. Serious termination options reinforce efforts to re-negotiate scope, price, and other terms. Retaining counsel and consultants, starting work on a request for proposals, or inviting the competition in for a chat are unmistakable signals that the customer is considering its options.

Often, some combination of repair, reconciliation, and re-negotiation is the best choice among unpalatable options—if only because the alternatives are worse. When customers decide to persevere, they should consider how best to both repair the relationship and resolve outstanding financial, contractual, and operational issues. Are both sides willing to face uncomfortable facts, make hard decisions, acknowledge mistakes, be honest with one another, and move forward? If not, the results may disappoint, even if 'worst-case' outcomes are avoided.

For suppliers, the analysis and process are similar, if less likely to involve outside advice, since suppliers are supposed to know their business (preferably without too much experience with failed contracts, contract termination, or proceedings). Suppliers may have claims of their own, for services performed outside the strict scope of the contract, or for the recovery of termination charges, if default termination proves unjustified. Generally, they have every incentive to retain business, and are often willing to exert serious efforts, such as personnel changes, adjustments to contract terms, and operational improvements in order to retain the customer's business.

11.3 'MARRIAGE COUNSELING'

To repair tattered but not irreparable relationships, parties may wish to consider engaging in a process that resembles marriage counseling. This is not group therapy or a weird California ritual conducted by Druids in redwood groves, but a serious effort to air, comprehend, and resolve differences. An experienced facilitator can be very helpful, and there are good consultants who do this for a living. Experienced lawyers who respect one another and enjoy the respect of both sides can also do this successfully (and may have the advantage of knowing not only the contract, but where the proverbial bodies are buried). Ground rules should be agreed in advance and may include the following:

- To be effective, the process must be confidential. Whatever may be said in these sessions should stay there, without exception, and should not be shared elsewhere within either company. The point is to listen, learn, and reconcile, not build a record or case.
- Attendance should be limited to account leadership on both sides, their superiors, and perhaps executive sponsors. The lawyers may observe, listen, and perhaps help to facilitate discussion, but their role is secondary.
- Both sides should prepare, considering honestly what has gone wrong and might be improved; but the process should be informal, without prepared remarks, minutes, note-taking, or Power Point slides.[2] Preparation should include some soul-searching, uncomfortable as that process may be. What might *we* have done differently? What have *we* done that most disturbs the other party? What questions would *we* least care to answer? What skeletons hang in whose closets?
- Focus must be limited to the relationship, communications, conduct, and the like, rather than immediate operational, scope or financial issues. This is not the place for sales talk, negotiation, or recapitulation of past sins and pending disputes. Avoid personalities. We all have them, and all of us have warts.
- The tone should be candid, but courteous, respectful and constructive. Accusatory or inflammatory remarks will raise temperatures, blood pressures, and ire to no good purpose.
- Listen. Think about what is said, rather than any rejoinder. Allow everyone to speak his or her mind.
- Come prepared to question one's own assumptions, face awkward facts, and admit errors. We all make them, frequently. Responsibility is always shared. Come prepared to say and hear what has previously been unmentionable, and may come as a surprise.
- Each side should say its piece. Often, the parties take turns—one person from each side, alternating back and forth until everyone has spoken. Wisdom does not necessarily correlate with rank and insight may come from

---

[2] Slides reduce eye contact in a darkened room, and focus preparations for the session on a set-piece presentation by one person, often a leader, to whom others may defer. They may therefore inhibit rather than stimulate communication and fresh thinking.

surprising sources. This kind of process is more likely to stimulate discussion and hold attention than longer group presentations by each side.

Facilitators should keep the process moving within the agreed ground rules, commenting now and then, in order to crystallize discussion, summarize or probe, and articulate implicit views or assumptions. Toward the end, the facilitator may attempt to identify potential understandings, differences that need attention and suggest further steps toward resolution. Generally, facilitators should not (unless asked) comment upon the relative merits of the parties' views or (like settlement judges and mediators) recommend compromise solutions. The point of this exercise is for the parties to communicate, recognize their own shortcomings, understand the other side's perspective and interests, and appreciate that—whatever the merits or disposition of any particular controversy—unless they also change, difficulties are likely to persist, in one form or another. Neither side should expect to gain any advantage over the other, but ideally the air will clear and both sides will listen and learn. Changes in contract terms and personnel (or even changing suppliers) may change less than is commonly supposed, without changes in behavior. In other words, to repair the contract, repair the relationship too.

11.4 FAILING CONTRACTS

Occasionally, relationships go so badly wrong that such drastic measures as termination or legal proceedings must be considered. What then? None of the customer's options is attractive. Living with a bad contract has few charms. So-called 'convenience' termination is a misnomer that may cost millions in termination charges, to say nothing of the indirect costs of disruption and distraction. Default termination may mean litigation, with its delights and costs. Disengagement may take months and, all the while, the customer must depend upon an unsatisfactory (and by then unhappy) supplier, whose staff is eagerly searching for other opportunities. Divorcing couples may separate quickly, but outsourcing suppliers and customers must continue to live together for some time—not a pleasant prospect.

Unhappy customers sometimes respond angrily, threatening termination and litigation. Tough tactics may seem invigorating, but drastic measures (even when justified) are not always effective or wise. The supplier might capitulate, fearing liability and tarnish upon its reputation. But the supplier has probably been through this before, and may respond in kind: demanding compensation for services it contends are out-of-scope, limiting service to the bare letter of the contract, seeking damages for alleged breaches, and asserting that the customer's claims are pretexts, meant to avoid convenience termination charges, which the supplier promptly demands.

If battle is joined, both sides may lose. Neither is likely to win a clear victory and, as most participants privately recognize, both sides usually share responsibility for the underlying trouble. Legal proceedings are a costly, unpredictable, and expensive distraction. Complete vindication is rare. More often, after prolonged aggravation and expense, the parties settle, or have compromise imposed upon them when a court or arbitrators award half a loaf.

Again, the divorce analogy seems apt. The unhappy couple can carry on in misery, negotiate separation and settlement, or have a nasty, destructive fight, and split assets three ways: one-third to each, and the remaining third to their lawyers. Or they may attempt reconciliation, before any drastic, irreversible action is taken that shatters remaining trust, fixes positions in concrete, and lets legal strategy dictate decisions.

What should a customer executive do when faced with these dilemmas? Above all, avoid dithering. Procrastination rarely brings improvement. Left alone, troubles may grow worse. Facing unpleasant facts sooner rather than later is usually wise. Dissatisfied customers should reconsider, if they have deferred, the steps suggested above, including the engagement of counsel to conduct an internal investigation, and then evaluate both sides' potential claims, defenses, and exposure.

Remedial measures short of termination or proceedings may be available and advisable. Customers may (depending upon contract terms) audit performance, take issues to senior management, withhold payment, or assess financial sanctions for poor performance. Strangely, these contract mechanisms are often neglected, when their use might forestall more serious difficulties. If the situation is already serious, one must consider what grounds, if any, exist for one party or the other to claim breach. Is the breach sufficiently serious to justify termination? What claims might the supplier assert? What defenses exist? These legal issues matter in court, but also affect bargaining strength. For example, the supplier who risks default termination and a public rupture with a major customer, may prefer an orderly retreat, dressed up as a convenience termination, even without large termination fees. The dissatisfied customer who has received mediocre service, without suffering severe disruptions, may be reluctant to attempt default termination, and risk a court determination that the termination was really for convenience, for which a large termination fee is due. If some services are deficient, and others are acceptable, partial termination may permit both parties to climb down (and 'restructure' their relationship).

Customers must consider ultimate goals, whether separation, scope adjustment, financial accommodation, or some combination of measures calculated to salvage the situation. Business objectives must drive strategy and, in most organizations, the strategy chosen will need strong executive support. This is especially true when contemplating the uglier options of termination and litigation, with their costs, uncertainties, and risks of disruption.

Strategy should be developed and executed to achieve those goals. Often, people forget that termination, partial termination, legal proceedings, re-negotiation, and other options may be alternatives. The preferred option may change over time. Pursuing multiple paths is good contingency planning that (coincidentally) provides leverage. For example, the supplier who learns that his customer has retained counsel, engaged consultants, begun writing a request for proposals, formed a working group, and contacted competitors will instantly recognize that the customer is dead serious. A serious termination option may complement efforts to re-negotiate scope, price, and other terms.

Cost-benefit analyses are helpful when weighing options. Replacing a supplier, for example, means turmoil, distraction, and substantial hidden costs—notably, loss of unwritten knowledge and accumulated experience—in addition to the initial payments to a new supplier, and the costs of a formal selection process. Litigation may be uneconomic, if one considers the real costs of transition, and adjusts potential recovery to reflect probabilities of success, delays in ultimate payment, legal costs, contractual limits upon the supplier's liability, and the hidden costs of legal proceedings (especially the diversion of valuable time and attention from the company's business).

Strategies may vary depending upon the situation, contract terms and, customer goals. Where the customer intends, or at least hopes, to re-negotiate the contract and salvage the relationship, it might propose that a joint working group should discuss all issues, in confidence, with an agreement that nothing said or proposed will later be used in evidence. Confidentiality helps to assure frankness, and minimize posturing by assuring both parties that nothing said will later become evidence in any proceeding. Senior executives from both sides, without day-to-day responsibility for the relationship, may bring a different, more independent perspective to discussions. An experienced mediator can help the parties to find common ground, and assess their positions realistically, despite accumulated frustrations on both sides. Throughout, each side should consider the other side's position and perspective.

For suppliers, the process is similar. They must determine what went wrong. Independent advice is often available within the company, rather than from outsiders. Suppliers too can profit from counsel's privileged and confidential investigation and assessment as they consider their strategy. For the supplier, however, there are some significant differences:

- Suppliers prefer to avoid nasty, public divorces from major customers, which may affect reputations. If possible, they hope to preserve relationships and revenue, so long as there remains some prospect of eventual profit.
- So long as the customer has paid undisputed bills, the supplier may have no ground to terminate for default. Suppliers possess other leverage. The supplier who formerly accommodated miscellaneous requests may work to the letter of the contract, and let loose a flurry of change requests. The customer's own delays and errors may establish defenses against customer claims or permit the supplier to seek compensation for additional services performed.
- If the customer's grounds for claiming breach are debatable, the supplier will almost certainly claim that the customer's default notice is really a 'convenience' termination, and demand a termination charge. Contracts sometimes treat unjustified default terminations as terminations for convenience, obliging the customer to pay termination charges.

For suppliers, this kind of thinking is a disagreeable but unavoidable (if infrequent) part of their business. Their experience with the process—with change orders, claims, and the rest—may give them some tactical advantages over many of their customers, especially those more accustomed to managing IT or other operations than to managing contracts.

The supplier's liability for damages is often limited; but even so, the potential liability on large contracts can be very substantial—even before accounting for operating losses from troubled contracts, or the direct and indirect costs of termination or proceedings, or the impact on reputation and future opportunities.

Usually, though not inevitably, dispassionate analysis of the risks and potential costs to both sides will confirm that some resolution—to re-negotiate, restructure, phase out some services, or even negotiate an early termination—is the most palatable choice on an unappetizing menu. It is therefore helpful, if possible, to keep these situations free from personal antagonism, and maintain civil relations, so that resolution is possible and day-to-day performance can continue largely unaffected by any controversy. Both sides have legitimate interests. Both sides usually share responsibility for whatever difficulties exist; and usually, it is better to salvage than to scuttle.

12

THE FINE PRINT—RISK ALLOCATION
AND REMEDIES

Buried in the back of most contracts are complex, arcane provisions bearing such labels as representations, warranties, indemnities, and liability limits. The reader's eye tends to glaze over. If ever they are invoked, something dreadful may have occurred. So they matter, and deserve care and attention at the outset, lest difficulties yield unpleasant surprises.

Companies negotiating major contracts enjoy a good deal of freedom concerning their obligations to one another, but statutes and regulations circumscribe their freedom in all countries—and more so in Europe, generally, than in the US. Americans doing business elsewhere are often surprised by the extent to which parliaments and public agencies in other countries have prescribed the terms on which business is done.

Choice of law therefore matters. Contract law principles are broadly similar in common law countries, but details may vary according to statutes and precedents (even within the US) and similar words or concepts do not necessarily have identical meanings wherever English is spoken. No comprehensive survey is attempted here. For practitioners, the essential thing is to choose the governing law, stick with that choice, and research relevant law when necessary. What works in the author's native California may not necessarily work in quite the same way (or at all) in Illinois or New York, let alone other common law countries. Choices of law should usually be supported by sufficient factual nexus to sustain jurisdiction, although some jurisdictions permit choice of their law and jurisdiction regardless.[1]

12.1 REPRESENTATIONS, WARRANTIES, AND COVENANTS

The terms representation and warranty are often used inseparably and almost interchangeably, like salt and pepper. In fact, they have different meanings and are often confused with 'covenants' or 'obligations,' which are affirmative commitments to perform (for example to produce a report, process a transaction, or install a computer). Representations are statements of fact (for example that the transaction has been approved or that no proceedings are pending). Warranties are statements concerning quality, quantity, title, and the like (for example that software will be free from serious defects) and may be coupled with obligations or covenants to repair, replace, or perform other corrective work. Representations, if false, may give rise to tort claims for misrepresentation, which may be innocent, negligent, or intentional and even fraudulent.

Suppliers asked to furnish extensive representations and warranties prefer to pare them back, reduce their scope and introduce other qualifications. They prefer to limit their exposure and, more subtly, to reduce the basis for any future allegation of intentional, fraudulent, or reckless misrepresentation that might fall outside usual contractual limits on a supplier's liability.[2]

For similar reasons, suppliers prefer to curtail warranty obligations. Customers are equally squeamish if asked, for example, to represent that equipment to be transferred is in good condition or premises to be occupied by the supplier are free from environmental contamination.[3]

For the customer, representations and warranties serve multiple purposes. Fundamentally, they position the customer to invoke appropriate remedies if, for example, software deliverables fail within the warranty period. Equally important, the mere request for extensive representations and warranties

---

[1] eg NY Gen Oblig Law § 5-1401–1402 (jurisdictional amounts US$250,000 for choice of law, US$1,000,000 for NY courts) ; Cal Code Civ Proc §410.40 (US$1,000,000 jurisdictional amount) and California's enactment of the UNCITRAL model arbitration law, Cal Code Civ Proc § 1297.281, obliging arbitrators to respect the parties' choice of substantive law.

[2] Liability for intentional misrepresentations or fraud is often unlimited. See 12.3 below. In the event of litigation, fraud claims—which are factual—may be difficult to dismiss short of trial, and so raise the stakes and potential settlement value of claims.

[3] In the US, mere occupants of facilities on contaminated sites may be liable for existing contamination.

should prompt disclosure and discussion. If a customer requests representations concerning the absence of proceedings or infringements, and claims have been asserted, a discussion will follow. When the lawyers settle on compromise language—for example that to management's knowledge no proceedings are pending or threatened, other than those that have been disclosed—there can be an informed discussion of risks.

12.1.1 Mutual representations, warranties, and covenants

Many outsourcing contracts contain reciprocal representations and warranties concerning corporate power and authority; good standing; authorization by appropriate corporate action; and the absence of defaults or conflicts with any law, judgment, or other obligation. Similar language appears routinely in many corporate transactions, and is rarely controversial, although some commitments may be limited to material issues within management's knowledge. As in other complex transactions, these provisions assure accountability in the unlikely event that corporate formalities have not been observed, or the transaction violates some other legal or contractual obligation.[4]

Often, each side provides some proprietary software or intellectual property, so there may be mutual representations and warranties concerning the absence of infringements and claims of infringement (or at least known infringements or claims). Like some other representations and warranties, this is often coupled with an indemnity, and a corresponding covenant to refrain from infringements. Many companies, mindful of the costs of patent litigation and the risks of unknown claims by 'trolls' who build portfolios for enforcement rather than commercial use, eschew representations and warranties, but will offer indemnification against claims actually asserted.[5]

Occasionally, one side or the other may request representations to the effect that customer disclosures or supplier proposals are complete, accurate, and without material omissions. These are rarely acceptable. Customer data and disclosures are never complete. For their part, suppliers do not warrant sales presentations, and few thoughtful customers would expect supplier proposals—prepared with limited time and information—to meet the more exacting standards that might apply to a prospectus.[6] Suppliers' proposals also evolve

---

[4] In some countries, the authority of company officers may be confirmed from public records.

[5] In some countries, certain statutory warranties cannot be disclaimed or omitted.

[6] General scope or sweep clauses (discussed at 5.1 above), are another way to manage and allocate the risks associated with undocumented responsibilities or assets. Suppliers often condition pricing upon assumed conditions, such as consumption data, that, if inaccurate or unfounded, will justify additional charges.

during negotiations, so that they are unlikely to align with ultimate statements of work, service levels, pricing, and other contract documents. Integration clauses commonly provide that the contract and related exhibits supersede everything that came before, including the supplier's proposal. Integration clauses do not, of course, entirely absolve suppliers from responsibility for their proposals if, for example, there were any misrepresentations. In the event of legal proceedings, the proposal and other records of negotiation may be considered as evidence to interpret the agreement or resolve ambiguities.

12.1.2 Customer representations, warranties, and covenants

Suppliers as well as customers may request representations and warranties. Where assets change hands and employees are transferred, the representations and warranties resemble those seen in acquisitions. Typical requests include:

- Clear title to transferred assets, free from liens and security interests. Customers unwilling to warrant the quality or condition of those assets will usually warrant clear title in order to effect a transfer to the supplier. In England, such a warranty is implied by law.[7] Since computers depreciate rapidly, these representations and warranties have modest importance and are rarely controversial.[8]
- Transferred equipment is in good working condition, excluding wear and tear. Customers universally prefer to unload assets as they are, without warranties, on an 'as is' basis (where permitted by applicable law), asserting that the supplier is free to inspect equipment, or review operational records and maintenance contracts.[9] The supplier may request instead a representation and warranty that the equipment has been maintained to manufacturer's specifications under a maintenance contract. If the customer's operations are in reasonable order, and major items are in good condition—facts that suppliers can verify with reasonable confidence—many suppliers are willing to do

---

[7] Supply of Goods and Services Act 1982, s 2.

[8] When suppliers purchase data centers or other facilities, they generally request the same representations, warranties, and indemnities as other purchasers of real estate, notably concerning title, environmental contamination, compliance with laws concerning land use, and the condition of facilities, among others. Since sales of facilities are commonly documented separately, as real estate transactions, apart from the basic services agreement, they are not treated here.

[9] 'As is' terms may not be valid in European countries. English law implies warranties of good title and satisfactory quality (Supply of Goods and Services Act 1982, ss 2 and 4). In commercial contracts, statutory liability may be avoided or limited by contract, but limitations must be reasonable (Unfair Contract Terms Act 1977, s 2(2)). In practice, limitations are more likely to be respected if the contract provides adequate remedies.

without the added contractual protection of representations and warranties concerning the condition of transferred assets.

- There are no material, uncured defaults under leases, maintenance contracts, software licenses, and other third party contracts assigned or otherwise transferred to the supplier. The supplier may also request an assurance that it has received complete sets of all transferred licenses, leases, and other agreements, including all amendments. If the customer has endured repeated mergers, acquisitions, reorganizations, or relocations, this may be easier said than done, although the customer's base case and financial records should usually provide a reliable guide to actual expenditures under the various contracts.

- Operational, consumption, and similar data used to determine charges are accurate. Customers resist this representation, since data may be incomplete or inaccurate, and they never agree to blanket assurances that all disclosures are complete, accurate, and current. Suppliers may protect themselves indirectly, by conditioning their charges upon explicit assumptions, with adjustment rights if baseline assumptions prove incorrect. Their concerns include the risks that performance data and customer 'base cases' may contain inaccuracies or reflect perceptions and agendas within the customer's organization.

- There are no violations of law or pending or threatened proceedings concerning transferred facilities, assets, contracts, and employees. When large numbers of employees are displaced and transferred, employment claims are a particular concern. When the supplier operates customer facilities, or the customer provides office space for the supplier's staff, suppliers may request detailed representations and warranties concerning compliance with health, safety, and environmental laws, and the absence of any proceedings.

12.1.3 Supplier representations, warranties, and covenants

For the customer, representations, warranties, and covenants are, among other things, ways to transform sales talk into binding commitments that, like service levels, have consequences. Service levels are precise and binary. Systems are either available during 99 per cent of business hours, or not. When service levels are missed without excuse, a specific sum must be paid or credited, but service levels can measure only a limited number of metrics. Representations, warranties, and covenants apply across the board, but must be phrased in general terms so they are difficult to apply to particular situations. Such familiar phrases as 'best practices,' 'good industry standards,' and the like defy precise or specific meanings and call to mind Justice Potter Stewart's oft-quoted observation that, although pornography may be difficult to define, he knew it when he saw it.[10]

In practice, quality and other commitments dressed up as contractual representations and warranties rarely become sources of contention in outsourcing relationships, or grounds for the exercise of termination and other remedies. Suppliers generally deliver acceptable service. Dissatisfaction tends to surface in other ways, over scope, cost, and other issues. Customers nevertheless insist upon whatever protection contractual assurances can provide, difficult as it may be to enforce imprecise quality standards. Extensive written commitments do provide some practical leverage: language to which customers can point and, if necessary, invoke in the event of proceedings. Few suppliers relish the prospect of courtroom debates with unhappy customers about quality standards, efficiency, and the rest in which the suppliers are almost bound to appear defensive. In negotiations, suppliers tend to accept their customers' desires for fairly extensive written commitments. They have confidence in their ability to deliver, and regard practical risks as remote, so long as the written commitments are not laden with superlatives or other excesses.

Customers often request the following:

- *Quality.* Covenants and warranties to the effect that the supplier will deliver good professional service that meets or exceeds good industry standards (or some similar form of words). English law implies obligations to perform services 'with reasonable care and skill.'[11] Customer drafts may be replete with references to quality, reliability, efficiency, and other imprecise terms to which suppliers may object (even when they seem to echo sales presentations). Suppliers are on better ground when they object to glittering superlatives, such as 'world class' (whatever that means) or 'superior' (which might be ascertainable, but rarely corresponds to customer desires for commodity pricing). Customers usually agree that, whatever the language, general quality standards do not alter or supersede agreed service level commitments. Service levels alone are not a sufficient quality commitment, since they can only measure a limited number of metrics. In practice, commitments to meet good industry standards mean that, except where some different, specific standard has been adopted as a service level, the supplier must meet the standards of its competitors—standards that could, if necessary, be proved through expert testimony in the event of a dispute.

---

[10] *Jacobellis v Ohio*, 378 US 184, 197 (1964) (Stewart J, concurring) ('I shall not today attempt further to define . . . But I know it when I see it . . .').

[11] Supply of Goods and Services Act 1982, s 13.

- *Current technology.* Covenants to maintain equipment and software, and keep them up-to-date through regular replacements (or 'refresh' as it is known). Suppliers sometimes contend that this should be up to them, so long as they meet agreed service levels (which cannot measure all aspects of all services). Customers fear older, failure-prone equipment and the possibility of inheriting museum pieces when the contract expires. The final language may be qualified by reference to any agreed commitments to replace or upgrade systems, and maintenance commitments may be limited to more important and expensive items (inexpensive equipment may simply be replaced). Similarly, many suppliers will agree to upgrade their methods, processes, tools, and technology when upgraded for all customers. Investments outside the normal course of business, above and beyond specific commitments built into cost models and pricing, are likely to cost more.

- *Efficiency.* Covenants to perform efficiently and minimize charges. Many charges are consumption-based, and may depend, in part, upon efficient tuning and management by the supplier. Customers fear that the supplier will just run the meter and maximize revenues, like a taxi taking a roundabout route. Suppliers have misgivings about guaranteeing efficiency, which involves judgment and may not become contentious until the relationship is in difficulty, when circumstances invite second-guessing. Moreover, efficiency is not always the supplier's exclusive responsibility. In recent years, the market has moved toward more granular, quantitative pricing, driven by customer usage and demand. Efficiency commitments can be tempered by references to reasonable efficiency, good industry standards, and a limitation to matters within the supplier's control.

- *Rights to use software.* Representations, warranties, and covenants to the effect that the supplier has authority to use all required software. Suppliers often wish to qualify this commitment, bearing in mind the hazards of obtaining consent and litigation risks—including claims concerning open-source systems and certain patents upon call center technology. Some suppliers, as targets of those claims, attempt to limit representations, warranties, and indemnities concerning these issues. They point out that some customers' own operations may already bear these risks, because of technologies the customers have adopted and expect suppliers to retain.

- *Viruses.* Covenants or warranties concerning the detection and eradication of viruses. In a sense, viruses, like vandalism or other crimes, are a kind of *force majeure* event, and the introduction of viruses may depend in part upon users. However, customers want, if not ironclad guarantees, at least an assurance that the supplier will use commercial tools and best practices to prevent the introduction of viruses, and, when necessary, will cleanse infected systems and data. Sometimes, the parties agree to share financial responsibility for virus attacks, either proportionally, or above some 'deductible' built into the price. Suppliers are generally willing to covenant that they will not knowingly introduce viruses and other malicious code, but prefer to treat virus prevention and remediation as a service obligation, based upon use of standard commercial products and tools and both sides' adherence to rigorous operational controls. Suppliers resist open-ended commitments to eradicate viruses, unless outbreaks are attributable to their failures to perform.

• *Improprieties.* Representations and warranties that the supplier has not offered improper inducements to win the customer's business and covenants to refrain from kickbacks, bribery, and other improper payments prohibited by such laws as the US Foreign Corrupt Practices Act.[12] These may be coupled with obligations to comply with ethical standards. Suppliers rarely object— everyone opposes sin—but ethical standards developed for employees, or for domestic use, may have to be adapted if applied to a supplier or a supplier's offshore operations. Often, compliance with the supplier's own ethical standards will suffice.

• *Product warranties.* Warranties concerning the quality of hardware and software products supplied follow the pattern in other sales of similar products. Suppliers limit their commitments concerning third party hardware to transferable warranties from manufacturers and disclaim implied warranties. Suppliers whose lines of business include hardware and software invariably offer their products to service customers with standard warranties. Warranties for newly developed software are generally brief, and limited to significant flaws. When scope includes applications development and maintenance, post-warranty support is essentially the same as support for other proprietary software. Support for third party software commonly consists of configuration, tuning, coordination with the third party licensor, and the installation of updates and fixes supplied by the licensor. One party or the other is commonly required to contract with the licensor for support, in order to assure access to telephone support, updates, and other maintenance.

• *Software documentation.* In software maintenance and development contracts, customers sometimes request extensive commitments concerning the quality of technical and user documentation. No one doubts that, in an ideal world, software should be thoroughly documented, in ways intelligible

---

[12] Pub L No 95-23, 91 Stat 1494 (1977), 15 USC §§ 78m, 78dd-1–78dd-2, 78ff, as amended by International Anti-bribery and Fair Competition Act of 1998, Pub L 105–366, 112 Stat 3302, 15 USC §§ 78dd-1–78dd-3, 78 *et seq* (1998).

to others who may later use, maintain, or modify software developed or supported by an outside supplier. In practice, not everyone rigorously applies textbook methodologies or can afford to do so, given time, cost, and resource constraints. Suppliers often inherit operations where documentation is of uneven quality or lacking. When asked to warrant the quality of documentation, suppliers therefore seek to limit these commitments. For example, new developments prepared by the supplier may meet agreed standards, while a lesser standard (such as compliance with past practice) may apply to existing software applications (especially if they are scheduled to be phased out). The rain dance about warranties and contract language is a bit of a charade. The real issues are scope and cost, not words. If documentation really matters, especially documentation of older systems, the parties must decide what is needed and what the customer is prepared to pay.

- *Corporate social responsibility.* In multinational transactions, many customers now seek commitments concerning corporate social responsibility— prohibitions of employment discrimination, child or prison labor; adoption of labor, environmental, and other standards; and diversity commitments, among others. These are more than matters of good citizenship. They affect the customer's corporate reputation, for good or ill. An outsourcer's practices pose the same risk of embarrassment that a manufacturer or retailer might experience when reporters discover that an obscure offshore subcontractor employs child labor or pays sweatshop wages. Suppliers tend to view these requests sympathetically. They too have reputations to protect. Both sides should take pains to be sure that commitments expressed in agreements or announced to the public will be observed and can be enforced. Some policies favored in the US or European countries conflict with customs and laws elsewhere, and it is not always practical or possible to police worldwide networks of suppliers.

12.1.4 Disclaimers

Suppliers generally propose to disclaim:

- Implied warranties, including (in the US) merchantability or fitness for a particular purpose, which sections 2-314 and 2-315 of the Uniform Commercial Code imply into all sales of goods.[13] Although warranties for sales of goods

---

[13] The Uniform Commercial Code (UCC) is the most important of a number of uniform laws recommended to the 50 states by the Uniform Law Commission and the American Law Institute. All 50 states have adopted the UCC, with variations. Art 2, concerning sales, has not been adopted in Louisiana, which retains a civil law system.

have limited or no application to services, suppliers universally disclaim implied warranties, whose extent, duration, and effect are uncertain matters for a court to determine. In England, a statute implies obligations to deliver satisfactory goods and perform services with reasonable care and skill.[14] Limitations and disclaimers may be valid, if reasonable,[15] and are more likely to be upheld if the contract provides other adequate protection.

- Warranties concerning the accuracy of any advice, reports, or data delivered to the customer, or business results from action the customer may take based on the supplier's advice, reports or data. This complements and reinforces restrictions upon the recovery of consequential damages. Suppliers deliver a service, and may be fairly expected to warrant its quality, but not business results, any more than a practicing lawyer can guarantee a winning trial strategy or the financial results from a joint venture agreement.

- Any warranty or assurance that any service or the operation of any computer, network, or other system will be uninterrupted or error-free. Suppliers reason that technology is imperfect (as most users know only too well). Even the most stringent service levels (such as 99 per cent plus availability) leave some slight margin for error.

Customers naturally prefer to avoid, or at least pare back, any disclaimers. If service levels and express warranties are robust, customers usually agree to dispense with implied warranties and accept some other disclaimers. In the event of legal proceedings, disclaimers and other exculpatory language tend to be construed against the interests of those seeking their protection.

12.2 INDEMNITIES

Representations and warranties are often paired with corresponding indemnities, or there may be a general indemnity against third party claims related to breaches of representations and warranties. Indemnities are commitments to pay another party's losses. Many familiar insurance policies are indemnities, and the usual contractual indemnities in an outsourcing contract commit the parties to defend and pay claims, in much the same way that an insurance carrier might in the event of an accident or other insured claim.

Often, the principal indemnities are reciprocal. Both sides are supposed to obey laws, refrain from infringements, use reasonable care, and defend third

---

[14] Supply of Goods and Services Act 1982, ss 4 and 13.
[15] Unfair Contract Terms Act 1977, s 2(2).

party claims related to their acts, omissions, contracts, and other obligations. Occasionally, as in other transactions, one party or the other may propose to indemnify, but without giving a corresponding representation or warranty. Given the costs and uncertainties associated with infringement claims, a supplier may, for example, decline to represent that no such claims exist, but undertake to indemnify and defend the customer against certain infringement claims. The customer may welcome the indemnity, but still wish to be sure that no claims are known. There are, of course, a variety of possible compromise positions. For example, a supplier unwilling to provide a blanket representation against infringements may be willing to affirm that, to the knowledge of its general counsel, no proceedings are pending or threatened, and it has received no notice of any claim of infringement. This is something less than ideal from the customer's standpoint, but limits the supplier's duty of inquiry and affords some assurance that the supplier's lawyers (who would be likely to know about serious claims) are concealing nothing.

Customers sometimes propose that indemnities embrace bilateral claims between the parties (that is, losses attributable to the other party's performance) in addition to the usual (and more typical) obligation to indemnify, defend, and hold the other party harmless from and against various claims by third parties. Suppliers resist such breadth, contending that: (i) damages for breach, termination rights, and other usual remedies are sufficient; and (ii) additional indemnification for bilateral claims could largely defeat limitations on liability (which may exclude some or all indemnified claims). If ordinary performance disputes are covered by indemnities, and liability for indemnified claims is unlimited, then contractual ceilings on bilateral liability may matter very little. Suppliers therefore prefer to limit indemnification to third party claims.

12.2.1 Mutual indemnities

Many indemnities are mutual and symmetrical, or nearly so. Each side, for example, usually indemnifies the other against personal injury and property damage claims. These particular claims are often insured. A customer may, for example, accept the risk of loss for supplier equipment located on its premises, or vice versa. In the event of a fire or accident, the relevant party will either pay the claim (if it is within the deductible under its insurance policy) or submit the claim to its carrier.

Indemnities allocate risk, and sometimes parties are inclined to use indemnities to shift risk—in effect, to position the other side as an insurer against particular risks, either because the other side is better situated to manage the risk, or because the party seeking indemnification enjoys bargaining leverage (as customers often do in competitive selection). Some customer forms request extensive indemnities from the supplier, while offering minimal indemnification, or none, to the suppliers. Many suppliers would cheerfully reverse this imbalance, but in large, competitively bid contracts, suppliers rarely hold the power of the pen and must start from the customer's form documents.

The desire to push risks across the table is understandable, but may be short-sighted. Suppliers are not, in fact, insurers. Their cost models do not include actuarially-based allowances or reserves for risks outside the scope of their operational responsibility; and if they did, costs might be significantly higher. Risks and costs go together like salt and pepper. If one party or the other accepts excessive risks, without either the ability to manage the risk or adequate financial reserves, the business relationship will be in jeopardy if ever a claim arises—no matter what the contract says. The more prudent course may be to align financial responsibility with the parties' actual responsibilities and their ability to manage particular risks. When this approach is taken, and claims arise, there is less danger to the business relationship. Most people will accept, however unhappily, responsibility for unpleasant contingencies within their control, in much the same way that parents accept responsibility for errant offspring. Conversely, most people dislike paying for problems that others have created and might have prevented (whatever the contract may say). Reciprocity has practical as well as intuitive attractions.

Typical reciprocal indemnities include:

- *Infringements.* Claims of infringement concerning software and other intellectual property provided to the other party. Since many services involve combinations of customer and supplier systems, these are usually reciprocal and reasonably balanced. Each party accepts responsibility for what it brings to the business relationship. Each indemnitor enjoys reasonable flexibility to defend claims, settle claims by procuring a license, or provide a non-infringing substitute. If no practical substitute exists, infringing technologies may be withdrawn or replaced, and scope, charges, and service levels are adjusted accordingly. If no replacement is available, the customer may insist upon a right to terminate relevant services. Indemnitors, however, are not responsible for an indemnitee's unauthorized uses or modifications, or for infringements attributable to the indemnitee's instructions or specifications. If a customer modifies supplier systems, uses them with incompatible systems, or provides specifications, it assumes the infringement risk.
- *Transferred employees.* The customer is generally responsible for claims by transferred employees that arise before transfer or relate to their employment by the customer. Thereafter, the supplier bears responsibility for

compensation and all the rest. The supplier should also be responsible (under this indemnity and its obligation to obey the law) for acts or omissions in its selection of transferred employees before the contract was signed (assuming for the moment that there is selection, rather than automatic transfer under the EU's Acquired Rights Directive).[16] Each side should answer for its own compliance with employment laws.

- *Third party contracts.* Claims concerning equipment leases, software licenses, maintenance agreements, and other contracts related to the services, including contracts transferred to the supplier. Again, the customer is responsible before transfer, and the supplier thereafter. Since many of these contracts may be software licenses, this indemnity may overlap the indemnity against infringements. Claims by subcontractors are the supplier's exclusive responsibility.

- *Breaches of confidence.* This may overlap with infringement claims, since software and other licenses contain strict non-disclosure provisions. It may also embrace privacy and data protection claims—a point where suppliers increasingly seek absolute limits upon liability.[17]

- *Violations of law.* Each side generally indemnifies the other against claims concerning its violations of applicable law. When complex allocations of responsibility for compliance are negotiated, those allocations are likely to be reflected in the indemnities. A supplier adhering to the customer's instructions and policies for regulated transactions will decline responsibility for non-compliance attributable to those instructions and policies and instructions. For its part, the customer will want protection against supplier violations of laws governing the supplier's business. When assets and employees are transferred, the supplier uses customer facilities, or particular regulations apply, there may be additional or more specific representations, warranties, and indemnities concerning particular laws and regulations (such as compliance with employment or environmental laws, and the absence of claims). Suppliers sometimes seek absolute ceilings on liability under security breach and privacy laws, because of large potential liabilities when personal data are compromised.[18]

- *Taxes.* Taxes are another legal obligation. Each side is generally obliged to pay taxes on its own properties and net income and to withhold payroll taxes. Taxes, if any, upon the services themselves may be absorbed or passed

---

[16] See 9.6.2 above.

[17] See 12.3 below.

[18] See Ch 13 below, concerning compliance, and in particular 13.4 concerning privacy, security breach, and data protection laws.

through to the customer (usually, the latter). Whatever the allocation, each side usually agrees to indemnify the other against claims for taxes, penalties, and interest that the indemnitor is obliged to pay. Where one party reimburses taxes paid by the other (as when customers reimburse sales and use taxes imposed by US states on suppliers of taxable services), there may be elaborate provisions for collaboration in tax proceedings in order to assure that the party with ultimate financial responsibility is a full participant.

• *Tort claims.*   Each party may agree to indemnify the other against negligent and other tortious acts and omissions, particularly claims of personal injury and property damage.

12.2.2 Supplier indemnities

Customers sometimes request indemnities from their suppliers that go beyond the mutual indemnities discussed above. For example:

• *Insured claims.*   Customers sometimes propose that suppliers should indemnify them against claims covered by whatever insurance the contract may require. Suppliers object to this broad indemnity, especially if commercial general liability or umbrella coverage is required. In practice, many indemnities are supported by insurance (for example concerning personal injury and property damage), and contracts often require suppliers to obtain particular kinds and amounts of insurance from reputable carriers and provide proof of coverage. Insurance coverage, however, is a source of payment rather than an independent basis for liability, and its coverage will rarely align perfectly with contractual indemnities.

• *Shared resources.*   Where services are provided from facilities and computing environments shared with other customers, customers may require indemnification against any claims by other customers arising from shared use.

12.2.3 Customer indemnities

When suppliers buy assets, and especially facilities, they seek (as noted earlier) representations and warranties concerning title to those assets, the assets' condition, and the facilities' compliance with health, safety, and environmental laws. They also request corresponding indemnities or blanket indemnification against all claims related to the representations and warranties. Apart from asset sales, infringements, and the various mutual indemnities discussed above, suppliers generally have less need for indemnity protection than their customers. Customers are not passive after signing, but their primary obligations are for payments, rather than performance.

12.2.4 Indemnification procedures

The procedures for indemnification resemble those in other contracts. Coverage generally encompasses a variety of losses (such as costs of investigation, defense, and settlement, as well as any damages ultimately paid)[19] and claims against the other company's officers, directors, agents, and affiliates, as well as the companies themselves. When claims occur, the indemnified party must give prompt notice, with full particulars, sometimes within time limits, and in any event without prejudicial delay, then cooperate in the investigation and defense of claims. To defend claims, the indemnitor generally engages lawyers acceptable to the indemnitee. One firm may defend all parties, unless conflicts require separate counsel. The indemnitee may engage separate counsel, at its own expense, even where the indemnitor provides a defense, but the indemnitor should not be required to pay for separate counsel, unless conflicts between the parties' interests require separate counsel. Settlements require the indemnitee's approval, which should not be unreasonably withheld or delayed, at least insofar as settlement means the payment of money without any admission of liability. Greater discretion may be reserved where resolution involves equitable relief, concerns confidential information or intellectual property, or involves anything more than a cash payment and mutual releases. After payment, an indemnitor is usually subrogated to the indemnitee's claims, but insurance carriers are sometimes asked to waive subrogation rights.

The extent of the indemnitor's liability may depend upon applicable law and the contract's language. Some jurisdictions limit liability proportionally, where others impose joint and several liability, at least for some kinds of claims, thus exposing an indemnitor to liability for the entire loss. Many contracts, mindful of the collaborative relationship between customer and supplier, limit liability proportionally, to the extent of the indemnitor's responsibility. Neither party indemnifies the other against its own negligent or wrongful acts or omissions, and in many jurisdictions, indemnities against a party's own wrongdoing may in any case be invalid. For similar reasons, indemnities against infringement do not apply to the extent that claims concern unauthorized modifications or uses of an indemnitor's software or other products.

12.2.5 Insurance

Customers often require that suppliers' indemnities be backed by insurance coverage. Lawyers, unless expert in insurance, generally do not advise clients

---

[19] As 12.3.1 below, explains, contractual limits on liability generally bar the recovery of lost profits and consequential damages, but not consequential damages paid or payable to third parties upon indemnified claims.

what policies or amounts of coverage are appropriate, leaving that business decision to their clients' risk managers. Whatever the coverage requirements, customers may ask that they: (i) be additional insureds (at least for some policies); (ii) approve carriers (often based upon published ratings); (iii) receive proof of insurance; and (iv) notice of any cancellation or reduction in coverage. Suppliers would, of course, prefer simply to maintain what the law requires (in the US, workers' compensation coverage) and such other coverage as prudent businesses maintain. Most policies have substantial deductibles, for which the supplier is responsible, and some suppliers self-insure. Insurance coverage can help to protect the business relationship, since at least some of the risk shifts to a third party insurance carrier.

12.3 LIABILITY LIMITS

Outsourcing contracts invariably limit the supplier's liability (and usually, both parties' liability) by: (i) precluding recovery of lost profits, indirect, punitive, and consequential damages; and (ii) imposing a ceiling on recovery of actual damages; subject to (iii) some narrow, and often intensely negotiated, exceptions for infringements, wrongdoing, and other remote, but serious risks. Newcomers to outsourcing may find the practice surprising, for in many other transactions, liability is unlimited. Suppliers say they cannot afford to assume unlimited liability, especially if they must deliver service at lower cost than the customer's own internal operations. Supplier cost models include no risk premium to insure customers against business interruptions, outages, or similar contingencies—costly coverage that few, if any, customers have for internal operations. If cost models included appropriate risk premiums, charges to customers would increase. Suppliers are unwilling to assume risks that customers already bear, or to bet their companies on individual contracts. For these reasons, limitations on supplier liability are virtually universal, but they vary a good deal according to the situation and the parties' bargaining leverage. Liability limits are intensely negotiated.

In common law jurisdictions, compensatory damages—payment of money—are the usual remedy in civil cases. When contracts are breached, damages are supposed to provide the benefit of the bargain—a kind of rough financial equivalent to performance. Damages for negligence and other torts are also compensatory, but premised upon fault, to compensate innocent parties for wrongs they suffer. Various labels are applied to different kinds of damages and, as so often, case law is less than ideally clear.

General, actual or direct damages compensate the non-breaching party for the foreseeable consequences of breach, based upon circumstances known to both parties at the time of the contract. These may include costs of substitute services or 'cover.'

Consequential or *special* damages compensate the non-breaching party for secondary consequences of breach that would not be foreseen unless special or unusual circumstances are communicated at the time of the contract.

Incidental damages are, as the label suggests, incidental costs related to the breach, such as costs of inspection and transportation of defective goods, and incidental costs of effecting 'cover' (that is, obtaining substitute goods or services in order to mitigate the breaching party's liability).

In the US, *punitive* or *exemplary* damages may be awarded in cases of fraud or other malicious or intentional misconduct, in order to punish or make examples of wrongdoers, and not for breach of contract.[20] Even in the US, they can rarely be claimed in commercial cases; and in outsourcing contracts, punitive or exemplary damages are, as a practical matter, unobtainable and routinely excluded.[21] Outside the US, punitive damages are rarely available.

Throughout the common law world, damages for breach of contract tend to follow the rule in *Hadley v Baxendale*.[22] Hadley milled grain with a steam engine and shipped the engine's broken crankshaft to the manufacturer for use as a pattern in making a replacement. The shipper took a full week to effect delivery, rather than the usual two days, so Hadley claimed lost profits for the five additional days when the mill was idle. The court famously denied the claim for lost profits, reasoning that damages should be those 'as may fairly and reasonably be considered [as] either arising naturally ... from [the] breach of contract, or such as may reasonably be supposed to have been in the contemplation of both parties at the time they made the contract, as the probable result of the breach of it.' In other words, general damages must be *foreseeable*. If special circumstances 'were communicated ... and thus known to both parties' (as evidently they were not) then the plaintiff might recover damages that 'would ordinarily follow from a breach of contract under [the] special circumstances

---

[20] See, eg, Cal Civ Code § 3294, allowing additional damages 'for the sake of example and by way of punishing the defendant' in actions 'for the breach of an obligation not arising from contract,' where 'oppression, fraud or malice' are proven by 'clear and convincing evidence.'

[21] Punitive or exemplary damages are not contract damages, so exculpatory clauses may be invalid in some US states as matters of public policy insofar as they limit liability for intentional acts. See, eg, *Apache Bohai Corp LDC v Texaco China BV* 480 F 3d 397, 406 (5th Cir 2007) (limitations inapplicable to intentional or grossly negligent acts under New York law).

[22] [1854] EWHC Exch J 70, 9 Ex Ch 341, 156 ER 145.

so known and communicated.' Since the carrier could not have known the consequences of delay, unless so advised, it was not liable for lost profits. Many lawyers suppose that the rule in *Hadley* excludes all lost profits, although if profits were foreseeable, they might be recoverable even without notice of special circumstances—as, for example, when a supplier of outsourced services sues to recover unpaid fees that presumably include some margin for profit.

12.3.1 Consequential damages

Outsourcing contracts uniformly restrict, and often prohibit, the recovery of lost profits, lost revenues, and consequential damages. Sophisticated customers with sufficient bargaining leverage sometimes secure limited rights to recover consequential damages, up to a negotiated ceiling, in situations where the only damages are virtually certain to be consequential, such as misappropriations of confidential information and intellectual property. Contracts more frequently (i) permit recovery (as indemnified losses) of consequential damages paid to third parties on indemnified claims and (ii) classify various costs related to corrective action as direct, rather than indirect or consequential damages. In this way, a customer may be made whole for indemnified claims and costs of corrective work, without metaphysical debates about whether particular costs may be 'consequential' damages.

12.3.2 Limits on recovery of actual damages

Ceilings on actual damages are sometimes fixed sums, as in an insurance policy. More often, ceilings equal total charges during an agreed number of months. If, for example, the parties decide that twelve months' worth of charges is an appropriate overall limit, the contract will limit actual damages to: (i) charges during the twelve months before the claim arose; or (ii) for claims spread over longer periods, the greatest total paid for any twelve months during the longer period; or (iii) for claims arising before twelve months elapse, estimated charges during those first twelve months.

No hard and fast rules govern resolution of this issue. Suppliers have their own internal policies, and deviations from those policies may require executive-level approvals. Customers naturally prefer higher limits, with as many exceptions as possible. For the customer, the questions are similar to those surrounding limits on insurance coverage. How much is sufficient for dire contingencies: breakdowns in service or project failures, related corrective work, substitute service, and costs of unwinding the relationship by engaging another supplier or bringing the functions back in-house?

Liability limits are sometimes the last major issue to be decided, and resolutions vary, depending upon the scale of the transaction, the parties' bargaining leverage, the presence or absence of competition, the number and extent of exceptions, and the resolution of other major (but unrelated) issues. In recent years, twelve months' worth of charges has become a common standard, but lesser or greater figures may also be agreed (and be appropriate) in particular cases. Sometimes, customers propose and suppliers accept 'waiver' clauses to the effect that if recoveries ever exceed a substantial percentage of the agreed limit, the supplier must either increase the limit—and open itself up to additional liability—or risk termination of the contract without payment of a termination charge. In practice, this right could be academic, as claims large enough to meet the threshold may well trigger termination.

For the very worst contingencies, such as intentional wrongdoing, liability may be unlimited (as discussed below). The existence of limits upon recovery makes other remedies—notably termination—all the more important to the customer. If unable to recover all losses, a customer must be able to cut its losses and end the relationship.

12.3.3 Exceptions—greater or unlimited liability

Usually, a few claims are at least partly exempt from overall limits on liability. Exceptions are intensely negotiated and resolutions vary for all of the usual reasons. Generally, the higher the basic limit on actual damages, the stingier a supplier will be about exceptions. The lower that basic limit, the harder the customer will press for more and broader exceptions.

Not all exceptions mean liability without any limits. Sometimes liability for actual damages is unlimited, or subject to a higher ceiling, but consequential damages are barred. Sometimes consequential damages are recoverable, up to an agreed limit, where the likely damages are consequential; but liability for actual damages is unlimited. Sometimes, liability for both actual and consequential damages is unlimited.

The following exceptions are, if not typical, at least common:

- Infringement, provided the indemnitor enjoys reasonable flexibility to procure a license, provide a non-infringing substitute or take other, reasonable measures. For the indemnitor, infringement claims concerning important products or systems are often 'life or death' cases, where no expense will be spared, so this exception may be fairly readily agreed.
- Liability for some other indemnified claims may also be unlimited, or subject to higher ceilings. Suppliers naturally prefer that liability for indemnified claims be limited, just like general damages for breach. Customers ask why

this is fair, if the supplier's acts or omissions expose them to liability above the basic limit. Indemnitees can usually recover consequential damages actually paid to a third party, despite the usual prohibition on recovery of consequential damages for a party's breach of the contract.

- Breaches of confidence, intentional torts, violations of law, and other willful misconduct. Few attempt to defend the indefensible, or contend that liability limits should shift costs of culpable wrongdoing to an innocent party. Breaches of confidence—often meaning security breaches and privacy claims—are another matter; and so are minor, unintended, or accidental violations of law. Suppliers sometimes propose that liability be unlimited only for intentional wrongdoing. Accidental or immaterial breaches of confidence or regulatory requirements should not, they contend, carry unlimited liability. Especially in regulated industries, where the risks of unintentional violation are not negligible, the contention has some merit, although the term 'intentional' begs complicated questions concerning proof of intentions, acquiescence, imputed knowledge, and potential responsibility for rogue employees. Customers sometimes insist that consequential damages be available for breaches of confidence, infringement, and certain other wrongdoing where the only significant damages may be lost profits or other consequential damages. Suppliers tend to seek absolute ceilings, in excess of the usual limits, where they might be at risk for runaway liability.

Often, the most sensitive and contentious exceptions are those that may embrace privacy and data protection issues, such as exceptions for indemnitites, breaches of confidence and violations of law. Both sides fear claims related to security breaches that may release sensitive personal data and expose consumers to identity theft. No clear consensus has emerged, or seems likely to emerge anytime soon, given the potential liability and the evolution of the law. Both sides fear ruinous claims. Suppliers are less willing than before to agree that liability for breaches of confidence or security, or violations of law should be unlimited in the event of a security breach or privacy claim. Customers, naturally, prefer that the suppliers' liability be unlimited.

Suppliers prefer to contain that liability through absolute limitations on liability for privacy, data protection, and related statutory claims—limits that may be greater than the basic limitation upon liability for breach of the contract, perhaps with narrow exceptions limited to intentional wrongdoing condoned by management. For example, a supplier might propose that: (i) the basic limit of liability be x months' worth of charges, plus (ii) an additional y months' worth of charges for breaches of confidence, violations of privacy laws, and related indemnities.

Thorough discussion of practical security measures for sensitive data may sometimes help the parties to find a satisfactory resolution, particularly where one party or the other has primary responsibility for the storage of personal data. From the customer's standpoint, privacy and security risks may be much greater when a supplier runs the customer's data center than in many software maintenance or development contracts, where suppliers use test data, without access to consumer or employee records that the customer retains on its own systems.

12.4 SET-OFF AND WITHHOLDING

Dissatisfied customers sometimes withhold payment. Few measures are better calculated to assure immediate attention, or to apply pressure. Suppliers fear abuse, and the possibility that they may not be paid, even though they must perform, and most contracts oblige the supplier to continue to perform while disputes are pending. These differences may be reconciled through:

- Commitments to continue both payment and performance while disputes are pending. Come what may, the parties will carry on until the dispute is resolved. Service continues uninterrupted, and the customer pays the bills (less any permitted withholding).
- Limitations upon withholding, which may be a gross total (such as one month's charges) or a modest percentage ceiling upon withholding from any single invoice, or both. If monthly withholding is capped, several months may be required to recover the entire disputed amount. There may also be an overall ceiling on total withholding (ie x per cent of monthly invoices, up to a maximum amount). Sometimes, larger disputed amounts are placed in escrow, pending resolution of the dispute, but they may also be paid to the supplier, under protest and subject to a reservation of rights. Suppliers naturally prefer to be paid, and escrows can be cumbersome.

Whatever withholding may be permitted (and withholding provisions may be more common in the US than elsewhere), expedited arrangements to involve senior management and resolve the dispute are both common and well advised.

12.5 DEFAULT TERMINATION

Termination, like litigation, is a drastic measure. The termination of long-term services contracts is so disruptive, complex, and costly that an ugly, expensive divorce is usually the very last resort. Sometimes, there is no alternative and, in severely troubled relationships, willingness to terminate may be required in order to find a satisfactory resolution.

12.5.1 Asymmetrical rights

Many commercial contracts contain reciprocal termination rights. If either party fails to cure a material breach within an agreed period after notice, the other party can walk away. In outsourcing, by contrast, termination rights are often asymmetrical. Customers may terminate for a variety of reasons—indeed, virtually anything that might be characterized as 'material breach.' Customers may also terminate without cause for their 'convenience.' Suppliers' termination rights, by contrast, are often limited to non-payment and, perhaps, certain kinds of intentional wrongdoing, such as intentional infringement or misappropriation of the supplier's intellectual property. As a practical matter, suppliers must carry on so long as their bills are paid.

Why is this so? To begin with, the customer's primary obligation is to pay the bills. The customer may have few other responsibilities. Customers contend that if the suppliers' termination rights were coextensive with theirs, suppliers could exercise overwhelming and inappropriate leverage by threatening to cut off service, and bully the customer into submission. They imagine a supplier graciously advising them that all service will cease unless particular change orders are approved. Few sane suppliers would actually jeopardize their reputations with such brazen tactics, but the perceived operational risks to the customer are greater, especially when consequential damages can rarely be recovered. The supplier, by contrast, can usually be made whole with money. A court or arbitrators can compensate the supplier for out-of-scope service, deficiencies in the customer's performance, short payments, and other ills.

12.5.2 Default termination by the customer

Most outsourcing contracts permit the customer to terminate for 'material breach,' unless the breach is cured to the customer's satisfaction within a reasonable cure period, which may be subject to extension when corrective action requires more than the usual 30, 45, or 60 days. When the breach is incurable—for example following disclosure of a trade secret—there may be no cure period.

Occasionally, contracts attempt to define 'material breach,' but piling on verbiage rarely adds clarity. Suppliers sometimes propose to limit 'material breach' to a discrete set of circumstances, such as specific failures to meet critical service levels. Customers rarely agree. They prefer the general phrase 'material breach,' relying on judges, jurors, or arbitrators to decide whether circumstances warrant contract law's answer to the death penalty. 'Material breach' is another term that resembles Justice Stewart's description of pornography as something recognized when seen, but difficult to define. 'Material breach' is, in a sense, a label for a conclusion—default sufficiently serious to justify termination—and a factual issue effectively immune from appeal.

Contracts frequently define subsets of 'material breach'—circumstances that are agreed to justify termination—such as breaches of confidence, infringement, misappropriation of intellectual property, failure to execute disaster recovery plans following a calamity, or various combinations of unexcused failures to meet critical service levels.[23] These are, in effect, 'unsafe harbors'—conditions so grievous that the customer may terminate. It may be difficult to agree upon specifics. How many failures are too many? Suppliers are wary of low thresholds, fearing hair-triggers. Customers are wary of any implication that lesser numbers of failures are acceptable. If four consecutive failures are unacceptable, are three tolerable? Good drafting can accommodate these concerns, at least in part, by reciting that agreed combinations of failures are without prejudice to contentions that more or fewer failures, or different combinations, may or may not constitute material breach. One can imagine circumstances where a single failure—such as a network outage or system failure lasting several days—might, by itself, constitute material breach.

Rampant mediocrity is a greater risk than wrongdoing and a more frequent source of dissatisfaction. Many contracts therefore include language to the effect that material breach includes numerous, lesser deficiencies that may be immaterial by themselves, but are material in the aggregate. This helps to protect the customer against the hemorrhage of a thousand small cuts.

12.5.3 Default termination by the supplier

Suppliers' termination rights are often limited to non-payment—generally meaning non-payment of material, undisputed sums in excess of an agreed threshold, such as one or two months' worth of charges. These provisions, coupled with limitations on the customer's right to withhold payment, help to assure that the supplier receives sufficient revenue to maintain good service. In the worst case, the supplier has a remedy (though one that may, in practice, be subject to the vagaries of bankruptcy laws if the customer is in dire financial condition). Suppliers sometimes secure rights to terminate for certain other

---

[23] eg x failures in a single month, y consecutive failures to meet the same critical service level, z failures in any rolling 12-month period, or liability for some large sum of service credits within a period of months.

remote, egregious contingencies, such as intentional infringements or misappropriation of the supplier's intellectual property rights. Customers often ask suppliers to waive any common law or other rights to terminate contracts or suspend performance. Suppliers generally insist that if they terminate for non-payment, the customer must pay in advance for subsequent service, including termination assistance.

12.6 CONVENIENCE TERMINATION

In outsourcing, as in construction and some other businesses, customers reserve rights to terminate at will, without cause, for what is misleadingly called 'convenience.' Convenience termination rights are most likely to be exercised: (i) after fundamental changes in a company's operations, strategy, or affairs; (ii) when the customer is dissatisfied, but prefers to avoid hostilities (for example because the grounds for claiming material breach are debatable, or the supplier has serious counterclaims); or (iii) the business terms have become sufficiently unattractive to justify the costs and disruption of termination.

Some contracts provide that if default termination is attempted, but the court or arbitrators ultimately find insufficient cause, the contract will not be reinstated, but deemed terminated for convenience. This term (which is less common outside the US) assures the supplier some compensation for an unjustified termination, but imposes a ceiling on the customer's liability, and precludes any judicial or arbitral decision to reinstate the contract after a decision to disengage. However, the advisability of such a provision largely depends upon the size of the termination charge. When the termination charge is substantial, a supplier may respond to a default termination notice by contending that, whatever the customer's complaints, termination is actually for convenience and then demand payment of the termination charge. If grounds for claiming default are problematic or subject to credible defenses, the dynamics of the dispute may be transformed, since both parties have something to lose.

Suppliers rarely dispute the customer's right to terminate for convenience. Negotiations commonly revolve around such important secondary issues as: (i) the length of the notice period; (ii) the duration of any 'lock-in' period; and, above all, (iii) the amount of the termination charge:

• The length of the notice period may depend in part upon the time required to disengage and either repatriate operations or shift to another supplier. Transformed business processes may require more time (because of technical and operational differences among competing solutions) than basic

IT services (which most suppliers provide using standard methods and technologies). Suppliers tend to prefer longer notice periods, in order to maximize revenue, and allow time to re-deploy people and other resources. Often, the notice period is a practical question rather than a contentious issue.

- Suppliers prefer to prohibit convenience terminations during the first year or two, in order to recoup their investment in bid, proposal and marketing costs, transitional expenses, and any assets dedicated to the customer's account. Customers want maximum flexibility, but understand that: (i) the supplier's investment and transition costs may mean large termination charges during the first year or two; and (ii) they are, in any event, unlikely to exercise convenience termination rights immediately after signing. If things go so badly wrong that termination is warranted, they might terminate for default (although that, too, is unlikely during the early going). For these reasons, deferring convenience termination rights for up to a year or two may be palatable to many customers.

- Termination charges are often the most important, contentious, and vigorously negotiated issue. From the customer's standpoint, lower termination charges provide maximum flexibility and leverage during the contract term, if termination is relatively inexpensive. Customers would be content to pay reasonable shutdown costs (such as relocation and severance) in order to send the supplier on its way. Suppliers want to recoup their initial investments, transitional expenses, shutdown costs, and at least a portion of their anticipated profit for the remaining contract term. Substantial termination charges tend to deter termination, but they decline over time, as revenues amortize stranded costs. Suppliers rarely disclose how the figure is computed. Bargaining often boils down to horse-trading over a table of lump sum figures, which decline to zero over the contract term.[24] Customers may minimize termination charges by paying transition costs when incurred, at inception, but doing so may erase immediate savings. Spreading those costs over the term (with the supplier's cost of funds) may actually be more expensive, if less obtrusive. To minimize termination charges, the customer's best option is to pay transition costs when incurred, make whatever capital investments are needed, then offer to reimburse severance, relocation, and other shutdown costs in the event of convenience termination.

---

[24] On both sides, parties tend to prefer agreement on a schedule of fixed payments, rather than compiling unamortized costs and actual shutdown expenses at the time of termination. Agreement on set figures (though approximate and compromised) forecloses the risk of contentious accounting disputes at a time when the business relationship may be strained.

Convenience termination is the customer's option. Suppliers rarely have any corresponding right. However, some contracts allow suppliers to terminate if relationships prove uneconomic because of adverse changes in taxation, laws, or regulations. This suggestion defies conventional wisdom, and the customer's instinctive desire to hold its supplier to the contract. However, uneconomic or unprofitable contracts work poorly for both parties. The supplier will feel severe pressure to cut costs through every feasible expedient, even at some risk to quality and performance. The supplier may work to the strict letter of the contract, requesting change orders for any service not expressly required. Dissatisfaction may lead to re-negotiation, adjustments to scope and price, or even the negotiated termination of some or all services. In a sense, permitting the supplier a way out may simply provide a framework for unavoidable discussion of these realties. Offshore suppliers often request rights to make equitable adjustments, re-negotiate, or (in an extreme case) terminate if future legislation or taxes should render their offshore service delivery model uneconomic or unlawful. Customers recognize that no supplier can absorb losses indefinitely, so they are generally willing to entertain these requests.

12.7 OTHER GROUNDS FOR TERMINATION

12.7.1 Changes in control

Customers frequently seek rights to terminate following a change in control of the supplier, contending that they contracted not merely for services, but with a particular organization, because of its distinctive philosophy, culture, and leadership. Customers worry that their chosen supplier may change its spots if acquired by other owners with uncongenial or incompatible ways of doing business. The sale of the supplier's business may well mean the departure of key executives and senior members of the account team, along with some discontinuity in operations. Suppliers would prefer to treat any such termination as a convenience termination, for which termination charges must be paid. The subtler concern, especially for smaller suppliers, is the effect of liberal termination rights on the value of the supplier's business, which consists of future revenue from a portfolio of contracts. If customers can terminate contracts quickly, easily, and cheaply, the supplier's business is less attractive to buyers and investors. There is no easy or conventional answer for this issue, but compromises may involve: (i) well-defined 'windows' for the exercise of termination rights following an announcement or completion of any sale or merger; and (ii) discounts from the usual convenience termination charge. For their part, suppliers attempt to preserve as much flexibility as possible through liberal rights to assign the contract to affiliates, successors, or a buyer of the business (especially if the buyer has adequate net worth, retains the account team, and is committed to continue the business). Reasonable approval rights give the customer some comfort, but as a practical matter, may oblige the customer to consent, if the successor is reputable, has adequate financial strength, and commits to continue the business and honor the contract.

Occasionally, customers seek a right to terminate if there is a change in control of the customer. From the supplier's standpoint, this is nothing more than convenience termination, for which the customer (or, more precisely, the buyer of the customer's business) should pay. The real issue is the potential effect on a sale of the customer's business. A buyer inclined to terminate the contract may pay less. The rationale is economic, and less persuasive than for termination after a change in control of the supplier, which may affect service to the customer.

When customers are permitted to terminate following a change of control, attention must be paid to conditions and mechanics. Decisions and disengagement are not instantaneous. Customers require months to weigh their alternatives (while also evaluating the incumbent's performance under new ownership) and then a reasonable period to disengage, select another supplier, and complete the transition. Notice and other periods are generally measured from the date when the change of control is either announced or completed.

12.7.2 Force majeure

Many outsourcing contracts permit the customer to terminate the contract (or at least affected services) if the supplier is unable promptly to restore service after a fire, earthquake, or other calamity. Sometimes the customer may have a right to obtain alternate service on an interim basis either: (i) at its own expense, with charges abated; or (ii) at the supplier's expense, so long as normal charges are paid. Since emergency service may be costly, the latter alternative is usually more attractive to customers. Suppliers often seek to limit their exposure by imposing time limits or cost ceilings on any premium they are prepared to absorb, or both. Time periods are generally predicated on the probable time required to restore service, measured in weeks or months.

If the supplier cannot restore service promptly, the customer may have a right to walk away for little or no termination charge (other than the purchase of dedicated assets transferred to the customer). However, the real usefulness of this termination right may be a matter of leverage, rather than actual exercise. Suppliers often have greater ability than customers to find scarce resources in a tight market after a catastrophe, even if they must stretch to serve all customers' competing demands. If nothing else, the right to terminate may help to assure that a customer can demand and receive urgent attention. The actual exercise of termination rights after a *force majeure* event may not be very attractive, especially if spare capacity is scarce after a calamity.[25] If the supplier is unable quickly to provide or obtain temporary facilities and service, it does not necessarily follow that the customer will succeed. Customer termination rights may be limited to services affected by the calamity, unless it is impractical to continue because most or all services were affected, or remaining services depend upon those interrupted by the calamity (for example when a call center is the hub on which IT services depend).

12.7.3 Changes in taxation

Tax changes, such as the imposition of tax upon the services, could erase anticipated savings from outsourcing. Customers may therefore ask the supplier to absorb future taxes (a risk that suppliers are rarely willing to assume) or request a right to terminate in the event of a material change in taxation—such as an increase in rates, or the extension of existing taxes to the particular outsourced services—that cannot be offset or mitigated in some other way (for example by relocating operations). Suppliers regard any such termination as one for the customer's convenience, subject to payment of the full termination charge, but that position may be negotiable, particularly if the supplier seeks corresponding rights if the event tax or legislative changes affect its offshore service model.

12.8 DISPUTE PROCEEDINGS

Sometimes, proceedings are unavoidable. The troubles may be irreparable, or drastic action may be required. Even then, it is wise to exhaust diplomacy before commencing hostilities.

12.8.1 Preliminaries

Many contracts refer disputes to a joint steering committee, to disinterested executives, or perhaps a mediator—a kind of shuttle diplomat who attempts to

---

[25] Rights to terminate following *force majeure* events should be distinguished from failures to execute required disaster recovery plans. The latter is almost always a material breach, if the customer has contracted for disaster recovery services (unless *force majeure* conditions prevent execution of the plan). Well-drafted contracts often list failures to perform disaster recovery obligations as defaults, and define *force majeure* to exclude failures that might have been prevented, or substantially mitigated, by performance of the plan or use of such precautions as emergency power. Good disaster recovery plans, kept current and regularly tested, are the customer's best protection against calamities.

reconcile the parties' differences and resolve the dispute. Where immediate issues are symptomatic of deeper difficulties with working relationships, the parties might engage a neutral facilitator to listen to both sides, evaluate the underlying difficulties, and make recommendations to repair the relationship and restore effective communication.[26]

Negotiation and mediation often yield good results and prevent occasional, and perhaps inevitable, differences from becoming more serious controversies that threaten the business relationship. Nonetheless, many managers seem reluctant to invoke disputes clauses, whether from fear of drawing attention to difficulties, or from reluctance to face unpleasant facts or appear hostile to their counterparts. Whatever the reasons, stated or unstated, this reluctance may allow difficulties to grow worse.

12.8.2 Confidentiality

To assure frank discussions and minimize posturing and other gamesmanship, settlement discussions between the parties, or within the steering committee, should be confidential. The parties may agree (in the contract or later, when a dispute arises) that settlement talks and communications are confidential and inadmissible in evidence for any purpose.[27] When things go wrong, both parties have usually erred, and resolution is difficult, even impossible, if the parties are unable to speak frankly and admit errors without any concern that the other side is building a record for use in later proceedings. Mediation, when used, is protected by law in some jurisdictions and generally by contract or the rules of neutral agencies providing mediation services.[28] Mediators, like judges and arbitrators, generally cannot be called as witnesses.

12.8.3 Court or arbitration

Sometimes proceedings cannot be avoided, and good contracts should in any event agree upon particulars—whether to arbitrate or litigate, if so where, and under what law. Otherwise, there is the risk of conflicting proceedings in various places, compounding costs and uncertainties.

---

[26] The process resembles marriage counseling. See 11.3 above.

[27] Under US rules of evidence, settlement offers are generally inadmissible to prove liability, but they may be admitted in evidence for other purposes. See, eg, Fed R Evid 408. Broader confidentiality agreements are therefore helpful.

[28] eg Cal Evid Code § 1119; Uniform Mediation Act § 5 (in effect in the District of Columbia, Idaho, Illinois, Iowa, Nebraska, New Jersey, Ohio, South Dakota, Utah, Vermont, and Washington); and the American Arbitration Association's Commercial Mediation Procedures, rule M-10.

Preferences vary from one practitioner or company to the next, and sometimes reflect their most recent satisfactory (or unsatisfactory) experience. Some prefer courts (and in the US, with or without juries) where others prefer to arbitrate disputes. There is no single correct answer.

In multinational transactions, binding arbitration in a neutral location is often recommended, because arbitration agreements and arbitral awards rendered in any country that has signed the New York Convention on Recognition and Enforcement of Arbitral Awards are readily enforceable virtually worldwide, subject only to severely limited defenses. US court judgments may not be easy to enforce abroad, and in any event, foreign companies have as many misgivings about US juries as US companies do about proceedings abroad. The New York Convention and modern arbitration statutes also provide good grounds to stay and dismiss (or better yet, deter) legal proceedings that might otherwise be filed for tactical reasons in many jurisdictions. In multinational transactions, each side usually harbors misgivings about proceedings in other countries, especially on the other side's home turf, so binding arbitration is a good compromise. Generally, the party with leverage—meaning, in competitive selection, the customer—attempts to secure its preference, and whatever venue (or 'seat' of arbitration) it regards as most convenient and advantageous.

If the parties agree to litigate, they should agree upon governing law, jurisdiction, and venue. Whatever the chosen means, everyone prefers 'home cooking.' In multinational transactions, often involving local or companion agreements for particular countries, claims may be assigned upstream for resolution between the parent companies. This helps to avoid multiple (perhaps 'tactical') proceedings, conflicting results, and wasteful legal expense. Parent companies sometimes reinforce these arrangements by indemnifying one another against claims by their affiliates.

In the US, the parties should consider whether the loser should pay attorneys' fees and whether to waive jury trial (where it can be waived).[29] Suppliers, aware that outsourcing may be controversial, often prefer to waive jury trials. Again, views of these familiar issues vary according to circumstances and individual experience.

Arbitration is supposed to be faster and cheaper than court. Sometimes it is. Above all, arbitration is different. To some extent, arbitral hearings can be scheduled to suit the parties' convenience (though arbitrators are busy too). The

---

[29] Contractual jury waivers are invalid in California: *Grafton Partners LP v Superior Court*, 36 Cal 4th 944, 116 P 3d 479, 32 Cal Rptr 3d 5 (2005). After litigation begins, juries may be waived in accordance with Section 631 of the California Code of Civil Procedure. In the US, unlike England, legal costs are not recovered unless the contract so provides.

parties may pick arbitrators based in part upon expertise or experience, unlike trial judges chosen by lot. Arbitration takes time to get started, permits little discovery (unless the contract so provides), and has relaxed rules of procedure and evidence. Since arbitrators' jurisdiction is consensual and contractual, they have no power to join third parties. Arbitrators need not be judges, have no juries, and may (some believe) tend to impose compromise results. They are likely to be expensive. Their proceedings (unlike court sessions and files) are private (though perhaps not totally confidential) and their decisions are, as a practical matter, final. Except in rare circumstances, such as corruption, appeals are futile. An arbitration clause should cover the following:

- Scope (all disputes, or most disputes, with exceptions for intellectual property, confidentiality, and claims related to third party litigation, discussed below).
- Rules, such as those of the International Chamber of Commerce (ICC), London Court of International Arbitration (LCIA), the American Arbitration Association (AAA), and the UNCITRAL rules (an excellent set of rules, developed under UN auspices, which most arbitral agencies will follow if the parties so specify).[30]
- Governing law for both the substance of the dispute and procedural matters.
- A neutral administrative agency (such as the AAA, ICC, or LCIA) to oversee the proceedings.[31]
- Language for the proceedings (and fluency requirements for the arbitrators).
- Place of arbitration, which can have important legal consequences, including the choice of procedural law and enforceability. In international contracts, most practitioners favor convenient, neutral sites in countries that are parties to the New York Convention, where local laws permit provisional remedies, ready enforcement, and the like. Actual hearings may take place elsewhere for the convenience of the parties or arbitrators, but well-drafted agreements specify a 'seat' for arbitration, generally in a neutral country that is a party to the New York Convention. Parties with substantial leverage often press for arbitration near their headquarters, for reasons of convenience and tactical advantage.
- Number of arbitrators (usually, one or three), means for selection, and any special qualifications (for example former judges, accountants, or IT professionals). Panels of three cost more, and prolong the proceedings (since there

---

[30] There are significant differences among the various rules concerning such matters as costs and selection of arbitrators, among others, so selection of rules should not be an afterthought or a matter of indifference.

[31] Neutral agencies cost money, and are not required, but serve a valuable function (analogous to a court clerk) at a time when parties may have trouble agreeing on anything. The imprimatur of such respected agencies as the AAA, the London Court of Arbitration, or the ICC tends to enhance prospects for enforcement.

are more schedules to coordinate), but are often recommended for very large cases. Typically, each side picks one arbitrator, and the nominated abitrators pick the panel's neutral chairman. If the nominated arbitrators cannot agree, arbitration rules govern selection of the remaining arbitrator.[32]

- Possible variations upon rules of procedure (for example concerning witnesses, cross-examination, evidence, availability of discovery, recovery of costs). Internationally, many popular rules are based upon civil law rather than common law traditions. Lawyers from common law countries often write cross-examination and other procedures into the contract.
- Reasoned opinions, in order to allow for the correction of miscalculations or other obvious errors, enforcement proceedings, and appeal (although appeals are rarely possible).
- Possible limitations on the arbitrators' power to amend or supplement the contract, reinstate a terminated contract, award consequential or punitive damages, fashion remedies not contemplated by the contract (such as compulsory licenses), or exercise general equitable powers.[33] Without these limitations, the arbitrators may enjoy an essentially free hand. Courts rarely second-guess arbitrators' discretion, so long as they follow the rules, and respect contractual limits on their jurisdiction.

Disputes concerning intellectual property rights or confidentiality may be reserved for the courts, whose decisions can be appealed, and equitable orders are more easily enforced after proceedings conclude. Arbitrators go home afterwards, and panels are not easily reconstituted, whereas courts are always open and may retain continuing jurisdiction. The arbitration clause may provide that either party may litigate those issues, and that upon commencement of any such proceeding, arbitration will be stayed, insofar as it concerns issues before the court. Arbitration statutes generally allow the parties to obtain provisional remedies from a court.

Well-drafted arbitration clauses may also permit the litigation of disputes involving third parties—for example when a third party sues the customer or supplier and there are related cross-claims or indemnities. This protects both

---

[32] The AAA selects arbitrators from lists circulated to the parties. The ICC's Court of Arbitration generally relies on relevant national committees. The LCIA's Court appoints neutrals. AAA Commercial Arbitration Rules and Mediation Procedures (including Procedures for Large, Complex Commercial Cases), rule 11; ICC Rules of Arbitration, rule 9; LCIA Arbitration Rules, rule 5.

[33] Sometimes described by the phrases *ex aequo et bono* ('in equity and good conscience') or and *amiable compositeur* ('amiable composition'). Arbitrators so empowered enjoy wide discretion to decide the matter as they think appropriate in the circumstances, without necessarily following the letter of the law or the strict terms of the contract. Where applicable law and contract terms are unfavorable, this may be attractive, but introduces additional uncertainty.

parties against the risk of inconsistent results in different proceedings, as well as the expense of multiple proceedings.

12.8.4 Limitation periods

Contracts occasionally impose abbreviated limitation periods. Bringing matters to a head quickly is generally wise. However, practitioners should remember: (i) the risks of continuing breaches or recurring events, and start the clock from the last event constituting the claim (although this kind of formulation may invite debate); and (ii) the possibility that a year or two or more may elapse before frustrations ripen into willingness to act. The customer finally poised to consider drastic action will not want to discover that significant claims are barred by the passage of time. Customers should not sleep on their rights for long periods, lest they invite arguments that: (i) claims were waived; or (ii) problems must not have been serious, since little was said, so that any termination can only be convenience termination, which may bear a substantial charge.

Customers sometimes seek the best of both worlds by saying nothing about shorter statutes of limitations, but imposing a short cut-off period for charges. Charges for services must be billed within, say, sixty to ninety days or not at all (with time measured from the end of the relevant month or completion of relevant billing milestones, and exceptions for such occasional items as tax reimbursements). This can effectively bar many claims for out-of-scope work that the supplier might assert in order to offset, at least in part, a customer's damage claims. In virtually all complex outsourcing relationships, the supplier at least occasionally does both more and less than the contract requires. Suppliers are likeliest to propose shorter limitations periods, which may not be valid in all jurisdictions, or in the customer's interest.

12.9 AUDITS AND AUDITORS

Proceedings are comparatively rare, but audits are an annual affair (and potentially, a remedy in some situations). Customers invariably require rights to audit their data, processes and systems, as well as the supplier's charges, service levels, performance, security, and controls, among other things. Suppliers keep their own costs confidential and often propose to charge for support of more than the customer's usual annual audit. Suppliers do generally agree to cooperate with auditors, comply with audit findings (unless seriously disputed), and refund overpayments. Auditors should not be supplier competitors, and may have to comply with the supplier's confidentiality, technical and other requirements while avoiding any disruption of operations. Customers often request copies of the outsourcer's own audits. Suppliers usually refuse, but may provide summaries of relevant, adverse findings and corrective action. Customers' audit rights may survive expiration or termination of the contract for at least a year or two. Records may have to be retained for longer periods.

For companies whose shares are publicly traded in the US, audit requirements became more complex with enactment of the Sarbanes-Oxley Act, which requires an annual assessment of internal controls.[34] Suppliers may implement the customer's controls, or propose their own as alternatives, particularly when offering a comprehensive or standard service. US customers require annual service auditor's reports with tests of operating effectiveness under Statement of Auditing Standards No. 70 (known as SAS-70, Type II). Many suppliers routinely furnish these reports for standard controls within the supplier's systems and facilities. If a customer needs more, it may either pay or send its own auditors. To support required certifications of financial statements and assessments of controls, customers may request factual certifications concerning the accuracy of charges, inventories and reports; disclosures of security or other incidents; and compliance with required ethics and record retention policies.[35] These resemble the certifications that an internal department would provide, and may be limited to material matters within the supplier's knowledge.

---

[34] 15 USC §7262.

[35] Ethics policies written for US operations and employees may not necessarily apply as written to outsourced operations, or comply with privacy and other laws elsewhere. Suppliers' ethics policies may offer comparable protection, and, if written for global operations, avoid some of these complexities. Record retention requirements may outlast storage media and technologies, so periodic testing and review are advisable. When complex processes are outsourced, a thorough review of records management and related compliance issues may also be in order. For example, laws written before the digital era may require ink signatures on paper copies rather than on-screen responses.

13

COMPLIANCE

Not long ago, compliance meant a brief provision buried in the back of the agreement amid the 'boilerplate' to the effect that both parties would comply with applicable laws and regulations. Today, compliance provisions are lengthier and vigorously negotiated for several reasons. Governments and regulatory agencies are watching more closely because outsourcing has become a widespread, occasionally controversial trend. Many countries have enacted laws and regulations to protect citizens' identities and personal data, and outsourced services often involve the collection, processing, and transmission of data about employees, consumers, and other individuals. Finally, most outsourcing now involves at least some offshore performance, so that compliance involves much more than relatively familiar domestic laws.

To survey the entire regulatory maze would range far beyond our scope. Whole treatises are devoted to such subjects as privacy, data protection, or the regulation of particular industries. Instead, this chapter will address: (i) basic allocations of risk and cost; (ii) the essentials of US and European data protection law, as they pertain to outsourced services; and (iii) regulatory guidance in the US, the UK, and Europe for financial services. Banks and stockbrokers are among the most stringently regulated consumers of outsourced services, so regulations for financial services illustrate what others may experience or anticipate in other sectors, as well as strategies for allocating and managing regulatory obligations.

In this sphere, as with tax, employment, and pensions, the reader undertaking or advising on a particular transaction should seek specialist advice appropriate for the jurisdiction, industry, and situation.

13.1 ALLOCATIONS OF RISK AND COSTS

Compliance is neither optional nor negotiable. Supplier and customer alike must obey the law. Both prefer to avoid legal trouble and minimize compliance costs. Their interests diverge or collide when allocating financial and other responsibilities. Customers prefer to avoid, or at least minimize, increases in suppliers' charges and their own retained costs. To preserve margins, suppliers must recover the costs of both effecting changes and operating under more stringent regulations. To assure consistency and reduce costs, suppliers prefer standard or common approaches for all affected customers, just as customers seek, so far as possible, uniform policies worldwide. How can their competing interests be accommodated or reconciled?

13.1.1 Conventional strategies—shifting risks

To reduce exposure, there is a natural tendency to draw bright demarcation lines, then push responsibility to the other side. Alas, this approach is neither wholly satisfactory nor practical. Many 'standard' forms of agreement divide the legal universe into 'customer laws' (affecting the customer's business) and 'supplier laws' (governing the supplier). Often, these definitions are skewed, at least in first drafts. The supplier's form will limit 'supplier laws' to those affecting its provision of services. Everything else enacted anywhere is a 'customer law' and thus, the customer's problem. Customer-oriented forms invert this, limiting customer responsibility to laws governing the customer's particular business. Responsibility for everything else rests with the supplier. Neither extreme is very attractive to the people across the table. Some laws do apply primarily to one side or the other—in regulated industries, for example. More often, reality is not neat and demarcation lines are unclear. Some privacy laws, for example, apply to both parties, but in different ways to customers who compile and use data, and outsourcers who store and process that data for them (or, in European parlance, to 'controllers' and 'processors'). Some statutes apply to regulated businesses. The US Health Insurance Portability and Accountability Act, for example, requires hospitals, medical insurance companies, and other 'covered entities' to 'push down' information security and other controls onto service providers ('business associates') who process payments and claims.[1] Sarbanes-Oxley applies to all companies whose shares are publicly traded in the US and, in practice, private companies with aspirations to 'go public' in the US. Attempts to classify or segregate laws affecting one party or the other may merely postpone, rather than answer, the real questions.

Shifting financial responsibility is another common tactic. Some supplier forms treat regulatory changes as just another reason to write change requests, with costs to be determined when the time comes. Customer-oriented forms may assert that suppliers assume all risk of legal and regulatory change for the base price. Whatever legislators may do, the price remains fixed. In fact, suppliers are no more willing to write insurance against legislative whims than to dispense legal advice. For their part, customers are wary of open-ended liability for unknown changes, especially after they are effectively locked in to long-term contracts. As so often, neither extreme is entirely fair, or a realistic negotiating goal.

13.1.2 Analysis in depth

So the question persists: how best to reconcile the parties' interests? One path to compromise is to break complex questions into manageable pieces. Analysis begins by considering what laws apply and examining present compliance policies:

- Which laws matter most for the particular customer's business and out-sourced function? HR services, for example, often start with payroll, and laws concerning wages, hours, vacation, sick leave, overtime, and withholding taxes.
- Do present practices comply? If not, the customer has work to do before handing over to an outsourcer, or immediately afterwards. This is especially likely with privacy, since many companies' policies have not kept pace with the law's evolution.
- For each category of law or regulation, should one party or the other have primary responsibility? Does one party have particular expertise, or statutory responsibility? Bankers, for example, must answer to the bank examiners, a central bank, and other regulators, whatever functions they may entrust to outsourcers.
- Where one party assumes primary responsibility for compliance, what responsibilities may fairly be allocated to the other party? With HR services, for example, an employer will want to determine its own policies concerning vacations, compensation, sick leave, hiring, and much else; but would expect

---

[1] See 13.4.1 below.

the supplier to compute payroll taxes. Suppliers of payroll services (who prepare the paychecks) are supposed to know the rules, calculations, and payment mechanics. They will therefore accept responsibility for the calculation of payroll taxes, provided the customer supplies accurate information about wages, hours, salaries, and the rest.

- Is compliance at or near the core of the customer's business? Few companies outsource functions closely related to core competencies. For similar reasons, in such industries as banking or insurance, where compliance is a condition of doing business, the regulated customer is likely to decide key compliance issues. Suppliers of service to such regulated industries as banking, insurance, health care, and pharmaceuticals know a good deal about regulatory compliance, but they do not take deposits, lend money, or write insurance or prescriptions—nor do they possess charters, licenses, permits, or accreditation that may be at risk in the event of regulatory displeasure.

Answers to these questions may vary with context. Usually, a common understanding of relevant laws and requirements will expedite a sensible, negotiated resolution. It is also helpful to break down compliance into component activities, such as monitoring legal developments, crafting and revising compliant policies, executing those policies, and responding to violations or other incidents. Suppliers of services to regulated industries may forswear responsibility for monitoring the law or writing and revising compliant policies, even if their customers were willing to delegate responsibility. Yet suppliers will accept responsibility for compliance with the customer's instructions, policies, and procedures. For that, and not the interpretation of the law, they can be held accountable through contract requirements and indemnities.

IT infrastructure services often involve the operation of systems chosen and managed by the customer. An outsourcer may fairly contend that compliance is largely the customer's concern, so long as it performs the contract and adheres to customer policies applying legal requirements. Banks, for example, cannot delegate their statutory responsibilities to manage risks. Regulatory agencies treat outsourcers as an extension of the bank's own organization, and examine them accordingly. Banks may require outsourcers managing data centers and networks to comply with bank policies, based upon the bank's interpretation of regulatory standards. This does not, however, absolve the outsourcer of all responsibility; quite the contrary. The outsourcer must comply with bank policies, answer for errors, report violations, and be familiar with applicable law. Violations arising from non-compliance with bank policies may be subject to indemnification, unless lapses are attributable to bank errors or the bank's misinterpretations of legal requirements. In this context, following orders may be a defense.

Suppliers may assume greater responsibility for business process services. Many suppliers market more or less complete or 'turn-key' solutions, and some services involve activities subject to complex legal requirements. Customers expect such services to be compliant; otherwise, why outsource? An employer outsourcing HR services will, as noted above, expect its supplier to compute payroll taxes accurately and pay them punctually. The successful performance of other HR services—such as benefits administration—requires the supplier to understand and comply with laws concerning benefits, privacy, record retention, and employment, even if the customer retains ultimate responsibility for its policies. Suppliers of recruiting services must understand laws and regulations concerning employment discrimination, background checks, and personal privacy, even though employers determine their own policies and select candidates. In much the same way, a supplier of finance and accounting services may be expected to be familiar with laws and regulations governing financial reporting, as well as accounting rules and practice. Suppliers of procurement services should understand and comply with laws concerning price-fixing, bid-rigging, kickbacks, imports and exports. In these realms, suppliers are expected to be knowledgeable, and could not operate successfully without a sophisticated understanding of regulatory requirements. However, they supply service and neither write insurance nor give legal advice, but defer to their customers' policies, procedures, and instructions.

Where both sides have ongoing responsibilities, the parties are well advised to map those responsibilities in sufficient detail (often through a chart or matrix) to achieve genuine understanding, and then commit sufficient resources to follow through after signing. An employer may prescribe HR policies, for example, but expect its supplier of HR services to advise it of regulatory developments affecting its customers generally. If, as in the example, an outsourcer assumes primary responsibility for payroll tax calculations, the employer may retain responsibility and prescribe policies for wages, hours, overtime, leave, severance, and a host of other matters—all of which must comply with relevant laws and regulations. Pains taken to unpack these requirements and allocate responsibilities may save time, money, and grief later on. Operational details may wait until after signing, but bland commitments to comply with applicable laws are rarely sufficient.

13.2 PAYING FOR CHANGE

As so often, the touchiest questions concern costs, especially the costs of unpredictable future changes in laws and regulations. In a sense, legislative and regulatory changes resemble *force majeure* events, such as embargoes, national emergencies, or other official acts beyond either party's foresight or control.

The supplier's charges and cost models should include known costs of compliance at the time of the contract. When costs increase because laws change, suppliers naturally seek to recover those costs, plus a reasonable margin. Customers view compliance as one of the supplier's costs of doing business, especially if that supplier serves many companies in the customer's industry. They fear bearing disproportionate costs if they are 'pioneers.'

Negotiated resolutions of these issues vary, depending upon circumstances, bargaining leverage, and other factors. But here again, breaking down costs and issues into smaller, manageable pieces can be a catalyst for workable compromise. For example:

- Separate initial costs of effecting changes (such as modifying systems, writing new processes, and testing) from costs of ongoing operations thereafter. Where charges are based upon consumption, normal pricing metrics may compensate the supplier fairly for future service. The customer pays for net additional machine cycles, data storage, transactions, staff time, and other resources. Where legal changes require additional service or capabilities for which no rate or price has been agreed, additional costs and resources can be identified and priced, using objective criteria, as for any change order. Modifications to systems and processes may be treated as projects, and priced accordingly.
- Separate customer-specific changes or compliance programs from changes affecting customers generally, or whole industries. If regulations impose new privacy requirements on hospitals, for example, individual hospitals may be perfectly willing to pay for their own compliance projects, so long as costs for system changes affecting service to all hospital clients are apportioned fairly, capped, or (ideally from the customer's standpoint) absorbed as a cost of doing business.

Since regulatory changes and their consequences are unpredictable, sophisticated parties sometimes adapt 'equitable adjustment' provisions like those commonly used to adjust charges following mergers, acquisitions, or other unexpected events. Charges are adjusted based upon the net change in costs of performance, or the net change in staff, equipment, facilities, and other resources, with appropriate allowances for one-off costs and investments. This does not provide a formula for calculation so much as a framework for negotiation, but with objective criteria.[2]

---

[2] See 6.5.3 above.

Controversy surrounding offshore outsourcing, and the risk of restrictive legislation, has aroused concern among suppliers, especially offshore suppliers, whose business models depend upon comparatively inexpensive Asian or Eastern European workers. If the US Congress were to prohibit offshore services, impose punitive taxes, or severely restrict offshore transfers of personal data, they could not profitably serve US customers. This issue is too new for any consensus to have emerged, but some recent contracts contemplate an adjustment process based upon: (i) the relocation of affected operations (if feasible) and (ii) equitable adjustment of charges, or (iii) orderly termination if no mutually satisfactory, practical onshore alternative seems feasible and offshore performance is either unlawful or uneconomic.

13.3 MANAGING COMPLIANCE RISKS

Lawyers tend to think of compliance as a legal problem (as it is), but it is also a management challenge. Wise managers prefer to anticipate—rather than merely survive—trouble. Reactive management is hazardous. Reaction means responses to incidents, violations, and claims after they happen, often with little time, while under unwelcome scrutiny from customers, public officials, and the news media. Contingency plans are best prepared before trouble erupts and reporters with television cameras arrive at headquarters. Good compliance programs for outsourced services often include the following elements:

• The mapping of responsibilities before signing and in still greater detail during the transition period in order to identify relevant legal requirements, regulatory filings, systems, policies, processes, databases, and data flows, and be sure that operations comply. Outsourced operations are different, and may require adjustments in familiar methods, processes, and policies.
• Building compliance and review of regulatory requirements into governance, change management, and other procedures. When systems or processes change, someone should consider whether changes comply, affect internal controls, or require changes in disaster recovery arrangements.
• Periodic review of regulatory compliance issues, by monitoring trends, consulting with counsel and other experts about developments in the law and relevant 'best practices,' auditing or testing compliance, and, when necessary, adapting processes and procedures.
• Regular compliance training for key personnel on both sides, starting with the account or project managers. Leadership matters. So does contingency planning for 'worst cases.' Too often, immediate operational, financial, or

other issues consume all attention and leave management unprepared for unpleasant contingencies.

On both sides, account management should include a compliance function. For larger relationships or customer project management offices, this may mean a full-time compliance officer or regular attention from internal corporate experts in privacy, security, audit, and other relevant fields. Neither side will assume disproportionate risk or insure the other, but active collaboration can reduce the unavoidable risks associated with the increasingly stringent regulation of outsourced services.

13.4 PRIVACY AND DATA PROTECTION

Scarcely a week passes without news reports of some breach of security—hackers siphoning sensitive data, a misplaced laptop computer, or a disc full of sensitive, unencrypted personal data left in a taxi. Few issues attract more interest from reporters (or sympathy from legislators) than identity theft, which can ruin credit ratings and create other miseries for innocent citizens. For companies whose data are compromised, the dangers include liability to customers and public authorities, plus serious damage to reputations and share prices. Since most outsourced services involve some collection, transmission, or processing of the personal data of consumers, employees, or other individuals, these risks are virtually universal—and as serious for the average company as, for example, an oil spill for an oil company.

Personal data are always at some risk, whether or not a company outsources any functions that use, process, and maintain personal data. Outsourcing to a reputable supplier may actually improve security. Major suppliers who serve the armed forces and intelligence agencies, for example, know something about robust security; but for the customer, shifting operations outside and especially offshore may increase the numbers of potential points of failure and thus the risk (or perceived risk) that sensitive personal data may be compromised. Privacy therefore lies at the heart of almost any discussion of compliance. No comprehensive survey of privacy laws is intended or attempted here. Instead, we survey selected US and EU privacy laws and regulations, as they pertain to outsourcing, and offer suggestions concerning contractual allocations of risk and responsibility for compliance with those laws and regulations.

The US and the EU have approached privacy in different ways. US companies must contend with a variety of federal laws and regulations for particular sectors of the economy, such as banking and health care, as well as a welter of state laws, notably concerning security breaches. Laws may be enforced by sundry public agencies or through private litigation, including class actions in appropriate cases involving large numbers of individuals with essentially similar claims. Europe, by contrast, has adopted a comprehensive Data Protection Directive, implemented (with some important variations) through legislation in EU Member States, and administered by national data protection authorities. One pattern is consistent with Europe's *dirigiste* traditions, the other with America's untidy federalism and litigious tendencies. Beneath these differences lie many common themes, so that companies may and often do develop robust policies that, with some variations, go far toward satisfying most substantive requirements on both sides of the Atlantic. In practice, compliance involves (among other things) a search for common denominators. Industry-based regulations vary among member countries. For example, the UK's Financial Services Authority (FSA) imposes its own requirements on financial services businesses that wish to outsource. Substantial fines have been imposed for security breaches (although not yet involving outsourced services).[3]

13.4.1 US federal laws

In the US, federal laws protect citizens' privacy where they bank, borrow, receive medical care, or purchase health insurance. Apart from financial services and health care, there is relatively little federal protection, although the Federal Trade Commission (FTC) treats the deficient protection of consumer data, or any violation of a company's promises concerning that data, as an unfair or deceptive practice under section 5(a) of the Federal Trade Commission Act.[4] Violations of FTC rules or cease and desist orders bear substantial financial penalties.

The privacy provisions in the Gramm-Leach-Bliley Act, enacted in 1999, apply to financial institutions, defined very broadly to encompass all companies engaged in 'financial activities' under the banking laws.[5] The law therefore applies not only to banks and thrifts, but also to insurance companies, real estate and mortgage brokers, retailers, debt collectors, and, indeed, virtually any business that extends credit to consumers. The statute authorized regulatory agencies (including the FTC, Federal Reserve, Federal Deposit Insurance Corporation

---

[3] See 13.4.4 below.

[4] 15 USC § 45(a).

[5] 15 USC § 6809(3)(A). See the FTC's Privacy Rule 16 CFR § 313.3(k)(2) for some examples (eg retailers who issue credit cards, appraisers, car dealers engaged in leasing, career counselors who advise concerning careers in finance, accounting, and audit; printers of checks; check cashing and money transfer agencies, accountants and others who prepare tax returns, travel agents, mortgage brokers, investment advisors).

(FDIC), Comptroller of the Currency (OCC),[6] Office of Thrift Supervision (OTS), Securities and Exchange Commission (SEC), and state insurance departments) to establish 'appropriate standards' for administrative, technical and physical safeguards to: (i) insure the security and confidentiality of customer records and information; (ii) protect against anticipated threats or hazards to their security and integrity; and (iii) protect against unauthorized access to or use of customer records and information. In addition, financial institutions must give consumers notice of privacy policies when relationships are established, and annually thereafter. Non-public personal information (broadly defined)[7] generally cannot be disclosed to unrelated third parties unless the practice is disclosed and the customer declines to opt out. Statutory exceptions apply for various legitimate purposes, such as dealings with reporting agencies, completion of transactions for the consumer, mergers, disclosures to regulators and others as required by law.[8]

Guidelines issued by federal bank regulators require board and management oversight of information security programs, which must include risk assessment, management of those risks, oversight of outside service providers, adjustments to meet changing circumstances, and periodic reporting to the board.[9] Security measures may include access controls for facilities and systems, encryption, dual control procedures, segregation of duties, background checks for employees who have access to customer data, monitoring systems to detect attacks or intrusions, and response programs following incidents, among others. When security breaches occur, notice must be given to regulators and affected customers in a manner that resembles notice requirements under state security breach laws (discussed below). When financial institutions outsource, they must select service providers with 'appropriate due diligence;' require providers to implement 'appropriate measures designed to meet the objectives' of regulatory guidelines; and, where indicated by risk assessments, monitor providers 'to confirm that they have satisfied their obligations.' In other words, good outsourcing contracts should impose the same or essentially similar standards and measures on suppliers, although there is ample room to adjust details concerning particular measures and their technical details, so long as they are appropriate

---

[6] The US Treasury office that regulates national banks.

[7] 15 USC § 6809(4).

[8] 15 USC § 6802(e).

[9] 12 CFR Part 30, app B (OCC); 12 CFR Part 208, app D-2 and Part 225, app F (Federal Reserve); 12 CFR Part 364, app B, Part II(B) (FDIC); 12 CFR Part 570, app B (OTS). For a good discussion of the guidelines, see the banking agencies' 'Small Entity Compliance Guide', available at (among other places) <http://www.federalreserve.gov/bankinforeg/interagencyguidelines.htm> (accessed 14 January 2009).

for risks identified through risk assessment, the sensitivity of the information, the size and complexity of the institution's business, and statutory goals.[10]

Gramm-Leach is not the only pertinent federal statute. The Fair and Accurate Credit Transactions Act of 2003[11] amended the Fair Credit Reporting Act by, among other things, requiring risk-based programs to prevent identity theft. The statute applies to financial institutions and other creditors (including finance companies, car dealers, mortgage brokers, public utilities, and telecommunications companies, all of whom regularly extend credit) who open 'transaction accounts' such as mortgages, consumer loans, car loans, cell phone and utility accounts, among others. Financial institutions and creditors subject to the Act must develop written programs to identify and detect identity theft, respond appropriately to incidents, and update the program periodically, all under board or executive supervision, with appropriate training and oversight of service providers. Detection measures should be based upon relevant indicators, known as 'Red Flags,' including: (i) various kinds of alerts and warnings; (ii) suspicious documents, activities, and patterns; and (iii) notices from customers, victims, and law enforcement of possible identify theft.[12] When related services are outsourced, contracts with suppliers should require compliance—for example by requiring policies and procedures to detect and report incidents and take other appropriate action.

Health care is another principal focus of federal legislation, principally through the privacy provisions of the Health Insurance Portability and Accountability Act and related regulations.[13] The Act applies not only to hospitals, physicians, health plans, and clearinghouses (so-called 'covered entities'),[14] who must give notices and comply with various requirements to protect patients' data, but indirectly (through contractual obligations imposed by covered entities) to third parties (known as 'business associates'), who perform related services (such as billing, payments, and claims processing, among

---

[10] SEC regulations for broker-dealers, investment companies and investment advisors are, for the time being, simpler. Regulation S-P, 17 CFR § 248.30 merely requires written policies to meet the statutory objectives of preserving confidentiality and protection against anticipated threats and unauthorized access. However, in March 2008, the SEC proposed extensive amendments that would, if adopted, require comprehensive security programs similar to those required of banks, and including a requirement to give customers and regulators notice in the event of a breach of security.

[11] 15 USC §§ 1681 *et seq.*

[12] Joint regulations appear in 12 CFR Part 41 (Comptroller); 12 CFR Part 222 (Federal Reserve); 12 CFR Parts 334 and 364 (FDIC); 12 CFR Part 571 (OTS); 12 CFR Part 717 (National Credit Union Administration); and 16 CFR Part 681 (FTC). On 'Red Flags,' see in particular App J to the regulations, Interagency Guidelines on Identity Theft Detection, Prevention, and Mitigation.

[13] 42 USC § 1320d-2; 45 CFR §§ 164.308(b)(1) and 164.314.

[14] 45 CFR § 160.103.

others) and 'create, receive, maintain or transmit electronic protected health information.'[15] Disclosures to business associates are permitted only if the covered entity obtains 'satisfactory assurances' in the form of a business associate contract or similar arrangement.[16] Regulations spell out the essential requirements for these agreements,[17] which must:

- describe the permitted and required uses and disclosures of protected health information;
- require appropriate administrative, physical, and technical safeguards to protect the confidentiality, integrity, and availability of protected health information;
- require the extension of similar requirements to the business associate's subcontractors and agents;
- oblige the business associate to report security breaches and similar incidents to the covered entity;
- allow the covered entity access to records if affected individuals exercise their rights to obtain an accounting of disclosures;
- allow the Department of Health and Human Services full access to books, records, and internal practices in order to assess compliance; and
- permit the covered entity to terminate the contract if the business associate commits a material breach.

If it is aware of any pattern or practice that constitutes material breach, the covered entity must take 'reasonable steps' to cure, and, if those are unsuccessful, terminate the business associate's contract. If termination is not feasible, the matter must be reported to the Department of Health and Human Services.[18] Whenever and however the contract expires or terminates, protected health information should be returned or destroyed.[19] Amendments and regulations enacted during 2009 impose notice requirememts similar to state security breach notice laws if unsecured personal health information (such as unencrypted data) is compromised through improper use, disclosure or similar breaches of security. Business associates must give notice to the covered entities, which must then notify affected individuals, and if more than 500

[15] 45 CFR § 164.308(b)(1). 45 CFR § 160.103 defines protected health information as 'individually identifiable health information' transmitted or maintained electronically or in any other medium, with exclusions for certain employment and educational records.

[16] 45 CFR §§ 164.308(b)(1) and 164.502(e)(1–2).

[17] 45 CFR §§ 164.314(a)(2)(i) and 164.504(e)(2)(ii).

[18] 45 CFR §§ 164.314(a)(1)(ii) and 164.504(e)(1)(ii).

[19] Otherwise, contractual protection must be extended, and further use of protected data restricted to whatever uses render return or destruction infeasible (45 CFR § 164.504(e)(2)(ii)(I)).

individuals' data are compromised, the news media and the Department of Health and Human Services.[20]

In practice, hospitals, health plans, and other 'covered entities' have standard forms for business associate agreements and require them as a matter of course from all manner of contractors (although appropriate terms may be and sometimes are incorporated in master service contracts). Suppliers understand perfectly well the sensitivity of personal health data, its importance to customers, and the potential exposure to both parties in the event of a lapse in security. Sensitive negotiation issues include termination rights (particularly materiality thresholds), indemnification against claims concerning incidents and violations, and costs associated with future regulatory changes (which are commonly covered by master contract provisions concerning compliance, changes in law, and changes in related customer policies).[21]

The FTC may be the single most important federal agency enforcing privacy laws and regulations. Established during the early twentieth century to police mergers and unfair or deceptive business practices, the FTC has: (i) adopted privacy and security regulations under Gramm-Leach-Bliley; (ii) treated deficient security for consumer data as an unfair or deceptive practice, subject to enforcement action; and (iii) assumed responsibility for violations of companies' 'safe harbor' self-certifications under an agreement with the EU permitting data exports from the EU to the US, where recipients (data importers, as they are known in Europe) adopt certain policies generally consistent with EU privacy legislation.[22]

FTC privacy regulations govern issuance of privacy notices by financial institutions regulated by the FTC (that is, financial institutions other than banks, thrifts, credit unions, and others regulated by the usual bank regulators).[23] Many businesses and services not normally considered financial institutions may fall under these regulations (for example car dealers, tax preparers, appraisers, and retailers, among many others).[24] Customers must receive notice of privacy policies, particularly concerning collection, disclosure, and the use of non-public personal information, when customer relationships are established and annually thereafter. Disclosures to unaffiliated parties are generally prohibited, unless notice is given and the customer declines to opt out. Once notices have been issued, policies may not be altered without further notice and another

---

[20] 45 CFR Parts 160, 164; PL 111–5, §§ 13400–13404, 123 Stat. 258–263, 42 USC §§ 17921, 17931–17934. On state security breach laws, see 13.4.2.

[21] See 13.2 above.

[22] See 13.4.3 below.

[23] 16 CFR § 313.

[24] 16 CFR § 313.3(k)(2).

opportunity to opt out. Happily for outsourcing, rights to opt out are not required when companies engage third parties to perform services on behalf of a financial institution, provided the service contract prohibits disclosure or use of personal data 'other than to carry out the purposes' for which the information was disclosed, such as the execution of transactions for individual customers.[25]

The FTC's standards for safeguarding customer information govern the protection of personal information for 'financial institutions' overseen by the FTC.[26] Requirements parallel those imposed on banks and other traditional financial institutions regulated by the banking agencies. Board and management oversight, risk assessment, appropriate safeguards, training, evaluations, updates, and the rest are required. When services are outsourced, reasonable steps must be taken to select providers capable of maintaining appropriate safeguards, which service contracts must then require.[27]

Section 5(a) of the Federal Trade Commission Act[28] empowers the FTC to commence proceedings and issue cease and desist orders against 'unfair methods of competition' and 'deceptive acts or practices' affecting commerce (though not against banks, thrifts, airlines, and meat packers, who fall outside FTC jurisdiction). In recent years, the FTC has obtained consent orders against a number of companies for security lapses and deficient protection of consumer data.[29] FTC consent orders typically require: (i) a rigorous information security program, with appropriate leadership, risk assessments, and safeguards; (ii) semiannual audits for twenty years; and (iii) commitments to comply with relevant laws and regulations, discontinue errant practices, and inform present and future officers, directors, and executives of the consent order. None of this comes cheap, and the effect on reputations and share prices may be still more costly.

13.4.2 US state security breach laws

Statutes in virtually all US states and the District of Columbia now require notice to consumers when personal data are compromised. Most state laws are modeled on California's, which took effect during 2003.[30] Individual statutes vary, but in general, these statutes require private businesses to notify state residents

---

[25] 16 CFR § 313.13.

[26] 16 CFR Part 314.

[27] 16 CFR § 314.4(d).

[28] 15 USC § 45(a).

[29] See, eg, *The TJX Companies, Inc* No 072-3055 (2008) (weaknesses in retailer's network security contributed to compromise of millions of credit cards).

[30] Cal Civ Code §§ 1798.82(a) *et seq.*

when breaches of security disclose personal information. Key provisions of California's statute include the following:

- The law applies to any business that 'conducts business in California' and keeps personal information about California residents on computers. The scope is imprecise, but companies with customers or employees in California should assume that it applies, whether or not they qualify to do business in California or have offices there.
- 'Personal information' includes unencrypted names, together with social security numbers, driver's license numbers, account numbers, credit card details, and codes or passwords for access to financial accounts.
- 'Breaches of security' encompass any 'unauthorized acquisition' of data 'that compromises the security, confidentiality or integrity of personal information.' Notice must be given in cases of reasonable belief as well as confirmed incidents.
- Notice must be given 'in the most expedient time possible and without unreasonable delay,' but may be deferred to accommodate criminal investigations (if the police so request) or 'any measures necessary to determine the scope of the breach and restore the reasonable integrity' of affected systems.
- Companies that maintain computerized personal information for others (such as suppliers of outsourced services) must inform their clients, as owners of the data, 'immediately following discovery' of a security breach. In outsourcing arrangements where suppliers hold personal data, this gives the customer time to investigate, react, and prepare to give notice to individuals expediently and 'without unreasonable delay.' The statutory obligation to give notice to individuals remains with the customer.
- Notice may be given by mail, by electronic mail (subject to the federal e-signature law, which requires prior consent),[31] or (in very large cases, or when contact information is insufficient) through a combination of electronic mail, web posting, and notice to statewide news media. Notice may also be given under notice procedures in a company's own information security policy.
- Violations invite civil liability and injunctions, as well as unfavorable media attention with consequent damage to corporate reputations.

Some statutory provisions are imprecise; but the Office of Privacy Protection in California's Department of Consumer Affairs has published helpful *Recommended Practices* concerning protection, prevention, preparations

---

[31] 15 USC § 7001.

for notice, and actual notice.[32] They are not binding regulations or mandates, but intended as 'a contribution to the development of "best practices."'[33] As authoritative guidance from a major US state (and the handiwork of an able public-private committee), California's guidelines are likely to be influential, and an indicator of best practices.

Since these statutes are relatively new, their interpretation by the courts remains to be seen, but given legislative and public concern about identity theft and computer fraud (often expressed in legislative recitals), companies who possess or process personal data should fairly expect liberal construction to carry out statutory purposes, including the protection of consumers and deterrence. Where so many states have acted, many observers anticipate federal legislation pre-empting individual state laws and eliminating inconsistencies (which can complicate notice and other compliance measures when incidents occur), but at the time of writing (spring 2009), Congress has yet to act.

How do security breach statutes apply to outsourcing? The basic answer is obliquely and indirectly. Outsourcers must, as noted above, inform their clients immediately after a security breach. The obligation to give individual notice to consumers, however, belongs to the owner of the data—the retailer, bank, insurance company, or other business that collects personal information in order to transact business with individual consumers. Statutory protections cannot be waived, nor can they be transferred or delegated. Consumers' claims for violations lie against the companies with whom they do business, not third party outsourcers.

However, this does not absolve the outsourcers from responsibility and liability. If a security breach occurs in the outsourcer's systems or facilities, imaginative plaintiff's counsel may craft allegations or legal theories that create credible claims against an outsourcer (despite contract provisions denying any intention to create third party beneficiaries). If class action suits are filed, the outsourcer may fairly expect to be named as a defendant. Even if the outsourcer avoids direct liability to consumers, or obtains the dismissal of imaginative claims, it may face substantial liability to its client for breaches of contract requirements (which typically include obligations to maintain confidentiality and observe agreed security procedures) and perhaps to indemnify its client against third party claims. One way or another, the outsourcer will be invited to join the festivities.

Most of these statutes do not require specific safeguards, although an obligation to detect may be implicit in the obligation to report security breaches

---

[32] Recommended Practices on Notice of Security Breach Involving Personal Information (June 2009), available at <http://www.oispp.ca.gov/consumer_privacy/pdf/COPP_Breach_Reco_Practices_6-09.pdf> (accessed 18 October 2009).

[33] *Recommended Practices*, 6–7.

(and Massachusetts and Nevada require encryption of personal data when transmitted).[34] After all, one must be on the alert in order to sound an alarm. Other laws and regulations may, at least arguably, require detection systems. In California, for example, businesses that disclose residents' personal information to third parties must require those third parties to 'implement and maintain reasonable security procedures and practices appropriate to the nature of the [personal] information, to protect the information from unauthorized access, destruction, use, modification or disclosure.'[35] Federal 'Red Flag' regulations may require scrutiny of unusual patterns of activity—patterns most likely to be detected using sophisticated software and other technologies.

Outsourcing contracts typically require protection for client data, confidential information, and personal data, and often specify security requirements in some detail. Outsourcers and their customers are well advised to be specific, lest they fall back on amorphous commitments to 'meet industry standards' or keep personnel, customer, and other individual data confidential. These general obligations are fine, as far as they go, but leave the parties (or, in the worst case, judges and jurors) to decide just what they mean. They also leave in doubt what kinds and levels of security the supplier must provide for the contract price, which party's standards apply, and other important particulars.

California's guidelines include a good list of 'best practices,' including preventive measures, preparations to give notice, and procedures for giving notice if and when the need arises. For businesses that outsource, the most important recommendation is to require third parties who possess and handle personal data to follow appropriate security policies and procedures. Where outsourcing is extensive, or involves large volumes of data, one could go further and recommend that the development and regular review of a detailed security plan be a collaborative effort. Leading suppliers, experienced with sensitive national defense, medical, or financial information, have much to offer and may be better equipped to prevent and detect breaches than many of their customers.

Key recommendations in the California guidelines may be summarized as follows, and apply in somewhat different ways to both suppliers and customers:

- Collect the minimum data reasonably necessary, classify data by sensitivity, and consider more stringent safeguards for particularly sensitive data (such as medical or financial information).

---

[34] Mass Gen Laws ch 93H, 201 Code Mass Reg § 17.03 (effective 1 January 2010); Nev Rev Stat § 597.970 (effective 1 October 2008). The two states' standards differ. Massachusetts' is more rigorous (requiring the use of algorithmic encryption, including transmission and storage in portable devices). Outsourcers must comply, and companies that outsource the processing of personal data must have comprehensive security programs similar to those required by federal Gramm-Leach-Bliley legislation.

[35] Cal Civ Code § 1798.81.5(c).

- Keep good inventories of records, systems, and storage media that contain personal data (paying particular attention to laptops and other portable devices, for which special provision may be made through encryption or restrictions on use or storage of sensitive data).
- Install appropriate physical, technical, and organizational safeguards to protect personal information, as well as detection systems for intrusions. (To be fully effective, intrusion detection systems must be monitored regularly.)
- Educate users and train employees who have access to personal data or maintain and operate related systems.
- Use encryption for more sensitive data. (In California and some other states, compromises of encrypted data need not be disclosed, since the data should remain protected and inaccessible; and, as noted above, Massachusetts and Nevada now require the encryption of personal data.)
- Dispose of records, equipment, and media appropriately.
- Develop a good security plan, review it regularly and keep it current.
- Be fully prepared to respond in the event of a security breach. This typically includes an immediate report by the outsourcer to the client (when the breach concerns systems operated or managed by the supplier), notices to management, credit reporting agencies, and law enforcement, and notice to affected consumers.

Preparation for media inquiries, though not required, is prudent and should be coordinated between customer and supplier, generally with the customer in the lead. Where customers' accounts, financial records, or credit cards may be compromised, one should also consider remedial measures that might help both to reduce exposure and preserve the company's reputation. When operations are outsourced, both the supplier and the customer put their checkbooks and reputations at risk.

Since these statutes are recent, many existing contracts say nothing specific about state security breach laws. As new contracts are written, and older ones re-negotiated, that will change. Many, perhaps most, sophisticated agreements already contain provisions for compliance with customer security requirements, as well as customary provisions for protection of confidential information and compliance with laws. Detailed, joint security plans are increasingly common; in newer contracts, so are detailed clauses allocating financial and other responsibility for security breaches and compliance with state notice statutes. The outsourcing customer cannot avoid its statutory duties or its potential liability to consumers and employees, but it can allocate financial and other responsibility to the supplier of outsourced services. Common provisions include obligations to give the customer prompt notice (as California's statute requires), cooperate in investigations and remedial measures, and pay costs associated with notices and other remedial action, at least to the extent of the supplier's responsibility for the security breach. Many customers also seek indemnification against claims by third parties (such as individual consumers and employees) and representations concerning the absence of past incidents, pending claims, or litigation about breaches of security.

Even when the contract lacks any specific reference to security breach laws and consumer notice obligations, many provisions common in outsourcing contracts may come into play, including:

- general obligations to protect confidential information or customer data, and comply with customer technical standards, security, and other policies;
- commitments to meet or exceed good industry standards;
- indemnities for breaches of confidence and security, violations of privacy, and other laws, and errors and omissions in performance (including obligations to cooperate in the investigation of claims); and
- limitations on liability, and exceptions where limits may be greater or liability may be unlimited (such as breaches of confidence and violations of law).

13.4.3 The EU Directive

Where US legislation is a jumble of state and federal legislation, the EU has adopted a comprehensive framework for the collection, use, disclosure, and processing of personal data, in all forms, throughout the twenty-seven Member States and neighboring members of the European Economic Area.[36] Each Member State has its own data protection authority, and there are (as in employment) significant variations among Member State legislation and practices (variations outside the scope of this introductory survey). In keeping with European traditions, there is greater reliance on notice to and enforcement by public authorities, than on private litigation and liability, as in the US.

The foundation for EU data protection and privacy laws is a 1995 Directive,[37] written with two goals in mind: (i) to establish a mandatory minimum level of protection for individual 'right[s] to privacy with respect to the processing of personal data,'[38] and (ii) to facilitate the free movement of goods, persons, services, and capital within the EU. The Directive proceeds from the premise that collection, processing, disclosure, and other uses of personal data are forbidden, unless permitted by the Directive on a basis consistent with its principles.

---

[36] Iceland, Liechtenstein, and Norway.
[37] Directive (EC) 95/46 [1995] OJ L281/31.
[38] ibid Art 1(1).

The Directive has its own vocabulary. 'Personal data' means 'any information relating to an identified or identifiable' individuals. Those individuals are 'data subjects.' 'Processing' means virtually any collection, use, or disclosure of personal data. Even storage or deletion of data is 'processing.' 'Controllers' are those who 'determine the purposes and means of the processing of personal data'; where 'processors' process personal data on behalf of the controller.[39] In outsourcing, this means that in general (although not in all circumstances) the customer is the 'controller' and the supplier is the 'processor.' As a processor, the supplier may have little or no direct liability under applicable regulations (at least in some countries), but its customers invariably require appropriate provisions to mitigate risk, comply with legal requirements, and indemnify the customer (or controller) against liability.[40]

Generally, the processing of personal data is only permitted if: (i) the data subject gives 'unambiguous consent;' (ii) processing is necessary to perform contracts with or for the data subject; (iii) for the data subject's 'vital interests,' or the controller's 'legitimate interests' (unless outweighed by individual privacy interests); or (iv) performed for responsible authorities in the public interest.[41] Personal data must be collected for specific, explicit, and legitimate purposes only, processed 'fairly and lawfully,' and maintained (in identifiable form) 'no longer than is necessary.' Data should be relevant, not excessive, accurate, and subject to erasure or correction if they are inaccurate or incomplete.[42]

The processing of sensitive personal data (concerning race, political opinions, religious and philosophical beliefs, union membership, health, and sex lives) is prohibited except in strictly limited circumstances: (i) when 'explicit' consent is given; (ii) when applicable law (with safeguards) so permits; (iii) for the legitimate activities (again, with safeguards) of unions, churches, and similar organizations related to their members; or (iv) in other, very limited circumstances.[43] As under some US laws, data subjects are entitled to notice concerning data collection, its purposes, and data controllers and third party recipients.[44] Data subjects are entitled to access to their data, and to information concerning processing, correction of errors, and the erasure of data. They may also object to processing (unless authorized by law) and processing for marketing purposes.[45]

---

[39] Definitions appear ibid Art 2.

[40] The analysis is not always so straightforward, and in some complex operations (eg the processing of such transactions as mortgages) a supplier might operate as a data controller, with direct liability for breaches of data protection laws and an obligation to register as a controller.

[41] Directive (EC) 95/46, Art 7.

[42] ibid Art 6.

[43] ibid Art 8.

[44] ibid Arts 10–11.

[45] ibid Arts 12 and 14.

Controllers must 'implement appropriate technical and organizational measures to protect personal data' against loss, destruction, alteration, unauthorized disclosure or access, and all unlawful processing. When processors are engaged, a contract must impose these requirements on the processor and direct the processor to act 'only on instructions from the controller.'[46]

Enforcement is entrusted to national data protection authorities, with whom notices must be filed for some activities. National laws in Member States must provide judicial remedies for data subjects, including the right to receive compensation from the controller when they suffer damage as a result of unlawful processing.[47]

Personal data may not be transferred to third countries outside the European Economic Area unless the third country 'ensures an adequate level of protection.'[48] So far, only a very few countries have been approved—Argentina, Canada, and Switzerland, as well as the two Channel Islands, Guernsey and Jersey, and the Isle of Man.[49] The US 'safe harbor' program (discussed below) has also been approved as providing adequate protection. For the rest, data transfers are permitted:

- when data subjects consent;
- when necessary for contracts with data subjects, at their request, or under contracts in their interest between controllers and third parties;
- to protect the data subject's vital interests;
- when legally required on public interest grounds or for legal claims; or
- when the 'controller adduces adequate safeguards. . . in particular result[ing] from appropriate contractual clauses.'[50]

For outsourcing and similar large scale activities, obtaining consent from hundreds or thousands of employees, customers, and other individuals is rarely practical. Someone is bound to refuse and, in any event, European data protection authorities may regard employee consents in particular as invalid, given the parties' unequal bargaining power. For large companies transferring data outside the EU there are, in practice, the following options:

- The adoption of standard clauses or agreements approved by the European Commission and data protection authorities. These include agreements for

---

[46] ibid Art 17.
[47] ibid Arts 22 and 23.
[48] ibid Art 25.
[49] For a current list, see <http://ec.europa.eu/justice_home/fsj/privacy/thirdcountries/index_en.htm> (accessed 26 June 2009).
[50] Directive (EC) 95/46, Art 26.

transfers between controllers and (more important for outsourcing) between controllers and processors.

- For transfers to the US, the adherence to safe harbor principles negotiated between the EU and the US Government. These require public self-certification to the US Department of Commerce, adoption of principles essentially consistent with the directive's protections, and acceptance of related liabilities, including oversight by the FTC or (for airlines and ticket agents) the US Department of Transportation. Safe harbor protection is not available for banks, thrifts, telecommunications, and certain other industries outside FTC jurisdiction.

- Corporate groups may adopt 'binding corporate rules' for data transfers among group members—a complex, expensive process that (for the time being, at least) requires individual filings and negotiation with data protection authorities in all Member States where group members operate (although the authorities are trying to iron out a 'mutual recognition' process where acceptance by one authority is effectively acceptance by all). For the largest global companies, this can be an attractive choice, affording greater flexibility than other alternatives. Policies and procedures may be aligned with the group's particular needs; but binding corporate rules are impractical for smaller companies without the patience, scale, or budget for the effort required.

This analysis may vary, depending upon Member State legislation. For example, the UK's Information Commissioner's Office has taken the view that data exports outside the European Economic Area by UK controllers need only have a contract requiring the processor to implement security measures and process data as directed by the controller. Other Member States, however, have more stringent policies, so that multinational companies exporting from several EU states may be forced to adopt a 'highest common denominator,' in order to comply with the most stringent applicable legislation and interpretations.

For companies with European operations who plan to outsource, the Directive and Member State legislation pose two sets of issues: local compliance within Member States and restrictions on transfers to countries outside the EU. For controllers, local compliance obligations include: (i) restrictions on the collection, use, and disclosure of personal data (especially sensitive data); (ii) respect for data subjects' rights of access, review, and the rest; and (iii) formal requirements for filings with data protection authorities, notices to data subjects, the appointment of privacy officers, and consultation with works councils, unions, and other representatives. All of these may vary, at least in detail, among the Member States. For global companies, there are the added complexities of data transfers to the US and other countries without equivalent laws reckoned to provide 'adequate' protection. Preparation to outsource begins with a thorough review of existing arrangements, data flows, and policies, which may have to change as operations relocate or are transformed by outsourcing—for example by the relocation of data or service centers to other countries, especially outside the EU. New or amended filings and notices may be required. Preparation does not end with review of the customer's internal arrangements. The customer should (and in many regulated industries, must) also satisfy itself that the supplier has appropriate mechanisms in place to protect personal data, generally through a combination of pre-contract due diligence and contract terms, including warranties, indemnities, and audit rights.

Often, the most significant challenges concern data exports outside the EU (if, for example, operations relocate to the US or the customer has US operations). The EU has approved model contracts for data transfers between controllers and—more important for outsourcing—a model contract between controllers and processors.[51] The processor undertakes, among other things, to process data only in accordance with the controller's instructions and to implement agreed technical and organizational security measures. This commitment matters a great deal to controllers, since they (and not the processors) are responsible for the consequences of any infringement of data protection laws and must include these provisions. Controllers ('data exporters') undertake to comply with applicable laws, including the provision of 'sufficient guarantees' through technical and organizational security measures. Processors must notify controllers in the event of unauthorized access to personal data, or receipt of inquiries from data subjects or data protection authorities. In case of violations of the clauses, data subjects are entitled to compensation from the controller, or from the processor—if the controller is insolvent, has disappeared, or has ceased to exist. Left to their own devices, controllers and processors alike might prefer different terms (suppliers particularly dislike the liability provisions), but, apart from indemnification and a few details, the language is immutable. Variations do not necessarily provide adequate protection, so must be filed and negotiated with individual data protection authorities (essentially defeating the point of an exemption from the basic export prohibition). In the circumstances, the model clauses have become a common, even preferred (if not exactly popular) approach to these issues.

Although the clauses themselves are effectively set in stone, appendices describing data transfers, processing operations, and technical and organizational security measures are generally for the parties to determine (although at

---

[51] For the text, see Commission Decision (EC) 2002/16 [2001] OJ L6/52.

least one Member State, Spain, has highly prescriptive requirements). The parties decide what level of security is appropriate. Each side seeks indemnification against the other's errors, omissions, and violations. In an ideal world, customers would prefer suppliers to deliver fully compliant solutions (especially if, as is often the case, the customer's own arrangements are flawed). Suppliers, for their part, seek representations, warranties, and covenants concerning the customer's compliance with privacy laws. Well-advised customers may request supplier representations and warranties concerning the compliance of the supplier's systems and facilities and especially the absence of any recent security breaches, other incidents or proceedings. In other words, compliance with privacy laws presents another variation on the usual rain-dance around all manner of compliance issues. Each side might prefer that the other bear most or all of the risk, but, in practice, the usual negotiated outcome is some rough equilibrium where each bears primary exposure within its own sphere of responsibility.

When data are transferred from EU Member States to the US, the parties may wish to consider safe harbor protection, available through a process of public self-certification with the US Department of Commerce, although the process was designed for transfers between companies (for example between parents and subsidiaries) rather than between controllers and processors.[52] Adherence involves the acceptance of seven principles (concerning notice, consent, onward transfer, access, data security and integrity, and enforcement) and fifteen 'frequently asked questions.' In case of violations, the FTC or (for airlines and ticket agents) the Department of Transportation may act. Safe harbor certification does not, by itself, invite private litigation. Data subjects enjoy no rights as third party beneficiaries, although safe harbor companies must offer a mediation or arbitration remedy and data subjects might have other grounds for court proceedings. In the event of a serious incident, the public listing of safe harbor certifications invites official scrutiny and FTC proceedings leading to a cease and desist or consent order. These may involve greater cost, unfavorable publicity, and risk to reputation than the usual private lawsuit, which might be settled confidentially and without fanfare.

13.4.4 Security breaches in Europe

Although Europe does not yet have legislation comparable to the US security breach notification laws, the issue is a sensitive one with the public, news media, and public authorities. An EU directive will, when implemented by Member States, require telecommunications carriers and internet service

---

[52] For details, see the US Commerce Department's website, <http://www.export.gov/safeharbor>.

providers to notify affected customers and regulators of security breaches.[53] There have been calls for more general notice requirements, and the UK's Information Commissioner has published guidance requesting voluntary notice to the commissioner's office, as well as guidance on the management of security breaches.[54] Similarly, although there is no requirement that financial services firms give notice of security breaches, the FSA Handbook recommends giving notice to the regulatory agency so that, in reality, giving notice to responsible public agencies and affected consumers is a best practice.[55] From an enforcement perspective, European financial service regulators treat information security as a high priority and, in the UK, the FSA has (and has exercised) the authority to impose substantial fines for information security lapses, notably for failures to implement adequate measures to control the risk of information security lapses.[56] So far, none of these cases involved outsourced services, but in Europe, as in the US, customers are well advised to require suppliers to give prompt notice, permit audits of security measures, and cooperate in both the investigation of incidents and remedial action, with appropriate indemnification for incidents caused by the supplier's errors and omissions.

13.4.5 Privacy and data protection in general

The US and the EU are scarcely the whole story, although EU practice has been influential elsewhere, and US security breach notification laws have attracted interest as one approach to that risk. A number of other countries have rigorous privacy laws. As concerns grow about privacy generally and identity theft in particular, laws and regulations everywhere seem likely to grow more stringent in the years ahead.

How, then, should a company approach these issues when preparing to outsource? There is no formula. Risks and legal requirements vary from one situation to the next, depending upon the outsourced function, the places where services are performed and received, the parties' capabilities, and other factors. The following—based in part upon the comprehensive security programs

---

[53] Directive (EC) 2002/58 [2002] OJ L201/37, Art 4.

[54] The ISO guidance is available at their website, <http://www.ico.gov.uk/upload/documents/library/data_protection/practical_application/guidance_on_data_security_breach_management.pdf> (accessed 18 October 2009).

[55] For the FSA's principles, see <http://fsahandbook.info/FSA/html/handbook/PRIN/2/1> (FSA Handbook). Notification requirements appear at <http://fsahandbook.info/FSA/html/handbook/SUP/15/3> (accessed 18 October 2009).

[56] In February 2007, the FSA assessed a £980,000 financial penalty against Nationwide Building Society following the theft of an employee's laptop computer that contained confidential customer information. The Final Notice is available at <http://www.fsa.gov.uk/pubs/final/nbs.pdf> (accessed 26 June 2009).

required by some laws and regulations—may provide a framework for the development of a strategy and appropriate contract terms:

- Review existing arrangements in depth. What personal data are collected, for what purposes? How long are data retained? What notices have been given? Have consents been obtained, where appropriate? What policies, procedures and safeguards are in place? What filings have been made with public agencies (if filings are required)? Data flows within and among business units and locations should be mapped in order to help determine what laws apply. Specialist lawyers and consultants can help with, among other things, detailed questionnaires tailored to legal requirements.

- Survey relevant legal requirements to determine whether or not current policies comply, identify deficiencies (if any), and, wherever possible, formulate 'common denominator' policies and practices that comply with relevant requirements in most (or ideally all) relevant jurisdictions. Within the US, attention must be paid to state laws, including variations among security breach statutes and other state privacy laws. Federal statutes do not necessarily pre-empt state laws. The Gramm-Leach-Bliley law, for example, expressly permits more stringent state statutes, so long as they do not conflict with the federal statute.[57]

- After surveying current practice and relevant law, conduct an assessment of practical and legal risks in order to identify appropriate security measures, safeguards, and contract requirements.

- When evaluating potential suppliers, review their security capabilities and offerings. Many suppliers can deliver excellent security (although more robust protection, like better service, costs money). Where both sides have security experts, arrange for them to talk to one another, rather than confine discussion to formal comments on written requirements, which are sometimes extravagant or unrealistic.

- Write essential elements of a comprehensive security program into the contract documents, including required safeguards, policies, and procedures; regular testing, audit rights, periodic review, and ongoing supervision. Unless someone takes responsibility and can be held accountable, little may be accomplished.

---

[57] 15 USC § 6807. HIPPA also permits more stringent state laws protecting personal health information, subject to certain conditions. See 45 CFR Part 160 implementing §1178 of the Social Security Act, as ammended by HIPAA PL 104–191 §262, 42 USC §1320d–7. California, for example, has enacted statutes requiring safeguards for medical records and imposing fines and other sanctions for unauthorized access. Cal Health & Safety Code §§130200–130205.

- Prepare to respond effectively in the event of an incident, so that effects can be contained, causes determined, corrective action taken, and (if necessary) notices given to affected customers and responsible officials.

Key contract terms include:

- Confidentiality and information security for personal data (even when available from public sources, with particular attention to any sensitive data concerning such matters as ethnic origin, beliefs, health, and personal finances).
- Allocations of compliance responsibilities (including interpretation of relevant laws and regulations, developments in the law, and related changes in security policies and procedures).
- Financial responsibility for costs related to future changes in relevant laws, regulations, and policies, including objective metrics for adjusting charges.
- Rights to audit and test security arrangements and controls, and require corrective action where indicated.
- Indemnification against third party claims. Customers seek protection against supplier errors. Suppliers seek similar protection, including protection against errant customer instructions or interpretations of legal requirements.
- When personal data are transferred from EU Member States, obtain an exemption from the prohibition on exports of personal data (most often, by requiring adherence to model processor agreements with appropriate technical and organizational security measures, which are—unlike the model contract terms—matters for negotiation).
- Reporting obligations, including notice of actual and attempted security breaches and results of periodic tests of security systems. Where notice to public agencies or affected individuals is either legally required or recommended by regulatory agencies, customers often require collaboration with investigations and the provision of (or at least financial responsibility for) remedial measures (such as notices to individuals and credit bureaux, improved security measures, telephone support for affected consumers, and credit reporting services, among others).
- Liability limits, which may be (with indemnities) the most vigorously negotiated issue. Customers would prefer that liability for both general and consequential damages be unlimited for any violation of privacy laws, breach of security, or breach of confidentiality. Suppliers increasingly seek to limit their exposure through narrowly drawn exceptions to liability limits and absolute ceilings (perhaps higher than basic liability limits) for claims concerning privacy, however characterized. This is a difficult issue. Both sides fear runaway liabilities, particularly where the underlying business involves large numbers of individual records. Experience suggests that liability limits are best resolved

as part of a wider discussion of security arrangements, supplier solutions, and related costs, rather than abstract legal debate about 'worst cases.' For example, practical risks and the supplier's potential responsibility may be limited if personal data remain on customer systems, at customer facilities, or supplier access to personal data is incidental and occasional (for example when responding to help desk calls or service requests, as opposed to the storage and processing of large volumes of personal data).

13.5 OUTSOURCING FOR REGULATED INDUSTRIES—FINANCIAL SERVICES

Banking has long been the leading private user of computer technology and outsourced services. Outsourcing for banking and financial services has understandably attracted legislators' and regulators' attention. Here again, there are differences among regulations on both sides of the Atlantic, but most regulations and regulatory guidance are broadly consistent with good commercial practice familiar to any experienced professional (and, for that matter, any reader who has made it this far).

13.5.1 US Regulations

In the US, outsourcing by financial institutions is comparatively lightly regulated, although the regulatory climate could change as regulatory laws are reviewed in the aftermath of the financial markets' collapse during the autumn of 2008. At the time of writing, in mid-2009, regulators still exercise a relatively light touch. No permissions or filings are required before outsourcing, and, apart from some restricted activities, financial institutions are free to outsource. However, ultimate responsibility for an institution's soundness and safety, and protection of customers' data, cannot be delegated or otherwise transferred. Outsourced operations are treated as extensions of an institution's own operations, and are subject to examinations and other scrutiny, even when operated by an outside supplier. So far as regulators are concerned, the name on the building matters not at all. Regulatory guidance concerning diligence, contracts, governance, and much else adheres to good commercial practice.

Much of that guidance appears in the bank examiners' IT Examination Handbook,[58] issued by the Federal Financial Institutions Examination Council

---

[58] FFIEC, *Outsourcing Technology Services, IT Examination Handbook* (June 2004), available at <http://www.ffiec.gov/ffiecinfobase/html_pages/it_01.html#outsourcing> (accessed 5 February 2009).

(FFIEC), an interagency group that prescribes principles and procedures for the various banking agencies.[59] Financial institutions 'should have a comprehensive outsourcing risk management process' including 'risk assessment, selection of service providers, contract review and monitoring of service providers. . . To help insure [that] financial institutions operate in a safe and sound manner, the services performed by [technology service providers] are subject to regulation and examination.'[60] When preparing to outsource, financial institutions should assess risks, involve stakeholders in the development of written requirements, and thoroughly investigate prospective suppliers' capabilities, financial strength, and commitment to service. Offshore suppliers merit particular scrutiny, in order to evaluate political and other risks, including the ability to comply with US export controls and Gramm-Leach-Bliley requirements, and the possible effects of distance, language, local laws, business practices, and accounting standards on performance.[61]

As for outsourcing contracts, the bank examiners recommend a wide range of protections, including specific service level commitments, clear definitions of the parties' responsibilities, robust controls and audit rights, protection of confidential information, indemnification, termination rights, and other remedies and protections. Regulators must, of course, have full access to outsourced functions. Certain provisions or inducements that may increase total cost or reduce flexibility are frowned upon, such as very long contract terms, deferred transition charges, large termination charges, asset purchases at book value, and the 'bundling' of products and services for a single price. Ongoing monitoring of service level performance, supplier financial condition and controls are also recommended. Business continuity plans should be kept current and tested regularly. Contracts with offshore suppliers should require compliance with US privacy laws and regulations, assure that US regulators may examine services, and include provisions concerning choice of law, jurisdiction, and resolution of disputes (so that enforceability may be assessed under applicable laws). Oversight should be as stringent as for domestic suppliers, and monitor both the supplier and conditions within relevant countries.

---

[59] These include the Federal Reserve Board (for members of the Federal Reserve System), Comptroller of the Currency (for national banks, chartered by the federal government), Federal Deposit Insurance Corporation (for institutions whose deposits are insured), Office of Thrift Supervision (for thrift institutions such as savings banks and savings and loan associations), and the National Credit Union Association. Representatives of corresponding state agencies also participate.

[60] FFIEC, *IT Examination Handbook* (n 58 above) 2.

[61] ibid App C; see also, OCC Bulletin 2002-16 (15 May 2002) and FDIC Financial Institution Letter FIL 52-2006 (21 June 2006) for further regulatory guidance concerning offshore outsourcing.

The regulations and guidance cover all this and more in detail, emphasizing matters of particular concern to regulatory agencies, such as audit and compliance. Regulatory guidance is not, strictly speaking, binding but bankers disregard official guidance at their peril. Anything examiners may consider when evaluating an institution's safety and soundness has self-evident importance, and in any event the agencies' guidance encapsulates a great deal of sound advice and good practice.

The same is true in the securities business. Rules and guidance restrict the outsourcing of certain 'covered functions' (such as executing trades) to registered clearing broker-dealers. Other functions may be outsourced pursuant to written supervisory procedures and a supervisory system.[62] Outsourcing does not, of course, relieve securities firms from primary responsibility for compliance. After a survey disclosed deficiencies in written procedures, business continuity plans, and formal diligence to screen suppliers' proficiency, official guidance emerged requiring: (i) the investigation of current and prospective suppliers' capabilities; (ii) continuing oversight, supervision, and monitoring of performance; (iii) 'complete access' to work product for regulators (just as for a firm's internal operations); and (iv) policies and procedures to determine whether functions are appropriate for outsourcing, based upon (a) an assessment of risks to operations, finances, and reputation from possible failure, and (b) impacts upon customer service and regulatory compliance.[63]

13.5.2 EU regulations

Across the Atlantic, the position is similar: regulators recommend or require contractual and other protections broadly consistent with good commercial practice. For those doing business on both sides of the ocean, many of the same sorts of contract terms and practical measures may help to satisfy regulatory requirements in Europe as well as the US; although regulated firms must be alert

---

[62] See NASD Notice to Members 05-48 (July 2005). NASD, the National Association of Securities Dealers was consolidated with the regulation, enforcement, and arbitration functions of the New York Stock Exchange to create the Financial Industry Regulatory Authority (FINRA). Its rules and policies are generally consistent with the 'Principles on Outsourcing of Financial Services for Market Intermediaries' (February 2005), published by the Technical Committee of the International Organization of Securities Commissions, and available at <http://www.world-exchanges.org/reports/regulation/iosco-principles-outsourcing-financial-services-market-intermediaries> (accessed 26 June 2009).

[63] In 2005, the New York Stock Exchange proposed a more stringent rule that would have prohibited the outsourcing of certain functions and permitted others considered material to broker-dealer functions, subject to detailed diligence requirements and after prior notice to the exchange. The proposal was amended in 2007, but not adopted.

to differences between the US and Europe, and among local laws and regulations in EU Member States.

Within the EU, two directives concerning markets in financial instruments (known popularly as 'MIFID') govern outsourcing by a broad subset of financial services firms. Even where MIFID does not apply, many regulators expect adherence as a matter of best practice. The first directive, issued in 2004, lays down the fundamentals. When outsourcing 'operational functions' that are 'critical for the provision of continuous and satisfactory service to clients. . . on a continuous and satisfactory basis' firms must take 'reasonable steps to avoid undue operational risk.'[64] Outsourcing must neither impair the quality of internal controls nor the regulators' ability to monitor compliance. Sound administrative and accounting procedures, internal controls, effective risk assessment, and effective controls for information processing are also essential.

The second directive, issued in 2006, elaborates upon these principles and imposes more detailed requirements (often referred to as 'Level 2'), including the following:

- service providers must have sufficient ability and capacity to perform 'reliably and professionally;'
- regulated firms must have methods to assess 'the standard of performance,' 'properly supervise' performance, and retain sufficient expertise for effective supervision;
- if service providers do not carry out their functions 'effectively,' the firm must take 'appropriate action;'
- an investment firm 'must retain the necessary expertise to supervise the outsourced functions effectively and manage the risks;'
- service providers 'must disclose' to their investment firm customers 'any development that may have a material impact' on its ability to perform 'in compliance with applicable laws and regulatory requirements;'
- an investment firm 'must be able to terminate the arrangement. . . where necessary without detriment to the continuity and quality of its. . . services to clients;'
- the service provider 'must cooperate' with regulatory agencies;
- those agencies, and the firm's auditors, must have 'effective access to data related to the outsourced activities;'
- the service provider must 'protect any confidential information relating to the investment firm and its clients;'

---

[64] Directive (EC) 2004/39 [2004] OJ L145, Art 13(5).

- there must be a 'contingency plan for disaster recovery and periodic testing of backup facilities;' and
- all this should be clearly documented and must not delegate senior management responsibilities, alter the firm's obligations to its clients, or affect its licenses, charter, or other authorization to conduct its business.[65]

Local regulators impose their own interpretation of the MIFID directives as well as additional requirements. For example, the UK's FSA imposes restrictions on outsourcing by financial services businesses through the FSA Handbook. This compliance requirement operates in addition to the MIFID-specific compliance requirements which are now also included in the Handbook. Outsourcing obligations appear in various sections of the FSA Handbook. Most of the generic provisions apply to all regulated businesses but additional requirements apply to banks, building societies, investment firms, and insurers. Therefore, one must work through the FSA rules to ascertain which rules apply to a particular firm. Detailed analysis of the FSA rules and their application is beyond the scope of this book, but they broadly reflect (often in more general terms) the requirements described above. In addition, they emphasize that a firm must conduct its business with due skill, care, and diligence and take reasonable care to organize and control its affairs responsibly and effectively, with adequate risk management systems. Regulated firms must therefore ensure that their outsourcing suppliers do the same. Additional specific obligations allow FSA representatives access to business premises, with audit rights. Suppliers under material outsourcing arrangements must deal in an open, cooperative manner with the FSA. Regulated firms must require from their suppliers cooperation essentially similar to that required from the firm itself. The FSA will normally seek information from a firm in the first instance, but reserves the right to seek information from a supplier under a material outsourcing arrangement, if it considers this to be appropriate.

There is a requirement to notify the FSA of certain types of outsourcing (but approval is not required, apart from certain controlled functions). Regulated firms (except insurers, managing agents, and Lloyds) must notify the FSA when they intend to rely on a third party for the performance of operational functions which are critical or important for the performance of relevant services and activities on a continuous and satisfactory basis. This rarely presents difficulties, for in practice regulators rarely quibble with sound contracts, but negotiation timetables must allow for notification.

The requirements in both MIFID directives are based in part upon the guidelines and principles laid down in two earlier reports, one from a committee of the

---

[65] Directive (EC) 2006/73, Art 14.

Bank for International Settlements and the other from the Committee of European Banking Supervisors.[66] Reduced to their essence the directives simply prescribe good business practice: thorough investigation of supplier capabilities, good service levels and reporting, robust governance, termination and other remedies, the protection of client data and other confidences, audit rights for regulators and the customer firm's own auditors, good disaster recovery planning and testing, and other, similar protections. Regulated firms contemplating new outsourcing engagements should, of course, scrutinize all applicable laws and regulations to be sure that their plans, practices, and eventual contracts meet every requirement; but in general, on both sides of the Atlantic, the kinds of best practices and contract terms recommended by this author and other knowledgeable advisors are likely to pass muster—although one must always be alert for local variations, idiosyncrasies, and lore, as well as the known attitudes of particular agencies.

13.6 SUMMING UP

No more than an introduction has been attempted. Companies must reckon with laws and regulations affecting their operations in countries where they do business. Many industries—pharmaceuticals, health care, insurance, energy, and many others—face distinctive, even unique, requirements. National laws concerning such things as immigration, export controls, corporate social responsibility, financial reporting, environmental compliance, corruption, business practices, and many others may have to be examined, depending upon the particular function outsourced, the customer's business, and the places where services are performed or received.

Whatever the situation, the ultimate responsibility for compliance cannot be delegated to an outsourcer, but practical responsibilities may be allocated and suppliers may be held accountable for violations of laws within their competence and responsibility or violations of the customer's policies and procedures. Where outsourcing itself is subject to regulatory scrutiny, attention to those requirements is essential but, in general, good practice is likely to satisfy many, even most, regulatory requirements.

---

[66] Committee of European Banking Supervisors, 'Guidelines on Outsourcing' (2006), available at <http://www.c-ebs.org/getdoc/f99a6113-02ea-4028-8737-1cdb33624840/GL02OutsourcingGuidelines-pdf.aspx> (accessed 3 May 2009); and Basel Committee on Banking Supervision of the Bank for International Settlements, 'The Joint Forum: Outsourcing in Financial Services' (February 2005), available at <http://www.bis.org/publ/joint12.pdf> (accessed 3 May 2009).

Whatever the extent of climate change, there is little question that the regulatory climate has changed since the collapse of world financial markets during the autumn of 2008. When this was written, midway through 2009, the US Congress was considering sweeping changes in the regulation of banking and financial services, as well as 'cap-and-trade' legislation intended to reduce emissions of greenhouse gases. Other governments may also revamp laws and regulations to address recession and potential environmental dangers in ways that affect outsourcing. Protectionist pressures might lead to more direct restrictions, particularly on offshore outsourcing. In other words, much written here may change in the immediate future.

Of these trends, the one with the most interesting, if indirect, effects may be climate change legislation. Computing consumes enormous amounts of energy—as much as aviation, according to some estimates—and thus immense quantities of fossil fuels burned to generate electricity. Many outsourced services are based upon technology and thus, energy. Already, customers seek efficiencies, and suppliers offer efficient equipment, 'green' facilities, and other measures meant to reduce effects upon the environment that all mankind shares. Some contracts already allocate carbon credits between supplier and customer. In the future, if regulations grow more stringent, new contract terms may emerge. There may be 'green' service levels, continuous improvements tied to reductions in power consumption, gain-share opportunities from savings, new reporting requirements, audit rights, and complex attribution rules concerning the worldwide carbon footprints of outsourced operations (which are extensions of the customer's operations and part of the supplier's business). No predictions are offered here, but these possibilities, in their complexity, bear more than a passing resemblance to complexities associated with the Sarbanes-Oxley statute or privacy legislation.

14

FLAVORS AND VARIETIES

Outsourcing contracts and relationships have much in common, no matter what the industry or outsourced function. Services must be described, measured and priced. Risks must be allocated, remedies provided, and the relationship governed. Open any outsourcing contract, and the table of contents recites a familiar litany; but behind the captions lie some important, occasionally subtle, differences. Familiar practices and contact terms devised for IT (and especially IT infrastructure) may not necessarily translate directly to other spheres. For customers, experience outsourcing one function (such as IT) is not always a sure guide to outsourcing other functions, with different requirements, internal constituencies, and risks. This is true even when extending an existing relationship, for suppliers usually entrust distinct lines of business to separate business units— each one a profit center with its own management.

In this chapter, we examine peculiar issues associated with some common varieties of outsourcing—applications development and maintenance (ADM), human resources (HR), finance and accounting (F&A), procurement, and legal support.[1] These are not, of course, the only functions that may be outsourced, but they illustrate approaches premised upon understanding the underlying business function, supplier solutions, sources of savings, and commercial realities on both sides of the relationship.

---

[1] Sometimes referred to as LPO for 'legal process outsourcing.'

14.1 APPLICATIONS DEVELOPMENT AND MAINTENANCE

During the 1990s, many companies outsourced essentially all IT functions, transferring responsibility for data centers, networks, help desks, PC support, and the maintenance and development of software applications.[2] More recently, companies have tended to contract separately for applications development and maintenance, often with offshore suppliers who caught the market's attention in the rush to rewrite old code before the millennium. Thus, most terms of a contract for comprehensive IT services apply also for applications, excluding those that apply only to data centers, networks, and other infrastructure. Often, key issues for software include pricing, service levels, intellectual property, and transitional issues, among others.

14.1.1 Outsourcing or staff augmentation

Customers may obtain application service in two ways: by (i) outsourcing the function to an outside supplier, who hires and manages programmers, then delivers fixes, preventive maintenance, enhancements, or new developments; or (ii) augmenting staff by engaging a supplier to provide skilled programmers to write requirements, code, and documentation under the customer's supervision. The latter arrangement is much simpler, and does not differ fundamentally from supplementing staff with temporary help engaged through an agency—although the temporary help may work thousands of miles away, on the supplier's premises. The customer obtains skilled manpower and enjoys savings from labor arbitrage, but otherwise retains essentially all risks. The supplier merely serves as a 'body shop.' With outsourced or managed services, by contrast, the supplier assumes primary responsibility to manage the effort and deliver results, rather than skilled staff.

14.1.2 Pricing for ADM services

Historically, applications and other labor-intensive services have tended to be priced based upon the level of effort, measured by man-hours, man-days, full-time equivalents, or other measures of time expended rather than results achieved. There may be different classifications and methods for the pricing of corrective and preventive maintenance, larger and smaller enhancements or

---

[2] Sometimes referred to as 'applications development and maintenance' (thus the inevitable acronym, ADM).

new developments, long-term and short-term assignments, but at bottom, most metrics are driven by levels of effort and the relevant mix of skills. These methods have all of the defects of time and materials charges, which reward inefficiency, but which are easy to measure and objective—unlike function points, standard work units, and other attempts to measure programmers' outputs and efficiency. None of those alternatives has proved wholly satisfactory or gained wide acceptance. Since savings derive from labor arbitrage—programmers cost less in India—and, to a lesser extent, from standardization and improved methods, attention tends to focus on rates, staffing, and possible reductions in numbers of supported applications, which reduce staffing requirements.[3]

Sometimes, the parties attempt to fix monthly or annual charges, but these easily become problematic as portfolios of supported applications evolve. Replacement applications may be more or less difficult to support, or require larger or smaller teams and different skills for newer technologies. A customer may easily pay too much (if the workload contracts) or too little (if more, or more highly skilled, staff are required, and the supplier must make do with fewer, less skilled or less experienced staff in order to maintain margins). Fixed charges work best when subject to frequent adjustment based on net changes in levels of effort and the skills mix—meaning in practice that charges are only fixed in the short term. In essence, these methods resemble pricing built upon baseline numbers of full-time equivalents or hours, with incremental charges and credits to reflect swings in demand and changes in the seniority and skills of the workforce.

When charges for software development are tied to deliverable software (as on fixed-price projects), special attention should be paid to acceptance procedures. Suppliers often propose 'deemed approval' clauses: deliverables are approved unless they are rejected within a limited time. Their legitimate concern is to avoid expensive delays when working within a limited budget. Customers dislike automatic approvals, and the risk that brief review periods may elapse without any adequate opportunity for review and testing, and compel them to accept and pay for substandard work. Suppliers, for their part, fear rejection for subjective reasons, or on account of minor defects that do not seriously affect system performance. Suppliers commonly insist that actual production use constitutes acceptance, for the same reason that car dealers require payment before customers drive away. However, acceptance may be

---

[3] Better discipline and documentation may also improve efficiency. Consistent methods and better documents reduce the time and effort required to find, diagnose, and fix software bugs.

conditional, and a portion of the final payment may be withheld pending completion of corrective work or the delivery of missing components.

Compromise resolutions often include the following elements:

- The early development of test scripts by an independent set of analysts and programmers, working with end users. Independence helps to assure scrutiny from fresh eyes not blinded by original development work, as well as insights from front-line users, so that tests simulate actual usage.
- Reasonable review periods, sufficient for testing and review, and subject to extension for good cause.
- If systems pass tests successfully, without serious mishaps or defects, they should be accepted. Deficiencies are often classified by severity. Initial acceptance may be conditioned upon a period of successful production use sufficient to exercise all features (such as monthly or quarterly closings) with live data.
- Customer commitments to act reasonably. Approvals should not be unreasonably withheld or delayed. This is the lawyers' attempt to prohibit arbitrary rejection, or the use of minuscule faults as pretexts for rejection.

14.1.3 Intellectual property rights

With software, intellectual property rights are crucial. There is no need here to repeat the discussion in Chapter 8 above, but with applications services, the usual issues concern (i) rights in new developments, and (ii) rights in supplier technology, including code or components embedded in customer systems and rights to use the supplier's tools after the contract expires. Suppliers readily agree that further developments or enhancements of the customer's own proprietary systems belong with the customer. Suppliers are simply hired help. But the picture is more complex if, for example, some of the supplier's existing code should be embedded in a customer system. Suppliers are not accustomed to giving assets away, particularly when those assets are in use elsewhere, represent competitive advantage, or may be offered to other customers. So language is usually agreed that preserves the supplier's ownership, while allowing the customer full rights to use and even further develop the delivered system, but only for its own business, and not in competition with the supplier.

Wholly-new developments, such as projects to develop new systems, invite the debate described in section 8.3 above. Customers generally start by insisting that they must own what they pay for; and suppliers reply that they have businesses to run, built upon marketing accumulated skills, experience, and, at least to some extent, work product, to customers. There are many potential approaches to these issues, and no universal recipe for resolution. Sound, negotiated resolutions are most likely to emerge from a reasoned discussion of the parties' legitimate expectation and interests that goes beyond emotional notions of ownership to consider intellectual property rights in detail—not only formal protection by copyright or patent registration, but rights to use, exploit, and further develop technologies, whether as owner or licensee. Suppliers need to carry on after the work is complete, redeploy development teams, and re-use accumulated knowledge and work product. Customers generally recognize this, provided competition-sensitive technology is not supplied to their competitors, at least not immediately. Consequently, new developments owned by customers may be licensed back to suppliers, so long as the suppliers do not transfer either software or the development team to the competition.

When the outsourcing contract expires, the customer (or perhaps a successor supplier of software maintenance services) will need to maintain the systems. Customers therefore request rights to use the supplier's tools. Some suppliers have proprietary tools and methodologies that they will make available to customers (and even competing suppliers) as commercial products (for a price) when contracts conclude. They may be less willing to provide tools used internally that they do not market to third parties or support, except for internal use. In such cases, if the supplier is unwilling, the customer should be sure that commercial equivalents are available. Some customers insist that the suppliers either agree to make proprietary tools available after the contract expires or otherwise use nothing but standard commercial products. Whatever the particular supplier's policies regarding its proprietary tools, all reputable suppliers recognize the customer's legitimate need to maintain what it receives after the contract lapses. There must be a road map to reverse the initial transition.

14.1.4 Service levels

Service levels for IT infrastructure are relatively straightforward, since many are based upon reports automatically generated by machines or software concerning availability, response times, and other familiar metrics. Some customers have fairly extensive records of past performance; and suppliers usually have good records for their own performance and systems. Customer records concerning software maintenance may be scanty, and in any event suppliers cannot easily predict system performance, resolution times, or other metrics for a customer's proprietary applications, which are unfamiliar to the supplier and may not be particularly well documented. Some metrics—notably resolution times—are particularly difficult to determine without actual experience. The supplier's dilemma resembles that of the construction contractor engaged to remodel an older building for which there are no blueprints. No one really knows what wiring, plumbing, or other surprises lurk behind plaster walls. In practice, a good many service levels must be established through a validation process during the first few months after transition. Rather than leave everything for negotiation after signing, when the customer's leverage has largely evaporated, it is helpful to agree upon tentative or presumptive service levels. If those can be consistently achieved, there is no need for negotiation; and if not, the parties can lower the bar, change systems and procedures, or lay on additional personnel or other resources as they think best.

14.1.5 Transitional issues

With applications, crucial aspects of transition and eventual reverse transition include transfers of data, documentation, and knowledge. In order to assure effective initial transfers of knowledge—especially undocumented knowledge—knowledgeable staff must be retained at a time when many of them, understandably, seek new opportunities. If everyone abandons ship, the incoming supplier will operate at a handicap, possibly jeopardizing stable operation of crucial systems. Wise customers therefore treat displaced employees respectfully and generously. Amounts paid in retention incentives and other benefits may be money very well spent, quite apart from rewarding loyal service and maintaining goodwill. Money spent requiring the supplier to document systems, deliver that documentation to the customer, and thereafter keep documentation current provides excellent insurance against total dependence upon the supplier and is sure to ease eventual disengagement.

When the relationship concludes, all this is reversed, as knowledge must be transferred back to the customer or onward to another supplier. The customer or successor supplier may wish to recruit knowledgeable staff, but incumbent suppliers and especially Indian suppliers resist this, although they may make knowledgeable staff available after the contract expires at hourly or daily rates. One way or another, knowledge must be transferred from the incumbent supplier's team to their successors. Since the same people cannot do both their usual work and brief their successors at the same time, something has to give, either through service level relief or by reinforcing the staff assigned to carry on normal operations. Customers may prefer to let this be an option that they may exercise when the time comes, either to live with a somewhat less responsive service, or to pay more money for additional support.

Good documentation provides protection against attrition and the discontinuities associated with transitions. Many existing systems are not well documented. Good statements of work should specify precisely what documentation the supplier must provide, whether for existing systems, upgrades, enhancements or new developments. Where existing documentation is weak or lacking, new documentation may be unnecessary if systems are slated for early retirement. Writing or rewriting documentation may be expensive. Clear documentation requirements can help to prevent unpleasant, potentially expensive misunderstandings. Going forward, documentation that other professionals can use will help to ease the transition to another supplier when the contract ends.

14.1.6 Privacy

Potential liabilities associated with security breaches and identity theft mortify both sides in these transactions, but, with applications support, risks can be reduced—and discussions of liability limits and indemnities simplified—if, for example, live or production data resides on the customer's systems and tests are performed with blind or simulated data without individual names, account numbers, and other particulars for actual employees and customers. If so, actual exposure to live data may be minimal and incidental.

14.1.7 Other issues

Since applications services are labor-intensive and rarely involve major investments in facilities and equipment, convenience termination charges are usually comparatively modest, since the supplier need not recover large front-end investments in order to be made whole (although some costs may be stranded in workstations and tools that have little further use).

Since skills are in demand, talent is always scarce, and many suppliers rely upon inexperienced, ambitious young people, attrition can pose challenges for suppliers and customers. To assure consistency and continuity, many customers require twelve-, eighteen-, or twenty-four-month commitments from at least some staff, and some customers subsidize incentive compensation, payable upon completion of assignments or projects. With applications services, as with many other offshore services, customers sometimes propose service levels tied to turnover, and many contracts require executive level consultations if turnover exceeds expectations.

For applications, disaster recovery rarely involves immediate recovery from an alternate location, using duplicate equipment and backup data. Instant recovery is rarely necessary or feasible. The essential thing is to relocate and reassemble staff at another facility, some distance away from the original site, with equipment and access to work in process, data, and the customer.

Accounting controls are important with applications (as for most outsourced services) but the usual issues involve logical, physical, and organizational security, especially at remote locations; so they are likely to be simpler than for comprehensive infrastructure services, or finance and accounting services (discussed below), which affect the company's books extensively and directly.

14.2 HR SERVICES

In a knowledge economy, people are many companies' principal asset, and so their recruitment, compensation, training, and management are critical functions. Some of those functions, such as selection of executives and other key personnel, have strategic importance; and others, such as compensation structures, are matters of basic policy that companies rarely, if ever, delegate. Routine HR administration, however, is another matter entirely. A whole range of activities can be done more cheaply and efficiently with advanced systems and integrated applications that replace on-site personnel with remote support, and paper forms with web pages or software. Here lie the attractions of HR outsourcing: superior service and lower cost through a combination of automation, remote or offshore support, economies of scale, labor arbitrage, and current technology (without inconvenient capital investments in a back-office function). For companies with obsolete systems that operate in isolation from one another and from corporate systems, and may differ across regions or business units, current technology may be very attractive. Since many of the HR suppliers' offerings are based upon technology, much of the logic of IT outsourcing, and many contract terms, translate straightforwardly. Service levels for an HR call center may look very much like those for an IT help desk, measuring how quickly calls are answered, how few are abandoned without being answered, and how many issues are resolved on the first call.

There are, however, differences.

14.2.1 Scope of HR services

Jim Madden, who led pioneering HR supplier Exult, used to say, in a nice nautical metaphor, that customers commanded the bridge, but outsourcing suppliers looked after the engine room: essential, unglamorous, grimy work below decks. In HR, such operations as payroll, benefits administration, HR data management and IT systems, recruiting, relocation training, and outplacement, among others, can be handed to an outsourcer. Since the outsourcer rarely takes over entire functions, let alone the entire HR function, conventional 'sweep clauses' encompassing everything formerly done internally may be problematic or heavily qualified. Staff may not transfer, and not every activity identified in the financial base case will be outsourced. Comprehensive statements of work are essential, and commonly include elaborate charts or matrices allocating responsibility between the parties for each and every function. Where the parties' responsibilities intersect, detail is helpful. With payroll, for example, the company must supply accurate information as well as sufficient funds so that the outsourcer may calculate payroll deductions, issue checks, and submit tax filings and payments. If scope includes severance and outplacement, decisions rest with the employer, who decides who must depart and on what terms, but an outsourcer may issue checks, administer severance benefits, and provide outplacement counseling. With IT, by contrast, the supplier is more likely to take over whole functions, such as data center operations (perhaps with minor exceptions). With HR (as with F&A) divisions of responsibility may be more complex. With many outsourced functions it is generally true that: (i) customers decide strategy; (ii) suppliers develop processes and programs for customer approval; and (iii) the supplier then implements and operates.

14.2.2 Pricing for HR services

HR services may be charged in the usual variety of ways, including time and materials and resource consumption, or may be based upon numbers of transactions or events, such as calls to service centers, numbers of payroll checks issued, or positions filled. Charges may also be tied to capitation (numbers of employees supported) or fixed, but subject to adjustment based on numbers of employees and transactions or other, similar criteria. As the market matures, there is some movement toward standard pricing elements and service levels, thanks in part to the work of the trade association HROA, with cooperation from customers, suppliers, and leading consultancies. Termination charges are usually substantial, in part because of investments in systems and infrastructure.

Transition periods at both ends of the relationship may be lengthy, because of complexities associated with transforming operations or, when the contract expires, adopting another supplier's procedures and systems. With IT, data centers use the same familiar hardware and operating systems (driven largely by the customer's applications and other requirements), where competing HR suppliers may deploy unique integrated systems which use different methods and technologies. Transition in and out may therefore take time, although disengagement should be faster than the original transition, because the successor can convert clean, comprehensive databases for employee information created and maintained by its predecessor.

14.2.3 Service levels for HR services

Since many HR services are driven by technology, some service levels may be adapted easily from familiar IT metrics, such as system availability, response times, accuracy of transactions, and reports or, as noted earlier, conventional metrics for call centers. Figures are readily available from standard software supporting those operations. Many customers lack good operating history, but services provided from the supplier's own facilities can be measured against the supplier's own standards and experience.

Move away from IT systems, and greater challenges arise. Many customers have few records of past performance of HR services, and even if they had, those records would provide little or no guidance for the calibration of appropriate service levels with wholly-new systems, methods, and procedures (although records may indicate volumes of activity, such as numbers of training or relocation requests). In the circumstances, some service levels must be fixed during or immediately after the transition period, through negotiation or validation processes like those described elsewhere.[4]

14.2.4 Intellectual property

HR services, unlike applications development, do not typically involve custom development. Nor do they rely upon systems chosen by the customer, as finance and accounting services may be tied to SAP, Oracle, or other systems chosen and installed by the customer. More often, the supplier of HR services deploys some combination of proprietary methods, software, and commercial products—combinations that they regard as proprietary, and do not offer to customers except in conjunction with service offerings, and never make available to their competitors. They are the chef's secret sauce, offered only to paying customers with a meal, and not otherwise. Suppliers may insist that they retain all rights in their systems, including rights in improvements, although there may be negotiated exceptions for unique enhancements created for particular customers (but not improvements in the supplier's basic service).

From the customer's standpoint, these policies are understandable, if in some respects unwelcome, but customers are not in the business of supplying HR services to others, and HR administration is rarely a source of competitive advantage. The customer must take pains to be sure that arrangements for disengagement or termination assistance allow sufficient time and cooperation for repatriation to the customer or, more likely, transition to another supplier.

---

[4] See 7.1.3 above.

14.2.5 Legal compliance

If intellectual property issues are simpler for HR than for IT, compliance issues may be more complex. Few relationships are more closely regulated than those between employers and employees, and neat divisions between employers' and suppliers' responsibilities are elusive. Laws abound concerning collective bargaining, wages and hours, pensions, fringe benefits, working conditions, discrimination, conduct in the workplace, and virtually every dimension of employment relationships. In recruiting, for example, laws concerning discrimination must be scrupulously observed in advertising copy prepared by the supplier, in initial screening by the supplier, and then in final interviews and decisions made by the employer. These are not 'supplier laws' or 'customer laws' but statutes that both sides must obey, at the risk of serious liability (to say nothing of damage to corporate reputations). For no other function is it more important to map legal responsibilities in detail, monitor developments in the law, and actively manage compliance on an ongoing basis, rather than simply react to incidents. Employment laws vary a great deal, even within the US. Early agreement on written policies with which the supplier must comply is excellent practice, especially in areas where the customer, as an employer, properly determines policies toward its employees.

14.3 FINANCE AND ACCOUNTING

Companies outsource finance and accounting functions in order to save money through a combination of efficiency and labor arbitrage. Indian or Filipino accountants and staff cost less. Accuracy, punctuality, and the integrity of controls are, of course, crucial; and outsourcing may be an agent of transformation, through consolidation or system changes; but saving money is the *sine qua non*.

14.3.1 Scope of service

Scope questions have particular importance with finance and accounting, because the entire function is rarely handed off. Outsourced finance and accounting operations require complex interactions between supplier and client. When accounts payable are outsourced, for example, the client usually inspects goods or accepts services and authorizes payment. Suppliers process invoices but rarely, if ever, spend the client's money. Demarcation lines and points of interaction must be clear. Allocations of responsibility between supplier and client vary from one situation to the next. As elsewhere, strategic functions tend to remain inside the client, along with operations that deal directly with customers or have unusual language requirements. Lower level transactions are often good candidates for outsourcing, along with middle-tier operations that use standard processes to support multiple business units. Since clients retain substantial responsibilities, the usual 'sweep' (or 'general scope') language may be less sweeping and less important.

14.3.2 Transition

Since companies' finance and accounting practices and procedures vary a good deal, transitions usually require extensive knowledge transfer at inception and when the contract later expires. In this respect, finance and accounting and other business processes may offer greater challenges than, say, IT infrastructure operations that use standard technologies in familiar ways. Therefore, pains are taken—and occasionally, incentives are paid—in order to retain key personnel through the period when they might otherwise be tempted to pursue other opportunities (for essentially the same reason that a company outsourcing applications support may pay incentives to retain, at least for a time, individuals who know undocumented systems).

14.3.3 Service levels

In finance and accounting, as in other outsourced operations, customers seek consistency, accuracy, reliability, and accountability, backed by service levels. Suppliers of finance and accounting services understand this, but may seek some margin for error, because their processes tend to be labor-intensive and less heavily automated than some other outsourced services. However rigorous the planning, documentation, and processes, human error is a fact of life. Suppliers therefore request reasonable tolerances, such as limited numbers of excused failures, or opportunities to recover any credits actually assessed through 'earn-backs' predicated on corrective action and later satisfactory performance.

Setting initial service levels poses challenges, since comparatively few companies have measured their own performance as comprehensively or rigorously as an outsourcer might. Without records of past performance, suppliers are reluctant to make specific performance commitments. On the other hand, clients fairly insist that some things—such as monthly, quarterly, and year-end closings—must occur on time, no matter what. Outsourcing suppliers reflexively object to 100 per cent standards, since perfection is rarely achieved; but it is usually possible to 'force' a timely closing—posting uncertain items into a holding or contingency account for later consideration. This is not desirable, of course, and should not happen often; but after some discussion a practical resolution is likely to emerge.

14.3.4 Pricing

Since people are the primary cost, many finance and accounting services are priced based upon man-hours, man-days, or headcount (generally expressed as numbers of full-time equivalents (FTEs)). Where the client's business is mature and stable, fixed pricing has attractions, particularly for such things as general accounting services that may not vary dramatically with the normal ebb and flow of business activity. Come what may, there can be only one general ledger, one annual closing, and four quarterly closings. When there are dramatic swings in effort and activity (following a merger, for example) charges may be equitably adjusted based upon net changes in staffing, facilities, and other inputs. Some services closely tied to volumes of transactions may be priced on a per-transaction basis—so much per invoice, for example—if baselines are well established. Charges then fluctuate with levels of activity. Ideally, supplier costs, charges to the client, and service volumes are effectively synchronized. Metrics must be chosen with care, however, to correspond with value delivered. With collections, for example, repeated calls to the same deadbeat may not accomplish much. Initial staffing requirements may be difficult to estimate, so parties may agree on a validation or stabilization period and pay initially on an hourly, daily, or FTE basis, before shifting to fixed or transaction-based charges.

14.3.5 Compliance—audit

Audit, Sarbanes-Oxley, and controls matter more in finance and accounting than in any other outsourced functions. Mercifully, since both suppliers and client accounting departments understand the requirements, discussion is usually straightforward. That discussion begins with a compilation of the relevant customer controls and, then (often after signing, during the transition phase) agreement on appropriate control activities. Sometimes, controls must change to match revised allocations of responsibility. Occasionally, adoption of the supplier's controls for its operations and facilities may be the most efficient solution. Some buyers find that suppliers' standards and consistency actually improve their controls. Suppliers accept that clients require annual service auditors' reports that comply with the relevant audit standard, SAS-70 Type II, and generally provide clients with a basic report concerning controls on their facilities and operations. Additional audits of customer-specific controls are at the customer's expense.

14.3.6 Compliance—privacy

For many companies—especially those that deal with consumers, their credit cards, and other personal data—finance and accounting services are likely to present ticklish questions concerning the security of personal data, as well as limitations on liability and indemnification. In this respect, they resemble HR services, which involve employees' personal data, or data center operations for companies with retail customers. Breaches of security may trigger notice requirements and expose the customer to substantial liability and unwelcome publicity. When suppliers are at fault, customers expect indemnification. The sensitivity and importance of this issue invite the kinds of discussions and resolutions suggested elsewhere.[5] Customers seek as much protection as possible; suppliers seek to contain their exposure; and both sides are well advised to consider practical measures to limit actual risk.

14.3.7 Compliance with laws

Finance and accounting services involve laws and regulations affecting companies generally (such as the securities laws) and the particular client's industry (such as banking, insurance, transportation, or hospitality). Regulatory responsibilities cannot be delegated, even if operations are outsourced, but companies can and do seek indemnification and other protection from outsourcers. Many laws affect both the client and its supplier (sometimes in somewhat different ways). To sort this maze, a matrix of legal requirements and responsibilities is often helpful, so that the parties proceed from a common understanding to sensible allocations of responsibility for monitoring, compliance, and potential liability based upon their particular competencies, operational responsibilities, and ability to manage risks.

Where compliance responsibility rests with the client (as it must in many regulated industries), the parties can protect themselves by developing detailed written procedures, approved by the client's lawyers, which the supplier must follow. Suppliers who (understandably) decline to give legal advice will generally accept that they must comply with customer procedures, and be accountable for failures to do so. Most also recognize obligations to be familiar with and abide by laws of general application affecting many or most customers, as well as local laws in the countries where they operate service centers.

---

[5] See 12.3 above.

14.3.8 Security

Suppliers of finance and accounting services are privy to some of their clients' most sensitive financial information, such as profitability and costs of production, which might be very valuable to competitors and is disclosed, if at all, only in compliance with securities laws. Customers therefore pay close attention to security arrangements, and the risk that personnel assigned to the client's account may perform services for competitors. In this respect, finance and accounting resemble other services. No client wants an account executive transferred to the competition (at least not immediately) or its data commingled with that of competitors. However, there may be little risk if lower level personnel performing routine tasks share work space or support other customers (excluding competitors), provided adequate technical and organizational security is in place. Dedicated staff or separate, secure working areas within the supplier's facility are likely to add cost, and may not always be necessary.

14.3.9 Intellectual property

The ownership of improvements and new developments is a thorny issue in contracts for software development and maintenance, because both sides have commercial interests in the supplier's work product. With finance and accounting this is much less likely, for the crucial technology often resides in third party systems or the client's own proprietary systems. Suppliers may be reluctant to let clients, or competing suppliers, use proprietary tools when the contract concludes, but the competitors have their own tools, and the tools are rarely critical or indispensable to these kinds of services.

14.3.10 Remedies—termination rights

Finance and accounting contracts generally provide the usual panoply of remedies, up to and including termination, both for breach and 'convenience.' Since finance and accounting transactions rarely involve major investments, termination charges should be lower than for some other kinds of services. Ideally, customers would prefer simply to reimburse reasonable shutdown costs.

14.4 PROCUREMENT

Some of the most interesting opportunities involve procurement: enlisting an outside supplier to manage purchasing in order to save money, not so much through efficiency (desirable as it may be) as through better buying at lower cost. Saving a million dollars in operations is all very well, but shaving a few per cent from spending may yield far larger dividends. In this sense, outsourcing procurement is about scale, for a small percentage of a very large number is still a large number. Not surprisingly, heads of procurement and finance are paying attention.

Many outsourced services offer savings through economies of scale (when operations transfer to a supplier's systems and facilities) or labor arbitrage (when operations relocate offshore). Procurement is another story. Suppliers do offer process improvements, efficiencies, and remote processing of transactions. These may be better and cheaper than most companies' internal operations, but far larger opportunities exist in spending reductions—securing better terms and lower prices for managed spending. Suppliers naturally hope to augment margins with a share of those savings. Shrewd customers recognize the value of rewarding performance from 'found money.'

Since the economic premises differ, so do the risks. Outsourcing procurement involves many of the same risks as other varieties of outsourcing: transitions can be bungled; service may be poor; sensitive information is at risk and must be protected; and relevant laws must be obeyed. There must be remedies if things go wrong. But for customers, the largest single risk is something else: the possibility that anticipated savings may not be achieved, even if the supplier fully performs. No one possesses a reliable crystal ball. Economic conditions change. Promising opportunities may prove to be mirages. In such circumstances the customer will want to end the contract and go in some other direction, with minimal disruption to its business and the supplier's cooperation (in other words, what practitioners call 'termination assistance').

14.4.1 How does it work?

This relatively immature market continues to evolve. Suppliers offer competing solutions, but, in general, procurement outsourcing means the management of a number of related processes by a supplier for one or more categories of spend over a term of years (as opposed to shorter-term consulting arrangements or outside assistance with the implementation of new tools and processes). Many service offerings involve some combination of the following:

- The identification of savings opportunities within particular categories, emphasizing the larger opportunities (the proverbial 'low-hanging fruit').
- The selection of vendors and negotiation of more advantageous terms through such familiar methods as competitive bidding, aggregation of

spending among business units (and, occasionally, among the supplier's other customers), and pruning vendor lists to a select few willing to offer volume discounts. Suppliers hope to take advantage of better knowledge of particular markets and improved tools, such as web-based catalogs, reverse auctions, and the like. Supplier teams are not necessarily more skillful than their customers' internal buyers, but may possess deeper knowledge because they specialize more narrowly, or deal regularly with the same suppliers on behalf of many customers.

- The processing of transactions, from issuance of purchase orders through payment of invoices, monitoring and reporting of vendor performance, and management of the relationship against agreed goals. Here too, suppliers may offer savings and efficiencies through superior methods, better technology, and remote or offshore operations. Equally important, putting these operations in one place helps to assure some control over scattered, 'maverick' spending in order to achieve the greatest possible savings.

Categories of spend entrusted to outsourcers are usually chosen from among goods and services that are not incorporated in the customer's own wares (so-called 'indirect spend'). A manufacturer, for example, may regard the procurement of critical parts, subsystems, and raw materials for its own products as a 'core competence'—something to keep inside the tent—but will let someone else buy office supplies, personal computers, furniture, and thousands of other items used by the business. In large companies, these less critical but essential items account for huge volumes of spending. In all cases, customers must honestly assess the strengths and weaknesses of existing operations in order to identify categories of spend where an outside supplier might achieve greater savings.

14.4.2 Scope and baselines

When whole functions are outsourced—for example when data center operations are handed off—customers invariably insist that the supplier should undertake whatever was formerly done by the customer's own staff. By contrast, most customers retain substantial purchasing organizations for both direct spending and a number of indirect categories. Only discrete functions are outsourced—particular processes for selected categories of spend. 'Sweep' clauses therefore matter less for procurement than for some other outsourced services, although the parties must still deal with activities related to or inherent in the (inevitably general) language of the statement of work or responsibility matrix.

With procurement, definitions of scope typically involve:

- matrices allocating responsibility for particular activities (such as customer approval of requisitions and supplier issuance of purchase orders); and
- the identification of relevant categories of spend entrusted to the supplier's management, and measurement of baselines, including such metrics as historic spending and numbers of transactions.

Since initial efforts focus on the largest savings opportunities—that 'low-hanging fruit'—customers fear that the supplier may lose interest or reassign its best talent to other accounts after the first year or two. Holding back some opportunities may provide ample incentives over the life of the relationship (although delay could postpone savings—a self-defeating strategy).

14.4.3 Pricing

Most outsourced services are priced in familiar ways—daily, hourly, or FTE rates for such labor-intensive services as software maintenance; usage or resource consumption for IT infrastructure; and per transaction for many business processes. Incentives, gain-sharing, and the rest are often after-thoughts of modest importance.

With procurement, by contrast, incentive fees are the crucial issue—often more important than rates for personnel or transactions. Suppliers seek shares of savings as incentive compensation. Their margins (to say nothing of bonuses for account teams and executives) depend upon incentive fees. Customers accept the importance of motivating and rewarding suppliers. The challenge for both sides is to strike an appropriate balance between monthly charges for service (determined in the usual ways) and incentive payments (based upon savings achieved). Base charges for service may correlate with quality. Better-paid, specialized buyers may make better deals, save more money, deliver better service, and please skeptical users scattered among the customers' business units. Load too much into incentive compensation, and buyers may chase bargains at the expense of service and quality—a false economy. On the other hand, bonuses paid for savings achieved may motivate suppliers (and their account teams) to redouble their efforts (particularly if supplier compensation plans reward account teams for results achieved and customer satisfaction).

There are no pat answers. One must seek a reasonable balance between savings and incentives sufficient to motivate the supplier to find savings, without disregarding quality, performance, or delivery. The parties must collaborate to identify and exploit opportunities in the marketplace, and divide the rewards in ways that motivate desirable outcomes—generally, a combination of lower cost, fair compensation for service performed, operational efficiency, and superior performance, all measured and reported with greater transparency than before. In legal terms, outsourcing contracts are not partnerships or joint ventures; but successful, collaborative pursuit of opportunities requires thinking (as partners might) of both parties' legitimate interests and overall success.

Since incentives are tied to savings, savings must be measured. This is easier said than done. Savings may be measured against historic performance, and paying less tomorrow than yesterday is surely ideal. However, this is not always realistic. Fuels and lubricants are crucial commodities, but when crude oil soared above $120 a barrel during 2008, no one paid less for fuels and lubricants than the year before. The following year, crude prices fell by three-quarters, to less than $40 a barrel, and pump prices fell almost as dramatically—no matter what the buyer's skill. In some circumstances, savings should be measured against the current marketplace as 'costs avoided.' Suppliers' tools and metrics for measuring and reporting savings may or may not align with the customer's familiar methods. Here again, there are no pat answers. The challenge is to find something that works acceptably, and then to measure trends against accurate baselines (yet another challenge).

Since incentive fees are tied to savings, the supplier's opportunity to earn incentive fees depends in part upon a continuing volume of purchases. Suppose the customer's consumption declines, or falls to negligible levels? Suppose that, for whatever reason, a company declines to pursue opportunities identified by its supplier—for example to retain an historic source for particular products, even though lower cost alternatives have been identified? Should the supplier be paid any incentive fee for 'might-have-beens'? Suppose that a company decides (for cost and environmental reasons) to move toward paperless offices, removes printers and copiers, and then buys no replacements and far less paper and toner. The supplier can claim no credit for those savings, and to the extent that money is saved on small volumes, incentive fees will be far less than originally anticipated.

What should be done? A supplier may request, and a customer may agree, to pay some minimum revenue, based upon initial scope and anticipated spending. Below that level, surcharges may apply or the customer may be required to 'top up' or terminate. Customers may also make a commitment that, come what may, there will be some minimum volume of spending under management. If (in the example above) the customer buys fewer toner cartridges and less paper, there may be corresponding increases in spending for other items (computer screens, for example) or some additional spending category may be entrusted to the supplier. There is no formula, and no known substitute for intelligent collaboration.

This brings us to another area where procurement presents distinctive challenges.

14.4.4 Governance

Disappointment with outsourced operations often derives, in part, from weaknesses in governance. Simply turning things over to someone else does not, by itself, assure good results; and successful management of a contractor is not the same as managing operations. Many companies now have capable organizations to manage portfolios of outsourced operations, with layers of joint oversight, strong executive leadership and common processes for change management, budgeting, and much else. Procurement adds some distinctive wrinkles, because procurement tends to be dispersed, organizationally and geographically. Many outsourced IT, HR, and other operations are centrally directed. Former operations are transferred elsewhere, onshore or offshore, and may be transformed, but as before, they remain largely centralized and subject to central direction. Purchasing, by contrast, is often scattered among business units, which purchase distinctive ranges of products and services, often in local or regional markets. Some of the best opportunities for savings arise from aggregation and coordination across an entire organization. Desired savings are unlikely to be achieved if business units and regional offices go their own way. Successful governance therefore requires full participation and a strong consensus among all business units, across all geographic regions, backed, if necessary, by sufficient organizational clout or discipline to compel adherence. To sustain that consensus, the entire business must be consistently engaged in governance. If the program succeeds, and saves money, even skeptics may become believers; but without consensus, results are likely to disappoint.

Some outsourced operations are relatively stable (except during transitions or transformations). In finance and accounting, quarterly closings come four times a year; annual closings and audits come just once a year. Many accounting practices and principles are relatively stable (apart from such exercises as the implementation of Sarbanes-Oxley). Many IT services are relatively mature and stable. Many technologies evolve fairly predictably, at least in the near term.

Procurement, however, involves many moving parts and uncertainties. Baselines are rarely entirely accurate. Business conditions change, erasing some opportunities for savings but creating new ones. Spending patterns are not predictable. Neither are prices. Savings targets involve some more or less educated guesswork. No contract, however painfully constructed, can anticipate and provide for every contingency. Success, as in marriage, requires collaboration, goodwill, plain speaking, the willingness to make adjustments, and even improvise, all the while respecting both parties' legitimate interests. None of this can be dictated by written rules. Intelligent collaboration is essential, and sound governance—beginning with effective, frequent communication at all levels—is imperative. Periodic reviews of the entire relationship—scope, pricing, performance, governance, contract terms, and all the rest—are a best practice.

14.4.5 Suppliers as agents

Legally, customers and suppliers are not partners (desirable as it may be for them to think and behave as partners might). Rather, the supplier is a contractor, performing a service for a fee; but in some respects, suppliers of procurement services may be agents, notably when they negotiate prices and terms with vendors and oversee the vendors' performance. The agency, however, is narrowly circumscribed. Customers prescribe or approve the terms and conditions on which they are prepared to do business. They properly reserve rights to approve variations on those terms. No supplier places orders for the customer's account without customer approvals. Liability for authorized purchases rests with the customer, who must look to vendors and manufacturers if products are defective or arrive late. The supplier performs a service, but does not guarantee the third party products and services.

14.4.6 Service levels

Buyers of all outsourced services seek quality, consistency, and accountability— preferably measured and reported through service levels with teeth. In this respect, buyers of procurement services are no different from other customers. The purchasing professionals who typically lead customer teams are accustomed to holding vendors and suppliers accountable. However, there are important differences. Familiar IT metrics have limited usefulness, and few customers have measured their own performance as rigorously or comprehensively as they propose for the outsourcer (who may, in any event, perform the service with different processes and technology). Without records of past performance (that may not exist) suppliers are reluctant to make specific, binding performance commitments. Service levels may have to be established through a validation process during or immediately after the initial transition to outsourced operations.

The service levels themselves tend to include, among others: the speed and accuracy of transactions and reports; timely completion of particular tasks or processing of anticipated volumes; compliance with process requirements;

timely completion of sourcing initiatives; the availability and performance of hosted tools and applications; and the usual call center metrics (where scope includes, as it often does, a call center for inquiries from buyers within the customer's organization).

14.4.7 Intellectual property and confidentiality

With procurement services, both sides are concerned to preserve confidences. Suppliers are no more willing to expose their methods to competitors than customers are willing to disclose their internal costs. The suppliers' effectiveness, however, may depend in part upon the expertise of buyers who specialize in particular products, commodities, and services; serve many customers; and rely on market data accumulated from dealings on behalf of the supplier's entire clientele. How then to square this circle? Rigorous confidentiality terms are only a start. Customers may require that supplier personnel sign confidentiality agreements, and insist on rigorous internal security within the supplier's organization, but permit the 'blind' use of quotations received and other information in databases that support all of the supplier's clients.

Suppliers are equally keen to protect their intellectual property, and are unlikely either to leave tools behind when the contract expires or to allow customers (let alone competitors) to recruit key staff. For them, talent is, if anything, more important than any toolset or proprietary database (although those also remain with the supplier).

Intellectual property rights are less likely to be a bone of contention for procurement than for many other services, especially those that involve the development of software or other technology. Suppliers of procurement services, like suppliers of other business processes, routinely insist on exclusive ownership of the proprietary tools, methods, databases, and software used in their outsourced 'solutions,' including any improvements developed from time to time. Customer-specific recommendations, reports, and the like may belong to the customer, but never the underlying templates and tools used to create them.

14.4.8 Remedies—termination rights

With procurement, as with other services, the crucial issue is the termination charge payable for a convenience termination. In the event of premature termination, all suppliers of outsourced services hope to be made whole through the recovery of initial investments, shutdown costs, and anticipated (but unachieved) returns. With procurement, that last item—anticipated returns—is complicated, because savings accrue over time. Customers are most likely to exercise convenience termination rights when they change strategic direction or are dissatisfied, but grounds for dissatisfaction may not constitute material breach. With procurement services, the likeliest possibility—and the largest risk—is failure to achieve savings targets. The supplier may fully perform, yet miss the targets. Or, after picking the 'low-hanging fruit,' the supplier could lose interest, redeploy its best people, and let results stagnate or erode. What then?

Suppliers fret about other 'worst cases.' Suppose they launch a series of initiatives that seem certain to achieve substantial savings (and incentive fees) over a period of years, and the customer pulls the plug in the hope of avoiding incentive fees? Their predicament resembles that of the sales agent or broker, whose prospects buy after the agency or listing expires, yet understandably believe they have earned at least some commission.

How can these competing interests be reconciled on a basis that respects both sides' legitimate interests? Termination charges may include a declining component for unamortized initial expenses and investments that the supplier expected to recover over the contract term and built into the price. Since procurement services rarely, if ever, involve transfers of assets or large investments in facilities and equipment, these costs are likely to be comparatively modest. Similarly, such shutdown costs as relocation and severance can be estimated or, for that matter, reimbursed, if ever the time comes.

Negotiation may therefore focus on two related issues: (i) the supplier's desire to reap at least some of what it has sown, if initiatives undertaken before termination yield savings afterwards; and (ii) the customer's desire not to pay large bonuses for mediocre results, if savings are substantially less than anticipated. No settled formula exists to reconcile these competing perspectives. Termination charges may be heavily discounted if termination occurs following failure to meet some minimum threshold for savings. The supplier may receive some diminishing share of savings achieved through its efforts for a reasonable period after termination. To avoid accounting and other controversies, the parties may agree on a fixed sum. Simplicity and rough approximations may trump acrimony.

14.4.9 Other issues

For the rest, contracts for outsourced procurement contain terms familiar in other contexts—occasionally, with a twist. For example disaster recovery arrangements matter at the supplier's service center. If disaster strikes, essential services must resume promptly. Invoices have to be paid and, in an era of 'just-in-time' inventories, facilities may close without regular orders and deliveries. Immediate recovery may not be necessary (as it is for a bank or an internet retailer), but time horizons for critical services are likely to be measured in hours or days rather than weeks.

Customer auditors will want the right to examine billings, service levels, and records of purchasing activities. If suppliers issue purchase orders, process invoices, and manage vendor relationships, controls may have to be implemented, examined, and tested. Customers may require the usual service auditor's report, in compliance with SAS-70, including tests (the so-called 'SAS-70 Type II' report).

Purchasing activities must comply with relevant laws and avoid such potential hazards as price-fixing, bid-rigging, kickbacks, and bribes. Given the agency relationship, customers may be at some risk if the service provider goes astray. If service includes procurement from sources overseas, compliance obligations should include export controls, customs requirements, the Foreign Corrupt Practices Act, and similar laws. Customers require adherence to rigorous ethical policies (for example restricting or prohibiting acceptance of hospitality or other favors from vendors). Customers who do business with public agencies must comply with additional requirements (for example concerning veterans' preferences, diversity requirements, and the engagement of companies owned by minorities and women).

Benchmarking—the right to measure supplier charges against the marketplace—is useful, but less so than in more mature markets, where more data are available, competing solutions are comparable (indeed, sometimes interchangeable), and pricing more nearly standardized than in procurement, which involves a negotiated combination of service charges and incentive fees. Total cost is more difficult to gauge and compare, and subject to variations depending upon the spending categories under management. Pricing, moreover, may be less important than savings.

These are merely examples. Companies outsource procurement in order to reduce spending, rather than just the cost of performing a critical, non-strategic function. Since the context and value proposition are different, so are the contracts. Conventional thinking, developed from experience with data centers, networks, and call centers, is not necessarily a sure guide.

14.5 LEGAL SUPPORT SERVICES

Outsourcing has transformed many businesses. It could do the same for (or to) the legal profession, but with variations dictated by the nature of legal work, licensing requirements for law practice, and lawyers' ethical obligations. With legal support, engagements tend to be comparatively brief, lasting only as long

as the internal investigation, lawsuit, patent search, or other specific assignment. However, good results and working relationships between attorneys and
service firms may mean a series of assignments and a long-term relationship.
In that respect, the commercial dynamics resemble those of longer-term outsourcing arrangements. The real differences flow from the peculiarities of legal
work, and the rules governing legal practice.

In an August 2008 opinion, the ABA's Standing Committee on Ethics and
Professional Responsibility ruled that, under the Model Rules of Professional
Conduct, US lawyers are free to outsource legal support services offshore, so
long as ethical rules are respected. Lawyers who outsource remain fully responsible for the work—not only for its quality, but also for compliance with ethical
standards. Errors may expose careless or inattentive lawyers to professional
discipline as well as professional liability. Ethical rules vary among common
law jurisdictions, and even within the US, but, very broadly speaking, lawyers
may delegate work to an offshore company in much the same way as they
might use a legal assistant, trainee, or law clerk, so long as the work is properly
supervised and ethical proprieties are observed. US and English lawyers
practice under different rules and regulatory frameworks, but the essential
ethical obligations are similar. Offshore outsourcing of legal work appears to be
growing on both sides of the Atlantic, and affecting the performance of much
routine legal work and support for large practices.

Once upon a time, document review was a rite of passage. Careers began with
due diligence on large transactions or document production in large cases.
Documents came in cartons or, occasionally, on reels of microfilm. That world is
changing. Documents are digital and may be transmitted offshore in the blink of
an eye, for review by lawyers or paraprofessionals in such places as India, using
search engines and tools that would have seemed like science fiction not so
many years ago. Document review as once known may go the way of riding
circuit on horseback, or long nights of proofreading and pizza at the financial
printer while rotary presses whirred in the background.

The relentless logic, efficiency, and economics of outsourcing have collided
with the settled ways of the legal profession, whose methods have not changed
fundamentally since typewriters and telephones first appeared in the late nine-
teenth century. Until quite recently, most work in law offices would have been
perfectly recognizable to Horace Rumpole or Clarence Darrow. No more.
Outsourcing scatters functions formerly housed within law firms or company
law departments. Legal documents can be reviewed or prepared almost as easily
in Bangalore or Manila as downstairs, and at lower cost to corporate clients
pressed to do more with less. Labor arbitrage means large savings, and those
savings have attracted great interest among corporate law departments and

practicing lawyers. Analysts predict that within a few years, offshore companies offering legal support services will employ tens of thousands of people, and reap hundreds of millions of dollars in revenues. This trend seems to be part of a larger transformation of law practice and the market for legal services, driven by disruptive technology and commercial pressures, including the tendency to commoditize much legal work.[6]

Lawyers and law departments may outsource or pursue offshore opportunities by:

- Engaging any of the growing number of service companies based in India or elsewhere who offer document review, legal research, and a host of other services, generally performed by foreign lawyers, but often overseen by lawyers admitted to practice in the US, the UK, or other relevant jurisdictions.
- Creating captive operations overseas. Many law firms have overseas offices, although Indian operations are limited to service centers that, under existing rules of practice, provide document management and other administrative services. Some US companies have established offshore legal support centers in India, the Philippines, and elsewhere. Some UK law firms have outsourced routine litigation support to South Africa.
- In addition, various intermediaries will provide lawyers directly to corporate clients, who pay for the lawyers rather than the legal service. Agencies do this and so, occasionally, do law firms, generally as an accommodation to reinforce client relationships.

With these (and other) arrangements, savings are the primary attraction, but there may be other advantages—such as sophisticated tools for document review, or the ability to revise documents while Europe and North America sleep.

14.5.1 Ethical considerations and constraints

Lawyers have long relied upon trainees, law clerks, temporary or contract lawyers, legal assistants, and others not licensed to practice. So long as they are closely supervised, do not appear in court, or otherwise practice law, ethical obligations are satisfied. The lawyer who delegates and oversees non-lawyers' work remains responsible for the quality of the work and for compliance with ethical obligations to provide competent advice and representation for a

---

[6] The book to read on these trends is R Susskind, *The End of Lawyers? Rethinking the Nature of Legal Services* (Oxford: Oxford University Press, 2008).

reasonable fee, protect clients' confidences and avoid conflicts between clients with adverse interests, among others.

The ABA opinion referred to above is only the most recent in a series of opinions from respected US bar committees applying these familiar principles to outsourced or offshore legal support. The ethical analysis remains essentially the same, although the engagement and oversight of remote or offshore services is, as a practical matter, much more complicated.

Within the US, ethical rules vary among the states, although most (except California) resemble the ABA's Model Rules of Professional Responsibility, and all incorporate, in some form, the following essentials:

- *Licensing.* Only licensed lawyers may practice law, and they cannot condone or assist unlicensed practice.
- *Competence.* Lawyers must provide 'competent representation,' meaning requisite legal knowledge, skill, thoroughness. and preparation. Associates, legal assistants, and others must be effectively supervised to assure not only competence and quality, but compliance with ethical rules and professional obligations.
- *Confidentiality.* Lawyers must keep their clients' secrets, unless the client authorizes disclosure (with rare exceptions for such situations as prevention of serious crimes). This is among the lawyer's most solemn obligations. California, for example, requires every lawyer to maintain client confidences 'inviolate and, at every peril to himself or herself to preserve the [client's] secrets.'[7]
- *Conflicts.* Lawyers must avoid the representation of adverse interests, although in many non-contentious situations, a lawyer may advise adverse parties after first obtaining the parties' informed consent.
- *Fees* must be reasonable. Fees should not be divided between lawyers in different firms without client consent and may not be shared with non-lawyers. For this reason, contingent fees cannot be shared with those providing support services. Support charges billed as disbursements must be passed through at their actual cost but may include a reasonable overhead allocation.

Elsewhere, rules and obligations are similar. In England, only authorized (or exempt) persons may engage in 'reserved legal activities,' including the conduct of litigation, conveyance of real estate, and exercise of rights of audience in the courts. Authorization is not required for some 'legal activities,' including the provision of legal advice and representation in disputes (although those activities

---

[7] Cal Bus & Prof Code § 6068(e)(1).

could be reclassified as 'reserved' by the Lord Chancellor, on a recommendation from the Legal Services Board).[8] English solicitors are therefore free to delegate a wide range of support work to trainees or send that work offshore, so long as they meet ethical obligations. These include obligations to act with integrity, independently, in clients' best interests, provide a good standard of service, avoid conflicts of interest, and keep client confidences.[9] Solicitors should agree with clients on an appropriate level of service, disclose the names of persons dealing with and supervising client matters, and supervise subordinates, including staff who are not qualified to practice.[10] A Law Society practice note concerning client care letters (engagement letters, in US parlance) emphasizes the potential risk to client confidentiality, and recommends that lawyers obtain non-disclosure agreements from outside suppliers, disclose any outsourcing to clients in writing, and invite clients to object if they have reservations about confidentiality.[11]

Rules vary among common law jurisdictions, but wherever the common law applies, lawyers must pass examinations, keep their clients' secrets, avoid conflicts, and deliver competent advice and service. The ABA opinion calls outsourcing a 'salutary' trend for the global economy, offering cost savings and other potential benefits: 'there is nothing unethical about a lawyer outsourcing legal and non-legal services, provided the outsourcing lawyer renders legal services to clients with the "legal knowledge, skill, thoroughness and preparation reasonably necessary for the representation."' Supervision is crucial, and the ABA opinion notes some of the potential challenges and complexities associated with performance in remote places, by lawyers who may not be fully familiar with relevant standards and practice, even in India and other common law countries.

Each of these ethical requirements merits a closer look, and precise rules may vary a good deal from one jurisdiction to another. So may their application to particular situations; thus the following general discussion is only that, and not a substitute for an analysis of actual facts under relevant rules.

14.5.2 Licensing

No one can practice law without a license—paralegals, law students, offshore companies, foreign lawyers, or anyone else. Indeed, unlicensed practice may be

---

[8] Legal Services Act 2007, ss 12, 13, and 24.
[9] Solicitors' Code of Conduct 2007, rules 1–5.
[10] ibid rules 2 and 5, and Guidance at paras 2.02, 19, and 5.01(1)(a), 8.
[11] Client care letters practice note (19 May 2009) s 4.1.7 (outsourcing of work), available at <http://www.lawsociety.org.uk/productsandservices/practicenotes/clientcareletters/2810.article> (accessed 19 June 2009).

a criminal offense. Licensed attorneys should neither condone nor assist unauthorized practice. What constitutes the 'practice of law' is less clear under US rules, particularly in comparison with the English statute's lists of 'legal activities' and 'reserved legal activities.' In the US, law practice generally includes representation of others in the courts or other proceedings, giving advice about the law or rights secured by law, and the negotiation and preparation of contracts that secure or affect legal rights; but neither these activities nor their boundaries are well defined. Where legal judgment is required, so, in all probability, is a license to practice, especially when the rights of others are involved. Anyone can negotiate his or her own contract or, if competent, represent him or herself in court. He who acts as his own lawyer may have a fool for a client, but needs no license. Representing someone else requires a license.

Without clear demarcation lines, lawyers are well advised to read limits conservatively, and closely supervise all services performed by law clerks, legal assistants, legal support firms, or others not licensed to practice. Good supervision is in any event required to comply with the ethical obligation to practice competently.

14.5.3 The duty of competence

Competence involves, among other things, appropriate knowledge, skill, thoroughness, and preparation. When non-lawyers are supervised—as they must be—the supervising lawyer must make 'reasonable efforts to ensure that the [non-lawyer's] conduct is compatible with the professional obligations of the lawyer.'[12] The broad reference to professional obligations embraces both quality and compliance with ethical rules. Secrets must be kept and conflicts avoided, not only by lawyers, but by those who work with them.

Well-run law offices assure competence among law clerks, legal assistants, contract lawyers, and others by taking pains in their selection—interviews, reference checks, reviews of transcripts and writing samples, and so on—and then through good training and active, ongoing supervision. No experienced lawyer would simply file court papers prepared by a green associate, assistant, or law clerk without reviewing drafts, editing, and rewriting where appropriate, and making sure that the final product meets the supervisor's standards and those of the firm. The partner whose name appears on any court filing assumes responsibility for every word.

---

[12] Model Rules of Professional Conduct, rule 5.3(b). The rule for supervision of lawyers is essentially similar. The supervising lawyer must make 'reasonable efforts to ensure that the other lawyer conforms to the Rules of Professional Conduct.' (ibid rule 5.1(b)).

When work is performed offshore the same rules apply, so, in a sense, nothing changes except geography, distance, time zones, culture, and communication. In other words, a great deal changes. Offshore personnel must be qualified, interviewed, and the rest, if not by the domestic law firm or corporate counsel, then by the offshore service company, using appropriate standards and criteria. They must be adequately trained, and that training must include training in applicable legal principles and ethical standards. Lawyers trained in common law traditions have much in common, but there are significant differences. For example, someone reviewing contracts for a US client might be concerned about potential third party beneficiaries—a concept not formally recognized in India.

When time zones and geography preclude immediate or 'hands-on' supervision, the responsible lawyer, firm, or law department must find other ways to provide effective supervision, such as:

- regular reports, conference calls, or video conferences, supplemented by occasional site visits where the scale and duration of the engagement will justify the costs;
- on-site supervision by lawyers qualified in the home country;
- training, including periodic 'refreshers' in relevant laws and practices, including ethical obligations;
- checklists, forms, templates, instructions, software tools, and other, similar guides to assure consistent quality and anticipate likely questions from those who perform the work;
- regular feedback to both individuals and offshore management, including periodic reviews of quality; and
- where quality can be measured easily and objectively (for example numbers of errors or turnaround times), service levels may be defined, measured, and reported continuously through 'dashboards' or periodic reports. When they are missed, liquidated damages or credits may be assessed.

14.5.4 Confidences and conflicts

Delegation does not transfer ethical obligations. Rather, the lawyer who sends work offshore must make reasonable efforts to assure that offshore services comply with ethical rules. If not, the lawyer might be held accountable for lapses on agency, negligence, or other grounds.

Among ethical obligations, preservation of confidences and avoidance of conflicts may rank foremost in the minds of practicing lawyers and their clients. Offshore suppliers of support services should therefore apply essentially the same policies and procedures as any law office, including rigorous physical and electronic security, 'need to know' disclosure of confidential information, periodic training in ethical requirements, and the implementation of robust systems to monitor and track conflicts, including assignments of individuals to particular transactions or cases. The prevention of adverse representations means more than an initial 'snapshot.' Adverse representations must not be accepted after an engagement is accepted. Exit interviews for departing staff should include appropriate admonitions about conflicts and confidences, for those obligations outlast individual employment. All this is familiar, but when working overseas, there are some differences. For instance:

- Offshore personnel must be trained, and occasionally reminded, of distinctive aspects of practice in the responsible lawyer's jurisdiction. Conflicts and other rules may differ. [13]
- Lawyers' professional obligations to maintain confidences are more stringent than the usual non-disclosure agreement, so that with licensed lawyers, non-disclosure agreements may be unnecessary, but they may be advisable with non-lawyers, including foreign lawyers engaged by a service company, and with temporary staff. Written non-disclosure agreements are recommended, and in India they are generally enforceable by preliminary injunctions, which can be obtained within a reasonable time (despite legendary delays in obtaining final judgments from Indian courts).

14.5.5 Disclosures, consents, and costs

Most offshore legal support services are performed on an hourly, time and materials or similar basis. Calculations of charges and invoices are straightforward. Complications do arise from ethical rules. Client consent may be required before delegating substantial work to an outside service, or disclosing clients' confidential information. Whatever the rules require, disclosure is good practice and good client relations, especially where substantial charges will be passed through. Keeping clients informed is a best practice.

Rules may vary concerning fees and fee agreements, but universally limit fees to reasonable amounts. Fee agreements, whether or not required, are always advisable and should clearly describe all arrangements concerning fees and costs. Whatever the rules may require, this is just good client relations and, for

---

[13] Securities laws are not canons of ethics, but, for essentially similar reasons, training programs may usefully cover such things as insider trading, which expose all concerned to embarrassment and potential liability.

that matter, common sense. The ABA opinion explains that charges for temporary or contract lawyers may include a profit margin, so long as the total fee is reasonable; but when charges for outside support services are passed through as disbursements, 'the lawyer may bill the client only [the] actual cost plus a reasonable allocation of associated overhead' (unless of course the client agrees to some other arrangement). For US lawyers to include offshore support services in their fees might violate rules against the sharing of fees with non-lawyers and, to make matters worse, invite vicarious liability under agency or similar theories.

For these reasons, the prudent course is to make full disclosure, secure client consent, and pass through charges from outside suppliers at their actual cost, plus any applicable overhead allocation (if appropriate and permitted), but without any margin. In any event, it may be more convenient for all concerned if offshore suppliers bill clients directly, expediting payment to the supplier and freeing the law firm from any need to advance substantial costs.

Many of these issues are simpler, or even disappear, when a multinational law firm charges for work performed by its own foreign offices or offshore service centers. Services that the firm performs offshore are part of the firm's overall service, and clients understand and expect that charges (like those for associates and paralegals) include a profit margin.

14.5.6 Suitable services

Practical and ethical considerations dictate the kinds of work that may go offshore. Much work will never go offshore—for example face-to-face interaction with clients, experts, and other witnesses. No one is likely to prepare expert testimony by video conference from Chennai—any more than a medical group will perform physical exams remotely (although they might have x-rays read overnight and overseas).

In general, offshore legal support should: (i) scrupulously avoid work for which a license or authorization is required; (ii) involve discrete, self-contained assignments requiring little 'real-time' interaction with the domestic client or on-site presence; and (iii) consist of standard, repeatable activities that can be performed from checklists, forms, or templates, and are suitable for relatively inexperienced lawyers and paraprofessionals working remotely, without immediate or 'real-time' access to the responsible attorney. Outsourcing to offshore companies in other spheres has been most successful when the work is repetitive and process-driven. Examples might include:

- patent applications (subject to export control requirements);
- basic legal research, such as surveys of relevant laws;

- the preparation and management of large scale filings (for example related to intellectual property portfolios, or routine corporate filings for large groups of related businesses);
- the preparation of draft contracts and related documents;
- the management of large portfolios of agreements, such as licenses or leases;
- monitoring legal developments in many jurisdictions;
- litigation support, including document review, coding, and management;
- documentary due diligence, including the review of large numbers of contracts, filings, and other records, preferably from good checklists and clear instructions; and
- preparing first drafts for pleadings, briefs, and other filings, especially in situations where there are numerous related cases (for example mass torts), although without primary or ultimate responsibility (lest there be avoidable issues concerning unauthorized practice).

This list is illustrative and by no means exhaustive.

14.5.7 Risks—look before you leap

For lawyers engaging offshore support, offshore support services involve significant risks, as the lawyers may be accountable for offshore suppliers' ethical and other lapses. Lawyers, like physicians and other professionals, are target defendants held to high standards who may not anticipate much sympathy from many courts (and in the US, jurors). In serious cases, lawyers and their firms risk substantial liability under negligence, agency, and other legal theories—to say nothing of the risk of professional discipline in the event of ethical infractions by overseas suppliers working under their supervision.

To minimize ethical and other risks, an investigation or due diligence is essential, as for other outsourcing relationships. Many key questions are the same as for other offshore services—for example, concerning infrastructure quality, physical security and electronic security, and disaster recovery planning and testing. Some others are unique to legal work or have distinctive wrinkles, such as:

- *Conflicts.* Does the supplier have effective systems to identify potential conflicts? How are data kept up-to-date and rules enforced? Will they turn down assignments for potential adversaries? Do conflicts or time-keeping systems track assignments to individuals?
- *Management.* Are the supplier's executives and management capable, competent, ethical, and closely engaged in operations? Do they understand (and are they prepared to enforce) the rigorous standards that apply to legal work?

Do they appear more interested in strong relationships than in current revenues or exit strategies? Will they turn down paying work on ethical grounds? Do their supervisors include lawyers licensed to practice in the home country for purposes of supervision, quality control, and ethical compliance? In the event of urgent requirements—for example, to respond to a subpoena—how quickly can they add staff, equipment, and other support? What do their references say? Do they receive repeat business from demanding customers? Who will take charge of the particular engagement, and will he or she remain committed 'for the duration'? Are they well-capitalized? Are they adequately insured, particularly for errors and omissions, by reputable carriers?

- *Legal system and culture.* What are the significant differences in professional training, discipline, and culture? What are local customs and practices concerning conflicts, client confidences, and other matters of professional integrity? In the event of a breach of confidence or security, are effective remedies available within a reasonable time? Are local courts regarded as impartial and honest?
- *Personnel.* Does the offshore company recruit capable, qualified staff? Interviews are always helpful. What are their credentials? What do those credentials mean, and how do they compare with standards in the referring lawyer's country? Do they perform background checks or reference checks? Does training include relevant US, UK, or other laws, ethical standards, and practices? Is training updated periodically? How do they provide engagement-specific training? Have any staff studied or practiced law outside their home countries? Do staff sign strong non-disclosure agreements? What about attrition and turnover (often an issue with offshore services)? Do the staff communicate easily and effectively in English, including the use of professional and other idioms?[14]
- *Practice management.* How do the suppliers manage work flows, timekeeping, and other reporting? How are staff supervised? Is their work reviewed for quality and consistency? Are they willing to undertake 'pilot' or test exercises, to confirm the capabilities of systems and personnel? What are their policies and practices when engagements conclude, or staff leave project teams?

14.5.8 Contracting for offshore services

Contracts for offshore legal support involve many issues common to other contracts for outsourced or managed services, such as objective service

---

[14] Lawyers sending work offshore must be prepared to work across cultures, and become accustomed to accents and idiosyncrasies in English as spoken in India, the Philippines, and elsewhere.

levels, well-defined billing metrics, disaster recovery, and robust security, among others. Some topics that are contentious in other contexts are very straightforward. Charges, as noted, use familiar methods. Clients' information belongs to those clients, so there are few issues concerning intellectual property; but in order to meet professional obligations, some additional refinements are useful, including the following:

- Scope should exclude anything that might require admission to practice.
- Subcontracting should be prohibited, or subject to stringent approval requirements, because of quality and security risks.
- Effective supervision across long distances requires frequent reports and regular conference calls or video conferences (often at inconvenient hours for all concerned). For efficient management, prompt decisions, and the resolution of issues, day-to-day operations are often overseen by project or contract managers empowered to decide most questions.
- Key staff, such as the project manager or any lawyer overseeing the work, should be committed to the project for agreed minimum periods (preferably, the duration of the project). Ideally, the project manager or another supervisor directly engaged in performance should be admitted to practice in the referring lawyer's home country.
- Termination rights must be asymmetrical. Lawyers engaging offshore suppliers should reserve rights to terminate 'for convenience' and for material breach. Offshore suppliers should have no right to terminate unless their bills remain unpaid after notice and a reasonable cure period. Withdrawal as trial approaches, for example, simply cannot be an option. When the contract expires or terminates, the contractor should support orderly disengagement, including transfers of data and knowledge and full cooperation with the corporate client, referring lawyer, and other service providers as required to effect a successful transition.
- Suppliers should be asked to indemnify their clients against potential third party claims for infringement, errors, and omissions, breaches of contracts with third parties, negligence and legal violations, and those indemnities should be backed by substantial net worth and adequate insurance from reputable carriers. Suppliers of legal support services, like suppliers of other outsourced services, may propose to limit their liability by contract. US lawyers generally cannot limit their own liability to clients for professional negligence, so indemnification is all the more important.
- Confidentiality obligations should be rigorous, and include individual non-disclosure agreements, in an approved form, for all staff assigned to the project. When dealing with Indian suppliers, separate non-disclosure

agreements, enforceable by preliminary injunction in India, are recommended. When contracting with the domestic affiliate of an Indian company, it may be wise to require the Indian parent performing services to sign such an agreement with the corporate client or law firm.

- When underlying cases or transactions involve multinational companies, all concerned may have to comply with applicable privacy laws. When large numbers of records are collected and reviewed, chances are high that at least some records contain personal data protected by law in many countries. Where personal data concerns citizens and residents of EU countries, transmission outside the EU (to the US or India, for example) requires an exemption from the usual prohibitions (for example by the adoption of an EU standard model processor agreement).
- Contracts should explicitly require compliance with applicable professional standards and approved policies implementing those standards—excellent security, approved conflicts systems, frequent reporting, oversight by qualified domestic lawyers, good practice management processes, and other similar policies, practices, and procedures along the lines suggested above.
- Compliance with professional standards should be subject to inspection and audit, along with record-keeping and billing. Technical standards should include rigorous electronic security, disaster recovery and testing, regular data backups, the remote storage of data, and regular transmissions of data and work product to a secure domestic facility. Since professional standards may change, the responsible lawyers should require compliance with future changes in law and practice (bearing in mind that there may be costs if, for example, more rigorous security or better infrastructure should be required). Rigorous policies against insider trading are also highly recommended.

A generation ago, many companies relied primarily on outside lawyers and few companies attempted to match the scale or breadth of leading outside firms. All that has changed, and law departments required to do more with less now have a constellation of choices, not only the familiar outside firms and in-house team, but offshore service companies, their own captive offshore operations (or those of their law firms), staff augmentation, contract lawyers, secondments, and the like. One challenge will be to manage all of this successfully—to get value for money and coordinate scattered activities in many time zones, yet assure consistency, quality, and confidentiality, and meet deadlines. The challenge for law departments resembles the challenge their companies face when outsourcing related functions to different contractors—the data center to one company, the network to another, HR administration to someone else, and back-office finance and accounting to yet another contractor. All must collaborate, use the same systems and meet a host of common standards. This is not as easy as many people suppose, and may make project management a core competence for company lawyers overseeing large transactions, controversies, and investigations.

15

OUTSOURCING AMID ECONOMIC UPHEAVAL

This book was conceived, and much of the text was written, before financial markets collapsed late in 2008. As this is written, during the aftermath, no one knows how long the ensuing recession may last or whether it represents something more profound than other post-war swings of the economic pendulum. Barring a return to protectionism and siege economies, or the imposition of punitive taxes, outsourcing seems likely to remain an attractive way for companies to save money—especially companies pressed by business conditions or competitors. As before, outsourcing may be counter-cyclical; but it also seems likely that this sharp, severe, and worldwide experience will have lasting effects on outsourcing and on much else. Regulation, for example, which has tended to mean insistence on good commercial practice, might become more rigorous and intrusive, particularly around such sensitive issues as privacy or in such industries as financial services, where the market collapse may lead to more stringent regulations. This concluding chapter will consider possible repercussions, as they affect new and existing relationships in light of recent, often painful, experience.

15.1 DEAL-MAKING

Hard times have, if anything, increased pressures for speed and efficiency, while compounding companies' frustration with selection and negotiation processes that, as they see it, take too long, cost too much, and produce unwieldy contracts that are as difficult to administer as they are to read. Fewer companies have the time, patience, or budget for the consultants' and lawyers' meticulous and time-consuming ways. Haste has its own hazards; so does the haphazard use of form documents intended for other purposes. Complex documents and procedures may contribute to an unfortunate tendency toward micromanagement by contract. How then can lawyers meet client demands and still protect their clients' interests? Several practical steps come to mind:

- Strive for brevity, simplicity, and clarity in the process and documents. Often, basic, relatively simple provisions will suffice. Where savings come from labor arbitrage, simple time and materials or FTE charges (whatever their limitations) may assure significant savings without administrative complexity. Simpler selection processes can save time and accelerate potential benefits. Simpler contract documents take less time to negotiate, and less effort to comprehend and administer. Willingness to set aside familiar forms, methods, and processes and start afresh from a clean sheet of paper can focus attention on essentials and yield creative solutions.
- Eschew extremes. In contract negotiations, taking reasonable positions can save time, aggravation, and expense.
- Concentrate on the issues that matter most. Attention to detail matters, but usually only a few issues will make or break the relationship: scope, charges, changes, service levels, remedies, compliance, employment and a few others, depending upon the circumstances.
- Not every contingency can be imagined, let alone provided for in advance. What goes wrong rarely occurs quite as expected, and may be completely unforeseen. So rather than attempt to write detailed provisions for all imaginable possibilities, build sound procedures for governance, escalation of disputed issues through senior management, and management of unanticipated, especially unwelcome, changes. Allocate risks and rewards so that when trouble arises, the relationship is worth preserving and destructive, purely self-serving measures have consequences.
- Collaboration between customer and supplier, and especially between their lawyers, during negotiations can help to solve knotty compliance problems by balancing risks equitably and assigning responsibility to the party best equipped to manage particular risks. Usually, one side or the other has done this before and avoided serious trouble. In difficult times, when both customers and suppliers face financial and other challenges, both sides' appetite and tolerance for risk may be less than before.
- Lawyers and consultants serve their clients, and must take instructions. Clear, consistent direction from executives on both sides to collaborate, get things

done, keep them as simple as reasonably possible, focus upon essentials, and play fair can help to prevent some of the posturing, positioning, and quibbling that too often infect (and prolong) negotiations. Leadership means setting the right tone from the outset, then following through.

15.2 EXISTING CONTRACTS—CUSTOMER PERSPECTIVES

Outsourcing contracts often languish unread in drawers or on shelves. Tough times prompt customers to dust off binders and read their contracts with fresh eyes. Some provisions long overlooked, or even forgotten, may be useful (although there is some risk that neglected rights have been inadvertently waived).

15.2.1 Business terms

Outsourcing is supposed to save money, especially when times are hard and pressures to cut costs and conserve cash are severe. Saving money involves much more than rates and charges. Scope, performance standards, payment terms, and a variety of other provisions may be equally important.

Ideally, invoices for outsourced functions should allocate charges among services, locations, and business units, and serve as management tools that permit attentive, informed customers to manage consumption and thus costs. Too often, reality falls short of this ideal. Invoices confuse rather than inform. Customers are unsure of usage and charges, pending time-consuming adjustments or reconciliation. There may be many reasons for this state of affairs, including poor planning, mismatches between client needs and supplier tools, and fitful customer attention, among others. Prompt, detailed, accurate invoices permit customers to allocate costs to users based upon actual usage, and so motivate efficiency. Costs formerly buried in customer overheads become real when billed every month and passed through to users. Many contracts already require invoices in sufficient detail to satisfy customers' chargeback and other requirements. Those that do not, should. Meeting these requirements (where they exist) or introducing them (where they do not) can be an excellent way to reduce costs through good management without reducing rates or unduly squeezing supplier margins.

Many contracts permit the customer to engage an outside firm to compare contract pricing and service levels with current market standards.[1] If charges exceed current market rates, charges may have to be reduced or the customer may enjoy other rights (such as a right to terminate benchmarked services for a

---

[1] See 6.6.2 above.

reduced termination charge). Benchmarking takes time, and can be both expensive and contentious. However, the mere existence of the right to benchmark charges may provide leverage, especially when coupled with some preliminary market data and, for that matter, the supplier's own knowledge of its markets. Suppliers regard benchmarking as something best avoided. Preliminary market data from a reputable outside firm, obtained without the time and expense of a full-blown benchmark, can be a good way for customers to start a conversation about price—although they should bear in mind suppliers' legitimate concerns about benchmarking and the limitations of the analysts' methods and data. When customers seek price concessions, they are more likely to make headway when they are open to changes in the supplier's delivery methods and service commitments that accommodate reductions in the supplier's costs.

Charges are not, of course, the whole story. Usually they are supposed to be all-inclusive, but reality may not be so neat and tidy. A customer may carry on paying for products, services, or support that are no longer needed, or properly within the supplier's responsibility. The comparison of actual expenditure with contract requirements may reveal some costs that can be transferred or cut.

Few expenses are less welcome than taxes. In some places, outsourced services are subject to sales, use, or value added taxes. Usually, those taxes are passed through to the customer, but even when suppliers absorb them, taxes add to the supplier's costs and affect price indirectly. Opportunities may exist to reduce tax costs legitimately, through good planning. For example, when some kinds of service are performed locally in many countries, local invoicing and payment for services may permit the customer to recover value added tax paid for local service.

Finally, many contracts contain provisions for gain-sharing. Most are long on generalities, but short on specifics—endorsing the principle but without specific commitments. Lean times, when customers press for concessions, may be an ideal time to motivate suppliers to seek efficiencies through incentive payments from actual savings achieved. Payments from 'found money' still mean net savings to the customer, while aligning the parties' interests.

15.2.2 Service and delivery

Many contracts contain so-called 'sweep' (or 'dragnet') clauses obliging the supplier to deliver more than the literal requirements of the service description, such as related, incidental, or inherent services, services formerly performed by the customer or covered by financial models disclosed to the supplier before signing. The fine print may contain exceptions and limitations. If years have passed without mention of related services formerly performed, the customer may have waived its rights. Still, comparisons or gap analyses may reveal additional services that might be covered by base charges.

Ten or fifteen years ago, many outsourcing contracts were exclusive. Many incumbents still enjoy a practical monopoly, but most contracts allow the customer to engage other suppliers or perform services itself, if it is so inclined (subject sometimes to minimum volume or revenue commitments). If a supplier's service leaves something to be desired, or costs more than it should, the customer may have alternatives. Mere mention of those alternatives is sure to get the incumbent supplier's attention, and for its part, the supplier may be perfectly prepared to shed responsibility for services that are less profitable than anticipated or otherwise problematic.

15.2.3 Service levels

In negotiations, few topics arouse more interest (or angst) than service levels. In practice, service levels are usually achieved and credits for failures are rarely paid (even, somewhat surprisingly, when they might be assessed). Many contracts call for a joint review of service levels at regular intervals and 'continuous improvement,' which may mean either specific commitments or general obligations that are subject to interpretation or negotiation. In practice, these provisions are often neglected or forgotten. When more savings are needed, it may be time for both a fresh look and some idiosyncratic thinking. Customers seek outstanding, indeed ever-increasing quality, but quality costs money. In hard times, stringent standards may be luxuries. Customers who review service levels may usefully ask questions like the following:

- If service levels were eased, could charges be reduced? Not everyone really needs gold-plated service. Ninety-nine per cent, twenty-four hours a day sounds impressive, but customers who do the arithmetic may find that they do not actually need a particular system for 42,768 minutes a month.[2] Fewer may suffice. On the other hand, easing service levels or other standards related to security, legal compliance, or audits may be hazardous, because of the risk to corporate reputations, brand images, and share prices.
- Does everything now measured and reported need to be measured and reported? If not, and assorted tools and reports are no longer required, what could be saved?
- If existing service suffices, are 'continuous improvements' needed? If not, what could be saved?

---

[2]   24 hours × 60 minutes × 30 days × 99% = 42,768 minutes.

- Might any upgrades or investments be deferred, without serious risks to reliability or performance, or would deferral be a false economy, leading to future trouble and expense?

15.2.4 Relocation and operational changes

Suppliers have become a migratory species, seeking lower costs in faraway places. Many contracts permit suppliers to relocate, but there may be conditions, such as uninterrupted service, maintenance of service levels, commitments to absorb any related costs (such as additional telecommunications charges), and, often, prior customer approval. Sometimes, the customer may condition that approval on an adjustment of charges so that both sides share anticipated savings. Even when there are no contractual approval rights, challenging times may be an ideal occasion to explore offshore opportunities, such as additional savings from relocation to cheaper locations or increasing the portion of service performed offshore.

Apart from relocation, restructuring outsourced solutions may offer opportunities for savings. For example, sharing services with other customers is usually cheaper than staff or facilities dedicated to one customer. Junior staff may replace some experienced staff without sacrificing quality. A fresh look at contract requirements may reveal specific obligations that add costs without corresponding benefits.

15.2.5 Errors and corrective work

Even the best suppliers make mistakes. Contracts often provide that there is no charge for corrective work. Billing software, however, may not have been switched off. Timekeepers' records may or may not deduct corrective work. When services include any significant rework or other corrective effort, the attentive customer may want to confirm that charges have been excluded or (if paid in error) refunded. If necessary, audit rights may be invoked.

15.2.6 Mergers, acquisitions, and divestitures

In changing times, many companies realign, reorganize, merge, or sell business units—urged on, occasionally, by creditors, regulators, central banks, or governments. When those companies have outsourced major functions, several contract provisions may come into play, including:

- Adjustments of charges based upon swings in consumption. When those swings exceed the thresholds originally priced, the contract may provide for an 'equitable adjustment' based upon changes in cost or resources, including one-off outlays or savings.[3]

- Provisions for service to newly-acquired or recently-divested business units, generally on existing contract terms (although there may be an obligation to pay the supplier for one-time transitional costs and efforts).

When businesses are combined, customers may enjoy an opportunity to re-negotiate with suppliers, assuring them larger volumes in exchange for price and other concessions and optimizing terms to suit new conditions and support the combined business.

15.2.7 Inputs

Customers often provide their suppliers with office space, equipment, or other resources. They do so without charge, lest the supplier build rent and other costs into its charges, then add overheads and margin. Customers can sometimes save money by consolidating operations, moving the supplier to cheaper quarters, or relocating away from expensive national capitals or coastal cities.

Many outsourced services involve numerous third party contracts: equipment leases, software licenses, hardware and software maintenance agreements, service contracts, and others. Some of those contracts may be assigned to the supplier; others remain the customer's responsibility but are managed by the supplier (who calls for support, orders spares, and approves or rejects orders). These contracts may present opportunities for savings through re-negotiation, consolidation, and other measures. In challenging times, such arrangements deserve the same scrutiny as the main outsourcing contract. Savings achieved may be shared, providing an incentive for the supplier and a potential reward to offset reductions in rates or consumption.

Software is a major expense. Some software costs are built into the supplier's charges. Others may be retained by the customer. Savings can be achieved by, among other things, consolidation, deferring upgrades, or even by replacing commercial products with inexpensive 'open source' software. Commercial support is available for many open source applications, but the potential legal effects of 'viral' open source licenses must be carefully considered. Open source software is not copyright-free, but licensed under unusual

---

[3] See 6.5.3 above. Equitable adjustment (or 'extraordinary event') clauses provide a framework for negotiation, rather than a precise method or formula for calculating changes, and so leave something to be desired and would profit from some creative thinking in the years ahead.

public licenses that include source code and throw open programs in which open source code may be embedded.

Many contracts oblige the supplier to use up-to-date hardware and software. Software is supposed to be current; equipment may have to be replaced (or 'refreshed') at regular intervals of three years or less—even if it is working normally and in excellent condition. There are, of course, good reasons for these commitments, but in difficult times, deferring replacements may save money, in much the same way that motorists save money by keeping well-maintained, serviceable cars.

With most services, people are the largest single cost. Suppliers properly enjoy considerable latitude in staffing. However, many contracts include provisions that: (i) specify qualifications and credentials; (ii) require that certain work be performed onshore or even on-site; or (iii) permit the customer to approve overall staffing levels. Savings may be achieved by delegating routine work to junior personnel (properly supervised), moving additional work offshore or reducing overall staffing (often with some corresponding reduction in service levels or other obligations).

Legal compliance has received ample attention recently on account of such issues as privacy, identity theft, data protection, and breaches of security. Regular attention to this rapidly-changing area of the law is a best practice, but attention to regulatory compliance often focuses on compliance alone, rather than related cost considerations. For many companies, the concern is not simply to avoid violations, but to develop and adhere to standard practices that meet legal requirements and do so without excessive costs. To the extent possible, well-advised business people look for 'common denominators'—practical solutions that meet relevant standards in most (if not all) relevant jurisdictions at reasonable cost. In this sphere, as in others, the parties should be alert for possible duplication of effort that might be eliminated.

Record retention policies raise complex questions. They must satisfy auditors and lawyers, as well as management, for whom records are part of institutional memory. Laws written before the digital age may require the retention of paper originals for long periods, or at the company's headquarters, or both. When companies outsource, they often pay large sums to preserve tons of paper, miles of tape, and acres of disc storage. Not all of this is necessarily required by law or even desirable as corporate policy. When reviewing an outsourcing contract with an eye for potential savings, storage charges are an obvious candidate for scrutiny, especially in organizations that appear to save enormous volumes of data more or less indefinitely. For suppliers of IT services, digitized record systems can be opportunities for substantial, profitable projects that save customers money in the long run while rationalizing scattered and jumbled paper records.

Close reading of an existing contract may identify opportunities for further savings—opportunities that customers will want to consider and perhaps pursue—but two risks should be considered.

- First, rights may have been lost through neglect, inattention, or lapse of time under various legal doctrines. Where different interpretations of contract requirements are possible, long acquiescence in the other side's interpretation may waive any right to object later on, urge a more stringent interpretation, or insist upon strict compliance. Informal understandings may, even unwittingly, amend contract terms.
- Second, two can play at the strict interpretation of contracts. Suppliers may invoke provisions that serve their interests or perform in a literal-minded manner that adheres to the letter of contract requirements, and charges more or issues change requests for everything else.

Outsourcing is, among other things, an exercise in collaboration. In difficult times, supplier and customer alike face financial and other challenges. Often, the best course may be first to review the agreement, financial results, operations, and business relationship, and then engage in a joint review of the relationship as a whole through a process of mutual accommodation. Suppliers have their own interests and agendas, and will be most receptive to requests for reductions in charges when corresponding adjustments in scope, service levels, or operations permit reductions in their costs or they are offered new opportunities through extensions of time or scope—opportunities they can earn with flexibility and good performance.

15.3 EXISTING CONTRACTS—SUPPLIER PERSPECTIVES

Suppliers are not passive participants. They too have businesses to run and face financial pressures in difficult times. Customers squeezed by recession have obvious concerns, but suppliers have concerns of their own, including their own cost reduction campaigns as well as their customers' financial condition and the hazards of bankruptcy proceedings. If asked for concessions, suppliers will expect accommodations in return, such as:

- An extension of the contract, especially if only a year or two remain. In return for concessions, suppliers may want a firm, ongoing commitment from the customer. Changes in delivery models, relocation, and other measures take time, cost money, and require management attention. Suppliers will seek something in return, including an opportunity for a return on their investment.

- Changes to reduce costs of performance (for example through the standard-ization of services, consolidation, or relocation of operations, or reductions in service levels). Price is not an independent variable. If the supplier receives substandard margins or loses money, price concessions may be unobtainable without major changes in scope, performance standards, and operations.[4]

- Accelerated payment terms, such as billing in advance against estimates, with payment on the 15th or 30th of the month and later reconciliation against actual consumption, rather than billing in arrears for payment in thirty, forty-five, or sixty days. For the supplier's finance department, this may be the indis-pensable *quid pro quo* when customers plead financial strain or concern exists about the customer's financial condition.

- Expansion to new regions, business units, or kinds of service or, conversely, the withdrawal of marginally profitable or unprofitable services.

- The amendment of contract terms that have, for one reason or another, adversely affected performance or profitability or, from the supplier's stand-point, present unusual risks. Suppliers' willingness to take risks has receded, and they may wish to revisit liability limits, indemnities, and other exposure (for example concerning privacy claims and identity theft). Some suppliers' preferred positions on these issues are more conservative today than they were only a few years ago.

- The resolution of any disputed charges, change requests, or other outstanding financial or operational issues. Usually, there are at least a few open or dis-puted issues. Suppliers asked to cut charges will seek a favorable resolution of those issues, including releases from claims and liability.

No two situations are the same, but when customers seek savings amid economic stress, and suppliers attempt to protect relationships, margins, and volumes of business, resolutions may involve some combination of elements from each party's 'shopping list' that reduce risks, together with both the supplier's cost to perform and charges to the customer, such as the following:

- reductions in rates (including unit rates and the incremental charges or credits for changes in consumption);

- the reduction of corresponding service levels and other performance require-ments, in order to reduce the supplier's costs and preserve acceptable mar-gins, while cutting the customer's charges;

---

[4] Anecdotal evidence suggests that some suppliers have responded to the recession by trimming deliv-ery staffs. This may indicate margin pressures and, if carried too far, staff cuts may affect service quality.

- the transfer of more delivery offshore or to lower cost locations;
- the replacement of dedicated facilities and staff with shared services or experienced, relatively expensive staff with lower cost, less experienced personnel for routine services;
- the replacement of 'continuous improvement' commitments with opportunities to reduce cost;
- the elimination of unprofitable or marginally profitable services through operational changes or reductions in scope;
- the extension of contract terms or, occasionally, contract scope in order to preserve the relationship's value to the supplier, build backlogs, and offset financial concessions;
- provisions for more rapid payment (customers asked to pay more quickly may seek discounts for early payment); and
- tighter limits on unusual or exceptional liabilities, such as privacy claims, which have the suppliers' attention and the parties can manage to some extent through security improvements.

We live in interesting times—as the phrase was used in the famous Chinese curse, 'may you live in interesting times'—but interesting times create opportunities to strengthen relationships, improve performance, and save money.

15.4 THE FAILING SUPPLIER

Amid other disconcerting news came the collapse of Satyam, a leading Indian supplier of outsourced services, amid admissions of executive malfeasance. This appeared at first to be every customer's worst nightmare—an outsourcing supplier disgraced by scandal, like Enron, WorldCom, or any number of other once reputable names. There were fears that the episode might tarnish the reputation of outsourcing generally, and especially outsourcing to India. India's government stepped in promptly to replace management and directors, who soon sold the business without, it would appear, lasting adverse consequences for customers or for the industry as a whole. Nonetheless, the experience has given observers, customers, and potential customers pause to reflect. What lessons can be learned?

The industry appears to have acted responsibly, recognizing the risk to outsourcing generally, in somewhat the same way that banks avoid comment about failing competitors because of the overriding need to maintain public confidence. Competing suppliers have surely pursued opportunities with worried Satyam customers, but without grandstanding or taking public advantage of Satyam's troubles. Conspicuous by its absence has been any advertising or whispered commentary about risks peculiar to Indian companies or India (where the Indian companies' Western competitors also have major operations). Predatory behavior that might discredit outsourcing generally seems to have been avoided. Satyam's difficulties concerned executive integrity—a potential risk in all businesses, rather than anything unique to offshore outsourcing or, for that matter, India.

Looking forward, customers are likely to give greater consideration to the perceived or potential risks of doing business with lesser-known offshore companies and other newcomers. Prudence begins with a thorough investigation of the potential supplier's management, capabilities, experience, reputation, financial condition, and the rest. There are no known substitutes for executive interaction, site visits, interviews, reference checks, and other diligence, even though these steps cannot be guaranteed to spot all potential troubles. Nonetheless, the effort must be made, and should include an assessment of the prospective supplier's professionalism, organization, and integrity. Integrity is all.[5] Serious troubles may lurk behind a façade of respectability, apparent success, and outward bonhomie. Just ask anyone who invested with Bernie Madoff. How then can a customer protect itself against the risk—remote but not non-existent—that a supplier of critical services might implode?

Many customers now seek financial covenants, of the kind common in loan agreements, that would permit a customer to terminate the contract if the supplier's financial condition or credit rating deteriorates. Having seen the headlines about Satyam, and other dire corporate news, customers and their advisors want robust protection against corporate calamities that could jeopardize the customer's own operations. They fear being left in the rubble after an implosion, and effectively without any recourse because defunct companies can neither honor indemnities nor pay judgments.

Suppliers resist these requests. As they see it, good contracts already provide ample remedies for actual performance issues. Suppliers are rarely willing to put major contracts at risk simply because analysts' assessments erode after a tough quarter or year. Some leading suppliers have carried on without material effects on service to customers, despite troubled contracts, management changes, slender or non-existent margins, and failures to meet anticipated earnings. Indeed, anecdotal evidence suggests that some Satyam customers received better

---

[5] In December 1912, when called before a congressional committee, JP Morgan was asked whether commercial credit was based primarily upon money or property. 'No, sir,' came the classic reply, 'the first thing is character . . . Before money or property or anything else. Money cannot buy it . . . because a man I do not trust could not get money from me on all the bonds in Christendom.' Quoted in J Strouse, *Morgan: American Financier* (New York: Random House, 1999) 13.

service after the company's troubles erupted, in part because employees understood that their livelihoods were at risk. For the supplier, agreeing that customers may walk away on account of soft earnings or analysts' ratings may risk transforming difficulty into disaster if a poor earnings report or less favorable rating could trigger widespread contract terminations. For this reason above all, most suppliers have been unwilling to agree to the kinds of financial covenants that many customers now request. If and when the supplier's financial condition affects performance, they contend, customers have their remedies. Where this issue will come to rest in the marketplace remains to be seen, although this writer expects that the better established suppliers will rarely, if ever, agree to the sorts of covenants and termination rights that some of their newer and lesser-known competitors might reluctantly accept.[6]

Financial covenants require disclosures, but suppliers whose shares are publicly traded cannot offer more information to customers than they disclose to the public. Privately-held suppliers may be more forthcoming. Whether the supplier is public or private, occasional executive level consultations between senior management may be opportunities to seek and receive some comfort about the supplier's stability and prospects (although not any non-public information about a public company).

When suppliers implode, or seem poised to do so, customers ask whether they can terminate the contract. The usual answer is the proverbial lawyer's answer: 'perhaps.' Termination, if feasible, is a drastic, disruptive, and expensive remedy, especially if the troubled supplier is unable to support an orderly transition. Scandal alone may not necessarily provide a basis for termination. Customers may terminate contracts for material breach, but venality in executive suites may not affect routine delivery of service. Customary provisions for termination on insolvency are essentially useless. Once proceedings commence, everything is drawn into the maw of bankruptcy, where the exercise of contract rights may require court approval, creditors' consent, and time. Under US law, bankruptcy filings trigger an automatic stay so that termination rights become unenforceable.

Where contracts explicitly require compliance with laws, and the supplier's difficulties involve serious violations of law, the customer may have grounds to terminate for breach; but covenants to comply with law are often tied to performance (for example 'comply with laws applicable to the performance

---

[6] For essentially similar reasons, customers rarely welcome supplier requests for financial covenants, or rights to terminate in the event of a 'material, adverse change' in the customer's financial condition or credit rating. Requests for financial covenants and related termination rights by one side may prompt requests for reciprocity, so this is not an issue to be raised casually. In the event of default termination by the supplier for non-payment, contracts commonly permit suppliers to require prepayment or other security for further performance, including support for disengagement.

of services'). Accounting improprieties like those that felled Satyam may not breach such narrowly-drawn commitments. Customers may now seek broader commitments, including assurances regarding compliance with securities and other laws of general application, but suppliers are unlikely to embrace provisions that amount to 'termination upon impropriety.' The topic is awkward to raise ('suppose your management is led away in handcuffs?') and improprieties, when they occur, may be isolated affairs that do not affect the health of the business, let alone the unfortunate supplier's survival. Many reputable, successful companies have survived scandals and continued to perform for their customers.

Changes in control may sometimes offer customers a way out, if the contract permits termination after a change in control of the supplier's business. If changes of control are defined broadly to include replacements in senior management or the boardroom as well as majority ownership or voting control of the board, the customer may be able to act sooner rather than later. In Satyam's case, new board members appeared almost immediately after trouble erupted, but several months passed before a sale could be completed.

For customers concerned about these risks, some of the best protections take the form of good contingency planning, including the following:

- The retention of sufficient operational knowledge within the customer's organization so that, if need be, the company may rebuild internal operations or successfully engage another supplier.
- Spreading outsourced operations (even within functional areas) among two or more suppliers so that, if one fails, operations may shift more easily to another company with whom the customer already has a contract and working relationship. Managing two suppliers and splitting related operations may mean some costs and inefficiencies, but all forms of insurance require premiums.
- Retaining critical software and data and requiring frequent transmission of work product to the customer so that, if troubles erupt, the customer has possession, data cannot be held hostage to events, and security is less likely to be compromised, exposing the customer to security breach and other liabilities. Contracts should, and often do, provide for the immediate return of all data at the customer's request—a useful prerogative in the event of all manner of difficulties. For similar reasons, it may be wise for the customer to retain ownership, control, and possession of critical equipment and other tangible assets that might otherwise become part of the bankruptcy estate, subject to court jurisdiction and the claims of other creditors.
- Making provision for rapid disengagement, at the customer's option, in the event of contract termination. Typical termination assistance arrangements contemplate a comparatively leisurely transition, spread over months.

In the ordinary course of business that is the prudent approach, as it allows time for thorough planning, knowledge transfer, rehearsals, and tests; but if the supplier is in genuine distress there may not be time before operations unravel and knowledgeable staff take to the lifeboats. A faster contingency plan—almost akin to a disaster recovery plan—may be useful in urgent cases, especially if acting quickly permits the customer or a successor supplier to hire staff who have supported the customer. Even when suppliers are willing (and many offshore companies resist any provision for recruitment of their staff), there may be legal complexities, including employment laws and, for onshore staff of offshore companies, visa requirements. In the US, many onshore staff hold visas tied to their original employer and cannot easily go to work for another employer, at least not without fresh applications.

15.5 INSOLVENCY—DOOMSDAY?

Each side regards the other's bankruptcy with dread, and not without reason. Contracts may be swept up in an unpredictable, protracted legal process, where usual contract remedies are either unavailable or usable only with the permission of courts concerned to achieve rough justice among competing claims on an estate that is, by definition, insufficient to satisfy all creditors. Ideally, these risks may be minimized or avoided by a thorough, clear-eyed investigation and assessment before the contract is signed and vigilance thereafter, including regular reviews of the other party's financial statements.[7] Suppliers are rightfully cautious about troubled companies, however impressive the management or turn-around plan. Customers should look past the new supplier's innovative solution, attractive terms, and marketing skills to ask hard questions about the supplier's management, capitalization, and staying power. Bankruptcy cases, like so many legal proceedings, tend to be exercises in damage control.

Bankruptcy, like employment, intellectual property, taxation, and a number of other legal disciplines, is the preserve of specialists. When insolvency risks are serious, or proceedings seem likely, there is no substitute for specialist advice. What follows is a very general introduction, based on US law. Laws and procedures vary worldwide. When operations and facilities are scattered, legal issues may be an order of magnitude more complex.

---

[7] If the other party's shares are publicly traded, financial information will be limited to public disclosures. Privately held suppliers or customers often request and provide annual or quarterly financial information.

Under the US Bankruptcy Code, service contracts are 'executory contracts'—incomplete or ongoing agreements—that the debtor (or its trustee in bankruptcy) may accept or reject in their entirety. The election is an 'all-or-nothing' proposition, meant to allow the debtor to shed burdensome contracts. The debtor cannot, however, 'pick cherries,' taking some benefits and obligations, but not others, from a particular contract. Assumption or rejection requires court approval, and if the debtor chooses to accept, it must cure any outstanding defaults. Only after court approval and cure can the debtor assign the contract (for example in connection with a sale of the business). The debtor need not accept or reject the contract until final confirmation of the plan of reorganization—a process that can take years.

Until the contract is either assumed or rejected with Bankruptcy Court approval, both parties' obligations to perform may be suspended. During the so-called 'limbo period' before acceptance or rejection, the Bankruptcy Court may compel performance and use the contract terms as a measure of the reasonable terms on which services should be performed during the bankruptcy proceeding. In this way, bankrupt US airlines, have continued to operate—paying for fuel, salaries, and outsourced IT and reservation services—while operating under bankruptcy protection. The supplier must stand ready to perform, and any rights to terminate on insolvency are unenforceable. If the bankrupt customer defaults, the supplier cannot terminate without court permission; and withdrawing service without court approval may expose the supplier to liability for damage to the debtor's properties and rights. If the customer rejects the contract, it is not clear to what extent a supplier could be compelled to provide termination assistance services, although one may expect the Bankruptcy Court in its discretion to require some basic support sufficient to prevent catastrophic interruption or disruption of the customer's operations (and a reputable supplier might not, in any event, want its good name associated with any such calamity, whatever the circumstances). The Bankruptcy Court has wide discretion to determine what services should be performed, and on what terms. Here again, the contract terms may provide a useful point of reference. Alongside bankruptcy proceedings, there may be efforts to re-negotiate the contract on a basis appropriate for the reorganized company's needs after conclusion of the bankruptcy case.

If the supplier, rather than the customer, seeks bankruptcy protection, the analysis is inverted, but essentially similar. The bankrupt supplier could accept or reject existing contracts, and so enjoy theoretical termination rights it might not possess outside bankruptcy (where contractual termination rights are often limited to non-payment and a limited number of extreme situations). However, since customer contracts are among a service company's principal assets, one may wonder whether a supplier in bankruptcy would jeopardize its remaining value (to say nothing of its reputation) by rejecting many customer contracts (other than those that are hopelessly unprofitable). Customers otherwise inclined to terminate would find themselves stymied by the bankruptcy code's automatic stay, although convenience termination charges might provide incentives for bankrupt suppliers (and their creditors) to cooperate in seeking approval for a negotiated or convenience termination that would inject additional cash into the bankruptcy estate. The bankrupt supplier's practical concern would be to reassure customers and the marketplace of its reliability and continuing ability to perform at a time when competitors may be only too willing to step in.

For the customer, supplier bankruptcy is an ugly contingency. When risks appear serious, the customer may obtain some protection through financial disclosures and covenants (described above) as well as ownership of equipment, data, and other intangibles, so that these do not become assets of the bankruptcy estate and, so far as possible, are either in the customer's possession or subject to seizure. Service credits and set-offs should be withheld from payment or paid into escrow, so that funds are not poured into the bankruptcy trough for the benefit of other creditors.

15.6 POLICIES, POLITICS, AND REGULATION

Outsourcing offshore—or as some say, 'exporting jobs'—became an issue during the US Presidential election in 2004. Legislative proposals flew like confetti. Dozens of bills were introduced in Congress (and many more in state legislatures) but few became law. Four years later, few candidates had anything good to say about outsourcing, but the political focus had shifted to trade generally, the North American Free Trade Agreement, the financial collapse, and other issues. The Obama administration has taken a full legislative program to Capitol Hill, and serious proposals to curtail outsourcing are nowhere in sight. Outsourcing's critics in organized labor appear to have other priorities, at least for the time being.

However, policy trends are notoriously difficult to predict. Even one week is a long time in politics.[8] Unexpected events can steer policy in new directions. More stringent regulation of financial services seems inevitable after the markets' collapse during 2008. What form new regulatory arrangements may take remains to be seen. As this concluding chapter is written (midway through 2009),

---

[8] Saying attributed to British Prime Minister Harold Wilson (1916–95) ('a week is a long time in politics').

it is certainly possible that regulatory agencies in the US and elsewhere may impose tighter reins on outsourced operations. Tax changes might trim anticipated savings from offshore outsourcing. Privacy legislation might restrict offshore transfers of personal data, make such transfers more costly, impose consent or reporting requirements, or increase potential liabilities. Notice and other requirements concerning displaced workers may become more extensive and rigorous. These speculations by no means exhaust the possibilities for restriction or scrutiny. On the other hand, the risk of drastic restrictions upon outsourcing, and even offshore outsourcing, seems comparatively modest. Behind the sound bites about outsourcing, exporting jobs, and globalization, many in public service, including elected officials, understand perfectly well that outsourcing helps domestic companies to compete and has modest effects on overall levels of employment. The economics of comparative advantage among nations is widely understood, if not often publicly acknowledged. Leading outsourcers include such US companies as Accenture, Hewlett-Packard, and IBM, which operate worldwide; and no US administration will lightly undermine one of the marquee industries of democratic India—increasingly seen as a US ally and partner. Faced with these imponderables, what should business people do?

First, they should pay attention and either directly or through their trade associations, watch the progress of whatever proposals emerge and, when appropriate, engage in the debate and legislative advocacy. The fine print matters, and bills ultimately passed are often milder than the sponsors' initial press releases.

Second, when negotiating, reviewing, or renewing contracts, they should pay attention to contract provisions that might be affected by shifts in public policy in the US and elsewhere, such as:

- change management, including the pricing of changes to meet new circumstances;
- compliance with laws and, in particular, the costs of effecting changes to meet regulatory requirements or perform under more stringent regulations;
- taxation, including future changes in taxation and, in extreme cases, possible termination rights if tax changes make outsourcing unattractive or uneconomic;
- provisions for the equitable adjustment of charges, relocation of operations, or (in extreme cases) termination if outsourced or offshore operations become unlawful or uneconomic;
- rights to subcontract or relocate outsourced operations (suppliers seek flexibility to save money, where customers want to share savings and preserve control); and

- *force majeure* clauses that excuse performance on account of various circumstances beyond the parties' control, often including some kinds of official action. If declarations of war or national emergency, embargoes, or quarantines excuse performance, what about protectionist legislation?

Fundamentally, these contingencies reflect a basic dilemma in outsourcing contracts and relationships. The contracts themselves, once written, are relatively stable, even static; but change is continual—in business conditions, technologies, customer requirements, both parties' businesses, and the political, legal, and regulatory environment in which they operate. There is no formula or recipe, and there are no known substitutes for prudence, good judgment, attention to detail, or a sense of fair play. Making these deals and making them work is not easy, but it is interesting and in keeping with these interesting times.

APPENDICES
CONTENTS

INTRODUCTION—FORMS

This is not a form book, but includes sample forms to supplement the text. They should not be thoughtlessly cut and pasted as 'boilerplate' or 'standard' language suitable for all occasions. Quite the contrary. They are meant to inform and illustrate, but they are not substitutes for legal or other professional advice. Nor do they provide a complete set of contract documents for any transaction.

All forms were written to comply with California and US federal law in effect during 2009. Commercial and contract law principles are similar throughout the US (apart from Louisiana, with its French heritage) and in other common law countries, but there are significant differences in substantive law. Some provisions enforceable in the author's native California or the US may be inadvisable or invalid elsewhere. Even in the US, the enforceability of particular provisions may depend upon a variety of circumstances and the application of various statutes and legal principles.

Apart from such legal questions as enforceability and variations in custom and terminology among common law countries, each form contains many provisions that may be heavily negotiated and must be tailored to particular situations, especially client goals and priorities. Although there are common themes in most outsourcing relationships, there are (as Chapter 14 explains) important differences among industries and the varieties of outsourced services.

The forms are moderately customer-oriented, but not overwhelmingly so, consistent with the belief that reasonably balanced contracts yield better results. However, there are few absolutes, and in particular situations different terms, or combinations of terms, might be advisable for any number of reasons. Many lawyers and clients will prefer different, more or less stringent or elaborate provisions, at least for some critical issues.

To minimize bulk, the forms included are relatively short. The contract form in particular is much shorter than many commonly used in large transactions, but sufficiently detailed to illustrate essentials. For large transactions, longer documents often merit the additional time, trouble, and expense. Shorter documents provide basic protections in fewer words; but these are matters of judgment that vary to some extent according to tastes and circumstances, including time and budgetary constraints, the scale of particular transactions, and the parties' tolerance for risk. At the time of writing, the market seems increasingly to prefer shorter, simpler documents in order to expedite negotiations and save money.

Finally, none of the forms—and for that matter, none of the commentary anywhere in the book—necessarily represents the opinion of the author's firm or clients. Legal and contract interpretations, suggested courses of action, contract language, and other matters of professional judgment may vary depending upon client preferences and interests, the functions outsourced, the customer's industry, the parties' bargaining leverage, and other circumstances.

The following forms are included:

- *Term Sheet.* This form, designed for inclusion in a Request for Proposals, contains basic terms for an IT services contract, but can easily be adapted for other outsourced services. Some will prefer more detailed terms, or invite suppliers to comment upon and mark up a complete contract, rather than complete a term sheet. Greater detail reduces the room for quibbling during contract negotiations, but also reduces the customer's flexibility, while increasing the time consumed by contract terms during preliminary discussions before selection of a supplier, when scarce time might be better allocated to price, performance standards, solution, transition, and other business and operational issues.
- *Letter of Intent.* This short form letter of intent confirms the parties' agreement to negotiate based upon the supplier's proposal and term sheet responses, as supplemented at the negotiating table. Only a handful of provisions concerning costs and confidentiality are enforceable, but preliminary terms, once agreed in a letter of intent signed by senior executives, tend to be settled and cannot easily be disavowed. Letters of intent without specific commitments usually have little value from the customer's standpoint.
- *Master Service Agreement.* The short form included is for IT services, but easily adapted for use with business process services, with attention to specific requirements and the business context. For larger transactions, much longer contracts are often used, but this form illustrates most essentials (but without provisions for asset transfers and local or companion agreements to support global operations).[1]
- *Service Description (or Statement of Work).* Two templates are included. One is for IT infrastructure services, and the other (though written for business process services) could be adapted for a variety of different IT or business process services. Both are limited to the introductory language that lawyers provide, without matrices, lists, or detailed descriptions of any service. The text merely provides an overview of the service, its basic scope, limitations, and goals. Whatever the form of the statement of work, a clear introduction, free from technical jargon and comprehensible to ordinary business people, provides a useful guide to interpretation.
- *Service Levels.* Two templates are included, one for comprehensive IT services and another for finance and accounting services, as an example of business process services. Neither includes specific service level commitments (such as accuracy, response times, or system availability) since these are specific to the transaction, and matters for business people and experts to determine. Lawyers' drafts provide the framework for

---

[1] Attached to the agreement is a glossary of defined terms. Other definitions, particularly those related to service levels and charges, appear in those documents. A single consolidated glossary has much to recommend it, but it may be more convenient for readers (and, for that matter, users of actual documents) to have self-contained documents, including relevant definitions.

establishing, measuring, and reporting service levels, calculating credits assessed for unexcused failures, adjustments, and other administrative matters.

- *Charges.*   Three examples are provided: for IT infrastructure, applications development and maintenance, and finance and accounting. All three illustrate the application of common pricing methods and metrics for IT and business process services. None of the forms includes accompanying tables of rates and adjustments, which are transaction-specific.

- *Standard Terms for Projects.*   Many outsourcing relationships involve large volumes of project work, particularly in IT, where regular upgrades to infrastructure and software are facts of life. Unless ground rules are agreed in advance, projects may be documented erratically, or with general purpose forms that may conflict with the master agreement. Customers find that suppliers' standard paperwork favors the suppliers, and so prefer to negotiate terms before signing a master agreement and relinquishing much of their negotiating leverage. The form provides a framework for authorization of projects, payment of charges, acceptance of deliverables, project management, and termination.

- *Governance.*   The example included illustrates the approach suggested in the text: governance in layers, from executive sponsorship at the top, through joint committees that set direction and oversee operations committees and other joint working groups. In practice, these basic provisions may be supplemented by detailed responsibility matrices. Governance arrangements may be more complex or simpler, depending upon the scale and complexity of the relationship.

- *Cooperation Agreement.*   Many companies now engage a variety of suppliers who must collaborate to support the customer's business. Suppliers of HR or finance and accounting services may, for example, rely upon networks and data centers operated by a third company. All must collaborate in reasonable harmony. Agreements like the sample included provide a framework for that cooperation—allocating responsibility, sharing technical and other confidential information, implementing adjustments, and resolving issues that are bound to arise, all in a manner consistent with the suppliers' individual service contracts. If those service contracts are derived from the same form, and use consistent nomenclature and processes, so much the better.

Appendix 1

IT TERM SHEET

TERM SHEET
(IT Infrastructure and Applications)[1]

FOR

[CUSTOMER]

Note: Term sheets are ordinarily prepared with wide columns for supplier comments, and presented in landscape orientation—like spacious spreadsheets. To allow still more room, they may be printed on long paper. Here, for the reader's convenience, the text appears conventionally oriented, with minimal blank space; but this is just a matter of presentation in print on a compact page, and not a clever tactic designed to deter extensive comments!

---

[1] Although written for IT infrastructure and applications, this form can be easily adapted for a variety of IT services, or for business process services.

TABLE OF CONTENTS

Instructions

Customer seeks long term, mutually beneficial relationships with one or more suppliers of outsourced IT services.

Customer and its advisors are working with potential suppliers to identify appropriate service solutions that will meet Customer's needs. This document describes Customer's current thinking concerning probable key terms in the contract and invites potential suppliers' responses.

For each term below, please indicate whether your company "Agrees" or "Disagrees." Where you disagree, please explain with specific reasons and, in appropriate cases, propose an alternative that you believe will meet the substance of the requirement, while accommodating your concern. Please propose any additional terms your company thinks important, based upon successful experience with other clients.

Customer and its advisors recognize that a successful contract should respect both parties' legitimate interests, allocate risks fairly, and permit both parties to succeed. Customer believes the terms proposed are consistent with mutual success and current market standards. Suppliers are encouraged to be thorough in their responses. Our evaluation of proposals will not fault any respondent for raising issues of real concern that affect a supplier's ability to perform, manage its costs, or earn a reasonable return from successful performance. Our evaluation will consider working relationships and effective collaboration, as demonstrated during the selection process.

After evaluation, Customer and its advisors will develop a form of agreement that will reflect the principles set out in this Term Sheet and accompanying documents. Customer reserves the right to modify and supplement the proposed terms described below at any time, which are not to be construed as an offer or in any way binding upon Customer.

	Requirements	Agree or Disagree	Issue/ Concern (if Supplier disagrees)
	AGREEMENT STRUCTURE		
1. International	The Master Services Agreement ("Agreement") will include local or regional Companion Agreements for implementing the transaction at the local or regional level in applicable jurisdictions in order to minimize overall tax expenses, comply with applicable employment and other laws, accommodate variations in local practice and requirements, provide efficient governance and dispute resolution procedures for the relationship as a whole.		
2. Modular	The Agreement will include a master contract, with separate schedules describing the Services, Service Levels, Charges and other service specific provisions. (For convenience, the Agreement, Companion Agreements and schedules are sometimes referred to below as "contract documents.")		
3. Parent Guaranty	Supplier's parent company will, simultaneously with execution of the Agreement, enter into a written guaranty of all of Supplier's performance and financial obligations (including those of all subsidiaries and affiliates of either Supplier or its parent).		
4. Services to Customer Group Members	Supplier will provide Services to Customer or Customer Group Member(s), as Customer from time to time requests, including (i) newly acquired business units and (ii) divested business units for a period of at least twenty-four (24) months after the divestiture.		

Requirements	Agree or Disagree	Issue/Concern (if Supplier disagrees)
OBJECTIVES		
5. Recitals — The contract will recite Customer's goals, including achievement of high standards of performance, continuous improvement in performance, reductions in cost, effective governance, and flexibility to adjust to changing needs, among others. These goals will not be construed to alter the scope of obligations, but contract terms will be interpreted to give effect to the goals.		
SCOPE OF SERVICES		
6. Specific — Supplier will provide all services described or contemplated in its proposal, which will be the basis for service descriptions describing both parties' responsibilities in reasonable detail, including any dependencies.		
7. General — In addition to functions and responsibilities expressly stated in service descriptions, the scope of service ("Services") will include functions, tasks and responsibilities not specifically described by the service descriptions but: • Now performed by affected personnel; • Contemplated by Customer's base case; • Related tasks and activities inherent in or necessary for the performance of tasks and activities referred to in service descriptions; and • Other miscellaneous activities. requested from time to time by Customer, to the degree that the requested activities do not require additional Supplier resources or affect agreed performance standards.		

	Requirements	Agree or Disagree	Issue/ Concern (if Supplier disagrees)
8. Nonexclusive	The Agreement will be nonexclusive. Supplier will cooperate with other Customer contractors, who must comply with reasonable technical, security and confidentiality requirements. Customer reserves the right to engage others to perform similar services, or to perform services internally. Reductions in the scope of the Services will be administered through written Change Control Procedures (described below).		
9. Priorities	Customer will retain final discretion over the priorities in scheduling performance of the Services, including any Projects, and may change priorities from time to time. Customer recognizes that changing priorities may affect ongoing Service delivery, Project cost, pricing and price reductions. The parties will cooperate to minimize cost and other effects.		
10. Reporting	The Agreement will describe, in reasonable detail, monthly and other periodic reports concerning Supplier's performance. Periodic reports may be based upon Supplier's standard forms of reports to its customers, if they provide the information that Customer reasonably requires. Reporting requirements will include read-only online access for responsible Customer management to tools used to manage delivery of service (eg, "dashboards" for Service Level performance and trouble-ticket systems).		

Requirements		Agree or Disagree	Issue/ Concern (if Supplier disagrees)

11. Change Control	Customer or Supplier may propose changes, including changes occasioned by acquisitions or divestitures. All Changes will be implemented pursuant to a written Change Control Procedure consistent with the following: • Routine changes, including all Changes that do not require material, net additional cost, effort or resources, or that can be accommodated with the staff and other resources ordinarily available for performance, will not result in any increase or decrease in Supplier's Charges. • Charges for changes or new services that do require material, net additional cost, effort or resources, or that cannot be so accommodated, will be priced at the applicable rate or metric and otherwise at the most favorable rates Supplier then offers for similar services. Customer will have approval rights over any change that may adversely affect its receipt or use of the Services, or increase Supplier's Charges or Customer's other costs.		
12. Projects	The Services may include certain Projects (discrete, separately authorized and administered activities, in addition to basic service) either taken over during the initial transition or authorized from time to time in writing (as changes or otherwise).		

	Requirements	Agree or Disagree	Issue/ Concern (if Supplier disagrees)
Projects *(contd.)*	There will be no additional charge for project management or other Project-related Services provided by the staff ordinarily assigned to the performance of Services for Customer.		
	When Supplier proposes additional staff or resources for Project-related Services, Customer may, at its option: (A) temporarily relieve Supplier of Service Level or other obligations, so that Services may be performed with available resources, without additional Charge or undue impact upon operations or user satisfaction; or (B) authorize additional staff and resources, for which Customer will pay at the appropriate contract rates.		
13. Terms for Projects	The Agreement will include standard terms for Projects, and appropriate rates or other metrics for Projects, related services and new services. The standard terms may include, among others, procedures for: (i) authorization of Projects; (ii) acceptance upon delivery or completion; (iii) change management; (iv) Project planning and management; (v) charges; (vi) payment; (vii) reimbursable expenses (if any); (viii) termination of Projects for Customer's convenience, Supplier's breach, or nonpayment by Customer; and (ix) templates for statements of work, Project plans and other Project documents.		

Requirements		Agree or Disagree	Issue/ Concern (if Supplier disagrees)
14. New Services	New services outside the scope of the service descriptions will be authorized as changes or otherwise in writing, and performed in accordance with the terms of the Agreement, at applicable rates for base services, or if no such rate applies, then at the most favorable rates Supplier then offers for similar volumes of similar services. [Optional: The Parties will consider gain sharing opportunities with respect to any new services.] [Optional: Customer proposes that savings in direct costs attributable to new services be apportioned as follows . . . . unless otherwise agreed for a particular new service.]		
TRANSITION			
15. Transition Services	Supplier will manage and perform all functions necessary for successful transfer of operations and performance of the Services in accordance with a mutually acceptable transition plan. The transition plan will include expected milestones for the transition of each service and milestone credits that may be assessed in the event that Supplier fails to achieve milestones within the time periods specified in the transition plan. The Supplier will designate a transition manager responsible for the overall success of transition, who will act as a single point of contact for Supplier pending the successful completion of transition. The transition plan will also include an acceptance testing procedure, which Customer will		

		Requirements	Agree or Disagree	Issue/ Concern (if Supplier disagrees)
	Transition Services *(contd.)*	use to determine whether or not the transition has been successfully completed. Transition Charges shall be apportioned among milestones for payment when milestones are successfully completed (less [percent] retention, which shall be released upon successful completion of the final transition milestone).		
16.	Relocation of Operations	Any relocation of Supplier's operations requested by Supplier will be subject to Customer's prior written consent, which may be conditioned upon (i) approval of a migration plan that assures continuous operation and compliance with Service Level and other performance, and (ii) in the case of relocation to another country, agreement upon adjustments in Charges to share anticipated savings. Supplier will bear all costs of relocation, and any cost increases associated with relocation (eg, for additional bandwidth or telecommunications circuits).		
	OPERATIONS			
17.	Operation	In performing the Services, Supplier must adhere to Customer's applicable corporate standards, guidelines and policies. Supplier will comply with any changes in and to such standards, guidelines and policies. Key policies include, among others [list].		

Requirements		Agree or Disagree	Issue/ Concern (if Supplier disagrees)
18. Current Technology	Supplier's tools, utilities, methodologies, and procedures for performing the Services will be upgraded and enhanced to keep pace with technological advances and advances in the methods of delivering similar services, at no additional cost or expense to Customer. In particular, and subject to any express commitments concerning currency, upgrades or refresh, Supplier will:		
	• Make improvements in its tools, utilities, methodologies, and procedures as and when they are introduced into Supplier's own operations or its service to other commercial customers.		
	• Keep software on current or near-current supported releases as reasonably determined by Customer.		
	• Keep material hardware for which Supplier has financial responsibility under warranty and/or manufacturer's service contracts.		
	• Refresh hardware for which Supplier has financial responsibility as and when specified by the contract documents, and, where no time period is specified, at reasonable intervals, consistent with good industry practice and as required to achieve agreed performance standards and avoid obsolescence.		

	Requirements	Agree or Disagree	Issue/ Concern (if Supplier disagrees)
19. Procedures Manual	Supplier will be responsible for preparing a procedures manual that documents the Supplier's procedures for performing the Services. Customer will have the opportunity to review, comment upon, and approve the procedures manual. Supplier will update and maintain the procedures manual throughout the term of the Agreement.		
20. Language	All records and invoices will be maintained in and all oral and written communications will be conducted in the English language (except as otherwise specified in the Agreement or required by applicable law). All Supplier personnel will be fluent in the English language, and those who interact with Customer employees, customers and vendors in the US must be readily understood by Customer's employees and users. Service descriptions or Companion Agreements may contain additional language requirements.		
21. Subcontracts	Supplier must obtain Customer's approval before subcontracting the performance of any material portion of the Services to a third party.		
	Subcontracts must conform to relevant terms of the prime contract, including, among others, Service Levels, audit, termination, intellectual property,		

	Requirements	Agree or Disagree	Issue/ Concern (if Supplier disagrees)
Subcontracts *(contd.)*	legal compliance and confidentiality, and be transferable to Customer or a successor supplier upon expiration or termination of the Agreement. Supplier will remain responsible for the perform-ance of all subcontracted services. Customer may revoke its approval of any subcontractor whose performance Customer reasonably believes to be defi-cient, or that is acquired by a competitor of Customer. In such cases, Supplier shall discontinue use of the subcontractor's products and/or services for Customer and provide substitutes.		
22. *Force Majeure*	*Force majeure* events will excuse performance, except failures to execute disaster recovery plans, or to use normal precautions, such as emergency power systems. If *force majeure* condi-tions interrupt or disrupt significant portions of the Services, Supplier will obtain alternative service at its expense, pending restoration of normal service; or, at Customer's option, Supplier's Charges will be abated, and Customer will be free to obtain alternative service from other sources, pending restoration of normal service. If the interruption or disruption lasts more than a brief, mutually agreed period, then Customer may terminate the Agreement, wholly or partially, without paying a termination charge.		

	Requirements	Agree or Disagree	Issue/ Concern (if Supplier disagrees)
23. Disaster Recovery	Supplier will prepare a disaster recovery plan, that meets Customer requirements contained in a schedule attached to the Agreement. Those requirements will include a business impact analysis, adoption of approved recovery strategies sufficient to meet Customer requirements (including recovery times for systems and/or processes), regular training, testing and interaction with and dependencies between and among the disaster recovery plan and related business continuity plans. Initially, disaster recovery plans will be based upon existing plans for the Parties' respective facilities. Long term arrangements will be put in place during the transition period in accordance with an agreed schedule. Supplier will keep the disaster recovery plan up to date, test it periodically (and at least annually), provide test results to Customer, permit Customer and its auditors or other representatives to observe tests and examine results, and repeat any unsuccessful tests or portions thereof, until they are successfully completed.		
24. Excused Performance	Supplier's performance may be excused to the extent attributable to Customer's acts or omissions or *force majeure* events, provided Supplier gives prompt notice, and makes diligent efforts to mitigate costs and other adverse consequences.		
25. Malicious and Disabling Code	Supplier will protect against viruses, remediate infections, and prevent the introduction of malicious or disabling code into Customer's systems.		

Requirements	Agree or Disagree	Issue/ Concern (if Supplier disagrees)
SERVICE LEVELS		
26. Basic Performance Standard — Supplier will meet or exceed (i) applicable Service Levels and (ii) where they do not apply, (A) standards achieved by Customer's own operations before transition and (B) good industry standards for first tier suppliers of similar services.		
27. Root-Cause Analysis & Corrective Action — After any Service Level failure, Supplier will promptly perform a root-cause analysis to investigate the reasons for the failure, report the results to Customer, and recommend and undertake appropriate corrective action to prevent recurrence.		
28. Service Credits — If Supplier fails to provide the Services in accordance with the applicable Service Levels, Customer will receive the Service Credits specified by an accompanying schedule. Service Credits will not limit or preclude Customer's right to recover other damages incurred by Customer, or to seek other remedies under the Agreement or applicable law.		
29. Service Credit Limitations — The total amount at risk for payment of Service Credits will not exceed ____% of monthly Charges (excluding any expense reimbursements). The gross total of all potential credits shall not exceed ____% of the amount at risk.		
30. Service Credit Adjustments — Customer may reclassify Service Levels (from critical to non-critical, or among other relevant categorxies) and adjust potential credit amounts so long as (i) no single Service Credit exceeds __% of		

	Requirements	Agree or Disagree	Issue/ Concern (if Supplier disagrees)
Service Credit Adjustments *(contd.)*	the amount at risk; (ii) the gross total of all potential credits does not exceed the percentage specified above; and (iii) the amount at risk remains fixed.		
31. Excused Failures	No Service Credits will be payable for failures attributable to Customer's acts or omissions (or those of its agents or third party contractors) or to *force majeure* events (excluding failures attributable to failures to perform disaster recovery obligations or use reasonable precautions, such as emergency power systems).		
32. Periodic Review	The Parties will review Supplier's performance against Service Level commitments at agreed intervals. The Parties will also meet formally each [month/quarter] to review operational and management issues. At least once each year, the parties' joint management committee (or their designees) will have a face-to-face meeting to review Service Levels and the results of the Customer Satisfaction Surveys.		
33. Continuous Improvement	Supplier's performance of the Services is expected to improve continuously and become more efficient over the term of the Agreement. These improvements will be reflected in the pricing and in the continuous improvement of Supplier's Service Level commitments over the term of this Agreement. [Insert further particulars, if desired.]		

Requirements		Agree or Disagree	Issue/ Concern (if Supplier disagrees)
34. Customer Satisfaction	The Parties will measure customer satisfaction through a Customer Satisfaction Survey, which may include both written surveys and personal interviews. The Parties will agree upon the content, recipients and timing of such surveys. The Parties agree that the results of the Customer Satisfaction Survey will trigger real consequences, including Service Credits and corrective action if Supplier's performance, as measured by Customer Satisfaction Surveys, falls below reasonable expectations.		
HUMAN RESOURCES			
35. Transferred Employees	Supplier will make offers of employment to [number/substantially all] of Customer's affected personnel, subject to interviews and other normal procedures. The terms of each individual offer must be at least comparable in aggregate salary and benefits to the affected personnel's total salary and benefits at Customer. Supplier must retain all transferred employees for at least twelve (12) months. If any transferred employees are discharged by Supplier before that period elapses (other than for cause), Supplier will pay them severance in amounts at least equal to those that would be paid under Customer's severance policies. Customer may designate transferred employees with specialized knowledge who must continue to provide services for Customer for agreed periods (unless they resign voluntarily or are discharged for cause).		

	Requirements	Agree or Disagree	Issue/ Concern (if Supplier disagrees)
Transferred Employees *(contd.)*	Affected personnel in jurisdictions subject to legislation under the EU's acquired rights directive (or similar legislation in any jurisdiction) that makes them eligible for transfer to Supplier will be provided employment in accordance with applicable law.		
36. Qualifications	Supplier will appoint a sufficient number of individuals to perform the Services in accordance with good industry practice. Supplier will only appoint individuals with suitable education, training, experience and qualifications to perform the Services. Supplier agrees that a limited number of specific positions will require specific educational, qualification or training backgrounds to be specified in the Agreement.		
37. Key Personnel	Customer will have the right to interview and pre-approve key Supplier operations management including the account executive, delivery manager, director of operations, transition manager and [specify others, if any]. Key personnel assigned to Customer's account will remain on the Customer account for minimum periods of twenty-four (24) months from the date they are first assigned (except in cases of disability, resignation, retirement or dismissal for cause). The specific roles and positions of key personnel will be identified in the Agreement.		

	Requirements	Agree or Disagree	Issue/ Concern (if Supplier disagrees)
38. Key Personnel— Services to Customer Competitors	Supplier will not assign any key personnel to perform services for any Customer competitor for a period of at least two (2) years after they cease performance of Services for Customer (unless Customer consents in its sole discretion).		
39. Certain Replacements	Upon request, Supplier will remove any staff member (including key personnel) whose performance falls below accept-able standards, or whose participation Customer deems not in its best interests.		
	OTHER RESOURCES		
40. Managed and Assigned Agreements	Certain agreements may be assigned to or administered by Supplier in connec-tion with its performance of Services. • Charges for assigned agreements will be Supplier's responsibility from and after assignment. • Supplier will comply with the terms of assigned and managed agreements. • Supplier will review invoices for managed agreements in a timely manner and work with relevant third parties in order promptly to correct any errors discovered and assure good performance for Customer. • Supplier will request products and services, oversee performance, and recommend appropriate action concerning renewal and other options under managed agreements.		

Requirements		Agree or Disagree	Issue/ Concern (if Supplier disagrees)
41. Facilities	Supplier staff assigned to perform at Customer facilities will: (i) comply with applicable Customer policies and the terms of any applicable leases, (ii) use reasonable care with Customer facilities, personnel and other property, and (iii) bear any unusual or additional cost associated with Supplier's use (eg, excess utility charges). Customer will provide office furniture, custodial service, network access, local telephone service, office supplies and other reasonable support. Customer facilities and equipment are provided solely for the purpose of providing Services to Customer and incidental related activities. Supplier will acquire no rights in Customer facilities, as tenant, subtenant or otherwise.		
42. Asset Transfers	[Alternative 1: In the event that any assets will be transferred to the Supplier, the Agreement will include a separate asset transfer schedule with bills of sale for such transfers. No asset transfers are currently identified.] [Alternative 2: Supplier will purchase the hardware, equipment and other assets listed on (cross-reference) ("transferred assets") for [insert particulars, eg, their then-current book value, as of the date of transfer], plus applicable sales and other taxes, if any, which Supplier shall pay or reimburse.] Assets will be transferred "as-is", without warranties (other than good title).		

	Requirements	Agree or Disagree	Issue/ Concern (if Supplier disagrees)
FINANCIAL TERMS			
43. Charges All-Inclusive	Supplier's Charges will include all hardware, software, personnel and other resources required to perform the Services. Customer will pay no other amounts, other than retained or pass-through costs specified by the contract documents. All assumptions, limitations, qualifications and conditions ("conditions") will be identified in the contract documents, as well as the consequences of failure to satisfy any of those conditions. The contract documents will identify (and where possible, estimate) all third party costs to be passed through to Customer. All other costs are included in Supplier's Charges. Customer will pay no administrative charge or markup upon expenses passed through or reimbursed.		
44. Invoices and Payment	Supplier will bill in arrears, on or before the [number] day of the succeeding month, and receive electronic payment within [number] days after receipt of the invoices. Invoices will contain such detail as Customer may from time to time require in order to (i) validate calculations and (ii) allocate charges among Customer business units.		
45. Most-Favored Customer	Throughout the term of the Agreement, Supplier's rates and Charges will be at least as favorable to Customer as the most favorable rates and charges then offered or provided to any of Supplier's other customers for similar services. For these purposes, "similar" will take into		

	Requirements	Agree or Disagree	Issue/ Concern (if Supplier disagrees)
Most-Favored Customer *(contd.)*	account the geography served, service locations, in-scope processes, volumes, systems used, service level requirements, and other appropriate criteria.		
46. Benchmarking	At any time after completion of the transition period but not more than once per year, Customer may benchmark the Supplier's price and performance levels for some or all services against then-current market standards. The benchmark will be performed by a third party chosen by Customer from an agreed list (excluding Supplier's competitors). The benchmarker will normalize comparable transactions to account for differences in volumes of service, complexity, service levels, investments in assets, transfers of personnel, start-up costs, variations in configurations, unique or unusual requirements, geography, and other appropriate criteria. If the benchmarking results indicate that the Charges paid by Customer, as normalized by the benchmarker, are higher than the average costs paid by the quartile of the benchmarked sample receiving the most favorable rates and charges, then (unless the parties otherwise agree within a reasonable, mutually agreed period) Customer will be entitled to a reduction in fees to equal the average of the most favorable quartile, retroactive to commencement of the benchmark assessment. If Supplier fails to make required adjustments, Customer may terminate the Agreement, or benchmarked Services, at its option, without paying any termination charge.		

Requirements		Agree or Disagree	Issue/ Concern (if Supplier disagrees)
47. Gain-Share	The Agreement will include a process to identify opportunities for additional savings or other benefits. In particular, the Parties will consider gain-share opportunities with respect to any Project or new service outside then-current scope. This gain-share procedure will provide the Parties with the opportunity to share the investment, implementation, and risks and potential rewards related to the opportunity and the potential rewards that may result from such opportunity. This process is in addition to any efficiency gains that Customer will achieve through the Supplier's continuous improvement commitments.[1]		
48. Withholding	Customer may withhold or set off amounts owed to Customer, or Charges that Customer disputes in good faith, from amounts otherwise payable to Supplier. When any material payment is withheld, Customer will inform Supplier of the reasons, and immediately consult with Supplier. [Optional: The right to withhold disputed amounts will be limited to an agreed percentage of fees due, and an overall cap above which the disputed amounts must be paid in an escrow account. Disputed amounts in excess of the ceiling may be withheld from later monthly payments. Escrowed amounts, plus interest earned, less reasonable		

---

[1] Note: optional provision intended to stimulate discussion and prompt creative proposals. More or less specific variations may be desirable, or the provision may be omitted.

	Requirements	Agree or Disagree	Issue/ Concern (if Supplier disagrees)
Withholding *(contd.)*	escrow charges, shall be disbursed as the parties may agree and instruct, or as determined by arbitrators or a court through disputes proceedings.]		
49. Taxes	Charges include (i) taxes upon Supplier's own assets and income, (ii) goods and services purchased for use in connection with provision or receipt of the Services, and (iii) all taxes (other than recoverable VAT) imposed upon the Services.		
50. Cost of Living Adjustments	Supplier must indicate in its response whether or not cost of living adjustments (COLA) are included in its price. If included in the price, Supplier should indicate what percentage was used. If excluded from the price, Supplier may include its proposal for making pricing adjustments for COLA that is tied to a specific index and limited to an annual maximum increase. Supplier should include any regional variations applicable to personnel in Supplier's various delivery locations.[2]		
51. Prepayments, Refunds, Prorations	The Agreement will contain conventional provisions for prepayments, refunds, and prorations so that financial responsibilities correspond with the commencement and expiration of the Agreement.		
52. Equitable Adjustments	In the event of an increase or decrease of [eg, thirty-five per cent (35%)] or more in consumption of any chargeable resource, or the volume of any service (other than exceptional situations that are not reasonably anticipated to persist for at least twelve [12] months), then either Party may request an equitable		

[2] Note: Many variations are possible, depending upon customer preferences.

	Requirements	Agree or Disagree	Issue/ Concern (if Supplier disagrees)
Equitable Adjustments *(contd.)*	adjustment of relevant Charges to account for (i) net increases or decreases in costs of performance, (ii) costs of acquisitions or dispositions of assets, (iii) one-time costs associated with effecting changes, (iv) a reasonable allowance for profit, and (v) other ordinary and necessary costs directly related to the change in circumstances or conditions. Convenience termination charges shall also be adjusted to reflect changes in scope, investments in and dispositions of assets, and other related changes in unamortized costs to be recovered thereby in the event of termination.[3]		
	COMPLIANCE AND AUDIT		
53. Regulatory Compliance	Supplier will comply with all laws, including regulatory requirements, applicable to Supplier's delivery of the Services and its performance of this Agreement, including, without limitation, those imposed on Customer but applicable to activities that Supplier undertakes pursuant to this Agreement. Customer will comply with all laws applicable to Customer's receipt of Services and its performance of this Agreement. Supplier will be responsible for identifying and becoming familiar with any changes in laws that are related to Supplier's delivery or performance of the Services or Customer's use or receipt of the Services. In particular, Supplier will (i) comply with applicable privacy laws in all jurisdictions; (ii) enter into EU model processor agreements when reasonably required by Customer, and cause its subcontractors to do so.		

[3] Note: Delete final sentence if shutdown costs are to be paid in lieu of convenience termination charge.

	Requirements	Agree or Disagree	Issue/ Concern (if Supplier disagrees)
54. Changes in Laws	If and when changes in applicable laws, regulations and treaties ("regulatory changes") adversely affect Supplier's cost to perform, then:		
	• Supplier shall bear costs associated with (i) regulatory changes affecting its business as a supplier of services, (ii) changes in Supplier's standards, methods, practices and procedures for customers generally, and (iii) regulatory changes affecting its customers generally.		
	• Costs attributable to changes in laws and regulations affecting Customer, its businesses and other customers in Customer's industry (that do not similarly affect Supplier or its other customers generally) shall be apportioned among Supplier's affected customers (with the apportionment to be subject to audit).		
	• Costs attributable to changes in Services that are specific to Customer shall be at Customer's expense, subject to applicable contract provisions concerning change control, pricing of changes and audit. (In order to minimize costs to Customer, Customer reserves the right to adjust priorities and schedules for relevant activities in order to minimize costs while assuring continuing compliance with regulatory and performance requirements.)		

Requirements		Agree or Disagree	Issue/ Concern (if Supplier disagrees)
Changes in Laws *(contd.)*	[Customer is prepared to discuss mechanisms for adjustments and, in the absence of commercially reasonable alternatives, termination of affected Services if and to the extent that future changes in laws or taxes may render performance uneconomic, impractical or unlawful.][4]		
55. Audit	Customer's auditors and regulators shall have the right to audit all Customer data, all systems used to support Customer, Supplier's performance, Charges, procedures, security, backup data and systems, and disaster recovery plans and tests. Supplier will cooperate with Customer's auditors and, in particular: • Implement specific controls that Customer may have in place or from time to time require for outsourced functions (or Supplier's equivalent or superior controls, if approved by Customer).Provide all reasonable assistance for Customer and its auditors to comply with applicable laws and regulations (including, without limitation, the Sarbanes-Oxley Act and regulations thereunder). • Provide certifications, at agreed intervals and upon request, concerning the accuracy of inventories, Charges, and reports; the absence of unasserted claims; reporting of security and other incidents, the absence of unreported weaknesses in controls and such other		

[4] Note: Final paragraph is optional, but provides a basis for equitable adjustment or termination in the event future restrictive legislation makes offshore performance unlawful or uneconomic.

Requirements		Agree or Disagree	Issue/ Concern (if Supplier disagrees)

		Agree or Disagree	Issue/ Concern (if Supplier disagrees)
Audit *(contd.)*	factual matters as Customer may reasonably request. Certifications may be to the best of Supplier's knowledge, after reasonable inquiry, and subject to reasonable materiality standards approved by Customer. • Provide an annual "Type II" service auditor's report in compliance with SAS-70 (or any successor auditing standard) in form and substance acceptable to Customer. • Make available the results of all audits of Supplier's operations, to the extent relevant to the Agreement and Services.		
	REPRESENTATIONS, WARRANTIES AND COVENANTS		
56. Supplier	Supplier will provide various representations, warranties and covenants, including, among others: (i) power and authority, authorization, binding effect and other customary matters; (ii) the absence of any known claims of infringement concerning Supplier software, systems, assets, methods and processes used to perform the Services, and (iii) efficient, high quality performance in accordance with generally accepted industry practices.		
57. Customer	Customer will provide various representations, warranties and covenants, including, among others, power and authority, good standing, authorization, binding effect and other customary matters.		

	Requirements	Agree or Disagree	Issue/ Concern (if Supplier disagrees)
58. Quality of Deliverables	Supplier will warrant that software and other deliverables will be free from material defects or nonconformities for a period of at least one hundred and twenty (120) days after their first production use. Hardware, when supplied, will be subject to normal manufacturer's warranties (unless otherwise agreed).		
59. Ethical Standards	Supplier will have in place and comply with ethical standards that meet or exceed those contained in Customer's ethical standards.		
60. Compliance With Laws	Both parties will comply with applicable laws, regulations and treaties in all relevant jurisdictions.		
	TERM AND TERMINATION		
61. Term	The Agreement term will commence on the effective date and will continue for [number] years [from the effective date of the Agreement/commencement of Services]. Customer will have the right to extend the contract term for up to three (3) additional years upon the terms then in effect, subject to applicable volume and other adjustments.		
62. Termination by Customer for Default	Customer may terminate the Agreement, or one or more Companion Agreements, wholly or partially, for cause if Supplier fails to cure a material breach within an agreed period following notice. Material breach will include: (i) the numbers or combinations of unexcused failures to meet Service Levels that are agreed to constitute unacceptable service; (ii) repeated or multiple breaches that may		

Requirements		Agree or Disagree	Issue/ Concern (if Supplier disagrees)
Termination by Customer for Default *(contd.)*	be minor individually, but are material in the aggregate; (iii) material failure to perform disaster recovery responsibilities; (iv) failure or delay in meeting transition milestones, as well as (v) material breach of any obligation. Customer may terminate for any of these reasons without paying a termination charge.		
63. Termination by Customer for Change in Control of Supplier	Customer may terminate the entire Agreement generally in the manner contemplated for convenience terminations, but without paying a termination charge, by giving at least [number] days' notice within six (6) months after consummation of a change in control of Supplier.		
64. Termination by Customer for Convenience	Customer may terminate the Agreement (or specific categories of service or Companion Agreements) for convenience at any time, by giving at least [number] days' notice and paying [an agreed termination charge/reasonable shutdown costs (such as severance and relocation for affected personnel, subject to reasonable mitigation)]. No termination charge shall be payable for convenience termination during any renewal or extension period.[5]		

[5] Note: If shutdown costs are to be paid in lieu of a termination charge, edit other references to termination charges appropriately throughout the text.

	Requirements	Agree or Disagree	Issue/ Concern (if Supplier disagrees)
65. Termination by Supplier	Supplier may terminate for cause if (i) Customer fails to pay material, undisputed invoices, after an agreed notice period or (ii) Customer, with management's actual knowledge, commits a material, intentional misappropriation of Supplier's proprietary rights. Supplier may not otherwise terminate the contract or suspend performance.		
66. Termination Generally and Termination Assistance	Upon expiration of the Agreement, or any total or partial termination, Supplier agrees to facilitate the transition of the Services away from Supplier to one or more alternate suppliers ("successor") or to Customer.		
	Supplier will continue to provide Services during the transition and for up to eighteen (18) months following the termination or expiration of the Agreement in order to ensure a smooth transition. Thereafter, Supplier will provide reasonable post-termination assistance on a time and materials basis.		
	The contract documents will describe in detail the services that Supplier will provide to effect a smooth transition when the contract either expires or terminates for any reason ("termination assistance"). Supplier's base Charges will include all such termination assistance performed before expiration or termination of the Agreement.		

Requirements		Agree or Disagree	Issue/ Concern (if Supplier disagrees)
Termination Generally and Termination Assistance *(contd.)*	Termination assistance will include, at minimum, the following: (i) provision of data and other reasonable support for bidding or other selection processes, (ii) transfer to the successor of Customer data, data bases or compilations, software, working documentation (eg, procedures and other manuals), knowledge bases, work-in-process, work product, and, at Customer's option, dedicated assets (at [book/market] value); (iii) familiarization in Customer-specific procedures and operations; (iv) reasonable consultation about Customer procedures, data, transition arrangements and other matters reasonably necessary to assure a smooth transition; (v) reasonable assistance to the successor in the review, implementation and performance of a written plan for transition to the successor; and (vi) reasonable assistance with the review, testing and execution of the successor's transition plan. Customer or successor suppliers(s) of similar services may, with Supplier's full cooperation, interview and offer employment to Supplier's staff engaged in performance of Services for Customer. Within EU member states, Supplier will comply with applicable acquired rights and employment legislation.		

	Requirements	Agree or Disagree	Issue/ Concern (if Supplier disagrees)
Termination Generally and Termination Assistance *(contd.)*	Terminations, including partial terminations, may be effected by category of service or as Customer otherwise reasonably determines, bearing in mind operational dependencies among services.		
	INTANGIBLE PROPERTY AND RIGHTS		
67. Customer Data	Supplier must comply with Customer's IT security policy and data privacy policies. Upon request, given at any time, Supplier will return some or all Customer data and other Customer intangible property, in the form reasonably requested by Customer. This obligation will be unconditional, and is not subject to any liens or other claims.		
68. Confidentiality	Each party will protect the other's confidential information and cooperate (at the disclosing party's cost) in legal defense of confidentiality. Supplier will keep Customer's confidential information in strict confidence. Security for proprietary information, personal data and other sensitive data will be at least as stringent as for Supplier's own similar data. Supplier will meet or exceed Customer's technical and organizational security protocols. Supplier will cause its key personnel and staff providing services to Customer to execute written confidentiality agreements in favor of Customer. Upon expiration or termination, after completion of transition to a successor, each party will return or destroy the other party's confidential information.		

	Requirements	Agree or Disagree	Issue/ Concern (if Supplier disagrees)
69. Security Breaches	Supplier will give Customer immediate notice of any breach or suspected breach in security for personal data or other Customer data from time to time in Supplier's possession, and undertake such remedial action as Customer may reasonably determine (or, alternatively, reimburse Customer's costs associated with remedial action) and pay or reimburse all costs of remedial action, including notices to affected individuals, that may be necessary or advisable under applicable law.		
70. Separate Facilities	Supplier must segregate Customer data and information, logically and physically, from its other customers' data and operation. Supplier must establish and maintain separate processing areas within its facilities for delivery of Services to Customer. In particular, applications development and maintenance activities shall be performed in separate, secure facilities by staff dedicated to Customer. Supplier will not permit its personnel (or subcontractor personnel) to provide Services to Customer competitors while assigned to the Customer account.		

Requirements		Agree or Disagree	Issue/ Concern (if Supplier disagrees)
71. Intellectual Property— New Developments	All rights in documentation, custom software development, data, data compilations, manuals (including the procedures manual), reports and other work product, and all related intellectual property developed by Supplier in the performance of the Services or developed or paid for by Customer, will be the property of Customer (with Supplier to retain rights in its templates, methods, techniques, and other intellectual property, except to the extent that they contain Customer confidential information). During contract negotiations, the parties will consider licensing or other arrangements to permit each party to make reasonable use of the other party's intellectual property.		
72. Proprietary Software	Customer will license Supplier to use Customer proprietary systems to the extent necessary to perform the Services during the term of the Agreement. Supplier will license Customer to use Supplier's proprietary systems to the extent necessary to receive the Services, and after expiration or termination of the Agreement, will license those proprietary systems to Customer and/or the successor upon commercially reasonable terms. If Supplier's proprietary systems are not assured to be available to Customer after expiration or termination, Supplier will use third party products that are transferable to or available to Customer after expiration or termination. Supplier will not deploy any of its proprietary software without Customer's prior written consent.		

	Requirements	Agree or Disagree	Issue/ Concern (if Supplier disagrees)
73. Third Party Software	Customer expects to retain current applications licenses, and obtain licenses for any new applications that it may adopt during the term of the Agreement. Supplier will, at its expense, obtain all other third party software necessary to perform the Services, and pay all license, upgrade, maintenance and similar charges. Customer may, in its discretion, hold certain of those licenses in its own name. Supplier will obtain, in cooperation with Customer, and at Supplier's expense, all consents necessary for any assignments, rights of access and use, or other rights and approvals necessary for (i) the use of any third party software currently licensed to Customer; and (ii) transfer of any other third party contracts that are, in either case, contemplated for use in the performance of Services for Customer.		

GOVERNANCE

74. Collaborative Management	A joint management committee will oversee the relationship, and will meet periodically to review progress of transition, ongoing performance, continuous improvement and other matters of mutual interest. Supplier's approved full-time contract executive and Customer's contract executive will have primary responsibility for day-to-day management of the relationship and performance of Services. A detailed governance schedule will provide for:		

	Requirements	Agree or Disagree	Issue/ Concern (if Supplier disagrees)
Collaborative Management *(contd.)*	• Executive oversight through the joint management committee. • Management of the relationship by the parties' respective contract executives and their immediate subordinates through regular meetings and other interaction. • Working level management of operations through committees and other working groups for particular services, business units, locations and activities. • In appropriate cases, participation in committees and working groups involving Customer and/or other Customer suppliers whose responsibilities relate to or interact with services performed by Supplier for Customer. Appropriate agreements concerning confidentiality, cooperation among suppliers, and compliance with common standards may be required. There will be no additional Charge for reasonable cooperation with Customer and other suppliers to Customer.		

	Requirements	Agree or Disagree	Issue/ Concern (if Supplier disagrees)
	REMEDIES		
75. Indemnities	Each party will indemnify the other against various potential claims by third parties, including (among others) personal injury, property damage, infringement of intellectual property rights, disclosures of confidential information, claims by transferred employees or Supplier personnel concerning their employment by the respective parties, breaches of the Agreement or agreements with third parties, violations of law and claims arising from a party's gross negligence, recklessness, fraud or willful misconduct. Indemnities will contain customary provisions concerning notice of claims, cooperation in their investigation and defense, approval of settlements, resolution of infringements by license, substitution, and modification or withdrawal of allegedly infringing matter, and other appropriate measures. Neither party will be responsible to indemnify against an indemnitee's own wrongdoing.		

	Requirements	Agree or Disagree	Issue/ Concern (if Supplier disagrees)
76. Liability Limit	The parties' aggregate liability to one another for damages during the entire term will be limited to the lesser of actual, proven direct damages or the total Charges for the eighteen (18) months immediately preceding the event that gave rise to the claim (or estimated Charges for claims arising during the first eighteen (18) months of the term).		
77. Consequential Damages	Generally (except as otherwise provided below) neither party may recover lost revenues, lost profits or indirect or consequential damages. (Costs of work-arounds, cover, reconstruction of lost data, transition or disengagement costs, fines or penalties assessed by public authorities and other, similar costs of corrective action will be deemed actual, direct damages.)		
78. Exceptions	Damages shall be unlimited for (i) Supplier's abandonment of this Agreement or termination of this Agreement other than in strict accordance with its terms, (ii) either Party's indemnification obligations, (iii) either Party's breach of confidentiality or security obligations, (iv) Supplier's failure to provide termination assistance, (v) death or personal injury, and (vi) a Party's gross negligence, recklessness, fraud, willful misconduct or violations of law. (Liability limits do not limit Customer's obligation to pay Supplier's Charges.)		

	Requirements	Agree or Disagree	Issue/ Concern (if Supplier disagrees)
79. Insurance	Customer will require Supplier to obtain and maintain workers' compensation, commercial general liability and other appropriate insurance coverage, of kinds and in amounts to be agreed upon during contract negotiations. During contract negotiations, the parties' risk managers will determine the contractual requirements related to proof of insurance, notice of cancellation, non-renewal and/or material reduction in coverage and naming of Customer as an additional insured on required policies (other than workers' compensation) where appropriate and reasonable.		
80. Disputes	Disputes will be resolved by escalation or consultation with the joint management committee or senior executives and if necessary, through proceedings as provided below. Consultations, settlement proposals and other communications will be confidential. Supplier must continue to perform Services while disputes are resolved. If the parties are unable to resolve a dispute, the dispute will be decided by binding arbitration in [location], with the right to litigate disputes concerning intellectual property, confidentiality or claims related to third party claims.		

Requirements		Agree or Disagree	Issue/ Concern (if Supplier disagrees)
Disputes *(contd.)*	Equitable remedies will be available in appropriate cases and provisional remedies may be obtained from competent courts. Permitted legal proceedings shall take place in [location] (excluding proceedings to obtain provisional remedies, enforce arbitral awards or proceedings commenced by third parties).		
81. Governing Law	[State] and applicable US federal laws.		
	GENERAL PROVISIONS		
82. Assignment	Supplier may not assign the Agreement or any of its responsibilities without Customer's prior written consent. Customer may assign its rights under the Agreement, but will remain responsible for payment to Supplier (except in connection with a merger, reorganization, sale of substantially all of Customer's assets, or other, similar transaction effecting a change in control of Customer's business).		
83. Non-solicitation	After transition, and except as agreed, Supplier may not offer employment to Customer employees. If it should hire any Customer employees (other than in response to general solicitations), Supplier will pay liquidated damages sufficient to pay costs of recruitment and training of successor staff.		

Requirements	Agree or Disagree	Issue/ Concern (if Supplier disagrees)
84. Miscellaneous The Agreement will contain customary provisions concerning, among other things, notices, severability, the parties' relationship, good faith, and the absence of third party beneficiaries.		

Appendix 2

LETTER OF INTENT[1]

[Date]

[Supplier
Address]
Attention: [Name]

Gentlemen and Ladies:

This letter of intent ("Letter of Intent") summarizes the terms on which [name], a [state] corporation ("Customer") and [name], a [state] corporation ("Supplier") have agreed in principle that Supplier will provide [describe] and related services for Customer. This letter of intent is a statement of intention only, and is not intended to be legally binding (apart from paragraph 3, below).[2] The parties intend to incorporate the substance of these terms in a Master Services Agreement, supporting schedules and exhibits describing services, service levels, charges, project work and other particulars (collectively, "Contract Documents").

1. The terms of the Contract Documents will be consistent with Supplier's Proposal and term sheet responses dated [date], each as supplemented in writing by [cross-references].[3] However, the parties reserve to themselves the exclusive right to negotiate a further agreement. Nothing contained in this Letter of Intent shall be construed to require them to reach any further agreement.

2. This Letter of Intent is a statement of intention concerning the terms of Contract Documents contemplated by the parties, but is not intended to be binding, and is

---

[1] This is a customer-oriented letter of intent for a long-term contract for IT services based upon the companion term sheet.

[2] Some letters of intent authorize preliminary work for which the customer will pay in accordance with the eventual contract or on a time and materials or similar basis if no final agreement is reached. In such cases, those provisions would also be binding.

[3] There are often supplementary responses (eg 'best and final' proposals or term sheet responses).

not a contract. The parties anticipate that their mutual intentions may evolve during contract negotiations, based upon changes in Customer's requirements and the results of further investigations into Customer's current operations. Neither party will be legally bound until execution and delivery of definitive Contract Documents by both parties' authorized representatives, after: (i) conducting a reasonable investigation with due diligence; (ii) obtaining all appropriate corporate approvals; and (iii) negotiation of the material terms of the Contract Documents (including those described in the Proposal, term sheet, Supplier's term sheet responses and other documents referred to above, and others that the parties may deem advisable).

3. Neither party may claim legal rights against the other by reason of actions taken in reliance upon non-binding portions of this Letter of Intent, including preliminary or transitional activities or any partial performance. The parties are, however, bound by their Nondisclosure Agreement dated [date] and the terms of this Letter of Intent, which shall be treated as confidential information thereunder. Each party will continue to bear its own costs.

Both sides will make every effort to complete negotiations and sign the Contract Documents by [date]. We look forward to working with you. Please confirm our understanding by signing and returning one copy of this letter.

Very truly yours,

[Customer]

By:
Name:
Title:

Accepted and agreed:
[Supplier]

By:
Name:
Title:

Appendix 3

MASTER SERVICES AGREEMENT

MASTER SERVICES AGREEMENT

between

[CUSTOMER]

and

[SUPPLIER]

For

INFORMATION TECHNOLOGY SERVICES

[Date]

TABLE OF CONTENTS

SCHEDULES

MASTER SERVICES AGREEMENT[1]

This Master Services Agreement (the "Agreement") is entered into as of [month] __, 201_ (the "Effective Date") between [name] ("Customer") and [name] ("Supplier").

RECITALS

A. Customer has engaged Supplier to provide information technology services described by this Agreement.
B. Supplier has agreed to provide the Services in accordance with the terms of this Agreement, for an initial term of [number] years, subject to renewal as provided below.

In consideration of the foregoing recitals, and the obligations stated below, Customer and Supplier agree as follows:

AGREEMENT

1 TERMS AND INTERPRETATION

1.1 Definitions
In this Agreement, capitalized terms shall have the meanings indicated in the accompanying Glossary, unless the context clearly requires some other meaning. Other terms used in this Agreement have the meanings assigned where they first appear. All defined terms include both plural and singular.

1.2 Goals and Objectives
The Parties acknowledge that their goals and objectives are to:

(a) Reduce Customer information technology (IT) costs through [specifics];
(b) Improve the quality and performance of Services through improvements in Service Levels, innovation and [specifics . . .];
(c) Allow Customer to focus on its core competencies;
(d) Provide Customer with the flexibility to adapt rapidly to changes in requirements, technology and operations; and
(e) Permit Supplier to earn a reasonable return through delivery of good service to Customer and performance of its obligations.[2]

The foregoing objectives are (i) intended as a general statement of purposes for this Agreement; (ii) are not intended to expand or contract the scope of the Parties' obligations or to alter the plain meaning of this Agreement's terms and conditions. However, the

---

[1] This is a moderately customer-oriented short form for outsourced services, written for IT, but adaptable for other kinds of services.
[2] Goals are illustrative and should be edited to suit transaction.

Parties do intend that the Agreement be interpreted and performed in a manner consistent with these objectives.

1.3 Interpretation of Contract Documents

All exhibits and schedules are incorporated by reference into this Agreement. The main body of the Agreement, the exhibits and schedules shall be construed consistently, to the extent practicable, to give effect to the entire Agreement. To the extent that any conflict may appear between the main body of the Agreement, on the one hand, and the exhibits and schedules on the other, the Agreement shall supersede exhibits and schedules, except to the extent that the exhibits and schedules may describe particular services, Service Levels, Charges or other particulars in greater detail, in which case the more detailed description shall supersede any conflicting general terms of the main body of the Agreement. Both Parties are sophisticated companies and have been represented by counsel, so no presumptions shall operate against the presumed author of any document or provision.

1.4 Particular Terms

Unless otherwise specifically provided:

(a) In the computation of a time period, "from" means "from and including" and "to" and "until" each mean "to but excluding." In the event that any action to be taken under this Agreement falls on a day which is not a business day, then that action shall be taken on the next succeeding business day.

(b) Unless otherwise expressly stated, words such as "hereunder" refer to the Agreement as a whole.

(c) Words such as "include" and "including" shall not be construed as terms of limitation.

(d) Unless otherwise stated, references to "writings," or "written" documents may mean hard copy (including facsimiles, where receipt is acknowledged), or electronic mail (where receipt is acknowledged) but exclude voice-mail recordings.

2 PERFORMANCE OF SERVICES

2.1 Supplier Account Executive

Supplier shall designate, as of the Effective Date, an individual to whom all communications from Customer may be addressed, and who has the authority to act for Supplier in connection with all aspects of this Agreement, including management, supervision and direction of Supplier's day-to-day performance (the "Supplier Account Executive"); but any written notice, demand or other communication in respect of matters other than the day-to-day performance of the Services shall be addressed to the person or persons specified in Section 13.2. Supplier's Account Executive may designate an alternate or deputy to act in his or her place in case of illness, vacation or other absence.

2.2 Provision of Services

During the Term, Supplier shall provide the Services to Customer, its Affiliates and other recipients from time to time designated by Customer.

2.3 Level of Effort

Unless the Agreement specifies some other standard (such as "best efforts") Supplier shall use reasonable efforts to perform and deliver Services and carry out its other obligations.

2.3.1 Reasonable Efforts

For purposes of this Agreement, reasonable efforts, commercially reasonable efforts and similar expressions mean diligent performance in a manner consistent with good standards in Supplier's industry and the quality and performance standards in this Agreement, but shall not be construed to require unusual or exceptional expenditures or use or engagement of facilities, resources and staff not ordinarily available for performance of Services.

2.3.2 Best Efforts

For purposes of this Agreement, "best efforts" means use of all of Supplier's available facilities, staff and other resources and capabilities in order to respond to emergencies and other urgent situations (such as, for example, execution of a disaster recovery plan, Force Majeure Events or major outages, interruptions in service and corrective action) but without materially impairing Supplier's ability to serve other customers or its financial condition.

2.4 Transition Services

Supplier will, in cooperation with Customer, undertake an orderly, timely transfer of operations, personnel and related matters and, in particular, perform its responsibilities under the Transition Plan. In the event that Supplier fails to meet any of the milestones in the Transition Plan for reasons other than those excluded by Section 2.18, then Customer may recover the Transition Credits specified in Schedule C (which are reductions in Charges reflecting the diminished value of inferior service, rather than liquidated damages or penalties).

2.5 Nonexclusive Contract

This Agreement is nonexclusive, and unless otherwise agreed, Customer may obtain Services, and similar or related services from third parties or its own resources. Supplier shall cooperate with Customer and its contractors to allow the proper performance of any such services.

2.6 Current Technology

In performing the Services, Supplier shall, without additional Charges, and in addition to any specific commitments concerning currency, upgrades and refreshment of equipment: (i) use current, proven technologies and methodologies, and (ii) implement changes from time to time approved by Customer to take advantage of improvements in technology (including, without limitation, periodic improvements in Supplier's methods, practices and procedures). In particular, Supplier will, without additional Charges, upgrade its tools, methodologies, processes and other normal procedures for performing similar Services as they may be upgraded from time to time for the operation of its business and the support of its customers generally. Software, tools and utilities used to perform Services will be maintained on current, or near-current, supported releases.

2.7 Performance Standards

Supplier's performance of the Services will: (i) be workmanlike and professional; and (ii) meet or exceed (A) all Service Levels in Schedule B (as they may be amended, modified and supplemented from time to time); and (B) the standards of quality, accuracy, completeness, timeliness and efficiency of other sophisticated companies providing similar services. Immediately after each failure to meet any of these performance standards, Supplier shall investigate the root causes of the failure, report its findings to Customer in writing, and take all appropriate action to correct any deficiencies and prevent recurrence. Upon Customer's request, or promptly following its own discovery, Supplier shall, without additional Charge to Customer, correct any errors in reports, transactions, Customer Data, processing or other Services attributable to its acts, errors and omissions, or to failures or malfunctions of systems, networks or other resources or facilities that Supplier manages or operates.

2.8 Review and Revision of Service Levels

Periodically, as appropriate, or as agreed in the relevant Schedules, and at least once during each calendar year, the Parties shall review the Service Levels and, if they agree, adjust the Service Levels to reflect appropriate changes in circumstances, including improvements contemplated by Section 2.6, above. Any such mutually agreed changes shall be authorized in accordance with the Change Control Procedures or other written agreement amending Schedule B.

2.9 Service Credits

Supplier recognizes that its failure to meet the Service Levels identified in Schedule B may have a material adverse impact on Customer's business and operations and that the damage may be difficult to measure precisely. Accordingly, in the event that Supplier fails to meet Service Levels for reasons other than those excused by Section 2.18, then Customer may recover the Service Credits specified in Schedule B (which are reductions in Charges reflecting the diminished value of inferior service, rather than liquidated damages or penalties). Service Credits shall be paid to Customer in cash or, at Customer's option, deducted from the next succeeding invoices or other amounts due to Supplier. Customer reserves all rights to other legal, equitable and contractual remedies. Awards of damages shall be reduced, dollar-for-dollar, by Service Credits paid or credited for the same incident(s).

2.10 Operational Changes

Supplier may not make any changes to the Services (except in case of emergencies) that would materially and adversely affect the quality of the Services, increase Customer's direct or indirect costs, or adversely affect Supplier's ability to meet the Service Levels (as they may be amended from time to time) without Customer's prior written consent. Supplier reserves the right to make any changes it may deem advisable in the event of any emergency, but will give Customer notice as soon as practicable.

2.11 Relocation of Operations

Supplier may not relocate operations from its Service Center or other approved facilities without Customer's consent, which may be conditioned upon: (i) approval of a transition or migration plan; (ii) reasonable assurances that relocation will be accomplished without any interruption or degradation of the Services, or any additional cost to Customer; and (iii) in the case of relocation of any operations from one country to another, upon mutually-agreed reductions in Charges for affected Services.

2.12 Project Services

The Services may include Projects, to the extent described by Schedule A or as authorized from time to time by change orders or otherwise in writing. Personnel assigned to perform Project Services shall possess the training, education, skills and competence necessary to perform their assigned responsibility, and unless Customer otherwise agrees, shall not be chosen from personnel ordinarily assigned to the performance of Services for Customer. To the extent that personnel ordinarily assigned are authorized to perform Project Services, (i) they shall be replaced with others with comparable skills; or (ii) Customer may, in its discretion, relieve Supplier from Service Level or performance obligations related to those persons' ordinary responsibilities, so as to minimize or avoid additional Charges and Charges for Services shall be equitably reduced in the manner described by Section 6.3 to reflect any net reduction in the level of effort.

2.13 Services to Third Parties

Customer recognizes that Supplier personnel providing Services to Customer under this Agreement may perform similar services from time to time for other customers of Supplier, and this Agreement shall not prevent Supplier from using such personnel (or any equipment or facilities not dedicated to Customer's use) for the purpose of performing similar services for other customers. However:

(a) Similar services for others may not adversely affect Supplier's ability to provide Services to Customer and meet the Service Levels;
(b) Supplier must comply with its obligations concerning Customer's Confidential Information and Materials (including, without limitation, applicable security policies and protocols); and
(c) Personnel filling Key Supplier Positions and those with access to competition-sensitive Customer's Confidential Information of Customer may not perform any services for any competitors of Customer for a period of two (2) years after they cease to perform Services.

2.14 Unidentified Contracts[3]

If any third party contract related to performance of the Services is not listed on the relevant schedule, was not disclosed to Supplier during its investigation preceding

---

[3] Where charges are tied to numbers of devices, such as servers or PCs, consider provisions (here or in the pricing schedule) for unidentified resources or devices, so that baselines or charges are adjusted if

execution of this Agreement and could not reasonably have been discovered (an "unidentified third party contract"), then: (i) the unidentified third party contract shall be added to the appropriate schedule when identified; and (ii) Supplier shall obtain, at its expense, any required consents.

2.15 Managed Agreements

When authorized by Schedule A or otherwise in writing, Supplier shall manage, administer and maintain certain agreements with third parties for the provision of products or services (including, without limitation, the Managed Agreements listed on Schedule D-3). Supplier shall provide Customer with reasonable prior notice of any renewal, termination or cancellation dates, options or elections. Supplier may order products or services in the normal course of business and may inspect and accept products delivered and services rendered. Supplier shall not renew, modify, terminate, or request or grant any consents or waivers under, any Managed Agreements without Customer's approval. Supplier shall receive all invoices for Managed Agreements (unless Customer otherwise instructs), review them, correct errors, and submit them to Customer for payment within a reasonable time prior to the due date (or if a discount for payment is given, then at least two (2) business days before the deadline for any such discount). Supplier shall be responsible for any late charges or for any discount not received because of Supplier's delays.

2.16 Subcontracts

Supplier shall be and remain fully responsible for all subcontracted Services.

2.16.1 Approval of Subcontractors

Except as otherwise provided below, Supplier may not delegate performance of any of its duties, obligations and responsibilities hereunder to any of its Affiliates or to any subcontractor without Customer's prior written approval in each instance. Customer approvals shall not be required for: (i) engagement of individuals as subcontractors, directly or through an agency, or (ii) subcontracts for support services (such as security at Supplier's facilities) that do not involve performance of Services. Customer hereby approves the following subcontractors: [list subcontractors and scope of subcontracted services, eg, ABC Company, field support]. If Customer gives Supplier notice that the continued engagement of any subcontractor is not in Customer's interests, then Supplier shall remove the affected subcontractor and either perform relevant services directly or engage another subcontractor approved by Customer to do so.

---

inventories taken after signing reveal discrepancies. Customer-oriented forms may provide for adjustment of charges to the extent that additional devices were not disclosed, directly or indirectly, or could not have been discovered with reasonable diligence. Suppliers prefer simply to adjust charges at agreed rates if additional devices are discovered after signing.

2.16.2 Subcontract Terms

All subcontracts shall permit assignment to Customer upon any early termination of this Agreement, and contain provisions consistent with, and at least as stringent as, the provisions of this Agreement concerning compliance with laws and policies, audit, confidentiality, intellectual property, use of Customer facilities, and replacement of personnel. Supplier shall require its employees and subcontractors (including individuals engaged as subcontractors) to enter into nondisclosure agreements consistent with the terms of this Agreement either with Customer or for Customer's express benefit.

2.17 Corporate Development

2.17.1 Divestitures

In the event of a divestiture, spin-off or other, similar transaction ("divestiture"), Supplier agrees to consult with Customer concerning provision of uninterrupted Service to divested Affiliates or business units and, as Customer may reasonably direct: (i) provide Services to successor entities under this Agreement for at least twenty-four (24) months after the divestiture; (ii) phase out and discontinue some or all Services in an orderly manner generally similar to that contemplated for partial convenience terminations (including provision of appropriate Termination Assistance); or (iii) negotiate in good faith with the successor entities for continuing provision of Services to them, with charges and service levels at least as favorable as then in effect hereunder, and without further Customer liability (provided that the successor has reasonably satisfactory assets and credit).[4] Supplier shall be compensated in accordance with the Change Control Procedure for material, additional costs incurred and services performed in connection with planning, implementation and related transitional activities associated with divestitures, disengagement from or continuing service to divested business units.

2.17.2 Mergers and Acquisitions

In the event of a merger, acquisition or other similar transaction, Supplier agrees to provide Services to acquired businesses upon the terms of this Agreement as and when Customer may reasonably direct. Supplier shall be compensated in accordance with the Change Control Procedure for material, additional costs incurred and services performed in connection with planning, implementation and related transitional activities associated with mergers, acquisitions and extension of service to newly-acquired businesses.

2.18 Excused Performance

Supplier will be excused from failures to perform, and no Service Credits shall be paid or credited for failures to meet applicable Service Levels to the extent that any such failure is attributable to any Force Majeure Event or to the acts or omissions of Customer or its agents, employees and contractors (excluding those under Supplier's supervision), if, in

---

[4] Optional provision. Suppliers often prefer that the original customer remain financially responsible, so parenthetically represents a reasonable compromise.

each instance: (i) Supplier gives prompt notice, with full particulars, and (ii) uses reasonable efforts to mitigate the effects of the failure.

2.19 Force Majeure

2.19.1 Force Majeure Events

Neither Party shall be liable for any default or delay in the performance of its obligations if and to the extent such default or delay is caused by any of the following (each, a "Force Majeure Event"):

(a) fire, flood, earthquake, elements of nature or acts of God, acts of war, terrorism, riots, civil disorders, rebellions or revolutions; strikes, lockouts, or labor difficulties (including in the case of either Party's performance, labor difficulties affecting the other Party or third parties, but excluding the affected Party's own labor difficulties), malicious acts of third parties, interruption of telecommunications service; or any other similar cause beyond the reasonable control of the affected Party; that

(b) the affected Party could not have prevented by: (i) execution of a disaster recovery plan, (ii) use of alternate sources, work-around plans or similar means, or (iii) reasonable precautions and safeguards (including, without limitation, standard commercial anti-virus products[5] and procedures, emergency power supplies, required back-up systems, fire-suppression systems, or other measures that are standard in the industry).

2.19.2 Restoration of Service

If a Force Majeure Event delays, disrupts or interrupts performance of Services, then Customer shall continue to pay Supplier's Charges and Supplier will use its best efforts to restore Service at its expense. If Force Majeure Event or disaster requires Supplier to allocate limited resources among customers, performance of Services for Customer shall enjoy a priority at least equal to any other customer.

2.19.3 Alternative Service

If Supplier is unable substantially to restore critical Services (so designated by Customer in advance) within three (3) days after a Force Majeure Event, then [Alternative 1: Customer may, upon notice to Supplier, abate payment to the extent Services are not performed and obtain similar Services from another supplier at Customer's expense] [Alternative 2: Customer may obtain or Supplier shall provide substitute service from an alternate source, at Supplier's expense, provided Customer continues to pay Supplier's normal Charges]. The foregoing remedies are in addition to all other remedies, and do not excuse Supplier's obligation to provide disaster recovery services.

2.19.4 Failures to Restore Service—Termination

If Supplier fails for any reason substantially to restore all Services within thirty (30) days after a Force Majeure Event, Customer may terminate the Agreement or affected Services,

---

[5] Service description should spell out obligations concerning anti-virus products, procedures, and responsibilities of both parties.

at its option, in the same manner as for any convenience termination, but without paying any Termination Charge.

3 COMPLIANCE AND AUDIT

3.1 Compliance with Laws and Policies[6]

Each Party will comply with all applicable laws, regulations and treaties in all relevant jurisdictions ("applicable laws"). In particular, Supplier and its subcontractors shall comply with: (i) applicable privacy, immigration and export control laws and regulations in all countries; and (ii) Customer's [list] and other policies in effect from time to time, and disclosed to Supplier. Upon request, Supplier and its subcontractors shall enter into model processor or other, similar agreements concerning transfers of data to, from and among the member states of the European Union.

3.2 Changes in Laws and Policies

If and to the extent that changes in applicable laws or Customer policies affect performance of Services, there shall be no additional Charges for changes that: (i) can be accommodated using the personnel and other resources ordinarily assigned or available for performance of Services or (ii) affect Supplier's customers generally or (iii) its customers in the [name] industry. Customer-specific changes or Projects related to compliance that require material, additional personnel or other resources shall be charged on a basis consistent with Section 6.2.3 (concerning Charges for changes).

3.3 Audit

3.3.1 Audit Procedures

Supplier shall maintain complete and accurate records of the performance of Services, Charges and any reimbursable expenses in accordance with good industry practice and generally accepted accounting principles, consistently applied. Upon request, at reasonable times during and after the Term, Customer and its auditors shall have access to all Customer Data, and to the Supplier's facilities, personnel, equipment and records concerning the Charges, Services, and Supplier's performance in order to audit Supplier's practices and procedures; charges; general, internal and other controls (including the Customer Controls listed in Exhibit H); security practices; disaster recovery procedures and tests; Service Level performance, and any other matters pertinent to Customer (including, for example, regulatory requirements and compliance). Customer and its auditors shall have no access to Supplier's internal cost data (except to the extent costs may be reimbursable) and data of other Supplier clients.[7] Customer's auditors shall observe procedures and enter into nondisclosure agreements as appropriate to protect Supplier's proprietary information, and that of its clients. Customer's audit rights shall survive expiration or termination of this Agreement for a period of two (2) years.

---

[6] This is a very basic provision. Depending upon the customer's industry, the scope of services, and other circumstances, many other variations may be appropriate.

[7] This limitation is inappropriate for the (comparatively rare) 'open book' or 'cost-plus' contract.

3.3.2 Certain Certifications

Upon request, Supplier's Account Executive will provide such factual certifications as Customer or its auditors may reasonably request (eg, concerning the accuracy of Charges and reports, compliance with applicable Customer or Supplier ethics and other policies, reporting of incidents reportable under those policies) in connection with Customer's audits or certifications required to be given by Customer's auditors or executives.[8]

3.3.3 Audit Adjustments

If an audit reveals that Supplier has overcharged Customer for Services, Supplier shall reimburse Customer for the overpayment [, plus interest from the date of payment at (rate),] [9] and the cost of the audit within thirty (30) days after Customer's written request. Any audits conducted pursuant to this Article shall otherwise be at Customer's expense.

3.3.4 Supplier's Audits

Supplier shall make available to Customer the results of any internal or external review or audit conducted by Supplier relating to Supplier's operating practices and procedures or the Services, as well as an annual service auditor's report on controls placed in operation and tests of operating effectiveness in compliance with SAS-70 (or any successor audit standard) concerning [scope of SAS-70].[10] In particular, and without limiting the generality of its obligations, Supplier shall (i) provide Customer with full particulars of any breach or weakness in processes or systems mentioned in its SAS-70 or internal audit reports, and (ii) undertake immediate, diligent corrective action pursuant to a corrective action plan approved by Customer.

4 CUSTOMER RESPONSIBILITIES

4.1 Customer Representative

Customer shall designate, as of the Effective Date, an individual to whom all communications from Supplier may be addressed, and who has the authority to act for Customer in connection with all aspects of this Agreement (the "Customer Representative"), but any written notice, demand or other communication concerning matters other than the day-to-day provision of the Services shall be addressed to the person or persons specified in Section 13.2. Customer's Representative may designate an alternate or deputy to act in his or her place in case of illness, vacation or other absence.

4.2 Customer Third Party Software

Customer shall make available to Supplier, for the sole purpose of providing the Services, Customer Third Party Software used by Customer to perform similar services and listed

---

[8] Customer policies written for employees and domestic operations may not be appropriate for suppliers or offshore operations. Some suppliers have sophisticated policies suitable for worldwide operations.

[9] Optional provision. Requesting interest invites the supplier to request interest on late payments.

[10] Many suppliers provide their customers with a standard SAS-70 Type II report, with tests, concerning IT, security, and other controls at their facilities. All audit clauses should be reviewed with the customer's auditors.

on Schedule D-2. Supplier agrees to obtain, at its expense, all required licenses, maintenance, and consents from third parties necessary to enable Supplier to have access to and use of such Customer Third Party Software. If for any reason Supplier is unable to obtain any such consent, then the Parties will consult and cooperate concerning alternative arrangements to provide access to, or use of, the Third Party Software, or if appropriate, substitute software with substantially equivalent or superior functionality. Supplier will not use any Third Party Software in performance of Services unless the license and other contracts therefor are transferable to Customer, or Customer approves in writing. Customer may condition its approval upon assurances that the Third Party Software is transferable, or available to Customer upon commercially reasonable terms.

4.3 Supplier Use of Customer Facilities

To enable Supplier to provide the Services, Customer shall provide, at no charge to Supplier, regular use of reasonably furnished office space, related utilities and janitorial service at Customer's facilities. Supplier, its employees and subcontractors shall comply with Customer's reasonable policies and procedures governing access to and use of Customer's facilities. Supplier shall be responsible for its own office supplies, long distance telephone service, photocopying, administrative support and other costs associated with occupation of Customer's facilities. Supplier shall refrain from any nuisance or waste, and return the facilities to Customer in the condition received, subject to normal wear and tear, when the Agreement expires or terminates. Supplier shall not make any alteration or improvement to Customer's facilities without Customer's prior written consent, which may be given or withheld in Customer's sole discretion. Supplier acquires no right, title, leasehold or other interest in Customer's facilities. Rather, its permitted use is a license, revocable by Customer at any time.

5 PERSONNEL

5.1 Employee Transfers[11]

5.1.1 Offers of Employment

On or before the Effective Date, Supplier shall have offered employment to each Customer employee it has agreed to employ, as listed on a separate list dated [date]. Supplier's offers shall be given in writing, conditioned upon execution of this Agreement and: (i) provide compensation at least equal to the affected employees' current total compensation; (ii) recognize length of service for purposes of vacation and other benefits; and (iii) immediately make all employees eligible for health and other benefit programs commensurate with their positions and length of service.

5.1.2 Employees on Leave

Transferred Employees on leave for family, medical, military or similar reasons on the Effective Date may commence work for Supplier upon: (i) completion of their leave previously authorized by Customer; or (ii) the [number] day following the Effective Date,

---

[11] These are very basic provisions for transfer of US employees. Details will vary, and expert advice may be required concerning employment law, benefits, and other issues. Outside the US, very different legal requirements apply. See Ch 9 above, at 9.6.

whichever first occurs, provided that Supplier must in all cases comply with applicable laws concerning family, medical, military and similar leave.

5.1.3 Key Transferred Employees

Supplier acknowledges that the Transferred Employees identified on a separate list dated [date] ("Key Transferred Employees") are critical to the provision of Services. Accordingly, Key Transferred Employees shall work on Customer's account on a substantially full-time basis (or such other basis as may be agreed) for at least the time periods specified on the list. Supplier shall not, for a period of [time] after the Commencement Date, transfer or reassign Key Transferred Employees to serve other customers without Customer's consent (which Customer may give or withhold in its sole discretion) or discharge them (other than for cause).

5.2 Key Supplier Positions

Supplier acknowledges that the personnel serving as Account Executive, [list others] and Transition Manager and ("Key Supplier Positions") are critical to the provision of Services, and will be assigned to the performance of Services on a full-time basis for at least [number] months, or in the case of the Transition Manager, until successful completion of all transition activities. Replacements for personnel filling Key Supplier Positions shall be subject to Customer's prior approval, following review of *curriculum vitae*, an interview, reference checks and other appropriate procedures.

5.3 Removal of Personnel

If Customer gives Supplier notice that the continued assignment of any individual to the performance of Services is not in Customer's interests, then after consultation between the Parties, if the issues are not resolved to Customer's reasonable satisfaction, Supplier shall remove the affected individual from Customer's account (but no such removal shall be deemed to require Supplier or any of its subcontractors to terminate any individual's employment or take disciplinary action).

5.4 Nonsolicitation of Employees[12]

5.4.1 No Solicitation

Except as otherwise expressly agreed concerning Termination Assistance, neither Party shall, without the other Party's prior express consent, solicit or offer employment to an employee of the other Party during the Term, and for one (1) year thereafter. This restriction shall not apply to offers extended in response to: (i) advertising; (ii) other, similar, general solicitations not directed toward the other Party's personnel; or (iii) unsolicited applications submitted upon an individual's own initiative.

---

[12] Optional provision. Policies and preferences vary concerning these commitments, and whether or not they should be reinforced by obligations to pay liquidated damages for breach.

5.4.2 Liquidated Damages

Any failure to comply with the foregoing obligations would have a material, adverse effect on the affected Party, but the actual damages sustained would be difficult to estimate. Accordingly, in the event of any breach of this provision, the breaching party shall be obligated to pay the other Party liquidated damages in an amount equal to [per cent] of the affected employee's total annual compensation as of the date of breach, including salary, applicable fringe benefits and payroll taxes. The Parties agree that these liquidated damages are reasonable estimates of actual damages, and are reasonable in the circumstances existing on the Effective Date. The Parties agree that such liquidated damages are not penalties, but reasonable estimates of actual damages that are reasonable in the circumstances existing on the Effective Date.

6 CONTRACT MANAGEMENT

6.1 Governance

The Parties will govern their relationship in accordance with Schedule G, Governance. Each Party will appoint duly qualified, employees to represent its interests in the applicable governance positions identified in Schedule G, and cause its representatives to devote the time necessary to meet their respective responsibilities.

6.2 Change Management

If and when Customer desires changes in the Services, or either or both Parties desire to add, delete or modify Services or make other changes in the terms of this Agreement, those changes shall be documented and approved in accordance with this Section 6.2 (the "Change Control Procedures").

6.2.1 Change Requests and Change Proposals

Customer shall propose changes through written requests to Supplier ("Change Requests"). Within [number] days after receiving a Change Request, Supplier shall, at its expense, prepare and deliver to Customer a detailed change proposal in a mutually agreed format ("Change Proposal") describing the change in reasonable detail, including any effect on Charges, other costs to Customer, Service Levels, performance, time schedules or other reasonably anticipated effects upon the Services. Supplier may submit Change Proposals to Customer on its own initiative. A Change Proposal shall constitute an offer, irrevocable for at least thirty (30) days after receipt, and shall be subject to discussion by the Parties and modification as appropriate.[13]

---

[13] Suppliers often request compensation for preparation of change proposals, especially when they require substantial effort, as they may for large projects. In such cases, it is good practice to require prompt submission of a brief preliminary estimate, including a preliminary and approximate (or 'rough order of magnitude') estimate of the probable scope, scale, cost, and impact, together with a binding estimate of the cost to prepare a detailed proposal. The preliminary estimate can help the customer to decide whether to go further and authorize preparation of a major proposal.

6.2.2 Effect of Approved Change Proposals

If Customer elects in writing to accept the Change Proposal, the Agreement and affected Schedules shall be deemed amended to the extent necessary to reflect the change. If Customer declines to accept the Change Proposal, the Schedules and Agreement shall remain unchanged. If the Parties are unable to agree upon a change, related Charges or other matters related to the proposed change, and Customer reasonably believes the change is legally required or otherwise urgent, then Customer may direct Supplier to perform, Supplier shall perform as directed and receive the payment Customer reasonably believes due, pending resolution of disputed charges and other matters in accordance with Sections 11.9 and 11.10, below, concerning disputes.

6.2.3 Charges for Changes

There shall be no additional Charges for changes that can be accommodated using the personnel and other resources ordinarily assigned or available for performance of Services. If and to the extent that changes require material, incremental effort, Charges therefor shall be based upon the net additional effort, priced at the applicable rate or other metric (if any) specified by Schedule C and otherwise at the most favorable rate Supplier then offers for similar volumes of similar services.

6.3 Equitable Adjustment

In the event of any extraordinary change in Customer's business because of acquisitions, divestitures, mergers, or other material changes in circumstances that increase or decrease volumes of Services by more than [eg, twenty-five per cent (25%)][14] above or below anticipated baselines, measured on an annual basis that [Customer] [either Party] reasonably expects to persist, then upon [Customer's] [either Party's] request, Supplier's Charges for the affected Services and relevant Termination Charges shall be equitably adjusted to reflect:

(a) the net increase or decrease in Supplier's aggregate costs of performing the Services that are caused by the extraordinary change;

(b) acquisitions or dispositions of assets and other similar costs of additions to or reductions in service; and

(c) a reasonable allowance for profit (not to exceed fifteen per cent [15%]) upon the net change in costs.

Equitable adjustments shall be effective as of the date of the request. Wherever this Agreement contemplates equitable adjustment of any Charges, they shall be adjusted generally in the manner contemplated by this Section.[15]

---

[14] Percentage generally corresponds to the range priced through incremental charges and credits (often referred to as additional resource charges (ARCs) and reduced resource credits (RRCs)).

[15] If the supplier prefers not to disclose costs, this provision can be rephrased to refer to net changes in staff and other resources, rather than costs (which can be estimated based upon known costs for staff, hardware, software, facilities, bandwidth, and the rest).

6.4 Acceptance of Deliverables[16]

Customer will designate one or more persons ("Acceptor") to (i) accept or reject Deliverables (in whole or in part) and (ii) communicate Customer's comments, objections or responses concerning any Deliverable, testing, review or prototype demonstration.

6.4.1 Acceptance Criteria

Acceptance criteria for Deliverables will be developed and agreed to at least thirty (30) days before the date of the relevant testing, delivery or milestone date. To the extent practicable, acceptance criteria will be objective, measurable and repeatable tests that are based upon Customer's anticipated production use of the Deliverables.

6.4.2 Acceptance Procedures

(a) In the case of Deliverables (or portions of Deliverables) consisting of documentation ("Documentary Deliverables"), the Acceptor will review the Deliverable and make any comments, objections or responses within the period specified in the relevant documents or if no period is specified, within ten (10) business days after receipt ("Review Period").

(b) In the case of hardware, software or infrastructure components of a Deliverable, Supplier will conduct the acceptance tests as prescribed in the relevant documents after giving Customer notice and an opportunity to observe the acceptance tests. Supplier will provide the Acceptor with any documentation or other record of the results of the acceptance tests.

6.4.3 Customer Review

The Acceptor will review the Documentary Deliverables and the record or results of acceptance tests for other Deliverables within the Review Period and then deliver to Supplier either: (i) written acceptance of the relevant Deliverable or (ii) a written response specifying in detail how the Deliverable fails to conform to applicable acceptance criteria. No Deliverable will be accepted for purposes of payment unless and until Customer formally accepts the Deliverable in writing, or approves its use in a production environment (other than on a qualified, conditional or other limited basis).

6.4.4 Reasonable Approval

Customer may not unreasonably withhold or delay acceptance of Deliverables.

(a) Customer will accept a Documentary Deliverable if it: (i) satisfies the scope of the work in all material respects, and (ii) contains the functionality or other content described in the relevant documents.

---

[16] Optional provision. Useful when applications maintenance and development are outsourced, or in other situations where extensive deliveries or Projects are anticipated. Similar language appears in the accompanying form standard terms for projects, and need not appear in both places.

(b) Customer will accept a hardware, software, infrastructure or other Deliverable if (i) it satisfies relevant acceptance criteria or tests in all material respects and is free from material faults; or (ii) it is put into production by Customer or upon Customer's approval (other than on a qualified, conditional or other limited basis); or (iii) the Acceptor signs the relevant acceptance documents without qualification or conditions.

6.4.5 Resubmission of Rejected Deliverables

In the event the Acceptor notifies Supplier in writing that all or any part of a Deliverable is unacceptable, Supplier will modify and return to Customer the entire Deliverable for review of the modified portions within five (5) business days (or such other period as may be agreed). If and to the extent that any deficiencies remain, these procedures may be repeated as necessary to correct the deficiencies that remain (or others revealed by further testing or review after corrective work). Upon review and approval of the corrected Deliverable by the Acceptor, the Deliverable will be considered accepted; but acceptance may be revoked at any time prior to completion of the last milestone or related Deliverable, if testing of a later Deliverable reveals material deficiencies in a previously accepted Deliverable.

7 CONFIDENTIAL INFORMATION

7.1 Customer's Confidential Information

Supplier shall take reasonable measures to keep Customer's Confidential Information and Confidential Materials in confidence and shall, at a minimum, protect Customer's Confidential Information and Confidential Materials with the same degree of care as Supplier's own Confidential Information and Confidential Materials. Except as authorized by Customer or as required by law, Supplier shall not disclose any of Customer's Confidential Information or deliver any of Customer's Confidential Materials to any person other than its own employees, consultants, permitted subcontractors and agents to the extent reasonably necessary to provide the Services. Supplier will not use, and will not permit its Affiliates, employees, subcontractors, consultants or agents to use any of Customer's Confidential Information or Confidential Materials for any purposes other than those contemplated by this Agreement. Upon expiration or termination of this Agreement, Supplier shall return all Customer Confidential Information and Customer Confidential Materials to Customer, retain no copies, and erase all media containing Customer Confidential Information (other than reasonable archival data authorized by Customer). Supplier's obligations to protect Customer's Confidential Information and Confidential Materials shall survive expiration or termination of this Agreement.

7.2 Supplier Confidential Information

Customer shall take reasonable measures to keep Supplier's Confidential Information and Confidential Materials in confidence and shall, at a minimum, protect Supplier's Confidential Information and Confidential Materials with the same degree of care as Customer's own Confidential Information and Confidential Materials. Except as authorized by Supplier or as required by law, Customer shall not disclose any of Supplier's Confidential Information or deliver any of Supplier's Confidential Materials to any person other than its own employees, consultants, contractors and agents to the extent reasonably necessary for normal use of Supplier's Services, governance, administration of the Agreement and related purposes. Customer shall not use, or permit its Affiliates, employees, contractors, agents or consultants to use any of Supplier's Confidential Information or Confidential Materials for any purposes other than those contemplated by this Agreement. Customer's contractors shall keep Supplier's Confidential Information and Materials in confidence, and upon request, enter into nondisclosure agreements reasonably satisfactory to Supplier. Upon expiration or termination of this Agreement, Customer shall return all Supplier Confidential Information and Supplier Confidential Materials to Supplier, retain no copies, and erase all media containing Customer Confidential Information (other than reasonable archival data and any Supplier Confidential Information and Supplier Confidential Materials that Customer may otherwise be permitted to use after expiration or termination). Customer's obligations to protect Supplier's Confidential Information and Confidential Materials shall survive expiration or termination of this Agreement.

7.3 Certain Disclosures

Disclosures of the other Party's Confidential Information compelled by subpoena or other legal process ("subpoena") shall not breach this Article 7, provided, that immediately after receiving any such subpoena, the recipient advises the other Party, and cooperates with the disclosing Party's efforts to obtain a protective order (at the disclosing Party's expense), or other reasonable and lawful measures to protect the other Party's Confidential Information and Confidential Materials.

7.4 Security Breaches

In the event that any data concerning individuals ("personal data") is disclosed by Supplier (or its employees, subcontractors or agents) contrary to applicable laws or security procedures, or Supplier (or its employees, subcontractors or agents) discovers, receives notice of or suspects that unauthorized access, acquisition, disclosure or use of personal data has occurred or is likely to occur ("incident"), then Supplier shall give prompt notice to Customer, with full particulars, and cooperate in the investigation of the incident. If applicable laws require notice to authorities or individuals, or other remedial action, or Customer determines that notices or other remedial actions are warranted, then Supplier shall undertake such remedial action as Customer may reasonably direct, at Supplier's expense or, at Customer's option, reimburse Customer for the expense of remedial action undertaken by Customer in its discretion. (For purposes of this Section, remedial action may include, without limitation, improvements to security measures; notice to individuals, credit reporting agencies, public authorities and other entities; customer service support; credit monitoring and defense and satisfaction of third party claims.) Supplier represents and warrants to Customer that, except as disclosed to Customer in writing, during the five (5) years preceding the Effective Date, Supplier and its Affiliates have not suffered or experienced any such incident, nor have any customers of Supplier or its Affiliates been required to give notice to individuals related to any such incident.

8 INTELLECTUAL PROPERTY

8.1 Customer License

During the Term, and subject to the terms and conditions of this Agreement, Customer hereby grants to Supplier a nonexclusive, royalty-free license to use, execute, reproduce, display, and modify[17] Customer Software identified by the accompanying Schedules or from time to time used in Customer's own operations, solely for the purpose of performing the Services for Customer. Customer may sublicense Customer Software to permitted subcontractors to the extent reasonably necessary for performance of approved subcontracted services. All sublicenses shall be in writing, and shall contain provisions consistent with this Agreement. Supplier acquires no right, title or interest in any Customer Software, other than the rights of use authorized by this Agreement, which shall expire on expiration or termination of the Agreement.

8.2 Supplier Licenses

Supplier shall, at its expense, install, operate and maintain any Supplier Software needed to provide the Services. Supplier shall not use in performing the Services any Supplier Software that is not available to Customer or a successor supplier of services upon commercially reasonable terms, unless otherwise expressly agreed in advance and in writing in each instance. Supplier hereby grants to Customer, its contractors and subcontractors, a worldwide, royalty-free, nonexclusive license to use, execute, reproduce, and display the Supplier Software during the Term for Customer's benefit, to the extent necessary or desirable for Customer or its contractors and subcontractors to perform any services related to this Agreement, or to receive and use the Services. Upon expiration or termination of this Agreement, Supplier agrees to license Customer or a successor supplier to use, execute, reproduce, and display the Supplier Software as (i) Supplier may use to perform Services at any time during the Term, and (ii) is reasonably necessary for Customer's continuing operations and the performance of similar services. All such licenses shall be in writing, in form and substance reasonably satisfactory to both Parties, and contain customary provisions for the protection of Supplier's intellectual property consistent with this Agreement. If Customer desires ongoing support following expiration or termination of this Agreement, and Customer offers such support, Customer shall be required to pay standard maintenance and support charges.

8.3 Third Party Software

8.3.1 Third Party Systems Software

Supplier shall, subject to any specific obligations contained in the Schedules: (i) maintain and adhere to third party systems software licenses used by Customer on the Effective Date (or equivalents); (ii) upgrade, enhance, and implement new versions of the third

---

[17] If applications maintenance and development are out of scope, rights to modify are unnecessary.

party systems software; and (iii) replace or add to third party systems software used by Customer on the Effective Date, so that all systems software is on a current, or near-current and supported release. Supplier shall not use any third party systems software in performing the Services unless either: (a) the license therefor is assignable, or a new license is available to Customer at Customer's request without transfer, upgrade or similar fees; or (b) the third party systems software is a standard commercial product, available to Customer, or a successor supplier of similar services, on commercially reasonable terms.

8.3.2 Third Party Applications Software

During the Term, Customer shall be the licensee of all third party applications software used to provide the Services, and shall be a party to any associated maintenance agreements. Supplier shall be operationally responsible for all such software during the Term, but Customer shall retain financial responsibility. Supplier shall comply with the use restrictions and nondisclosure obligations imposed on Customer by the licensors of third party applications. Supplier shall not introduce any third party applications software without Customer's prior written consent. Supplier shall install, operate and support additional third party applications software designated by Customer from time to time during the Term in accordance with the Change Control Procedure.

8.4 Work Product

All software, documentation, inventions, works of authorship and intellectual property developed by Supplier (or its subcontractors) in connection with the performance of Services ("Work Product") shall be Customer's exclusive property and are "works made for hire" under US copyright laws. If any such Work Product is not considered a work made for hire under applicable law, Supplier hereby irrevocably assigns to Customer, without further consideration, all of Supplier's right, title and interest in and to the Work Product. Supplier shall execute any documents and take any other actions reasonably requested by Customer to accomplish the purposes of this Section. Customer may apply for patent, copyright or other intellectual property rights with respect to such newly developed intellectual property in all countries, and Supplier will extend reasonable cooperation in order to obtain and retain such registrations and other protections as Customer deems advisable. Customer grants Supplier a nonexclusive license to use all such Work Product in the performance of Services for Customer during the Term. All Work Product shall consist of: (i) wholly original works of Supplier; and (ii) matter that Supplier may use and transfer to Customer without breach of any legal or contractual obligation, or infringement of any third party's proprietary rights. Unless otherwise agreed to the contrary in writing, Customer may make, use, sell, copy, distribute and make derivative works from all Work Product delivered to Customer, free from any restriction, consent requirement, or royalty obligation to Supplier or any third party.[18]

---

[18] If the supplier may embed any of its own software components or other intellectual property in work product, there may be additional language concerning customer consent and rights to use.

8.5 Infringements

Each Party will perform its responsibilities under this Agreement in a manner that does not, to the Knowledge of the applicable Party, infringe, or constitute an infringement or misappropriation of, any patent, trade secret, copyright or other intellectual property right of any third party.

8.6 Open Source

Supplier will make no use of any open source software or code in any Work Product, operations or other Services of any kind without Customer's prior written consent in each instance. Customer may give or withhold its consent in its sole and absolute discretion.

8.7 Rights in Residuals

Nothing contained in this Agreement shall restrict either Party from the use of any ideas, concepts, know-how, methodologies, processes, technologies, algorithms or techniques relating to the Services which either Party, individually or jointly, (i) owns prior to the Effective Date, or (ii) develops or discloses under this Agreement, (iii) develops or obtains independently during the Term, or (iv) incidentally learns or develops in the course of performance and retains in the unaided memories of its personnel, provided that in doing so such Party does not breach its obligations of confidentiality or infringe the intellectual property rights of the other Party, or third parties, who have licensed or provided materials to the other Party. Except for the license rights contained in this Article 8, neither this Agreement nor any disclosure made hereunder grants any license to either Party under any patents or copyrights of the other Party. Each Party reserves all rights in its ideas, concepts, know-how, methodologies, processes, technologies, algorithms, techniques and other intellectual property of every kind and description (except as otherwise expressly agreed in writing) and no provision of this Agreement shall be construed to transfer any of such Party's rights in such intellectual property.

9 CHARGES AND PAYMENT

9.1 Invoices for Services

Supplier will invoice Customer monthly in arrears for Supplier's Charges. Each invoice will separately state Supplier's Charges as well as reimbursable expenses and applicable taxes owed by Customer, in such detail as the Schedules require, or Customer may reasonably request for chargeback or other purposes.[19] Invoices for Services must be submitted, if at all, within sixty (60) days after the end of the month in which they were performed, or within sixty (60) days after completion of the relevant delivery, milestone, billing date or other billing event. Thereafter, Customer's payment obligations shall be excused.

9.2 Charges All-Inclusive

Supplier's Charges are all-inclusive. Payment of the Charges specified by Schedule C constitutes full payment for all Services, including provision of all hardware, software,

---

[19] To avoid misunderstandings, it is helpful to discuss invoices during negotiations and agree upon the level of detail and form of invoice, which may be attached as an exhibit.

facilities, personnel and other resources required to perform the Services. Unless otherwise expressly agreed in writing, Customer shall have no responsibility to pay or reimburse any other charge, expense or amount.

9.3 Payment

Customer shall pay all amounts set forth on Supplier's invoices within [number] (__) days after receiving Supplier's invoice. [Amounts not paid when due shall be subject to a late charge of (percent) per month, or the applicable legal maximum, whichever is less. Late charges are intended as liquidated damages, to compensate Supplier for delays in payment, and not as penalties or interest upon a loan or forbearance. The Parties agree that these late charges are reasonable estimates of actual damages, and are reasonable in the circumstances existing on the Effective Date.][20]

9.4 Proration

All periodic charges are to be computed on a monthly basis, and will be prorated for any partial month, unless specifically stated otherwise in this Agreement. Any charges payable to third parties for periods before commencement or after termination or expiration of the Term shall be prorated as of the Effective Date or date of termination or expiration, as appropriate.

9.5 Disputed Amounts

Customer may withhold payment of invoiced amounts that Customer disputes in good faith, or otherwise withhold or set off amounts otherwise owed to Customer, pending resolution of the matter [,but if the disputed amount exceeds (threshold amount) then Customer shall pay further disputed amounts into an escrow account established under an agreement with a national bank approved by both Parties. Amounts held in escrow shall be invested in US Government securities, certificates of deposit of the bank acting as escrow holder, or other high quality, short term liquid investments acceptable to both Parties. Amounts held in escrow, plus accrued interest shall be paid to Customer or Supplier, or in portions to both Parties, as determined or agreed, within ten (10) business days after final resolution of the dispute by agreement, arbitral award or judgment (unless stayed, in which case payment shall be due when the judgment becomes final after any appeal). Amounts withheld and placed in escrow with respect to any month shall in no event exceed [per cent] of Supplier's Charges (excluding expense reimbursements) for that month. If the disputed amount exceeds the amount permitted to be withheld, then Customer may withhold the remainder in successive months until the entire disputed amount has been withheld and paid into escrow.] [21] Failures to withhold or set off shall in no event be construed as waivers of Customer's rights.

---

[20] Optional language, not generally proposed by customers, but inserted to illustrate a common approach to the issue.

[21] Optional language, not generally proposed by customers in the first instance. Suppliers generally resist unlimited, fully discretionary withholding. Bracketed language illustrates a possible compromise resolution.

9.6 Taxes

[Alternative 1, Customer pays: Customer agrees to pay, or reimburse Supplier for, all taxes, assessments, fees and other governmental charges of any kind (including, without limitation, sales, use, excise and, value-added, business license and gross receipts taxes) (collectively, "taxes") that may be imposed upon the Services, any amount paid to Supplier hereunder, or this Agreement.] [Alternative 2, Supplier absorbs current taxes: Supplier's charges include all sales, use, gross receipts, excise, value-added, withholding, personal property or other taxes attributable to goods and services used in performing the Services, or that are imposed upon the Services on the Effective Date ("current taxes"). Supplier's charges exclude taxes thereafter imposed, or later increases in current taxes, which Customer shall pay or reimburse.] Each Party bears sole responsibility for all taxes and assessments upon its own real and personal property and net income. The Parties shall cooperate with the other to comply with their respective tax obligations, and make available any resale certificates, exemption certificates or other information reasonably requested by a Party.

9.7 Reimbursable Expenses

If, when and to the extent that Customer may agree in writing to pay or reimburse any expenses, Supplier shall (i) provide such documentation and supporting information as Customer may reasonably request and (ii) comply with applicable travel, expense and other policies specified by Customer. Customer shall have no obligation to pay any overhead allocation, administrative charge or other markup upon any reimbursed expense. If, when and to the extent that the Schedules may call for Supplier to pass through to Customer any costs paid to third parties, then Supplier shall review the third party's invoice and performance, approve or disapprove the invoice, and promptly transmit the invoice to Customer for payment (insofar as approved) in sufficient time for Customer to pay the invoice in a timely manner.

9.8 Most-Favored Customer

Charges payable from time to time by Customer under this Agreement shall not exceed those then paid by other Supplier customers for services similar to the Services in their duration, scope, and volume. Within thirty (30) days after the beginning of each Contract Year, or upon Customer's request (made no more than twice in any Contract Year), [Supplier's chief financial officer] [a Supplier officer with executive responsibility for outsourcing operations] shall certify in writing to Customer that Supplier's Charges to Customer comply with this Section. If the prices charged to another Supplier customer are lower than the Charges to Customer, then the Charges to Customer shall be equitably adjusted to provide Customer the benefit of such lower Charges, retroactive to the first date on which such lower Charges to the other customer first became effective. Upon request, Supplier shall provide to Customer's independent auditors the inform ation reasonably necessary for Customer to verify compliance. The auditors shall inform Customer and Supplier whether Supplier's Charges comply with this Section, but shall keep in information disclosed to them for this purpose in strict confidence.

9.9 Benchmarking

Customer may [at any time] [once in every Contract Year] measure the quality, efficiency and cost of some or all Services against the market using an independent benchmarking firm retained by Customer ("Benchmarker"), which may not be a Supplier competitor. Benchmarker shall submit its draft findings to both Parties for review and comment by both Parties, consider comments received, and then deliver its final report in writing to both Parties. If the Benchmarker determines that Supplier's Charges materially exceed market rates for similar volumes of similar services (normalized, as provided below), then the Parties' representatives shall meet to discuss adjustments of the Charges. If the Parties are unable to agree upon adjustments in Supplier's Charges within sixty (60) days after receiving Benchmarker's report, then Customer may, at its option, terminate some or all relevant Services, or this Agreement for convenience, as provided below, but no Termination Charge shall be paid. Customer's right to terminate shall expire one hundred eighty (180) days after receiving Benchmarker's final report. For purposes of this Section, "materially exceed" shall mean that total charges for benchmarked Services exceed the [least expensive quartile/median] of the benchmarked sample. Comparisons with market measures of quality and cost shall be normalized to account for investments in assets, transfers of personnel, variations in configurations, transition charges, reasonable overheads and profit, the place of performance, differences in service levels, unique or unusual Customer requirements and other, similar factors. Comparisons shall disregard unusual or uneconomic terms (such as introductory discounts).

10 REPRESENTATIONS, WARRANTIES AND COVENANTS

10.1 Mutual Representations, Warranties and Covenants

Each Party represents and warrants to the other as follows:

(a) It is duly organized and validly existing under the laws of its jurisdiction of organization.
(b) It is qualified to carry on its business wherever qualification is necessary for the conduct of its business.
(c) It has all necessary organizational power to carry on its business, enter into this Agreement and perform its obligations hereunder.
(d) The execution, delivery and consummation of all transactions contemplated in this Agreement have been duly authorized by all necessary organizational action on its part.
(e) This Agreement constitutes a legal, valid and binding obligation of the relevant Party, enforceable against it in accordance with its terms.
(f) Its execution and performance of this Agreement will not, to its Knowledge: (i) violate any law or regulation, or breach the terms of any judgment, instrument, agreement, charter or by-law provision, authorization or license to which it or its assets are subject; (ii) violate or infringe any proprietary rights of third parties; or (iii) create circumstances that would, with notice or lapse of time, or both, constitute violation, breach or infringement of any of the foregoing.

10.2 Supplier Representations, Warranties and Covenants

(a) Supplier represents and warrants to Customer that Supplier's use of the Supplier Software, Supplier Third Party Software and other methodologies, practices and procedures do not, to the Knowledge of Supplier, violate any copyright, patent, or other proprietary right of any third party and Supplier has no Knowledge of any such claim or potential claim.

(b) Supplier shall not infringe the copyrights, patents, trade secrets or other proprietary rights of any third party.

(c) Supplier's performance of Services will comply with all applicable laws and regulations.

(d) Supplier will comply, and cause its officers, directors, employees, agents and subcontractors to comply, with ethical standards approved by Customer and at least as stringent as Customer's in effect from time to time, and disclosed to Supplier in writing. Supplier will promptly report to Customer any: (i) violations or attempted violations of those ethical standards; (ii) theft, fraud or other, similar misconduct; or (iii) breaches of confidentiality, security or controls of which Supplier becomes aware during the performance of Services.

(e) Supplier has not violated any applicable laws or regulations or any Customer policies regarding the offering of inducements in connection with this Agreement.

10.3 Disclaimers

THERE ARE NO WARRANTIES BY EITHER PARTY, OTHER THAN THOSE STATED IN THIS AGREEMENT, AND SUPPLIER DISCLAIMS ANY IMPLIED WARRANTIES, INCLUDING, WITHOUT LIMITATION, ANY IMPLIED WARRANTIES OF MERCHANTABILITY AND FITNESS FOR A PARTICULAR PURPOSE.

11 REMEDIES

11.1 Insurance

Supplier shall carry and maintain the insurance required by Schedule I. Policy limits in Schedule I: (i) apply to this Agreement; (ii) are not intended to state Supplier's overall insurance coverage for its business (which is greater, individually and in the aggregate); and (iii) shall not be construed to limit Supplier's liability, or to modify any provision of this Agreement limiting liability, or providing exceptions from any such limitation.[22]

11.2 Risk of Loss

Each Party shall be responsible for risk of loss of, and damage to, any equipment, software or other tangible property in its possession or under its control, whether owned or leased.

---

[22] Schedule should spell out insurance requirements in detail: kinds of coverage, policy limits (for individual claims and in the aggregate), carrier ratings, proof of insurance requirements, notice requirements (eg of reductions in coverage or policy cancellation), etc.

The Parties shall look to their own insurance or self-insurance with respect to all such loss or damage. Each Party shall promptly notify the other of any damage to or destruction of the other Party's tangible property in its possession, whether owned or leased. The Parties shall cause their respective insurers to issue appropriate waivers of subrogation for their respective property insurance policies (or, alternatively, advise the other Party in writing if no such waiver is obtainable, or is obtainable only at material additional expense).

11.3 Limited Remedy
11.3.1 Recovery of Actual Damages
Except as otherwise expressly provided below:

(a) The Parties shall not be liable to one another in contract, tort, for breach of warranty or otherwise, for any lost revenues, lost profits, lost goodwill or special, consequential, exemplary or punitive damages arising from any act or omission of the relevant Party, or its Affiliates, officers, agents, employees, or subcontractors, even if advised of the possibility of such losses or damages. However, costs associated with mitigation of losses and damages, substitute products or services or other corrective or remedial measures reasonably undertaken by Customer shall in no event be considered consequential damages.

(b) The Parties' total liability (in contract or tort) for any acts or omissions arising from or relating to the performance of this Agreement shall be limited to payment of actual damages, up to an aggregate maximum equal to Supplier's Charges (excluding expense reimbursements, if any), during the [number] months preceding accrual of the last claim asserted by Customer, for all claims that arise under or relate to the Agreement. If a claim arises during the first [number] months after the Effective Date, the limitation shall equal projected Charges through the end of that period, or [amount] ($_____), whichever is greater. Amounts paid or credited as Service Credits or Transition Credits shall not count toward the foregoing limits.

11.3.2 Certain Exceptions
The limitations in Sections 11.3.1(a) and (b) shall not apply to Customer's payment obligations, or to acts or omissions of a Party or its Affiliates, officers, agents and employees that constitute, involve or relate to: (i) gross negligence or recklessness; (ii) intentional misconduct; (iii) violations of law; (iv) indemnified claims; (v) misappropriation or infringement of intellectual property rights; (vi) breaches of confidentiality obligations; or (vii) abandonment of any or all performance or wrongful termination of the Agreement.

11.4 Customer's Indemnity
Customer agrees to indemnify, defend and hold the Supplier Indemnitees harmless from and against any and all Losses arising from or related to claims by unrelated third

parties that arise from or relate to any act or omission of Customer, its officers, directors, employees, consultants or agents, and concern actual or alleged:

(a) Breach of any agreement with any third party that relates in any way to Customer's performance of Services before the Effective Date;

(b) Infringement of any patent, trade secret, copyright, trademark, service mark or other proprietary rights related to: (i) equipment, software or other resources provided to Supplier by or on behalf of Customer; or (ii) Customer's acts or omissions under or related to this Agreement (but specifically excluding claims arising from Supplier's failure to obtain any consents it is required to obtain from third parties);

(c) Breach of Customer's obligations concerning Supplier's Confidential Information;

(d) Taxes, penalties, assessments or interest assessed against Supplier with respect to any of Customer's tax obligations; and

(e) Violations of laws or regulations (including tax laws and regulations) by Customer or any of the Customer Indemnitees related to Customer's performance hereunder.

11.5 Supplier's Indemnity

Supplier agrees to indemnify, defend and hold the Customer Indemnitees harmless from and against any and all Losses arising from or related to claims by unrelated third parties that arise from or relate to acts or omissions of Supplier, its officers, directors, employees, consultants or agents, and concern actual or alleged:

(a) Breach of any agreement with any third party that relates in any way to Supplier's performance of Services (including, without limitation, Managed Agreements and agreements assigned or otherwise transferred to Supplier);

(b) Infringement of any patent, trade secret, trademark, service mark, copyright or other proprietary rights alleged to have occurred because of (i) equipment, software, deliverables or other resources provided to Customer by or on behalf of Supplier; (ii) Supplier's acts or omissions under or related to this Agreement, including performance of Services;

(c) Breach of Supplier's obligations concerning Customer's Confidential Information;

(d) Taxes, penalties, assessments or interest assessed against Customer with respect to any of Supplier's tax obligations;

(e) Violations of laws or regulations (including tax laws and regulations) by Supplier or any of the Supplier Indemnitees related to Supplier's performance hereunder;

(f) Breaches of or inaccuracies in any of Supplier's representations, warranties, or covenants;

(g) Supplier's failure to obtain or abide by any required consent;

(h) Supplier's errors, omissions or failures to perform;

(i) Shared use of facilities, hardware, software or other resources with other Supplier customers;

(j) Any claims by or on behalf of Customer employees relating in any way to selection of the Transferred Employees, representations to or communications with Transferred Employees, or Supplier's offers of employment; and

(k) Any claims by or on behalf of Transferred Employees or other persons employed or engaged by Supplier or its subcontractors that arise from or relate in any way to their employment with Supplier or its subcontractors or to the termination of their employment with Supplier or its subcontractors.

11.6 Mutual Indemnity—Personal Injury, Property Damage

Each Party agrees to indemnify, defend and hold the other party harmless from and against any and all Losses related to claims by unrelated third parties that arise from or relate to:

(a) Death of or bodily injury to any agent, employee, customer, invitee, visitor or other person to the extent caused by the conduct of the indemnitor, its Affiliates, or their respective agents, employees or contractors; or

(a) Damage to, or loss or destruction of, any real or tangible personal property to the extent caused by conduct of the indemnitor, its Affiliates, or their respective agents, employees or contractors.

11.7 Indemnification Generally

With respect to indemnification under Sections 11.4, 11.5 and 11.6:

11.7.1 Proportional Liability

Each indemnitor's liability to pay or reimburse any Losses shall be limited to the extent of the indemnitor's proportional contribution to such Losses. Neither Party shall have any liability to the extent that any Losses are attributable to acts or omissions of the other Party or its indemnitees. In cases of infringement, an indemnitor shall have no liability to the extent that the claims of infringement concern: (i) infringing matter supplied by an indemnitee; (ii) unauthorized modifications or uses of hardware, software or other intellectual property supplied by the indemnitor; or (iii) acts or omissions of an indemnitee (other than use of infringing matter supplied by the indemnitor).

11.7.2 Subrogation

In the event that either Party shall be obligated to indemnify any of the other Party's indemnitees pursuant to this Agreement, the indemnitor shall, upon full payment of the indemnity, be subrogated to all rights, claims and defenses of the indemnitees.

11.7.3 Indemnification Procedures

Each indemnified Party agrees to give the indemnitor prompt written notice, with full particulars, of all claims and to cooperate, at the indemnitor's expense, in the investigation and defense of indemnified claims. After receiving notice, the indemnitor shall defend any action or other proceedings by counsel reasonably satisfactory to the indemnitee (but the indemnitor shall have no obligation to provide separate counsel for the indemnitee, except to the extent that conflicts or potential conflicts between the Parties' interests may require.) An indemnitee may, at its own expense, participate in the investigation and defense of such claim by separate counsel.

11.7.4 Settlement of Indemnified Claims

No indemnitor shall have any obligation to pay or reimburse any amounts paid in connection with any settlement or compromise reached without the indemnitor's prior written consent. Settlements or compromises reached by an indemnitor shall be subject to the prior written consent of the indemnified Party. In cases of claims of infringement, the indemnitor may in its sole but reasonable discretion: (i) procure a license authorizing use of disputed intellectual property by and for Customer; or (ii) develop or obtain and implement a non-infringing substitute with equivalent functionality. If none of the foregoing alternatives is commercially practicable, then, the allegedly infringing matter shall be withdrawn from the performance of Services, and related Charges, Service Levels and performance obligations shall be equitably adjusted to reflect that withdrawal. An indemnitor or indemnified Party may, in its sole but reasonable discretion, withhold consent to settlement of claims of infringement affecting its proprietary rights.

11.7.5 Certain Limitations

No indemnitee may assert directly against an indemnifying Party any claim for punitive, exemplary or similar damages; but this limitation shall not limit an indemnitee's rights hereunder to be indemnified against any Losses (including punitive or exemplary damages) arising out of a third party claim against the indemnitee.

11.8 Continued Performance

Except where clearly prevented by the issue in dispute, both Parties agree to continue performing their respective duties, obligations and responsibilities under this Agreement (including, among others, their respective obligations to perform and pay for Services) while the dispute is being resolved in accordance with this Article, unless and until such obligations are lawfully terminated or expire in accordance with the terms of the Agreement.

11.9 Management Review and Settlement of Disputes

Unless urgent circumstances or imminent expiration of limitation periods require a Party to commence proceedings or seek provisional relief from the courts, neither Party may commence any legal proceedings concerning any dispute without first submitting that dispute: (i) to the Supplier Account Executive and Customer Representative, then, if they are unable to resolve the matter within thirty (30) days; (ii) to one executive designated by senior management for each Party, and not directly engaged in day-to-day oversight or management of the Services, who shall consult together concerning possible resolution of the Parties' differences. Proposals, counter-proposals, negotiations and information exchanged during any such consultations or any later settlement negotiations shall be privileged, confidential, and inadmissible as evidence for any purpose in any subsequent proceedings (but otherwise admissible evidence, such as business records, shall not be rendered inadmissible merely because it may be transmitted or referred to in connection with settlement consultations or negotiations).

11.10 Disputes

11.10.1 Arbitration of Disputes

Except as otherwise expressly provided below, any dispute concerning the validity, interpretation, performance, breach, threatened breach, or termination of this Agreement shall be submitted to binding arbitration at [place], California in accordance with the Commercial Arbitration Rules and Mediation Procedures (including Procedures for Large, Complex Commercial Disputes) of the American Arbitration Association then in effect (the "Rules"). If the amount in dispute is Two Million Dollars ($2,000,000) or less, there shall be a single arbitrator, chosen by agreement of the Parties, or if they are unable to agree within thirty (30) days after the respondent receives the demand for arbitration ("demand"), then in accordance with the Rules. If the amount in dispute exceeds Two Million Dollars ($2,000,000), each Party shall nominate an arbitrator within thirty (30) days after the respondent receives the demand, and the two nominees shall select a third arbitrator, who shall act as chairman of the panel. If they are unable to agree, or either Party fails to nominate an arbitrator, the missing arbitrator(s) shall be chosen in accordance with the Rules. The arbitral award shall be final and binding, state reasons therefor, and may be confirmed by the judgment of a court of competent jurisdiction. The arbitrator(s) shall have no power or authority to award damages in excess of applicable limits, compel licensing of any intellectual property, award other remedies or relief not contemplated hereunder or authorized by applicable law, reinstate the Agreement (or any portion thereof) following exercise of termination rights, or to alter, amend or supplement any term, condition or other provision of this Agreement.

11.10.2 Legal Proceedings

Each Party reserves the rights to: (i) seek provisional remedies from a court of competent jurisdiction; (ii) litigate disputes concerning Confidential Information, intellectual property or Termination Assistance; and (iii) litigate claims against one another arising in litigation involving third parties who are not amenable to arbitration hereunder. In the event of any such litigation, the court or arbitrator, as appropriate, shall stay any arbitral proceedings then pending to the extent that they concern the foregoing. The Parties consent to exclusive jurisdiction and venue in competent California or federal courts in the [name] District of California for all legal proceedings contemplated or permitted hereunder (but without prejudice to either Party's right to seek provisional remedies or enforce an arbitral award, or judgment entered thereon, in any court with jurisdiction over the relevant Parties or their assets).

11.10.3 Costs of Proceedings

The prevailing Party shall be entitled to recover, in addition to all other relief, its reasonable attorneys' fees, court costs and costs of arbitration, including fees and costs related to enforcement of an arbitral award.

11.11 Governing Law

All questions concerning the validity, interpretation, performance, termination, breach, threatened breach or termination of this Agreement shall be governed by, and decided in accordance with, the law of California (excluding principles relating to the conflicts of law) and applicable US federal laws.

12 TERM AND TERMINATION

12.1 Term and Renewals

The Term shall commence on the Effective Date and shall end (unless renewed or terminated in accordance with this Article) on [date], but this Agreement shall not become effective unless and until the transactions contemplated by the Asset Purchase Agreement are consummated.[23] Customer may renew this Agreement for up to two successive terms of one year each ("Renewal Term(s)"), upon the terms then in effect by giving written notice of its election to renew at least one hundred eighty (180) days before the Agreement would otherwise expire.

12.2 Termination by Customer

Customer may terminate this Agreement, or one or more Categories of Service, in whole or in part, upon written notice if:

(a) Supplier materially breaches any of its obligations concerning disaster recovery; or
(b) Supplier fails to cure any material breach of its obligations hereunder within thirty (30) days after receipt of written notice; or
(c) Supplier's material breach is not reasonably subject to cure within thirty (30) days, and Supplier fails to submit a plan to cure reasonably acceptable to Customer within that period, or thereafter fails to use best efforts to prosecute the approved plan to completion within sixty (60) days; or
(d) Supplier commits numerous breaches that may be immaterial individually, but are material in the aggregate, and fails, within thirty (30) days after receiving notice, to cure the breach and complete a corrective action plan to prevent recurrence; or
(e) Supplier fails to cure any material weakness in relevant controls identified by any auditor within thirty (30) days; or
(f) Supplier's material breach is not reasonably subject to cure within sixty (60) days; or
(g) There are unexcused failures to meet Service Levels or Service Credit liability that exceed the thresholds for Unacceptable Service in Schedule B (but identification of those thresholds as Unacceptable Service is without prejudice to any contention that lesser liability or fewer failures may also constitute material breach); or
(h) Supplier files, or has filed against it, any petition or action under any bankruptcy, reorganization, insolvency, arrangement or similar law for the relief of debtors if such petition or action is not dismissed within ninety (90) days after filing.

Customer shall exercise its termination option by delivering Supplier a written notice identifying the scope of termination and the termination date (which shall be subject to the provisions of this Agreement concerning Termination Assistance).

12.3 Termination by Supplier

Supplier may terminate this Agreement only if Customer fails to pay undisputed amounts in excess of [amount] [one month's Charges] when due, and thereafter fails to cure its

---

[23] Delete reference to Asset Purchase Agreement if no assets are transferred.

failure within thirty (30) days after receiving written notice from Supplier.[24] Supplier hereby waives any other rights it may have under this Agreement, at law, or in equity to suspend performance or to terminate this Agreement for any reasons or in any circumstances other than those expressly permitted by this Section. Supplier shall exercise its termination option by delivering Customer a written notice specifying the termination date (which shall be subject to the provisions of this Agreement concerning Termination Assistance).

12.4 Termination for Convenience

Customer shall have the right to terminate this Agreement, or one or more Categories of Service, in whole or in part, prior to the end of the Initial Term without cause for its convenience upon (i) one hundred twenty (120) days' prior written notice to Supplier and (ii) payment [on or before the effective date of termination, of a Termination Charge in the amounts specified by Schedule C] [of Shutdown Costs within forty-five (45) days after receipt of Supplier's invoice therefor, including reasonable backup information]. No [Termination Charge] [Shutdown Costs] shall be paid if notice is given within one hundred eighty (180) days after announcement or consummation (whichever is later) of any transaction(s) effecting a change in Control of Supplier.[25] If a purported termination for cause by Customer is determined pursuant to Section 11.10 (Disputes) to have been improper, that termination shall be deemed a termination for convenience subject to this Section. Payment of [the applicable Termination Charge] [Shutdown Costs], if any, shall be Supplier's sole compensation for all convenience or other terminations for which [a Termination Charge] [Shutdown Costs] may be payable.

12.5 Partial Terminations

If Customer exercises any of its partial termination right, then:

(a) Services shall be terminated by Service Category, region, business unit, location or logical segment(s) or component(s), reasonably determined by Customer.
(b) The scope of particular remaining Services, and any affected Charges or Service Levels shall be equitably adjusted (generally in the manner contemplated by Section 6.3) to the extent necessary to allow for operational dependencies and phased reductions in Service (or introduction of new or substitute services) all in order to assure orderly, continuous operations with consistent quality of service.
(c) Termination Charges, if applicable, shall be in proportion to the value of the Services then terminated.[26]

---

[24] Where withholding is limited, or disputed payments are paid into escrow, wording should be revised accordingly, so that failures to pay material additional amounts in excess of relevant limitations, or to pay into escrow, may permit the supplier to terminate.

[25] Alternatively, there may be a reduced termination charge upon a change in control, and no termination charge if the supplier's business is sold to one of the customer's competitors. If shutdown costs are paid in lieu of termination charges, references to termination charges throughout the agreement should be edited accordingly.

[26] Omit if shutdown costs are paid in lieu of termination charges.

12.6 Disengagement

12.6.1 Termination Assistance Services

During the [number] month period before expiration of the Agreement, or following receipt of notice of termination (the "termination assistance period"), Supplier will cooperate with Customer and provide Customer with all reasonable assistance requested by Customer in order to assure the orderly transfer of Customer's data, systems and related operations to Customer or to a new third party supplier of services. That assistance ("Termination Assistance") includes but is not limited to the assistance described by Schedule E. Customer reserves the right to phase out one or more Services or Service Categories, change the sequence of particular activities and take other reasonable action that it deems advisable to effect an orderly transition. In cases of partial termination, all of the foregoing provisions shall apply to the terminated Services.

12.6.2 Assets and Personnel

During the termination assistance period, Supplier shall not dismiss, reassign or replace personnel, adjust their compensation, change their terms of employment, take other material personnel action, or redeploy or dispose of any assets otherwise transferable to Customer (other than in the normal course of business, or consistent with Schedule E) without Customer's prior written consent in each instance. Upon request, Supplier shall waive any contractual or other restrictions and permit Customer or a successor supplier to interview and offer employment to Supplier and subcontractor employees primarily performing Services for Customer.[27]

12.6.3 Charges, Extension

Supplier's Charges include Termination Assistance through the expiration or termination date of this Agreement. Thereafter, upon Customer's request, Supplier shall provide Termination Assistance (including performance of some or all Services) for a period of up to [number] months in accordance with Schedule C, or if no rates are specified for the relevant service, at Supplier's then-current standard rates. Upon any expiration or termination of this Agreement, Supplier shall pay all transfer and similar charges payable to third parties in connection with the legal, physical or electronic transfer of Customer Data and Customer Software.

12.6.4 Specific Performance

Supplier acknowledges that, if it were to breach, or threaten to breach, its obligation to provide Termination Assistance, Customer would be irreparably harmed and that money damages would provide no adequate remedy. Accordingly, in any such circumstances, Customer shall be entitled to proceed directly to a court of competent jurisdiction and obtain such injunctive, declaratory or other equitable relief as may be reasonably necessary to prevent such breach, compel performance and preserve the status quo by assuring continued performance of all Services (including Termination Assistance). Supplier irrevocably waives any requirement that Customer post any bond or undertaking, or demonstrate irreparable harm or the inadequacy of money damages.

---

[27] Provision written for US transactions. Under the EU Acquired Rights Directive and Member State legislation, employees may transfer by operation of law to the successor. See Ch 9 above at 9.6.

12.7 Bidding Assistance

Customer may obtain offers for performance of services similar to the Services at any time, during or after the Term. Upon request, Supplier shall provide to Customer such information and other cooperation as would be reasonably necessary for (i) Customer and/or its outside advisors to prepare requests for proposals or other, similar, documentation related to selection of a successor supplier and (ii) a third party to prepare an informed, non-qualified offer to perform similar services. The types of information and of cooperation to be provided by Supplier shall be at least as comprehensive as those initially provided by Customer to Supplier prior to the Effective Date.

12.8 Return of Data

Without limiting the generality of Section 12.6 or Schedule E, Supplier shall return all Customer Data, Customer Software, and Third Party Applications in the form maintained, or as otherwise reasonably requested by Customer, when required by Schedule E or otherwise requested by Customer at any time. Supplier acknowledges that Customer Data is Customer's exclusive property. Supplier has no right to retain (other than authorized archival copies), encrypt, corrupt or destroy any Customer Data or Customer Software, and waives any and all statutory or common law liens, claims of lien or similar rights, remedies or encumbrances that may now or hereafter exist and might limit or condition Supplier's obligations.

13 GENERAL PROVISIONS

13.1 Binding Nature and Assignment

This Agreement binds the Parties and their respective successors and permitted assigns. Unless otherwise agreed, neither Party may assign this Agreement without the prior written consent of the other Party. Customer may assign or transfer this Agreement in connection with any merger, sale of assets, reorganization or other similar transaction effecting a change in Control of Customer. Assignment of this Agreement shall not relieve a Party of its obligations hereunder, unless otherwise agreed by the Parties.

13.2 Notices

All notices required or contemplated hereunder shall be given in writing by prepaid certified mail, personal delivery (including express courier service with proof of delivery), or by facsimile or other electronic means with proof of delivery (if subsequently confirmed by certified mail or personal delivery). Notice by mail shall be deemed received three (3) days after mailing. Notice by personal delivery shall be effective upon receipt. Electronic notice shall be effective upon transmission and receipt of electronic confirmation. Actual receipt shall constitute effective notice in all cases. Notices shall be addressed as follows:

To Supplier: [Name]
                                             [Street Address]
                                             [City, State, zip]
                                             Telephone:
                                             Facsimile:
                                             Attention: General Counsel

To Customer: [Name]
                                       [Street Address]
                                       [City, State, Zip]
                                       Telephone:
                                       Facsimile:
                                       Attention: General Counsel

13.3 Entire Agreement, Amendment, Waiver

This Agreement, including all attached Schedules (which are incorporated by this reference) constitutes the entire agreement of the Parties, and supersedes any prior or contemporaneous understandings, agreements or representations. No supplement, modification, amendment or waiver of this Agreement shall be binding unless executed in writing by both Parties. No waiver of any of the provisions of this Agreement shall constitute a waiver of any other provision (whether or not similar) nor shall any such waiver constitute a continuing waiver unless otherwise expressly provided.

13.4 Further Assurances

The Parties shall with reasonable diligence do all things and provide all reasonable assurances as may be required to complete the transactions contemplated by this Agreement, and each Party shall provide such further documents or instruments requested by the other Party as may be reasonably necessary or desirable to give effect to this Agreement and to carry out its provisions.

13.5 Severability

Any provision in this Agreement which is prohibited or unenforceable in any jurisdiction shall, as to that jurisdiction, be ineffective to the extent of that prohibition or unenforceability without invalidating the remaining provisions or affecting the validity or enforceability of those provisions in any other jurisdiction.

13.6 Headings

The division of this Agreement into articles, sections, subsections and schedules and the division of schedules of this Agreement into sections and subsections and the insertion of headings are for convenience of reference only and shall not affect its construction or interpretation.

13.7 Survival

Notwithstanding the expiration or termination of this Agreement, those rights and obligations which are stated to survive pursuant this Agreement, or which by their nature are intended to survive such expiration or termination, shall so survive, including (without limitation) the following Articles and Sections: 3.3 (Audit), 5.4 (Nonsolicitation of Employees), 7 (Confidential Information), 8.2 (Supplier Licenses), 8.4 (Work Product), 9 (Charges and Payment), 11 (Remedies), 12.6 (Disengagement), 12.7 (Bidding Assistance), 12.8 (Return of Data), 13.9 (No Third Party Beneficiaries) and 13.10 (Duty to Act Reasonably).

13.8 Independent Contractors

The Parties are independent contractors and this Agreement shall not be construed to create any other relationship between the Parties, as principal and agent, joint venturers or otherwise. No Party is authorized to enter into agreements for or on behalf of the other, collect any obligation due or owed to any other Party, accept service of process for any other Party, or bind any other Party in any manner whatever.

13.9 No Third Party Beneficiaries

Nothing in this Agreement is intended to confer any rights, benefits, remedies, obligations or liabilities on any person (including, without limitation, any employees or Affiliates of the Parties) other than the Parties or their respective successors, permitted assigns and indemnitees.

13.10 Duty to Act Reasonably

Whenever this Agreement requires or contemplates any action, consent or approval, the Parties shall act reasonably and in good faith and (unless the Agreement expressly allows exercise of a Party's sole, or sole and absolute discretion) may not unreasonably withhold or delay its action, consent or approval.

13.11 Counterparts

This Agreement, including the Schedules, may be executed in one or more counterparts, each of which shall be deemed an original but all of which taken together shall constitute one and the same instrument.

Executed by the Parties' undersigned authorized representative as of the date first written above.

[Supplier]

By:
Name:
Title

[Customer]

By:
Name:
Title

GLOSSARY

"Affiliate" means, with respect to any Person, any Person directly or indirectly Controlling, Controlled by or under common Control with such other Person as of the date on which, or at any time during the period for which, the determination of affiliation is being made.

"Agreement" means this Master Services Agreement, including all schedules, exhibits and other attachments incorporated by reference, as they may be amended from time to time.

"Asset Purchase Agreement" means the Asset Purchase Agreement between Supplier and Customer dated as of [date].[28]

"Category of Service" (or "Service Category") means any of the following: [insert descriptions and cross-references].

"Charges" means the amounts payable by Customer to Supplier for Services, as described by and adjusted pursuant to the provisions of Schedule C and other applicable provisions of the Agreement.

"Confidential Information" means all of the business and financial information, source code, object code, business methods, business plans, procedures, know-how, trade secrets and other information of every kind that relates to the business of either Party (including information disclosed prior to the Effective Date) [optional: that is marked as such, promptly identified as such following disclosure, or disclosed in circumstances that would lead a reasonable person to recognize its confidential character]. Confidential Information excludes: (i) information in the public domain, (ii) generally known in either Party's industry, or (iii) independently developed or lawfully acquired (in either case, without breach of any legal or contractual obligation). Personal data concerning individuals are Confidential Information, even if available from public sources. The terms of this Agreement are Confidential Information of both Parties.[29]

"Confidential Materials" means all manuals, bulletins, computer programs (in any medium), databases (in any medium), printouts, reports, correspondence, memoranda, copies and other documentation and tangible things (in any medium) that contain or relate in any way to any Confidential Information.

"Contract Year" means the period beginning on the Effective Date and ending at the end of the twelfth (12th) complete month thereafter, and each twelve (12) month period thereafter.

---

[28] If no assets are transferred, this can be deleted. Separate agreement should cover transfers of facilities, hardware and other assets.

[29] Definitions of Confidential Information sometimes list specific categories of information that are particularly sensitive to either or both parties. Suppliers, for example, may be particularly concerned to protect methods or price quotations. Customers may be concerned to protect particular technology or trade secrets, depending upon their business.

"Control" means (i) the beneficial ownership or control of fifty per cent (50%) or more of the equity interest in any Person, or (ii) the ability to direct or cause the direction of the management or affairs of a Person, whether through the direct or indirect ownership of voting interests, by contract or otherwise.

"Customer" means [name] and its Affiliates.

"Customer Data" means all information entered on storage media or equipment by or on behalf of Customer and information derived from such information.[30]

"Customer Indemnitees" means Customer and, if applicable, its respective directors, officers, shareholders, partners, attorneys, accountants, agents and employees and their respective heirs, successors and assigns.

"Customer Software" means the applications and system software from time to time owned by Customer and used to provide the Services (including the software listed on Schedule D-1).

"Customer Third Party Software" means the third party applications and system software licensed to Customer and used to provide the Services (including the software listed on Schedule D-2).

"Deliverable" means hardware, software, documentation, goods, services and other matter furnished or to be furnished to Customer.

"Effective Date" means the date first written above.

"Force Majeure Event" has the meaning assigned by Section 2.19.1.

"Initial Term" means the initial term of [number] years beginning on the Effective Date as described by Section 12.1.

"Knowledge" or any similar word or phrase, means the actual knowledge of the management of Customer or Supplier, as applicable, responsible for the negotiation and performance of this Agreement or the Asset Purchase Agreement, or for management of the relationship between the Parties.

"Losses" means damages, claims, losses, charges, actions, suits, proceedings, deficiencies, taxes, interest, penalties, and reasonable costs and expenses (including reasonable attorneys' fees, court costs and expert witness fees).

"Managed Agreements" means the third party agreements from time to time managed by Supplier for Customer (including those listed on Schedule D-3).

"Party" means Supplier or Customer, and Parties means Supplier and Customer.

"Person" (whether or not capitalized) means an individual, a corporation, a partnership, an association, a trust or other entity or organization.

---

[30] Text contemplates IT services, where customer data are stored on the supplier's systems. Edit as appropriate.

"Project" means discrete, non-recurring tasks, deliverables or other Services that are not an inherent, necessary or customary part of day-to-day performance of Services and are not required to be performed in order for Supplier to meet the Service Levels.

"Project Services" means performance of services related to Projects.

"Renewal Term" means any of the renewals authorized by Section 12.1.

"Service Center" means Supplier's facility located at [location], or such other location as Customer may approve from time to time in accordance with Section 2.11.

"Service Credit(s)" are amounts payable for unexcused failures to meet Service Levels, determined in accordance with Schedule B.

"Service Levels" mean the various objectives, measurable performance standards identified as such in Schedule B.

"Services" means the [development, maintenance, operations, management, support, help desk and related][31] services, functions and responsibilities:

(a) described by Schedule A, as it may be amended and supplemented from time to time;

(b) inherent or implicit in, or necessary for proper performance of, services described by Schedule A;

(c) performed prior to the Commencement Date by persons or with assets either transferred or displaced by the transfer of operations and responsibilities to Supplier under this Agreement;

(d) services, functions and responsibilities performed by or for Customer under the [IT budget/base case (date)]; and

(e) Project Services, to the extent described by Schedule A or authorized by change orders or otherwise in writing.

"Shutdown Costs" means: (a) reasonable severance pay for Supplier personnel terminated; (b) reasonable relocation costs for Supplier personnel obliged to relocate; (c) cancellation costs for any subcontracts, leases or other contracts with third parties for products or services used solely to perform the Services; (d) unamortized costs of assets purchased by Supplier solely to perform the Services; and (e) other ordinary and necessary costs paid to third parties and associated with termination of the Agreement. Shutdown Costs *exclude*: (x) Supplier's general and administrative expenses; (y) unamortized costs attributable to useful lives or other amortization periods after the actual or scheduled expiration of the Agreement (whichever is later); and (z) costs avoided or avoidable through reasonable mitigation, such as reassignment of personnel or redeployment of assets to support other Supplier customers or Supplier's business generally. For purposes of clause (a) above, reasonable severance pay shall be limited to reasonable

---

[31] Edit as appropriate.

amounts actually paid attributable to: (i) for severance based upon length of tenure, years of service performing Services for Customer; (ii) for personnel not wholly dedicated to performance of Services, that portion of their work dedicated to Customer; and (iii) in all cases, terminations carried out with fair and proper procedures, in compliance with all laws, regulations (including collective redundancy regulations) and contractual requirements.[32]

"Supplier" means [name], a [state] corporation.

"Supplier Indemnitees" means Supplier, its Affiliates, and, if applicable, their respective directors, officers, shareholders, partners, attorneys, accountants, agents and employees and their respective heirs, successors and assigns.

"Supplier Software" means the software from time to time owned by Supplier and used to provide the Services.

"Supplier Third Party Software" means the software from time to time licensed to Supplier by third parties and used to provide the Services.

"Term" means the term of this Agreement, as described by Article 11, consisting of the Initial Term and any Renewal Terms.

"Termination Assistance" has the meaning assigned by Section 12.6.1.

"Termination Charge" means the amount payable under Schedule C upon certain terminations of this Agreement, as provided in Section 12.4.[33]

"Third Party Software" means the applications and system software from time to time owned by third parties and licensed to Customer or Supplier (Customer Third Party Software and Supplier Third Party Software, respectively) listed on Schedule D (as it may be amended from time to time pursuant to this Agreement) and used to provide the Services.

"Transferred Employees" are employees of Customer who accept offers of employment from Supplier in accordance with the terms of this Agreement.

"Transition Credits" are amounts payable for unexcused failures to meet agreed transition milestones, determined in accordance with Schedule F.

"Transition Plan" means the plan for commencement of Services, transfer of operations, [personnel, assets][34] and related matters attached as Schedule F.

---

[32] Optional definition, where Shutdown Costs are paid for convenience termination, rather than a lump sum termination charge.

[33] Omit if Shutdown Costs are paid in lieu of a Termination Charge.

[34] Edit as appropriate.

Appendix 4

SERVICE DESCRIPTION—INFORMATION TECHNOLOGY SERVICES

INTRODUCTION

TO
SERVICE DESCRIPTION
(IT Infrastructure and Applications)[1]

1 INTRODUCTION

The Services include the services, functions and responsibilities described in this Schedule __ that Supplier has agreed to perform, as well as the additional services, functions and responsibilities described throughout the Agreement and the other Schedules, each as required to meet or exceed the specific Service Levels identified in the Agreement and Schedule __ [Service Levels] (as they may evolve in accordance with the Agreement and Schedule __).

This Schedule __ also describes related responsibilities of Customer, which are in addition to the Customer responsibilities described throughout the Agreement and the other Schedules, as they may be supplemented, enhanced, modified or replaced in accordance with the Change Control Procedures or otherwise in writing.

General descriptions in this Introduction are subject to the more detailed descriptions, qualifications, limitations, and exclusions in the Agreement and this Schedule __.

The Services include:

- Applications Services, as described in Section 2;
- Data Center Services, as described in Section 3;
- Help Desk Services, as described in Section 4;
- Desktop Services, as described in Section 5;
- Network Services, as described in Section 6;
- Cross-Functional or General Services, as described in Section 7; and
- Projects, as described in Section 8.

---

[1] Since actual descriptions of particular services are technical and specific to transactions, none appear. The introduction merely provides an overview, in simple terms, together with guidance for interpretation.

In accordance with Section __ of the Agreement (General Scope):

- The Services include all services, functions and responsibilities (i) specifically described in the Agreement and Schedules as Supplier responsibilities; (ii) identified in this Schedule __ as Supplier responsibilities; and (iii) not specifically described, but required for the proper performance of, and inherent in or necessary sub-tasks for, the functions described as Supplier functions or responsibilities (unless specifically excluded by the text or matrices).[2]
- Customer responsibilities include all functions, services and responsibilities (i) specifically described in the Agreement and Schedules as Customer responsibilities; and (ii) not specifically described, but required for the proper performance of, and inherent in or are necessary sub-tasks for, the functions described as Customer responsibilities (unless specifically excluded by the text or matrices).[3]

The Services *exclude*:

- [List categorical exclusions, eg, voice, etc. as appropriate];
- Services expressly excluded by this Schedule __ or excluded by operation of Section __ (General Scope) of the Agreement;
- Services, functions and responsibilities that are described as Customer services, functions and responsibilities, or are implied by or included within the scope of Customer's responsibilities (except to the extent they are expressly stated to be joint responsibilities).

Services provided hereunder are (except as otherwise expressly stated) based upon:

- Supplier's standard service offerings, methods, tools, and reports as they may from time to time evolve during the Term;
- Use of technologies described below, including evolutionary derivatives (eg, successor versions of supported operating systems) and other improvements contemplated by Section __ of the Agreement concerning current technology; and
- Use of Equipment and Software that conforms to Customer's then-current applicable technical standards (as provided in the Procedures Manual), such as current generation, standard servers and personal computers and current or near-current versions of all Software.

To the extent that Customer requests or requires Supplier to perform services inconsistent with the foregoing, Supplier reserves the right to propose changes, request equitable adjustment of its charges and adjustment of or relief from Service Levels, as appropriate, subject in all cases to Customer's right to determine, in its discretion, the most appropriate, least costly means of adjustment. None of the foregoing is intended to supersede any

---

[2] This largely duplicates the usual 'general scope' or 'sweep' clause, but may be worth repeating so that users referring to the document on both sides have a single self-contained scope document.

[3] Suppliers sometimes request a corresponding 'sweep' clause for Customer responsibilities. Where those are extensive, language like this may be both appropriate and acceptable to the customer.

specific, inconsistent provision of the Agreement and, in particular, any of the provisions concerning priorities, governance, change management or adjustments to Charges. Statements of purpose (e.g., to the effect that a particular service is intended to optimize performance) shall not be construed as guarantees of ideal or optimum performance; nor are they intended to alter any Service Levels.

For purposes of this Schedule __:

• All time references mean [Eastern/Central/Mountain/Pacific] Time (Standard or Daylight, whichever is in effect); and
• Capitalized terms have the meanings assigned by the Agreement, unless the context clearly requires some other meaning. Any capitalized terms not defined by the Agreement have the meanings assigned where they first appear.

Appendix 5

SERVICE DESCRIPTION—FINANCE AND
ACCOUNTING SERVICES

SCHEDULE __

SERVICE DESCRIPTION
FINANCE AND ACCOUNTING SERVICES

TABLE OF CONTENTS

1 OVERVIEW[1]

The Services include: (i) services, functions and responsibilities described below; and (ii) additional services, functions and responsibilities described by Section __[2] and other provisions of the Agreement, each as required to meet applicable Service Levels and other performance standards, and as each may evolve or be supplemented, enhanced, modified or replaced in accordance with the Change Control Procedures or other terms of the Agreement.

The Services generally consist of finance and accounting services designed to maintain Customer's general ledger accounts, and process accounts receivable and payable in accordance with Customer's applicable policies, procedures and instructions in effect

---

[1] This template is intended for business process services, with the bulk of the description and allocation of responsibilities contained in detailed matrices. A general description of exclusions (as in the accompanying IT template) may also be useful, depending upon the transaction and situation. For illustrative purposes, descriptive language has been included for outsourcing of some basic finance and accounting services—general ledger, accounts payable, and accounts receivable.

[2] The 'sweep' clause.

from time to time and applicable legal and regulatory requirements, all as more fully described below.

Capitalized terms have the meanings assigned by the Agreement, unless the context clearly requires some other meaning. Any capitalized terms not defined by the Agreement have the meanings assigned when the terms first appear.

2 MAJOR FUNCTIONS

Supplier's principal responsibilities include, without limitation, all of the following, each as more fully described in the Responsibility Matrix, and as supplemented by other provisions of this Service Description and the Agreement:

(a) General ledger accounting services (including setup and maintenance, processing, reporting, and monthly, quarterly and annual processing and closings);

(b) Accounts payable accounting services (including setup and maintenance, invoice processing, expense reporting and monthly processing and reporting); and

(c) Accounts receivable processing (including setup and maintenance, credit requests, invoice processing, collections, cash application, banking activities, and monthly processing and reporting).

3 DESIRED RESULTS

Listed below are certain of the results that Customer desires to obtain from Supplier's performance of certain finance and accounting Services. Supplier will be responsible for meeting or exceeding applicable Service Levels and other performance standards. Customer's primary business objective in outsourcing is to obtain high quality, stable, well controlled, efficient, and cost-effective processes for general ledger accounting, and the processing of accounts receivable and payable. Other business objectives include the following:

(a) Implement improved processes, based upon new or upgraded systems;

(b) Reduce processing and reporting times; and

(c) Improve and accelerate collection of accounts receivable.[3]

4 PROCESS REQUIREMENTS

Supplier's obligations to perform Services and meet or exceed applicable Service Levels for the Charges stated in Schedule ___ include compliance with all of the following requirements:

(a) Process all transactions on Customer's systems, in compliance with applicable laws and Customer policies, including closing requirements;

---

[3] Where goals are listed in the master services agreement, this may be unnecessary, or, alternatively, describe additional, specific or secondary goals for the particular services.

(b) Perform services at times and in a manner that supports Customer's business hours; and

(c) Provide essential services, respond to questions, book additional entries and issue or re-run reports on short notice during closings and other key periods.

5 RESPONSIBILITY MATRIX[4]

The Responsibility Matrix below indicates which Party is accountable for listed processes, activities and tasks as part of the Services. Entries in both columns indicate a shared responsibility or combined effort. Where responsibility is shared, Supplier shall have responsibility for completing the task and Customer shall have decision-making authority (unless the text expressly states some other allocation of responsibility). The Responsibility Matrix does not identify each and every process, activity or task to be performed by Supplier. Rather, Supplier is responsible for all services within the subject areas covered by this Service Description, in accordance with Section 1, above ("Overview") and other applicable provisions of the Agreement, whether or not the particular task or responsibility is expressly stated in the Responsibility Matrix or otherwise in this Service Description (subject to any express qualifications, limitations or exclusions contained in the matrices below).

No.	Description	Supplier	Customer

---

[4] Responsibility matrices may fill dozens of pages or more. The few lines above merely illustrate a typical layout. Sometimes, there is a third column for joint responsibilities, but one party or the other should be accountable. So it is generally better to assign primary responsibility to one party or the other, with the remaining party to be consulted, provide support or, in the customer's case, approve or disapprove particular recommendations or action. Varying responsibilities may be indicated with letter codes (eg, P for primary, S for secondary, C for consult, A for approval).

Appendix 6

SERVICE LEVELS—INFORMATION TECHNOLOGY SERVICES

SCHEDULE __

SERVICE LEVELS
INFORMATION TECHNOLOGY SERVICES

TABLE OF CONTENTS

INTRODUCTION

This Schedule __ defines Service Levels for the Services, and describes the manner in which they will be computed, reported and administered.

1 DEFINITIONS[1]

The following capitalized terms shall have the meanings assigned. All other capitalized terms shall have the meanings stated where the terms first appear, or assigned by the Agreement.

"Amount at Risk" means, with respect to any month during the Term, _____ per cent (__%) of the Monthly Charge.

"Availability" means with respect to a system, availability of the computer, operating system, intended functionality and peripheral devices stated as a percentage of Scheduled Uptime for the relevant system or item (ie, Availability = [Scheduled Uptime − (Excused Downtime + Unexcused Downtime)] ÷ (Scheduled Uptime − Excused Downtime)]). Other or different calculations may be specified in the accompanying tables for calculations of Availability for particular systems and services.

"Average Availability" means the individual system availability computed as an average percentage using the following equation: Average Availability = Cumulative Availability of all Systems ÷ Number of Systems.

"Business Day" means _____ A.M., to _____ P.M., [specify] time (or such other time zone as may be specified) on any Monday through Friday, excluding legal holidays.

"Call" means any inquiry, request for service or problem submitted to the [Help Desk] for assistance (by telephone, facsimile or electronic mail)[2] by an End User. Calls exclude (i) calls for systems status recording, (ii) calls routed through the Help Desk as a pass-through function (eg, calls logged by the Help Desk and then transferred to designated Customer or external organizations, but excluding calls referred to Level 3 support, in accordance with Schedule __, which are "Calls"),[3] (iii) follow-up calls for problem updates or closure, and (iv) multiple Calls placed about a single Incident.[4]

---

[1] Definitions may be combined in a glossary of all definitions, but it may be more convenient to place definitions related to service levels or pricing in relevant schedules. For discussion purposes, those related to Service Levels should be discussed in connection with review of this document. Some definitions (eg concerning calculations and measurements) may vary from one function to another because of differences in delivery, tools, the underlying service, etc.

[2] Edit as appropriate.

[3] Help desks often offer 'levels' of support. Typically, level 1 represents the analyst who takes the call; level 2 is the help desk's internal expert on the particular system; and level 3 is an outsider, such as support from the licensor of a software package.

[4] 'Call' is defined to include more than telephone calls (eg e-mail requests) but some references elsewhere (eg Call Abandonment Rate) are limited to telephone calls. 'Contact' is another term commonly used for all inquiries to a help desk, since it embraces both calls and e-mail messages. Definitions may vary for billing purposes. Multiple calls from many users about an incident may not be chargeable, or count for

"Call Abandonment Rate" means the percentage of telephone calls to the Help Desk that are abandoned after the system status message on the automatic call director ("ACD") but before an analyst answers the call, expressed as a percentage of the total number of telephone calls to the Help Desk during the relevant month or other Measurement Period.

"Closure" occurs (or a Trouble Ticket or Service Request is "Closed") when Supplier confirms with the End User that a Trouble Ticket or Service Request has been Resolved. If the End User indicates that the problem is not Resolved, or a work-around put in place, during these communications with the Help Desk, then the Trouble Ticket or Service Request remains open and is not Resolved. If Supplier reasonably believes that the Trouble Ticket or Service Request has been Resolved, *and* has made three (3) attempts to contact the End User during business hours to obtain Closure and has not been able to communicate with the End User regarding the Trouble Ticket or Service Request, then Supplier may deem the Trouble Ticket or Service Request Closed as of the time Supplier restored service or completed the Service Request, subject to its being reopened if the End User subsequently notifies Supplier that the problem is not Resolved. The interval between the time Supplier first attempts to contact the End User to obtain Closure and the time (prior to the third attempt to contact the End User) Supplier actually contacts the End User shall not be counted for any Service Level measurement purpose.

"Critical Fault" means an unexcused failure to meet a Critical Service Level (including Faults where performance equals or falls below the "Serious Impact" level).

"Critical Service Level" means each of the required levels of performance so designated in the accompanying tables, including Standard Service Levels or KPIs from time to time reclassified as Critical Service Levels by Customer in accordance with the terms of this Schedule.

"Cycle Time" shall mean the elapsed time in hours or Business Days between the commencement of a measurement task (eg, job execution time, receipt of order or request for service by the Help Desk) and the successful completion of the task.

"Downtime" means that period of time when a system, application or service is not available for normal business use.

"Eligible Recipient" means a third party (such as a supplier to Customer) authorized to receive Services (excluding Supplier's staff and subcontractors).

"End User" means an individual who receives Services (excluding Supplier's staff and subcontractors). End Users may be Customer End Users (such as employees or independent contractors of Customer and its Affiliates), or individuals engaged by an Eligible Recipient.

---

purposes of First Call Resolution, yet be measured automatically for purposes of measuring Average Speed of Answer and Call Abandonment Rates.

"Excused Downtime" shall mean periods of time when (i) mutually agreed scheduled maintenance actually occurs (generally, within agreed Maintenance Windows), (ii) Customer requests an outage, or (iii) time attributable to Incidents excused by Section __ of the Agreement.

"Fault" means an unexcused failure to meet a Critical Service Level or a Standard Service Level. Faults may be excused only for the reasons described by Section __ of the Agreement.[5] Faults include unexcused failures that meet the Serious Impact criteria defined below.

"First Call Resolution"[6] means the percentage of Calls Resolved during the End User's initial telephone call or upon the first response to inquiries received by facsimile or electronic mail. The following conditions apply to calculation of First Call Resolution:

(a) Calls are considered Resolved on the first Call if the problem or question or request for information or service is satisfied (i) while the End User is still on the line during the initial telephone call to the Help Desk or (ii) upon receipt of the first communication (other than an automatic acknowledgment) received from the Help Desk.
(b) Calls are considered unresolved on first call if: (i) a follow-up call to the End User or a return call or communication by the End User to the Help Desk is required; or (ii) the Trouble Ticket is dispatched to another Supplier service organization.
(c) Calls requiring hardware repair or IMAC[7] support for resolution (eg, orders for devices to be delivered to an End User) shall be excluded from calculations of First Call Resolution.
(d) Multiple Calls to report a single Incident affecting multiple users (eg, a network outage) shall be excluded from calculations of First Call Resolution.
(e) Calls that are properly passed through to a Customer retained function or a third party (other than Supplier's subcontractors) are excluded from calculations of the First Call Resolution.

"Incident" means a single event (such as failure of a device) or a series of substantially contemporaneous related events that result in the occurrence of one or more Faults.

---

[5] Contract terms generally excuse failures attributable to *force majeure* or acts and omissions of the Customer and its agents. One could revise to allow other grounds, such as unanticipated surges in volumes, failures attributable to customer failures to take action (such as investments in capacity or the customer's own infrastructure) recommended by the supplier as necessary to continue to meet Service Levels, and possibly others. However, some of these potential grounds for excuse are either subsumed within the basic grounds, or may vary among services and transactions.

[6] This metric is sometimes called 'First Contact Resolution' to include resolution of incidents reported by e-mail or facsimile, and worded accordingly. Here 'Calls' are defined to include e-mail messages and facsimiles as well as telephone calls. A customer might prefer separate measurements for telephone calls and other communications with the help desk.

[7] Installation, move, add or change to hardware, in this case for an individual user, rather than a group of users. Since IMACs require service calls, they cannot be resolved over the telephone and are excluded from the calculation.

"Key Performance Indicator" ("KPI") means each of those levels of performance so designated by the accompanying tables. Although KPIs are measured and reported in the same manner as Service Levels, unexcused failures to meet KPIs do not expose Supplier to payment of Service Credits (unless and until they may be reclassified as Service Levels, as provided below).

"Maintenance Windows" are mutually agreed time periods outside normal business hours (eg, weekend nights, holidays) when Scheduled Downtime may be scheduled for maintenance and similar purposes.

"Measurement Period" means monthly, unless otherwise stated below, in an accompanying table, or agreed in writing by the Parties.

"Monthly Charge" means the total amount of the Charges (excluding only reimbursable expenses, Project Charges,[8] pass-throughs, and taxes) to be paid by Customer to Supplier for Services performed during that month.[9]

"Problem Resolution Time" means the elapsed time between registration of a problem into Supplier's problem tracking system and its successful Resolution (as defined below). Supplier shall register all problems into its problem tracking system when first reported.

"Problem Response Time" means the elapsed time between registration of a problem into Supplier's problem tracking system (eg, through automatic notification, Help Desk Calls, or by on-site Supplier Personnel) and the commencement of resolution efforts.

"Resolution" or "Resolve" means the elapsed time between the time that a problem is registered in Supplier's problem tracking system and the time that Supplier restores service or completes the Service Request, measured in accordance with the definition of Closure, as described above. All relevant Service Level elapsed times are based on this definition of Resolution.

"Scheduled Downtime" means mutually agreed times when systems, applications or services are scheduled to be out of service for maintenance or similar purposes, generally within Maintenance Windows outside business hours (eg, weekend nights, holidays).

"Scheduled Uptime" shall mean that period of time (days of the week and hours per day) when a service or system is scheduled to be available to Customer for normal business use.

"Serious Impact" means levels of performance so specified by the accompanying tables, which are: (i) below the related Service Levels; (ii) agreed to represent inferior

---

[8] Calculations of Monthly Charges on which Service Credit calculations are based ordinarily exclude unusual charges such as projects.

[9] If Amounts at Risk and Service Credits are calculated separately for service categories (such as data center and help desk), this would be defined by service category, rather than for the Agreement as a whole.

quality service; (iii) have greater impact upon Customer's business; and (iv) for which greater Service Credits are payable when Supplier's performance equals or falls below the "Serious Impact" levels.

"Service Credit" means:

(a) For Critical Faults, the amount determined by multiplying the Amount at Risk for the month in which the Fault occurs by the Weighting Percentage for the relevant Critical Service Level, plus any applicable adjustments for Serious Impact Incidents and repeated or multiple Faults, as provided below; and

(b) For combinations of Standard Faults described by Section 5.4, below, __ per cent (__%) of the Amount at Risk for the month in which the last relevant Standard Fault occurs.

For convenience, these two categories of Service Credits are sometimes referred to below as "Critical Service Credits" and "Standard Service Credits," respectively. References to "Service Credits" generally refer to both categories.

"Service Level" means each of those levels of performance (eg, Availability) specified by the accompanying tables, as they may be modified or adjusted from time to time. Service Levels may be designated as "Standard" or "Critical." References to "Service Levels" include both categories.[10]

"Service Level Objective" means the levels of performance so specified by the accompanying tables. Service Level Objectives shall exceed related Service Levels. Although the Parties believe that Service Level Objectives represent reasonable expectations for actual performance, no Service Credits are payable for failures to meet Service Level Objectives.[11]

"Speed of Answer" means the elapsed time, measured in seconds, between the End User's connection to the Help Desk's ACD unit and the time when an analyst answers the telephone Call.

"Standard Fault" means an unexcused failure to meet a Standard Service Level.

"Standard Service Levels" means Service Levels that are not Critical Service Levels.

---

[10] These are the 'minimums' for which Service Credits are paid in the event of unexcused failures. Service Level Objectives are more stringent. 'Serious Impact' levels are lesser standards of performance, with greater impact upon the business, and larger financial consequences. For example, if the Service Level Objective for Availability were 99.5%, the Service Level might be 99% and 90–95% might represent Serious Impact.

[11] Briefly, metrics are classified as Service Level Objectives (targets, bearing no consequences), Critical Service Levels (comparatively few, but significant and costly, if missed), Standard Service Levels (which are more numerous, and bear modest financial consequences if missed repeatedly, or if large numbers of them are missed), and Serious Impact (low thresholds for Critical Service Levels, representing very poor performance and serious impact upon the customer's business). Key Performance Indicators (KPIs) are reported but do not bear financial consequences, unless and until reclassified as Service Levels.

"Transition Period" means the period commencing [date][12] and ending [date] or upon successful completion of the tasks contemplated by the Transition Plan, whichever is later.

"Trouble Ticket" means the record opened by the Supplier at the first report of a problem and tracked until Closure upon Resolution of the problem.

"Unacceptable Service" means any of the conditions or circumstances defined as such in Section 6, below.

"Weighting Percentage" means, with respect to any Critical Service Level, the percentage of the Amount at Risk to be paid as a Service Credit for a Critical Fault. Weighting Percentages reflect the probable severity of Incidents and the relative importance of Service Levels, determined and adjusted by Customer from time to time in its sole but reasonable discretion, as provided below.

2 CLASSIFICATION OF INCIDENTS

2.1 Severity Codes
The Help Desk shall classify all Incidents in accordance with the severity codes in [the accompanying tables] [cross-reference].[13]

2.2 Reclassification of Incidents
Customer's Contract Executive (or his or her designee) may, in his or her reasonable discretion, reclassify any Incident based upon the importance of a particular Incident or component, or the actual or potential impact upon Customer's operations. If Customer reclassifies any Incident into a higher category, response time calculations for the higher category shall commence upon receipt of notice of reclassification (which may be given by telephone, facsimile or electronic mail to the Help Desk supervisor then on duty). If Supplier disagrees with any such reclassification, and is unable promptly to resolve the matter to mutual satisfaction, then the dispute may be resolved, at either Party's initiative, pursuant to Section __ of the Agreement (concerning disputes).

3 EFFECTIVENESS AND VALIDATION OF SERVICE LEVELS

3.1 Timing
All Service Levels and KPIs shall be measured and reported beginning on the Commencement Date[14] or installation of relevant tools when specified by the Transition

---

[12] Generally, the Effective Date (signing) or Commencement Date (first date of service).

[13] This assumes a standard set of classifications (eg Severity 1, 2, 3, etc). Definitions vary, but generally, Severity 1 incidents are major failures or outages, affecting large numbers of users, whole facilities or business units that seriously interrupt or disrupt business operations. Severity 2 and 3 incidents have more modest effects—eg, upon small groups of users, or individual users, and work-arounds may be available, with less convenience and speed.

[14] Template presumes separate 'Effective' and 'Commencement' Dates for signature and commencement of Services. Edit as appropriate.

Plan, but shall not otherwise be effective (and no Service Credits shall be payable for Faults) until:

(a) the date specified by the accompanying tables, a mutually agreed plan, or otherwise agreed in writing, or

(b) for Service Levels validated pursuant to Section 3.2, below, when agreed or otherwise determined in accordance with that Section; or for those Service Levels subject to a corrective action plan, then ninety (90) days after approval of the plan by Customer, and in any event no later than [outside date].

3.2 Validation of Preliminary Service Levels[15]

(a) The Parties expect and intend that (except as otherwise expressly agreed) Service Levels are consistently achievable using the systems available on the Commencement Date (or for systems that transfer to Supplier facilities, relevant Supplier systems), if used in accordance with the practices used in well-managed operations performing similar services ("consistently achievable"). Certain of the Service Levels not previously documented are designated by the accompanying tables as "subject to validation" or Preliminary Service Levels. Preliminary Service Levels shall be validated in accordance with this Section.

(b) If Supplier's performance meets or exceeds a Preliminary Service Level for either (i) three (3) consecutive months or (ii) any four (4) months during the Transition Period,[16] then, in either case, it shall become effective for all purposes, including payment of Service Credits, during the month following achievement of the first threshold to be achieved. If Supplier is unable to meet or exceed a Preliminary Service Level with sufficient consistency to achieve either threshold, and Supplier reasonably believes that a Preliminary Service Level is not consistently achievable, it shall promptly give written notice to Customer proposing: (i) the Service Levels Supplier believes to be consistently achievable, and (ii) the additional resources, changes in practices or other measures that Supplier recommends in order consistently to achieve the Preliminary Service Levels. The Parties shall thereafter meet, confer and negotiate in good faith in order to agree upon a corrective action plan.

(c) To the extent that Customer declines to take corrective measures within its responsibility that are reasonably necessary in order consistently to achieve the Preliminary Service Levels, then Preliminary Service Levels shall be equitably adjusted to fix Service Levels that are consistently achievable.

(d) If the Parties are unable to agree promptly upon Service Levels, a corrective action plan or equitable adjustments, then any and all Preliminary Service Levels not then

---

[15] This paragraph is an approach to tentative or presumptive Service Levels that are believed to be reasonable, but require validation. If the supplier meets those levels consistently during a validation period, they take effect. If not, service levels are to be adjusted to those that can be consistently achieved.

[16] Template assumes transition period lasting approximately six months, so that four measurements is an appropriate indicator of consistent performance.

determined shall be determined in accordance with Section __ of the Agreement (concerning disputes).

(e) Preliminary Service Levels to which Supplier makes no objection by notice, as provided above, shall be effective when specified by the accompanying tables or, if no date is specified, then [date].[17]

4 SERVICE LEVEL MANAGEMENT AND ADMINISTRATION

4.1 Single Point of Contact

Supplier shall provide a single point of contact for inquiries, root cause analyses and corrective action related to all Incidents. Unless otherwise agreed in the Procedures Manual or other, mutually agreed working documents, the point of contact shall be Supplier's Contract Executive.

4.2 Service Level Reports

Supplier's monthly reports shall include a report of Service Level performance, in a form [based upon Supplier's standard reports and][18] approved by Customer, that includes at least the following information:

(a) performance of all Service Levels (including relevant calculations);

(b) summaries of root cause analyses and corrective action required by the Agreement (which are to be reported separately, in reasonable detail, including any alleged grounds for excuse under Section ___ of the Agreement);

(c) significant changes that have occurred or are anticipated that may affect Service Level performance; and

(d) management comments on Service Level performance and trends.

Supplier will make information concerning Service Level and Service Credit calculations available to Customer upon request. This obligation is in addition to Customer's audit rights under the Agreement.

4.3 Service Levels for New Services

(a) Service Levels for a new Service, system or function (a "New Service") shall be determined by mutual agreement through the Change Control Procedure and, if necessary and agreed upon, validation during the first six (6) months of production use, in accordance with the procedure described by Section 3.2 above, concerning validation of Preliminary Service Levels.

(b) Unless otherwise agreed, an initial production period of ninety (90) days (or such other period as may be agreed) shall apply before Service Levels apply and Service Credits become payable for (i) a New Service or (ii) extension of existing Services to a new location or business unit.

---

[17] Typically, the end of the transition period.

[18] Optional but typical provision.

(c) Customer may designate the Service Level for a New Service as a Critical Service Level and assign a Weighting Percentage (subject to the limitations in Section 4.6 below), effective sixty (60) days after notice or upon completion of any initial production period (as described above), whichever is later.

(d) Once a New Service has been put into production, any associated Service Level and Weighting Percentage shall be subject to all of the provisions of this Schedule __. If the designation of the Service Level for a New Service as a Critical Service Level would result in Customer exceeding the limitations in Section 4.6, below, Customer may re-designate a Critical Service Level as a Standard Service Level, adjust Weighting Percentages or take other appropriate action consistent with Sections 4.4 and 4.6.

4.4 Service Level Adjustments

Initial KPIs, Service Levels and Weighting Percentages are set forth in the accompanying tables. Customer may, in its sole discretion exercised no more than four (4) times during any Contract Year, and upon at least sixty (60) days' prior notice to Supplier: (i) re-designate KPIs, Standard Service Levels, and Critical Service Levels in the other respective categories; and (ii) increase or decrease the corresponding Weighting Percentages (subject to the limitations below).

4.5 Service Levels for Replacement Systems

If, as and when systems or processes may from time to time be replaced or modified during the Term, and except as otherwise agreed through the Change Control Procedure (or otherwise in writing), the Service Levels for the replacement systems or processes shall be at least as stringent as those that applied to its predecessor (unless the replacement system or process is incapable of achieving those Service Levels, in which case Service Levels shall be fixed at consistently achievable levels). There shall be corresponding adjustments in Service Level Objectives and Serious Impact levels. Weighting Percentages may be adjusted in the manner described above for New Services.

4.6 Certain Parameters

In no event shall: (i) more than [number] Service Levels be designated as Critical Service Levels at any one time; (ii) the Weighting Percentage for any one Critical Service Level exceed [per cent]; or (iii) the aggregate Weighting Percentages for all Critical Service Levels exceed [per cent].

4.7 Periodic Review

At intervals reasonably determined by Customer, upon either Party's request,[19] and at least annually, the Parties will meet and confer to discuss additions to, deletions from, or modifications of Service Levels and related standards to reflect improvements in

---

[19] This could also be synchronized with any annual or other periodic review of the entire relationship.

performance, changes in Customer's business requirements, objectives, operations or the manner or technologies used to deliver Services. Modifications from time to time agreed to will be approved in accordance with the Change Control Procedures, or through written amendment of this Schedule __ and related contract documents.

5 SERVICE CREDITS

5.1 Critical Service Credits

The Service Credit payable for any Critical Fault equals the Weighting Percentage for the relevant Critical Service Level times the Amount At Risk for the month in which the Critical Fault occurred (subject to the other provisions of this Schedule). Service Credits shall be paid or credited in accordance with Section ____ of the Agreement.

5.2 Repeated Faults

If the same Critical Fault occurs in successive months, or more than one Critical Fault occurs in any month, then the Service Credit(s) shall be one hundred fifty per cent (150%) of the Service Credit(s) otherwise payable (subject to the limitation in Section 5.6, below).

5.3 Serious Impact

If a Critical Fault occurs, and performance is equal to or less than the level specified as "Serious Impact", then the Service Credit otherwise payable shall be doubled (subject to the limitation of Section 5.6).

5.4 Standard Service Credits[20]

A Standard Service Credit shall be payable whenever:

(a) A Standard Fault occurs for the same Standard Service Level ____ (__) times within any [number] consecutive months; or

(b) ____ (__) Standard Faults occur in a single month; or

(c) ____ (__) Standard Faults occur in any rolling ____ (__) month period.

5.5 Multiple Faults from a Single Incident

All Faults attributable to a single failure of a component or similar Incident shall be considered a single Fault. If any such Incident causes a Critical Fault and one or more Standard Faults, Supplier shall be obligated to pay the Service Credit for the Critical Fault (and the Standard Fault may not be included in any aggregation of Faults pursuant to Section 5.4). If any such Incident causes two or more Critical Faults, Supplier shall be obligated to pay the largest Service Credit payable for any single Fault attributable to the particular Incident.

---

[20] As noted earlier, the supplier will pay a small credit (eg, 1% of the Monthly Charge) if it misses the same Standard Service Level repeatedly, or large numbers of Standard Service Levels. The purpose is to offer some protection against epidemic mediocrity.

5.6 Maximum Service Credits

The maximum amount payable as Service Credits for any single month shall not exceed the Amount at Risk. Service Credits in excess of the Amount at Risk do not carry forward into subsequent Measurement Periods.

5.7 Waivers

Customer may waive any Fault or failure to make any payment or allow any Service Credit, but no such waiver shall be binding or effective unless given in writing, and no such waiver shall constitute a continuing waiver of similar or other such Faults or failures. Customer may at any time direct future compliance with any waived requirement.

5.8 Cumulative Remedies

Subject to the provisions of Section ___ of the Agreement (concerning offset of Service Credits paid against related damage claims), Service Credits and other remedies contemplated or permitted by this Schedule __ are in addition to other remedies authorized by the Agreement or permitted by applicable law.

6 UNACCEPTABLE SERVICE

The following Faults or combinations of Faults constitute Unacceptable Service, and grounds for termination of the Agreement, in whole or in part, pursuant to Section __ of the Agreement:

(a) [Number] consecutive Critical Faults related to the same Service Level;

(b) [Number] consecutive Critical Faults related to the same Service Level and involving Serious Impact in each instance;

(c) [Number] Critical Faults related to the same Service Level within any rolling period of [number] months;

(d) [Number] Critical Faults related to the same Service Level and involving Serious Impact in each instance within any rolling period of [number] months;

(e) [Number] Critical Faults within any rolling [number] month period;

(f) [Number] Critical Faults within any rolling twelve (12) month period;

(g) [Number] Critical Faults involving Serious Impact within any rolling [number] month period;

(h) [Number] Critical Faults involving Serious Impact within any rolling twelve (12) month period;

(i) Occurrence of Faults for five per cent (5%) or more of the reported Service Level measurements within any rolling twelve (12) month period;[21]

(j) Supplier becomes obligated for [$ amount] or more in Service Credits during any rolling period of six (6) months or less; or

---

[21] For example, if there are fifty Standard and Critical Service Levels, and each is measured and reported monthly, there are six hundred (600) reported measurements every year, and thirty (30) Faults would equal five percent (5%).

(k) Supplier becomes obligated for [$ amount] or more in Service Credits during any rolling period of twelve (12) months or less. [22]

Identification of the foregoing circumstances as Unacceptable Service is without prejudice to contentions that other or different circumstances, individual Faults, greater or lesser numbers of Faults, different combinations of Faults, or lesser liability for Service Credits, may also, by themselves or in combination with other facts or circumstances, constitute material breach of the Agreement, and grounds for termination in accordance with Section ___ of the Agreement (concerning termination by Customer for Supplier's material breach).

---

[22] The form provides a variety of potential combinations of failures that might constitute 'Unacceptable Service' and justify default termination. Not all may be appropriate or relevant. Often, 'Unacceptable Service' is defined simply on the basis of gross liability for credits above an agreed threshold, on the theory that total liability is a fair proxy for frequency and severity. Many negotiated outcomes are possible.

Appendix 7

SERVICE LEVELS—FINANCE AND ACCOUNTING SERVICES

SCHEDULE ___

SERVICE LEVELS
FINANCE AND ACCOUNTING SERVICES

TABLE OF CONTENTS

INTRODUCTION

This Schedule __ defines Service Levels for the Services, and describes the manner in which they will be computed, reported and administered.

1 DEFINITIONS[1]

The following capitalized terms shall have the meanings assigned. All other capitalized terms shall have the meanings stated when the terms first appear, or those assigned by the Agreement.

"Amount at Risk" means, with respect to any month during the Term, _____ per cent (__%) of Monthly Charge.

"Business Day" means ___A.M. to ___P.M. [specify] time (or such other time zone as may be specified) on any Monday through Friday, excluding legal holidays.

"Fault" means an unexcused failure to meet a Service Level. Faults may be excused only for the reasons described by Section __ of the Agreement. Faults include unexcused failures that meet the Serious Impact criteria defined below.

"Incident" means a single event or series of substantially contemporaneous related events that result in the occurrence of one or more Faults.

"Key Performance Indicator" ("KPI") means each of those levels of performance so designated by the accompanying tables. Although KPIs are measured and reported in the same manner as Service Levels, unexcused failures to meet KPIs do not expose Supplier to payment of Service Credits (unless and until they may be reclassified as Service Levels, as provided below).

"Measurement Period" means monthly, unless otherwise stated below, in an accompanying table, or agreed in writing by the Parties.

"Monthly Charge" means the total amount of the Charges (excluding only reimbursable expenses, Project Charges, pass-through expenses, and taxes) to be paid by Customer to Supplier for Services performed during that month.

"Resolution" or "Resolve" means the elapsed time between the time that a problem is registered in Supplier's problem tracking system and the time that Supplier restores service or completes the relevant transaction, report or other activity to Customer's reasonable satisfaction.

---

[1] Definitions may be combined in a glossary of all definitions, but it may be more convenient to place definitions related to service levels or pricing in relevant schedules. For discussion purposes, those related to Service Levels should be discussed in connection with review of this document. Some definitions (eg concerning calculations and measurements) may vary from one function to another because of differences in delivery, tools, the underlying service, etc.

"Resolution Time" means the elapsed time between registration of a problem into Supplier's problem tracking system and its successful Resolution (as defined below). Supplier shall register all problems into its problem tracking system when first reported.

"Response Time" means the elapsed time between registration of a problem into Supplier's problem tracking system and the commencement of resolution efforts.

"Serious Impact" means levels of performance so specified by the accompanying tables, which are: (i) below the related Service Levels; (ii) agreed to represent inferior quality service; (iii) have greater impact upon Customer's business; and (iv) for which greater Service Credits are payable when Supplier's performance equals or falls below the "Serious Impact" levels.

"Service Credit" means the amount determined by multiplying the Amount at Risk for the month in which the Fault occurs by the Weighting Percentage for the applicable Service Level, subject to adjustment, as provided below for Serious Impact Incidents and repeated or multiple failures.

"Service Level" means each of those levels of performance specified by the accompanying tables, as they may be modified or adjusted from time to time.

"Service Level Objective" means the levels of performance so specified by the accompanying tables. Service Level Objectives shall exceed related Service Levels. Although the Parties believe that Service Level Objectives represent reasonable expectations for actual performance, no Service Credits are payable for failures to meet Service Level Objectives.

"Transition Period" means the period commencing [date][2] and ending [date] or upon successful completion of the tasks contemplated by the Transition Plan, whichever is later.[3]

"Unacceptable Service" means any of the conditions or circumstances defined as such in Section 5, below.

"Weighting Percentage" means, with respect to any Service Level, the percentage of the Amount at Risk to be paid as a Service Credit for a Fault. Weighting Percentages reflect the probable severity of Incidents and the relative importance of Service Levels, determined and adjusted by Customer from time to time in its sole but reasonable discretion, as provided below.

2 EFFECTIVENESS AND VALIDATION OF SERVICE LEVELS

2.1 Timing
All Service Levels and KPIs shall be measured and reported beginning on the Commencement Date or installation of relevant tools when specified by the Transition Plan,

---

[2] Generally, the Effective Date (signing) or Commencement Date (first date of service).
[3] Fixed date or completion of final transition milestone.

but shall not otherwise be effective (and no Service Credits shall be payable for Faults) until:

(a) the date specified by the accompanying tables, the mutually agreed plan, or otherwise agreed in writing; or

(b) for Service Levels validated pursuant to Section 2.2, below, when agreed or otherwise determined in accordance with that Section; or

(c) for those Service Levels subject to a corrective action plan, then ninety (90) days after approval of the plan by Customer, and in any event no later than [date].

2.2 Validation of Preliminary Service Levels[4]

(a) The Parties expect and intend that (except as otherwise expressly agreed) Service Levels are consistently achievable using the systems and processes available on the Commencement Date (or for systems and processes that transfer to Supplier facilities, relevant Supplier processes), if used in accordance with the practices used in well-managed operations performing similar services ("consistently achievable"). Certain of the Service Levels not previously documented are designated by the accompanying tables as "subject to validation" or Preliminary Service Levels. Preliminary Service Levels shall be validated in accordance with this Section.

(b) If Supplier's performance meets or exceeds a Preliminary Service Level for either (i) three (3) consecutive months or (ii) any four (4) months during the Transition Period,[5] then, in either case, it shall become effective for all purposes, including payment of Service Credits, during the month following achievement of the first threshold to be achieved. If Supplier is unable to meet or exceed a Preliminary Service Level with sufficient consistency to achieve either threshold, and Supplier reasonably believes that a Preliminary Service Level is not consistently achievable, it shall promptly give written notice to Customer proposing: (i) the Service Levels Supplier believes to be consistently achievable; and (ii) the additional resources, changes in practices or other measures that Supplier recommends in order consistently to achieve the Preliminary Service Levels. The Parties shall thereafter meet, confer and negotiate in good faith in order to agree upon a corrective action plan.

(c) To the extent that Customer declines to take corrective measures within its responsibility that are reasonably necessary in order consistently to achieve the Preliminary Service Levels, then Preliminary Service Levels shall be equitably adjusted to fix Service Levels that are consistently achievable.

(d) If the Parties are unable to agree promptly upon Service Levels, a corrective action plan or equitable adjustments, then any and all Preliminary Service Levels not

---

[4] This paragraph is an approach to tentative or presumptive Service Levels that are believed to be reasonable, but require validation. If the supplier meets those service levels consistently during a validation period, they take effect. If not, service levels are to be adjusted to those that can be consistently achieved.

[5] Template assumes transition period lasting approximately 6 months, so that 4 measurements is an appropriate indicator of consistent performance.

then determined shall be determined in accordance with Section __ of the Agreement (concerning disputes).

(e) Preliminary Service Levels to which Supplier makes no objection by notice, as provided above, shall be effective when specified by the accompanying tables or, if no date is specified, then [date].[6]

3 SERVICE LEVEL MANAGEMENT AND ADMINISTRATION

3.1 Single Point of Contact

Supplier shall provide a single point of contact for inquiries, root cause analyses and corrective action related to all Incidents. Unless otherwise agreed in the Procedures Manual or other, mutually agreed working documents, the point of contact shall be Supplier's Contract Executive.

3.2 Service Level Reports

Supplier's monthly reports shall include a report of Service Level performance, in a form [based upon Supplier's standard reports and][7] approved by Customer, that includes at least the following information:

(a) performance of all Service Levels (including relevant calculations);
(b) summaries of root cause analyses and corrective action required by the Agreement (which are to be reported separately, in reasonable detail, including any alleged grounds for excuse under Section __ of the Agreement);
(c) significant changes that have occurred or are anticipated that may affect Service Level performance; and
(d) management comments on Service Level performance and trends.

Supplier will make information concerning Service Level and Service Credit calculations available to Customer upon request. This obligation is in addition to Customer's audit rights under the Agreement.

3.3 Service Levels for New Services

(a) Service Levels for a new Service, system or function (a "New Service") shall be determined by mutual agreement through the Change Control Procedure and, if necessary and agreed upon, validation during the first six (6) months of production use, in accordance with the procedure described by Section 2.2 above, concerning validation of Preliminary Service Levels.
(b) Unless otherwise agreed, an initial production period of ninety (90) days (or such other period as may be agreed) shall apply before Service Levels apply and Service Credits become payable for (i) a New Service or (ii) extension of existing Services to a new location or business unit.

---

[6] Typically, the end of transition.
[7] Optional but typical provision.

(c) Customer may assign a Weighting Percentage for a New Service (subject to the limitations in Section 3.6 below), effective sixty (60) days after notice or upon completion of any initial production period (as described above), whichever is later.

(d) Once a New Service has been put into production, any associated Service Level and Weighting Percentage shall be subject to all of the provisions of this Schedule __. If the designation as the Service Level for a New Service as a Service Level would result in Customer exceeding the limitations in Section 3.6, below, Customer may re-designate a Service Level as a KPI, adjust Weighting Percentages or take other appropriate action consistent with Sections 3.4 and 3.6.

3.4 Service Level Adjustments

Initial Service Levels and Weighting Percentages are as set forth in the accompanying tables. Customer may, in its sole discretion exercised no more than four (4) times during any Contract Year, and upon at least sixty (60) days' prior notice to Supplier: (i) re-designate KPIs as Service Levels or vice versa; and (ii) increase or decrease the then-existing Weighting Percentages (subject to the limitations below).

3.5 Service Levels for Replacement Systems

If, as and when systems or processes may from time to time be replaced or modified during the Term, and except as otherwise agreed through the Change Control Procedure or otherwise in writing, the Service Levels for the replacement systems or processes shall be at least as stringent as those that applied to its predecessor (unless the replacement system or process is incapable of achieving those Service Levels, in which case Service Levels shall be fixed at consistently achievable levels). There shall be corresponding adjustments in Service Level Objectives and Serious Impact levels. Weighting Percentages may be adjusted in the manner described above for New Services.

3.6 Certain Parameters

In no event shall: (i) the Weighting Percentage for any Service Level exceed ____ per cent (__%), or (ii) the aggregate Weighting Percentages for all Service Levels exceed ____ per cent (__%).

3.7 Periodic Review

At intervals reasonably determined by Customer, upon either Party's request,[8] and at least annually, the Parties will meet and confer to discuss additions to, deletions from, or modifications of Service Levels and related standards to reflect improvements in performance, changes in Customer's business requirements, objectives, operations or the manner or technologies used to deliver Services. Modifications from time to time agreed to will be approved in accordance with the Change Control Procedures, or through written amendment of this Schedule __ and related contract documents.

---

[8] This could also be synchronized with any annual or other periodic review of the entire relationship.

4 SERVICE CREDITS

4.1 Service Credits

The Service Credit payable for any Fault equals the Weighting Percentage for the relevant Service Level times the Amount At Risk for the month in which the Fault occurred (subject to the other provisions of this Schedule). Service Credits shall be paid or credited monthly in accordance with Section ___ of the Agreement.

4.2 Repeated Faults

If the same Fault occurs in successive months, or more than one Fault occurs in any month, then the Service Credit(s) shall be one hundred fifty per cent (150%) of the Service Credit(s) otherwise payable (subject to the limitations in Section 4.5, below).

4.3 Serious Impact

If a Fault occurs, and performance is equal to or less than the level specified as "Serious Impact", then the Service Credit otherwise payable shall be doubled (subject to the limitation of Section ___, below).

4.4 Multiple Faults from a Single Incident

All Faults attributable to a single failure of a component or similar Incident shall be considered a single Fault. If any such Incident causes two or more Faults, Supplier shall be obligated to pay the largest Service Credit payable for any single Fault attributable to the particular Incident.

4.5 Maximum Service Credits

In no event shall the maximum amount payable as Service Credits for any single month exceed the Amount at Risk. Service Credits in excess of the Amount at Risk do not carry forward into subsequent Measurement Periods.

4.6 Waivers

Customer may waive any Fault or failure to make any payment or allow any Service Credit, but no such waiver shall be binding or effective unless given in writing, and no such waiver shall constitute a continuing waiver of similar or other such Faults or failures. Customer may at any time direct future compliance with any waived requirement.

4.7 Cumulative Remedies

Subject to the provisions of Section ___ of the Agreement (concerning offset of Service Credits paid against related damage claims), Service Credits and other remedies contemplated or permitted by this Schedule ___ are in addition to other remedies authorized by the Agreement or permitted by applicable law.

5 UNACCEPTABLE SERVICE

The following Faults or combinations of Faults constitute Unacceptable Service, and grounds for termination of the Agreement, in whole or in part, pursuant to Section ___ of the Agreement:

(a) [Number] consecutive Faults related to the same Service Level;

(b) [Number] Faults related to the same Service Level within any rolling period of [number] months;

(c) [Number] Faults related to the same Service Level and involving Serious Impact in each instance within any rolling period of [number] months;

(d) [Number] Faults within any rolling [number] month period;

(e) [Number] Faults within any rolling twelve (12) month period;

(f) [Number] Faults involving Serious Impact within any rolling [number] month period;

(g) [Number] Faults involving Serious Impact within any rolling twelve (12) month period;

(h) Faults occur for five per cent (5%) or more of the reported Service Level measurements within any rolling twelve (12) month period;[9]

(i) Supplier becomes obligated for [$amount] or more in Service Credits during any rolling period of six (6) months or less; or

(j) Supplier becomes obligated for [$amount] or more in Service Credits during any rolling period of twelve (12) months or less.[10]

Identification of the foregoing circumstances as Unacceptable Service (and subsequent identification of any other circumstances as Unacceptable Service) are without prejudice to contentions that other or different circumstances, individual Faults, greater or lesser numbers of Faults, different combinations of Faults, or lesser liability for Service Credits may also, by themselves or in combination with other facts or circumstances, constitute material breach of the Agreement, and grounds for termination of the Agreement, in whole or in part, in accordance with the terms of the Agreement.

---

[9] For example, if there are twelve Service Levels, and each is measured and reported monthly, there are 144 reported measurements every year, and eight Faults would exceed the five per cent (5%) threshold.

[10] The form provides a variety of potential combinations of failures that might constitute 'Unacceptable Service' and justify default termination. Not all may be appropriate or relevant. Often, 'Unacceptable Service' is defined simply on the basis of gross liability for credits above an agreed threshold, on the theory that total liability is a fair proxy for frequency and severity. Many negotiated outcomes are possible.

Appendix 8

CHARGES—INFORMATION TECHNOLOGY SERVICES

SCHEDULE __

CHARGES

INFORMATION TECHNOLOGY SERVICES

TABLE OF CONTENTS

1 INTRODUCTION

In consideration for the Services, Customer agrees to: (i) pay the Charges and (ii) pay or reimburse the costs specified below (subject to applicable terms of the Agreement). Customer has no obligation to pay or reimburse any amount in consideration for Supplier's performance of Services other than as expressly provided by this Schedule __, the Agreement, or otherwise agreed in writing.

Generally, after the Transition Period (defined below), Supplier's Charges consist of:

(a) Transition Charges; *plus*
(b) Base Charges specified below for Baseline Volumes of Resource Units; *plus or minus*
(c) Additional Resource Charges ("ARCs") or Reduced Resource Credits ("RRCs") for actual Resource Unit consumption (if consumption exceeds or falls below the thresholds of applicable [percentage] Dead Bands); *plus*
(d) Project Charges, as specified in Section 4.5 below; *plus*
(e) COLA adjustments for Services subject to Project Hourly Rates; *subject to*
(f) Annual minimum payment obligations for the Agreement as a whole and for certain Categories of Service.[1]

Supplier's Charges are also subject to equitable and other adjustment as provided below, or by the terms of the Agreement.

2 DEFINITIONS

The following terms shall have the meanings assigned:

"Additional Resource Charge" ("ARC") means the amount payable, in addition to the Base Charges, for additional Resource Units consumed above Baseline Volumes, computed monthly on a per-Resource Unit basis, but payable only when consumption exceeds the upper threshold of the applicable Dead Band.

"Base Charges(s)" means the total Charges to Customer for Services (or for a particular Service Category) for Baseline Volumes of Resource Units (adjusted from time to time, as provided below).

---

[1] Assumes minimum payment obligation, which is common but not usually proposed by customers.

"Baseline Volume" means the specific quantity of Resource Units for a Resource Category included within the Base Charges. (Initial Baseline Volumes are set forth in the attached tables.)

"Category of Service" (or "Service Category") means any of the following: Mainframe Services, as described by Section __ of Schedule __ ...; [list other categories]; and General [Cross-Functional] Services, as described by Section __ of Schedule __.[2]

"Contract Year" means, during the Term, the twelve (12) calendar month period from [date] through [date] of the following calendar year. (The first Contract Year includes the "stub" period between ..., plus the twelve (12) month period beginning [date].)[3]

"Dead Band" means a range between _____ and one hundred ____ per cent (eg, 95–105%) of Baseline Volumes within which no adjustment of Base Charges is required.

"Eligible Users" means Customer's end users and other persons authorized to receive Services, excluding Supplier personnel or subcontractors.

"Full-Time Equivalent" ("FTE") means [number] Productive Hours of work per annum.

"IMAC" means install, move, add and change, as described by Schedule __.[4] For purposes of this Schedule, IMACs exclude: (i) IMACs not satisfactorily completed; (ii) logical moves, adds and changes performed without dispatching a technician to move, add to, change or relocate any devices; (iii) preparation of devices for installations, removals, moves, adds, changes or relocation; and (iv) IMAC Projects.

"IMAC Projects" are groups of [number] or more IMACs that are authorized and performed at the same time, and administered as Projects (eg, for relocation of a department or large-scale new installations).

"Pass-Through Expense" means the actual invoiced amounts charged by third parties that Customer has agreed in writing to pay directly or for which Customer has agreed to reimburse Supplier. Pass-Through Expenses include any tax, insurance, shipping or other, similar costs actually paid to third parties or public agencies, but exclude any markup for overheads, administrative expenses, profit or any other purpose.

"Productive Hours" means time expended performing Services, measured in quarter hour increments, excluding: (i) holidays, vacation time, sick leave, military leave, meals or other personal time; (ii) education and training (other than as expressly required solely for Customer); (iii) travel time; (iv) time spent on administrative or management matters (eg, account and relationship management, internal meetings, matters unrelated to the Services, and internal reporting, except to the extent requested or required by Customer

---

[2] 'General' or 'Cross-Functional' Services generally include account management, reporting and other services that support the account as a whole, rather than any particular Service Category. Charges may be paid separately, or allocated among (and buried in) charges for various Service Categories.

[3] Note that term may run from the contract's effective date or from completion of transition and cutover to steady-state service.

[4] Service description or statement of work.

or directly related to performance of Services, rather than Supplier's business generally); and (v) marketing and sales activities, including preparation of change and other proposals (except to the extent authorized in writing to be paid for as Services).

"Reduced Resource Credit" ("RRC") means the reduction in the Base Charges when actual Resource Unit consumption falls below Baseline Volumes, computed monthly on a per-Resource Unit basis, but credited only when consumption falls below the lower threshold of the applicable Dead Band.

"Resource Category(ies)" and "Resource Units" refers to categories of resources, or particular kinds of resources (such as MIPS, numbers of devices, calls or other measurable items) used to determine Base Charges.

"Seat" means a Desktop or Laptop computer ("workstation") issued or assigned to an end user or otherwise supported by Supplier (*excluding* workstations assigned to Supplier personnel or subcontractors and workstations held in storage or identified as spares).[5]

"Shutdown Costs" means: (a) reasonable severance pay for Supplier personnel terminated on account of premature termination of the Agreement; (b) reasonable relocation costs for Supplier personnel obliged to relocate; (c) cancellation costs for any subcontracts, leases or other contracts with third parties for products or services used solely to perform the Services; (d) unamortized costs of assets purchased by Supplier solely to perform the Services; and (e) other ordinary and necessary costs paid to third parties and associated with termination of the Agreement. However, Shutdown Costs *exclude*: (x) Supplier's general and administrative expenses; (y) unamortized costs attributable to useful lives or other amortization periods after the actual or scheduled expiration of the Agreement (whichever is later); and (z) costs avoided or avoidable through reasonable mitigation, such as reassignment of personnel or redeployment of assets to support other Supplier customers or Supplier's business generally. For purposes of clause (a) above, reasonable severance pay shall be limited to reasonable amounts actually paid attributable to (i) for severance based upon length of tenure, years of service performing Services for Customer; (ii) for personnel not wholly dedicated to performance of Services, that portion of their work dedicated to Customer; and (iii) in all cases, terminations carried out with fair and proper procedures, in compliance with all Laws, regulations (including collective redundancy regulations) and contractual requirements.[6]

"Transition Period" means the period beginning on [date] and ending on [date], or upon successful completion of the tasks contemplated by the Transition Plan, whichever is later.

All other capitalized terms shall have the meanings assigned by the Agreement or given where the terms first appear, unless the context clearly requires some other meaning.

---

[5] Optional definition. PC services may be measured by device or by 'seat.' If the latter is used, there are sometimes classifications based on the sophistication of the device and level of support (eg power users, standard, limited use, training, etc) with variations in charges.

[6] Optional definition, where Shutdown Costs are paid for convenience termination, rather than a lump sum charge.

3 TRANSITION CHARGES

3.1 Milestone Payments

Supplier's Transition Charges shall be payable in increments, upon completion of Transition Milestones to Customer's reasonable satisfaction in all material respects, as provided in Table __, below. Supplier's invoices for payment of Transition Charges shall be presented promptly following completion of relevant Transition Milestones, and paid in accordance with Section __ of the Agreement.

3.2 Transition Credits for Delays

In the event Supplier fails to meet any Transition Milestone, Customer shall be entitled to receive the Transition Credits set forth in Table __. In the event that action or inaction of Customer or any agent or subcontractor (other than action or inaction undertaken at Supplier's direction or with its consent) prevents or delays any Transition Milestone, Supplier's performance will be excused for the period of the delay caused by Customer, if Supplier gives prompt notice and acts reasonably to mitigate the effects of any such delay. Where delays are partially excused, Transition Credits shall be proportionally reduced. Payment of Transition Credits is without prejudice to Customer's other remedies, but amounts paid as Transition Credits shall be deducted from any damages claimed or recovered by Customer for related breaches of Supplier's obligations.

4 RESOURCE UNITS

Certain adjustments to Base Charges shall be computed based upon Customer's consumption of the Resource Units identified below, which Supplier shall measure and report monthly beginning at the times specified by the Transition Plan.[7] The Parties will schedule installations, removals, IMACs and other activities in good faith, based on business requirements, availability of staff and other resources and other legitimate reasons, and not in order to maximize or minimize Charges. Devices, ports and certain other Resource Units shall be counted monthly for billing purposes, as provided below, on or about the __th day of each month (or the next succeeding business day, unless otherwise agreed). Counts shall be based upon Customer's actual inventory, performed during the Transition Period, as adjusted from time to time thereafter to reflect installations, removals, IMACs and other adjustments all as recorded on service requests, Trouble Tickets or other, similar records (excluding incomplete work or work rejected as deficient) or as updated by future inventories.

---

[7] Measurement and reporting may require installation of tools, so may not commence immediately.

4.1 Mainframe

Resource Unit	Unit of Measurement
MIPS [Alternative 1][8]	Average number of MIPS used for production workload, excluding re-runs on account of Supplier errors, system overhead and usage for purposes other than performance of Services, measured monthly
CPU Minutes [Alternative 2]	Processor minutes, excluding re-runs on account of Supplier errors, system overhead and usage for purposes other than performance of Services, measured monthly
Production DASD GBs	Average Number of GBs of disc storage used for production
Test environment DASD GBs	Number of GBs of disc storage installed for testing purposes

[MIPS/usage/CPU minutes] shall be measured as reported by the system management facility ("SMF"). Disc storage shall be measured based on monthly averages.

4.2 Midrange Services

Resource Unit	Unit of Measurement
Small Servers[9]	The number of servers installed that have [range, e.g., 1-2] CPUs [Add other criteria]
Medium Servers	The number of servers installed that have [range] CPUs [Add other criteria]
Large Servers	The number of servers installed that have [range] CPUs [Add other criteria]

---

[8] Generally, customers pay for either MIPS or CPU minutes but not both, as both measure processor usage. Separation of re-runs, overhead and other usage may or may not be practical. Clients should consider whether a provision to 'benchmark' usage is appropriate in the event of transition to a different mainframe computer. Usage is measured before and after change, with identical workloads, in order to isolate and adjust for system overhead and other non-chargeable consumption. Alternatively, conversion factors and formulae may be used.

[9] Classification by size (here, numbers of CPUs) is typical, but there are many potential classifications (eg based on operating systems, physical versus virtual devices, or classes of support—greater and more expensive for servers performing critical functions, less for others). Generally, the more complex and costly the device, and the greater the level of support, the more it will cost. Special arrangements are sometimes necessary for isolated, non-standard machines (eg, otherwise obsolete devices used to operate an older application).

Per-server Charges will be pro-rated on a per *diem* basis for partial months.[10]

4.3 Desktop Services[11]

Resource Unit	Unit of Measurement
Desktop Computers	Desktop computers supported by Supplier for Eligible Users at Customer Locations
Laptop Computers	Laptop computers supported by Supplier for Eligible Users ordinarily assigned to Customer Locations
Laptop Computers (Remote)	Laptop computers supported by Supplier for Eligible Users at Customer Locations other than its principal locations at [specify]
Laptop Computer (Virtual)	Laptop computers supported by Supplier for Eligible Users who are not located at fixed Customer Locations
Printers (Network)	The number of network printers supported by Supplier
Printers (Local)	The number of local printers supported by Supplier (excluding printers retained by Customer's remote or virtual users)
Help Desk	The number of telephone calls, facsimile messages, e-mail or voice messages received and logged by the Supplier Help Desk from Eligible Recipients (collectively, "calls")[12] excluding: (i) status calls satisfied by a broadcast message; (ii) repeated calls concerning the same Trouble Ticket; and (iii) calls by Supplier personnel or subcontractors (unless acting on behalf of a Customer Eligible Recipient)
E-Mailboxes	The total number of E-Mailboxes maintained by Supplier for Customer Eligible Recipients and Customer
IMACs	The total number of IMACs required by Customer (excluding IMAC Projects)

[10] Pro-ration of substantial per-server charges (hundreds or thousands of dollars per month) is more likely to be appropriate for servers than for relatively modest charges for each user, seat, PC, e-mailbox, etc.

[11] Resource units used (for various classes of devices, calls, electronic mailboxes, etc) are illustrative and typical, but may vary.

[12] Note that measurement of Calls for billing purposes is narrower than measurement for some Service Levels. Call abandonment, mean time to answer, and other, similar metrics are captured automatically for all telephone calls received, even if they are not chargeable. Other Service Levels (eg first call resolution) may include requests received by e-mail and facsimile, as well as telephone calls. Many Service Levels for help desks are computed from the time a trouble ticket is opened, however the call may have been received.

Supplier will make diligent efforts to reduce numbers of calls (including, without limitation, implementation of automated password reset processes, web-based or similar status references, automated messages to reduce the impact of multiple calls reporting outages and comparable methods and procedures, and implementation of self-help or web-based help tools). Devices and E-Mailboxes will be counted on the __th day of every month (or, if that date falls upon a weekend or legal holiday, the next succeeding business day) or such other date as may be from time to time agreed in writing. IMACs and installations shall be measured and reported based on trouble tickets, service requests and other similar records (excluding incomplete or deficient work).[13]

4.4 Network Services

Resource Unit	Unit of Measurement
Voice Ports	The number of active voice ports for either digital or analog connections supported by Supplier
Data Ports	The number of active connections to the local area and wide area networks supported by Supplier
IMACs (Telecom)	The total number of telecom IMACs required by Customer, excluding (i) logical voice moves, adds, and changes which do not require a corresponding physical IMAC and (ii) IMAC Projects

4.5 Project Services[14]

Resource Unit	Unit of Measurement
Productive Hours Worked on Projects	Productive Hours Worked in excess of Baseline Volumes

Additional Project Productive Hours, above and beyond those included in Base Charges, shall be charged in arrears at the applicable Project Hourly Rate, as stated in Table __.[15] Unless otherwise agreed, Project IMACs shall be billed based upon Productive Hours at applicable rates.

---

[13] Device counts are sometimes scheduled for the middle of the month. Devices installed before that date count for billing purposes, and devices installed after that date do not. So long as neither side "games" the timing, and per-device Charges are modest, this is fair. For more expensive devices (eg, servers) the Charges may be pro-rated on a daily basis.

[14] Assumes a basic volume of services or pool built into Base Charges. Generally, this is good for customers, as they can obtain volume discounts on usual time and materials rates, where a regular volume of Project work is anticipated.

[15] Rate card to contain appropriate detail concerning skill levels, long- and short-term rates, etc as may be appropriate and agreed.

5 BASELINES AND BASE CHARGES

5.1 Base Charges

Base Charges for all Categories of Service are as provided in Table __, below and reflect consumption of chargeable Resource Units in accordance with the Baseline Volumes contained in Table __.[16] During the Transition Period, Supplier shall invoice and Customer shall pay Base Charges in accordance with Table __, without any ARC, RRC or other adjustment (other than for approved Changes). Thereafter, Base Charges are subject to adjustment as provided below.[17]

5.2 Adjustment of Baselines

During the Transition Period, Supplier shall measure actual consumption of all Resource Units and recommend any changes to Baseline Volumes, if necessary, so that Baseline Volumes accurately reflect Customer's then-current consumption, allowing for any increases or decreases that are likely to continue thereafter, but excluding any unusual, exceptional or non-recurring conditions.[18] After completion of the Transition Period, this process shall be repeated during the final two (2) months of each Contract Year, beginning with the second Contract Year, with changes to be effective at the beginning of the next succeeding Contract Year and implemented in accordance with the reconciliation process described below. Base Charges shall be adjusted accordingly, using applicable ARC, RRC or other adjustments described by this Schedule or the Agreement. If the Parties are ever unable to agree upon adjusted Baselines (and related adjustments to Base Charges) in a timely manner, the matter shall be referred to the joint Executive Committee and if they are unable to agree, then resolved, if necessary, in accordance with Section __ of the Agreement (concerning disputes).[19]

---

[16] This template prices Services based upon Base Charges for Baseline Volumes, plus or minus incremental charges and credits (ARCs and RRCs), and other adjustments. Alternatively, Services may be priced on a pure consumption basis (unit charges x quantities), subject to minimum volume or revenue commitments. The net result is likely to be essentially similar.

[17] The text assumes that during the transition period, the customer pays both transitional charges (on a milestone basis, according to Section 3) and charges for normal service. This is just one possible arrangement when a supplier takes over daily operations while also effecting a transition and even relocating operations to the supplier's facilities. Unless there are reasonably accurate inventories, and tools in place to measure consumption, it may not be possible, initially, for the supplier to bill based on consumption, so the text makes no provision for adjustments during the transition period. Many variations are possible. For example, the supplier's transition charges could include costs for both operations and transition, and base charges could begin when transition ends, either for all services, or on a category-by-category basis when service begins. The text should be edited as appropriate to match the situation.

[18] This may be unnecessary if customer baselines are current and accurate. Edit as appropriate.

[19] The text contemplates annual adjustment of Baselines and Base Charges using ARC and RRC rates. If consumption falls outside priced bands, an equitable adjustment may be appropriate, since original ARC, RRC and other figures were presumably based upon expected consumption (and related economies of scale). Alternatively, Baseline and Base Charges may remain fixed. In such cases, the parties may consider billing based on estimated consumption, so that billings and payments approximate probable charges, adjustments are kept to a minimum, and neither side inadvertently becomes a lender. See Section 6.2 of the form concerning optional quarterly adjustments.

5.3 Incremental Charges and Credits

After the Transition Period, Customer shall pay Base Charges (as adjusted from time to time) plus ARCs (if consumption of Resource Units exceeds the upper limit of the Dead Band) or minus RRCs (if consumption of Resource Units fall below the lower limit of the Dead Band). ARCs and RRCs shall be determined and invoiced as provided below.

6 PERIODIC RECONCILIATIONS AND ADJUSTMENTS

6.1 Reporting and Payment of ARCs and RRCs

Within thirty (30) days following the end of each month, Base Charges for each Category of Service will be adjusted by Supplier based upon (i) positive or negative differences between actual usage of Resource Units for the preceding month and (ii) the upper or lower limits of relevant Dead Bands (as appropriate), (iii) times applicable ARCs and RRCs.[20] After calculation of all adjustments, Supplier shall deliver to Customer, a statement in reasonable detail specifying all adjustments for that month, and explaining their calculation. [Alternative 1 (monthly reconciliation): If there has been a net overpayment by Customer, the amount of the overpayment shall be credited against the next succeeding Supplier invoice(s) or paid by check when the Agreement expires or terminates.[21] Customer agrees to pay the net amount due, if any, within forty-five (45) days after receipt of Supplier's statement.] [Alternative 2 (quarterly reconciliation): Monthly statements concerning adjustments are informational only. Adjustments shall be cumulated for each calendar quarter, then invoiced or credited within forty-five (45) days after the end of each calendar quarter, or expiration or termination of the Agreement. Customer shall pay the net amount due, if any, within forty-five (45) days after receipt of invoice. If there has been a net overpayment by Customer, the amount of the overpayment shall be credited against the next succeeding Supplier invoice(s) or paid by check when the Agreement expires or terminates.]

6.2 Quarterly Adjustments of Base Charges

In addition, invoices for March, June, September and December may propose any adjustments in Base Charges for the subsequent calendar quarters based on those calculations and reasonably projected usage (allowing for any increases or decreases that are likely to continue thereafter, but excluding any unusual, exceptional or non-recurring conditions)

---

[20] The text calculates adjustments from the outer limits of the Dead Band, so that if the Dead Band is plus or minus 5%, the base charge is $100, the unit charge and ARC are $1 per resource unit, and the customer consumes 106 units, it would pay $101 for 106 units. Alternatively, when consumption exceeds the Dead Band, the customer would pay for all 6 additional units, and the first sentence might read: 'Within thirty (30) days following the end of each month, Base Charges for each Category of Service will be adjusted by Supplier based upon (i) positive or negative differences between actual usage of Resource Units for the preceding month and (ii) *then-current Baseline Volumes*, (iii) times applicable ARCs and RRCs, *provided that there shall be no actual adjustment unless actual consumption falls outside the Dead Band.*'

[21] This contemplates monthly reports, invoices and payment or credit. In practice, quarterly adjustments may be more convenient as an administrative matter, especially if Base Charges approximate actual consumption so that actual adjustments are small.

in order to minimize the amount of any net payment or credit following periodic reconciliation. Adjustments in Base Charges shall be subject to Customer's approval but do not affect Baseline Volumes, which are to be adjusted in accordance with Section 5.2.

6.3 Cost-of-Living Adjustment ("COLA") for Project Hourly Rates[22]

Project Hourly Rates shall be subject to an annual cost-of-living recalculation, equal to the percentage change in the [specify index: eg, Consumer Price Index (CPI), Employment Cost Index (ECI)] published by the US Department of Labor's Bureau of Labor Statistics (or a successor index published by the US Government)[23] during the preceding Contract Year. COLA adjustments shall be computed annually, during the first sixty (60) days of each Contract Year (beginning with the second Contract Year), and effective from the beginning of the relevant Contract Year, with any adjustment for that initial sixty (60) day period to be paid as part of the reconciliation and adjustment process described above. If the Bureau of Labor Statistics redefines the base year for the [price index], calculations will be adjusted using an appropriate conversion formula.

6.4 Annual Minimum Payments[24]

If total payments for all Services (including all additional Service performed for approved changes, Projects and otherwise, excluding expense reimbursements) in any Contract Year are less than the amounts specified in [cross-reference][25] for specific Categories of Service or the Agreement as a whole, then promptly following the end of the Contract Year, Supplier shall deliver to Customer an invoice for the shortfall, computed as follows:

(a) First, for each Category of Service, by deducting actual payments for the relevant Category from the applicable minimum, then adding all positive remainders together to determine the total shortfall (if any) for all Categories of Service; *and*

---

[22] If Base Charges do not include an allowance for inflation, COLA could apply to Base Charges, ARCs, RRCs, etc.

[23] The choice of an appropriate price index is often a negotiated term. The Employment Cost Index (ECI) is regarded as a good measure of labor costs. Changes in prices for hardware, software, bandwidth, like labor rates, may or may not align well with the better-known Consumer Price Index, which is tied to a 'basket' of consumer goods. When services are performed offshore, a portion of the charges may be indexed based on an appropriate, agreed index for the relevant country. Within the US, there may be significant differences between national indices and those for particular regions or metropolitan areas.

[24] Common provision, heavily negotiated, and not generally proposed by customers. Suppliers will prefer to adjust minimums upward to match scope increases. Customers prefer lower thresholds, and generally prefer a single overall minimum to per-Category minimums. Suppliers prefer higher thresholds, and per-Category minimums, lest any single service (or internal delivery organization) operate on an uneconomic basis. For the supplier, margins may vary considerably among various services. Customers sometimes propose declining minimums (eg 85% in the first year, 70% in the second year, and so forth) on the theory that (i) supplier internal thresholds are based upon gross value of the entire contract, and (ii) scope and volume are more likely to contract gradually, so that (iii) greater flexibility during the final years of the term is more useful. See Ch 7, at 6.12 above.

[25] Table of minimum payment obligations, usually based on an agreed percentage of projected revenues. This template contemplates a two-tier minimum, for Service Categories and the entire Agreement.

(b) Second, if total payments for all Categories of Service plus the sum of all per-Category shortfalls (calculated as provided above) are less than the aggregate minimum for the entire Agreement in the relevant Contract Year, then Customer shall also pay the difference so determined (the "remaining shortfall").

7 EXPENSES

7.1 Retained Expenses

Customer agrees to pay the retained expenses listed in Table __,[26] and as otherwise specified by the Agreement or agreed to from time to time in writing.

7.2 Pass-Through Expenses

Customer agrees to pay costs of [insert list or reference to a financial responsibility matrix] and the other Pass-Through Expenses specified by the Agreement or agreed to from time to time in writing. Products and services may not be purchased from or through Supplier's Affiliates or members of the Supplier Group without Customer's prior written approval of the terms in each instance. Supplier will: (i) review the corresponding invoiced charges to determine whether they are valid and proper and (ii) provide Customer with a reasonable opportunity to review the invoice and confirm its determination before the invoice is due and in sufficient time to obtain available discounts. Supplier will use reasonable efforts to minimize Pass-Through Expenses. Customer reserves the rights to (a) obtain products and services obtained on a Pass-Through basis directly; (b) designate the third party sources for such products and services; and (c) approve the terms of purchase.[27]

7.3 Travel and Living Expenses

Supplier's Charges generally include all travel, living and other, similar costs related to performance of Services.[28] However, if, when and to the extent that Customer agrees to reimburse reasonable out-of-pocket expenses incurred by Supplier in connection with the performance of Project-related Services or other additional Services outside the scope of Schedule __, Service Description, Customer shall do so at actual cost and without any markup, to the extent authorized in advance by the relevant Project Documents or otherwise in writing. Invoices shall describe reimbursable expenses in reasonable detail. Upon request, Supplier shall provide reasonable backup documentation. Travel, living and other expenses shall comply with Supplier's reasonable written policies, in effect from time to time, and approved by Customer.

---

[26] Insert reference to appropriate table or financial responsibility matrix.

[27] Note that this calls for the Supplier to review and submit invoices, rather than review, pay and obtain reimbursement (a less common practice, because of suppliers' desire to add overheads and profit to all costs they pay).

[28] Where transition involves transfers of operations offshore, be sure that text is clear (here or relating to Transition) concerning costs of travel related to transition. Charges generally include costs of periodic home leave for onshore staff, visits to customer sites by supplier management and other predictable travel.

8 CONVENIENCE TERMINATION

8.1 Termination Charges [Shutdown Costs]

[Alternative 1—Fixed, Declining Termination Charge: Table __ specifies Termination Charges payable upon convenience termination pursuant to Section __ of the Agreement. During any Contract Year, Termination Charges shall decline monthly by an amount equal to one twelfth (1/12) of the difference between the Convenience Termination Charge for that Contract Year and the Convenience Termination Charge for the subsequent Contract Year.[29] Convenience Termination Charges are payable on or immediately after the effective date of termination. In cases of partial termination for convenience, Convenience Termination Charges shall be proportionally reduced, based upon the reduction in Charges.]

[Alternative 2—Shuttdown Costs: Within sixty (60) days following the effective date of any convenience termination pursuant to Section __ of the Agreement, Supplier shall prepare and submit to Customer an invoice for its Shutdown Costs, together with such supporting documentation and detail as Customer may reasonably request. Customer shall pay the invoice within sixty (60) days, subject to its rights to audit and to withhold any amounts disputed in good faith, and its other rights under the Agreement.][30]

8.2 Convenience Termination—Change in Control of Supplier

No Convenience Termination Charge [Shutdown Costs] shall be paid if Customer terminates the Agreement for its convenience by giving notice within six (6) months after consummation of any merger, acquisition, reorganization, sale of stock, sale of assets or other, similar transaction or transactions that effect a change in Control of Supplier.[31]

8.3 Option to Purchase Assets

Concurrently with any termination or with expiration of the Agreement, Customer may, at its option, purchase any and all hardware and other assets then used to provide Services that are used [primarily/exclusively] to support Customer (including, without limitation, any assets transferred by Customer, or replacements therefor) for their then-current [book value] [market value, as reasonably determined by agreement or, if the Parties are unable to agree, by an independent appraisal by a third party engaged by Customer and acceptable to Supplier].[32]

---

[29] Contracts sometimes preclude convenience termination during transition and an initial 'lock-in' period.

[30] When this alternative is chosen, references to termination charges should be edited accordingly in this document and the agreement.

[31] Alternatively, the parties may agree to a reduced termination charge following a change in control, or no termination charge in the event the supplier is sold to one of the customer's competitors.

[32] If termination charges include unamortized cost of transferred assets, only nominal consideration may be paid.

9 PROJECT CHARGES

Supplier's Base Charges include the Baseline Volumes of Project Work specified by Table __.[33] When Project Services exceed those Baseline Volumes, computed on a monthly/annual basis, Customer will pay those Project Charges specified in Price Table __ or other Charges as specified in the Project Documents and applicable provisions of Schedule __ (Project Terms) and the Agreement.

10 GENERAL PRICING CONDITIONS AND ASSUMPTIONS

Supplier's Charges are based upon the following general conditions and assumptions. In the event of any material deviation from the following assumptions, and subject to Section __ of the Agreement (concerning excused performance, notice to Customer, mitigation and potential compensation upon the conditions specified), then relevant Charges shall be adjusted through the Change Control Procedure to compensate Supplier for the net additional Service performed (if any) and, to the extent not otherwise compensated by such adjustments, reimbursement of net, documented additional costs actually paid to third parties for products, services and related charges paid to third parties, such as taxes, shipping and insurance:

(a) Customer will provide facilities as described in [name document].
(b) Customer will continue to conduct business in [locations].
(c) Customer will perform all of the various functions identified in Schedule __ (Service Description) as Customer responsibilities.
(d) Services will be performed in the English language.
(e) All material hardware provided to Supplier by customer is under warranty and manufacturers' (or equivalent) maintenance contracts.
(f) All material Software applications furnished by Customer or within its financial responsibility are under maintenance and support agreements with relevant licensors.[34]
(g) [Others].

---

[33] Text assumes that some level of Project work is built into Base Charges. Edit as appropriate.

[34] Listed assumptions are illustrative and typical, but actual assumptions vary depending upon circumstances.

Appendix 9

CHARGES—APPLICATIONS, DEVELOPMENT AND MAINTENANCE SERVICES

SCHEDULE __

CHARGES

APPLICATIONS, DEVELOPMENT AND MAINTENANCE SERVICES

TABLE OF CONTENTS

1 INTRODUCTION

In consideration for the Services, Customer agrees to: (i) pay the Charges and (ii) pay or reimburse the costs specified below (subject to applicable terms of the Agreement). Customer has no obligation to pay or reimburse any amount in consideration for Supplier's performance of Services other than as expressly provided by this Schedule __, the Agreement, or otherwise agreed in writing.

Generally, after the Transition Period (defined below), Supplier's Charges consist of:

(a) Transition Charges; *plus*
(b) Base Charges specified below; *plus or minus*
(c) Additional Resource Charges ("ARCs") or Reduced Resource Credits ("RRCs") for actual Resource Unit consumption (if consumption exceeds or falls below the thresholds of applicable [percentage] Dead Bands); *plus*
(d) Project Charges, as specified in Section 8 below; *plus*
(e) Cost-of-living (COLA) adjustments; *subject to*
(f) Annual minimum payment obligations.[1]

Supplier's Charges are also subject to equitable and other adjustment as provided below, or by the terms of the Agreement.

2 DEFINITIONS

The following terms shall have the meanings assigned:

"Additional Resource Charge" ("ARC") means the amount payable, in addition to the Base Charges, for additional Resource Units consumed above Baseline Volumes, computed monthly on a per-Resource Unit basis, but payable only when consumption exceeds the upper threshold of the applicable Dead Band.

"Base Charge" means the total monthly Charge to Customer for Services (or for a particular Category of Service) as adjusted in accordance with the terms of this Schedule __ and other provisions of the Agreement.

"Baseline Volume" means the specific quantity of Resource Units for a Resource Category included within the Base Charges. (Initial Baseline Volumes are set forth in the attached tables.)

"Category of Service" (or "Service Category") means any of the following: [list categories, eg, by computing platform, operating system or other relevant technology or group of applications]; and General [Cross-Functional] Services, as described by Section __ of Schedule __.[2]

---

[1] Assumes minimum payment obligation, which is common but not usually proposed by customers.

[2] 'General' (or 'Cross-Functional') Services generally include account management, reporting and other services that support the account as a whole, rather than any particular Service Category. Charges may be paid separately, or allocated among (and buried in) charges for various Service Categories.

"Contract Year" means, during the Term, the twelve (12) calendar month period from [date] through [date] of the following calendar year. (The first Contract Year includes the "stub" period between. . ., plus the twelve (12) month period beginning [date].)[3]

"Dead Band" means a range between _____ and one hundred ____ per cent (eg, 95–105%) of Baseline Volumes within which no adjustment of Base Charges is required.

"Full-Time Equivalent" ("FTE") means [number] Productive Hours of work per annum.

"Pass-Through Expense" means the actual invoiced amounts charged by third parties that Customer has agreed in writing to pay directly or for which Customer has agreed to reimburse Supplier. Pass-Through Expenses include any tax, insurance, shipping or other, similar costs actually paid to third parties or public agencies, but exclude any markup for overheads, administrative expenses, profit or any other purpose.

"Productive Hours" means time expended performing Services, measured in quarter hour increments, *excluding*: (i) holidays, vacation time, sick leave, military leave, meals or other personal time; (ii) education and training (other than as expressly required solely and for Customer); (iii) travel time; (iv) time spent on administrative or management matters (eg, account and relationship management, internal meetings, matters unrelated to the Services, and internal reporting, except to the extent requested or required by Customer or directly related to performance of Services, rather than Supplier's business generally); and (v) marketing and sales activities, including preparation of change and other proposals (except to the extent authorized in writing to be paid for as Services).

"Reduced Resource Credit" ("RRC") means the reduction in the Base Charges when actual Resource Unit consumption falls below Baseline Volumes, computed monthly on a per-Resource Unit basis, but credited only when consumption falls below the lower threshold of the applicable Dead Band.

"Resource Baseline" means Baseline Volumes projected forward over time, as reflected in Table __, and as adjusted from time to time.

"Resource Category(ies)" and "Resource Units" refers to categories of resources, or particular kinds of resources (such as FTEs) used to determine Base Charges.

"Shutdown Costs" means: (a) reasonable severance pay for Supplier personnel terminated on account of premature termination of the Agreement; (b) reasonable relocation costs for Supplier personnel obliged to relocate; (c) cancellation costs for any subcontracts, leases or other contracts with third parties for products or services used solely to perform the Services; (d) unamortized costs of assets purchased by Supplier solely to perform the Services; and (e) other ordinary and necessary costs paid to third parties and associated with termination of the Agreement. However, Shutdown Costs *exclude*: (x) Supplier's general and administrative expenses; (y) unamortized costs attributable to useful lives

---

[3] Note that term may run from the contract's effective date or from completion of transition and cutover to steady-state service.

or other amortization periods after the actual or scheduled expiration of the Agreement (whichever is later); and (z) costs avoided or avoidable through reasonable mitigation, such as reassignment of personnel or redeployment of assets to support other Supplier customers or Supplier's business generally. For purposes of clause (a) above, reasonable severance pay shall be limited to reasonable amounts actually paid attributable to: (i) for severance based upon length of tenure, years of service performing Services for Customer; (ii) for personnel not wholly dedicated to performance of Services, that portion of their work dedicated to Customer; and (iii) in all cases, terminations carried out with fair and proper procedures, in compliance with all Laws, regulations (including collective redundancy regulations) and contractual requirements.[4]

"Transition Period" means the [number] month period ending on [date], or upon successful completion of the tasks contemplated by the Transition Plan, whichever is later.

All other capitalized terms shall have the meanings assigned by the Agreement or given where the terms first appear, unless the context clearly requires some other meaning.

3 TRANSITION CHARGES

3.1 Milestone Payments
Supplier's Transition Charges shall be payable in increments, upon completion of Transition Milestones to Customer's reasonable satisfaction in all material respects, as provided in Table __. Supplier's invoices for payment of Transition Charges shall be presented promptly following completion of relevant Transition Milestones, and paid in accordance with Section __ of the Agreement.

3.2 Transition Credits for Delays
In the event Supplier fails to meet any Transition Milestone, Customer shall be entitled to receive the Transition Credits set forth in Table __. In the event that action or inaction of Customer or any agent or subcontractor (other than action or inaction undertaken at Supplier's direction or with its consent) prevents or delays any Transition Milestone, Supplier's performance will be excused for the period of the delay caused by Customer, if Supplier gives prompt notice and acts reasonably to mitigate the effects of any such delay. Where delays are partially excused, Transition Credits shall be proportionally reduced. Payment of Transition Credits is without prejudice to Customer's other remedies, but amounts paid as Transition Credits shall be deducted from any damages claimed or recovered by Customer for related breaches of Supplier's obligations.

4 BASELINES, BASE CHARGES AND ADJUSTMENTS

4.1 Resource Units
Certain adjustments to Base Charges shall be computed based upon Customer's consumption of FTEs, Productive Hours and other Resource Units, which Supplier shall

---

[4] Optional definition, where Shutdown Costs are paid for convenience termination, rather than a lump sum fee.

measure using tools acceptable to Customer and report monthly in such detail as Customer may reasonably require.

4.2 Base Charges

Base Charges for all Categories of Service are as provided in Table __, below, and reflect consumption of chargeable Resource Units in accordance with the Baseline Volumes contained in Table __.[5] Base Charges, as adjusted by operation of this Schedule __ and other applicable terms of the Agreement, fully compensate Supplier for providing the Services. Base Charges commence upon [completion of the Transition Period] [completion of Transition-related activities and completion of the final Transition Milestone for the relevant Category of Service.]

4.3 Baseline Volumes

Baseline Volumes are set forth in Table __. If usage is more or less than applicable Baseline Volumes, an ARC or RRC, respectively, may apply, as provided below. Supplier shall provide for the flexibility to respond to changes in Customer's demand on a day-to-day or month-to-month basis (using staff ordinarily assigned and available) particularly for those Services where Customer experiences fluctuations in demand. Unless otherwise provided in the Agreement, and subject to Schedule __ (Governance), and applicable work authorization procedures, if compliance with the Service Levels or other performance standards requires more dedicated support, additional staff or other resources, or extended hours of service, Supplier shall provide that support at no additional charge to Customer (other than for ARCs, if applicable).

4.4 Adjustment of Baselines

Baseline Volumes (and the corresponding Base Charges) may be adjusted by the Parties, as mutually agreed, at the beginning of each Contract Year (or as otherwise agreed by the Parties) using applicable ARC, RRC or other rates or adjustments to reflect the anticipated future consumption, based on (i) usage during the twelve (12) months preceding the date of calculation, and (ii) any significant changes in usage reasonably anticipated by Customer. If the Parties are ever unable to agree upon adjusted Baselines (and related adjustments to Base Charges) in a timely manner, the matter shall be referred to the joint Executive Committee[6] and if they are unable to agree, then resolved, if necessary, in accordance with Section __ of the Agreement (concerning disputes).

4.5 Incremental Charges and Credits

Customer shall pay Base Charges (as adjusted from time to time) *plus* ARCs (to the extent that consumption of Resource Units exceeds the upper limit of the Dead Band) or *minus*

---

[5] This template prices Services based upon Base Charges plus or minus incremental charges and credits (ARCs and RRCs), and other adjustments. Alternatively, Services may be priced on a pure consumption basis (unit charges times quantities), subject to minimum volume or revenue commitments. The net result is likely to be essentially similar.

[6] Joint steering committee or equivalent.

RRCs (to the extent that consumption of Resource Units fall below the lower limit of the Dead Band). ARCs and RRCs shall be determined monthly. Base Charges, plus or minus applicable ARCs and RRCs, if any, shall be invoiced monthly in arrears, on or before the __ th day of the succeeding month, and paid within forty-five (45) days thereafter.

4.6 Committed Productivity Gains

Supplier has committed to achieving certain productivity gains by increasing the productivity of the Supplier staff so that support for Customer's portfolio of supported applications requires fewer FTEs over time. Such reduced staffing levels are reflected in the Resource Baselines in Table __. Customer will not be charged for any additional FTEs to support the portfolio, except to the extent that (i) Supplier's failure to achieve such reductions is excused by operation of the Agreement or applicable law, or (ii) changes are approved to reflect changes in the portfolio, and related changes in the size, skill and composition of Supplier's staff. To the extent that Supplier may achieve greater productivity gains than anticipated, so that still fewer staff than anticipated are needed to support the portfolio, then Supplier shall, as Customer reasonably determines after consultation with Supplier, either (a) further reduce the number of FTEs as appropriate (and reduce Charges accordingly) or (b) reassign FTEs no longer required to Projects or other Services, at no additional cost to Customer.

4.7 Cost-of-Living Adjustment ("COLA")

Service rates for Productive Hours, FTEs, Projects, ARCs, and RRCs shall be subject to an annual cost-of-living recalculation, equal to the percentage change in the [specify index: eg, Consumer Price Index (CPI), Employment Cost Index (ECI)] published by the US Department of Labor's Bureau of Labor Statistics (or a successor index published by the US Government)[7] during the preceding Contract Year. COLA adjustments shall be computed annually, during the first sixty (60) days of each Contract Year (beginning with the second Contract Year), and effective from the beginning of the relevant Contract Year, with any adjustment for that initial sixty (60) day period to be paid as part of the monthly reconciliation and adjustment process described above. If the Bureau of Labor Statistics redefines the base year for the [price index], calculations will be adjusted using an appropriate conversion formula.

5 ANNUAL MINIMUM PAYMENTS[8]

If total payments for all Services (including all additional Services performed for approved changes, Projects and otherwise, excluding expense reimbursements) in any Contract

---

[7] The choice of an appropriate index is often a negotiated term. The Employment Cost Index (ECI) is regarded as a good measure of labor costs, but has often exceeded the Consumer Price Index (CPI), which is based upon a 'basket' of consumer goods. When work goes offshore, indices from relevant countries may apply to offshore services, so there may be an apportionment based upon the ratio between onshore and offshore services. Within the US, there may be significant differences between national indices and those for particular regions or metropolitan areas.

[8] Common provision, heavily negotiated, and not generally proposed by customers.

Year are less than the amounts specified in Table __⁹ for the Agreement as a whole, then promptly following the end of the Contract Year, Supplier shall deliver to Customer an invoice for the shortfall, which Customer shall pay within forty-five (45) days thereafter.

6 EXPENSES

6.1 Retained Expenses

Customer agrees to pay the retained expenses listed in Table __,¹⁰ and as otherwise specified by the Agreement or agreed to from time to time in writing.

6.2 Pass-Through Expenses

Customer agrees to pay costs of [insert list or reference to a financial responsibility matrix] and the other Pass-Through Expenses specified by the Agreement or agreed to from time to time in writing. Products and services may not be purchased from or through Supplier's Affiliates or members of the Supplier Group without Customer's prior written approval of the terms in each instance. Supplier will: (i) review the corresponding invoiced charges to determine whether they are valid and proper and (ii) provide Customer with a reasonable opportunity to review the invoice and confirm its determination before the invoice is due and in sufficient time to obtain available discounts. Supplier will use reasonable efforts to minimize Pass-Through Expenses. Customer reserves the rights to: (a) obtain products and services obtained on a Pass-Through basis directly; (b) designate the third party sources for such products and services; and (c) approve the terms of purchase.¹¹

6.3 Travel and Living Expenses

Supplier's Charges generally include all travel, living and other, similar costs related to performance of Services.¹² However, if, when and to the extent that Customer agrees to reimburse reasonable out-of-pocket expenses incurred by Supplier in connection with the performance of Project-related Services or other additional Services outside the scope of Schedule __, Service Description, Customer shall do so at actual cost and without any markup, to the extent authorized in advance by the relevant Project Documents, or otherwise in writing. Invoices shall describe reimbursable expenses in reasonable detail. Upon request, Supplier shall provide reasonable backup documentation. Travel, living and other expenses shall comply with Supplier's reasonable written policies, in effect from time to time, and approved by Customer.

---

⁹ Table of minimum payment obligations, usually based on agreed percentage of projected revenues.

¹⁰ Insert reference to appropriate table or financial responsibility matrix.

¹¹ Note that this calls for the Supplier to review and submit invoices, rather than review, pay and obtain reimbursement (a less common practice, because of suppliers' desire to add overhead and profit to all costs they pay).

¹² Where transition involves transfers of operations offshore, the text should be clear (here or relating to transition) concerning costs of travel related to transition. Charges generally include costs of periodic home leave for onshore staff, visits to customer sites by supplier management and other predictable travel.

7 CONVENIENCE TERMINATION

7.1 Termination Charges [Shutdown Costs]

[Alternative—Fixed, Declining Termination Charge: Table __ specifies Termination Charges payable upon convenience termination pursuant to Section __ of the Agreement. During any Contract Year, Termination Charges shall decline monthly by an amount equal to one twelfth (1/12) of the difference between the Convenience Termination Charge for that Contract Year and the Convenience Termination Charge for the subsequent Contract Year.[13] Convenience Termination Charges are payable on or immediately after the effective date of termination. In cases of partial termination for convenience, Convenience Termination Charges shall be proportionally reduced, based upon the reduction in Charges.]

[Alternative—Shutdown Costs: Within sixty (60) days following the effective date of any convenience termination pursuant to Section __ of the Agreement, Supplier shall prepare and submit to Customer an invoice for its Shutdown Costs, together with such supporting documentation and detail as Customer may reasonably request. Customer shall pay the invoice within sixty (60) days, subject to its rights to audit and to withhold any amounts disputed in good faith, and its other rights under the Agreement.][14]

7.2 Convenience Termination—Change in Control of Supplier

No Convenience Termination Charge [Shutdown Costs] shall be paid if Customer terminates the Agreement for its convenience by giving notice within six (6) months after consummation of any merger, acquisition, reorganization, sale of stock, sale of assets or other, similar transaction or transactions that effect a change in Control of Supplier.[15]

8 PROJECT CHARGES

Supplier's Base Charges include the Baseline Volumes of Project Work specified by Table __. When Project Services exceed those Baseline Volumes, computed on a [monthly/annual] basis, Customer will pay those Project Charges specified in Table __ or other Charges as specified in the Project Documents and applicable provisions of Schedule __ (Project Terms) and the Agreement.[16]

9 GENERAL PRICING CONDITIONS AND ASSUMPTIONS

Supplier's Charges are based upon the following general conditions and assumptions. In the event of any material deviation from the following assumptions, and subject to

---

[13] Contracts sometimes preclude convenience termination during transition and an initial 'lock-in' period.

[14] When this alternative is chosen, references to termination charges should be edited accordingly in this document and the agreement.

[15] Alternatively, the parties may agree to a reduced termination charge following a change in control, or no termination charge in the event the Supplier is sold to one of the customer's competitors.

[16] This paragraph anticipates that volume pricing is based upon transfer of ongoing projects to the Supplier.

Section __ of the Agreement (concerning excused performance, notice to Customer, mitigation and potential compensation upon the conditions specified), then relevant Charges shall be adjusted through the Change Control Procedure to compensate Supplier for the net additional Service performed (if any) and, to the extent not otherwise compensated by such adjustments, reimbursement of net, documented additional costs actually paid to third parties for products, services and related charges paid to third parties, such as taxes, shipping and insurance:

(a) Customer will provide facilities as described in [name document].
(b) Customer will continue to conduct business in [locations].
(c) Customer will perform all of the various functions identified in Schedule __ (Service Description) as Customer responsibilities.
(d) Services will be performed in the English language.
(e) User documentation and technical documentation will conform to [describe standards].
(f) [Others].

Appendix 10

CHARGES—FINANCE
AND ACCOUNTING SERVICES

SCHEDULE __

CHARGES

FINANCE, ACCOUNTING AND SERVICES

TABLE OF CONTENTS

1 INTRODUCTION

In consideration for the Services, Customer agrees to: (i) pay the Charges and (ii) pay or reimburse the costs specified below (subject to applicable terms of the Agreement). Customer has no obligation to pay or reimburse any amount in consideration for Supplier's performance of Services other than as expressly provided by this Schedule __, the Agreement, or otherwise agreed in writing.

Generally, Supplier's Charges consist of:

(a) Transition Charges; *plus*
(b) Base Charges specified below; plus *or minus*
(c) Additional Resource Charges ("ARCs") or Reduced Resource Credits ("RRCs") for actual Resource Unit consumption (if consumption exceeds or falls below the thresholds of applicable [percentage] Dead Bands); *plus*
(d) Cost-of-living (COLA) adjustments, *subject to*
(e) Annual minimum payment obligations.[1]

Supplier's Charges are also subject to equitable and other adjustment as provided below, or by the terms of the Agreement.

2 DEFINITIONS

The following terms shall have the meanings assigned:

"Additional Resource Charge" ("ARC") means the amount payable, in addition to the Base Charges, for additional Resource Units consumed above Baseline Volumes, computed monthly on a per-Resource Unit basis, but payable only when consumption exceeds the upper threshold of the applicable Dead Band.

"Base Charge" means the total monthly Charge to Customer for Services (or for a particular Category of Service) as adjusted in accordance with the terms of this Schedule __ and other provisions of the Agreement. Certain Base Charges are fixed, subject to adjustment as provided below, and other Base Charges are variable and consumption-based, determined by numbers of Resource Units consumed times applicable rates.

"Baseline Volume" means the numbers of transactions or quantities of Resource Units included within the Base Charges. (Initial Baseline Volumes are set forth in the attached tables.)

"Category of Service" (or "Service Category") means any of the following: [list categories, eg, Accounts Payable, Accounts Receivable, General Ledger Accounting and Reporting, etc]; and General [Cross-Functional] Services, as described by Section __ of Schedule __.[2]

---

[1] Assumes minimum payment obligation which is common but not usually proposed by customers.

[2] 'General' or 'Cross-Functional' Services generally include account management, reporting and other services that support the account as a whole, rather than any particular Service Category. Charges may be paid separately, or allocated among (and buried in) charges for various Service Categories.

"Contract Year" means, during the Term, the twelve (12) calendar month period from [date] through [date] of the following calendar year. (The first Contract Year includes the "stub" period between . . . , plus the twelve (12) month period beginning [date].)[3]

"Dead Band" means a range between _____ and one hundred ____ per cent (eg, 90–110%) of Baseline Volumes within which no adjustment of Base Charges is required.[4]

"Full-Time Equivalent" ("FTE") means [number] Productive Hours of work per annum.

"Pass-Through Expense" means the actual invoiced amounts charged by third parties that Customer has agreed in writing to pay directly or for which Customer has agreed to reimburse Supplier. Pass-Through Expenses include any tax, insurance, shipping or other, similar costs actually paid to third parties or public agencies, but exclude any markup for overheads, administrative expenses, profit or any other purpose.

"Productive Hours" means time expended performing Services, measured in quarter hour increments, *excluding*: (i) holidays, vacation time, sick leave, military leave, meals or other personal time; (ii) education and training (other than as expressly required solely for Customer); (iii) travel time; (iv) time spent on administrative or management matters (eg, account and relationship management, internal meetings, matters unrelated to the Services, and internal reporting, except to the extent requested or required by Customer or directly related to performance of Services, rather than Supplier's business generally); and (v) marketing and sales activities, including preparation of change and other proposals (except to the extent authorized in writing to be paid for as Services).

"Reduced Resource Credit" ("RRC") means the reduction in the Base Charges when actual Resource Unit consumption falls below Baseline Volumes, computed monthly on a per-Resource Unit basis, but credited only when consumption falls below the lower threshold of the applicable Dead Band.

"Resource Baseline" means Baseline Volumes projected forward over time, as reflected in Table __, and as adjusted from time to time.

"Resource Category(ies)" and "Resource Units" refers to categories of resources, or particular kinds of resources (such as FTEs) used to determine Base Charges.

"Shutdown Costs" means: (a) reasonable severance pay for Supplier personnel terminated on account of premature termination of the Agreement; (b) reasonable relocation costs for Supplier personnel obliged to relocate; (c) cancellation costs for any subcontracts, leases or other contracts with third parties for products or services used solely to perform the Services; (d) unamortized costs of assets purchased by Supplier solely to

---

[3] Note that term may run from the contract's effective date or from completion of transition and cutover to steady-state service.

[4] Where fixed charges are agreed, dead bands may be very wide (eg 10–20%). Many accounting activities (eg quarterly and annual closings) are relatively stable, and unlikely to vary in the absence of extraordinary circumstances, such as dramatic growth through an acquisition.

perform the Services; and (e) other reasonable, ordinary and necessary costs paid to third parties and associated with termination of the Agreement. However, Shutdown Costs *exclude*: (x) Supplier's general and administrative expenses; (y) unamortized costs attributable to useful lives or other amortization periods after the actual or scheduled expiration of the Agreement (whichever is later); and (z) costs avoided or avoidable through reasonable mitigation, such as reassignment of personnel or redeployment of assets to support other Supplier customers or Supplier's business generally. For purposes of clause (a) above, reasonable severance pay shall be limited to reasonable amounts actually paid attributable to: (i) for severance based upon length of tenure, years of service performing Services for Customer; (ii) for personnel not wholly dedicated to performance of Services, that portion of their work dedicated to Customer; and (iii) in all cases, terminations carried out with fair and proper procedures, in compliance with all Laws, regulations (including collective redundancy regulations) and contractual requirements.[5]

"Transition Period" means the [number] month period ending on [date], or upon successful completion of the tasks contemplated by the Transition Plan, whichever is later.

All other capitalized terms shall have the meanings assigned by the Agreement or given where the terms first appear, unless the context clearly requires some other meaning.

3 TRANSITION CHARGES

3.1 Milestone Payments

Supplier's Transition Charges shall be payable in increments, upon completion of Transition Milestones to Customer's reasonable satisfaction in all material respects, as provided in Table __. Supplier's invoices for payment of Transition Charges shall be presented promptly following completion of relevant Transition Milestones, and paid in accordance with Section __ of the Agreement.

3.2 Transition Credits for Delays

In the event Supplier fails to meet any Transition Milestone, Customer shall be entitled to receive the Transition Credits set forth in Table __. In the event that action or inaction of Customer or any agent or subcontractor (other than action or inaction undertaken at Supplier's direction or with its consent) prevents or delays any Transition Milestone, Supplier's performance will be excused for the period of the delay caused by Customer, if Supplier gives prompt notice and acts reasonably to mitigate the effects of any such delay. Where delays are partially excused, Transition Credits shall be proportionally reduced. Payment of Transition Credits is without prejudice to Customer's other remedies, but amounts paid as Transition Credits shall be deducted from any damages claimed or recovered by Customer for related breaches of Supplier's obligations.

---

[5] Optional definition, where Shutdown Costs are paid for convenience termination, rather than a lump sum fee.

4 BASELINES, BASE CHARGES AND ADJUSTMENTS

4.1 Resource Units

Certain adjustments to Base Charges shall be computed based upon Customer's consumption of FTEs, Productive Hours and other Resource Units, which Supplier shall measure using tools acceptable to Customer and report monthly in such detail as Customer may reasonably require.

4.2 Base Charges

Base Charges for all Categories of Service are as provided in Table __, and reflect consumption of chargeable Resource Units in accordance with the Baseline Volumes contained in Table __.[6] Base Charges, as adjusted by operation of this Schedule __ and other applicable terms of the Agreement, fully compensate Supplier for providing the Services. Base Charges for [list Service Categories] are fixed, subject to adjustment as provided below; while Base Charges for [list Service Categories] are variable and consumption-based, determined by numbers of Resource Units consumed times applicable rates set forth in Table ___ (as adjusted from time to time). Base Charges will commence upon completion of Transition-related activities and completion of the final Transition Milestone for the relevant Category of Service.

4.3 Baseline Volumes

Baseline Volumes are set forth in Table __. If usage is more or less than applicable Baseline Volumes and outside the Dead Band, then (a) an ARC or RRC, respectively, may apply, as provided below (where Base Charges are fixed); and (b) where Base Charges are variable, they shall be based upon actual monthly consumption times the relevant rate. Supplier shall provide for the flexibility to respond to changes in Customer's demand on a day-to-day or month-to-month basis (using staff ordinarily assigned and available) particularly for those Services where Customer experiences fluctuations in demand. Unless otherwise provided in the Agreement, and subject to Schedule __ (Governance), if compliance with the Service Levels or other performance standards requires more dedicated support, additional staff or other resources, or extended hours of service, Supplier shall provide that support at no additional charge to Customer (other than for ARCs, if applicable).

4.4 Adjustment of Baselines

Baseline Volumes, Resource Baselines (and the corresponding fixed Base Charges or rates for variable Base Charges) may be adjusted by the Parties, as mutually agreed, at the

---

[6] This template prices Services based upon a combination of (i) fixed Base Charges plus or minus incremental charges and credits (ARCs and RRCs), and (ii) consumption-based charges (based upon numbers of transactions, hours or FTEs, subject to minimum volume or revenue commitments. Where workloads are stable and predictable (as for general ledger accounting) fixed prices may be appropriate (subject to adjustment in the event of large swings). Variable pricing is more appropriate when workloads may fluctuate (eg based on numbers of invoices for accounts receivable). When initial workloads are uncertain, the parties sometimes agree to hourly or FTE-based charges initially, then convert to transaction-based charges.

beginning of each Contract Year (or as otherwise agreed by the Parties) using applicable rates, ARC, RRC or other adjustments to reflect the anticipated future consumption, based on (i) usage during the twelve (12) months preceding the date of calculation, and (ii) any significant changes in usage reasonably anticipated by Customer. If the Parties are ever unable to agree upon adjusted Baselines (and related adjustments to Base Charges or rates) in a timely manner, the matter shall be referred to the [name] Committee and if they are unable to agree, then resolved, if necessary, in accordance with Section __ of the Agreement (concerning disputes).

4.5 Adjustment and Payment of Base Charges

Customer shall pay:

(a) Fixed Base Charges (as adjusted from time to time) plus ARCs (to the extent that consumption of Resource Units exceeds the upper limit of the Dead Band) or minus RRCs (to the extent that consumption of Resource Units falls below the lower limit of the Dead Band); and

(b) Variable Base Charges, as computed monthly based upon actual consumption of Resource Units times the applicable rate (subject to Section 4.6).

Base Charges shall be invoiced monthly in arrears, on or before the __th day of the succeeding month, and paid within [number] days thereafter. ARCs and RRCs shall be determined [monthly] [quarterly], within [number] days after the end of the relevant [month/quarter], and reported in such detail as Customer may reasonably require. Net amounts due shall be invoiced simultaneously with Supplier's report, and net credits shall be applied to the next succeeding invoice or paid in cash when the Agreement expires or terminates.

4.6 Committed Productivity Gains

Supplier has committed to achieving certain productivity gains by increasing the productivity of the Supplier staff so that fewer FTEs are required over time. Such reduced staffing levels are reflected in the Resource Baselines for anticipated volumes of transactions and other activities. Customer will not be charged for any additional FTEs to support the same Resource Baselines except to the extent that Supplier's failure to achieve such reductions is excused by operation of the Agreement or applicable law. To the extent that Supplier may achieve greater productivity gains than anticipated, so that still fewer staff than anticipated are needed to perform Services, the Parties shall, as Customer reasonably determines after consultation with Supplier, either (a) further reduce the number of FTEs as appropriate (and reduce Charges accordingly) or (b) reassign FTEs no longer required to Projects or other Services, at no additional cost to Customer.

4.7 Cost-of-Living Adjustment ("COLA")

Service rates for Productive Hours, Projects, ARCs and RRCs shall be subject to an annual cost-of-living recalculation, equal to the percentage change in the [specify index: eg, Consumer Price Index (CPI), Employment Cost Index (ECI)] published by the

US Department of Labor's Bureau of Labor Statistics (or a successor index published by the US Government)[7] during the preceding Contract Year. COLA adjustments shall be computed annually, during the first sixty (60) days of each Contract Year (beginning with the second Contract Year), and effective from the beginning of the relevant Contract Year, with any adjustment for that initial sixty (60) day period to be paid as part of the reconciliation and adjustment process described above. If the Bureau of Labor Statistics redefines the base year for the [price index], calculations will be adjusted using an appropriate conversion formula.

5 ANNUAL MINIMUM PAYMENTS[8]

If total payments for all Services (including any additional Service from time to time performed for approved changes, Projects and all other Services, but excluding expense reimbursements) in any Contract Year are less than the amounts specified in Table __[9] for the Agreement as a whole, then promptly following the end of the Contract Year, Supplier shall deliver to Customer an invoice for the shortfall, which Customer shall pay within forty-five (45) days thereafter.

6 EXPENSES

6.1 Retained Expenses

Customer agrees to pay the retained expenses listed in Table __,[10] and as otherwise specified by the Agreement or agreed to from time to time in writing.

6.2 Pass-Through Expenses

Customer agrees to pay costs of [insert list or reference to a financial responsibility matrix] and the other Pass-Through Expenses specified by the Agreement or agreed to from time to time in writing. Products and services may not be purchased from or through Supplier's Affiliates or members of the Supplier Group without Customer's prior written approval of the terms in each instance. Supplier will: (i) review the corresponding invoiced charges to determine whether they are valid and proper and (ii) provide Customer with a reasonable opportunity to review the invoice and confirm its determination before the invoice is due and in sufficient time to obtain available discounts. Supplier will use reasonable efforts to minimize Pass-Through Expenses. Customer reserves the rights to: (i) obtain products

---

[7] The choice of an appropriate index is often a negotiated term. The Employment Cost Index (ECI) is regarded as a good measure of labor costs, but has tended to exceed the Consumer Price Index (CPI), which is based upon a 'basket' of consumer goods. When work goes offshore, indices from relevant countries may apply to offshore services, so there may be an apportionment based upon the ratio between onshore and offshore services. Within the US, there may be significant differences between national indices and those for particular regions or metropolitan areas.

[8] Common provision, heavily negotiated, but generally not proposed by customers in first drafts.

[9] Table of minimum payment obligations, usually based on agreed percentage of projected revenues.

[10] Insert reference to appropriate table or financial responsibility matrix.

and services obtained on a Pass-Through basis directly; (ii) designate the third party sources for such products and services; and (iii) approve the terms of purchase.[11]

6.3 Travel and Living Expenses

Supplier's Charges generally include all travel, living and other, similar costs related to performance of Services.[12] However, if, when and to the extent that Customer agrees to reimburse reasonable out-of-pocket expenses incurred by Supplier in connection with the performance of Project-related Services or other additional Services outside the scope of Schedule __, Service Description, Customer shall do so at actual cost and without any markup, to the extent authorized in advance by the relevant Project Documents, or otherwise in writing. Invoices shall describe reimbursable expenses in reasonable detail. Upon request, Supplier shall provide reasonable backup documentation. Travel, living and other expenses shall comply with Supplier's reasonable written policies, in effect from time to time, and approved by Customer.

7 CONVENIENCE TERMINATION

7.1 Termination Charges [Shutdown Costs]

[Alternative 1—Fixed, Declining Termination Charge: Table __ specifies Termination Charges payable upon convenience termination pursuant to Section __ of the Agreement. During any Contract Year, Termination Charges shall decline monthly by an amount equal to one twelfth (1/12) of the difference between the Convenience Termination Charge for that Contract year and the Convenience Termination Charge for the subsequent Contract Year.[13] Convenience Termination Charges are payable on or immediately after the effective date of termination. In cases of partial termination for convenience, Convenience Termination Charges shall be proportionally reduced, based upon the reduction in Charges.]

[Alternative 2—Shutdown Costs: Within sixty (60) days following the effective date of any convenience termination pursuant to Section __ of the Agreement, Supplier shall prepare and submit to Customer an invoice for its Shutdown Costs, together with such supporting documentation and detail as Customer may reasonably request. Customer shall pay the invoice within sixty (60) days, subject to its rights to audit and to withhold any amounts disputed in good faith, and its other rights under the Agreement.][14]

---

[11] Note that this calls for the Supplier to review and submit invoices, rather than review, pay and obtain reimbursement (a less common practice, because of suppliers' desire to add overhead and profit to all costs they pay).

[12] Where transition involves transfers of operations offshore, text should be clear (here or relating to transition) concerning costs of travel related to transition. Charges generally include costs of periodic home leave for onshore staff, visits to customer sites by supplier management and other predictable travel.

[13] Contracts sometimes preclude convenience termination during transition and an initial 'lock-in' period.

[14] When this alternative is chosen, references to termination charges should be edited accordingly in this document and the Agreement.

7.2 Convenience Termination—Change in Control of Supplier

No Convenience Termination Charge [Shutdown Costs] shall be paid if Customer terminates the Agreement for its convenience by giving notice within six (6) months after consummation of any merger, acquisition, reorganization, sale of stock, sale of assets or other, similar transaction or transactions that effect a change in Control of Supplier.[15]

8 GENERAL PRICING CONDITIONS AND ASSUMPTIONS

Supplier's Charges are based upon the following general conditions and assumptions. In the event of any material deviation from the following assumptions, and subject to Section __ of the Agreement (concerning excused performance, notice to Customer, mitigation and potential compensation upon the conditions specified), then relevant Charges shall be adjusted through the Change Control Procedure to compensate Supplier for the net additional Service performed (if any) and, to the extent not otherwise compensated by such adjustments, reimbursement of net, documented additional costs actually paid to third parties for products, services and related charges paid to third parties, such as taxes, shipping and insurance.

(a) Customer will provide facilities as described in . . . [16]
(b) Customer will continue to conduct business in [locations].
(c) Customer will perform all of the various functions identified in Schedule __ (Service Description) as Customer responsibilities.
(d) Services will be performed in the English language (and such other languages as may be required or contemplated by the Service Descriptions or other terms of the Agreement).
(e) [Others].

---

[15] Alternatively, the parties may agree to a reduced termination charge following a change in control, or no termination charge in the event the supplier is sold to one of the customer's competitors.

[16] Assumptions listed are illustrative. These may vary a good deal or (ideally from the customer's standpoint) there may be none.

Appendix 11

STANDARD TERMS FOR PROJECTS

SCHEDULE __

STANDARD TERMS FOR PROJECTS

TABLE OF CONTENTS

1 INTRODUCTION

Unless otherwise agreed in writing, the following terms and conditions, together with applicable provisions of the Agreement (the "Agreement"), shall govern performance of the Projects described by Schedule __, and such [infrastructure, development, consulting][1] and other Projects as may be authorized from time to time by change order or otherwise in writing.

2 DEFINITIONS

All capitalized terms shall have the meanings assigned below, or by the Agreement, unless the context clearly requires some other meaning.

3 PROJECT DOCUMENTS AND DELIVERABLES

3.1 Project Plans

Each Project will have a plan or description developed by Supplier (the "Project Plan") and, upon approval by both Parties, the Project Plan will be assigned a sequential number and will be attached to, and become a part of, this Schedule (e.g., Project Plan __-1/Title, Project Plan __-2/Title, etc).

---

[1] Edit as appropriate for outsourced functions and probable projects.

3.2 Project Documents and Deliverables

Supplier shall provide to Customer and Customer shall acquire from Supplier, the hardware, software, documentation, goods, services and other documentary or other deliverables (collectively, "Deliverables") specified in the relevant Schedules, Project Plans, change orders, or other pertinent documents (collectively, "Project Documents") for each Project. Unless otherwise agreed, the Project Documents shall further specify, as applicable, the work plan, project organization, assumptions, criteria for acceptance of Deliverables ("Acceptance Criteria"), Customer and Supplier responsibilities, Project-specific warranties, pricing and payment terms, delivery schedule, and any amendments or supplements to these Standard Terms and Conditions (the "Standard Terms") and the Agreement.

3.3 Interpretation of Agreement, Standard Terms and Project Documents

The Agreement, Project Documents and Standard Terms shall be construed consistently, but in the event of any conflict, these Standard Terms shall supersede inconsistent terms of the Agreement, and the Project Documents shall supersede any inconsistent provisions of these Standard Terms or the Agreement, to the extent applicable to the relevant Project.

4 CHARGES AND PAYMENT

4.1 Milestones, Retention

[Alternative 1—Mandatory Retention: Customer shall pay for Project-related services and Deliverables ("Project Services") in accordance with the relevant Project Documents and Section __ of the Agreement. Unless otherwise agreed, payments for Project-related services and Deliverables will be contingent upon acceptance of Deliverables or completion of specific tasks, or both (collectively "Milestones") and subject to retention of [percentage] (__%) of each payment until completion of all Milestones for the particular Project ("Retention"). Retention shall be released to Supplier upon completion of all Milestones, including successful completion of all acceptance tests, and corrective work identified through inspections and acceptance tests. The final portions of Retention may be reserved for release upon successful completion of initial production use during the applicable warranty period described below or such other period of initial production use as may be specified by the Project Documents.]

[Alternative 2—Optional Retention: Customer shall pay for Project-related Services and Deliverables ("Project Services") in accordance with the relevant Project Documents and Section __ of the Agreement. When Project Documents so specify, payments for Project-related Services and Deliverables will be contingent upon acceptance of Deliverables or completion of specific tasks, or both (collectively "Milestones") and subject to retention of an agreed percentage of each payment until completion of all Milestones and final acceptance of the particular Project ("Retention"). Retention shall be released to Supplier according to an agreed schedule, or upon successful completion of all Milestones, any required corrective work, and final acceptance. The final portions of Retention may be reserved for release upon successful completion of initial production use during the applicable warranty period described below or such other period of initial production use as may be specified by the Project Documents. Milestones, Retention amounts and apportionment shall be agreed on a case-by-case basis in Project Documents.]

4.2 Fixed Price Projects

When the Parties agree upon fixed prices for Projects, the fixed price shall be reasonably apportioned among all Milestones, and invoices (less any applicable Retention) shall be submitted to Customer following completion of Milestones, all as provided below or specified by the Project Documents.

4.3 Time and Materials Projects

4.3.1 Rates and Invoices

When the Parties agree upon payment based on hourly, daily, FTE or other rates, professional time shall be charged at the rates specified by Schedule __ ("contract rates") unless other rates are agreed for particular Project(s). Invoices (less any applicable Retention) shall be submitted to Customer monthly, in arrears (or as otherwise agreed in relevant Project Documents).

4.3.2 Overruns

[Alternative 1—Mandatory "No Fault"/Shared Overruns] When the Parties agree upon payment based on contract or other hourly, daily or FTE rates, invoices (less any applicable Retention) shall be submitted to Customer [monthly in arrears] [upon completion of relevant Milestones], all as provided below or specified by the Project Documents. Services shall be valued (i) as the Parties may from time to time agree, and (ii) otherwise, at contract rates, or (iii) if no rate is specified for relevant skills, at Supplier's then-current standard hourly, daily or FTE rates. If actual Charges so determined exceed the agreed budget for any reason (other than approved changes), then Customer shall pay one-half of the overrun, and Supplier shall absorb the remainder, regardless of the Parties' relative responsibilities for the overrun. (For example, if the Project budget is $500,000, and actual time charges are $700,000, Customer would pay $600,000—that is, the original price of $500,000 plus one-half (1/2) of the $200,000 overrun.)[2]

[Alternative 2—Optional "No Fault"] When the Parties so agree through Project Documents that expressly adopt the provisions of this Section 4.3.2, (i) a budget shall be agreed after requirements are defined, and (ii) if actual Charges exceed the agreed budget for any reason (other than approved changes), Customer shall pay one-half of the overrun, and Supplier shall absorb the remainder, regardless of the Parties' relative responsibilities for the overrun. (For example, if the Project budget is $500,000, and actual time charges are $700,000, Customer would pay $600,000—that is, the original price of $500,000 plus

---

[2] Many variations are possible (eg discounts according to the extent of the overrun and, above some agreed upper threshold, a 100% discount—effectively, a 'not-to-exceed' ceiling).

one-half (1/2) of the $200,000 overrun.) Project Documents may specify greater or lesser percentages, as mutually agreed.

4.3.3 *Time and Materials Services Generally*
[If the Parties do not agree to share overruns, as provided above, or otherwise agree in writing], [Unless otherwise agreed in writing,] Customer shall pay for Project Services undertaken on a time and materials basis by paying invoices for Services rendered (and authorized reimbursements) monthly, in arrears, and generally in accordance with Section __ of the Agreement. Supplier will use reasonable efforts to perform Project Services and deliver all Deliverables in accordance with a mutually agreed budget and estimated price ("Estimated Price") set forth in the relevant Project Documents, but does not guarantee that the Project Services can be completed or the Deliverables can be delivered within the Estimated Price. Estimates of numbers of hours by skill category are provided for information only, and Supplier may, in its reasonable discretion, use greater or lesser numbers of hours in any labor category as it deems appropriate to perform the Project Services. Supplier will give Customer prompt written notice whenever it (i) makes material increases or decreases in the staff assigned to a Project, or the mix of labor categories, or (ii) reasonably foresees that Deliverables cannot be completed within the Estimated Price, or within the time schedule in the relevant Project Documents. In any event, Supplier will submit revised estimates of the total cost to complete, and estimated time to completion at regular intervals (and unless otherwise agreed, at least every three (3) months) during performance of each Project.

4.3.4 *Overruns Generally, Suspension and Termination*
If at any time any Project is reasonably estimated, by either Party, to cost more than one hundred ten percent (110%) of the Estimated Price (or other budget or estimate of total cost), the Project shall be subject to suspension or termination (as provided below), in Customer's discretion, as well as further review and re-authorization by Customer's responsible management.

4.4 Expense Reimbursement
Customer agrees to reimburse reasonable out-of-pocket expenses incurred by Supplier in connection with the performance of Project Services, but only to the extent authorized in advance by the relevant Project Documents, or otherwise in writing. Invoices shall describe reimbursable expenses in reasonable detail. Upon request, Supplier shall provide reasonable backup documentation. Reimbursable expenses will in all cases exclude Supplier's internal costs and overheads and comply with Customer's reasonable written policies, in effect from time to time, and disclosed to Supplier concerning travel, living and other expenses. [To the extent reasonably practicable, Supplier shall staff Projects with personnel who ordinarily reside near (locations).][3]

---

[3] Optional provision, intended for use when services are performed at the customer's site, particularly in major cities where the supplier may have knowledgeable staff.

4.5 Invoices

Invoices (less any applicable Retention) shall be submitted to Customer: (i) monthly, in arrears; (ii) promptly following completion of Milestones; or (iii) as may otherwise be agreed in relevant Project Documents. Disputed Charges for Project Services may be withheld in accordance with Section __ of the Agreement.

5 PROJECT MANAGEMENT

5.1 Project Management Generally

Supplier's Contract Executive will have overall responsibility to meet agreed upon quality, cost, schedule and technical objectives of all Projects. In addition, each Party will assign an individual to each Project to act as its representative with responsibility for specific operational roles as described below and supplemented by the Project Plan (each a "Project Manager"). Based upon the scope of the work and the Deliverables to be provided for a Project, a Project Manager may be assigned to oversee more than one Project at a time.

5.2 Charges for Project Management

Supplier's Base Charges include project management services provided by the Supplier Contract Executive and other Supplier personnel, to the extent that such services can be provided within the resources ordinarily assigned to performance of Services for Customer. If, for a particular Project, additional personnel are required for project management or other purposes, Customer may, at its option, (i) temporarily relieve Supplier of Service Level or other obligations, so that the Project Services may be performed within the available staff, without additional charge or undue impact upon operations or user satisfaction, or (ii) authorize additional staff, for which Customer will pay at the appropriate contract rates.

5.3 Supplier Project Manager

Supplier's Project Manager will have full authority to act on behalf of Supplier in all matters pertaining to a Project. Supplier's Project Manager shall possess appropriate business, process and technical experience, as well as agreed minimum certifications. The Supplier Project Manager shall provide project management services, including the following:

(a) manage the Project, including planning, directing and monitoring all Project activities;
(b) develop the detailed Project Plan with the assistance of the Customer Project Manager;
(c) maintain files of the Project Plan and any associated documentation;
(d) establish the Project team and, in cooperation with the Customer Project Manager, orient team members regarding the Project Management process and the Project Plan, including individual responsibilities, Deliverables, schedules, etc;

(e) be the primary point of contact to Customer for establishing and maintaining communications through the Customer Project Manager;

(f) define and monitor the support resources required for the Project so that these resources are available as scheduled;

(g) measure, track and evaluate progress against the Project Plan;

(h) obtain and provide information, data, decisions and approvals within three (3) days following Customer's request, unless otherwise mutually agreed;

(i) resolve deviations from the Project Plan with the Customer Project Manager;

(j) administer and, in cooperation with the Customer Project Manager, be accountable for Project change control;

(k) plan, schedule and participate in Project planning and status meetings, as required;

(l) plan, schedule and participate in periodic Project reviews, including reviews of Work Product;

(m) provide periodic written status reports to Customer that provide information such as schedule status, technical progress, issue identification and related action plans; and

(n) establish and maintain the necessary financial controls for those areas of the Project for which Supplier has responsibility.

5.4 Customer Project Manager

Customer will assign a Project Manager who will have the authority to act on behalf of Customer in all matters pertaining to each Project. The Customer Project Manager will assist the Supplier Project Manager with project management. He or she will:

(a) be the single point of contact for the management of Customer's obligations under the Project;

(b) serve as the principal point of contact between the Project team members and Customer's business functions, units or Affiliates participating in the Project;

(c) define Customer's business and technical requirements for each Project;

(d) work with the Supplier Project Manager to develop a detailed Project Plan and verify that the Project Plan meets Customer's business and technical requirements;

(e) assign Customer personnel to the Project as required by the Project Plan and in cooperation with the Supplier Project Manager, orient team members regarding the project management process and the Project Plan, including individual responsibilities, Deliverables and time schedules;

(f) provide operational guidance to manage and be accountable for the performance of Customer personnel assigned to the Project;

(g) administer and, in cooperation with the Supplier Project Manager, be accountable for Project change control;

(h) attend Project planning, review and status meetings, as required;

(i) obtain and provide information, data, decisions and approvals reasonably requested by Supplier;

(j)   coordinate and schedule the attendance of Customer personnel, as appropriate, at planning, review and status meetings;

(k)   assist in the resolution of Project issues and escalate as needed;

(l)   establish and maintain the necessary financial controls for those areas of the Project for which Customer has responsibility; and

(m) review and confirm that the Deliverables meet the Acceptance Criteria set forth in the applicable Project Plan.

5.5 Stability

Customer shall use reasonable efforts to ensure that its Project Manager continues to direct and manage the relevant Project. Supplier may not reassign or replace its Project manager until the Project is complete (except in cases of disability, death, resignation, retirement or termination for cause). Customer shall have an opportunity to interview and approve any prospective Supplier Project Manager.

5.6 Project Steering Committee

Where appropriate, the Project Documents shall establish a Project Steering Committee consisting of each party's Project Manager and an equal number of other representatives from each Party with responsibilities relevant to completion of the Project and/or use, support and maintenance of related Deliverables. The Project Steering Committee shall meet at such intervals as the Project Managers deem advisable (and unless otherwise agreed, at least monthly) to discuss and evaluate the progress of the Project, including, without limitation, any pending change requests. Members of the Project Steering Committee may participate by conference telephone call. The Supplier Project Manager shall prepare and distribute (i) an agenda before each meeting of the Project Steering Committee, and (ii) minutes summarizing matters discussed and action taken promptly following the meeting.

5.7 Project Change Control

Either Party may request a change to a Project subject to the Change Control Procedures in Section __ of the Agreement and such additional or supplementary procedures as may be agreed in the Project Documents.

5.8 Methods

In performing Project Services, and except as otherwise agreed in writing through Project Documents or otherwise, Supplier shall apply its standard practices, procedures, methods and methodologies (including, without limitation, [identify approved methodology], and successor upgrades, versions and products) as well as approved project management procedures.

5.9 Reports

For each Project, Supplier shall deliver written reports summarizing progress at the intervals specified by the Project Documents (and if no interval is specified, then every two (2) weeks). Each such report shall identify any potential or actual delays or overruns, or other significant unresolved problems in the Project along with Supplier's proposed plans for resolution and estimated additional Charges (if any) and other costs for resolution.

5.10 Delivery of Work Product

Project Documents shall require, at Customer's option, maintenance of electronic copies of all Work Product (including, without limitation, all drafts, source and object code and supporting documentation) on machines or media specified and controlled by Customer and/or [daily/weekly/monthly] delivery or transmission of electronic or paper copies, or both, of all such Work Product to Customer.

5.11 Delays

5.11.1 Notice of Delays, Mitigation

The scheduled completion dates set forth in the Project Documents shall be adjusted from time to time to reflect approved changes, delays caused by Force Majeure Events ("Force Majeure Delays"), and delays caused by the acts or omissions of Customer, its officers, directors, employees, agents, and third party contractors ("Customer Delays"). Supplier agrees to give Customer prompt written notice of all delays, however caused, and when giving notice, to identify known reasons therefor. Supplier will take reasonable measures to mitigate the effects of all delays, however caused.

5.11.2 Certain Delays—Equitable Adjustment in Fixed Price Projects

If and to the extent that delays in fixed price Projects may be attributable to Customer Delays or changes required by Customer's acts or omissions, then Supplier's Charges shall be equitably adjusted to compensate Supplier for such delays. There will be no adjustment in Supplier's Charges to the extent that delays may be attributable to Supplier's failure(s) to perform its obligations in a timely manner (including, without limitation, its obligations to give prompt notice of and mitigate the effects of delays) ("Supplier Delays"). If the delay cannot be solely attributed to Supplier or Customer Delays, then any equitable adjustment shall be proportional, taking into consideration all factors contributing to the delay. [There will be no equitable adjustment for Time and Materials Projects covered by Section __, above ("no fault" overruns)].

5.11.3 Certain Delays—Time and Materials Charges

If and to the extent that any delays in Projects priced on a time and materials basis are attributable to Force Majeure Delays, Customer Delays, or changes required by Customer's acts and omissions, then Customer shall pay for additional Services performed. To the extent that delays in such Projects are attributable to Supplier Delays, Supplier shall not be compensated. If delays cannot be solely attributed to Supplier or Customer Delays, then Supplier shall be compensated only for the portion of the delays attributable to Force Majeure Delays and Customer Delays.

5.11.4 Disputed Delays

In the event of any material delays in the schedule stated in the relevant Project Documents, the Parties' respective Project Managers shall meet and confer regarding measures to assure completion as expeditiously as reasonably possible. If the Parties' respective Project Managers or Contract Executives are unable to agree upon such measures, all unresolved issues shall be resolved in accordance with the provisions of Section __ of the Agreement (concerning disputes).

6 ACCEPTANCE OF DELIVERABLES

Except as otherwise agreed in relevant Project Documents, the following procedures shall govern acceptance of all Deliverables.

6.1 Authorized Representative

Customer's Project Manager (or his or her designee) shall be Customer's authorized representative (or "Acceptor") to (i) accept or reject Deliverables, in whole or in part, and (ii) communicate Customer's comments, objections or responses concerning any Deliverable, Change Request or review or prototype demonstration.

6.2 Acceptance Procedures

The following procedures shall apply upon delivery of a Deliverable for which Acceptance Criteria are specified in the Project Documents, or otherwise agreed to in writing:

6.2.1 Acceptance Criteria Generally

Acceptance Criteria shall be mutually developed and agreed to in, or when specified by, the Project Documents, and in any event, at least thirty (30) days before the relevant test, delivery or Milestone date. To the extent practicable, Acceptance Criteria shall be object-ive, measurable and repeatable tests that are based upon Customer's anticipated produc-tion use of the Deliverables.

6.2.2 Documentary Deliverables

In the case of Deliverables (or portions of Deliverables) consisting of documentation ("Documentary Deliverables"), the Acceptor shall review the Deliverable and make any comments, objections or responses within the period specified in the Project Documents or, if no period is specified, within ten (10) business days after receipt (the "Review Period").

6.2.3 Hardware, Software and Infrastructure Deliverables

In the case of the hardware, software or infrastructure components of a Deliverable, Supplier shall conduct the acceptance tests prescribed by the Project Documents, after giving Customer appropriate prior notice and an opportunity to observe the acceptance tests. Supplier shall provide the Acceptor promptly with any documentation or other record of the results of such acceptance tests. Acceptor shall respond as set forth below.

6.3 Acceptance Standards
Customer may not unreasonably withhold or delay any acceptance of Deliverables.

6.3.1 Documentary Deliverables
Customer shall accept Documentary Deliverables if they: (i) satisfy the scope of the work in all material respects, and (ii) contain the functions or other content described by the Project Documents.

6.3.2 Hardware, Software and Infrastructure Deliverables
Customer shall accept hardware, software and infrastructure Deliverables if they: (i) satisfy relevant Acceptance Criteria or tests in all material respects, and are free from material faults; or (ii) are put into production (other than on a qualified, conditional or other limited basis); or (iii) the Acceptor signs relevant acceptance documents, without qualification or conditions.

6.4 Customer Review
The Acceptor shall review the Documentary Deliverables and the record of results of acceptance tests for other Deliverables within the Review Period. Before the end of the relevant Review Period, the Acceptor shall deliver to Supplier either (a) written acceptance of the relevant Deliverable, or (b) a written response indicating the unacceptable portions. Deliverables are not deemed accepted for purposes of payment unless and until Customer formally accepts the Deliverable in writing, or approves its use in its production environment (other than on a qualified, conditional or other limited basis).

6.5 Procedure for Correction
In the event the Acceptor notifies Supplier in writing that all or any part of any Deliverable is unacceptable, Supplier shall modify and return the entire Deliverable to Customer for review of the modified portions within [number] (___) business days (or such longer or shorter period as may be agreed for a particular Project). If and to the extent that any deficiencies remain, those procedures may be repeated as necessary to correct those deficiencies (or others revealed by further testing or review after corrective work). On review and approval of the corrected Deliverable by the Acceptor, the Deliverable will be considered accepted (but acceptance may be revoked, at any time prior to completion of the last Milestone, if testing of a later Deliverable reveals material deficiencies in a previously accepted Deliverable.)

7 WARRANTIES

7.1 "Critical Fault" Defined
For the purpose of these Standard Terms, a "Critical Fault" shall be any failure of a component to perform substantially in accordance with its specifications set forth in the Project Documents which either (i) prevents the relevant component(s) from providing substantially all of one or more of the material functions identified in the Project Documents, or (ii) prevents the proper operation of other material

components or functions of the hardware and software environment into which it is to be installed.

7.2 Basic Warranty

Except as otherwise provided in Section 7.4 below, Supplier warrants to Customer that each hardware, software or infrastructure component of a Deliverable will perform free of Critical Faults when used in accordance with its specifications in a production environment for a period of ninety (90) days after acceptance by Customer. Supplier does not warrant that (i) Deliverables will be free from immaterial errors, or (ii) Software Deliverables will operate without interruption (other than the absence of Critical Faults during the warranty period). Supplier further warrants to Customer that documentary Deliverables will comply with applicable requirements in all material respects, and conform to the requirements of Section 7.3 below.

7.3 Services Warranty

Supplier will perform promptly, diligently, in a workmanlike manner and in accordance with good professional standards among well-managed firms engaged in similar consulting, development and services businesses.

7.4 Third Party and Supplier Products

Supplier may acquire certain Deliverables from independent or third party vendors. Other Deliverables may consist, wholly or partially, of Supplier commercial products subject to standard warranties. To the extent that third party Suppliers provide warranties to Supplier, and the third party products are delivered to Customer without (i) modification or (ii) incorporation into Deliverables, Supplier will pass such warranties through to Customer. Except for the initial Critical Fault warranty set forth above, Supplier makes no independent representations or warranties concerning third party products that are neither delivered without modification, nor incorporated into Deliverables. Unless otherwise agreed, all Supplier commercial products are sold, leased or otherwise supplied to Customer subject to their standard warranties then in effect.

7.5 Disclaimer

UNLESS OTHERWISE AGREED IN WRITING, IN THE PROJECT DOCUMENTS OR OTHERWISE, THE FOREGOING WARRANTIES ARE IN LIEU OF ALL OTHER WARRANTIES, EXPRESS OR IMPLIED, INCLUDING WARRANTIES OF MERCHANTABILITY AND FITNESS FOR A PARTICULAR PURPOSE.

8 PROJECT TERMINATION

8.1 Termination for Customer's Convenience

Customer may terminate any Project for convenience and without cause, at any time, on written notice to Supplier. Promptly following receipt of such notice, and in any event within [number] ___ business days, Supplier shall marshal its Work Product and stop work on all pending Deliverables and shall account for the amount of work it has performed on Deliverables which have not yet been delivered. Within thirty (30) days of receipt from Supplier of an accounting of amounts due, Customer shall pay to Supplier the following amounts: (i) for Projects undertaken on a time and materials basis, the amount which would be due for work satisfactorily performed and permitted reimbursable expenses (if any) through the date of cessation of work in accordance with the notice of termination, or (ii) for fixed price Projects, the amount due for work satisfactorily performed on account of all completed Milestones, plus, for incomplete Milestones, [an amount based upon the percentage of work satisfactorily performed, determined based upon the percentage of completion achieved and applicable rates] [compensation at applicable rates for additional work satisfactorily completed (but not to exceed the amount due and unpaid in the aggregate for the Milestone Deliverables in process in accordance with the agreed work schedule under the Project Documents)]. Retention shall be released upon final payment for work in process and delivery of all Work Product to Customer (unless Customer expressly waives its right to require delivery). No compensation shall be paid for idle time of Project staff pending reassignment to other Projects or Supplier customers.

8.2 Suspension of Projects

Customer may at any time direct Supplier to suspend work on any Project. Upon receipt of any instruction to suspend work, Supplier shall promptly suspend work in an orderly manner, and in such a way that work may be resumed promptly following further instruction from Customer. In consultation with Customer, Supplier shall take reasonable measures to mitigate continuing costs to Customer, but will not re-locate or reassign Project staff (other than for temporary assignments that do not materially prejudice prompt resumption of work) without Customer's consent. Supplier shall be compensated for the effects of suspension through payment for Project staff necessarily retained during the period of suspension, and reasonable, necessary costs paid to third parties (e.g., for equipment leased for a longer period than contemplated), all to the extent authorized or approved in writing by Customer.

8.3 Termination for Cause

8.3.1 Termination by Customer

Customer may terminate any Project (i) if Customer terminates the Agreement for cause as provided in Section ___ of the Agreement, or (ii) Supplier fails to deliver an acceptable Deliverable when required, or otherwise materially breaches its obligations with respect to a Project and, in either case, fails to cure its failure within thirty (30) days after receiving written notice from Customer.

8.3.2 Termination by Supplier

Supplier may terminate any Project if (i) Supplier terminates the Agreement for cause as provided in Section ___ of the Agreement, or (ii) Customer fails to pay any material, undisputed amount due, when due hereunder, and thereafter fails to cure its failure within thirty (30) days after receiving written notice from Supplier. (Failure to pay for Project-related work shall not entitle Supplier to terminate the Agreement.)

8.3.3 *Payment following Termination for Cause*
When Projects are terminated for cause, Supplier shall be paid in the same manner as for convenience terminations, less (i) any Charges and other costs or charges disputed in good faith, and less (ii) amounts reasonably believed to be due to Customer that are attributable to material breaches of Supplier's obligations to perform Project Services.

8.4 Termination Generally, Work Product
If a Project terminates before acceptance of all Deliverables, for Customer's convenience or Supplier's material breach, Supplier shall do the following (subject to provisions of the Agreement concerning intellectual property, and unless otherwise agreed in writing with respect to a particular Project):

(a) Deliver to Customer copies of all Work Product generated by or for Supplier, for which Supplier has received payment.

(b) Upon request, provide such technical assistance as Customer or its designated contractors (the "successor") may reasonably require to complete the Project (at contract rates).

(c) Grant Customer or the successor a royalty-free, nontransferable, nonexclusive license to use any software, tools or other Supplier intellectual property reasonably necessary to finish the Project and use the Deliverables for Customer's business, provided that the license shall: (A) include reasonable and customary terms to protect Supplier's intellectual property; (B) be revocable only for material breach; and provided further that (C) in case of convenience terminations only, Customer shall pay any unpaid amounts separately payable under the relevant Project Documents for use of the relevant Supplier intellectual property (such as, for example, an agreed license fee for a commercial software product); but (D) there shall be no additional charge therefor in connection with termination for Supplier's material breach; or (E) in any termination by Customer, for other Supplier intellectual property agreed to be reasonably necessary to finish the work and not separately priced (such as, for example, a proprietary tool not separately priced).

(d) Take such steps as Customer may reasonably request to protect Customer's rights in all Work Product. Unless otherwise agreed, all rights and obligations regarding Work Product shall be as specified in Sections ____ of the Master Agreement.

8.5 Limitation of Liability

Except as otherwise agreed with respect to a particular Project, the Parties' liabilities are limited in accordance with Section __ of the Agreement. Both Parties shall use reasonable efforts to mitigate damages for which the other Party is responsible.[4]

---

[4] Separate liability limits are often negotiated for individual projects. Suppliers prefer to limit their basic liability to the amount paid or the price of the project. Customers may not want unsuccessful projects to erode overall liability limits for the entire relationship. If they agree that liability is limited to the amount paid, customers may insist that there be a floor, lest liability be negligible before any substantial payments are made.

Appendix 12

GOVERNANCE

SCHEDULE __

GOVERNANCE

TABLE OF CONTENTS

1 INTRODUCTION

This Schedule __ describes a framework and processes for management of the Parties' working relationships and performance of Services through:

(a) Service management by the Parties' Contract Executives and their subordinates;
(b) Oversight by the Parties' Executive Sponsors, and joint Executive, Management and other Committees (supplemented by such other or special committees as the Parties may deem advisable from time to time);
(c) Participation in joint committees or working groups with other suppliers of related products and services to Customer;
(d) Resolution of Issues (as defined below) through orderly, mutually agreed processes; and
(e) Annual review of the Agreement, the scope of Services, Fees, Service Levels, Projects (completed, pending and planned), Customer and User satisfaction and other aspects of the Parties' business relationship,

all as more fully described below, in order to achieve the Parties' mutually agreed goals.

2 GOALS

Both Parties shall discharge their responsibilities in a manner reasonably calculated to advance and achieve the following goals:

(a) Efficient, low cost delivery of excellent Services to Customer and all other Eligible Recipients;
(b) Timely completion of Projects that meet or exceed performance goals and are within budgets;
(c) Compliance with all applicable Laws;
(d) Regular access to Supplier's skilled personnel, knowledge, best practices and other capabilities and resources;
(e) Continuous improvement in the quality of Supplier's solution and Services;
(f) Prompt, full and regular communication between the Parties at executive, managerial and operational levels on all matters of mutual interest pertaining to the Services;
(g) Effective, cordial collaboration between the Parties, and with third Parties;
(h) Regular review and (when necessary) adjustment of the Parties' relationship in order to improve performance and achieve mutually agreed goals; and
(i) Achievement of the business goals stated in Section __ and other provisions of the Agreement.

The foregoing goals, and the other provisions of this Schedule __ are not intended, and shall not be construed to alter, augment or diminish the Parties' respective rights and obligations contained in the Agreement or any Service Description or Statement of Work. In particular, none of the provisions below concerning Service Management, Committees or Resolution of Issues are intended to supersede or alter any provision of the Agreement concerning Changes, root cause analyses, reports, amendments, consents, approvals or other processes related to management and administration of the Agreement and performance of Services. Rather, the processes and provisions contained in this Schedule are intended, among other things, to assure effective communication concerning the Agreement and Services and to provide an organizational framework for consideration and resolution of all Issues, Incidents and other matters concerning the Agreement and Services.

3 DEFINITIONS

The following capitalized terms shall have the meanings assigned below, unless the context clearly requires some other meaning.

"Executive Committee" means the joint committee described by Section 6.1, below.

"Issue" means any question, difference of opinion or interpretation identified as such in writing by either Party, acting through one of its authorized representatives. ("Issues" may or may not concern actual or potential changes, problems or Incidents reported to the Help Desk, or Faults, and consideration of any such matters as described below is without prejudice to the Parties' other rights, obligations and recourse under the Agreement.)

"Management Committee" means the joint committee described by Section 6.2, below.

All other capitalized terms shall have the meanings assigned by the Agreement, or where the terms first appear, unless the context clearly requires some other meaning.

4 ADMINISTRATIVE MATTERS

4.1 Charges All-inclusive
Charges for Services include performance of all of Supplier's obligations hereunder, including, without limitation, travel and living expenses for attendance at meetings.

4.2 Notice, Agendas and Minutes
One Party or the other, as reasonably determined by Customer, shall prepare and distribute notices and agendas for Committee and other meetings, draft and circulate minutes for review and approval, and maintain complete records of all meetings (including agendas, proposals, action taken, minutes and the like). Records shall be maintained centrally and electronically, using a web-site, e-room or other, similar means equally accessible to Committee members and other responsible management of both Parties.

4.3 Committee Action
The Parties will (i) deal in good faith, and (ii) use reasonable efforts to reach agreement on Issues and other matters from time to time considered, but (iii) changes and other Issues from time to time considered shall be decided in accordance with applicable terms of the Agreement, by mutual agreement, or action of one or the other Party, with or without the other Party's consent, as the Agreement may specify in each instance.

4.4 Meetings

Meetings shall be scheduled at the intervals specified, as otherwise agreed, and at any reasonable time, upon either Party's request. Unless otherwise agreed, meetings shall take place at Customer's offices at [location], but the Parties nevertheless intend to schedule at least [number] Executive [and/or Management] Committee meetings at Supplier's offices in [location]. Committee and other meetings may (with both Parties' consent) be conducted by conference telephone call, video conference, or other means that permit all participants to hear one another and to speak.

4.5 Appointments

The Parties reserve the rights to designate such persons as they may from time to time deem advisable to fill Committee and other positions designated by this Schedule and the Agreement, subject to the provisions of the Agreement concerning qualifications, designation, approval, tenure and removal of Key Personnel, subcontractors and other Supplier personnel. Alternates may be designated to attend and act in case of illness, vacation or other unavoidable absence. Replacements and alternates shall have comparable seniority, experience and authority.

5 SERVICE MANAGEMENT

5.1 Executive Sponsors

Each party shall appoint one or more Executive Sponsors, who shall be Senior Vice Presidents or other corporate officers of at least equal rank with executive responsibility for relevant functions and oversight of this Agreement and the Parties' relationship. Customer's initial Executive Sponsor shall be [name, title] and Supplier's initial Executive Sponsor shall be [name, title]. The Parties may designate successor Executive Sponsors from time to time in their reasonable discretion, but acknowledge the importance of continuity, active participation and appropriate seniority to effective governance of the Parties' relationship.

5.2 Contract Executives

In accordance with Sections ___ of the Agreement, the Parties' respective Contract Executives, supported by Supplier's Key Personnel and account team (in the case of Supplier) and Customer's Project Management Office ("PMO") (in the case of Customer), and their respective subordinates and designees shall have primary responsibility for day-to-day performance of the Agreement, including performance and management of Services, including, without limitation:

(a) Management of the relationship;
(b) Supervision of the delivery and receipt of Services;
(c) Reporting;
(d) Invoicing, payment, budgets, financial plans, estimates and other financial matters;
(e) Investigation and resolution of Incidents (including root cause analyses);
(f) Quality assurance;
(g) Compliance with applicable policies, procedures and Laws;

(h) Recommendation, consideration, authorization of Changes;

(i) Planning; and

(j) Other responsibilities described by any Service Description, Statement of Work or other portion of the Agreement.

6 OVERSIGHT—JOINT COMMITTEES

Promptly following the Effective Date, the Parties shall establish the following Joint Committees to oversee performance of the Agreement and delivery of Services, with the membership and responsibilities specified below.

6.1 Executive Committee

Executive Committee	
Membership	Executive Sponsors Contract Executives Supplier Delivery Manager Customer Director of Operations Others by invitation of the Executive Sponsors
Term	Contract Term
Responsibilities	1. Review performance reports for the most recent quarter; 2. Review Supplier's overall performance; 3. Manage strategy, policies and the relationship; 4. Resolve any outstanding Issues (including those unresolved by the Management Committee and the Parties' Contract Executives, and other matters that they may refer); 5. Consider long-term strategies for the Services; 6. During the Transition Period, oversee successful, timely completion of Transition activities; and 7. Such other matters as the Parties desire.
Meetings	Quarterly (and upon request)

6.2 Management Committee

Management Committee	
Membership	Contract Executives Supplier Delivery Manager Customer Director of Operations [other Customer and Supplier representatives] Both Parties' Transition Managers (during Transition) Others by invitation of either Contract Executive
Term	Contract Term
Responsibilities	1. Review performance reports; 2. Oversight of operations and performance (including, without limitation, Service delivery, proposed and approved Changes, Projects, Service Levels (including Service Level Failures, Service Credits, root cause analyses and corrective action); 3. Review invoices, budgets, trends and other financial questions; 4. Review and, when necessary, adjust working level procedures; 5. Review plans (including, among others, annual plans, Disaster Recovery and Business Continuity Plans and test results, capacity plans); 6. Discuss and, if possible, resolve any outstanding Issues referred by the Parties' Contract Executives, the Operations Committee or its members; 7. During the Transition Period, manage successful, timely completion of Transition activities; and 8. Such other matters as the Parties desire.
Meetings	Weekly, during the Transition Period; monthly thereafter and upon request.

6.3 Other Committees

The Parties, acting through their Contract Executives, or any of the foregoing committees may from time to time establish such other committees or other joint working groups as they may deem advisable to review and manage transition, user communications, planning, technical standards, operations, Projects, budgets or other matters of mutual interest.

7 COORDINATION WITH THIRD PARTIES

Supplier acknowledges that Customer does now, or may from time to time during the Term, engage third party contractors to perform services related to the Services that will require cooperation among Customer, Supplier and such third party contractors in order effectively and efficiently to serve Customer and achieve the goals set forth above and contained in the Agreement.

7.1 Operating Agreements

Upon request, Supplier shall negotiate in good faith and agree upon one or more operating or cooperation agreements, in form recommended by Customer and reasonably acceptable to Supplier, concerning:

(a) Cooperation among Customer and contractors;
(b) Participation in joint committees or working groups to coordinate related activities and services;
(c) Adoption and adherence to common technical standards, processes and procedures;
(d) Planning for related services and activities;
(e) Disaster recovery planning and testing;
(f) Compliance with applicable Laws, policies and procedures;
(g) Protection of all parties' confidential information and intellectual property;
(h) Resolution of disputed matters by Customer (subject to the parties' respective rights under bilateral service agreements between Customer and the service providers, including applicable limitations upon liability);
(i) Such other matters as Customer may reasonably require; and
(j) Other customary, commercially reasonable terms and conditions.

7.2 Multilateral Committees

Customer may from time to time require Supplier, acting through its Executive Sponsor, Contract Executive, and their designees to participate in one or more joint committees or working groups together with representatives of Customer and other contractors for the purpose of coordinating related activities, planning, technical standards and other, similar matters that Customer may deem advisable in order to assure efficient, effective delivery of Services and related services, and otherwise to achieve the goals listed above, and Customer's other business goals. Initially [insert particulars here] [1]

8 ANNUAL REVIEW

Beginning [time], and thereafter, during the first quarter of every subsequent Contract Year, the Parties' Executive Sponsors and the Executive Committee shall meet in person and undertake a joint review of the Agreement and the Parties' relationship, considered as a whole, including:

---

[1] Where Service Levels include user satisfaction, consider a survey of Customer management to assess the quality of cooperation among and between service providers in order to deter 'turf fights' and other inappropriate or counter-productive conduct.

(a) Service quality, as measured through surveys of user satisfaction, Service Levels and other appropriate means;

(b) Financial performance, measured against projected expenditures and consumption and (if available) any benchmark reports or other market data;

(c) Outstanding Issues;

(d) Actual or potential changes and Projects;

(e) Effectiveness of governance procedures in this Schedule and other provisions of the Agreement;

(f) Extensions, reductions or adjustments to the scope of Services;

(g) Possible adjustments of Service Levels and related Service Credits;

(h) Possible amendments to the Agreement;

(i) Anticipated consumption trends, improvements in Services, changes in Supplier's methods, procedures and solution; and other developments anticipated to affect performance of Services and the Parties' relationship; and

(j) Such other matters as either Party may wish to review.

Review by the Executive Sponsors and Executive Committee shall be based upon a joint report, prepared by the parties' Contract Executives and their designees, and reviewed by the Operations and Management Committees which shall summarize the Parties' views concerning the foregoing. Where the Parties differ, their respective views shall be summarized for discussion and further consideration. Neither Party shall be obligated to amend the Agreement, approve any Change or take any other action as a result of the foregoing review (unless required by other provisions of the Agreement) but each Party shall consider the other Party's concerns and proposals in good faith.

9 RESOLUTION OF ISSUES

Either Party may identify an Issue to the other through written notice, delivered to the other Party's Contract Executive (or his or her designee) describing the Issue with reasonable particularity, including any proposed resolution. Disputed issues that the Parties are unable to resolve through consultation by the Executive Committee shall be referred to the Executive Sponsors (unless otherwise agreed, and if either or both Executive Sponsors were direct participants in disputed matters the relevant Parties shall designate other knowledgeable executives of comparable seniority). Issues not resolved shall be resolved in accordance with Article __ of the Agreement, concerning disputes (subject to the Parties' obligations to continue performance pending resolution of any dispute). Proposals, counter-proposals and other communications related to disputed matters shall be confidential (and inadmissible as evidence) in accordance with the terms of Section __ of the Agreement. The provisions of this Section 9 are in addition to and do not derogate from (i) the provisions of any Service Description(s) concerning classification and resolution of operational matters reported to the Help Desk in the ordinary course of performance, and (ii) the provisions of the Agreement and Schedule __ concerning Service Levels, Service Credits and root cause analyses.

Appendix 13

COOPERATION AGREEMENT

COOPERATION AGREEMENT

between and among

CUSTOMER

SUPPLIER A

and

SUPPLIER B

[Date]

TABLE OF CONTENTS

SCHEDULES

COOPERATION AGREEMENT

This Cooperation Agreement is entered into as of [date] between and among [name] ("Customer"), [name] ("Supplier A") and [name] ("Supplier B") with reference to the following facts:[1]

RECITALS

A. Customer has outsourced its [describe functions] to Supplier A under a master services agreement dated [date] (the "Supplier A Bilateral Agreement")
B. Customer has outsourced its [describe functions] to Supplier B under a master services agreement dated [date] (the "Supplier B Bilateral Agreement")
C. All parties recognize the importance of proper and effective cooperation to successful performance of the Suppliers' respective Bilateral Agreements and the conduct of Customer's business and have therefore entered into this Cooperation Agreement.

NOW, THEREFORE, in consideration of the foregoing recitals and the mutual promises set forth below, the Parties agree as follows:

1 INTERPRETATION

1.1 Definitions
The following terms shall have the meanings assigned (unless the context clearly requires some other meaning):

"Agreement" means this Cooperation Agreement, including any amendments, extensions, variations, ancillary agreements or any replacements therefor.

"Bilateral Agreement(s)" means the Supplier A Service Contract, the Supplier B Service Contract, or both, as the context requires.

"Confidential Information" means all of the trade secrets, business and financial information, source codes, machine and operator instructions, business methods, business plans, procedures, know-how and other information of every kind that relates to the business of a Party (including information disclosed prior to the Effective Date) [optional: that is marked as such, identified as such at or immediately after the time of disclosure, or disclosed in circumstances that would lead a reasonable person to recognize its confidential character]. Confidential Information includes, without limitation, all such information so identified or defined pursuant to any Bilateral Agreement. Confidential Information excludes information in the public domain, generally known in any Party's industry, or independently developed or lawfully acquired (in either case, without breach of any legal or contractual obligation). The terms of this Agreement are Confidential Information of all Parties.[2]

---

[1] Drafted for two suppliers, but the number could be larger.
[2] If desired, add specific examples of particularly sensitive matter (eg 'Customer's Confidential Information includes, without limitation,. . ..').

"Confidential Materials" means all manuals, bulletins, computer programs (in any medium), databases (in any medium), printouts, reports, correspondence, memoranda, copies and other documentation and tangible things (in any medium) that contain or relate in any way to any Confidential Information.

"Disclosing Party" means the Party disclosing Confidential Information.

"Financial Responsibility Matrix" means the matrix attached as Schedule A, as it may be updated or amended from time to time.

"Functional Responsibility Matrix" means the matrix attached as Schedule B, as it may be updated or amended from time to time.

"Party" or "Parties" means one or more of Supplier A, Supplier B and Customer, as the context requires.

"Recipient" means the Party receiving Confidential Information.

"Services" means services performed (or required to be performed) by a Supplier under a Bilateral Agreement.

"Supplier A Bilateral Agreement" means the master services agreement entered into, or to be entered into, between Supplier A and Customer concerning the [describe functions], including any amendments, extensions, variations, ancillary agreements or any replacements therefor in effect from time to time.

"Supplier B Bilateral Agreement" means the master services agreement entered into, or to be entered into, between Supplier B and Customer concerning the [describe functions], including any amendments, extensions, variations, ancillary agreements or any replacements therefor in effect from time to time.

"Supplier(s)" means either Supplier A, Supplier B, or both, as the context requires.

Other capitalized terms have the meanings assigned where they first appear, unless the context clearly requires some other meaning.

1.2 Relationship to Bilateral Agreements
This Agreement governs cooperation among the Parties related to their respective performance under the Bilateral Agreements, but is not intended to make any Supplier responsible for any other Supplier's obligations under its respective Bilateral Agreement. Nothing in this Agreement shall affect the Parties' respective obligations under the Bilateral Agreements.

1.3 Headings and References
References to laws or regulations include any amendments, consolidations, codifications or replacements in effect from time to time. The masculine, feminine or neuter gender respectively includes the other genders and any reference to the singular includes

the plural (and vice versa). Headings are for convenience only and shall not affect the interpretation or construction of this Agreement.

2 COOPERATION

2.1 Cooperation Generally

Each Supplier confirms to Customer that it shall cooperate reasonably and in good faith with Customer and the other Supplier(s) in order to ensure successful performance of all Suppliers' respective Services for Customer's benefit, and shall provide all such information and assistance as Customer or the other Suppliers may reasonably require in connection with performance of this Agreement and the Bilateral Agreements. The Suppliers acknowledge that reasonable cooperation with Customer and other Suppliers is an incidental service, included within the scope of Services they perform under their respective Bilateral Agreements, without additional charge to Customer.

2.2 Specific Functional and Financial Responsibility

In particular, and without limiting the generality of the foregoing Section 2.1, each Supplier shall:

(a) Perform those functions designated as its responsibilities in the Functional Responsibility Matrix;[3]
(b) Be liable to Customer under and to the extent set forth in its respective Bilateral Agreement for any failure to perform its designated responsibilities;
(c) Cooperate with and provide reasonable assistance to other Suppliers in connection with performance of their respective responsibilities;
(d) Provide such technical and other information to other Suppliers as they may reasonably require in order to perform their obligations under this Agreement and applicable Bilateral Agreements (subject to their confidentiality obligations hereunder and any applicable nondisclosure agreements);
(e) Give such access to its systems as may be reasonably requested by Customer or other Suppliers for performance of their respective responsibilities under the Functional Responsibility Matrix and their respective Bilateral Agreements (subject to compliance with reasonable technical and security standards);
(f) License proprietary systems and technologies to other Suppliers as reasonably requested by Customer or other Suppliers for performance of their respective responsibilities under the Functional Responsibility Matrix and their respective Bilateral Agreements, upon commercially reasonable terms and without additional charge;

---

[3] Matrix to spell out responsibilities in detail (eg participation in governance committees or working groups, adherence to relevant technical standards, access to networks and other resources, planning, collaboration on disaster recovery and other shared responsibilities, compliance with security and other standards).

(g) Participate in joint committees or working groups from time to time designated by Customer in order to coordinate or plan related activities, operations and services or for other appropriate purposes (including, without limitation, disaster recovery, business continuity and [list others]);

(h) Adopt and comply with common or standard processes, procedures and technical standards from time to time designated by Customer for related activities, operations and services;

(i) Be liable to Customer under and to the extent set forth in the respective Bilateral Agreements for any failure to perform its responsibilities in a timely manner; and

(j) Refrain from any act or performance for which Customer consent is required without first obtaining Customer's consent.

2.3 Customer Responsibilities

Customer shall:

(a) Perform those functions allocated primarily to Customer in the Functional Responsibility Matrix;

(b) Be liable to either or both Suppliers, as appropriate, under and to the extent set forth in the respective Bilateral Agreements for any failure to perform its responsibilities; and

(c) Cooperate with and provide reasonable assistance to the Suppliers in connection with performance of their respective responsibilities.

2.4 Disputed Responsibilities

In the event of any dispute concerning a Supplier's responsibility for any functions described by or related to the Functional Responsibility Matrix, the matter shall be resolved in accordance with the dispute resolution procedure in Section 5. Pending resolution of the dispute, Customer may in its sole discretion require a Supplier to perform the disputed function promptly in accordance with the Functional Responsibility Matrix as if it were responsible for such function. If, after resolution of the dispute, it should be determined that the particular Supplier directed to perform was not responsible, then (i) if another Supplier was responsible, that Supplier shall thereafter bear responsibility and pay or reimburse all charges paid or payable, and any reimbursable costs; or (ii) if no Supplier was responsible, the Supplier required to perform shall be deemed to have done so pursuant to a change, and be compensated accordingly under its Bilateral Agreement (but Customer reserves the right thereafter to discontinue such additional services).

2.5 Financial Responsibility

Each Supplier and Customer shall be responsible for making the payments and/or incurring the costs described by the Financial Responsibility Matrix. No additional payments or other consideration shall be due or payable to the Suppliers for performing their obligations under this Agreement (including those contained in the Functional and Financial Responsibility Matrices). All Supplier obligations hereunder constitute Services within the scope of the Bilateral Agreements, for which normal charges thereunder constitute full payment.

3 GOVERNANCE

3.1 Changes Affecting One Supplier

Modifications or amendments of the Functional or Financial Responsibility Matrices affecting Customer and only one Supplier shall be authorized and implemented pursuant to change control procedures under the applicable Bilateral Agreement. Customer shall thereafter provide an updated Functional or Financial Responsibility Matrix to the other Supplier(s).

3.2 Changes Affecting Multiple Suppliers

Modifications or amendments of the Functional or Financial Responsibility Matrices affecting Customer and multiple Suppliers shall be authorized and implemented pursuant to change control procedures under the applicable Bilateral Agreements, insofar as reasonably practicable, but (i) the Parties shall cooperate in order to coordinate related changes, as Customer may reasonably request; and (ii) if particular changes require agreement of all Suppliers, they shall not be effective unless and until Customer and all Suppliers so agree in writing.

3.3 Representatives of the Parties

The Suppliers' respective contract executives under the Bilateral Agreements shall have authority to act for the Suppliers in connection with all aspects of this Agreement, including management, supervision and direction of Supplier's performance; but any written notice, demand or other communication in respect of matters other than the day-to-day performance of the Services shall be addressed to the person or persons specified in Section 7.11. Customer's representative shall be [name or title], or his or her successor(s) designated from time to time. Customer's representative and the Supplier contract executives may designate alternates or deputies to act in their places.

4 CONFIDENTIALITY

4.1 Standard of Care

The Parties shall keep confidential all Confidential Information obtained from any of the other Parties pursuant to or in connection with this Agreement. Each Party may only disclose Confidential Information relating to another Party to those of its personnel who require the Confidential Information in order to perform under this Agreement or the relevant Bilateral Agreement. Each Recipient shall exercise the same care to protect and prevent disclosure of other Parties' Confidential Information that it exercises to protect Customer's Confidential Information under its Bilateral Agreement and, in all cases, at least the care it exercises to protect its own similar Confidential Information.

4.2 Permitted Use of Confidential Information

No Party may use any other Party's Confidential Information for any purpose other than the performance of its obligations or enforcement of its rights under this Agreement or the relevant Bilateral Agreement. No Party may disclose another Party's Confidential Information to any third party (such as an approved subcontractor), except to the extent approved in writing by a Disclosing Party (for example, by Customer for its Confidential Information, under the relevant Bilateral Agreement), and that approval may be conditioned upon the third party's agreement to a nondisclosure agreement acceptable to the Disclosing Party. Each Party may disclose this Agreement to its attorneys, auditors and other professional advisors (subject to appropriate confidentiality obligations or agreements) as well as auditors or regulatory agencies (from whom they shall request confidential treatment). Disclosing Parties retain all right, title and interest in and to their respective Confidential Information and Confidential Materials, and Recipients have no rights therein, other than the limited rights of use provided above.

4.3 Compulsory Disclosures

Disclosures of another Party's Confidential Information compelled by subpoena or other legal process ("subpoena") shall not breach this Section 4, provided that immediately after receiving any such subpoena, the recipient so advises the Disclosing Party, and cooperates with the Disclosing Party's efforts to obtain a protective order (at the Disclosing Party's expense), or other reasonable and lawful measures to protect the Disclosing Party's Confidential Information.

4.4 Return of Confidential Information

Upon expiration or termination of this Agreement, each Recipient shall: (i) return, erase, shred or otherwise destroy (as the Disclosing Party may reasonably direct) all Confidential Information and Confidential Materials in Recipient's possession, power or control in a manner that assures the Confidential Information is rendered unrecoverable (excluding only archival copies maintained for the benefit of Customer); and (ii) provide written confirmation to the Disclosing Party that Recipient has complied with the requirements of this Section.

5 DISPUTES

5.1 Bilateral Disputes

Resolution of bilateral disputes between Customer and the respective Suppliers shall be resolved pursuant to relevant provisions of the applicable Bilateral Agreement(s).

5.2 Other Disputes

Disputes between and among Suppliers or among Customer and one or more Suppliers shall be referred to [the [name] committee] [executives of all relevant Parties, nominated by the respective Parties, and not engaged in day-to-day performance of this Agreement or the Bilateral Agreement] for discussion and resolution. If the [committee/executives] are unable to resolve the dispute within thirty (30) days after the matter is first referred, then the affected Parties may commence proceedings as provided below. All Parties reserve the right to commence proceedings immediately, if reasonably necessary in order to obtain provisional remedies or avoid expiration of applicable statutes of limitation. If Customer reasonably believes that the unresolved matter has serious effects upon performance under either a Bilateral Agreement or upon Customer's operations, the Parties shall use diligent efforts to expedite resolution.

5.3 Confidentiality
Proposals, counter-proposals, negotiations and information exchanged during any such consultations or any later settlement negotiations shall be privileged, confidential, and inadmissible as evidence for any purpose in any subsequent proceedings (but otherwise admissible evidence, such as business records, shall not be rendered inadmissible merely because it may be transmitted or referred to in connection with settlement consultations or negotiations).

5.4 Applicable Law
All questions concerning the validity, interpretation and performance of this Agreement shall be governed by and decided in accordance with the internal laws of California and applicable federal laws (without reference to principles of conflicts of laws).

5.5 Jurisdiction and Venue
The Parties hereby submit and consent to the exclusive jurisdiction of the [name] County Superior Court and the United States District Court for the [name] District of California. They irrevocably agree that all actions or proceedings arising under or relating to this Agreement (other than (i) proceedings to obtain provisional remedies or enforce judgments or (ii) proceedings arising in or related to litigation involving third parties) shall be litigated in those courts. Each of the Parties waives any objection which it may have based on improper venue or forum non conveniens to the conduct of any such action or proceeding.

5.6 Consolidation of Proceedings
To the extent that applicable Bilateral Agreement provisions, arbitration rules or procedural rules or law may permit consolidation, intervention or joinder (collectively, "consolidation") of related proceedings involving common issues of law or fact, no Party may object to consolidation of related proceedings where another Party or other Parties reasonably believe consolidation would prevent inconsistent results, avoid duplicate proceedings and otherwise serve the interests of justice.

5.7 Fees and Costs
In any legal action, the prevailing Party shall be entitled to recover, in addition to its damages (which are subject to limitations stated elsewhere in this Agreement), its reasonable attorneys' fees and costs, as determined by the court. Those costs include, without limitation, attorneys' fees and costs of any legal proceedings brought to enforce a judgment or decree.

6 REMEDIES

6.1 Equitable Remedies

The Parties agree that in the event of any breach or threatened breach of any provision of this Agreement concerning Confidential Information or intellectual property rights, money damages would be an inadequate remedy. Accordingly, those provisions may be enforced by the preliminary or permanent, mandatory or prohibitory injunction or other order of a court of competent jurisdiction.

6.2 Liability Limits

Liabilities under the Bilateral Agreements are limited in accordance with their terms. In the event of any breach of this Agreement, each Party shall be responsible for the other Parties' actual damages but, no Party shall be liable to any other Party (or its affiliates or agents) for any lost profits, lost revenues, special, indirect, consequential or punitive damages, whether in contract or tort, and even if advised of the possibility of such damages.

6.3 Certain Operational Failures

If a Supplier causes another Supplier to breach its obligations to Customer under a Bilateral Agreement; and the failure would result in payment or assessment of liquidated damages or service credits under the other Supplier's Bilateral Agreement then the responsible Supplier shall, as appropriate, reimburse the other Supplier or pay to Customer the liquidated damages paid or service credits due (without regard to any limitations upon the responsible Supplier's liability for similar failures under its own Bilateral Agreement).

6.4 Indemnification

(a) Suppliers and Customer indemnify one another to the extent stated in or contemplated by the Bilateral Agreements.

(b) Each Supplier agrees to indemnify, defend and hold the other Supplier (and its respective affiliates and agents) harmless from and against all claims, demands, causes of action and other liability (including, without limitation, reasonable attorneys' fees) that arise from or relate to claims by Customer or other unrelated third parties concerning: (i) breaches of this Agreement or agreements with third parties; (ii) acts or omissions of the indemnitor that disrupt, interrupt or otherwise adversely affect the indemnitee's performance of Services for Customer; (iii) breaches of confidentiality; (iv) infringements of intellectual property rights; (v) damage to or destruction of tangible property; (vi) injury to or death of persons; or (vii) acts or omissions of the indemnitor that constitute negligence, gross negligence, recklessness, willful misconduct, or violations of law.

(c) Each Party agrees to give the other prompt notice, with full particulars, concerning all claims subject to the foregoing indemnities, and to cooperate in the investigation and defense of any claim. Payment of attorneys' fees shall be limited to the reasonable fees and disbursements of a single firm of attorneys, except to the extent that applicable rules of professional conduct reasonably require separate counsel. No indemnitor shall have any obligation to pay or reimburse any settlement reached without the indemnitor's prior written consent. Settlements or compromises reached by an indemnitor shall be subject to the prior written consent of the indemnified Party. In cases of claims of infringement, an indemnitor may, in its reasonable discretion, procure a license, develop or obtain a non-infringing substitute, implement work-arounds, settle or compromise the claim, take other appropriate action, or (in the absence of any other commercially reasonable course of action) withdraw the allegedly infringing matter from use. In such cases of withdrawal, the relevant Parties' functional obligations shall be adjusted accordingly. An indemnitor or indemnified Party may, in its sole but reasonable discretion, withhold consent to settlement of claims of infringement affecting its proprietary rights, or admitting liability (other than monetary settlement payments paid by the indemnitor). Consent to monetary settlements may not be unreasonably withheld or delayed.

7 GENERAL PROVISIONS

7.1 Entire Agreement, Amendment, Waiver

This Agreement (including all attached exhibits and Schedules) constitutes the entire agreement of the Parties concerning its subject matter and supersedes any prior or contemporaneous understandings, agreements or representations (but is not intended, and shall not be construed to amend any Bilateral Agreement or to alter the scope of any performance or other obligations thereunder). No supplement, modification, amendment or waiver of this Agreement shall be binding unless executed in writing by both Parties. No waiver of any of the provisions of this Agreement shall constitute a waiver of any other provision nor shall any such waiver constitute a continuing waiver unless given expressly and in writing.

7.2 Further Assurances

The Parties shall with reasonable diligence do all things and provide all reasonable assurances as may be required to complete the transactions contemplated by this Agreement, and each Party shall provide such further documents or instruments required by the other Party as may be reasonably necessary or desirable to give effect to this Agreement and to carry out its provisions.

7.3 Relationship of the Parties

The Parties are independent contractors, and nothing in this Agreement or the Bilateral Agreements shall be construed to create any other relationship between or among them, as joint venturers, partners, principal and agent or otherwise (except to the limited extent that any Bilateral Agreement may, by its express terms, create an agency relationship).

7.4 Assignments

As between Customer and either Supplier, a Party may assign its rights and obligations under this Agreement where and to the extent that there has been an effective, permitted assignment under the relevant Bilateral Agreement. This Agreement shall then operate as between such assignee and the other Parties to this Agreement. This Agreement may not otherwise be assigned without the consent of all Parties.

7.5 Replacements, Additional Suppliers

Upon Customer's request, any Supplier shall enter into a new agreement, consent to additions or substitutions of Suppliers or to assignments of their rights and obligations (with related amendments to the Functional and Financial Responsibility Matrices reasonably determined by Customer that do not materially or adversely alter the affected Supplier's then-existing responsibilities) on terms substantially similar to this Agreement. Customer shall use reasonable efforts to secure accession to this Agreement or entry into a similar agreement by any such additional or replacement supplier. Material or adverse changes in Functional and Financial Responsibility Matrices affecting Supplier(s) shall be authorized in accordance with the provisions of this Agreement concerning changes.

7.6 Term

This Agreement shall automatically terminate (i) with respect to a Supplier, upon expiration or termination of its Bilateral Agreement, and (ii) with respect to Customer, upon expiration or termination of the last Bilateral Agreement to expire or terminate (subject to Section 7.10 below, concerning survival of certain provisions).

7.7 Publicity

No press release or other public communication concerning this Agreement, its terms, the transactions and Bilateral Agreements referred to in this Agreement, or (in the case of any Supplier) in connection with Customer, shall be made without the prior written consent of the other affected Parties unless required by applicable laws or regulations, and then after consulting with all affected Parties as to the form of notice and taking appropriate action to protect the affected Parties' Confidential Information. This Section shall not prevent any announcement permitted or authorized by a Bilateral Agreement that does not refer to other Parties.

7.8 Duty to Act Reasonably

Whenever this Agreement requires or contemplates any action, consent or approval, the Parties shall act reasonably and in good faith and (unless the Agreement expressly allows exercise of a Party's sole, or sole and absolute discretion) may not unreasonably withhold or delay such action, consent or approval.

7.9 Severability

Any provision in this Agreement which is prohibited or unenforceable in any jurisdiction shall, as to that jurisdiction, be ineffective to the extent of such prohibition or unenforceability without invalidating the remaining provisions or affecting the validity or enforceability of such provisions in any other jurisdiction. The Parties shall seek in good faith to agree to amendments to this Agreement to reflect the original commercial intent as closely as legally permissible.

7.10 Survival

Sections 4.4, 5, and 6 shall survive expiration or termination of this Agreement, together with any other provisions that expressly survive, or by their nature are intended to survive.

7.11 Notices

Notices to be given by Customer to Suppliers (or vice versa) under this Agreement must be made in the manner provided by the relevant Bilateral Agreement. Suppliers may give notice to one another in writing by prepaid certified mail, personal delivery (including express courier service with proof of delivery), or by facsimile or other electronic means with proof of delivery (if subsequently confirmed by certified mail or personal delivery). Notice by mail shall be deemed received three (3) days after mailing. Notice by personal delivery shall be effective upon receipt. Electronic notice shall be effective upon transmission and receipt of electronic confirmation. Notices shall be addressed as follows:

To Supplier A:

[Name]
[Street Address]
[City, State, zip]
Telephone:
Facsimile:
Attention: General Counsel

To Supplier B:

[Name]
[Street Address]
[City, State, zip]
Telephone:
Facsimile:
Attention: General Counsel

To Customer:

[Name]
[Street Address]
[City, State, zip]
Telephone:
Facsimile:
Attention: General Counsel

7.12 Counterparts

This Agreement, including the Schedules, may be executed in one or more counterparts, each of which shall be deemed an original but all of which taken together shall constitute one and the same instrument. The Agreement shall be effective when all Parties have executed an original or counterparts.

Executed by the Parties' undersigned authorized representatives as of the date first written above.

[Supplier A]   [Supplier B]

By: By:
Name: Name:
Title   Title

                                              [Customer]

                                              By:
                                              Name:
                                              Title

Index